ROLE THEORY

Perspectives for
Health Professionals

Second Edition

ROLE THEORY

Perspectives for Health Professionals

Second Edition

Margaret E. Hardy, Ph.D.
Professor
College of Nursing
University of Rhode Island
Kingston, Rhode Island

Mary E. Conway, Ph.D.
Professor and Dean
School of Nursing
Medical College of Georgia
Augusta, Georgia

APPLETON & LANGE
Norwalk, Connecticut/San Mateo, California

R690 .R6 1988
Role theory.

0-8385-8472-1

Copyright © 1988 by Appleton & Lange, © 1978 by Appleton-Century-Crofts
A Publishing Division of Prentice Hall

88 89 90 91 92 / 10 9 8 7 6 5 4 3 2 1

Prentice-Hall of Australia, Pty. Ltd., Sydney
Prentice-Hall Canada, Inc.
Prentice-Hall Hispanoamericana, S.A., Mexico
Prentice-Hall of India Private Limited, New Delhi
Prentice-Hall International (UK) Limited, London
Prentice-Hall of Japan, Inc., Tokyo
Prentice-Hall of Southeast Asia (Pte.) Ltd., Singapore
Whitehall Books Ltd., Wellington, New Zealand
Editora Prentice-Hall do Brasil Ltda., Rio de Janeiro

Library of Congress Cataloging-in-Publication Data

Role theory.
    Bibliograpyy: p.
    Includes index.
    1. Medical personnel.   2. Social role.   3. Professional
socialization.   I. Hardy, Margaret E.   II. Conway,
Mary E., 1923–   .   [DNLM: 1. Health Occupations.
2. Role. 3. Socialization.   W 21 R745]
R690.R6 1988 305'.961 88–19236
ISBN 0-8385-8472-1

Production Editor: Michael Duford, Bellamy Printz
Design: Kathleen Peters Ceconi

PRINTED IN THE UNITED STATES OF AMERICA

Contributors

Bonnie Bullough, Ph.D.
Dean, College of Nursing
SUNY/Buffalo
Buffalo, New York

Joy D. Calkin, Ph.D.
Professor and Dean
Faculty of Nursing
The University of Calgary
Calgary, Alberta, Canada

Mary E. Conway, Ph.D.
Professor and Dean
School of Nursing
Medical College of Georgia
Augusta, Georgia

Margaret E. Hardy, Ph.D.
Professor
College of Nursing
University of Rhode Island
Kingston, Rhode Island

William L. Hardy, Ph.D.
School of Medicine
Boston University
Boston, Massachusetts

Ada Sue Hinshaw, Ph.D.
Director
National Center for Nursing Research
National Institutes of Health
Bethesda, Maryland

Barbara Ann Hurley-Wilson, Ph.D.
Director, Shapero Institute for
Nursing Excellence/Research
Sinai Hospital of Detroit
Detroit, Michigan

Phyllis Beck Kritek, Ph.D.
Professor
School of Nursing
Marquette University
Milwaukee, Wisconsin

Jean L. J. Lum, Ph.D.
Professor and Dean
School of Nursing
University of Hawaii at Manoa
Honolulu, Hawaii

Mary-'Vesta Marston-Scott, Ph.D.
Associate Professor
Department of Public Health Nursing
College of Nursing
University of Illinois at Chicago
Chicago, Illinois

Margaret M. McGrath, DNSc
Assistant Professor
College of Nursing
University of Rhode Island
Kingston, Rhode Island

Afaf Ibrahim Meleis, Ph.D.
Professor
School of Nursing
University of California at San Francisco
San Francisco, California

Contents

Introduction

As with the first edition of *Role Theory: Perspectives For Health Professionals,* we are indebted to our students for important questions and insights. These questions have prompted us to enlarge upon several areas for this second edition. These insights include the knowledge base relevant to symbolic interaction and the theory and research related to gender roles.

We have found that for students using the first edition, symbolic interaction is a new and exciting theoretical perspective, one they identify as particularly relevant for studying clinical problems. We have determined, however, that students have difficulty identifying the works on symbolic interaction, primarily because these are not systematized to the same extent as those on structural role theory. Therefore, we have made a special effort to include well-documented sections on symbolic interaction in the new and many of the revised chapters where such information is relevant and particularly in Chapter Two that traces the historical development of symbolic interaction ideas.

Interest among students in knowledge related to gender roles is partly a response to the relevance of the knowledge but also to the need for systematic study in this area. We have attempted to integrate knowledge of gender roles into each chapter and have added a new chapter, authored by Kritek, to present the theory and research on gender roles in a coherent manner.

In the second edition of *Role Theory* we decided to strengthen the theoretical ideas and integrate both symbolic interaction and structural role theory into several chapters. Chapter One by Margaret Hardy and Two and Three were developed to establish the theoretical groundwork for this book. The second chapter includes a discussion of the development of role theory and identifies symbolic interaction and structural role theory as the major branches of role theory. This theoretical view has been purposefully extended by Conway in Chapter Three and by Margaret Hardy and William Hardy in Chapter Seven. In Chapter Two the authors trace the development of symbolic interaction in detail in order to illustrate the notion of stages of theory development. Symbolic interaction is also used extensively in Chapter Four by Hurley-Wilson and Chapter Nine by Lum.

References have been updated throughout the text in order to provide the student with extensive sources for further study. Recent critiques by scholars in the fields of symbolic interaction, structural role theory, health belief models, and organizational analysis have also been included in this edition. A few of the chapters have required very little updating since the first edition, reflecting the gradual incrementing of the underlying knowledge base.

We have left the basic organization of the book unchanged from the first edition. It seems worth repeating here that we still find no common agreement among so-called role theorists on a metaparadigm for role theory. Role theorists, however, are now more frequently combining the symbolic interaction perspective with the structural perspective of role theory (as in the first edition) to provide a theoretical knowledge base for structural and interactional analysis of phenomena. Thus, as before, we have organized knowledge about role development and role theory to include those major concepts that have commanded the attention of other scholars and for which there is the strongest empirical support. We have retained the emphasis on theory development in general and the two prevailing approaches to roles and role development, that is, to structuralism and symbolic interaction. We have also attempted to expand the discussion of the relevance of certain role interactions for the health care professional.

OVERVIEW

In Chapter One, Margaret Hardy discusses the general characteristics of scientific knowledge; special attention is given to the characteristics of the norms of science that guide human social activity and the characteristics that distinguish these norms from the norms that guide the practice of health professionals. She identifies the importance of the relative contribution each norm makes to knowledge and draws attention to the connection between theory-as-knowledge and theory-as-practice in a practice discipline. In this introductory chapter, Hardy reviews such criteria as semantic adequacy, empirical adequacy, and logical adequacy—all criteria that scientists use to analyze and evaluate knowledge. Furthermore, she identifies additional criteria that may be needed by practicing health professionals.

In Chapter Two, Margaret and William Hardy develop the notion of stages of scientific knowledge development and suggest that the type of theoretical work and research activity at each stage is determined by the level of knowledge development. The authors identify four major stages of theory development: (1) conceptualization, (2) systematic knowledge development, (3) systematic theorizing, and (4) formal theory development. They then proceed to draw upon symbolic interaction to illustrate each of these stages. To provide the essential background for understanding the illustrations, the authors describe the early development of symbolic interaction and trace its evolution. The authors identify important social, cultural, and political factors and the social context of the newly created University of Chicago that influenced the development of symbolic interaction.

A 1985 publication by a German social scientist, Joas, presents a systematic study of the development of Mead's ideas. This publication, through an analysis of Mead's notions relative to symbolic interaction, identifies Mead's theorizing as creative, purposeful, and unusually systematic. This same publication is a source of major insights and new information relative to Mead and to symbolic interaction. Only a few recent publications of American scholars identify some segments of this more complete and more comprehensive work.

Mead's theoretical work was directed by his commitment to the value of scientific methodology and his intent to develop a scientific knowledge base for symbolic interaction. His creation of concepts that were empirical, relevant, and readily observable differentiated his work from that of the dominant theories in psychology and psychiatry which focused on subjective phenomena (i.e., internal to persons). The concepts developed by Mead had observable counterparts and therefore could be measured. The newer and more comprehensive analysis of Mead's theoretical work provides a remarkable illustration of scientific knowledge development.*

Chapter Three by Conway continues the development of the theoretical background introduced in Chapters One and Two, but concentrates specifically on role theory. Conway provides an extensive overview of the two major perspectives under which roles historically have been studied, the structural (sometimes known as functional) and symbolic interaction perspectives. Consistent with the scientific knowledge which has been generated on organizations and systems, the utility of describing organizations as being comprised of systems of roles is discussed. In this perspective, roles are not viewed as fixed, precisely defined entities, but rather, as having a flexibility permitting the maintenance of open evolving systems. The symbolic interaction perspective is treated in greater length by Conway in this new edition of *Role Theory*. To illustrate the important potential inherent in a similar shift in social science publications in general, Conway selects "definition of the situation," a fundamental concept in symbolic interaction, and develops a subtheory by drawing on current theoretical and empirical works. Conway's review of the literature illustrates the convergence between the structuralist and symbolic interaction views of individuals, roles, and society. This convergence, important to health professionals, was initially proposed in the first edition of *Role Theory* (1978).

Chapter Four continues the logical sequence as Hurley-Wilson provides an in-depth discussion of the theoretical notions basic to an understanding of socialization. Here, as in Chapter Two, symbolic interaction is discussed extensively and is also integrated with the notions of structural role which places its focus on the needs of society. Hurley-Wilson carefully develops and documents the theoretical notions on socialization unique to symbolic interactionists and to structural theorists. The extensive theoretical development in the literature that is explicated by Hurley-Wilson reflects Mead's introduction of a theoretical focus on conditions and processes that make it possible for society to be influential on the development of human nature and individuals. Hurley-Wilson brings to the readers' attention the capability of generalizing Mead's notions on socialization by explicating the nature of this concept and its relevance to children and adults. In addition she explores the nature of the continuities and discontinuities that occur when role transitions are made from childhood roles to adult roles. Hurley-Wilson provides numerous references to encourage the student to explore primary sources to learn more about this important and continuously evolving aspect of role theory.

In Chapter Five Conway explores the concept of professional autonomy within the bureaucratic setting. This chapter has been expanded to include *contingency* theory with a brief critique of the assumptions underlying this model of

---

*The perspective provided by the discussions in Chapter Two is important for gaining a fuller understanding of the subsequent chapters in the book.

organizations. Major contradictions in findings based on research about effectiveness as a measure of the contingency model are discussed. Retained in this edition are the salient features of bureaucratic organizations that may influence autonomy in the process of actualization of professional roles. Findings from some of the more recent research publications on professional role enactment in bureaucratic settings are cited. Contrary to a pervasive notion that the need of organizations to maintain their routine is a barrier to the work autonomy of professionals, Conway notes that the burden of evidence from recent research suggests that the organization may actually enhance the autonomy of professionals.

In Chapter Six, Calkin explores two general views of organizational thought, the rational and the political. The rational school of thought contains the ideas of the structural-functional and contingency theorists. In contrast the ideas of the political theorists are reflected in the focus of the Marxist, political-economic theorists, and others. The views of the political school are offered as a counterpoint to the culturally dominant view of the rationalists and the associated ideas of the political school are developed to account for role behaviors of health care professionals. In this latter perspective the issue is the politics of organizations rather than the administration of organizations for unitary goals. The point of view taken in this chapter is that the study of complex organizations and their environments provides a basis for understanding that is critical for the study of social behavior of organizational members. This chapter offers the student a contextual background against which to assess the more normative and individualistic view of roles and role enactment.

The student will find that Chapter Seven (by Margaret and William Hardy), in which theoretical assumptions about role stress and strain are analyzed, provides a rich source of references related to role enactment problems. Most of the content of Chapter 7 is new. This chapter includes the development of a strong theoretical base for understanding role stress and the types of role stress. This base comes from symbolic interaction, structural role theory, and social exchange theory. The authors carefully identify the contrasting theoretical views of role stress held by proponents of symbolic interaction and structural role theory. Another addition to this chapter is a discussion of social changes external to the health care system and changes in health care roles, both of which provide new sources of role stress. The authors note that both technology and changes in gender roles have combined to make the nurse/physician/patient interaction more problematic than heretofore. The basic typology of role stress developed by Margaret Hardy (1978) is used to organize the discussion of role stress but the discussion has been strengthened and expanded significantly. Two new bodies of knowledge have been included for their value in extending our knowledge of role stress and role strain. These are stress related to women's roles and stress related to nurse's roles. The authors have assumed in developing this chapter that the role stress and role strain model and the stress typology, introduced in the previous edition, together with the extended theoretical analysis, and discussion of the types of role stress would provide insight and useful knowledge for understanding roles and role stress in the health care system.

The theoretical orientation which Margaret and William Hardy developed in Chapter Seven is carried over to Chapter Eight to provide a basis for their discussion of managing role strain. The chapter begins with the assumption that the symbolic interaction view of role stress as a "problematic situation" and the related tension associated with an increased level of awareness are similar to role strain. The notions of role bargaining and negotiation are introduced as a constructive means of reducing role strain. Social exchange theory is used to augment these theoretical notions and to provide access to an empirical body of knowledge on bargaining. Structural role theory is used to identify conditions that may alter the nature of role bargaining. The chapter concludes with an analysis of the consequences that prolonged role stress may have on role performance in organizations.

In Chapter Nine the concept of socialization is enlarged from the previous edition by Lum through the inclusion of theoretical notions related to reference groups. Lum perceives that the role occupant looks beyond his or her immediate others for an evaluation of personal behavior and chooses as his or her evaluative reference point selected other persons or groups who provide cues for behavioral responses. While emphasizing that professional socialization is a life-long process, Lum brings out the complexity of the task facing the neophyte professional. Following Lum's review of selected research in which students preparing for medicine and nursing careers were the subjects of study, one is prompted to ask: does a learning environment that accepts the student as a junior "colleague" offer a superior socialization experience to the one which treats the student as a "novice"?

In Chapter Ten, McGrath re-examines the Queen Bee Syndrome. In updating the Queen Bee chapter the author explores and extends the notion of the Queen Bee Syndrome initially developed by Halsley (1978) by including significant theoretical thinking related to this syndrome and by using appropriate concepts from both symbolic interaction and structural role theory.

The Queen Bee Syndrome, McGrath points out, portrays an intriguing pattern of role conflict resolution by females in administrative positions. McGrath describes Halsley's work in some detail. She follows this with a description of a recent study of nurse educators in which some of Halsley's research is replicated. The major strength of this chapter is the sound knowledge base that is developed to account for the dynamics of the Queen Bee Syndrome. McGrath concludes her chapter with the intriguing notion that the conditions that foster leadership behavior and the Queen Bee Syndrome may preclude the development of mentoring, a notion which nurses have proposed as important for the development of professional nurses.

Chapter Eleven by Bullough reviews the concept of stratification and traces its implications for the health care systems. She identifies gender and race as irrational variables that influence the nature of stratification. Any analysis of health care systems is complicated by the steep power gradient which is comprised of high-status, high-paid physicians at one end and many low-status, low-salaried persons at the other. This steep power gradient complicates interaction by replacing potentially collegial roles with superordinate and subordinate roles. The emergence of physicians as high status professionals interferes with the functioning of the bureaucratic health care institution.

A significant characteristic of the system is the wide discrepency between salaries at the top and those at the bottom of the status hierarchy. The would-be professional should understand that it is not one's competence alone that determine one's location within a hierarchy of professionals, but that other variables such as social class or gender may be important determinants.

In Chapter Twelve, Kritek traces the origins of sexually ascribed roles, drawing on anthropologic, psychological, and feminist literature to show how, historically, gender has relegated women to less important roles in health care. She raises and discusses an all important question relative to women's expected contributions in the health care field: if being female is associated with "unwellness," what are the implications for nurses as health care providers? The position of *dominants* versus *subordinates* (i.e. generally men versus women) in society is explored. She traces the influence of a large body of research in psychology that, she asserts, is based on the unquestioned assumptions that gender typing and adjustment to society's gender role ideology are both desirable and "healthy" for women. More recent perspectives on women's roles and emerging new roles are provided. Kritek points to an apparent paradox, that of women who in their eagerness to challenge male dominance structures, find themselves co-opted by these structures and ultimately utilize male values to perpetuate male norms.

In Chapter Thirteen, as in the first edition, Hinshaw addresses the issue of how to empirically study roles. She raises two provocative questions: "Why are social attitudes and opinions related to health care roles and role performance important to study?" and "What are the problems in operationalizing measures of such role phenomena?" She proceeds to answer these questions by drawing on psychophysics and S. S. Steven's method of magnitude estimation. Stevens was able to use this method to establish psychophysical laws in the form of power functions relating sensation to stimulus magnitude. This method, which has been used extensively in psychology, has been adapted to measure emotions, social values, and attitudes. Hinshaw's research over the years has identified the value of the magnitude estimation scale in the study of role attitudes. The scale generates ratio data and can be used in computer-based theoretical modeling. Hinshaw's chapter provides useful information for advancing both research and theory related to roles. The author explains the value of the method of magnitude estimation to measure subjective attitudes, employing as the example for analysis the complexity of a set of tasks in patient care required of nurses. Hinshaw points out the importance of this type of measurement for health professionals, citing the fact that frequently the questions asked about quality of and satisfaction with health care are subjective phenomena that do not lend themselves to measurement by traditional quantitative methods. Although this type of scaling has not yet received wide acceptance by health professionals, its methodological and empirical implications should be of considerable interest to the serious student.

Meleis, the author of a new Chapter Fourteen, has a strong orientation to theoretical knowledge and research related to symbolic interaction. For these reasons, she was asked to develop a chapter combining the structural role theory notion of "sick role" (Parsons, 1955) with some of the symbolic interaction conceptualizations related to illness and to integrate into it important symbolic interaction notions such as the flexibility of interaction and the influence of the social context on interaction. Given these general directions Meleis has produced a brief chapter which combines structural role theory and symbolic interaction as a basis for understanding the patient vis-à-vis the health care system.

In the final chapter, Marston-Scott reviews the conditions under which individuals may take, or fail to take, action to maintain health. The author reviews Becker's Health Belief Model and its major assumptions. She then presents several more recent studies in which these assumptions are investigated. The findings of these studies have particular relevance for health professionals, especially nurses, since many of them were tests of experimental interventions using subjects with known health impairment. Of special interest is a section on the potential of behavior modification and contingency contracting with individuals who wish to modify their health behaviors but have difficulty doing so.

We believe that for the health practitioner the practical value of greater knowledge about self and other roles cannot be overestimated. We have not intended that this role theory text be considered exhaustive, but rather that it be a meaningful stimulus for the reader. We believe that serious students will discover for themselves the exciting possibilities of drawing from the theoretical constructs and practical examples in this text knowledge that they can then test and apply in the development of their own professional role.

Acknowledgments

The editors wish to thank those who made significant contributions to this book and made the second edition of *Role Theory* possible. We are particularly indebted to our authors for their superior work and their contribution to make this a quality publication.

Margaret Hardy wishes to acknowledge the extent to which the master's and doctoral degree students from Schools of Nursing at Boston University and the University of Rhode Island influenced the content and nature of this, the second edition of *Role Theory*. Similarly, Mary Conway owes thanks to students at the Medical College of Georgia. It has been a pleasure to be present when these emerging scholars express surprise and excitement with the insight, new perspective or meaning that they gain through the use of role theory. For the master's students from Boston and Rhode Island the excitement often came when frustrating and often impossible work became comprehensible and even manageable. For the doctoral students, the insight came in working analytically with role theory, and finding that the notions of typology, taxonomy, and theory were no longer elusive.

Some of the doctoral candidates from Boston University, including Eileen Murphy, Barbara Whitmyer, Ann Hurley, Margaret McGrath, Pat Burbank, and Nancy Wells contributed individually and in a special way to this book; their ideas and dedication were invaluable. Nancy deserves a special thanks for the comprehensive and theoretically based index found in this edition.

Margaret Hardy also credits the doctoral students who formed the committee responsible for the Boston University Nursing Science Theory Development Colloquia over the last five years for raising and sustaining a new and higher level of knowledge on meta-theoretical issues among doctoral students across the country. The scholarly interests of the committee members and those who attended the annual colloquium necessitated that the strong orientation towards the research literature which characterized the first edition be balanced by a fuller development of theory. This has been undertaken for this edition. Clearly, the 110 plus who attended the yearly colloquium would soon be among the faculty in academe who would use this book.

Not coincidentally, the First Doctoral Colloquium Committee was comprised of sudents in a Theory Seminar in which Professor Hardy proposed for the first time that doctoral students use role theory systematically as a means of illustrating some of the more abstract and difficult ideas in their meta-theoretical readings.

The group of students found the class stimulating; they worked with terminology they had never used before and enjoyed the challenge of new ideas. The group wished to continue learning about theory and decided that this could best be done through a colloquium. The doctoral students who spearheaded this effort were Christine Bridges, Bianca Chambers, Margaret McGrath, Francine Brim, Toni McKenna, Trish Gibbons, Ann Hurley, Nancy Wells, and Kathy Simon. Many other doctoral students were active participants over the last five years.

The editors are particularly appreciative of the work of Bill Hardy on this book; he is the hidden editor. His editing and masterful use of the computer helped create this book as it stands today. Although he is cited as co-author on three chapters, he has made invaluable contributions to other chapters.

The editors recognize the important help of Marion Kalstein-Welch, the Executive Editor, Nursing at Appleton & Lange, in enabling this edition of *Role Theory* to reach our readers.

The writing of the chapter "Role Stress and Role Strain" was supported in part by a summer fellowship to Margaret Hardy from the University of Rhode Island (1986).

1

Perspectives on Science

Margaret E. Hardy

PERSPECTIVES ON DEVELOPING A
SCIENTIFIC KNOWLEDGE BASE

The prevention of illness and the promotion and maintenance of health are goals for all health professionals. To meet these goals, health professionals frequently draw upon the steadily evolving knowledge of the social sciences. This knowledge base, although relatively new, is already a resource that may be used to improve the management, delivery, and effectiveness of the services offered by each of the health care professions. Since a health care professional who is to use scientific knowledge must often go to documents and publications that scientists have developed for their own use, it is appropriate that we explore the nature of the scientific community and its work before considering the application of its product. Furthermore, a discussion of the characteristics of scientific knowledge will make it possible for the professional to be a more discerning and critical reader and user of such scientific knowledge as role theory.

Although most health professionals are well aware that science is a continuous, self-correcting enterprise involving theory development, research for empirical testing, and subsequent refinement of theory, they are usually less aware that science is a social activity with its own standards of behavior and goals. The goals of science and the associated norms of the scientific community are not necessarily congruent with the goals and norms guiding the clinical practice of health professionals.

The following sections discuss the characteristics of science as an organized activity guided by strong norms. This framework makes it possible to understand the activity of scientists and differentiate them from such action-oriented persons as nurses, physicians, and social workers. Next a brief historical overview of role theory and its branches is presented, followed by a discussion of how scientific knowledge progresses through identifiable stages. The branch of role theory with the longest history (85 years) will be used to illustrate this notion of stages of theory development.

Chapter 2 and subsequent chapters utilize two perspectives within role the-

The author is indebted to W. L. Hardy, Ph.D. for his thought-provoking ideas and his helpful editing of this chapter. He contributed to the shaping of this chapter in innumerable ways.

ory. One perspective is symbolic interaction, and the other is structral (role) theory. In Chapter 2 an overview of the theoretical strands of role theory will be discussed, and symbolic interaction will be examined in considerable historical detail. This will provide an opportunity to identify influential theoretical developments and the social scientists associated with each of them. In addition, a review of the development of this perspective should sensitize the reader to the time and work necessary to develop a scientifically based body of knowledge. Symbolic interaction will also be used to illustrate other general characteristics of scientific knowledge. In particular it will be used to illustrate the notion that there are identifiable *stages* of knowledge development.

This discussion of symbolic interaction should also increase the reader's awareness that institutions and social conditions can foster or inhibit the growth of scientific knowledge and the nature of that knowledge. In addition, analysis of the initial work in symbolic interaction illustrates how individuals can, at one time, function as empirically based scientists generating scientific knowledge, and at another time, function as citizens, actively working on projects aimed at improving social conditions and minimizing the devastating effects of social problems. It had become clear at the turn of the century that there was a major effort to separate the role of scientist from the role of social reformer or practitioner. Although science is usually presented as an objectively developed body of knowledge, it will become apparent in reading about the development of symbolic interaction that values, and continuous involvement with destructive social conditions and problems, can influence the nature of social knowledge. Furthermore, the work on symbolic interaction illustrates how time-consuming it is to develop a new science knowledge base and yet, how necessary it is at the same time, to maintain an overriding commitment to an enterprise, such as science, that in the long run can improve the human condition.

The early researchers in symbolic interaction deemed that progress in science was impossible if scientists did not separate their scientific role from their role as citizens, or if they were "committed to an approach." Dogma, ideologies and schools of thought were eschewed; time and energy were devoted to the development of empirical work which was closely guided by theory. For all these reasons it is valuable to examine the development of symbolic interaction.

The reason for discussing stages of knowledge development is to illustrate the idea that knowledge at various levels of development is different, examined differently, used differently, and evaluated differently. Early knowledge development usually involves identifying loosely connected clusters of concepts for which there is no real inter-subjectivity present. Such knowledge is found in descriptions of social phenomena (communication, interaction, influencing strategies) extant in a health care setting. Knowledge from the later stages of knowledge development typically consists of interrelated sets of statements and concepts. The relative precision of definitions and stated relationships makes prediction and clinical intervention possible. That is to say, more advanced scientific theory may provide a knowledge base for developing intervention strategies, whereas clusters of concepts cannot do so. For these reasons it is valuable to examine the development of symbolic interaction.

It is assumed that scientific knowledge-based rational decisions are both wanted and possible for clinical interventions. Most social scientists expect that their work will generate a cumulative knowledge base that can be used by others to improve the quality of human existence. The use of knowledge from the social sciences by health providers furnishes a rich opportunity to improve both the delivery of health care and the health and sense of well-being of the vulnerable sick. Possibly an existing set of scientific knowledge has not previously been used to deal with problems which are in the domain of the providers' responsibility, clinical skills, and interest. It is clear that scientifically skilled providers are in key positions to draw on an established body of knowledge and to use their unique perspective to work on the problems of concern. Of course, they are also in an excellent position to identify "problematic" areas requiring research. Clinicians encountering such problems and utilizing an interdisciplinary approach have often been very successful. Role theory has been particularly noted for interdisciplinary work; indeed it is the product of interdisciplinary work. It may be especially useful for the inventive.

A body of scientific knowledge that focuses on the reciprocal influence of interacting persons and their social environment is valuable for today's health care providers. The nature of the subject matter, with its focus or unit of analysis consisting of two or more persons, augments its potential for significant intervention strategies. The relatively lengthy history of role theory and the extent of cumulative scientific knowledge increases its potential as an invaluable resource.

SCIENCE AS A SOCIAL SYSTEM

There are at least three generally accepted meanings of the term *science*. Science may refer to a body of well-grounded knowledge, to a method of inquiry, or to a social system that generates knowledge. Science as a body of knowledge refers to cumulative theory and research findings that are generic, re-researchable, valid, and generalizable. Science as a method of inquiry refers to a rational, objective, repeatable, empirical method for developing cumulative analytical and generalizable knowledge—generally focusing on research methodologies. Finally, science as a social system involves focusing on the goals, norms, and activities of scientists as they "do" science.

Science as a social system comprises a network of roles. As such it can be viewed in terms of the interrelated social structures, processes, activities, and products that are common to groups of persons engaged in developing a substantive body of knowledge through the scientific method. Those in the health care professions utilizing the products of the social system of science find themselves trying to make sense of a body of scientific knowledge as they pursue their general goal of achieving desirable patient outcomes.

As groups of scientists with their special skills engage in generating knowledge, a system of roles and norms emerges. The social context within which scientists work has a marked influence on that work. The general social context for undertaking scientific work is discussed next, in terms of a community of scientists. Not all social systems generate a sense of community, but those that do create a shared culture of social order among their members.

Community of Scientists

The social nature of science has been discussed by several authors. Merton has introduced and discussed particularly important ideas concerning the social nature of scientific work. Storer (1966), working with the ideas of Merton, described the social characteristics of science rather fully. He linked the scientific ethos identified by Merton to a social systems description of the organization of scientists. The social system of scientists can be more fully understood through analyzing the structure in terms of the concepts of role theory. It can be described as a network of professionals who function within a set of interrelated roles and positions. Their role behavior is guided by a special set of universal norms. This strong normative structure is learned and internalized during the process of professional socialization. The perspective learned as a graduate student is the ethos of science. The ethos is the same for international scientists as for Americans. It is the same for physical, biological, and social scientists.

Scientists form a social group of professionals who value rationality over intuition and objectivity over subjectivity in the study of phenomena. Their scientific work attempts to minimize personal biases by making use of impartial, neutral methods of observation.

Science may exist in a supportive or a socially hostile environment. Merton (1968) identified hostility towards science as likely to exist when the results or methods of science are antagonistic to satisfaction of important values. A less rational source of hostility arises when there is a feeling that the values of the scientific ethos are incompatible with those of other esteemed institutions. Normally scientific theories are judged on their logical consistency, the reliability of their empirical base, and their generality. Merton initiated the systematic study of science in 1930 when he wrote of the problems scientists were encountering in Nazi Germany.[1] Characteristics of the researcher are expected to be considered irrelevant to the quality of the knowledge produced.[2]

He identified the ethos of science and its normative structure as the means by which science is able to remain *autonomous and progressive* in spite of changes and pressures from political, economic, and religious societal institutions. Science, just as any other social activity, is not immune from attack, restraint, and suppression.[3] Merton proposed that the norms of science were a significant force for the advancement of scientific theory. He saw scientists as gaining protection from external social pressures through the ethos of science and by the common social bond created among scientists in their endorsement of the norms of science.

T.S. Kuhn, in a much-discussed historical study of science, identified the importance of a community of scientists to the progress of knowledge. Like Merton before him, Kuhn has also described social factors which influence the development of scientific knowledge.[4] Two of his proposals are particularly important in any discussion of science and the development of scientific knowledge. He identified both a *community of scientists* and a *dominant paradigm* as essential for scientific progress (T.S. Kuhn, 1970). His perspective has influenced thinking in many scientific and applied disciplines, including sociology and nursing.

Kuhn claims that if a body of knowledge can be subsumed by a dominant paradigm, then the advancement of scientific knowledge is relatively nonproblematic. A paradigm, or what I term a *Research Tradition Based on Theory* (RTBT), provides a common perspective and approach for working with related theories. The relationship between a RTBT and the theoretical work it subsumes is depicted in Figure 2, Chapter 2. The bases for introducing this notion is discussed more fully in Chapter 2.

To work within an RTBT means that many aspects of doing science in a particular substantive area are not a problem for the majority of scientists. For scientists working on an RTBT it is very clear what methodological direction their work will take—even though the theory they work with may have serious ambiguities. The tradition determines the theoretical concepts, the research questions, the research methods, and the focus of study. In this book the RTBT of role is utilized. An RTBT may subsume several related theories; here the focus is primarily on two, namely, symbolic interaction, and structural role theory. These two theories have their own sets of concepts, appropriate research questions, and methods.

To make sense of the activities of scientists the notion of a "community of scientists" and the powerful normative structures of science need to be taken into account. The notion of community of scientists is discussed first.

The term *community of scientists* refers to a group of persons who have both a common bond and a common scientific perspective. Members of such groups are brought together by a shared commitment to the development of special knowledge in a specific area—through the use of the scientific method. One or more of these groupings may exist in any one discipline; sometimes they are interdisciplinary. Development of role theory has always been an interdisciplinary activity. The scientific community working on role-related theories is primarily composed of anthropologists, sociologists, and social psychologists. This group of people is aware of their unique and separate identity as a group. This identity is based on their consensus on a particular perspective that they endorse and the science they undertake, rather than on their originating disciplines. They have a sense of solidarity and purpose that separates them from other groups; this specialness or "we-ness" reflects their common bond, shared sets of values, interests, norms, and common commitment which operate as they work together to achieve a common goal of developing scientific knowledge of roles.

Scientists have specific expectations for the proper role behavior of their colleagues. This behavior is learned, as it is in other professions, through the process of professional socialization (see Chap. 9). This professional socialization requires long hours of intense work over many years. When the normative behavior of science is successfully learned and enacted, the elders in the scientific discipline acknowledge it through the granting of a doctoral degree. Subsequent scientific work is expected to be of high quality regardless of where the work of science is conducted. Much scientific work is conducted independently in the isolation of one's laboratory.[5]

In science the individual and the community are inextricably entwined. The ability to think differently than others, to see what others do not see, to use a body of knowledge differently all are functions of creative and informed minds. The value and success of work on creative ideas rest to a large extent on the acceptance and support the work receives in the community of scientists. The individual-group relationship has been depicted in terms of a dialectic process. Individual rationality functions within the scientific group; science is not seen as an individual activity.

Appropriate scientific behavior is sustained through the strong norms and sanctions enforced by the scientific community. The institutionalized scientific norms of universalism, organized skepticism, communality, and disinterestedness comprise the ethos of modern science and are very powerful (Merton, 1973, p. 270). Groups governed by these norms and having the characteristics just outlined form our scientific communities. Thus, science is not generally the product of individuals working on their own, but rather it is the product of a social group. These groups endorse what are considered to be appropriate scientific behaviors. The value of any knowledge generated is assessed in terms of the rational approach taken, the systematically controlled method utilized, and the appropriateness of the resulting data. The scientific study of roles and norms is incorporated in the idea of a community of scientists.[6]

The norms of science are discussed next. To facilitate a comprehension of scientific knowledge and the writings of scientists and to make possible the appropriate utilization of scientific work, it behooves the health professional to gain a general understanding of scientific activity, including a comprehension of the norms of science. The behavior of scientists and that of the health professional are complementary; different norms, however, promote different role behaviors.

THE NORMS OF THE SCIENTIFIC COMMUNITY: A COMPARISON OF THE ACTIVITIES OF HEALTH CARE PROFESSIONALS AND SCIENTISTS[7]

Persons working in the health care arena, such as physicians, nurses, physical therapists, and social workers, are usually identified as belonging to a profession. Scientists also are members of a profession. Accordingly, because both sets of persons have professionalism in common they are likely to share at least some common norms, namely, those that guide the activities of members of professions. There are, however, many norms they do not share because the *goals* of the two groups are quite different. The health care professional's function is to prevent or solve health-related problems; the scientist's function is to solve "answerable" scientific or knowledge-related problems. In seeking solutions to such problems scientists are guided by a universally accepted set of norms and standards consistent with the scientific method. Health professionals are also influenced by a set of norms that guide their choices and behaviors as they work to improve the health of patients. Health care professionals and scientists may differ in their modes of thinking and in their decision-making processes; they definitely do differ in their intended outcomes and in how they go about their work. Health care professionals are "doers"; they do things for people, they use things (technology) to "do" for people, they want things and ideas that "work." The effectiveness of an idea is judged by the resulting outcomes utilizing it, rather than by its explanatory power. There is concern with the improved functioning and health of the individual case and its unique needs and variability. Scientists, on the other hand, do things with words and ideas; they may use special equipment or technology to test ideas; they are concerned about the standardization of meaning and measurements and the empirical validity of knowledge. Their empirical findings are usually based on a theoretical foundation and are subject to scrutiny and to repeated examination by peers. Scientists have the ultimate goal of developing a cumulative body of valid knowledge and they are concerned about the general rather than the unique case. They look for counter cases or instances that may throw an hypothesis into question. Health care professionals, on the other hand, are encouraged to use knowledge that has reasonable empirical support; they look for a cumulative knowledge base. The knowledge that scientists develop may or may not be used (in the applied sense). Use of knowledge is usually determined by practitioners or those interested in applied science. Problematic areas in the health sciences may or may not attract the interest and attention of scientists from outside the health professions. Hence there is an increasing number of health-focused scientists—from the social sciences, medicine, nursing, or social work—who are able to bring their scientific expertise to health-related problems which are important to other health professionals.

Both scientists and health professionals write for publication, but the purpose and nature of their writings differ markedly. Health professionals write in their professional journals to share clinical expertise, often through case studies, whereas scientists write to share their ideas and other works, often based on generalizations derived from study of many subjects, and to have their works and ideas critiqued. Publishing is an integral part of scientists' work.

Because the goals of health professionals are different from those of scientists, it is not surprising to find that many norms governing their activities and interests are different. An examination of the dominant norms of science may help health professionals to better understand the characteristics of acceptable scientific work and may help them to more readily discriminate between potentially useful scientific work and work that is outside the realm of science. It also may make them better able to differentiate between problems that science can and cannot solve. Health care professionals should also be aware that scientists will often be more interested in minutiae and counter instances that go against a theory than in vast amounts of data that support it. Furthermore, an awareness of the incongruity between some norms of science and some norms guiding the conduct of health care professionals may decrease the frustration of the health care professional in dealing with scientific personnel and the scientific literature. Such an awareness may also increase health care professionals' skill in identifying problematic areas in the clinical setting that could benefit from scientific research.

The activities of scientists continue to be the subject of important studies by sociologists interested in understanding the development of knowledge. Major contributions to our understanding of the social behavior of scientists have been made by Barber (1952), Hagstrom (1965), Merton (1973), Mitroff and Kilmann (1978), Hargens (1975) and Bleier (1984). The analytic work of Merton and complementary work by Storer provide a particularly useful and sound basis for examining the norms of science. Merton has identified four institutional imperatives that form the basis of the scientific ethos. These are: *universalism, organized skepticism, communality,* and *disinterestedness* (Merton, 1973, p. 270). Storer (1966) seeks to extend Merton's ideas by studying science as a social system and incorporating the dynamics of social exchange to describe behavior between scientists. The social system is seen to provide normative expectations, costs, and rewards for the individual scientist. The norms prescribe that scientists be detached, skeptical, impersonal, self-critical, and open-minded in their use of objective data. Conformity by scientists to these norms makes a reliable, cumulative knowledge development possible.

Roles and Norms

Theory and research on roles have consistently shown that the rights and obligations (normative expectations) associated with particular positions evolve as occupants interact with others in related positions. General norms are also in operation—regardless of role specialization. Norms of science have developed over time as scientists have worked to achieve their ultimate goal, the development of objective knowledge about the nature of the external world. Scientific norms are evident in the behavior of the scientists and in the behavior of the scientific community. Through the occupancy of their roles, scientists internalize the norms of science and create or modify their organizational structure (Mitroff & Kilman, 1978).[8]

The dominant science norms, identified later in this chapter, form broad guidelines that define, determine, and delimit the activities of scientists. These norms are an essential part of the ethos of science since they are strong directives for all actions of scientists. They are expressed in terms of preferences, prescriptions, and proscriptions; they are transmitted by example and are enforced by sanctions and rewards.

Variability in role behavior. Enactment of roles is not solely a matter of conforming to existing rules; such enactments, may be subject to considerableva-riability. In depicting science as a social activity with a general set of norms, one must expect that individual scientists or groups of scientists may implement the norms in different ways. Variability in role behavior and the adherence to norms will be a function of several factors. Role behavior of scientists may vary as a function of the social conditions and the individual scientist's negotiation of reality given the presence of counter norms (Mulkay, 1979). Symbolic interaction studies suggest that individuals negotiate their own interpretation of the social order. Formal rules and obligations may be modified or replaced by others as role occupants negotiate a social order which will foster social activity, acceptable role behaviors, norms, and achievement of the organizational goals. The negotiated order usually fits within the broad social context of norms and role systems.

As in any study of human behavior, some science norms are found to be more mandatory than others. For example, severe sanctions are likely to follow discovery of the "fixing" of one's data in science, whereas the reporting of scientific knowledge in vague and general terms (or possibly in glowing terms) in popular nonscientific journals is likely to receive minimal sanction from the community of scientists.

Variation in behavior among scientists may be a function of responding to one or more of the strong counter norms that are associated with most dominant norms (Merton, 1968). For example, the dominant norm of disinterestedness coexists with the scientists' commitment to basic ideas, to their wish to have their own ideas acknowledged by peers, and to their emphasis on originality of ideas.

As in any social activity, some role occupants may violate the very norms which are considered important. If the violation is significant to the community, the person's behavior will be identified as deviant and sanctions will be applied by the group in an attempt to return the behavior of the deviant to a point that the group can accept.

NORMS

Universalism

The norm of universalism reflects a general orientation in science toward both knowledge and knowledge development. In this view there is an expectation that universal laws can be developed to explain, predict, and control phenomena in the external world.[9] This view is often extended to include a belief in the existence of underlying uniformities that can be summarized in empirical generalities and expressed in universal laws. This norm also reflects a commitment to the value of knowledge developed in an objective manner using the scientific method.

According to Merton (1973, p. 270) universalism means " . . . that all truth-claims are subjected to pre-established impersonal criteria consonant with observation and with previously confirmed knowledge." Merton goes on to say that personal and social characteristics of protagonists are not to be weighed in the determination of the value of their scientific contributions. This norm is reflected, for example, in the establishment of peer-review committees for the review of potential publications, the awarding of grants, and the making of university appointments.

The application of this norm means that the development of knowledge in diverse scientific fields is guided by a standard set of criteria and rules of evidence that transcend other differences among the contending intellectual traditions (Merton, 1975, p. 51). Pre-established standard scientific criteria of objectivity are rigorously applied to evaluate all knowledge claims in all disciplines before they are accepted as representing knowledge. Accordingly, in both the natural and social sciences the same principles of the scientific method of inquiry are taught to students. Advances of scientific knowledge in the social sciences and health fields, if to be accepted as "scientific," are expected to conform to the standards of science already established by the natural sciences because these sciences are acknowledged to be the mode for "successful" science.

The norm of universalism refers to the fact that there generally is agreement on the basic nature of science. Up to now, however, the social sciences have generated such soft or inconclusive data that theory developments has not progressed beyond elementary formulations and into laws (Benton, 1977).

The norm of universalism implies that the truth and value of scientific work depends only on the merit of the work. Merton proposed that the truth of scientific work is independent of the scientist's sex, prestige, nationality, political views, and professional allegiances. Some research, however, has identified that in the past the gender of the scientist may have influenced publication and the perceived value of the publication—which is a normative violation. Once identified, violations of the norms of science such as this are usually corrected. The value of scientific work is, according to the norm of universalism, unrestricted also by time and geographical location. Recognition is based on the credibility and significance of the work itself, not on the person, time, or place associated with the contribution. Also, personal values, gain, and other social factors, such as career advancement and influence, are not factors that should influence the work of scientists.

Scientific activity involves the search for empirically based laws; the scientist looks for lawful relationships between variables and looks for conditions under which these relationships vary. For example, recent scientific work has focused on the theoretical statement that role overload decreases the quality of work performed. This relationship is modified by the personality structure of the role occupants. The more rigid the personality, the less likely that role overload will interfere with the quality of work.

Work is currently being directed at the empirical testing of theory and on an accumulation of empirically based knowledge. Every effort is usually made to remove possible sources of distortion that might decrease the likelihood of having valid knowledge. Observations are standardized and quantified, providing data that are then available for critique by colleagues. The validity of the knowledge is judged only relative to the tenets of scientific inquiry. This assessment is made by peers, i.e., the community of scientists; there is no other generally accepted authority. The tentative acceptance of a piece of research by the researcher's peers awaits further testing through replication of the study.[10]

Organized Skepticism

This norm implies an independence and an attitude of disbelief in the absence of empirical proof on the part of each and every scientist. Opinions and impressions are not acceptable sources of knowledge. Scientists are expected to sustain a critical attitude toward their own work and the work of their peers. This norm typifies an approach to the work of each individual scientist as well as to the work of groups of scientists. All scientific work must be subjected to objective assessment—it must be examined for its logical consistency and for its empirical validity. Although the ideals of objectivity and of empirical validation are usually apparent, it might be less obvious that this is a norm that specifies that theories and research are made public explicitly for the purpose of being scrutinized and critiqued by others. If scientific communities do these critiques and come to similar conclusions, then the knowledge has credibility. Research studies must be open for replication by others for the express purpose of validation or refutation. This norm of organized skepticism further implies that the theoretical reasoning, the measurement tools, and the specific techniques utilized in conducting research should be purposely made available for critical analysis and subsequent improvement by peers. Accordingly, much of the scientific literature details these tools, techniques, and processes and presents extensive critiques of each. Advances in knowledge development, whether theoretical or empirical, and critiques thereof, whether published in refereed journals (where the audience is composed of potential critiquers or informed peers) or presented at meetings, require a public forum for the purpose of identifying biases and other errors which may make a particular piece of knowledge less than "true."

Although the detailed critical dialogues in scientific journals may not interest people in applied fields, they can often be of considerable general value beyond their original purpose. For example, nurses may not be interested in a discussion of specific questions in a questionnaire, or of procedures used for measurement of social support by reference groups and the relationship of such groups to the pain experienced by arthritic women. The issues of reliability and validity of measures, however, are of critical importance because they are instrumental in determining the soundness of knowledge; and soundness is important to any person wishing to apply such knowledge. Often measurement instruments can be used for a purpose other than that for which they were developed. A practitioner interested in examining variability among clients may use an existing research tool to measure the degree of social support and the level of pain experienced. In making the tool selection, the original reported reliability and validity of the tool along with the available critiques must be taken into account.

This norm of organized skepticism, according to Storer (1966, p. 78), holds that each scientist is individually responsible for making sure that the previous research by others, which forms a basis for his own work, is valid. Furthermore, scientists are obligated to make public the work of others they believe to be in error. This requires an honest, critical evaluation of one's own work and of the related work of others. This activity is necessary to ensure that a valid knowledge base is generated and accounts for the extensive critical analysis of the methods and techniques in the relevant literature which scientists must undertake before they publish their own work. It also accounts for the extensive reporting of such work in the early sections of their publications and the frequent publication of critical reviews in science journals. Health care providers may perceive such critiques as being unduly harsh. The problems identified in the critique, however, may preclude the testability of a theory or mar the accurate and unequivocal interpretation of empirical findings. Publications of this type may be used by the clinician for another purpose, namely, to determine if the knowledge is sufficiently sound for it to be used in health promotion or in a clinical intervention.

This norm of organized skepticism implies that research will be replicated and will be replicated with specific, controlled changes in conditions. This process of replication is designed to determine if the lawful relationship between variables initially reported by one scientist are found by other scientists and to determine if the identified relationships hold up or change under specific modification of conditions. This information is important for examining the validity of empirical support, for identifying sources of inaccuracy, for increasing the precision and generality of predictions, and for extending the range of empirically based cumulative knowledge. Replications increase the credibility of a body of knowledge. For the practitioner, the specification of the conditions of measurement has a major bearing on the relevance of findings to a specific situation.

Communality

The norm of communality[11] refers to a norm that directs scientists to share their work with colleagues. Scientific knowledge in its broadest sense is not the property of any one discipline nor any one individual. Such knowledge is not individually owned (even though such appellations as Selye's theory of stress and Caplan's crisis theory suggest otherwise). Knowledge is a product of social collaboration. Individual contributions to knowledge are recognized and valued, but the product of the competitive cooperation among scientists—scientific knowledge—is common property (Merton, 1975, pp. 273–274). This type of collegiality mandates not only the sharing of scientific findings, but also the sharing of techniques, new ideas, and failures. Such sharing refers to joint efforts and responsibilities as well as to communication. Sharing knowledge of unsuccessful endeavors, dead ends, and other theoretical and methodological problems reduces the likelihood of subsequent wasted effort. This type of collegiality, offered freely and without favor, accelerates the growth of scientific knowledge. The norms of organized skepticism and communality together state that scientists have something vital to share with others, namely the outcomes of their own work and their critiques of others' work.

Disinterestedness

The norm of disinterestedness, according to Storer (1966, p. 79), makes it improper for scientists to profit personally from their work; it encourages persons to do science for science's sake alone. Merton discounts claims that personal motivation, passion for knowledge, altruistic concerns, and other special motives are the primary determinants of what appears to be an unusual degree of moral integrity among scientists. Rather, he sees the normative characteristics of science itself as a more plausible explanation for this integrity. The norm of disinterestedness is supported by the ultimate accountability of scientists to their peers (Merton, 1973, p. 276).

Commitment to Progress of Knowledge Rather Than to a Specific Theory or Technique.

An expectation closely related to disinterestedness encourages scientists to be open to new developments and to new approaches whenever theory or research suggests this to be appropriate. Ideally, scientists should not be biased or committed to a specific theory or to one method to the extent that contradictory ideas, differing views, new methods, and conflicting empirical evidence are intentionally overlooked or excluded. Scientists are committed to seeking scientific truth wherever the search leads. This norm suggests that scientists must be flexible, that they must fairly evaluate the state of knowledge, and that they must be informed of the most recent developments in their field.

A basic assumption of science is that a rational approach to knowledge development will result in changes and progress in any Research-Tradition-Based-Theory. The theory, the accumulated scientific knowledge, and the methodological techniques are expected to change and progress over time. What remains constant is the standard of rationality in the approaches to both theory development and research. The selective use of scientific methodology involves eliminating as much irrationality from the theory-based research as possible. The norms of science can be viewed as scientific behaviors that have become established over time because they facilitate the systematic rational development of knowledge. The norms within the community of scientists fosters this approach among scientists.

Norms of Science Not Necessarily Congruent with Norms of Health Professionals.

The norms of science may not be fully operational or valued in the health professions. Although this thesis is not discussed in detail here, consider, for example, the suggestion that the sharing of ideas and the careful documentation of new strategies of care and the documentation of their effectiveness are not a prime concern among the majority of nurses. Subjectivity, authority, tradition, and uniqueness are frequently more prevalent and often are more valued in the health professions than are objectivity of knowledge, empiricism, and generality.

The general norms described here guide the activities of scientists in all fields. Their effects are seen in the debates over concepts and methods that commonly occur at scientific meetings, in scientific publications, in the day-to-day activities of working scientists, and in the teaching of those aspiring to be scientists. Science can be depicted as a continuous, self-correcting social activity; it currently is seen by the majority of scientists as the only reliable method for advancing knowledge.

Although there are never-ending methodological and metatheoretical debates about the nature of science, the process of science goes on. The cycle of developing ideas, re-creating and reformulating them, then testing hypotheses and refining theories and concepts in light of the empirical evidence, is a slow but dependable process. Unfortunately, the inconclusiveness of knowledge and this slow, self-correcting method may make the use of scientifically based knowledge difficult and may contribute to the frustration of individuals in applied fields. It is hoped, however, that practitioners who understand the nature of scientific knowledge production will be more tolerant of debate over the nature of science, the meaning of specific concepts, the various methodologic issues, and the tolerance of conflicting or ambiguous empirical findings. Knowing that the social system of science has both different norms and different goals than does the social system of the health professions may make the generation and utilization of knowledge more comprehensible.

This discussion of the norms of science has been undertaken to make explicit the nature of scientific activity. The reader can compare the norms of science systematically with the norms and activities of the health professions.

SCIENTIFIC KNOWLEDGE

The long range goal in scientific work is to generate precise theories which make prediction and control possible. This goal requires time and the combined efforts of many scientists to accrue the knowledge. The social sciences are still in the early stages of developing scientific theory. Accordingly, many of their publications are directed at proposing ideas which might lead to important scientific progress.[12] It is often difficult for those outside a particular scientifically oriented discipline to recognize important scientific work that is underway and to identify the specific theories being developed.

All scientific publications have the potential for contributing to important scientific theory but it requires skill to determine on a day-to-day basis which of these are the more valuable publications. There is some general knowledge about theory which can be used as a basis for establishing critical criteria for analyzing scientific work. These criteria, which can be called metatheoretical criteria, are universal scientific knowledge and therefore useful to persons who read scientific publications in all disciplines.[13] This information is standard to science but is difficult for those not in the typical scientific disciplines to acquire. The criteria provide a means of systematically assessing and later comparing relevant scientific publications for their value.

In the health professions, interventions and treatments are based on scientific knowledge. Since this knowledge is not static and has been growing at a phenomenally rapid rate, it becomes mandatory to monitor it on a continuous basis. The metatheoretical criteria provide a systematic method for analyzing and evaluating scientific publications for their relative scientific merit and for determining their potential for making significant interventions.[14]

In order to use the metatheoretical criteria it is necessary to understand the general nature of scientific theory. Only then will the basis for selective application of the different criteria make sense.

THE NATURE OF SCIENTIFIC KNOWLEDGE

A Theoretical Perspective

Initial theorizing entails the difficult task of determining which segment of reality is worth analyzing and then sharing this knowledge with peers. It is a major achievement in early scientific work to recognize that scientific theory deals with only a small part of reality and that the focus is selective. No scientific theory explains everything in a discipline's domain even though early theorists may write copious material about a unified theory. The scientific publications in a new discipline are often discursive accounts of a theoretical perspective bolstered by empirical anecdotes. This work is tentative but often makes a convincing argument as to the significance of the scientific ideas. These early accounts are particularly difficult for newcomers to judge in terms of their scientific merit. In the long run, very few of the early ideas are likely to stand the rigors of full scientific evaluation.

The early scientific activities in a field begin as a loose set of ill-defined ideas, broadly applied. With time, these ideas become refined as they are more closely related to the empirical world (the work on role theory illustrates many of the characteristics of a newly developing perspective). The new ideas are seen initially as applying to a broad spectrum of phenomena; early work is discursive and lacks scientific rigor; some systematic descriptive work is used to illustrate the value of the theoretical ideas. It takes a long period of time for ideas to be proposed, revised and ultimately serve as a basis for research in a scientific manner.

The publications on role theory illustrate this progression. Theoretical activity began with the emergence of a theoretical idea which was expressed orally. This was followed by a period of discursive writing using anecdotal illustrations, some definitional work was undertaken and then followed by systematic descriptive research which illustrated the value of the approach. Only after a long period of time, systematic empirical scientific work was undertaken. The evolution of "role theory" has spanned an 85-year period.

The development of role theory will be discussed more fully in the next chapter. The writings, however, on role theory are typical of those in any developing body of knowledge and illustrate the need for the fledgling scientist to acquire special knowledge and skill to make sense of the literature. As is typical of a developing body of knowledge, role theory is not found in a coherent set of readings, but is dispersed throughout a variety of journals and books.

The term *theory* is often used in referring to the role literature, although the work is a long way from being truly scientific. It would be more accurate to describe *role* as a conceptual framework or a theoretical perspective because it basically consists of a cluster of concepts. Furthermore, the knowledge base is understood and expressed in everyday language rather than in specialized terminology. Most importantly, the connection between the major ideas or concepts is unspecified or ambiguous. In the next section the characteristics of scientific theory will be discussed, primarily to provide a comparison standard for use when assessing scientific knowledge.[15]

Theory

Scientific Theory. A scientific theory is a set of interrelated concepts, definitions, and statements that can be tested empirically. The purpose of theory is to increase our understanding and knowledge about the empirical world through the processes of explanation and prediction. It is expected that society will ultimately use such accrued knowledge to its benefit. The main focus of scientific work is to develop empirically based knowledge, to systematize the existing knowledge, to improve the precision of the explanatory and predictive processes, and to minimize the "error" in predictions based on them. This can be done generally through the development of circumscribed, moderate-scope theories which are testable. Such theories are composed of sets of important interrelated concepts. These concepts are clearly defined and have valid empirical referents. Theoretical statements specify the relationship between the concepts; thus scientific theories are composed of concepts and the statements which interrelate the concepts.

Sound understanding of theory, together with the ability to work systematically with existing scientific knowledge of roles, are urgently needed by practitioners in the health care field. Of the available theories from the social sciences, role theory has the potential of becoming one of the most important and useful for health care providers.

A Useful Framework for Analyzing Theory. A theory is a method of sharing useful and empirically relevant ideas with others. For analytic purposes, a scientific theory can be viewed as a language and examined in terms of its linguistic elements. Theory, as a language, can be divided into two major units for analysis. The first is a set of discrete units called the *terms* or *concepts*. The second is the *structure* or *interrelationship* between the concepts; this structure is specified in the theoretical statements of the theory.

The set of concepts are called the *semantic* portion of the theory. They provide the subject of the theory; the meanings of terms do change over time but the meanings always relate to the central theme of the theory. The meanings of concepts are understood in terms of their verbal *definitions*, their empirical *referents*, and their *semantic context*.

Identifying an idea, that is, *naming* or providing a *label* for it, is an important part of any theoretical analysis. Also, it is a vital, ongoing process in science. For example, role theory still has many ill-defined or inconsistently defined terms. There still exist vague ideas that are never fully defined or have ambiguous, conflicting, or multiple meanings. Keeping track of the ideas involves analyzing the labels and their associated definitions.

The relationships between the concepts are identified in theoretical statements. This portion of a theory is termed its *syntax*. The interrelationships are specified by rules and are determined by looking at the logical connections between the key ideas.

THE COMPONENTS OF A THEORY

Concepts. Concepts are the fundamental elements of any scientific theory. They are the basic elements used for selectively identifying phenomena, for thinking about a segment of reality, and for communicating about it to all others. Concepts are not isolated entities; they have meaning in relation to all other concepts. That is, their interpretation is connected with a semantic field. The notion of mother only has meaning, for example, if the terms child, father, or family are considered. Meaning may change over time as a result of social changes and as the body of available theoretical knowledge advances.

Concepts are abstractions drawn from experience. As such they refer to selected common analytical properties rather than to concrete entities. Abstract theoretical terms summarize general patterns rather than describe events, things, or conditions in their entirety. For instance, *role expectations* and *role conflict* are concepts in role theory that selectively focus our attention on social positions and specifically on the normative and self-defining aspects of roles. Concepts identify similarities in otherwise diverse phenomena. For example, role conflict refers to a social pattern found in families, work groups, friendships, occupations, and deviant subcultures. The ability to connect diverse entities on the basis of common ideas contributes to the value of a theory, identifies the theory's substantive focus, and utilizes the abstract and general features distinctive to concepts and hence to theory. Concepts give a theory its substantive focus and thereby provide a selective view of reality.

Definition and Meaning of Concepts. An important requirement of concepts is that they be defined and have empirical referents. Identifying an empirical referent for an analytical notion makes it possible for the concept to be part of a scientific development. Once empirical referents are identified for a concept, then the concept can gain stronger empirical value through the development of operational definitions. A concept that has an operational definition is of stronger empirical import than one that has only an empirical referent.

Definitions are tentative proposals of meaning for terms in a theory; such proposals may be accepted, modified, or rejected. Definitions can not be tested, nor validated, nor can they be identified as true or false. These activities are reserved for hypotheses. This is because concepts are ideas abstracted from experience and there is no right way to abstract from experience and no one correct representation. As a selected representation of reality, a concept and its associated definition may be more or less congruent with its referent and be more or less useful.

Clarifying the meaning of a theory's terms is the fundamental activity in early theorizing. This can be a long and difficult process because the work entails specifying the meaning of one concept and differentiating it from closely related concepts. Since the terms initially arise from everyday language, their meanings are often similar or even identical to common dictionary definitions. This can mean that the semantic ambiguity found in conventional language is often also present in the scientific use of the same terms. Dictionary definitions may include multiple meanings and these may be vague, ambiguous, and contradictory. On the other hand, the goal of science is to define its terms clearly and precisely so that existing theory can be linked to the empirical world. Clarity in verbal definitions makes it possible to develop valid operational definitions.

Unfortunately, in early theorizing it is often assumed that the readers know the meanings of the concepts being used. Writings that lack clear definition require each reader to provide the meaning of terms and from these to infer the empirical referents, and ultimately the operational definitions. Loose theorizing results in further ambiguity and ultimately to conflicting ideas in the literature.

The major scientific theories all require major conceptual work in their early stages. This is always necessary for developing a rigorous, testable theory. Precise definitions are achieved through systematic analysis of the written and empirical works. The definitions of the concepts move slowly from implicit meanings and ordinary language toward theoretical definitions. The latter only make sense when they are considered within the context of the other concepts and other definitions which are also part of the theory. For example, the concept of role incongruity can only be understood within the set of terms dealing with role stress. As the meanings of concepts is explicated and refined, ordinary language is replaced by precise theoretical terminology.

In science, the meaning of a concept is established through a process of successive definitions. There is no exact definition nor is there any unchanging definition of any scientific concept. The meaning of a concept evolves over time as the network of ideas becomes more fully developed. Definitions are really agreements on how to use a term. Even with scientific terms, such agreements are always provisional.

Conceptual work requires more than identifying and naming significant ideas. The concept's meaning is further specified by identifying its *empirical referent*. Since concepts are selective representations of reality the concept's meaning can be conveyed to others through making the connection to the empirical world explicit.[16] As the concept becomes more clearly defined, its observable properties can be specified more precisely. Thus, refinement of verbal definitions make it possible to tighten the link to the empirical world. Rules are established for identifying when a phenomenon is an example of a theoretical concept and when it is not. These rules become part of what is known as the operational definition for a concept.

CONCEPTS OF ROLE THEORY. The role theory literature is difficult for a newcomer to identify and understand. Some of the reasons stem from the fact that role theory is more of a rudimentary perspective than a scientific theory. The fact that theoretical ideas are developed discursively and through many extensive theoretical discussions often makes it difficult for the neophyte to explicate the theoretical ideas. This difficulty is compounded by the fact that role theory publications are interdisciplinary and come from both clinical and academic settings. Accordingly, theoretical writing in a topical area may come from many different perspectives and can be found in diverse and scattered interdisciplinary publications. The interdisciplinary nature of the scientific work adds immensely to the richness of the conceptualizations, but it also adds to the conceptual confusion.

Despite these difficulties, health professionals are in a prime position to make important uses of role theory and to expand it by introducing new ideas and concepts which are germane to the health-care setting. In order to make valuable and usable contributions, the health professional needs to know how to analyze and evaluate existing knowledge. This requires making use of the accumulating knowledge in role theory. A scientific perspective and certain other scientific skills are also necessary. The focus in the following section is on providing you with the necessary background so that you will be able to dissect a theory into its essential parts, capture its meaning and potential, then select and use evaluative criteria to determine the usefulness of the theory. This knowledge will make it possible for you to more readily identify theoretical perspectives, work with key concepts and empirical referents, and recognize empirical generalizations.

THEORETICAL STATEMENTS

It has been pointed out that concepts are the basic units of any theory. Taken singularly or in combination, these units form the theoretical statements of a theory. Thus, a theory is a set of interrelated concepts, definitions, and statements. A theory is not just concepts, nor is it a single statement, nor a collection of unrelated statements; rather, the integrated relationships of both concepts and statements is a necessary characteristic of scientific theory.

In any theoretical formulation there are two major types of theoretical statements. One is an existence statement and the other is relational. Only the latter type of statement is empirically testable. We will look at each type of statement during the following discussion.

The *existence statement* defines the meaning of each theoretical term. The statement is true by definition and differs from other theoretical statements in that it makes no claims about the empirical world. A definition cannot be empirically tested.

The second type of statement is the *relational statement*. This statement specifies, with varying degrees of precision, the link or association between the concepts. This type of statement has the potential for being empirically tested. If it is derived from a core of theoretical knowledge, then an empirical test of the statement is an indirect test of the theory.

The following is an illustration of a relational statement. The greater the degree of *role ambiguity* in a position (e.g., that of critical care nurse) the higher the levels of *role strain*. Theoretical statements like this, when empirically supported, add to the credibility of a substantive theory. In this case the substantive theory is role stress.

Statements can also be analyzed in terms of both their relative truth and their level of abstraction. This requires arranging the statements in a hierarchy, ranging from the most true (those with the greatest empirical support) to the least true (those with the least empirical support), and from the most abstract to the most concrete. Arranging theoretical statements on the basis of either of these hierarchies produces the same list of statements, namely, laws, axioms, postulates, propositions, empirical generalizations, and hypotheses. Assumptions, axioms, and postulates are statements of *universal knowledge claims* and relate two or more concepts.[17] As such, they are the "givens"—that is, the knowledge believed to be true. Claims made in one set of statements serve as a foundation for deriving other statements. Accordingly, they form the core and make up the substantive content of a theory.

A common convention in the social sciences is to classify a statement derived from a set of postulates as a proposition, and if the statement is testable, it is called a *hypothesis*. Statements that summarize empirical findings from quite a large number of studies are termed *empirical generalizations*. An illustration of such a statement is: "Role ambiguity is inversely related to job satisfaction." The term *theoretical statement* is a general term encompassing all statements connecting theoretical concepts. These statements make substantive claims and specify the type of relationship between concepts. If the connection is fairly precise, then terms such as linear, curvilinear, or power relationship are used. If the connection is rather loose, then terms such as related, and associated are used to describe the relationship. The direction or form of the relationship in these other statements is usually unspecified.

CRITERIA FOR ANALYZING AND EVALUATING CONCEPTS

The meaning of a theoretical term is made explicit through a precise verbal or mathematical definition. With a precise definition it is possible to assess the properties associated with the semantic meaning and assess the relationship of the theoretical term to its empirical referent and operational definition. If the meaning of a term is implicit, then no real assessment can be made of the *semantic adequacy* of the term.

Concepts provide the substantive focus of theories. The analysis of concepts requires classifying the terms and their *associated meanings*. Early publications may use terms inconsistently and provide only vague definitions whereas more advanced work usually has clearly defined terms. A systematic analysis of concepts should include determining if there is consistency in the properties specified in the definitions. On the basis of this analysis it may be possible to draw some conclusions as to the necessary and sufficient properties of the concept. If there are a variety of properties identified in the definitions then some of the properties may be used more frequently than others.

In assessing the semantic aspect of a theory, one compares the concepts and definitions as they are used in the major publications. This comparison should involve an increasing specificity of the definitions published over time. A second part of the assessment of the meaning of a concept includes an analysis of the adequacy of the *empirical referent* of the concept. This necessitates an assessment of the meaning of the concept together with its link to the empirical world.

Determining *semantic agreement* requires an assessment of the meaning attributed to a term. This means making some judgment as to the extent to which there is agreement on the defining characteristics of the term, on the referent for the term, and on the conditions which must be present before the concept can be applied to empirical phenomena.[18]

In order to determine the *empirical import* of a concept, an assessment is made of the concept's connection to the world of observables. This connection may vary from a sense that one can ultimately link an abstract idea to the world of experience or to a clear specification of rules for applying the concept. The former is an assessment of the validity of the empirical referent whereas the latter refers to the validity of the operational definition. Stronger empirical import exists for a concept when there is a valid operational definition than when only an empirical referent exists. A concept that has an operational definition has empirical import.

The two criteria of semantic agreement and empirical import are combined to assess the semantic adequacy of a concept. As noted earlier, in the long run a concept is assessed for its usefulness. This judgment is based on the link to other concepts in the theory and on the extent of empirical import. A concept may be modified and refined on the basis of its contribution to an understanding of reality. The outcome of this judgment, initially for the concept, and ultimately for the theory, is termed the semantic adequacy of the concept.

Another significant characteristic of a concept that can be used as a criterion for evaluation has to do with its abstractness.

Abstractness. A desirable characteristic of scientific concepts is that they be universal. The extent of abstractness of a concept reflects its universality. An abstract concept is independent of time and place. The abstractness of a term is not to be confused with any notion of vagueness. Abstract concepts are valued in science, while vague ones are not. Concepts have limited application when they are restricted by time, place, or by both. For example, the notion of clinical nurse specialist as a type of nurse is unique to this country and has only been in existence for fifteen years. The analytic use of the concept, clinical nurse specialist, is restricted to a narrow period of time and a relatively limited geographical area when compared to the term staff nurse.

Scientists prefer to work with concepts of limited abstractness and with ideas that can be applied to a variety of phenomena or have a reasonable degree of generality. Early theorizing in the social sciences has been characterized as building grand theory. In this type of theory the concepts cannot be connected to reality. Later the focus shifted to theory which focused on a manageable segment of reality and concepts with limited abstractness. These partial or circumscribed theories made it possible to work with important concepts that have empirical referents. Thus, the criterion of abstractness is related to the semantic adequacy of a theory because a concept must not be too abstract to preclude identification of its empirical referent. The level of abstractness of a theory's concepts is important in determining its potential as a scientific theory.

CRITERIA FOR ANALYZING AND EVALUATING STATEMENTS

Theoretical statements and theories may be assessed in terms of the characteristics associated with their concepts. In addition, they may be analyzed by criteria that are specific to sets of theoretical statements and theories. Since theories themselves usually consist of sets of interrelated statements, the term *theory* will often be used in this section to refer both to such *sets* of statements and also to theories (this is a rather free usage of the term in that not all theoretical statements are theories).

The main criteria useful for analyzing a study, a theory, or several theories include logical adequacy, empirical adequacy, and predictive power.

Of major importance in analyzing theories is the determination of the internal consistency or *logical adequacy* of the set of theoretical statements making up the theory. This is a necessary prerequisite for determining the empirical adequacy and predictive power of the theory. In order to examine the logical adequacy of a theoretical formulation the relationships among the concepts and statements must first be identified and then examined. This process involves examining the *syntax* of a theory and not its substantive meaning.

Identifying a theory's syntax or structure can be accomplished through the technique of diagramming; this technique is illustrated in Figure 1. The structure of the theory in question is analyzed systematically. First, the concepts in the theoretical statements are represented by content-free symbols to make the analysis as objective as possible. Next, the existence of a relationship between concepts is identified along with the nature of that relationship. With this basic information in hand, it is then possible to diagram the structure of the theory. This procedure makes it possible to examine the structure relatively objectively. It is important that the logical structure of the argument or the theory's syntax be examined apart from its content. The process of determining logical adequacy is discussed more fully in Hardy, Theory: Components and Evaluation, *Nursing Research*, 1974. Here it is sufficient to note that diagramming is a vehicle for identifying gaps, overlaps, and contradictions within the theory. Conventions for diagramming theory and using sign rules exist in the literature (Blalock, 1969; Costner & Leik, 1964; Hardy, 1974). Abstract symbols are used to represent the theory's terms:

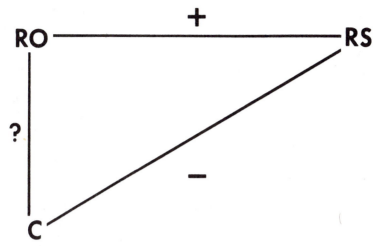

Figure 1. Demonstration of the relationship between concepts. RO = role over-load, RS = role strain, and C = cooperation. The + sign indicates a positive relationship exists between RO and RS; the − sign indicates a negative relation-ship exists between RS and C; the ? indicates the relationship between RO and C is unspecified.

+ means a positive relationship
− means a negative relationship
0 (zero) means no relationship
? (question mark) means that the relationship is unclear; it has not been specified

Consider the following formulation: an increase in role overload is associated with an increase in role strain, and an increase in role strain is associated with a decrease in cooperation. The syntax of this formulation can then be diagrammed to visually depict the theory's internal structure. The formulation can be readily assessed for its logical adequacy.

This type of diagramming facilitates an objective evaluation of the structure of a theory and the relationship of derived hypotheses to the theory itself. If these explicit steps are not taken, the practitioner or researcher may overlook internal weaknesses in the structure. This is especially likely to occur if the substantive focus or conclusions of the theory are in accord with the philosophy and experi-ence of the practitioner. A theory that is internally inconsistent or lacking in logical adequacy cannot be tested empirically, nor can deductions, generaliza-tions, or predictions be properly made with it.

The empirical adequacy of a theory is of importance to a practitioner. The evaluation of empirical adequacy is based on an examination of the existing research to determine the extent of the empirical support. This research will probably vary widely in the extent and quality of the support. A systematic analysis of the body of relevant research makes it possible to come to a conclu-sion as to the extent of the empirical support for the theory.[19] Recently meta–

analysis has been used to quantify the empirical research in a clearly bounded area (theoretical or clinical problem). This technique provides a means for quantifying the analysis of relevant research and for assessing the empirical adequacy of a theory. Accordingly, a judgment about the empirical adequacy may be based on systematic analysis of the pertinent research or on a meta–analysis of the same information.

Another important criterion for assessing a set of theoretical statements is *predictive power*. Prerequisites to providing predictive power are precise measurement of the concepts and specific information as to the conditions under which the predictions are expected to hold true. To achieve the desired theoretical outcome (prediction) it may be necessary to create specific conditions.

CRITERIA FOR ANALYZING AND EVALUATING THEORY

When the problem of evaluating a theory is broached, the problem is meta-theoretical rather than theoretical. The evaluation of a theory requires judgments to be made about how sound or "good" a theory is. It may also involve a judgment regarding which of two theories is "better." Evaluation implies the comparison of concepts and theoretical statements against some standard. Criteria are related to the structure of theory (discussed in the preceding section), the nature of the theory's concepts and theoretical statements, and the goals of the theory.

In assessing the "goodness" of a theory, one can examine the concepts used in the theory to determine the soundness of both their theoretical and operational definitions and the congruence of these two sets of definitions with each other and to the real world. The concepts may also be examined to determine the completeness with which they describe and classify the phenomena under study. In addition, the theoretical statements themselves may be examined for their plausibility and their predictive power. Of particular interest is the logical adequacy of the set of statements. Those which clearly specify the direction and form of the relationship between concepts and have adequate empirical referents for the concepts as well may serve as an indirect test of theory. These derived statements, with operational definitions of concepts, form the links between the theoretical world and the empirical world.

Although there are a variety of criteria utilized by theorists for assessing theory—such as scope, parsimony, abstractness, and testability—selected criteria for *evaluating* theory, such as the logical adequacy and empirical support for the theory, the plausibility of the theory, and exactness of prediction by the theory, are of importance to practitioners.

The scientist is interested in the expansion of knowledge while the practitioner's primary focus is usually on the applicability of the available knowledge. The use of theory to alter the health and lives of patients demands close analysis to see how empirically adequate the statements or theory are. The practitioner needs to ask whether there is sufficient empirical evidence to feel confident that the theory at hand is "sound." The empirical adequacy of a theory is of primary significance to anyone wishing to alter social events in accord with theoretical orientation; the strength of the empirical support indicates the validity of that particular theory.

Also of significance to the practitioner is the *plausibility* of a theory. The theory's statements, when taken as a whole, need to provide a reasonable and believable explanation concerning the phenomena of concern. The theory should present a credible and likely explanation. For instance, if role conflict is of concern, then the practitioner can ask if role theory provides a reasonable explanation for the occurrence of role conflict and the consequences of role conflict. The theory in hand can likewise be assessed for the degree of understanding it communicates; a plausible explanation associated with a sense of *understanding* is of prime importance to practitioners. A practitioner may need to read extensively to assess the plausibility of a theory.

Another important criterion for assessing a theory is the exactness of the *predictions* it provides. Theoretical statements that precisely identify the link between two or more concepts make exact predictions possible. In the earlier stages of theory development, theoretical relationships may be loosely stated; they may provide indefinite or imprecise links between concepts. For example, in role theory, there are statements such as "the more overload a person is exposed to, the more role strain he will experience." This type of statement links two concepts and indicates the linkage may be proportional. However, statements such as this one do not give a precise prediction of how may units of role overload will result in how many units of role strain. This is exactly the precision of prediction that is sought from theory. This preciseness of prediction can be found in some aspects of the health sciences. Reasonably precise drug dosages are given to produce a precise range of biochemical or physiological changes. Theories that could provide exact predictions of health-related social behavior do not exist at this time in the social sciences but are being actively sought. In the meantime, less precise statements that indicate the direction and form of a relationship can be tested. A statement that indicates that an increase in role overload is associated with an increase in role strain can be empirically tested and is of more value than a statement that indicates only that role overload and role strain are associated or that the two conditions coexist.

In determining the goodness of a theory, the health professional utilizes criteria used to evaluate theory and then makes some judgment as to how well the theory meets these criteria. This assessment is not an either/or activity; the judgment is neither that the theory is "good" nor that the theory is "bad," but rather an assessment using a number of criteria and judgment to determine the degree to which the theory adequately meets the criteria. Any final decision regarding the relative value of that theory should be derived from such an assessment.

The determination of which theory is the "best" to use requires an additional judgment on the part of the health professional. Any theory being considered for application must satisfactorily meet the standards for theory, but a question may still exist concerning which of two or more theoretical orientations should be selected and used. For example, a health practitioner working with a family may identify that the problem of concern is that a member of a family is not following a specified medical regimen. Role theory, social exchange theory, and the health belief model may be identified as theories that are relatively good ones for analyzing the problem at hand. Choosing the best theory may involve decisions regarding the following: (1) which theory deals most adequately with the variables of concern to the health professional, (2) which variables central to the theory are the ones that the health professional can alter or modify to bring about the desired change; and (3) would such changes be strong enough or significant enough to make it worth implementing a plan of action based on the theory.

Although only a brief overview of the process of evaluating theory is presented in this chapter so that the reader may have a perspective for reading and assessing the adequacy of role theory, it should be recognized that the health professional plays a vital role in making judgments about the soundness of theories, their appropriateness for modifying behavior, and their appropriateness for modifying the behavior in the predicted direction. Evaluating existing theory is a serious and significant activity for health professionals. They may also wish to contribute to the development of the body of knowledge relevant to health care. Most importantly, the health professional must have sufficient expertise to evaluate knowledge for its soundness and for its appropriateness in improving the quality of health care and, ultimately, of the quality of life.

CONCLUSION

It is important to make a distinction between science as a human social activity and science as a body of knowledge or as a method of inquiry. In looking at science as a social activity, certain important goals and norms can be seen to operate. These goals and norms are not identical to those of health professionals. Scientists work primarily to accumulate a body of knowledge that can help us to understand and explain the world around us. The health professional is primarily engaged in the delivery of care to clients and in the improvement of this care. The scientist's work is guided by the norms of scientific inquiry, while the health professional's work is guided by professional codes of ethics. Although scientists and the health professionals may have similar perspectives on theory, the relative importance of criteria utilized by them to assess theory may differ according to whether the goal is to develop a body of knowledge or to solve a specific health-related problem. Theory development is an activity that both scientists and health professionals engage in as they attempt to explain phenomena. An understanding of science, theory development, the structure of theory, and selected criteria for evaluating theory is necessary for both the health professional who is to contribute to the body of scientific knowledge and to the health professional who is utilizing existing scientific knowledge. This understanding facilitates the generation of a body of scientific knowledge relevant to health care and the utilization of appropriate knowledge.

This chapter has presented science as a social organization with its own goals, norms, and phases of theory development. The basic structure of theory and selected criteria for evaluating theory are also presented. The reader is encouraged to utilize material from this chapter to analyze and evaluate the subsequent chapters on role theory.

NOTES

1. At that time Merton identified the specific norms of science as crucial for the autonomy of science. The ethos and normative structure of science are identified as particularly important when science is threatened by other institutions, such as when political forces attempt to use the institution of science to further their own goals (such as

promulgating the superiority of the Aryan race). The progress, nature and direction of science in Germany was markedly altered in that era by the introduction of nonscientific goals and criteria for judging the acceptability of scientific findings. Energy was directed at obtaining knowledge of the supremacy of the Aryan race; the race, ethnicity, and political creed of the researcher became important criteria for accepting knowledge as scientific.

2. Since the time of Merton's work, the feminist movement has been confronting the problems of male scientists creating a discipline that does not take women into account. Some female philosophers and scientists have pointed out that the accrual of a scientific body of social science essentially has resulted in a body of knowledge on male behavior, and this knowledge is seen as normative. Some feminist thinkers propose that there is a distinctive feminist perspective and methodology for generating a feminist body of scientific knowledge. These feminists claim that since women's thoughts and experiences are different than men's, a different methodology is needed to identify this knowledge (see papers edited by Harding and Hintikka, 1983). It is clear that women have not taken part in generating much of the presently held scientific work; this omission has resulted in a biased, unbalanced knowledge base which can be corrected. For example, in the health field, problems peculiar to women such as breast cancer, osteoporosis, and depression have not *received* the *degree of* scientific study that heart disease, stroke, and other predominately male health problems have. Sound scientific research is needed in these predominately female-related fields.

It is not clear, however, why scientific studies of these areas would need to be conducted by women using any different method of inquiry or requiring a methodology other than the current scientific method of inquiry. Scientific knowledge is expected to be logical, empirically valid, and generalizable, and thus, the characteristics of the researcher, such as race, ethnic background or, in particular, gender, are not expected to bias the knowledge base (other than in personal values which influence the selection of the research project.) What is needed are scientific studies of human persons which include equal generation of knowledge on women, and on men, relative to their problems, experiences, and perspectives. It has been only recently that women have become aware of their invisibility in much of the scientific knowledge base.

3. Merton first discussed the norms of science as means of protecting the autonomy of science from the political forces of Nazi Germany. He saw both logical and nonlogical forces converging to curtail the activities of science. Normally scientific knowledge is assessed relative to its logical arguments, empirical evidence, and generality.

Merton wrote about how social institutions may attempt to influence the nature of science. He proposed two major sources of hostility towards science. One is the decision (not necessarily correct) that science is inimical to the satisfaction of important values. The second consists largely of nonlogical elements. It rests upon the feeling of incompatibility between the sentiments embodied in the scientific ethos and those found in other institutions. Whenever this feeling is challenged it is rationalized (Merton, 1968, pp. 591–592). Current attacks on science in general, and positivism in particular, may be an illustration of the belief that science does not support the prevalent social values of subjectivism.

4. The social factors identified by Merton were those that influence the focus of study. In his view, the nature of the knowledge generated is not altered by social factors. Kuhn, on the other hand, identifies social factors as altering the nature of the body of knowledge and proposes that, accordingly, there is an element of irrationality in science.

Among philosophers of science, the validity of the Kuhnian approach to understanding knowledge development is still controversial. The necessity of "revolutions" to advance scientific knowledge is one feature of Kuhn's work that causes controversy. A revolution in the dominant paradigm is expected to occur, according to Kuhn, when sufficient anomalies have accumulated to throw the dominate paradigm into dispute.

Depicting growth of knowledge as a slow evolutionary process, or a process of slow accumulation tends to be favored over Kuhn's idea of scientific revolutions. Although knowledge development is most likely to develop over time through a slow crescive process rather than through revolution, Kuhn's discussion of the nature of the preparadigm stage of science does seem to provide a reasonable explanation of the current state of scientific-related activities in nursing (Hardy, 1978, 1983). The term *research programs* (Lakatos, 1970) seems to be more meaningful to scientists then does the term *paradigm*. Lakatos' notion of research programs includes the study of empirical and conceptual problems.

5. Scientific work requires the capacity to be alone for extensive periods. Consider the years of isolation from peers, friends, and family experienced by the anthropologist Margaret Mead as she scientifically studied the culture of Samoa. Consider also the years of isolation and perceived social rejection of the Nobel laureate biologist-geneticist Barbara McClintock. Patiently and meticulously for more than 30 years she scientifically observed genetic changes in corn (Fox Keller, 1983).

6. Scientific communities are often composed of a number of subcommunities. Thus in the discipline of sociology, for instance, scientists work within different but identifiable theoretical orientations such as role theory and conflict theory. Likewise, within the theoretical area of role there are distinct subcommunities of scientists which work on various aspects of their framework. One group may focus on professional socialization, for example, and another group may study the conflict between social organizations and professional work. There are many such communities. A strong sense of community exists among those who work on a particular body of scientific knowledge which is very distinct from that of others.

In less mature scientific disciplines such as nursing, a sense of community may also develop among persons who are adherents to a school of thought or to a conceptual framework. However, until they begin to develop testable hypotheses, these less mature communities cannot grow through shared testing and development of formal ideas. Nevertheless, a sense of being part of a community of scholars does evolve as the supporters of an idea work to achieve common goals, such as fuller development of a model or work on developing means for establishing an empirical base.

7. Even though these norms of science were identified and analyzed by Merton in 1942, within the sociology of science these four norms are still acknowledged as dominant and central to the ethos of science (Mitroff, 1974; Mulkay, 1979). Mulkay (p. 23) claims that the vitality of this portrayal may be because it presents the accepted view of science.

8. Such a structure often is characterized as a negotiated (social) order; because it is created by current role occupants it usually is compatible with the broad social context of norms and role systems.

9. This norm lies at the core of science in that other norms of science can be traced to it. It is central to those who hold to the standard view of science and those who favor the revised view. A view that is held by the majority of the philosophers of science has been referred to as "the standard view of science" (Mulkay, 1979), the logical positivist view (Hempel, 1966), and the received view (Suppe, 1977). The norm of universality is held by both the social sciences and the natural sciences. The relatively limited accomplishments in the social sciences compared with the natural sciences are believed to be differences in degree, not in kind.

It would be misleading, however, to say that all scientists view science in this way. The nature of science is the focus of reassessment by those who hold the revised view of science. This questioning is occurring more by the social scientists, who see the basic axioms of science as being problematic, and for some of these scientists the axioms are untenable. There has been a greatly increased general awareness in the scientific community of the possible problems associated with a scientific study of human behavior since the late sixties. There is also much more frequent discussion of the problem in the literature.

10. The norm of universalism implies that the truth and value of scientific work depends only on the merit of the work. Merton proposes that the truth of scientific work is

independent of the scientist's sex, prestige, nationality, political views, and professional allegiances. Some research, however, has identified that the gender of the scientist may have, in the past, influenced publication and the perceived value of the publication, which is a normative violation. Once identified, violations of the norms of science such as this are usually corrected. The value of scientific work is, according to the norm of universalism, unrestricted also by time and geographical location. Recognition is based on the credibility and significance of the work itself, not on the person, time, or place associated with the contribution. Also personal values, gain, and other social factors (career advancement, influence) are not factors that should influence the work of scientists. The norm of universalism refers to the fact that there generally is agreement on the basic nature of science.

11. Merton originally termed this norm of communality, *communism*. It did not refer to a political orientation but to a norm of sharing.

12. Scientific knowledge and scientific theory will at times be used interchangeably in this chapter. Although research may not be specifically mentioned, all theories progress on the concurrent development of ideas and related research. Research is always carried out to advance scientific theory (knowledge). The numerous textbooks on research and methods may give the erroneous impression that it is an independent aspect of science.

13. "Meta-" means about; metatheory means knowledge about theory. The knowledge has to do with understanding such things as the development and structure of theories and does not focus on the substantive aspect of the theory. A parallel can be made between the initial learning of anatomy and physiology as a basis for understanding health and illness rather than only examining peoples' health-related problems.

14. These criteria are discussed more fully in Hardy (1974, 1986).

15. Burr (1974) and Heiss (1981) have systematized some of the knowledge on role theory. This is an important step toward establishing a scientific theory base. (See Chap. 7)

16. Even though the notion that ideas must have empirical relevance is found in elementary texts, it is common to find discussions of a concept's operational definition with no mention made of its empirical relevance.

17. These terms are often used interchangeably.

18. In this analysis the focus is on consistency in, and consensus on, the properties of a concept. In the analysis of the various meanings of the concept, the definitions are examined for clarity, consistency in usage, completeness, and accuracy. Variations in definitions, contradictions in use, the identification of essential properties, or incomplete definitions are identified separately.

19. There tends to be some confusion between the notion of empirical support for a testable hypothesis and empirical adequacy. These notions are quite different. In testing an hypothesis the empirical findings in a single research study are assessed to determine the extent to which the hypothesis has been supported. The assessment of the empirical adequacy of a theory is based on the analysis of *all of the relevant research studies* that have been generated from that specific theory. Such an analysis is only possible after some determination of the empirical support for each study has been made. Studies with major methodological defects and biases must be discarded from the analysis.

2

Development of Scientific Knowledge

Margaret E. Hardy
with William L. Hardy

PART 1: AN OVERVIEW OF ROLE THEORY

In this chapter we discuss the evolution of scientific knowledge as a multistaged process. There are several reasons for selecting this topic. One is that each stage seems to have specific strategies for advancing theoretical knowledge. Strategies at one stage may not be useful or relevant at other stages. Second, the criteria for evaluating a body of knowledge are determined to a large extent by the level of knowledge development. For example, in the conceptualization stage the semantic adequacy of the theoretical terms would be an important criterion to use whereas at the stage of formal theory development logical adequacy and predictive power would be more appropriate criteria. Third, an understanding of the evolutionary process of knowledge development and the nature of scientific work required at each stage may help clarify the type of theory development strategies and empirical work likely to be most productive at a given stage. Fourth, in presenting scientific knowledge as a cumulative process requiring both fundamental conceptual and empirical work, we hope to convey the idea of the close connection between theory and research. Usually research courses and theory development courses are taught independently, creating the impression that the two activities are completely separate. We hope that our discussion will show that they are indeed inseparable for the development of scientific knowledge—in any field. Finally, an overriding purpose of discussing scientific knowledge as a multistaged process is to convey a *sense of understanding* of science as a social process, with a general set of rules that are relevant to all stages of knowledge development. Scientific work is conducted by a community of scientists in a social context. Their shared work contributes over time to a cumulative body of scientific knowledge.

We have selected one branch of role theory, namely, symbolic interaction, as our primary source of illustrations. This body of knowledge has developed over the last 85 years and is a rich source of examples for illuminating the evolution of scientific ideas. Also, there are many similarities between this body of knowledge and some of the applied social science areas in the health sciences.

SYMBOLIC INTERACTION

In the first part of this chapter a brief overview is given of the development of role theory before focusing specifically on symbolic interaction as the analytic model. We briefly describe the sociohistorical context in which the theory developed and flourished in order to provide a background for Part 2, in which the stages of theory development are discussed.

In choosing symbolic interaction to investigate theory development we have chosen a theory whose substantive focus overlaps a large area of interest in the health sciences. Other similarities are described later, but what is of value here is that it has been a phenomenally successful area of work and its concepts have been developed over a long period of time. This longitudinal dimension of symbolic interaction may be a source of valuable insight into the development of a community of scientists, a theoretical perspective, and the process of theory development. Furthermore, the current work of some nurse scientists is based on symbolic interaction theory and, thus, a review of the development of the theory has additional value. It may provide an understanding in general for those engaged in developing theory in the health sciences.

The early conceptualization phase in symbolic interaction, together with the development of qualitative data and appropriate field research methods, was followed 40 years later by a very scientific approach with quantification that has led to empirically testable microtheories. This transition may provide important insights for health scientists who are working at both concept analysis and development of clinical research. The detailed empiric work by symbolic interactionists involved a specific type of field work, the use of ethnographic materials, observations, interviews, nonintrusive measurement, and private and public documents to provide data. This work can also provide a background for understanding the development of what Glaser and Strauss (1967) called *grounded theory*. Since symbolic interactionists' works have been both qualitative and quantitative and these aspects have been combined in their research strategies for developing theory, their work may provide useful insights on both theory development and general research strategies.

We make inferences about the influence of a particular point in time on the underlying assumptions and substantive focus of the theory, the questions being explored, and the concepts identified. These inferences also may be relevant for our development of theory in the health sciences. There may be additional similarities between sociology as a "science in training," as it was seen to be in the first part of this century, and in the applied health sciences today. This is clarified later in this chapter.

Additional reasons for choosing to focus on symbolic interaction include the relatively extensive metatheoretical and empirically based publications devoted to it, which make it possible to illustrate different intellectual orientations and diverse research methods. There are three reasons a symbolic interaction focus is especially relevant to the health care giver's role.

First, early theory development work involved a search for both a total theory and a unique theory that would explain all of human behavior—particularly social problems. This search was not successful, nor did it advance the development of scientific knowledge. A similar orientation exists today in "theories" that have captured the imagination of many nurse scholars and practitioners in the health sciences.

Second, as mentioned earlier, the focus of study in symbolic interaction is very similar to a focus in nursing. Thus the unity of person–environment, concern with persons, social integration, the development of meaning, the embeddedness of persons in a social context, and the reciprocal social processes engaging persons are foci of considerable interest in applied health science today. It took approximately 40 years of intense work by sociologists before these social conditions and processes could begin to be studied scientifically. Interestingly, again in the 1980s, questions arise as to whether a new type of science is required to study these processes.

Third, the intense methodological dilemmas faced in the period 1920 to 1932 in symbolic interaction arose as a result of an apparent incommensurability between a strong commitment to scientific methodology, with its related systematic, objective analysis, and an area of study (phenomenology) which is basically subjective in nature. Similar methodological dilemmas are the subject of much current debate in scientific circles.

Methods Used in Developing Part 1

The generalizations that are made about symbolic interaction are obtained from several types of scholarly works that include early theory and research, descriptive historical work, philosophical analyses, analytical critiques, and research.[1]

Part 2 of this chapter describes the stages of theory development illustrated by the activities associated with the development of symbolic interaction knowledge. The various theoretically related activities identified in diverse types of publications, such as historical and descriptive studies and the research-related studies of symbolic interaction, serve as the data base used to illustrate (and to some extent evaluate) the conceptualization or notion of stages of theory development.

Relevance of the Sociohistorical Context

Symbolic interaction emerged at the turn of the century and developed in a sociohistorical context that had many similarities to the social conditions of the present within which applied social-health science theory is emerging. Inference can be made as to the influence these factors had on the nature and course of the development of symbolic interaction in particular and theory development in general.

The historical development of symbolic interaction and structural role theory is briefly identified to provide background and to illustrate the development of branches within an overall theory. The sociohistorical context in which the theory developed is examined and its basic tenets identified.

ROLE THEORY

The body of knowledge that is termed *role theory* consists of clusters of concepts, emerging subtheories, and a diverse set of empirical research findings that address specific aspects of social behavior. It is made up of two major theoretical perspectives, both of which utilize the term *role* as a basic concept. These are symbolic interaction role theory and social structural (earlier known as structural–functional) role theory.

Both perspectives have as their goal the understanding and explanation of social order. At this point it is sufficient to note that symbolic interaction focuses on individuals in reciprocal social interaction who actively construct and create their environment through a process of self-reflexive interaction. Social processes and their outcomes that emerge as individuals interact, shape, and adapt to their social environment are studied. *Problematic situations* or situations that demand new interpretations or new lines of action are major foci of study. The theory initially dealt with change, dynamics, and the processes by which individuals creatively adapted to a society in flux. The process of creative adaptation is a reflection of evolutionary assumptions and has been used by pragmatists such as Mead and Dewey. Thus it can be seen as a focus which is a response to the sociohistorical context in which it developed.

In contrast, the structural–functional perspective focuses on the bigger picture—society, social systems, the social structure—and on other patterned behaviors that develop over time. Social structures are seen to shape and to a large extent determine individual behavior. Analysis is of the structure or of the aggregate rather than the individual in relation to the social environment. Major theoretical contributions to this field have been made by Parsons (1951), and Merton (1968). The latter has made both significant empirical and theoretical contributions.

Symbolic interaction and social structural role theory are the two major branches of role theory. They differ in level of analysis, unit of analysis, research, and theory development strategies, but they have in common such concepts as role, role behavior, norms, sanctions, and status.

Development of Role Theory

The development of role theory is presented briefly for the purpose of examining and increasing awareness of theory development. Why or how did these theories get started? Were there conceptual breakthroughs of significance?

Theoretical Beginnings. There are distinct strands of knowledge within role theory. In the 1930s, publications by several early social theoreticians formally created the basic knowledge area of role theory. These theorists defined three distinct theoretical areas that had come to the attention of social scientists. The discussion of their definitions that follows should give the reader a deeper appreciation of the early processes that occur as ideas are developed in a new and evolving social context. The historical development of role theory is depicted in Figure 1.

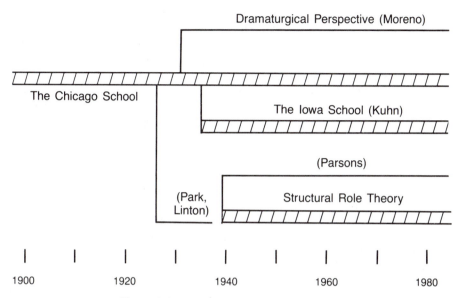

Figure 1. Historical development of role theory.

The Dramaturgical Perspective. Moreno was a psychiatrist who came to the United States from Germany in 1930 with experience in the theater of spontaneity in Vienna. He pioneered the innovative therapy of psychodrama—the use of groups and role playing in psychiatric treatment (Thomas & Biddle, 1979). Moreno's creative use of psychodramatic techniques was based on an assumption that artificially constructed groups and roles could provide opportunities for the sociocultural reintegration of disturbed patients. Inspired by Mead's concept of role taking, he was the first to introduce the idea of using role playing as an experimental procedure for learning to perform a role more adequately. In addition, he developed sociometry, the quantitative study of interpersonal attraction. Data were summarized in sociograms (Moreno, 1959). Of particular significance is the fact that he linked types of role behavior to different sets of expectations.

Moreno's work typifies that of the clinician. Important ideas were developed in response to patient problems but many of the ideas remain outside a theoretical body of knowledge. This reflects the ongoing problem of linking the theoretical world with the practical; of translating what appear to be useful ideas generated in the rich settings of practice into scientifically valid ideas that can contribute to the building of sound, empirically based theoretical knowledge.

Symbolic Interaction: The Emergent Self-Reflexive Model

George Herbert Mead, a social philosopher, is considered the originator of symbolic interaction. Mead's creative ideas and stimulating teaching had such a significant impact on his associates and students at the University of Chicago, particularly those in sociology, that a new school of thought emerged, namely, symbolic interaction (Thomas & Biddle, 1979, p. 6).

Mead's main interest was in mind, self and understanding human nature in terms of groups and society. His methods included the study of reciprocal social relationships and the response to rapid social change. He examined processes associated with adapting to change and finding one's social niche. He introduced the perspective that the human mind, the social self, and the structure of society all emerged through *reciprocal* social interaction. The mind and self, he postulated, developed simultaneously and reflexively. Mead explored social experience, with consciousness, language, and communication as "emergents" from the social process and examined the self in relation to social situations as well as to itself and to others. His contributions, in addition, ranged from novel ways of looking at social processes to development of a theory of perspectives (later picked up by W.I. Thomas in definition of the situation), to development of the concept of emergence, and a radical conceptualization of temporality (Natanson, 1973, p. 3). These latter perspectives appear to have received less initial attention relative to role theory than his ideas on the reflexive nature of self and his theory of perspectives (Goff, 1980; M.H. Kuhn, 1978; Natanson, 1973; Stryker, 1980; Thomas & Biddle, 1979).

The Structural Approach. Mead's work did not focus extensively on how individuals participate in society but he proposed that persons, acting together, can change the goals of groups and, thereby, ultimately shape society. The concept of *role* began to be a focus of work at the University of Chicago in 1920. Park, a colleague and dynamic early sociologist at the university, identified the fact that roles are linked to structural positions and ultimately the self is linked to playing multiple roles within the confines of these positions. Park proposed that the self emerges through playing these multiple roles. This new idea complemented the symbolic interaction perspective; it identified the importance of structure and other processes.

Linton (1936), an anthropologist and a member of the Chicago School, made a significant conceptual breakthrough along similar lines by further conceptualization of social organization and the individual's embeddedness in it. He was the first to propose a conceptual distinction between status—a collection of rights and duties—and role—the dynamic aspect of status. He identified analytic concepts related to the social structure (network of positions, status, and expectations), and made a clear distinction between structure and the individual (Thomas & Biddle, 1979; Turner, 1978).[2]

The ideas of social structure introduced by Park and Linton provided impetus and direction for work in symbolic interaction and for the development of theory and research on social structure. This theoretical approach, with its focus on society, totally dominated the sociological literature during the 1950s and 1960s and significantly influenced the applied social health sciences. Major theorists of this era were Parsons and Merton. Parsons developed the idea of social systems with complex conceptual schemes; Merton developed the analytic approach of functional analysis and preferred initially to work with middle-range theories rather than the "grand" theories of Parsons.

BRANCHES OF ROLE THEORY: VARIETIES AND SCHOOLS OF THOUGHT IN SYMBOLIC INTERACTION

As we have seen, in the development of role theory two main complementary bodies of knowledge about the same conceptual phenomena of role evolved, namely, symbolic interaction (and a subtheory of dramaturgy) and structural role theory. Work on these initial theories continues today. A renewed interest in phenomenology and the new area of ethnomethodology emerged in the 1960s. The theme of these perspectives is the "meaning" of everyday activities, but because each study is unique, the resulting lack of generalizability means that, unlike Mead's work on symbolic interaction, they fell outside the realm of normal science (Burr et al., 1979; Meltzer, Petras, & Reynolds, 1975, 1978).

Considerable early work on symbolic interaction occurred between 1920 and 1935 (the peak period for the Chicago School) whereas the bulk of the work in the structural branch occurred in the 1950s and 1960s. The turmoil of the late 1960s, with a heightened awareness of the ideological nature of social theory and the status quo assumptions of structural theory, dislodged it from its 20 years of dominance. Symbolic interaction, with its humanistic perspective, generated renewed interest to the extent that a journal and an annual review book became necessary in 1980. Only a few theorists since Mead have proposed combining the two perspectives as a means for obtaining a fuller comprehension of social behavior (Handel, 1979; Hardy & Conway, 1978; Heiss, 1981; Katz & Kahn, 1966).

Two Traditions within Symbolic Interaction

Symbolic interaction research and knowledge grew phenomenally in the era between 1920 and the 1940s, primarily in the sociology department at the University of Chicago. Because of this prominence, the research and associated traditions became known as the Chicago School (see Fig. 1). The research on symbolic interaction within this school was qualitative, descriptive work. In contrast, quantitative work was emphasized in the other research areas in the department. In 1934, after publication of Mead's book, a group of symbolic interactionists outside the University of Chicago who were committed to a quantitative, scientific approach to symbolic interaction began research. This group, frustrated with Blumer's focus at Chicago on fluid interaction, initiated objective, quantifiable research on core concepts under the leadership of Manfred Kuhn at the University of Iowa. Their work was also a response to a frustration with the general failure of symbolic interactionists to advance the theory (Buban, 1986). The empirical development of partial theories that occurred at Iowa has resulted in subtheories such as reference groups, self-theory, and other theories which go by a variety of names other than symbolic interaction. The resulting work has been called the Iowa School, even though many other universities, including Minnesota, Wisconsin, and the University of Washington, were involved in the research.

The two distinct types of research on symbolic interaction exist today. The qualitative work, in the tradition of the Chicago School, is represented by Blumer

(1940), who has used "sensitizing" concepts, also by Glaser and Strauss, who have developed grounded theory, and by Goffman, who has been a very skilled observer and a developer of important new theoretical ideas. The grounded theory methodology (Glaser & Strauss, 1967) presents qualitative research as a valid process for generating theory. The end product of such research is considered to stand on its own. Because of the philosophical underpinning of pragmatism, proponents of grounded theory believe repeated studies (for validity) and developmental quantitative research are inappropriate and unnecessary (Glaser & Strauss, 1967; Rock, 1979). In contrast, the quantitative branch of symbolic interaction considers its methodology important for the development of scientific symbolic interaction knowledge. This branch has fit easily into standard sociology; grounded theory has not.

Symbolic interaction, with its relevant knowledge base and its varied development and history, has the potential for providing a rich source for understanding theory development, the topic of the second part of this chapter.

George Herbert Mead and His Work

Any theoretical work can be understood best if the reader recognizes the fundamental question posed by the theorist. Moreover, it is important to recognize that a theory is also a product of the time and social context in which the originator works. An understanding of Mead's work may be facilitated by the knowledge that he struggled with the major question of how consciousness and thinking develop in humans and how they arise from both the individual and the social context (Dewey, 1932). Mead saw the mind as developing through interaction; thus he saw it as arising from social processes. Rationality (Kang, 1975) and intersubjectivity (Joas, 1985) are terms that have been used to describe Mead's work. His ideas have also been described as the development of a theory of motivation that takes into account the role of social forces (Meltzer et al., 1976). Mead, in considering the influence of social forces and perception on the development of the self, was actually working on ideas that provided alternatives to individualistic theories of motivation.

Meltzer et al. (1975) identify Mead's pragmatism as having a major influence on his views of motivation and the mind. For the pragmatist, the mind is a selective tool which seeks an adjustive relationship between the individual and the environment. In addition, Mead's concern with thinking and rationality led him to the central idea that science is the epitome of rationality and the only practical means for obtaining knowledge. Mead saw science as the supreme instrument for controlling and modifying the physical and social environment (Strauss, 1934, p. xix). The ability to manage the environment successfully is, in the symbolic interaction perspective, a primary indication of intelligence.

Even though it is now 90 or more years since its inception, Mead's work is still recognized for its originality. Unfortunately, his style of writing, in which he integrated his own ideas with existing thought, although invaluable for knowledge development, did not attract attention to the originality of his thinking during his lifetime. After Mead's death, Dewey noted that in retrospect much of the obscurity of Mead's expression was due to the fact that Mead saw something as a problem which had not presented itself at all to other minds. "The power of observing common elements which are ignored just because they are common, characterized the mind of George Mead" (Dewey, 1932, 1980). Unfortunately, Mead's mode of transmitting his new ideas via common terminology can be erroneously taken for repetition. Rather, as Miller (1973), a contemporary philosopher and specialist in Mead's works, has pointed out, Mead was often trying to say something from a new and a most revealing standpoint. Miller has also identified another factor which, for the superficial reader, may make Mead's writing seem repetitious. Mead, with his extensive interests in the biological, physical, and social sciences, had developed a whole system of philosophy, and to understand one part of it requires working with and understanding the whole (Miller, 1973, pp. xxix–xxx; p. 65). It is tempting now to take a contemporary approach and try to read just some of his subtheories—for instance his theory of self or of role taking—and to ignore his theory of the past, of time, and of relativity. However, Mead wrote in a manner in which his ideas were always presented as a system, rather than as independent parts—hence the appearance of repetition (Miller, 1973).

While Mead's ideas evolved over time, the core of his theoretical work had been almost completely developed by 1912 (Joas, 1985). Unfortunately, he never wrote a book in which he fully developed his philosophy (largely because he never felt he had his ideas sufficiently coherently worked out). A periodic criticism in the sociological literature has been that Mead did not publish. This comment is related not only to books but publications in general. It seems that for a number of years sociologists were not aware of Mead's publications in psychology and philosophy journals. Since we have no well-rounded view of symbolic interaction written by Mead, the main sources for understanding his perspective are his published papers (numbering over 100) and his unpublished personal papers (archived at the University of Chicago). The symbolic interaction perspective is taught primarily through the interpretations and writings of other symbolic interactionist social scientists.[3]

It appears that most of the publications and critiques of Mead's work (those authored by Americans) have looked primarily at the American influences on Mead, neglecting the European (especially German) influences, and accordingly only provide partial, incomplete, and often inaccurate representations of Mead's ideas (Joas, 1985).

Only recently Mead's work has been rediscovered by philosophers. They have read and analyzed articles which social scientists generally have not read. Consequently there are some new ideas and ideas that either extend or contradict the traditional social science views of symbolic interaction (see Baldwin, 1986; Hardy & Hardy, 1988; Joas, 1985; Kang, 1975). Some of the newer information is integrated into this chapter, but space limitations prevent a fuller discussion.

Mead, although originally interested in social philosophy, decided he could accomplish more by doing scientific work. While his interests lay initially in the area of physiological psychology, he was employed for most of his life in the social philosophy department at the University of Chicago. There he was one of a new breed of psychologists committed to using scientific methods for understanding and explaining social psychological phenomena and for providing the basis for implementing social action programs.

Like all of his departmental colleagues at the University of Chicago (except

Dewey), Mead studied the *new psychology* in Germany. This period of his education began with a visit to Leipzig where Wundt had founded the first experimental psychology laboratory (Joas, 1985).[4] Wundt's ideas strengthened Mead's personal commitment to science and helped shape his view of science as a rational process and the highest form of thinking. These ideas permeate his subsequent theoretical work. (See Baldwin 1986, and Kang, 1976, for lists of the numerous references Mead made to science and rationality.) Mead's observations of Wundt's simultaneous study of neurological and psychological phenomena at Leipzig and his attendance there at Wundt's lectures in philosophy strengthened his decision to reject dualism—the separate study of mind and body and the separation of knowledge and experience.

Mead subsequently studied at the University of Berlin, where he found that two of the principal resident philosophers held diametrically opposed views as to how human behavior should be studied and explained. One, Dilthey, believed that the study of human behavior was humanistic work employing interpretative methods (i.e., descriptive psychology). To Mead this work did not seem to be scientific. The other philosopher, Ebbinhaus, believed in experimental methods of science—the goal being explanation. However, Ebbinhaus endorsed the notion of reductionism whereby human behavior would be explained through more fundamental processes at the biochemical and biological levels. These two contrasting views on how human behavior should be studied sensitized Mead to possible problems that could arise in his own theoretical work. Mead's belief that the study of complex human systems should be done in their entirety (the basic assumption of holism) meant that the use of reductionism by skilled scientists would be suspect. Moreover, Mead's commitment to scientific methodology also meant that humanistic introspective data had no place in his work. His subsequent very careful theoretical work in developing the concepts of symbolic interaction obviated the use of these two inappropriate approaches (Joas, 1985, p. 80).[5]

When first introduced to the two opposing views on the study of human behavior at Berlin, Mead did not choose one over the other (Joas, 1985). Later in his theoretical work Mead carefully developed his theoretical perspective to ensure that the related research it would foster would be scientific. He achieved this goal by focusing on a functional psychology in which he saw humans as utilizing their minds to manipulate their environment. In a mutually reciprocal relationship, he saw the mind and the self as developing through social forces. The emergent theoretical concept of the social act, for example, was formulated as an objective, observable entity composed of social, psychological, and biological elements. Mead carefully identified the empirical units and approach to analysis and provided suggestions as to how to proceed with research.

In Mead's theorizing, concepts were carefully developed both to meet the theoretical requirements and also to prevent reductionist scientists from misconstruing his work to fit their model. For instance with regard to the *social act*, the *actual situation* in which the social act occurs was combined with the scientific notion of generalizable situations to further extend the analyses. His theoretical work was unusually sound and firmly linked to the empirical world, thus lending itself to scientific research (Joas, 1985; Kang, 1976). From a substantial analysis of Mead's theoretical work by Joas it is apparent that Mead's theorizing was sufficiently systematic that introspection and reductionism were clearly excluded.

There were similarities in the interests of Wundt and Mead in that both were interested in the use of gestures in communication. Indeed, Mead began his theoretical work by systematically analyzing gestures among animals. Thus he appraised the soundness of his ideas using data from animal studies and only after this did he turn to look at distinctly human characteristics, progressing to analysis of modes of communication among humans. Much of Mead's theoretical work is still considered unusually thorough, systematic, and unique (Joas, 1985).

Knowledge based on Mead's symbolic interaction perspective is now found primarily in the research and theory-related publications of social psychologists (in sociology). Another source of information consists of the few textbooks written by students of Mead. The basic social psychological views of Mead are presented in a book consisting of the posthumous publication of his lecture notes (taken in his social psychology class, taught in the sociology department at the University of Chicago). C.W. Morris edited these notes by students and published them in 1934 as George Herbert Mead's *Mind, Self, and Society*. Subsequently, there have been 17 reprintings of this book. There also have been several other publications of collections of selected papers by Mead.

Perhaps the major transfer of information about Mead's ideas took place orally—in classes, at meetings, and in other informal communications. Information passed orally came from those who were part of the symbolic interaction traditon (i.e., primarily members of the Chicago School) and also from those who had such persons as teachers or mentors. Publications arising from these sources, however, do not provide sufficient information on the theory for an outsider to develop a sound notion of symbolic interaction.

Rock (1979), an English sociologist who came to the United States for postdoctoral work in symbolic interaction, found that many aspects of symbolic interaction were not codified but were clearly part of an underground knowledge base. The limited availability of this information also poses a problem for current students (who are not sociology majors) when they try to discover the foundations and important ideas of symbolic interaction.

The strong friendships that developed among students and faculty who worked with symbolic interaction at the University of Chicago provided a powerful medium for knowledge transfer. The close-knit network minimized the need for codifying the basic ideas, but made it difficult for outsiders to gain knowledge of symbolic interaction. The ideas were so well internalized by the insiders that they had no need to refer to written works. Thus, the ease of communication among those in the network precluded a need for documentation of symbolic interaction and therefore contributed to prolonging the period of the oral tradition. Mead's death and the subsequent posthumous publication of his *Mind, Self, and Society* in 1934 terminated the period of the oral tradition (M. Kuhn, 1978).

The sociological version of symbolic interaction has been carried forward by Blumer, who is generally recognized as continuing Mead's work. Recently, Blumer's views have been severely criticized, primarily for their fragmentary nature and for not providing a good representation of the theoretical system—developed by Mead—which was the precursor for symbolic interaction. Blumer has been attributed with reducing Mead's concept of *action* to *interaction*, and linguistically attenuating Mead's concept of *meaning* (Joas, 1985, p. 7). Furthermore, Blumer has largely abjured adherence to a scientific focus (with its use of definitive concepts and variables) which actually permeated Mead's own theoretical work (Stryker, 1981, p. 11). Although Blumer now has much less of an impact than previously, his perspective has influenced 50 years of research.

Two recent critiques of symbolic interaction further address the nonscientific approach utilized by Blumer (Coser, 1984; Turner, 1986). Major critiques by Joas (1985) and by Meltzer et al. (1978) point out that much of Mead's original work is completely ignored or has been appropriated only fragmentarily into symbolic interaction theory. Furthermore, only indirect works, which are related to Mead's ideas (for example *Mind, Self, and Society*), have received major analysis.

In our view symbolic interaction theory presently is an incomplete and inaccurate representation of Mead's work. Partial information on Mead's theory has been accepted by sociologists for over 50 years without explication of his theoretical work in published articles. The traditional view has been passed on, based on the posthumous publication of notes on Mead's lectures and on the oral information transmitted by students of the Chicago School.

Newer information which is beginning to emerge on Mead's theoretical work suggests that many of the existing ideas are inaccurate and incomplete representations of his theoretical work. This material is exciting and identifies many ways of connecting symbolic interaction with reality. The explications make symbolic interaction theory much more amenable to scientific research and to further theory development than does the incomplete knowledge of the *established view* (carried forward by Blumer et al.). Indeed the problems that have been encountered in attempting to develop scientific studies based on symbolic interaction may be due, in part, to incomplete knowledge of Mead's original theoretical work. As more scholars begin to utilize Mead's own publications (rather than secondary publications based largely on student lecture notes) and as the literature grows, Mead's work is being clarified, discussed, and analyzed and his theoretical ideas are being much more fully explicated.

Many recent publications have brought the shortcomings of previously published material to light.[6] Several examples from Joas (1985) illustrate some of the problems. For instance, there is a common belief perpetuated in the literature that Mead did not publish. In fact, Joas notes that Mead was the sole author of over 100 articles. Joas also notes that the major influence German philosophy and psychology had on Mead's theoretical work has largely been ignored in American publications on Mead. Also, existing publications have not fully explored Mead's theoretical position; rather they have provided only fragmentary representations of his work.

The social act and the situation are central themes in Mead's theoretical work on human behavior. (It is in the *social act* where thinking occurs, and where intelligence, meaning, and the self develop.) Philosophical analysis of Mead's views on rationality reemphasizes the importance of the *social act* and the *actual situation* in Mead's work (Kang, 1976, pp. 30–35). A lack of research on these key concepts and on the notion of *social context* inherent in them has been the focus of major criticism of related research in social psychology. Miyamoto (1959) has reminded us that the keystone to symbolic interaction—the *social act*—needs to become the center of research. The related notion of the *social context* also needs to be reintegrated with the study of the *social act*.

The *social act*, in Kang's analysis, includes the notion that humans live and experience in a *social context*. This context includes the transactional relations persons undertake with various elements in their immediate setting or situation. Problems are solved, therefore, in terms of the *actual situation* in which objects or values emerge and can be meaningfully explained as part of the whole (Kang, 1976, pp. 30–36). Clearly, for Mead the situation or social context was connected directly to the social act. One could not be studied without consideration of the other.

Miyamoto's criticism of major omissions in the social psychological research and knowledge development directly relate to core ideas of Mead's symbolic interaction. Miyamoto points out that early work did indeed focus on Mead's core ideas. For instance, at the Chicago School, Thomas worked on the definition of the situation, and Park and Burgess worked on cooperation. Subsequently, systematic work on the social act was undertaken by Foote and Cottrell (1955), Weinstein and Deutschberger (1964), and Blumstein (1973). However, emphasis on negotiation in interaction, the fluid nature of social settings (Blumer), and the generally ascientific approach of Blumer may have resulted in deflection of energies from systematic study of the social act.

Kang (1976, pp. 30–36) has also examined Mead's notion of the *actual situation* as it relates to *the act*. Mead proposed using *the act* as a unit of analysis in the transactional context in which persons begin and end a task or face and solve a problem. Kang has noted that Mead's position was that any study of *the act* requires also an analysis of the *actual situation* in order to make generalization to a broader category of situations or social contexts possible. The notion of identifying *the situation* in which certain social acts take place enables a scientific researcher to move from a particular case to a more general principle. Kang uses this illustration to show how Mead integrated his theoretical thinking with his overriding belief in the methods of science.

Mead's Originality—Social Roles. Dewey noted at the time of Mead's death (1931) that Mead had been a remarkably creative and original thinker. Subsequent scholarly analysis of Mead's work supports this contention. This analysis provides us with a theory which has more potential scope and depth than was initially apparent in the immediate posthumous publications. For instance, Mead proposed that there is no separate self, rather that self only exists relative to others. The others "perform existentially different roles, each role being part of a more inclusive social act whose effect is a result of the different role performances" (Miller, 1973, p. 7). This notion, similar to the basic idea of social exchange, makes it possible to connect symbolic interaction to structural role theory (Hardy & Hardy, Chap. 7).

Miller (1973) has discussed Mead's proposal that persons may have a much broader perspective vis-à-vis role performance than the mere attainment of immediate goals. For instance, Mead proposed that the performance of social roles that are fully coordinated with the roles of others in society make for the development of moral excellence, self-realization, and self-actualization. Because persons are able to place themselves in the role of others and from this perspective judge and understand their own behavior, they can consciously and knowingly choose actions which will help determine the direction of group action as well as simultaneously influence their own and others' role performances.

The primary focus of study in symbolic interaction is on social interaction in which persons cooperate to achieve a goal or outcome. Such cooperative behavior requires reasonable consensus between (or among) persons on the nature of the situation. Only as agreement develops regarding the social context (including the anticipated outcomes) is it possible to then coordinate activities to obtain a shared goal.

Mead referred to *reality* in socially coordinated behavior as the outcome of a process entailing mutual interpretation and adjustment. He saw communication as central to this process. Development of the self, the experience of self-awareness, the development of various relevant perspectives, and role-taking all occur and develop in social interaction.

Mead's early theoretical work was on instrumental pragmatism, the notion of gestures, intersubjectivity, and the social origin of the self (Baldwin, 1986; Joas, 1985, p. 35; Miller, 1973). For Mead social activity was purposeful activity involving persons cooperating to achieve goals. Mead referred to this concept as *social action*. Joas (1985, p. 6–7) points out that this construct is much broader than the idea of *social interaction* used by Blumer.

Mead's model of the social act has four phases:

1. Impulse to action (source either internal or external)
2. Perception
3. Manipulation
4. Consummation

As noted earlier, the social act is the basic unit in both social action and in social behavior. Both social action and social behavior consist of a series of social acts for the persons involved in the action or behavior. Role-taking and the related social acts enable persons to mutually adjust their action to the *actual situation* as they engage in establishing a shared perspective. Reality and meaning emerge, as do changes in thinking, emotion, and various biological states. Through this process, socially coordinated goal-directed activity results.

Mead was interested in *subjective experiences* (but eschewed any dependence on nonscientific sources of data, such as introspection).[7] From his fundamental assumption that there is a reciprocal relationship between *mind* and *society* it follows that inner experience (consciousness) is *determined* during and *as a result of* involvement in *social processes*. Thus, to have knowledge of a person's external social experiences is to have (partial) knowledge of their *internal experiences*. The analysis of the social act makes it possible to assess this knowledge and the extent to which social experiences determine subjective experiences.

Thinking or *reflexive intelligence* requires the use of shared symbols or language. When an individual thinks, communication occurs internally. This process is the inner conversation of thinking. Reflexive intelligence makes it possible for persons to identify potential alternative behaviors and to select the best for themselves.[8] Human behavior was conceptualized by Mead as representing intelligent attempts to successfully manage existing conditions.[9]

A related notion that is important for the study of health-related problems is the relationship of *intelligence and problematic situations*.[10] Individual intelligence is related to the ability to solve problems successfully when confronted with new and unusual conditions. Such conditions are part of the immediate situation and require reflective thought and action. Active *mental processes* or *conscious problem-solving activities* are brought into play when an activity has been stopped and cannot be continued readily. Problem-solving efforts are initiated when "real problems are present in the immediate experience . . ." (Baldwin, 1986, citing Mead). Under these circumstances the thinking process becomes totally committed to finding a solution. Such conditions are called "problematic situations." In order to deal successfully with these circumstances, persons engage in reflexive thought, drawing on past experience, including their general knowledge and considerations of the future, as they contemplate possible alternative solutions and their consequences. Thus uncertainty and unpredictable conditions, from the perspective of symbolic interaction, provide valued opportunities for successful change and progress.[11]

The Sociohistorical Context of Symbolic Interaction Work

The influential work of Thomas S. Kuhn (1970) brought to the attention of a wide audience the possibility that both science and the development of scientific knowledge might not be totally objective and rational. They might be influenced by the social context in which they develop. This idea, although not new, was intriguing; it conflicted with the general, well-accepted belief that scientific knowledge is objective, value free, and exists independent of social factors. Participants at nurse scientist conferences have endorsed this perspective. The fascination for scholars that Kuhn's ideas have had seems related to the growing humanistic and antiscientific philosophies that developed in the 1970s.

Kuhn suggested a rationale for considering the environment in which a scientific idea arises. For example, the sociohistorical context within which the conceptualizations of Mead evolved was sufficiently tumultuous and stimulating to have significantly contributed to the identification and the originality of his conceptualizations. Furthermore, the relevance of his ideas for understanding the development of social problems as a response to rapid social change and the appeal of the approach over instinct theory probably hastened the development of his ideas.

Symbolic interaction ideas were being developed in the early 1900s by philosophers in Chicago and achieved remarkable preeminence in sociology during the years 1920 to 1932. The ideas have flourished ever since.

Critical factors marked the 1890s in Chicago—a city of rapid social change and an abundance of social problems. It was a city with a reputation for violence and corruption, a phenomenal rate of growth, and rapid industrialization. There was a rapid influx of immigrant groups seeking work but creating massive social problems. The feminist movement of the day made it possible for women to be active in social reform and for women to seek graduate education. Thus, women were active in social reform during their graduate education and in a focused, scientific manner upon graduation. These developments along with the social chaos, the enthusiastic, future-oriented and proud inhabitants, the depression of 1893, and the magnificence of Chicago's First World's Fair that same year, followed by the violence of the Pullman strike of 1894, served as the backdrop for the development of the University of Chicago (Faris, 1967).

To this tumultuous but rich and challenging environment came young faculty members. They came with a progressive reform orientation, a strong belief in the future of the city and the university, and above all else a strong belief in the value of science in solving human problems. To the university also came an increasing number of women seeking higher education.

CREATING THE UNIVERSITY OF CHICAGO

The University of Chicago, unlike any prior university, was established as a first-rank major university from its opening in 1892. This remarkable creation was made possible by the farsightedness, ambition, inventiveness, and the persuasive skills of its first president, William Harper, together with John D. Rockefeller's interest and wealth, which were invested in the institution. Harper, a young educational revolutionary who had orchestrated the Chatauqua experience in New York State, sought and got the best scholars in the natural and social sciences. He imbued them with his vision of teaching as a confrontation with superior minds steeped in a scientific milieu of ongoing research and publication (Bulmer, 1984; Faris, 1967; Martindale, 1976; Rosenberg, 1982). Commitment to high ideals, new ideas, action, and reform characterized these young, forward-looking faculty scholars and social reformers. Foremost among these was Mead, who joined Chicago's new Department of Philosophy in 1893 at the invitation of its chairman, his close friend and colleague, John Dewey.

Nature of the Academic Milieu

The early years at the University of Chicago were a time and place in which unrestricted theoretical discussions were valued. New theoretical ground was broken. Innovative theoretical discussions provided fertile ground for the growth of some of our current theories in the social sciences and education. Philosophers, sociologists, and psychologists generated the new ideas of pragmatism, symbolic interaction, behaviorism, functionalism, and urban ecology. These theories and their associated empirical work thrived. The simultaneous growth of such a variety of significant theories was unprecedented; a similar phenomenon in the social sciences has not occurred since in the United States.

In spite of the major breakthroughs establishing scientific theories at Chicago, there never developed a strong emotional or fanatical commitment to a cause, doctrine, or theory (Faris, 1967; Heidbreder, 1933). All schools of thought were "working schools." The leadership in philosophy, psychology, and sociology has been credited with creating a stable milieu which fostered diversity and created room for controversy.[12]

The core of philosophers and social psychologists, who were actually experimental psychologists, directed their interests and energies to conducting research and developing theory on social–psychological phenomena. They explored the reciprocal relationship between the individual and society, and the creative, adaptive functioning of humans in their natural and social environment. This focus is not surprising, given the context of Chicago, a frontier town.

The Milieu in the Sociology Department. The social–psychological ideas of Mead found fertile ground in Chicago's sociology department where students took his social psychology course. It was here that the initial work was begun which subsequently was to become the standard content for sociology curriculums. The first American department of sociology was established in 1893 at the University of Chicago. The department began with three members, with Albion Small (previously president of Colby College in Maine) as its chair.

W.I. Thomas, who was among the first students to earn a degree in this department, was subsequently appointed its third faculty member. During the next 25 years he became its most creative, productive, and influential member. Students remembered him for his unusual skill in combining research and theory in all of his work. He stands out as an ethnographer. During his studies in Germany he was influenced by the objective, meticulous scientific methods used in gathering comparative data on peasant groups. He conceptualized attitudes as the simultaneous mobilization of the cognitive and emotional faculties. His notion of personal and social "crisis" is still used in the applied health and social sciences. He made a greater contribution to sociology than did any of his earlier colleagues. His interest in folk sociology or ethnology and attitudes as well as his active participation in a developing sociologic tradition of exploiting ethnological material contributed significantly to the development of symbolic interaction. The style of research he initiated was and still is a dominant research method in symbolic interaction (Faris, 1967). Not surprisingly, over time his own research and that of his students included a symbolic interaction perspective. A major concept for which he is remembered is his *definition of the situation*. The idea for this came from his study with Znaniecki which began with the discarded letters of Polish immigrants and led him to the importance of *definition of the situation* to social behavior.

Establishing the Knowledge Base for the Discipline. A transition within the original sociology department occurred during the period from 1916 to 1920. Between 1920 and 1932 a renewed department became the nucleus for vigorous growth and productivity during which the basic subject matter of sociology was established. Of particular significance is the fact that the faculty were committed to *science* and the development of *basic* knowledge as compared to *applied* knowledge. It was expected that this approach in the long run would yield the greatest results. The justification for science was the potential service it might render to human welfare. Also of importance was the fact that faculty and students were encouraged to take diverse theoretical approaches and open exploration—not to develop or defend doctrine (Faris, 1967). The work of Mead, for example, was not named symbolic interaction until after his death—an illustration of the department's commitment to using important researchable ideas, wherever they came from, rather than restricting its work to a particular school of thought. It is apparent in the literature that the department abhorred the idea of a strong emotional commitment to any particular doctrine and saw such a commitment as destructive to the advancement of scientific knowledge. The issue of avoiding premature closure on ideas was discussed in the literature in terms of the overriding concern that it would inhibit systematic, objective, scientific work. During this period the basic subject matter of sociology was firmly introduced and the importance of qualitative methods in developing symbolic interaction established. It is hard to know now whether this was a requirement of the knowledge or a reflection of the particular interest and expertise of the faculty. Ideas related to symbolic interaction were identified as important enough to integrate into a variety of types of sociological research and to be included in mainstream sociological knowledge.

After the transition, the faculty in the newly rejuvenated and highly influential department were Park, Burgess, and Faris. Their interests, orientations, and expertise had a tremendous impact on the subsequent knowledge to be developed.

The first sociologic text (written by Park and Burgess) and Burgess' work on human ecology are credited as being key factors in the department's success.

The faculty, all strong teachers and very active researchers, were committed to the development of basic science and were an effective group that worked well together. As a team of three (plus Thomas for a few years) they had a phenomenal impact on knowledge development in their discipline.

Park had a unique ability to organize sociological knowledge for students and to stimulate extensive exploratory research. He frequently urged students, with whom he spent hours, to get inside their subject and to live their experience.

Burgess was a phenomenally productive person. He coauthored two highly influential texts while developing sociology of the family and transforming the field of social pathology and crime into objective and scientific disciplines. He was the second faculty member to earn his doctorate within the program.

Faris, the third member of the nucleus, was the departmental chair. He viewed the creation of conditions which made the department effective in both education and the production of new knowledge as his major achievement. The high faculty morale and productivity during this period attests to his success. Although educated as an engineer, idealism led Park to serve 7 years as a missionary. He went to Chicago to obtain his doctorate in philosophy, but his theological interests declined. The influential teachings of Dewey and Mead reportedly changed his life. A commitment to psychology (in which he took his doctorate) and to science replaced his previous commitment to theology. He was asked to join the department for his knowledge of the Dewey–Mead perspective. He taught the basic course on social psychology which originated with them.

Increasing the ferment at Chicago, the student body grew rapidly after the First World War. Veterans selected the school as *the* place to go. They were a mature group accustomed to work and enthusiastic for sociology and an academic career. Chicago was the social laboratory; it was the land of opportunity for scientists with a ready mind and a creative bent.

It was in this setting that a large number of original perspectives and research strategies developed which are still used today. From this context came symbolic interaction.

Opportunity in a Responsive Environment. Mead, along with other academics of similar orientation, worked and lived in Chicago in a world of progressive social reform (Fisher & Strauss, 1979). Interestingly, most of the social scientists came from intensely religious families, but they rejected religion in favor of science. Social problems and the potential for social reform seem, however, to have strongly influenced the direction of their work. The life they created for themselves made it possible to dovetail humanitarian efforts with scientific work. As social reformers, they were challenged by the myriad of social problems faced by the city's ethnic groups, the slums and social conditions in general. Academics and social reformers worked side by side. Mead, as a citizen, was an active participant in progressive efforts and social causes, giving speeches, writing for the mass media, and attending meetings. This social activity complemented his academic work (Fisher & Strauss, 1979).

A center for this social activity was Hull-House, the first Chicago settlement house established in 1889 by Jane Addams. It was a center where women college students and graduates and social scientists (primarily men) worked together.

Hull-House became a laboratory for the social scientists and a center for social reformers and political activists. Not surprisingly most of the social scientists were men and the social reformers were women; the mores of the time were supportive of women playing an active role in public life. It was as respectable to be a social reformer as it was to be an academician (Rosenberg, 1982, pp. 36–38). Mead, an activist, conducted educational research, a survey of social conditions, and proposed a central statistical bureau to serve social policy and action. Men and women, academicians and reformers, sometimes joined in their social reform activities.

This was an ideal setting for generating ideas on the reciprocal relationship between self and society. On the one hand there was intellectual stimulation and a challenge to be scientific. On the other hand there were major social problems and a public pressing for solutions. These two sets of demands were responded to by a strong emphasis on practical and empirical work. The openness and receptiveness to the development and expression of new ideas—which might not have occurred in less turbulent times (Rosenberg 1982)—provided a rich environment and impetus for Mead to integrate his social philosophy with work on social problems.

Intellectual Currents Influencing American Thought

Dewey, Mead, and their colleagues developed the philosophical ideas of pragmatism. Mead described pragmatism as the convergence of the scientific method and of Darwin's evolutionary theory. Both assume incremental change and a progressive character of life and emphasize the emergent nature of change rather than the absoluteness of change.

Besides the tumultuous but receptive social context in which new theoretical ideas were being generated, the intellectual currents of the time were probably equally disruptive and influential for Mead. For example, Darwin's ideas of evolution, Spencer's ideas on social evolution, and Hegel's notion of dialectical processes were fundamental to Mead's and Dewey's conceptual work. But probably the strongest influences on the development of Mead's ideas at that time were the German philosophies and his experience in Wundt's experimental psychology laboratory in Germany (Joas, 1985; Natanson, 1973, p. 1). Also, the newly developing philosophical ideas of functionalism and pragmatism and an emphasis on science were central to the department and a significant part of the intellectual milieu at Chicago.

The functionalists in that era viewed the mind as a natural object open to study. They saw the mind and mental activities as well as the environment (both natural and social) as having practical importance for the emergence of the individual (Rosenberg & Turner, 1981, p. 6). From pragmatism came the belief that knowledge should have a bearing on social problems and the source of that knowledge is science. Functionalists also had an explicit faith in the scientific method as a means for solving problems (Miller, 1973).

There are some similarities between the social forces encountered by social health scientists today and those encountered by the early contributors to symbolic interaction. Some of the parallels include the social unrest and activism of the 1960s, the economic depression of 1970, the associated increase in unemployment and social problems and reduced resources for dealing with them, the feminist movement which led to entry of women into traditionally male disciplines and, subsequently, a backlash that compromised the gains in equality made by feminists.

Relevance of Symbolic Interaction to the Health Sciences

Factors which we took into account in selecting symbolic interaction to illustrate the characteristics of a developing body of scientific knowledge include the relevance of the theory's concepts and methods to health care. In addition, the concepts and some of the basic assumptions are part of the health care provider's orientation. The dyad, the focus of study in symbolic interaction, along with the domain of the social situation in which the dyad is located, the meaning of events, and the integrity or inseparability of the person and environment all have been part of the orientation in nursing since Florence Nightingale's work.

Some of this theory's concepts and methods are used by current nurse scientists. Some of the concepts, such as the self, role making, socialization, meaning, definition of the situation, and reference groups are used extensively in the health science literature (Conway, 1974; Hardy & Conway, 1978; Tuckett & Kaufert, 1978; Twaddle, 1981). Benoleil (1983), for example, has worked with many symbolic interaction concepts. She has used body image, awareness contexts, status passage, role identity, turning point, deviant careers, and reference groups in her studies of patients with mastectomies, chronic illness, and diabetes.

The methods of symbolic interaction may be useful in developing a knowledge base. The long descriptive research period during which work was focused on concepts and case studies ultimately provided a basis for developing a scientific knowledge base. Health care providers may wish to look at the early work in depth to see whether it provides insight into useful work of social scientists working in this area. The tolerance of diverse ideas and open exploration in the early stage of symbolic interaction is another philosophical approach that potential health care providers may wish to examine and evaluate. The scientific work on symbolic interaction presents no special problem to health scientists since the underlying philosophy supports the use of scientific method; the approach is totally compatible with the approach in health care science.

Symbolic interaction theory combines physiological, psychological, and social aspects in its core concepts. It may be a source of insight to health scientists. The theory itself is relevant to phenomena of particular interest to nursing and may provide a better explanation and more predictive power than other current theoretical approaches (Murphy, 1985; Paige, 1980; Whitmyer, 1984). The value of the approach may be due to its long history of scientific development. Our interest now turns to theory development.

PART 2: STAGES OF THEORY DEVELOPMENT

Theories differ significantly in their levels of maturity. Theoretical ideas may range from being at a vague or elementary stage of development to being part of a precise and refined formulation. In the early stages of substantive theory development the characteristics of the available knowledge are quite different from those at later stages. The *level* of theory development is an important factor to take into account when working with a theory, when selecting a theory for directing research, and when selecting a theory for use in any practice setting. The type of knowledge available, the strategies which may be used for extending the theory, and the empirical work which is generally undertaken differ according to the stage of development. Also, the clarity, usefulness, and empirical support for theoretical ideas and the selection of criteria for evaluating them differ according to the extent to which the conceptualizations have been developed.

For understanding, evaluating, and applying scientifically developed knowledge, the responsible health care professional should be skilled in identifying and working with all levels of conceptualization. Any decision to implement an action based on creative but invalid ideas, on vaguely understood concepts, or on conceptualizations still awaiting empirical testing is likely to be potentially serious or even hazardous. Practice guided by scientific knowledge is the hallmark of a profession and is expected by consumers.

FOUR STAGES OF THEORY DEVELOPMENT

In the early development of a theoretical perspective scientific activities are primarily those of conceptualization and concept development. Identifying sets of interrelated theoretical statements and determining lawful relationships cannot be attempted in a meaningful way until concepts are clearly defined and made measurable through operational definitions. Thus, during the early stages of a theory's development the theorist's main concern is with conceptualizing ideas and relating these ideas to the world of reality by means of descriptive works. During later stages of development greater emphasis can be placed on identifying lawful relationships between concepts, including the development of testable statements, the development of theory-based predictions, and the accumulating of empirical evidence for support or refutation of such predictions.

If scientific theory and research in a substantive area are examined as they develop over a period of time, stages (which are not always distinct) can be identified. The first stage is one of *conceptualization*, which involves identifying and developing the basic ideas and concepts that typically are expressed in ordinary words. These ideas come from experience and observation. There then evolves a second stage, one of *systematic knowledge development*. During this stage work focuses on explicating the meaning of concepts, specifying and differentiating concepts, establishing empirical relevance, and finally, systematizing existing knowledge. This stage requires extensive time, effort, and person hours. Stage three involves *systematic theorizing*, and finally, stage four entails working with the *formal theory*.

The sequential stages are illustrated in Figure 2. Progress begins with conceptualization and gaining systematic knowledge through observation (stages one and two), continues through systematic theorizing, and ends with well-formulated theory and a formal scientific knowledge base (stages 3 and 4). This development is portrayed as ascending the staircase. However, in the ongoing work of science, it is common to move down a step or two or move up and down before an adequate scientific foundation makes the desired upward movement the only direction to go.

The goals of science are evident in the different stages of theory development. In the early stages the work is descriptive and gives only a general sense of

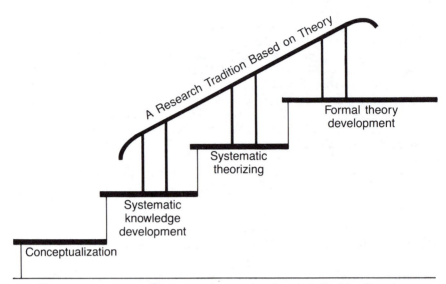

Figure 2. Stages of theory development and a Research Tradition Based on Theory (RTBT). The RTBT (or paradigm) guides and supports normal scientific activities.

understanding. This contrasts with the focus in the latter two stages when the major focus is on empirical testability and increasing the precision of the tests of theoretical formulations. Stage three—systematic theorizing—provides theory that is capable of both explaining and predicting. Knowledge at stage four— formal theory—has gained increased predictive capability. At this level of theory development the knowledge may be used to develop intervention strategies. A Kuhnian paradigm, that is, a Research Tradition Based on Theory (RTBT), does not emerge until the scientific work moves into the second stage—systematic knowledge development.[13]

The sequential model illustrating stages of development of scientific knowledge is not intended to reflect day-to-day scientific work; rather, it is a reflection of the stages of growth of scientific knowledge over time. The day-to-day scientific work may appear chaotic, with many false starts and much noncumulative and tedious work. Assembling a cumulative body of scientific knowledge requires the work of many scientists with many hours of effort. The work of the serious scientist is focused and ongoing. Accordingly, the knowledge base is likely to grow at an uneven rate, with periods of progress and periods of retrogression. Like other intellectual work of professionals, progress occurs in fits and starts with frequent missteps and wrong turns taken.

Even with extended groups working on a scientific body of knowledge, development occurs relatively slowly. For instance, work on symbolic interaction has been going on for more than 80 years and much of it is still at the conceptualization phase.

Stage One: Conceptualization

To illustrate the development of scientific theory, we have described the origin and development of symbolic interaction. The evolution of the theory of symbolic interaction can be understood more readily by considering it in terms of stages of theory development. The early stages of theory development are emphasized because that is the phase where most of the work in the health sciences and nursing science is still needed.

In the first stage, conceptualization, ideas are developed and expressed with varying degrees of clarity, utilizing associated sets of concepts. The early ideas may or may not develop into a theoretical perspective. Not infrequently, theoretical work which initially seems farfetched or unimportant becomes recognized as a significant scientific contribution. Scientists whose early work in the conceptualizing of social processes, through labeling what appeared to them to be important, regularly occurring phenomena, patterns, and diversities in social behavior, may not be readily identifiable as making major contributions to what we now call role theory. When new ideas are proposed to explain patterns of social behavior, the meanings of the major concepts may be unclear and may be used inconsistently. The basic ideas are usually only partially thought through. The usefulness of an early perspective for advancing knowledge is often unclear when such a perspective is first presented. There is no way of determining the potential scientific payoff of newly developing ideas.

Scientific theories, composed of networks of ideas, develop slowly. If new conceptualizations are to be used, the ideas need to be clear, plausible, and have increased potential for generating research (relative to ideas of existing theories). To move ideas from being vague conceptualizations to being a body of publicly discussed ideas requires both the original ideas and the skill to convey them to one's peers so they are convinced of their originality and usefulness. The visibility and productivity of his friend Dewey, his own reticence, the "behaviorism" shock wave initiated in 1913 by J.B. Watson (a student of Mead's) all contributed to Mead's theoretical and philosophical work going largely unnoticed during his lifetime. Mead's style of theorizing and writing, discussed earlier, precluded easy identification of his new and exciting theories by his readers. Also Mead's tendency to spend more time engaged in social action and political activities than scientific meetings may have restricted his influence. His work has only begun to be known, analyzed, and generally appreciated by philosophers since the 1960s (Miller, 1973).

In the early stages of theory development there is considerable looseness of expression in conveying the new notions. Novel ideas are generated from uncommon or different experiences and these ideas need to be conceptualized (i.e., encoded in words). At first, ordinary terms are used to represent the new ideas; such terms may be applied to very different phenomena from what the term normally stands for (such as in the case of Mead's theorizing, in which the term *the act* was used). Usually newly developing ideas are difficult to articulate but they gain clarity and intersubjectivity through the process of discussion and writing. Initially original ideas are very loosely formulated and as a result are difficult to explain. Consequently, everyone, other than the originator, has difficulty understanding the new notions. In part this problem exists because of the new meanings attached to common terms, but even more important is the fact that the experience upon which the originator's conceptualizations are developed are always somewhat different from that of others. The originator of new ideas needs to persist with trying to conceptualize the ideas so they become clearer in his own mind and carry the same ideas to those who read or hear of them. This is what is meant by developing intersubjectivity.

A lack of clarity in defining the new ideas is due partly to the complex theoretical notion being represented by an ordinary term to which it may be only marginally related. The theorist may have difficulty in articulating the meaning at this initial stage of the conceptual work since a precise vocabulary has not been developed.

Everyday Terminology in Symbolic Interaction. The sharing of ideas seems to be necessary for the originator to work out meanings of his new concept and to develop a link between the new "experience" and the linguistic terms that represent it best. Simple ordinary language, with all the ambiguity of dictionary definitions, is usually where communication starts. Mead developed some very complex notions which were represented by such everyday terms as *gestures, self, I,* and *me,* also *role-taking, perspectives, social act, situation, conversation of gestures, temporality,* and *generalized other.* The simplicity of the terms belies the complex notions Mead was creating. Mead's mode of restating his ideas was to try to convey to his listeners (usually students) the sense that the terms had a different meaning than their usual one (Miller, 1973).

Working with Ill-Defined Concepts. Attention now turns to working with ill-defined concepts, concepts which have vague or contradictory meanings. This process of clarifying the meanings of selected concepts or a cluster of concepts, known variously as explicating the meaning of a concept, concept analysis, linguistic analysis, and concept evaluation, involves untangling the meanings associated with a concept and subsequently selecting those meanings which are found to be relevant. The aim is to identify all significant properties—those that must be present for the concept to be applied or used. In the process of explication other concepts may be differentiated from the working concept. Also while establishing the meaning of terms, other terms may emerge or become differentiated from the working group of concepts. Empiricists draw their knowledge from the world through verifiable research. Thus additional information pertaining to the meaning of a concept is acquired through empirical observations (Kim & Schwartz-Barcott, 1986).

Global Theory—Loosely Formulated Ideas

Developing Scientific Theory. Work on theory at the early stage of conceptualizing consists of identifying and working on the basic concepts. This entails determining if the phenomena of interest exist, developing conceptual definitions, and determining appropriate empirical referents. The process of identifying concepts begins the delineation of the phenomena of interest.[14] These phenomena usually are seen as fundamental and unique to the discipline and to the "theory." At a minimum, scientific theory requires definable and measurable concepts, statements of relationships between the concepts, and a potential for empirical testing.

During this early stage of theory development, global theories often emerge.[15] Such theories are not really scientific theories and they may actually impede the development of scientific theory. As we have just discussed, much of the conceptualization in the beginning of theory development amounts to working with an amorphous collection of loosely formulated ideas that may have only vague connection to the empirical world. These ideas may be moved into an empirical realm and become the focus of true scientific activity or they may degenerate and be presented as a global theory.

Global theories are usually loose collections of very general ideas that are purported to describe and explain many vaguely identified phenomena. They may give the originator and the originator's disciples a sense of understanding, but in actuality they serve more as a basis for an ideology rather than a true scientific theory. Sociologists in the early days of the discipline searched for a unified theory that could explain all of human behavior. Underlying this search was a belief in a grand unity of knowledge that would generally be applicable in solving all of the problems of humanity. Faris has noted that there may be such feverish excitement in creating such all-inclusive and valuable systems of thought (in the face of ignorant and powerful rivals—other theorists) that slow, calm, objective research can hardly be expected to be undertaken (Faris, 1967, pp. 4–6).

Merton (1968, p. 7) and Mills (1959) have also extensively criticized global theories for their obscurity, unintelligibility, and general lack of relation to reality. Mills has described such schemes as expositions on the nature of man that are elaborate and arid formalizations composed of highly abstract and vague concepts. He noted that the general lack of definable concepts in such theories makes it impossible to move with them between different levels of abstraction. Merton (1968) noted that the early phases of most fledgling disciplines often are characterized by these all-encompassing formulations: "Extravagant claims, total systems of theory, adequate to the entire range of problems encompassed by the discipline." Merton was primarily concerned with the obtuse writings and conceptual schemes developed by Parsons which did not lend themselves to empirical testing. Merton urged the use of middle range or partial theories. Unlike global theories, the middle range theories are deductive theoretical formulations which can be subjected to empirical testing.

A global theory, although it may create an illusion for both the originator and beholder of an understanding of reality, actually prevents systematic research. Research is prevented because of the use of vague global concepts and a concomitant lack of specific, identifiable relationships between such concepts.

Efforts made in developing global theories may thwart appropriate attempts to

1. focus on specific, significant empirical problems
2. identify clearly the central concepts
3. develop conceptual or theoretical definitions
4. develop empirical links and operational definitions of concepts
5. develop a system of theoretical statements
6. develop testable hypotheses for making predictions
7. accumulate knowledge

Global theory development seems to be a fairly typical initial step by some theorists in establishing a knowledge base for newly developing disciplines. The creation of an overriding theory may, however, impede the development of scientific knowledge.

Development of Global Theory Related to Roles. The two major branches of role theory, structural role theory and symbolic interaction, both began as global theories.

Structural Role Theory. Parsons, a Harvard sociologist, studied in Europe in the 1930s. He developed a style of incorporating sociology and philosophy in the vein of the grand theorizing of European sociologists. His publication, *The Structure of Social Action* (Parsons 1937), was a landmark in setting a new course in sociology which dominated theoretical developments from the early 1940s to the mid-1960s (Coser, 1976). Parsons developed numerous abstract conceptual schemes for attempting to understand society. His writings were difficult to understand and other publications mushroomed as scholars tried to clarify the meaning of his theorizing. In his writings he developed the early ideas of the norms and values governing the social structure in which people were enmeshed. In *The Social System*, Parsons focused on both the importance of institutionalized values and norms and the development of differentiated social roles which correspond to differentiated status positions. He is credited with developing the major ideas of a normative structural role theory. The criticisms made by Merton and Mills were primarily directed at Parsons' voluminous, diffuse, abstract writings about society and the social structure. His ideas themselves were considered interesting. Because these ideas had all the characteristics of a global theory, however, they did not provide a basis for research. Merton, a one-time student of Parsons, was a social structuralist who rejected Parsons' attempt to develop a general, all-encompassing theory and opted for a more modest goal, namely, the development of theoretical propositions of the middle range to study a limited set of empirical phenomena (Merton, 1968).

The development of scientific middle range theories, with their associated cumulative research, was the immediate goal of Merton's plea to his colleagues. Structural sociologists began to respond—first by reporting focused, empirical work on problematic aspects of the social structure. For example, several early studies were published on role conflict, lack of role consensus (see Hardy & Hardy, Chap. 7), and adoption of nonconforming behavior (deviance) such as the sick role, presumed to be a consequence of structural problems.

Symbolic Interaction. The empirical work in symbolic interaction began in the early 1900s; focused theoretical research was initiated in the 1920s and 1940s. Symbolic interaction had the potential for developing into a global theory, but Mead's systematic theorizing and his careful linking of his developing ideas with empirical work kept the theory from degenerating. The milieu in which the theory developed further fostered a tight relationship between theory and research.

The first research based on Mead's developing ideas on symbolic interaction was undertaken at the Chicago School. It was descriptive research in general which focused on identifying the subjects' world view, the variety of perspectives the subjects held, and the shared communication occurring in identifiable (sub)-groups. Some of the studies[16] focused on "types" of human activity; this group included *The Hobo* (Anderson, 1923), *The Sales Lady* (Donovan, 1929), and *Taxi-Hall Girls* (Becker, 1930). Other studies looked at social behavior, including *Suicide* (Cavan, 1928), *Family* (Mowrer, 1929), and *Organized Crime* (Landesco, 1929). The Chicago tradition (symbolic interaction as a theoretical focus and utilization of field research methods) has continued to the present. Studies include observations of the changing of self-concept with changes in the situation (Goffman, 1963), observations of the negotiation and bargaining that occurs between physicians and patients (including the strategies both use to advance their view) (Goffman, 1959; Roth, 1963), and observations of negotiation relative to death and dying in different settings and situations (Glaser & Strauss, 1965; Sudow, 1967).

Advancing beyond observation, Weinstein and Deutschberg (1964) and Blumstein (1973) have utilized experimental studies to investigate negotiation during social acts and have looked at the strategies utilized by the subjects.

A Note on Methodology

The faculty in the University of Chicago sociology department were committed to the development of social *science*. The empirical work on Polish immigrants by Thomas is still cited today for the development of the concept *definition of the situation*. The strong empirical orientation in time was coupled with a strong commitment to develop theory; thus research and theory were closely allied. Furthermore, the faculty were committed to basic social science knowledge, not particularly to applied knowledge. This was a remarkable stance considering the abundance and urgency of social problems in their immediate community.

Research on Mead's ideas began in this milieu. Accordingly, the qualitative research conducted on Meadian ideas was also work that helped define the body of knowledge for the discipline.

The Chicago faculty's strong commitment to science—especially measurement and quantification—resulted in the almost unanimous agreement in the 1920s to bring to the department experts in statistical methods and scaling techniques. This introduction of quantitative methods provided a sound basis for examining the developing knowledge base for its scientific merit (Faris, 1967). The result was also to add to the diversity of the methodologies available in the department. Scaling techniques and quantification became an accepted part of research at the Chicago School.[17] Meanwhile, the department's collective spirit and commitment to ideas remained strong. However, for symbolic interaction, the strong tradition of field work research persisted.

As a partial outgrowth of the Chicago School, a strong positivist orientation to sociological knowledge developed in the late 1930s at the University of Iowa.[18] M.H. Kuhn, the chair at the Iowa School, initiated the use of quantitative research on partial theories with his own studies on the self. The work thus begun on partial theories at Iowa was successful in generating multiple empirically based *subtheories* (Kuhn, 1964).

Thus we see that the conceptualization phase in the development of both branches of role theory—symbolic interaction and structural role theory—began with loosely formulated, general ideas. As the basic ideas in symbolic interaction were being taught by Mead they became the focus of field studies conducted by both faculty and doctoral students. Even though the initial ideas were broad and not always precisely defined, they nevertheless provided a basis for empirical descriptions. Approximately 25 years after Mead introduced the new ideas, systematic quantitative research was initiated.

The history of the development of role theory illustrates the notion that the early stage of theory building tends to be one in which theoretical expositions are initially of the global theory type. This type of theorizing may then progress to other theoretical and scientific activities which, when considered in toto, characterize the stage of conceptualization.

Stage Two: Systematic Knowledge Development

Narrowing the Conceptual Focus: Refining the Concepts. As a perspective progresses beyond the initial conceptualization phase, changes in both the theoretical and research orientations become apparent. Scientists initially focus on developing the details of selected workable ideas and terms. The terms which are selected are likely to be those emerging in the conceptualization phase which have potential for inclusion in an empirically testable theory. Attention then turns to working with the selected concept or cluster of concepts. The work actually begins with explicating the meaning of concepts so that the basic properties are identified. This process not only clarifies the meaning of the working group of concepts but links each of them to existing knowledge bases and to each other. While establishing the meaning of the terms, other terms may emerge or become differentiated from the working group of concepts. For example, a study of role made it possible to differentiate a role from a social position. Subsequently role behavior, role expectations, and role performance were terms that gained clear meanings, distinguishing each of them from the others and from the previously undifferentiated term, *role*. Accordingly, where there was previously only one general concept, now there may be several, each of which is more specific. Thus, in attempting to clarify the meaning of a term the cluster of relevant terms increases and it may be possible to identify the relationship among some of them. This cluster of interrelated concepts, also known as a set or network, has the potential for being used in the formation of an empirically testable theory. During the literature review conducted to explicate the meaning of a working set of concepts, it may be possible to identify theoretical and empirical statements relating the working concept to other concepts. Of importance here is the development of a set of theoretical statements containing the working concept.

Depending on the nature of the knowledge base, it may be possible to identify or develop both general theoretical statements and some more precise ones. The interrelatedness of the concepts makes it possible to generate testable statements (hypotheses) but before empirical testing can occur it is necessary to develop empirical measures of the concepts which reflect the explicated meanings. Of course it is only necessary to develop such measures for the concepts included in the testable statement.

The work primarily involves an interplay between concept specifications and concept explication on the one hand (Hardy, 1985), and measurement of the defined concepts on the other. The result is a differentiated set of concepts which become defined with increased clarity and consistency, and measured with increased reliability, validity, and precision.

Early conceptual differentiation by Park (1920) and Linton (1936) demonstrates the conceptual and definitional work that must be done in the early stages of theory development. For example, in analyzing the nature of social organizations and the individual's embeddedness in them, Linton clearly differentiated the concepts of status, role, and individual. *Status* and *role* were taken to represent the social structure, and *individual* to represent the person.

Structuralists continued working with the structural aspects of role, and the symbolic interactionists were able to begin to develop concepts describing the individual *in interaction with* or *in negotiation with* the social structure. Again, this work on theory development primarily involved specifying and describing the conceptual ideas. More recent illustrations of concept differentiation can be seen in Turner's (1962) differentiation between role making and role taking and Lauer and Boardman's (1971) subsequent work on role taking.

Clear definitions become an important focus of scholarly work. The identification of a significant set of concepts and the explication of their meaning become the central tasks. Concepts in the working cluster may be used to define other concepts in the set. Thus the definitions move from common dictionary definitions to precise theoretical definitions. The scientific work may take considerable time and energy and be associated with frequent intellectual struggles with colleagues over the validity of the work before sufficient agreement within the community of scholars and scientists can be achieved. Once there is agreement on the set of concepts, however, and on their theoretical meaning, then productive, cumulative work becomes possible. This type of conceptual work did not occur to any major extent in symbolic interaction until recently. Several textbooks published since 1969 have focused on definitional work (Biddle, 1979; Biddle & Thomas, 1979; Heiss, 1981).

Classifying Existing Knowledge. Creating order among the diverse sets of knowledge (concepts, empirical generalizations, and propositions) that are generated during stage one and in the early work of stage two is an important activity in a discipline before systematic theorizing can be successfully undertaken. Typologies and taxonomies are the simplest most used forms of such classification. This work reduces the volume of empirical phenomena and establishes some sense of organization for studying them. The properties of the studied concepts are used in deriving the classification scheme. It is important that the classification system itself not be confused with the scientific theory it supports.

One important outcome of classifying empirical generalizations, propositions, and concepts is the identification of new areas for building theory. An important method for systematically organizing statements is on the basis of antecedents (independent variable) and their consequences (dependent variable) (Zetterberg, 1963). This type of codification has been carried out with many thousands of family studies to reduce the diversity and to look for commonalities (Burr et al., 1979). Systematizing the existing knowledge base makes it possible to develop it further through purposeful research generated from specific theories. This classification process takes us to the next stage of knowledge development.

Stage Three: Systematic Theorizing

Once a body of research has become well organized, it is possible to advance the knowledge base through systematic theorizing. This process results in a cumulative development of knowledge. One strategy that may facilitate this development is the use of theories that have a fair degree of generality. Generality promotes theories that can subsume many microconcepts and can be used in different substantive areas. Structural role theory and symbolic interaction have this characteristic of generality and both have been found useful for developing a knowledge base on families, organizations, health care, and illness. Systems theory has also served this function in the past. Social exchange theory, which has been carefully developed into a scientific theory, also has been used across a large number of problem areas and disciplines.

Other strategies for systematic theory development may include the use of a propositional inventory of antecedents and consequences. Small, partial theories may be combined to provide a larger network of ideas for scientific investigation.

In the third stage, the research is likely to be primarily correlational but will also include theoretical reasoning suggesting the direction of influence among the small set of variables.

Research becomes much more productive in this third stage. It is guided by a theory-based research program which provides a basis for ongoing normal research that may be on both conceptual and empirical problems. The existence of a research tradition implies that a "community of scientists" is working on facilitating the advance of theory and research. Research is not random but becomes cumulative, developing from other research and theory in the RTBT.

Such theory development becomes possible only after an empirical body of knowledge has been accumulated. Sufficient data sets must be gathered from numerous studies and from different areas to permit integration and synthesis. Theoretical formulations at this stage are expressed verbally (in contrast to the abstract calculus of a formal theory). Efforts are made to extract, collate, and organize empirical generalizations into a meaningful theoretical structure.

Partial Theories. By working with a limited number of concepts that can be linked to the empirical world via operational definitions and a series of focused research investigations of limited scope, a focused, circumscribed knowledge base can be developed. The theory must be logically sound before the empirical work of testing relationships between specific sets of statements can begin. The development of partial theories is an important procedure for working with portions of *grand theory* (which are otherwise unresearchable), thereby bringing subsets of these into the realm of scientific knowledge.

Concepts in the working cluster may be used to define additional concepts in the set. Thus the loosely defined concepts eventually acquire definitions within an overall set of concepts. This means they acquire *theoretical definitions*. The scientific work required to develop reasonable definitions and a collection of significant concepts may take considerable time and energy and be associated with frequent intellectual struggles with colleagues over the validity of the selections. Once concepts are explicitly defined, operationalized, and become the basis of a (small) body of coherent research, the antagonism or skepticism of colleagues may abate. Partial theories may be a useful theory construction strategy; if partial theories are closely related (both in substantive focus and semantically) they may be combined to generate new and broader propositions and a larger cumulative knowledge base.

Partial theories are often named according to their specific focus (e.g., role negotiation) rather than the global theory or more general orientation from which they evolved.

An illustration of systematic theoretical work to develop partial theories is found in family theory (Burr et al., 1979). There are over 20 specific substantive domains which utilize a number of general theoretical perspectives. Several new subtheories were formulated using the symbolic interaction perspective. They consist of clusters of interrelated propositions and their focus is circumscribed. Examples include *definition of the situation* and *role transition* (Burr et al., 1979). This work, carried out by scholars working on family theory, represents a particularly significant knowledge-building effort by a community of scientists.

Stage Four: Formal Theory

After a theoretical area has accumulated considerable empirical research and interest turns to formalizing a theory, the focus is directed to the theoretical syntax or relationships between the concepts. Work then centers on developing more precise specification of the relationships expressed in theoretical statements.

Thus the description of the relationship between concepts moves from verbal descriptions to precise numerical specifications. A theory may then be expressed abstractly in a mathematical equation. In formal theories, abstract symbols are often useful in the theory explication process (Blalock, 1969, 1970). (A publication by Kinch [1963] illustrates an early use of formal or axiomatic theory in symbolic interaction. A more recent application of such theory has been published by Hage [1980] for studying organizations.)

Scientific theory is expected to be parsimonious. Therefore, simplifying is an important part of formal theory development. Instead of including the complexity of social phenomena the *way* of representing it is simplified, either by making simplifying assumptions (limiting the explanatory variables) as is done in causal modeling (see Blalock, 1969, for illustration of these) or by creating simplified situations. The latter is used in the study of processes by through an examination in a controlled setting—either a field or laboratory setting. Extraneous, potentially contaminating variables are excluded; only the variables of interest are included and are manipulated to study their effect. Gradually a theory is developed utilizing both these simplifying procedures.

In this chapter the stages of theory development have been discussed and work in the area of symbolic interaction has been cited to illustrate the discussion. The use of symbolic interaction as a case to be analyzed by the theoretical stages proposed has hopefully been helpful, lending credence to the stages proposed. It is clear, however, that the theoretical work is not linear as the model would suggest: Work at several stages may occur simultaneously; also, work at one stage does not preclude retrogressing to a simpler level. The presence of a conceptually based research tradition evolves only after systematic knowledge development work on theoretical statements predominates.

SUMMARY—SYMBOLIC INTERACTION AND THE STAGES OF THEORY DEVELOPMENT

In the process of establishing, clarifying, and exploring a new idea or set of ideas, an oral tradition develops. This occurred in the development of symbolic interaction. If the ideas are sustained over a period of time and generate supporters, then a school of thought becomes identified with both the ideas and the proponents of the ideas. This also occurred: Mead's theorizing and teachings made a significant impact on sociology during his lifetime and in the years that followed. The impact was strongest between 1915 and 1935; the symbolic interaction orientation and phenomenal amount of research and research publications generated by the University of Chicago sociology department resulted in both work and workers being known as the Chicago School. The supporters of symbolic interaction endorsed diversity in ideas and research; they formed a spirited community of scholars and scientists.

The Chicago School relied heavily on the oral tradition for sharing. The Iowa School never attained the network connectedness of the Chicago School (Meltzer et al., 1978). Independent scientific work and impersonal communication through scholarly papers and journals at Iowa may have replaced Chicago's oral transmission of ideas. Scientific work is generally considered relatively independent work but for progress to occur scientists need to be part of a community. The scientific orientations of the two "schools" of symbolic interaction have been integrated into departments among many universities across the country.

The work in symbolic interaction was initiated at the Chicago School. Here, the early theory and research efforts focused on bolstering the general Meadian ideas by empirical illustration. The substantive domain of symbolic interaction was developed during this time. Work subsequently focused on further development of this knowledge base. Scaling and measurement techniques made it possible to differentiate concepts. Statistical techniques made it possible to measure the relationship between concepts and develop empirically grounded theoretical statements. Thus, quantitative methods made it possible for scientific work to move from the stage of *conceptualization* to one of *systematic knowledge development*. The work in these two stages is occurring simultaneously today on ideas originating from the Chicago School tradition. Serious work on systematic theorizing began with significant improvement in qualitative methods. Some noncumulative methodological work has been conducted on formal theory. The major focus of work has been more on developing appropriate investigative methodologies and less on role theory.

NOTES

1. R.E. Faris (1967) was a remarkably informative source. In his book Faris wrote about the Chicago School where his father, E. Faris, was chair and where he obtained his doctoral degree. Faris' personal connections to that time are not evident in the book; his account is dispassionate and well documented. Two sources, Meltzer et al. (1975) and Rock (1979), are both descriptive and critical of symbolic interactionism. Rock's critique is unusual in that, being English, he did not grow up with symbolic interaction as a standard part of the sociological curriculum and thus his perspective retains some of that valuable stance of a stranger. Emerson (1983) is an excellent source for an analysis of the research methodology (field research) that developed simultaneously with the ideas on symbolic interaction. The author makes clear distinctions between the ethnographic methodology, qualitative methodology which includes methods for dealing with reliability and validity, and "grounded theory" methodology. The latter methodology is used in health care research. Emerson reminds the reader that the grounded theory approach of Glaser and Strauss is based on the qualitative branch of the Chicago School and, like Blumer's

work, the focus is on the process of discovering and elaborating theory; the concern is with discovery and not with verification of theory. Rather, the end product stands by itself. Most of the background on Mead is based on the works of the following:

- Sociologists: Baldwin, 1988; Bulmer, 1984; Burr et al., 1979; Faris, 1967; Fisher & Strauss, 1979; Goff, 1980; Joas, 1985; Kuhn, 1978; Martindale, 1976; Meltzer et al., 1978; Rock, 1979; Thomas & Biddle, 1979
- Feminist theory: Deegon, 1985; Rosenberg, 1982
- Philosophers: Corti, 1973; Kang, 1975; Miller, 1973; Natanson, 1973.

2. Sources such as Biddle and Thomas credit Linton with the introduction of social structure. Crediting this breakthrough to Linton rather than Park may be a reflection of the tendency to portray role theory as an interdisciplinary enterprise. Park was a very productive faculty member of the sociology department while Linton, it seems, was a student in anthropology. Sociology and anthropology were one department until well into the 1930s, and even after anthropology became an independent department there were close ties between the two departments (Faris, 1967).

3. The social sciences have generated the body of knowledge we know as symbolic interaction theory. This common knowledge base was created and is shared by self-selected social psychologists, in particular those in sociology, and some in anthropology.

4. Wundt based his methods on those that had been used to develop the scientific knowledge base in physiology. The new methodological approach was established to replace the tradition of using "introspection" to obtain data on the mind.

Current publications in psychology draw attention to extensive misrepresentation of Wundt's work in American texts. Apparently, the problem arose from Tischner's erroneous comments on Wundt's work (Reiber, 1980). Also Hall, the first American psychologist to work with Wundt, failed to represent Wundt's work accurately (Reiber, 1980). (Hall was Dewey's mentor and also influenced Mead to travel to Berlin [Rosenberg, 1982].)

5. Reductionism is an approach used in science whereby complex phenomena (e.g., human behavior) are explained by moving to more basic levels of analysis (e.g., neuro-chemical). With this approach, animals will often be used as models for the study of mechanisms and processes in humans.

6. *Sources providing a new perspective on symbolic interaction.* Joas' (1985) work is the most comprehensive explication of Mead's theoretical position and Mead's social and political activities. Joas also identifies major limitations and biases in most publications on Mead and symbolic interaction. Baldwin (1986) adds support to Joas' work. He provides both a new perspective and new material on symbolic interaction, Mead's view of persons as whole entities (utilizing simultaneous assessment of biological, psychological, and social aspects), his commitment to science, and his work on a unified theory. The next two publications are concerned with the social context. Bulmer (1984) provides important information on the social context in which Mead worked—the University of Chicago and the institutional forces contributing to the success of symbolic interaction. Rosenberg (1983) discusses women in higher education at the University of Chicago, providing information on the females in academe, their work as activists, and their scholarly work with Mead and other social scientists.

7. Introspection is the major data source used by Blumer. The publication by Joas and Baldwin emphasize that Mead found introspection and other subjective sources of data unacceptable because they did not meet the criteria of science. Mead's strong scientific orientation and the unacceptability of nonobjective methods have not been identified in *American* publications prior to Baldwin (1986) and therefore are not part of the standard knowledge in this country.

8. Science, for Mead, represented the highest form of reflexive intelligence.

9. Pragmatism and social behaviorism together generate the view that human behavior is an intelligent effort to deal with the environment. If such behavior allows an individual to manage the existing condition successfully, then gratification is experienced. Subsequent behavior is directed at achieving similar gratification; thus gratifying behaviors are learned and repeated. Therefore, creative social change and progress, in Mead's view, was achieved through reflexive thought followed by intelligent choice and gratifying behavior.

10. The notions of stress and strain are reconceptualized in terms of "problematic situations" which cannot be solved. (See Hardy & Hardy, Chap. 7, "Stress and Strain.")

11. W.I. Thomas, a student of Mead's and an early symbolic interactionist, has used similar ideas to advance the notion of *crisis* at both the individual and societal levels. Consistent with Mead's perspective, Thomas proposed that the more *crises* (Thomas' term) or problematic situations a person encounters and handles successfully, the greater the social intelligence of that person. Thomas' view on crisis has similarities to the *crisis theory* so central to the work of some health professionals, particularly those in community mental health. (Thomas' view is discussed more fully in Hardy & Hardy, Chap. 7, "Stress and Strain.")

12. A comparison of these departments' leadership with that in less productive university departments provides the basis for concluding that a perceptive, supportive, and low-profile type of academic leadership contributes to scientific work and productivity. By comparison, leaders or developers of ideas who are overtly vocal, somewhat charismatic, and committed to a particular stance or doctrine actually inhibit scientific work by faculty (Faris, 1967; Heibreder, 1933; Martindale, 1976).

13. We have identified the basis of knowledge development in several areas. The model is intended to serve as a heuristic device that will aid an understanding of the progressive nature of science and the work undertaken on knowledge development.

14. The initial work at the Chicago School was primarily a process of identifying significant concepts and establishing consensus as to their importance. The empirical description of the concepts of symbolic interaction has been the major thrust of research in the Chicago School. This activity seems to have been relatively nonproblematic and has been associated with an abundance of empirical work which describes phenomena relevant to the concepts.

The conceptual work on specific symbolic interaction concepts at the time when the Chicago School was at its peak is now difficult to identify since it was such an integral part of many of the case studies and life histories, as well as the studies on urban behavior. The conceptual work was basically that of establishing the empirical relevance of the theoretical ideas. The work on conceptualization has continued over the years. Sensitizing concepts (Blumer, 1959) and grounded theory (Glaser & Strauss, 1967) are current methodologies being utilized.

15. *Global theory*, *grand theory*, and *conceptual frameworks* are terms used somewhat interchangeably to refer to loosely formulated ideas that are at a high level of abstraction.

16. For references, see Bulmer (1984).

17. The substantive domain of sociology developed simultaneously with the identification of role expectations and behavior and a system of positions within the department. The goals and values emerged as the system developed. Bulmer (1984) has summarized the Chicago School as having had a commitment to excellence in empirical research, as having considerable intellectual and methodological diversity, and being able to successfully sustain a collective research program combining theory and empirical research.

18. This orientation stressed formal, objective, quantitative research. There was a commitment in the department to quantitative measurement in which there is a tight connection between concepts and their operational definitions. The philosophers at Iowa had a strong commitment to scientific methodology.

3

Theoretical Approaches to the Study of Roles

Mary E. Conway

Following are definitions of important terms used in this chapter:

- *Interaction:* A situation in which at least two persons are involved in verbal or nonverbal communication (Kuhn, 1974, p. 139; Turner, 1962, p. 6)
- *Symbol:* A stimulus that has a meaning for individuals and calls forth a response based on meaning rather than on a physical object (Mead, 1934; Turner, 1962)
- *Interpretation:* The meaning an individual gives to the symbols used by another during the course of interaction (Biddle & Thomas, 1966; Blumer, 1962; Turner, 1962)
- *Role taking:* The reflection of an understanding of the generalized attitudes of others in one's actions (Turner, 1962) and directing self accordingly (Charon, 1979)

We have used the words *role theory* in the title of this book. To the serious student who has learned that a theory is a set of logically interrelated concepts from which can be deduced testable hypotheses, however, the term *role theory* may seem a misnomer. Role theory represents a collection of concepts and a variety of hypothetical formulations that predict how actors will perform in a given role, or under what circumstances certain types of behaviors can be expected. The word *role* has its roots in theatrical usage and refers to a part one plays or is assigned in a drama. It began to appear in behavioral science literature as early as the 1920s (Thomas & Biddle, 1979; p. 6), and from that time its usage has increased rapidly and an associated body of terminology has grown up around it.

The word *theory,* as it is used in this text and as it is construed by a number of authorities (Merton, 1968; Rose, 1962; Secord & Backman, 1964; Thomas & Biddle, 1979), refers to a large body of literature—much of it hypothetical discussion and somewhat less of it reporting empirical research—related to social behavior and both the overt and covert mechanisms that shape it. While the question of a single, unitary theory is debatable, it is unlikely that a coherent body of knowledge will emerge that is all-encompassing or a "unique and total system of theory" (Merton, 1968, p. 64). As noted by Thomas and Biddle (1979, p. 18):

> *The field of role consists of many hypotheses and theories concerning particular aspects of its domain, but these propositions like the knowledge to which they relate, have yet to be reviewed and integrated. And even if the propositions were brought together in some organized form, they would undoubtedly not constitute a single, monolithic theory of the sort that the appellation role theory implies, nor would they always be distinguishable from other theoretical statements in such disciplines as psychology, sociology and anthropology.*

In this chapter the two major perspectives from which roles and role performance have been studied in the behavioral sciences and their relevance for health professionals in particular will be considered. These two perspectives are structuralism and symbolic interaction (Table 1). The former derives its title from the underlying assumption that roles are more or less fixed positions within society to which are attached certain expectations and demands and, further, that these are enforced by sanctions, either negative or positive. In the structuralist view the possibilities for individual social interaction are determined by the structure of the society and the opportunities for individuals to alter the patterns of social structure are extremely limited (Stryker, 1980, p. 66).

The interactionist perspective is the one that will be more fully developed here. It derives its name from the interpretation of human behavior as a response to the symbolic acts of others—notably, gestures and speech—the response being in effect an interpretation of those acts. Symbolic interaction acknowledges society and its institutions as a framework within which actors make their roles explicit. This framework, however, is acknowledged only as a skeleton, so to speak, on which the actor constructs or *organizes* social action (Bolton, 1967, p. 104). A major difference between the two perspectives is that the former conceives of social action as learned responses that are communicated during the process of socialization and reinforced in the individual by the approval or disapproval of significant others such as parents, teachers, or employers (Goslin, 1969, p. 6; LeVine, 1969, p. 508), while the latter posits that the individual engages in interactions with others and selects certain cues for action which, for him, have more relevance than others. Bolton (1967) perceives the "elements" of organic behavior in the social context as learned; but he holds, in addition, that human beings *conduct* their actions. Thus, social action is construed not simply as learned responses but as an organizing and interpreting of cues in one's environment.

Mead (1934, pp. 154–155) expressed an almost identical viewpoint in his belief that the individual takes the attitudes of others toward himself as well as their general attitudes toward social institutions in constructing his own actions. Mead was the first social psychologist to introduce the idea of the self as *reflexive;* that is, the individual in the course of normal growth and development comes to take himself as both subject and object (Mead, 1934, pp. 136–137).

TABLE 1. TWO PERSPECTIVES ON SOCIAL INTERACTION

Functionalist View*	Symbolic Interactionist View
1. Objects and persons are stimuli that act on an individual.	An individual constructs objects on the basis of his ongoing activity. He gives meaning to objects and makes decisions on the basis of his judgments.
2. Action is a release or response to what the situational norms demand.	The individual decides what he wishes to do and how he will do it. He takes account of external and internal cues, interpreting their significance for his action.
3. Environmental forces act to "produce" behavior.	By a process of self-indication, an individual accepts, rejects, or transforms the meaning (impact) of such forces.
4. Prescriptions for action, or norms, dictate appropriate behaviors. They are social facts.	Others' attitudes are the basis for individual lines of action.
5. An act is a unitary, bounded phenomenon; i.e., it starts and stops.	An act is disclosed over time and what the end of the act will be cannot be foretold at the start.
6. The act (of an actor) will be followed by the response of an other with or without any interpretation taking place on the part of the other.	An act is validated by the response of another.
7. Persons act on the basis of a generally objective reality; i.e., learned responses.	Reality is defined by each actor; one defines a situation as he "sees it" and acts on this perception.
8. Group action is the expression of societal demands and shared social values.	Group action is the expression of individuals confronting their life situations.

*For a more detailed explanation of numbers 1, 2, and 8 see H. Blumer, Society as symbolic interaction. In Rose, A. (ed.), *Human Behavior and Social Processes.* New York: Houghton Mifflin, 1962, pp. 179–192.

FUNCTIONAL PERSPECTIVE

The structural perspective—termed *structural–functional* theory—holds that institutions arise in society because they fill a need for that society. An additional assumption of the functional perspective is that the division of labor within a given society is considered an expression of its state of development. That is, the more developed a society, the more complex are its structures and, accordingly, the more differentiated is its labor force (Caplow, 1954; Durkheim, 1964; Parsons, 1951). Durkheim, considered by some to be the earliest proponent of functionalism, made an analogy between the cohesiveness engendered by the division of labor and that which is characteristic of the biologic system. "Organic solidarity" is that patterning of roles and statuses that is characteristic of the division of labor (Durkheim, 1964, pp. 147–173). Inherent in the concept of a division of labor that is organic is the realization that as social forms evolve and change over time, so will the division of labor adjust or reconstruct itself to reflect these changes. An example in recent history of a profoundly reordered division of labor is the large body of professionals, technologists, and skilled laborers that grew up around the United States space exploration efforts.

In the structural–functional view of society, roles as well as institutions, culture, and norms are treated as *social facts*—facts that are transmitted to each succeeding generation in the process of socialization as objective, real entities (Berger & Luckman, 1966). The individual's place in this scheme of things has been described as an egoism-altruism dichotomy, with egoism held to be less functional for society and altruism more functional (Simmel, 1950). Altruism involves subordination of the individual to society; he is a "mere part" of the all-important organic whole (Simmel, 1950, p. 59) and, further, the individual is expected to subordinate his personal orientation to the collectivity (Parsons, 1951, p. 97). If roles are to be construed as social facts—as the functional view casts them—then the behaviors of actors can be considered to be structurally determined by the social forces dominant in a given society at any point in time (Bandura & Walters, 1963; Brim, 1966). While sanctions can be imposed for behaviors that violate norms, a consensual acceptance of these norms is the strongest force for maintaining adherence to them. This consensual acceptance has been called the "collective conscience" (Durkheim, 1964, pp. 287–297).

Roles, in the functionalist schema, are viewed as primary mechanisms serving essential functional prerequisites of the social system (Parsons, 1951, p. 115), and a relationship is held to exist between roles and the social structure that is similar to that which exists between organs and functions in the biologic system. While the conceptualization of roles as social facts suggests a kind of fixed or stable character, roles can be seen to change as the institutions of society evolve. Buckley holds that institutions undergo a developmental process over time in which they recreate themselves (Buckley, 1967, p.137).

The particular social structure of a given society is one important determinant of the process of socialization—perhaps the most important determinant. Those norms and values that characterize the society's culture are the "social facts," as Durkheim puts it, that the younger members of that society will be expected to adopt as they take on adult roles. Consistent with the conceptualization of roles as social facts is the view that those roles that are considered appropriate for the individual as one progresses from infancy to childhood are made relevant sequentially as one matures (Bandura & Walters, 1963; Brim, 1966; Goslin, 1969; LeVine, 1969).

The precise nature of the relationship between the norms of society that are presumed to be fixed and invariant and the individual's perception of those norms as one constructs one's actions is a source of both theoretical and practical debate. Stryker (1980), citing Cicourel's criticism of the assumed relationship between social process and social structure, comments that it is taken for granted that the content of statuses and roles is clear to all, but goes on to say the reality is that "concrete situations of action involve a dialectic between what *appears* to be structurally or institutionally invariant and what depends on actors' perceptions and interpretations" (p. 140). It is fairly obvious even to the layman that individuals who occupy higher statuses are freer to act in nonconforming ways than others, and often do so. Yet there is much evidence that individuals of lower status—miners, for one example—do take socially unapproved actions, often at great risk to themselves and their jobs.

THE SYMBOLIC INTERACTION PERSPECTIVE

In contrast to the functional perspective , the symbolic interactionist interpretation of roles and role behavior focuses on the *meaning* that the acts and symbols of actors in the process of interaction have for each other. The theoretical formulations of this perspective derive from the writings and research of such social psychologists as Blumer (1962), Cooley (1964), Goffman (1952), Mead (1934), Thomas and Znaniecki (1918), Turner (1962), and Webster and Sobieszek (1974), to name but a few. Symbolic interaction emphasizes the meanings that significant symbols have for actors, rather than the normative constraints presumed to be exerted by the social structure (Blumer, 1962, p. 180; Turner, 1962, p. 23). Not all symbols are equally significant for every actor. Symbols are selectively identified by each actor in any given situation. Symbols must be social in nature for them to have meaning for actors; as Charon (1979) noted, a horse is only an object when one rides it; it becomes a social symbol when one uses it to communicate "skill, prestige, wealth, or happiness to others." Significant symbols must also by definition have the same meaning for each actor in a situation if they are to serve as an integral part of the communication process. It is important to note that significant symbols arrest action as well as facilitate it; symbols control the actions of both actor and other. To take the role of the other "means to share the meaning of a gesture, and that meaning controls the behavior of the other as he performs his role" (Miller, 1981).

The formation of role identity is a complex process. It is a product of self-conception and the perspective of generalized others. As Stryker (1980) pointed out, each role identity has two aspects: the conventional and the idiosyncratic in varying proportions. And as he has further observed, "individuals are faced with the problem of devising perspectives that allow them to maintain their views of self, to legitimate their role identities" (p. 120). Mead, Cooley, and subsequent theorists attached great importance to the attitudes of others reflected toward the self in the development of self-identity. In modern, complex society where social identities are only fleetingly glimpsed by others and can hardly be said to be established in the minds of others, how much influence others' evaluations have on the self is called into question. Shrauger and Schoeneman (1979) conducted an extensive review of studies focused on the proposition that "individuals' self perceptions should be highly congruent with the way they see themselves as being perceived by others." In approximately half of the studies reviewed (N = 48) significant correlations were found between self-perceptions and others' evaluations. Findings in the other half of the studies were ambiguous. They concluded that "people do not accurately perceive others' opinions of them and that these opinions minimally influence self-judgments." Another possibility for lack of conclusiveness in the research—one related to the fleeting social contacts of a mobile society—is that many persons frequently do not know what others' views of them actually are.

The symbolic interactionist approach to the study of behavior clearly has taken precedence over structural theory in the continuing attempts to explain human behavior (Blumer, 1962; Handel, 1979; Meltzer et al., 1975; Rose, 1962; Stryker, 1980, 1981; Webster & Sobieszeck, 1974). One obvious reason for this is that functional theory, as it is generally understood, simply does not account well enough for the wide variations in behavior that take place within complex social structures. Presumably, if the social structure alone were the underlying determinant of behavior, all social action should be explainable and predictable on the basis of the norms governing the society in question. Developments in psychology, particularly those associated with the psychoanalytic tradition, have led to a recognition of the influence of individual personality and early socialization experiences as important determinants of the subsequent adaptive (or nonadaptive) behavior of individuals (Burr et al., 1979; Gewirtz, 1969; Piaget, 1968; Sullivan, 1953).

The argument between so-called structuralists and proponents of individualism goes deeper than asserting that only one method of study of society (structuralism) is scientifically justified. Structuralists, as Mayhew (1980) asserts, "do not attribute social or psychological characteristics to individual humans. Rather, structuralists view individual human beings as biological organisms." Taken to its logical extension, this view of human nature would suggest that persons respond only to objects in the environment without attaching any intrapsychic meaning to them.

DEFINITION OF THE SITUATION

Sociologists seek to make generalized predictions about the probabilities of certain behaviors occurring under similar, recurring situations. The difficulty in making such generalizations is that behaviors are usually studied after the fact; it is almost impossible to study behaviors in naturally occurring social situations with or without the knowledge of the subjects and without introducing investigator bias. And as Blumer (1980) has noted, "much of what develops in human group life, especially in complex societies is obscure, or hidden from immediate notice." A reason of theoretical and practical importance in the uncertainty of predicting outcomes of interactions is that an actor tends to construct a given situation *as it seems to him*. This is known as *definition of the situation* (Burr et al., 1979 p. 64; Stebbins, 1981; Thomas & Znaniecki, 1918; Turner, 1962). It is on the basis of each actor's definition that subsequent actions take place. Since such definitions are internal mental constructs for each actor, not all actors in a given situation will act on the same definition.

Stebbins (1981) has stressed the importance of distinguishing between *subjective* and *objective* situations in attempting to understand the orientation of actors. Subjective situations are those seen by the actor to affect any one of his or her action orientations, whereas an objective situation is one comprised of "the immediate social and physical surroundings and the current physiological state of the actor" (p. 348).

ROLE MODIFICATION AS RESPONSE TO KNOWLEDGE EXPANSION

The body of scientific knowledge has grown markedly in recent years, and concomitantly the field of health care has experienced a proliferation of roles. In addition, the health care system is one of the most rapidly expanding and complex systems within society. Because of both the exponential increase in technology that has occurred within an extremely short time and the expansion of the health care system itself, attempts to cope with related role changes have been identified as a major stressor. In coping with the demands associated with expansion of knowledge and the demands made by consumers seeking ready access to care, health professionals are faced with the continuing need to redefine and realign their roles. Role redefintion involves consideration of normative patterns of interaction in the relationships of professional to consumer and professional to professional. It is within the context of this impetus toward role redefinition and realignment that the theoretical framework of symbolic interaction offers a map for understanding the process of role change. This framework can be used to explain how roles evolve over time and, in addition, it suggests means by which present role patterns can intentionally be altered.

The term *role making* best describes the process that takes place when role modification is consciously entered into. There are at least five distinct phases that can be isolated in the sequential process of role making: (1) initiator behavior, (2) other response, (3) interpretation by actor and other, (4) altered response pattern, and (5) role validation (Table 2).

Both role taking and role making involve taking the attitudes of others who are involved in an interaction; that is, both actor and other endeavor to understand the meaning of each other's symbolic gestures (Charon, 1979, pp. 40, 98; Stryker, 1980, p. 62). What is unique to role making, however, is the structuring of the interaction in such a way as to modify it and, in doing so, to make explicit certain aspects of the role (Turner, 1962, p. 22). As we have already observed, consistency is a feature of roles and role participants can anticipate with a fair degree of predictability what the responses of their role partners will be. It is when the response of a role partner departs from the one anticipated in some phase of the interaction and the other in the interaction accepts that departure (i.e., reciprocates in such a way as to sustain the interaction), that role making can be said to take place. That is, some *part* of the role becomes modified. The word *phase* is used deliberately (Turner uses the term *segment* in a similar though not identical sense) to convey the idea that an interaction consists of a sequential pattern of successive action–response episodes and to emphasize that any single episode of action–reponse must be considered incomplete within the context of the entire interaction.

The notion of phase is an appropriate and meaningful term for the empirical study of interactions for the reason that neither observers nor participants in a given interaction can predict on the basis of one, or even several, act–response sequences what the eventual meaning of the completed interaction will be. Let us take an example from a multiprofessional health team. The physician (who perceives himself to be the leader of the team) gives a directive to the physical therapist who has been providing passive exercise to a patient who has suffered a

TABLE 2. ROLE MAKING AS A SEQUENTIAL FIVE-PHASE PROCESS

1st Phase *Initiator Behavior*	2nd Phase *Other-Response*	3rd Phase *Actor/Other* *Interpretation*
1. Actor initiates behavior. 2. Intent of actor may not be explicit. 3. Completion of interaction unpredictable.	1. Other responds on basis of established normative expectations. 2. Other may or may not be aware of actor's intent.	1. Act unfolds in successive symbolic expressions. 2. Successive act/ responses are based on interpretation of each prior act/ response unit.

4th Phase *Altered Response* *Pattern*	5th Phase *Validation*
1. Actor/other role relationship different from that which existed at onset of interaction.	1. Altered relationship acknowledged by behaviors of relevant others. 2. Revised normative expectations emerge for this altered relationship.

cerebral accident. The physical therapist (who perceives himself to be more knowledgeable than the physician about the extent of muscle atrophy that the patient has sustained) responds not by agreeing to follow the physician's directive, as might be expected, but instead suggests an alternative therapy. The physician (who momentarily may be surprised that his directive is not accepted) acquiesces to the therapist's suggested alternative. In this instance, role making can be said to have occurred. Let us examine what took place: (1) the initiator of the interaction exhibited a behavior generally consistent with that of physician; (2) the "other," i.e., physical therapist, responded with a behavior generally inconsistent with that of physical therapist—that is, his act "challenged" the authority of the physician; (3) the physician can be said to have interpreted the attitude conveyed by the therapist and on the basis of his response apparently accepted it as within the norms of his perception of physician–other role; (4) the therapist made explicit an aspect of his self-perceived role as an autonomous professional by defining the treatment he determined appropriate to the patient's need. If, over time, both physician and therapist were to continue in this altered pattern of response to the other's role and relevant others were to accept the realigned role relationship, it could be concluded that the therapist's evolved role was validated.

One example of a recently evolved professional role is that of the nurse practitioner—a role also referred to as the expanded role of the nurse (Andrews & Yankauer, 1971; U.S. Department of Health, Education and Welfare, 1971). The nurse practitioner is trained to provide health supervision and health assessment of individuals through performing history taking and physical examination of clients—role functions that have previously been restricted to the physician. In one study of nurse practitioners it was reported that clients were better satisfied with the health supervision provided by the nurse than that provided by the physician (Linn, 1976). Similarly, the role of occupational therapist is a role that is in the process of evolving from one of a dependent (vis-à-vis physician) provider of services to the disabled or mentally ill to a role in which the focus is on health promotion and prevention of disability within the community at large (Cermak, 1976). In addition, the role of the pharmacist shows a similar evolutionary trend. Pharmacists, emphasizing their in-depth knowledge of drugs and drug chemistry, are moving beyond their traditionally defined role of compounders and dispensers of prescriptions to one of educators of the consumer (Salisbury, 1977). It is conceivable that at some not too distant time the pharmacist, rather than the physician, will be the legitimate prescriber of drugs. Given what seems to be a momentum toward still further role realignments within the total system of health delivery, we can assume that, in addition to the roles alluded to above, other health provider roles are undergoing, or will soon undergo, similar altered role functions and relationships.

ROLE MERGER

In a society still much influenced by the Protestant work ethic, many individuals fuse their work roles with their self-identity. This phenomenon is known as role merger, a situation in which the individual enacts behavior appropriate to his work role in social situations where it is out of place (Heiss, 1981, p. 100; Turner, 1978). For example, the president of a large corporation who demands instant service in a busy supermarket check-out line is enacting the role of corporate chief rather than ordinary consumer. It is likely that persons who tend to merge roles experience more difficulty than others in adding successive or new roles.

Turner (1978) outlines 15 propositions related to how likely an actor is to be perceived by others as the person-revealed-by-the-role. Individuals most likely to be so perceived are those whose roles are more visible, more salient and whose roles have greater consequences for the community.

A MELDING OF TWO PERSPECTIVES

Recent literature reflects attempts at reconciling both the structural and interactionist perspectives. More recent analyses of Mead's writings and thought have prompted some to assert that Mead consciously placed role taking and the negotiation of roles within the context of the larger social structure (Handel, 1979; Joas, 1981; Turner, 1981) and that he recognized the limitations put on freedom to *make* roles by the social structure. For example, in highly structured institutions (the Army, for one) where behavior is formally prescribed there is little or no freedom to create roles. "The location of situations on a continuum of degrees of institutionalization affects the flexibility accorded participants and the very nature of their involvement in role conduct" (Handel, 1979). Handel further argues that courses of action for all actors are constrained by the normative structure, but since there are conflicting norms present in almost every social situation the actor in effect chooses a course of action and waits to see what response the other will make. In effect the *I* acts and his further actions are modified as responses to other's reciprocal response. The actor in such an instance is testing to determine which norms are applicable.

Turner (1981) supports a similar view of the structural aspects of Mead's conception of symbolic interaction. He notes that a complex society has "multiple generalized others" and that common symbols form a structure. Joas (1981) has termed Mead's philosophy a *practical intersubjectivity*. That is, the minded individual acts not simply from an intrapsychic conversation with himself, but from a recognition of the social context within which he acts and a background of mutuality of expectations. Joas insists that in these terms Mead must be seen as a supporter of social rationality.

Heiss (1981, p. 100) lends more support to the notion of rationality from the actor's perspective. He notes that this principle, although not explicitly stated, appears to be implicit in the work of both interactionists and structuralists. The plethora of recent attempts to find a rapprochement between the strict structuralist view of social behavior and the interactionist view suggests that such efforts will continue and that more research to test the fundamental assumptions of both positions will be done (Stryker, 1981, p. 8). It will be interesting to learn whether Handel's (1979) contention that symbolic interaction is *embedded* in normative social structure is supported by future research on the theoretical assumptions of each approach to human behavior.

SUMMARY

Two competing theoretical formulations for the study of roles and role behavior have been identified and briefly explicated. The point has been emphasized that, although many hypotheses have been advanced to explain the basis for social (role) behavior, empirical research in natural settings is still minimal and inconclusive; thus, caution must be exercised in drawing generalizations. It is obvious that neither the structuralist nor the symbolic interactionist theoretical perspective alone adequately accounts for the wide variety of human responses possible in the numerous and ambiguous situations where human actors confront each other. Recent interest in examination of the theoretical assumptions of both perspectives together with some attempts to build conceptual frameworks inclusive of each for the purpose of further analyses promises a greatly enlarged understanding of both role taking and role making.

4

Socialization For Roles

Barbara Ann Hurley-Wilson

THE NATURE OF SOCIALIZATION

Traditions in Socialization

The systematic study of the area known today as socialization emerged simulta-neously from three different traditions: anthropology, psychology, and sociology. Although the focus, theories, and methodologies used by each of these fields differ substantially, each has endeavored from its individual perspective to deline-ate some aspect of how the human person develops within the social and cultural milieu. Anthropology, for example, has distinguished itself by focusing upon the broader culture, viewing socialization as an enculturation process in which the learner passively absorbs and internalizes the cultural norms and contents trans-mitted by the society of which one is a member. In contrast, psychology has focused upon the processes of learning and development. Studies of the processes of identification, motivation, and cognitive, psychosexual, language, and con-science development have reflected psychologists' varied theoretical positions on the inherent nature of man as a passive learner requiring control of intrinsic negative tendencies. In contrast to the psychologist's position, sociologists have in large part focused on the agencies of socialization (family, peers, school, institu-tions) and the processes involved in the acquisition of social skills, including modes of social control, development of the social self, the influences of social structure and value orientation on child-rearing practices, and social roles and role training (Clausen, 1968a, pp. 22–48; Goslin, 1969, p. 1; Levine, 1969, pp. 505–510; Zigler & Child, 1969, pp. 451–473; Zigler et al., 1982, pp. 20–36).

Anthropology, psychology, and sociology have distinguished themselves by their divergent perspectives and approaches to a central phenomenon of interest, i.e., how is it that a human person acquires the prerequisite knowledge, skills, and motivation to become a functioning member of society? Anthropologists, psychologists, and sociologists have differentiated themselves from one another in several respects on this matter. The differentiation has included the theoretical and methodologic perspectives they adopt, the levels of analysis with which they treat the subject, the aspects of the socialization process upon which they focus, and, in particular, the positions they assume on major theoretical issues stemming from their adopted theoretical and methodologic approaches (Clausen, 1968a, pp. 47–52; Goslin, 1969, pp. 1–2; Zigler, Lamb, & Child, 1982, pp. 13–43, pp. 104–

73

106). Such issues (as summarized by Goslin, 1969, pp. 1–2) include the relative importance of early as opposed to later experiences on socialization outcomes; the relative emphasis attached to individual needs, motives, and drives as opposed to environmental determinants of behavior; the relative importance attached to process as opposed to content in predicting the outcomes of social behavior; the emphasis placed upon the unique aspects of the socialization experience as opposed to its common properties; and finally, the focus upon the processes promoting conformity to societal norms as opposed to the causes of deviations from these behavioral norms. Of particular relevance here are two further issues that have distinguished psychologists, anthropologists, and sociologists in studying the phenomenon of socialization; namely, differences in views regarding the characteristics of the learner and the learning process and differences in the conceptualization of socialization as an active or passive process (MacKay, 1973, pp. 5–24; Goslin, 1969, pp. 3–5; Miller, 1983; Schwartz, 1976, pp. vii–xviii; Zigler & Child, 1969, pp. 468–470; Zigler et al., 1982, pp. 6, 13–19, 37–44, 118–119). References to several of these issues will recur throughout this chapter.

The Concept of Socialization

Use of the Term. The term *socialization* has a history of varied use in the disciplines from which theory and research relevant to it emerged (Clausen, 1968a, pp. 18–46). First used in sociology in the mid-1890s by Simmel, the term socialization originally referred to "the process of group formation or development of the forms of association" (Clausen, 1968a, p. 22). From that time until the end of the 1920s the term was used with markedly varied meanings, but eventually it was used to refer primarily to "the 'shaping' of the person and to the mechanisms whereby individuals were transformed into persons" (Clausen, 1968a, p. 24). Prior to the 1930s, much of the research focusing on the development of the person and of the personality that we currently refer to as socialization research was classified under the rubric "culture and personality" (Clausen, 1968a, p. 24). Although the term socialization retained vestiges of earlier usages as evidenced in the writings of Park (1939) and Dollard (1939), it was not until approximately 1939 that it came to be used widely in its present sense (Clausen, 1968a, pp. 24–25).

Because the field of socialization has emerged from various traditions, it has been defined in numerous ways. Elkin and Handel (1984, p. 4) have defined socialization as "the process by which we learn the ways of a given society or social group so that we can function within it." For Zigler and Child (1973, p. 36), "socialization is a broad term for the whole process by which an individual develops, through transactions with other people, his specific pattern of socially relevant behavior and experience." For Inkeles (1969, pp. 615–616), who takes a sociologic and societal point of view, "socialization refers to the process whereby individuals acquire the personal system properties—the knowledge, skills, attitudes, values, needs and motivations, cognitive, affective and conative patterns—which shape their adaptation to the physical and sociocultural setting in which they live."

Various theoretical perspectives give the concept of socialization differing connotations. Despite this variety, all definitions seem to encompass basic elements of this process. Common to the definitions is an attempt to delineate what is learned, how it is learned, why it is learned, and what are its expected outcomes. Ultimately, all theories attempt to account for individual variation (differences) in characteristics or performance.

Views on Socialization

Perhaps one of the issues that has most clearly distinguished positions on socialization is the question of whether the socialized person is viewed as an active or passive agent in his own socialization. Those investigators who advocate the position that the socialized person is a passive recipient of cultural norms and contents assume that the effect of socializers is unidirectional. However, as Goslin (1969, pp. 5–10), MacKay (1973, pp. 5–24), and Zigler, Lamb & Child (1982, pp. 15–16, 44–45) point out, there has been a shift in emphasis from a passive to an active view of the socialized person as a result of empirical evidence gathered since the mid-1960s. Increasingly, socialization has come to be viewed as an interactional and reciprocal process in which the person being socialized and socializer are mutually influenced. Such an emphasis on the socialized person as an active participant in his own socialization is an issue that most clearly differentiates positions on socialization. Socioiogists, anthropologists, and psychologists who hold this position employ different theoretical and methodologic approaches in order to systematically study socialization as an interactive process.

Socialization can also be viewed from the perspective of both the individual being socialized and the society. From the individual perspective, the process of socialization encompasses the learning of motor and language skills, the acquisition of self-other systems, and the learning of social roles and moral norms and values, as well as affective and cognitive modes of functioning (Clausen, 1968b, p. 4; Inkeles, 1968, p. 83). From the societal perspective, the goals of socialization focus primarily upon the attainment of some form of competence that the society accepts as appropriate for adult performance, as well as an internalized commitment to continuing responsible participation in society (Elkin & Handel, 1984, pp. 35–38).

In order to attain these ultimate goals, society uses its socializing agents (family, peers, institutions) as means of transmitting to the person being socialized the kinds of social learning that ultimately have relevance for adult role performance, i.e., the development of motor and language skills, the teaching of social roles, the development of the social self, and the teaching of moral norms and values, as well as affective and cognitive modes of functioning. The word *transmitting* is used broadly here, since socialization has come to be viewed more and more as an interactional process in which the socializer and the individual being socialized are mutually influenced.

Viewed in this context, that is, socialization as an interactional process, individual and societal perspectives are interrelated, with both the socializers and the socializees influencing the acquisition of those types of social learning requisite for adequate and socially acceptable adult role performance (Clausen, 1968c, pp. 139–146; Inkeles, 1968, pp. 78–83).

Broadly conceived, socialization has been viewed as including a variety of processes that prepare the socializee for adult performance. Such an encompass-ing view takes the socialization process to be not only efforts of socialization agents to transmit existing norms, motives, and values to the socializee through child-rearing practices, but also as efforts to transmit the learning that is required for marriage, parenthood, and occupational roles, as well as the kinds of social learning leading the individual to acquire the knowledge, skills, and dispositions appropriate to an individual of a particular age, sex, and social status (Clausen, 1968b, p. 7; Elkin & Handel, 1984, pp. 38–40, 201–252).

Because socialization is viewed as the societal means of attaining and main-taining social and cultural continuity, the adequacy of the socialization process is assessed in terms of the criterion of adequate adult performance. Adequate adult performance is seen to include the attainment of socially accepted competencies, as well as a motivated commitment to continued participation in the society. From a societal perspective, the socialization process is seen as a method utilized to establish the standards by which the socializee is expected to pattern achieve-ments and developments in skills, emotional expression, intellectual activity, and relations with significant others (Clausen, 1968b, p. 5; Elkin & Handel, 1984, pp. 35–38; Inkeles, 1968, p. 75).

Frequently, the socialization process is viewed as implying that the socializee is induced in some measure to conform willingly to the norms and values trans-mitted to him by society's designated socialization agents. Inherent in this view is the assumption that norms and values transmitted to the socializee are internal-ized, becoming standards for behavior in the absence of internal or external sanctions (Clausen, 1968b, pp. 5–10).

Questions Socialization Addresses

There is no single theory of socialization. As previously indicated, the theories and research of the various traditions treat different aspects of the process at different levels of analysis, focusing upon various issues pertinent to their theoret-ical perspective and methodology. Thus, the various theoretical perspectives may be viewed as addressing different questions, which taken together comprise the whole area of socialization. These questions include some of the following:

1. What is learned, i.e., what is the content learned through the process of socialization?
2. How is the content learned, i.e., what is the learning process associated with the process of socialization?
3. Why is the content learned and subsequently enacted, i.e., what motivates the learner to both learn the content and subsequently utilize it in role performance?
4. What is the outcome of socialization desired by society?
5. What accounts for individual differences as opposed to conformity to social norms as a result of the socialization process?
6. What methods are used by society to ensure learning of social norms?
7. What are the preconditions for socialization?
8. What are the prerequisites for the learning of social roles?
9. What is the overall process through which socialization occurs?

THE NATURE OF SOCIALIZATION FROM A ROLE PERSPECTIVE

Socialization for Roles

Among sociologists, one of the traditions that has focused upon the phenomenon of socialization has been role theory. From the role theorist's perspective, the nature of socialization has been defined largely in terms of the learning of social roles that prepare the socializee for adult role performance. Role theorists studying the phenomenon of socialization have focused primarily upon adult socialization for occupational, marital, and parental roles. As Brim (1960, p. 127; 1966, p. 7), Clausen (1968c, pp. 133–138), and Goslin (1969, p. 6) point out, however, the conceptualization of socialization from a role perspective provides a mechanism for viewing socialization as a continuous and cumulative process. Studying from this view the way social roles are learned by children and adults permits the joining of these seemingly disparate areas of interest within the socialization literature (Brim, 1966, pp. 5–7; Brim & Kagan, 1980; Kagan, 1980; Maccoby, 1959, pp. 239–252; 1961, pp. 493–503; Sewell, 1970, pp. 568–572).

Brim (1960, 1966) has given us two definitions of socialization from a role perspective. In the first, he defined socialization "as a process of learning through which an individual is prepared with varying degrees of success, to meet the requirements laid down by other members of society for his behavior in a variety of situations" (1960, p. 128). In Brim's second definition (1966, p. 3), which is the most frequently quoted, socialization refers to the "process by which persons acquire the knowledge, skills, and dispositions that make them more or less able members of their society."

In each of these definitions, socialization refers to the learning of those social roles that facilitate the socializee's participation and adequate adult performance in the ongoing society of which he is a member. In his first definition, Brim identified the content of socialization, i.e., what is learned, as the "requirements laid down by other members of society," namely, role prescriptions and role behaviors. In his second definition, he more specifically identified the content of socialization or what is learned as the "knowledge, skills, and dispositions," i.e., role demands attached to positions or statuses within the social structure of the society. Thus, the content learned includes not only the role prescriptions and role behaviors with their associated feeling modes but additionally the positions or statuses to which these role demands are attached. In each definition, Brim specified that the content of socialization—"knowledge, skills, and dispositions" —is acquired through a process of learning that occurs within an interactional context. Further, each definition specifies that the socializees will learn the content of socialization with "varying degrees of success" and will fulfill the function and outcome of the socialization process by becoming "more or less able members of their society."

Brim's definitions of socialization and his discussion of the nature of socialization from a role perspective (Brim, 1960, pp. 127–159; 1962, pp. 176–180; 1966, pp. 1–50; 1968a, pp. 555–562; 1968b, pp. 182–226) address and elaborate upon many of the questions on which theorists and investigators from various disciplines in the area of socialization focus. Each of these aspects of socialization developed from the role perspective—including content, processes, motivation, outcomes, and individual differences—will be addressed in the discussion that follows. Brim's and other role theorists' conceptualizations of the nature of socialization will be used as the organizing framework for the discussion of each of these aspects. Contributions of theorists and investigators from various other disciplines will be included only as these deal with the process of socialization at different levels of analysis or focus upon aspects of the socialization process minimally addressed by the role perspective.

What Content Is Learned?

From a role perspective, the content or what is learned in the process of socialization includes both knowledge and understanding of the status structure of the society, as well as the role prescriptions and role behaviors attached to the various statuses or positions within the social structure (Brim, 1957, p. 345; 1960, p. 128; 1966, pp. 4–5).

Members of a society develop both prescriptive and performance aspects of roles in order to regulate the behavior of members so that the functions of the society will be successfully discharged. These normative prescriptions specify the feelings that the socializee occupying a particular status within the society should have, the behavior he should perform, and the effects he should produce (Brim, 1957, p. 345).

Since role prescriptions are based on implicit or explicit theories about human behavior, changes in role prescriptions will occur either when the underlying theory of human nature changes or when there are changes in the functions of society. Discrepancies or conflicts in what constitutes the content of role prescriptions result either from differences in underlying theories of human behavior or from differences in conceptions of what constitutes adequate, competent adult role performance (Brim, 1957, p. 345).

Role prescriptions for the occupant of a particular status not only explicitly specify how that individual is to behave, but implicitly specify as well the behaviors of persons in related positions toward the occupant of that particular status. It is generally the case that occupants of particular positions or statuses within the society know both the explicitly stated role prescriptions attached to their respective positions and the implicit reciprocal prescriptions guiding the role behaviors of others toward them (Brim, 1957, pp. 345–347).

Because the ultimate purpose of prescribed behavior is fulfillment of the functions of the society, societal role prescriptions are based on theories that incorporate into the role prescriptions the motives of the status incumbent, his or her overt behavior, and the effects of that behavior. Viewed in a causal sequence, motives are considered to result in behavior, which produces certain effects (Brim, 1957, pp. 348–349).

Whether role analysis involves motives, overt behavior, or effects of such behavior as the units of analysis, one or more descriptive properties of the role are required. Thus, one may analyze the amount of dependence or aggression shown or the degree to which some other characteristic is demonstrated. It is equally important to analyze roles in terms of such variables as sex, ordinal position within the family, size of family, absence of statuses within the family system, and so forth (Brim, 1957, pp. 350–354; 1960, p. 148).

The preceding discussion of role prescriptions may lead the reader to believe that roles are always clearly prescribed and perceived by occupants of different positions as congruent. Role prescriptions perceived by occupants of similar or different statuses, however, will differ considerably depending upon the source from which information about the role has been derived, i.e., formal laws, opinions, special interest groups, individuals, and so forth (Brim, 1957, pp. 351–354). Variations in role behavior may also emanate from individuals' personality needs, expressive features, or degree of proficiency in role performance (Colomy & Rhoades, 1983, p. 212). Thus, it may be concluded that while some positions or statuses within society have highly specified role prescriptions regulating motives, behaviors, and the behavioral effects of the occupant of the status and of the expected behavior of related status holders, there are many positions for which role prescriptions are extremely vague and open to wide variation in interpretation and enactment.

How Is The Content Learned?

The content of socialization, i.e., knowledge of the status structure of the society and of the role prescriptions and role behaviors attached to the various statuses, is acquired through two simultaneously occurring processes—interactional processes and learning processes—that involve different agents or agencies of socialization, such as family, peers, school, television, and other institutions.

Interactional Processes Through Which Socialization Occurs. Heiss (1976, p. 4) and Nye and Gecas (1976, pp. 4–7) make an initial distinction between two distinct role theory traditions: the structural tradition emerging from the work of Linton (1936, 1945) and the sociopsychologic branch emerging from the work of George Herbert Mead (1934). In essence, this distinction is made on the basis of whether or not socialization is viewed as a unidirectional or a two-way process. Linton, cited in Hollander and Hunt (1972, p. 112), used the term *role* to "designate the sum total of the culture patterns associated with a particular status by the society to any and all persons occupying this status." From this perspective, role performance consists of the enactment of a prescribed role, a socially agreed upon specific script in which the actor plays out a series of role behaviors that he has learned through the process of socialization.

As analyzed by Turner (1962, p. 32), this model of "role as conformity," based on Linton's definitions of status and role, specifies that the individual enacts the prescribed set of expectations appropriate to individuals in relevant other statuses, conforms to others' expectations, and receives in return some indications of approval (Turner, 1962, pp. 32–33). Viewed from this perspective, socialization is a unidirectional process in which the socializee is a passive recipient and enactor of cultural norms and contents.

In contrast to the "enacting of a prescribed role" inherent in Linton's perspective, a Meadian view of role similarly defined as "prescriptions for interpersonal behavior associated with . . . statuses" (Heiss, 1976, p. 3) emphasizes the principle of role reciprocity, in which the individual devises his role performance on the basis of the role that he imputes to the other, i.e., the individual improvises a performance based on immediate cues (Heiss, 1976, p. 13). From this symbolic interactionist or Meadian perspective, interaction proceeds as roles are identified and given content, that is, self and other roles are created and modified as the process of interaction unfolds (Turner, 1962, pp. 21–23). From this viewpoint the learning of roles or role making is a two-way process in which the socializee and the socializer are active participants in an interactional process in which they are mutually influenced (Colomy & Rhoades, 1983, pp. 211–213; Denzin, 1977, pp. 2–3; Goslin, 1969, pp. 5–10; Lewis & Rosenblum (1974; Rheingold, 1969, pp. 779–790; Turner, 1962, pp. 21–23).

Mead's concept of role learning through the process of interaction is described in more detail by Berger and Berger (1979, pp. 4–20), Brim (1958, pp. 1–16; 1966, pp. 7–17), Denzin (1977, pp. 1–14), Elkin & Handel (1984, pp. 33–76), Goslin (1969, pp. 5–10), Heiss (1976, pp. 16–25), Hewitt (1976), Kerckhoff (1972, pp. 17–38), and Turner (1968b, pp. 95–97). Role theorists following Mead make two assumptions: (1) that roles are learned in the process of social interaction, and (2) that in the interactional process the individual sees himself and the other as occupants of particular statuses and responds accordingly with appropriate role behaviors. But what is the mechanism by which roles are learned through interaction?

Through the process of interaction with members of the *primary group* (Cooley, 1962, pp. 23–31), the individual learns those role behaviors appropriate to his position within the group. The members of the primary group, holding normative beliefs about what constitutes the role, use reward and punishment to assist the individual to learn both the correct and incorrect actions appropriate to his role. The socializee becomes involved in a series of complex interpersonal relationships with a number of people who, because of their frequency of contact, their primacy, and their control over rewards and punishment, orient the child toward those role prescriptions and role behaviors that are expected outcomes of the socialization process (Brim, 1958, p. 1; 1966, pp. 8–9). Because of their intense contact and influence upon the socializee, the family members and particularly the mother are called *significant others*. When the child matures, the potential set of significant others enlarges, with teachers and peers becoming increasingly important to the socializee (Kerckhoff, 1972, pp. 18–20).

In essence, from a Meadian point of view, socialization for roles begins with the personal attachment established between mother and child. For the child the relationship with the mother is the first encounter with what it means to be human; it is through her that the child is presented with its first expectations of the social world and with her that the child first begins to experience a sense of self. Through being cared for and through evoking responses and being responded to by the mother, the child learns both the sense of self and that of another person (Elkin & Handel, 1984, pp. 40–44). Although the mother is usually the first emotionally significant person with whom the child may establish a relationship, additional significant others, including the father, grandparents, caretakers at day-care centers, siblings, peers, older children, and adults, will make different contributions to socialization because of their different statuses and roles within the social structure (Elkin & Handel, 1984, pp. 43–44; Lamb, 1976c, 1981, 1982; Lamb & Bronson, 1980, pp. 340–341).

Goslin's (1969, p. 6) conceptualization of socialization in role-developmental terms adds further to our understanding of socialization as a two-way process. Goslin proposes that the process of interaction through which socialization occurs is one of role negotiation in which each participant influences the behavior of each other participant in significant ways, with the result that the behavior of each is altered to some degree.

Even though socialization is viewed as a process of role negotiations, numerous factors affect the extent to which the behavior of individuals may be subject to negotiation (Goslin, 1969, p. 7). As an occupant of a particular social position, the individual is involved in responding both to the expectations of others and in exercising the right to expect certain behaviors from related status holders. In the interactional situation, this involves an agreement or *contract* between participants as to what one may expect of the other. Deviations from prescribed expectations may vary considerably, depending upon the institutionalized nature of the situation in which the participants interact. In the highly institutionalized situation, both participants have little opportunity for role negotiation because the rights and duties of each are specified in advance, allowing little room for negotiation of a new contract. Socialization under this highly institutionalized situation consists primarily in learning the existing role prescriptions for reciprocal roles (Goslin, 1969, p. 7).

When there are very general institutional prescriptions, such as in cases of friendships or casual social situations, societal norms or prescriptions are relatively unspecified and large variations in role enactment may be anticipated. For interaction to proceed in such situations, the pair of participants must create reciprocal roles through the process of role negotiation in which both must establish and maintain situational identities (roles) and recognize the identities (roles) of the other (Goslin, 1969, pp. 7–8).

With respect to role negotiation, Goslin (1969, pp. 8–10) makes several significant points that follow from his position that socialization is a two-way process. First, in the establishment of every interactional relationship, regardless of how highly institutionalized its roles may be, some negotiation is possible and necessary. This role negotiation goes on whether one or all the parties to the interaction are aware or unaware of the process and whether they perceive the possibility that aspects of their roles are subject to negotiation (Rheingold, 1969, pp. 779–790). Those participants able to assess accurately the negotiability of a situation are at a distinct advantage.

Awareness that roles can be negotiated is fostered by nonauthoritarian child-rearing practices in which children are encouraged to express their own feelings and in which their rights as children are given explicit recognition (Goslin, 1969, p. 8). In nonauthoritarian child-rearing situations not only does the child develop an awareness of the possibility of role negotiation, but the child also develops specific techniques for handling role-bargaining situations. There are distinct advantages and disadvantages for the child who acquires both the awareness that roles can be negotiated and the specific techniques of role bargaining, as well as for the child who learns neither of these skills. For those children who have experienced the freedom to utilize bargaining techniques in various situations with frequent success, situations in which role negotiation is not possible may be viewed as frustrating and intolerable. This is particularly true when these children have not learned to distinguish between situations in which role negotiation is and is not possible (Goslin, 1969, p. 9).

Those children who have had little experience in role negotiation, that is, have either not learned of the possibility or have not developed negotiation techniques, are at a distinct disadvantage when they become involved in situations where negotiation is necessary or desirable (Goslin, 1969, p. 9).

As Goslin further points out, the distribution of power in an interactional system is of extreme importance in role negotiation. With respect to power, control of resources is a particularly critical factor, as the member possessing the greater resources has considerably greater bargaining power, regardless of the formality or informality of the power structure (Goslin, 1969, p. 9).

Finally, Goslin makes the point that the absolute freedom to negotiate one's role may be significantly restricted by the individual's internalization of values and standards of conduct that inhibit his exercise of personal power in situations that are negotiable (Goslin, 1969, p. 10).

Through the process of interaction, the child learns not only the social structure of statuses and their accompanying role prescriptions and role behaviors but also the prerequisites necessary for learning of role demands. The outcomes of the interactional process which are also prerequisites for the learning of roles include (1) the learning of verbal or language skills, (2) the learning of role-taking skills, (3) the genesis or development of the self, and (4) the learning of the presentation of self or interpersonal competence. Because of the importance of each of these prerequisite outcomes or elements to the learning of roles, each will be discussed with respect to its importance in relation to role-learning and its interrelationships with the others (Brim, 1966, pp. 7–15; Denzin, 1977, pp. 76–169; Elkin & Handel, 1984, pp. 11–76; Goslin, 1969, pp. 10–12; Heiss, 1976, pp. 6–16; Hewitt, 1976, pp. 21–104; Kerckhoff, 1972, pp. 17–38).

Verbal or Language Skills. The acquisition of language, i.e., verbal skills, is a prerequisite for learning most roles (Goslin, 1969, p. 10) and plays an important part in socialization because it facilitates learning other skills required for role acquisition (Jenkins, 1969, p. 663).

Within the last 50 years, four models representing a range of views of psychologists regarding the acquisition of language have been popular: language as words, language as strings of words or classes, language as utterances, and language as a structural system (Jenkins, 1969, p. 663). Although it seems obvious that language is made up of words, word-based systems (with some notable exceptions; e.g., Chinese) have been replaced by more efficient alphabetic systems. If language is thought of as words, its acquisition is seen to consist of two processes: development of the motor skills involved in saying words and the cognitive skill of getting the words attached to meanings (Jenkins, 1969, p. 663). Viewed from this perspective, language involves a combination of instrumental learning and classical conditioning that permits the learning of both semantic and emotional meanings (Jenkins, 1969, pp. 663–669).

When language is viewed as a string of words, the sequences and the exact pattern of sequences in which words are ordered or combined are of critical importance (Jenkins, 1969, p. 667). Two general approaches have been proposed to account not only for the words but for their ordering in sentences, both as they are spoken and as they are understood. In the first approach, it is assumed that humans engage in probabilistic learning in which words subsequently become probabilistically linked in productive arrangements. The second approach proposes that words are learned as members of classes, with certain sequences of classes forming permissible sequences. It has been suggested that these two approaches can be fused into a joint model in which there is the probabilistic linking of classes of words with varying probabilities of words having memberships in classes (Jenkins, 1969, pp. 666–672).

Language viewed as utterances stems from B.F. Skinner's prospect that language is behavior reinforced by others. Language, like any other behavior, is seen as developing through operant conditioning. Skinner divides verbal behaviors into two functional classes, mands and tacts. *Mands* refer to verbal behaviors controlled by the organism's state of deprivation;, their purpose is to command some specific reinforcement for the organism. Mands, which are "shaped" and maintained by reinforcement, will be extinguished when no longer reinforced. *Tacts*, on the other hand, refer to verbal behaviors that report something about the state of the world and are maintained by generalized reinforcement (Jenkins, 1969, pp. 672-675).

The fourth model of language acquisition focuses on language as a rule system. This position, championed by modern linguistics, and Chomsky in particular, argues that since language is infinitely variable, productive rules rather than words of particular sentence orders are learned. The learning of these productive rules permits the individual to both produce and to understand a variety of sentences. (Jenkins, 1969, p. 675). However, little is known about how the child actually acquires the rules of language. It is suggested that the child starts with "pivot grammars" that subsequently become more complex (Chomsky, 1975; Jenkins, 1969, pp. 675–682).

From a sociological role perspective, language develops through interactional processes usually between mother and infant. Initially, social interaction between mother and infant is preverbal. Nonetheless, the infant and mother do communicate at a rudimentary level, with the mother interpreting the infant's cries and responding with activities that she hopes will restore the newborn to a state of comfort. Not only does the mother interpret the infant's cries, but subsequent to her intervention she evaluates from the infant's response whether her interpretation was correct. Although the mother possesses the capacity to interpret the infant's communication and to represent to herself what the infant may be trying to communicate, the newborn must develop this capacity through interaction with the mother. Gradually the infant becomes able to anticipate the mother's appearance, learning through the relationship with the mother how to emit meaningful sounds. Basically, this occurs through a process of operant learning in which the child learns to associate his or her vocal sounds and the mother's reinforcing responses. With his increasing capacity to emit vocal sounds, which are reinforced by the mother, the infant learns to make sounds in the mother's absence. Gradually, through vocal interaction between mother and child the child develops the ability to associate a specific sound with a specific desired circumstance, and this subsequently leads to a building up of vocabulary and to the use of an increasingly complex set of shared symbols (Damon, 1983, pp. 50–52; Denzin, 1977, pp. 83–85; Elkin & Handel, 1984, pp. 44–48; Kerckhoff, 1972, pp. 23–24).

The acquisition of language accelerates socialization and is of enormous importance as one of the component processes of role learning. With the gradual acquisition of language and the use of common gestures, the infant acquires the ability to symbolize, i.e., to specifically identify things, persons, and feelings to himself. Once he has acquired the ability to present to himself the same symbol for an object that is presented to others, the child makes great strides toward the regulation of his own behavior and simultaneously toward responsive participation with others. Having entered into the social world of shared symbols, the child has gained the capacity to move beyond the mother–infant relationship into the larger social world of family, peers, school, and so forth (Denzin, 1977, pp. 88–91; Elkin & Handel, 1984, pp. 44–48).

Role-taking. Another prerequisite to the learning of roles is the development of the capacity to take the role of the other. Turner (1956, p. 316) has defined role-taking in its most general form as "a process of looking at or anticipating another's behavior by viewing it in the context of a role imputed to that other." Role-taking has been defined also as "the process by which the actor imagines what the other person's response would be to any one of a number of things he might do" (Kerckhoff, 1972, p. 32); "the ability to imagine oneself in the place of the other and to see things as he sees them" (Heiss, 1976, p. 6); and "the imaginative construction of the other's role" (Turner, 1956, p. 317, after Coutu, 1951). Common to these and many other definitions of role-taking is the fact that the individual anticipates the response of the other to his own behavior, i.e., self-consciously views himself from the standpoint of the other in terms of relative social location (position, status), reflects upon his own performance or appraises his own behavior in view of the other's response, and enacts or performs his own role accordingly (Brim, 1966; Coutu, 1951; Denzin, 1977, p. 130; Heiss, 1976; Hewitt, 1976; Kerckhoff, 1972; Lauer & Boardman, 1971; Miller, 1981, p. 170; Sherohman, 1977). The role of the other may be inferred through observation of the behavior of the other, supplying in imagination the role of which the behavior is indicative. The role may also be inferred by knowledge of the situation through projection, i.e., imputing the role to the other, or through prior knowledge of the other obtained from previous experiences with the individual or those with behavior like the other's in similar situations, or with behavior of individuals in comparable situations (Denzin, 1977, p. 131; Turner, 1956, p. 318).

The manner in which the inferred other role shapes the enactment of the self role depends on what standpoint the individual adopts in taking the role of the other and on whether the role-taking is reflexive or nonreflexive (Turner, 1956, p. 319). Taking the role of the other need not include taking the standpoint of the other. When the standpoint of the other is adopted, however, one acts from the standpoint of the other in taking the role of the other. When the standpoint of the other is adopted in role-taking, various factors would then determine what influence taking the role of the other will have on the individual's behavior (Turner, 1956, p. 319).

"Taking the standpoint of the other" refers to one's ability to imaginatively take the role of the other while at the same time maintaining one's own personal identity (Turner, 1956, p. 319). This distinction between taking the *role* of the other and taking the *standpoint* of the other is not made by children in early role-taking activity. As the child gradually engages in more complex behavior, role-taking becomes divested of identification, i.e., taking the standpoint of the other.

Such situations arise when the individual becomes simultaneously concerned with multiple others and is unable simultaneously to take the standpoint of each; when there are conflicting standpoints in the varied roles with which the individual becomes involved; or when needs or purposes gradually lead the individual to adopt role-taking in an adaptive context (Turner, 1956, p. 319). Thus, in taking the role of the other one may adopt the other's standpoint as one's own with an automatically resulting identification with the other role, which serves as a guide to self behavior; the individual may adopt a third-party standpoint in which the role of the other is viewed from the standpoint of a personalized third party or depersonalized norm; or the individual may take, in an adaptive context, a standpoint consisting of a purpose or objective (Turner, 1956, p. 321).

The manner in which the inferred other role shapes the enactment of the self role is also determined by whether role taking is reflexive or nonreflexive. In reflexive role-taking the role of the other serves as a mirror reflecting the expectations or evaluations of the self as seen by the other, i.e., Cooley's "looking-glass-self." From this perspective, the role taker is focused upon the way he or she appears to the other and shapes the behavior of the self accordingly. More attention will be given to this aspect of role taking when we consider the genesis of the self. In nonreflexive role-taking, other attitudes, expectations, or evaluations are not directed toward the self and thus are not relevant to the determination of the individual's behavior (Turner, 1956, p. 321).

By using the concepts of reflexive and nonreflexive role-taking in combination with the three general standpoints which may be adopted in role-taking, we can more sharply delineate the different ways in which self-other relationships can determine behavior (Turner, 1956, p. 322). First, when role-taking is nonreflexive and involves taking the standpoint of the other, the individual's behavior is determined by identification with the standpoint of the other. When role-taking is reflexive and the standpoint of the other is adopted, the individual desires to conform to the other's expectations and shapes his or her self-behavior into conformity with the other. When role-taking and a third-party standpoint is adopted, the individual is able to act discriminately toward the other in determining which aspirations and attitudes to use for herself or himself. When role-taking is reflexive and the actor adopts the standpoint of the third party, the actor is enabled to react selectively to an audience, accepting some of its evaluations as legitimate while rejecting those expectations that lack legitimacy. When role-taking occurs in an adaptive context and is reflexive, the other manipulates his or her own self-image as a means of achieving ends. In contrast, when role-taking is nonreflexive, the other may endeavor to establish a false self-image so as to modify the behavior of the self in the anticipated direction (Turner, 1956, pp. 322–323).

These types of role-taking are important because in each, one finds oneself in a somewhat different relationship with the other whose role one is attempting to take, and in combination the effect on self-role behavior is different (Turner, 1956, p. 323).

Taking the role of the other occurs through the process of social interaction and is clearly related to cognitive development (Kerckhoff, 1972, p. 57; Selman & Bryne, 1981). Through interaction the individual learns both his own responses to others and the responses of those others with whom he interacts (Brim, 1966,

p. 10). In learning self-other roles, the individual gets needed information by direct instruction, by observing interaction as a participant, or by observing interaction as a bystander (Heiss, 1976, pp. 6–7). Television may also serve as a viable alternative source of potential significant others and as an additional training ground for the acquisition of role-taking skills through the process of vicarious role-taking (Ellis, Streeter, & Engelbrecht, 1983; Peterson & Peters, 1983).

How children acquire role-taking skills has been studied by a number of developmentalists (Cooper, Grotevant, & Condon, 1983; Feffer & Gourevitch, 1960; Flavell et al., 1968; Hoffman, 1977; Selman & Bryne, 1974, 1981; Shantz, 1983). Selman (1976, 1980) has delineated a developmental sequence of five general role-taking levels, which span the period from childhood to adolescence and which have been empirically related to several types of social knowledge, particularly moral judgments (Selman 1971; Kurdek, 1978; Selman & Jaquette, 1978; Muus, 1983).

Several factors affect the individual's role-taking ability and role-taking accuracy. The actor's role-taking ability, i.e., "the generalized ability to accurately imagine the roles of other people," is largely determined by

1. The extent of the individual's social experience
2. The extent of the individual's experiences with a particular role as actor, other, or observer
3. The adequacy of the individual's memory of those experiences
4. The recency of relevant experiences
5. The extent to which the individual "paid attention" during the interaction.

The actor's role-taking accuracy, i.e., "the degree of similarity between the estimate of another's role [plan of action] . . . and that other's actual role," may be influenced by the characteristics of (1) the role taker, (2) the other, (3) the relationship between the role-taker and other, or (4) the situation. When one finds oneself in a situation that has not been previously experienced, one must not only draw upon prior experience but apply information that has been previously obtained. Skill in perceiving the essential differences in situations previously experienced depends upon the ability of the individual to develop, through a process of trial and error, implicit hypotheses concerning the differences between past and present circumstances and to take the role of the other on this basis; usually, the role taken is that of the *generalized other*. The individual's ability to take the role of the generalized other is based upon an ability to take into account the statuses of the others involved in the interaction, take all of their roles in turn, and then develop a conception of the probable group reactions or responses (Heiss, 1976, pp. 7–8).

Development of the Self. The development or genesis of the self is both a product of social interaction and a prerequisite for social interaction and the learning of social roles. The self, which is not initially present at birth, arises through the process of interaction with significant others, particularly the mother. Preverbal social interaction that precedes the acquisition of language takes place through a process that Mead termed a *conversation of gestures* (Mead, 1934, pp. 135–141). Differential responses on the part of parents, siblings, and others communicate to the infant whether or not its behavior is appropriate and in so doing they lay the groundwork for the child's self-evaluation. Since language is essential for the development of the self, the child's increasing ability to use language enables the socialization process and the development of the self to proceed with greater rapidity and depth (Brim, 1966, p. 11).

From a Meadian viewpoint, the self is a process in which the individual first becomes an object to himself by taking the attitudes of others toward himself. This ability to take the attitude of others toward the self is made possible through the development of language. The self, which is essentially a social process, arises in social experience, allowing the self to be an object to himself (Mead, 1934, pp. 138–140).

The *conversation of gestures* that one comes to carry on within oneself is the beginning of communication. With the increasing ability of the child to use language, the symbol that the child uses arouses in the self the same response that it arouses in other individuals. As the child develops, she or he begins to use larger segments of behavior, even whole roles, and engages in what Mead has referred to as *play*. Through play the child may actively and dramatically act the role of parent, teacher, or policeman; as he or she plays each role the child builds up a repertoire of roles that assist him or her to participate in a variety of situations.

With encouragement from the culture to play roles that may subsequently be required for adult role performance, the child learns the statuses or positions within the social structure of the society as well as the role prescriptions and role behaviors required of occupants of specific positions. The child also learns those role behaviors and prescriptions that should be avoided. Since play occurs under conditions that are viewed as practice sessions for future role performances, the atmosphere is nonpunitive and there is little censure. This early role play, which occurs in learning situations that are usually unrelated, is essentially transient and unorganized.

As the child grows older, he or she becomes involved in more complex situations that require taking the roles of several individuals simultaneously so as to enact his or her role. Mead referred to this advanced state of development as the *game*. In contrast to the play situation, in the game the self must take into account the attitude of everyone else involved, noting as well the relationships of each of the varying roles to the other. Essentially, this period or activity that Mead calls the game is the situation through which the self incorporates the generalized other, i.e., the attitude of the whole community of which the self is a part.

It is under the conditions of play and the game that the self arises as an object to itself. To develop the self to its fullest extent one must not only take on the attitudes of the other individuals toward oneself and toward one another within the process of social interaction and bring the whole social process into one's individual experience, but one must also take on the attitude of the generalized other, which is the attitude of the whole community of which one is a part. It is through the process of incorporating the generalized other that the individual's behavior is influenced and the community exercises control over the conduct of its members.

Thus, the development of the self involves two general stages. The first, designated by Mead as *play*, involves the self being constituted through incorporating the attitudes of particular individuals toward oneself and one another in specific social acts in which the individual participates with those individuals. In the second stage, which Mead termed the *game*, the self is organized not only by the particular attitudes of individuals but also by the organization of the social attitudes of the generalized other, the social group, or community to which the individual belongs (Mead, 1934, p. 158). The game is simply an illustration of the process through which the self is developed by continually taking the attitudes of those about one, by taking the roles of those who in some sense are the controllers of one's behavior and upon whom one depends (Mead, 1934, p. 160).

Both the acquisition of language and the taking on of the role of the other are prerequisites for play, in which the individual takes the role of the individual other, and for the game, in which the individual incorporates the attitudes of the generalized other. Taking on the role of the other occurs essentially through the use of language, and it is through language that the individual is able to arouse in himself or herself the same attitudes that the individual arouses in the other (Mead, 1934, pp. 160–161).

What constitutes the self is viewed by Mead as the organization of the attitudes that are common to the group of which the individual is a part. By putting oneself in the place of the generalized other, one is guided and controlled by principles. It is only through the relationship of the self to other selves that the self can exist (Mead, 1934, p. 164). The individual becomes a self only in so far as he or she is able to take the attitude of the other and act toward himself as others act toward him (Mead, 1934, p. 171). This implies the preexistence of a group with whom the individual can interact. The self is a reflexive and cognitive phenomenon rather than an emotional one. Its essence lies in its capacity to carry on an internalized conversation of gestures, which constitutes thinking (Mead, 1934, p. 173). The *I* consists of the response of the individual to the attitudes of the other, whereas the *Me* is the organized set of attitudes, the generalized other, which the individual assumes (Mead, 1934, p. 175). The I and the Me constitute phases of the self. Essential to the self in its full expression are the I and the Me (Mead, 1934, p. 199). Although all selves are constituted by means of social interaction with significant others, the individual self has its own peculiar individuality and uniqueness.[1]

Elaborations of the Meadian theory of self have been proposed by Turner (1978), who developed the concept of "role–person merger" as a complement to the idea of self-conception; Lewis (1979), who extended and slightly reformulated Mead's theory within the social behaviorist interpretation of the *I*; and Bolton (1981), who followed the emergence implications of Mead's theory which lead to a more phenomenologic view of the self.

Presentation of Self and Interpersonal Competence. Equally important for the acquisiton of roles is the learning of interpersonal competence (Weinstein, 1969, pp. 753–775) and presentation of self (Goffman, 1959) through the process of social interaction. Interpersonal competence is the ability of the actor to control the response of the other through the use of interpersonal tactics, an ability which ultimately depends upon the development of language.

Intelligence and cue sensitivity underly the individual's capacities for developing interpersonal competence. Cue sensitivity, meanings of common gestures, facial expressions, and voice inflections are learned through a social conditioning process as part of language acquisition. Heightened cue sensitivity is necessary for the individual to be able to recognize and discriminate differences in meaning between individuals and for the same individuals in differing situations.

The genesis for developing interpersonal competence is found in the capacity that the individual develops to distinguish self from nonself. Projective and positional role-taking, personality stereotyping, individuation, and autistic projection are types of role-taking that have their beginnings during the early school years and continue developing subsequently.

Several conditions promote the development of interpersonal competence, including exposing the child to a breadth and variety of social relationships, role-playing, and parental practices that orient the child toward projective role-taking. Highly authoritarian child-rearing practices tend to inhibit role-taking accuracy.

Interpersonal competence, the "ability to control the responses of others" (Weinstein, 1969, p. 764), depends both upon the development of more self-conscious use of interpersonal tactics and upon the development of language. The learning of role prescriptions and role behaviors and how these are enacted in varying situations are fundamental to the learning of interpersonal tactics. The individual must learn the tactics of interpersonal bargaining as well as techniques for both establishing and maintaining his or her situational identity and *altercasting*, or assigning situational identity to others (Weinstein, 1969, p. 757).

Effective participation in social exchange requires awareness of exchange as an approach to the pursuit of personal goals, the learning of exchange tactics, and the development of the ability to differentiate situations in which tactics may not be equally effective for interpersonal control.

The development of reciprocity in exchange is believed to have its foundation early in socialization, peer influence probably having a major importance. Through interaction with peers the individual learns that advantageous exchange means maximizing one's outcomes in the balance of rewards and costs for the individual actor.

For the adult, much interaction focuses upon establishing and maintaining situational identities, which may change from encounter to encounter. Situational identities, or the ways in which one presents oneself to others, are the basis for lines of action and interpersonal tasks. In establishing which self is to be presented, the individual learns the cues that need to be given in establishing identity through direct claim, by adoption of the particular sets and demeanor associated with the desired identity, shading, and coloration, and by directing others to asssume or play roles through the use of sanctions or altercasting.

Several personal tendencies may enhance or inhibit the individual's ability and freedom to be interpersonally competent. Role rigidity, particularly as it relates to being rule bound, and rigidity in certain aspects of one's self-concept interfere with interpersonal competence. Personal motivations also affect the individual's motivation for interpersonal competence, with feelings of alienation resulting in low motivation, internal locus of control resulting in high motivation, and external locus of control resulting in reduced motivation. Failure also affects motivation for interpersonal competence. When an individual assumes a failure–avoidance orientation, the result is reduced flexibility in the bargaining process. The underlying basis for the failure–avoidance orientation is probably low self-esteem enhanced by parental rejection (Weinstein, 1969, pp. 753–775).

From the point of view of Meadian role theory, a socialization process is necessary to teach the individual what self he or she should present in specific situations and how to go about presenting an image of self that is consistent with his or her actual self-image. The processes by which the individual learns to present the correct self-image, sometimes termed management of impressions, are basically the same processes as those utilized in socialization for roles. The difference is essentially in the content learned rather than in the process by which the learning occurs.

According to Elkin (1976, pp. 356–358), the child goes through several stages in learning impression management or presentation of self. Using the work of Goffman (1959), Elkin proposed that through the process of socialization, i.e., interaction with significant others, the child learns the parts or roles that he should present before certain audiences and in certain settings as well as those behaviors permitted in "back regions" which are not open to the audience. Elkin maintains that the learning required for presentation of self, i.e., role performance behavior, begins very early in the child's life, even before the development of the self. Ultimately, the ability to learn to manage impressions requires both the development of the self and the ability to take the role of the other, i.e., to take the attitude of the other person with respect to one's own behavior. Once the child has developed a self and is capable of taking the role of the other, others take greater care in the presentation of the self that they enact before the child.

Learning Processes Through Which Socialization Occurs

The main emphasis of Meadian role theorists has been upon the interactional processes through which socialization occurs rather than upon the learning processes through which socialization is achieved. Although these theories conceptualize the learner as an active participant in his or her own socialization, they acknowledge that socialization involves both conscious and unconscious learning processes in which the socializee may be viewed under varying circumstances as either an active or a passive participant in the process of role learning and role enactment (Goslin, 1969, p. 12). In the earlier discussion of the interactional processes through which socialization occurs, several learning processes were identified as necessary for the learning of verbal or language skills, the learning of role taking skills, the genesis or development of the self, the learning of the presentation of the self or interpersonal competence, and the learning of social roles. These learning mechanisms included (1) operant learning; (2) direct instruction; (3) observational learning; (4) imitation; (5) role-taking; (6) role-playing; (7) modeling; (8) trial and error; (9) identification; and (10) role negotiation.[2] Although a theory of social learning is thus necessarily inherent in the role theorists' position that socialization occurs through interactional processes, this learning theory has not as yet been specifically delineated. Cahill (1980), however, has proposed directions for an interactionist study of gender development that incorporates a suggested sequence through which gender identity is learned.

As indicated earlier, psychologists have focused upon processes of learning and development, taking varied theoretical perspectives with respect to the processes of identification, motivation, and cognitive, language, psychosexual, and moral development. Learning theorists have also taken theoretical positions regarding the acquisition of sex role identities and sex role standards (Biller, 1971,

1976; D'Andrade, 1966, pp. 173–203; Emmerich, 1973; Fleishman, 1983a, 1983b; Hoffman, 1977; Honig, 1983; Kagan, 1964, pp. 137–167; Kohlberg, 1966, pp. 82–172; Maccoby 1966; Maccoby & Jacklin 1974; Mischel, 1966, pp. 56–81; Mussen, 1969, pp. 707–731; Simari & Baskin, 1983; Spencer, 1967, pp. 193–205; Zuckerman & Sayre, 1982) which are pertinent to the sociologist's interest in the mechanisms through which role prescriptions and role behaviors are learned.

With respect to learning theories and learning mechanisms in general, Gewirtz (1969, pp. 57–212) emphasizes the operant conditioning paradigm and uses imitation-identification and dependence-attachment as the two key social-learning processes (Gewirtz, 1969, pp. 136–182). In contrast, Bandura (1969b, pp. 213–262; 1977) proposes a social-learning theory of identificatory processes that is much in keeping with the Meadian role theorists' position on learning processes. In Bandura's theory, the terms " 'identification,' 'imitation,' and 'observational learning' are employed interchangeably to refer to behavioral modification resulting from exposure to modeling stimuli" (Bandura, 1969, p. 219). Bandura proposes that the basic learning process underlying identification is observational learning, which involves imagery formation and verbal coding of observed events. The proposed modeling phenomenon consists of four components: attentional, retentional, motoric reproduction, and incentive or motivational processes. In order to reproduce modeling stimuli, Bandura proposes that the individual must (1) attend to, recognize, and differentiate the distinctive features of the model's responses; (2) retain the coded modeling events over time through covert role practice of modeled responses that produce rewarding outcomes; (3) utilize symbolic representations of modeled responses in the form of imagery and verbal coding to guide overt role performances; and (4) respond to favorable or reinforcing incentive conditions (Bandura, 1969, pp. 220–225), which may be externally applied, self-administered, or vicariously experienced (Bandura, 1969, pp. 233–241). Bandura's theory (1969, pp. 241–247, 255) emphasizes the emulation of the behavior of models possessing distinctive characteristics. The result is that these models eventually function as discriminative stimuli for identificatory responses toward unfamiliar models in different social situations. Bandura's theory of identificatory processes differs significantly from psychoanalytic theories of anaclitic and defensive or aggressive identification, and from Whiting's status-envy hypothesis of modeling stimuli and social power theories (Bandura, 1969b, pp. 225–233). These latter theories will not be discussed here.

Motivation of the Socialized Person to Learn Content and Utilize It in Role Performance

Our previous discussion of the interactional processes through which socialization occurs emphasized both the roles of external and internal sanctions, i.e., rewards and punishment imposed by significant others, and the internalization of dispositions and values as two major motivational forces enhancing the learning of role prescriptions and role behaviors (Aronfreed, 1969, pp. 270–292; Brim, 1966, pp. 11, 15–17; Elkin, 1976, pp. 358–359; Elkin & Handel, 1984, pp. 40–44; Ferguson, 1970, pp. 59–79; Kerckhoff, 1972, pp. 26–28; and Parke, 1970, pp. 81–108).

Although there is some convergence of opinion among psychologists and sociologists that role learning and role enactment depend in part on the effectiveness of external and internal sanctions, the views of the learner taken by the psychologist and the sociologist lead to somewhat different interpretations of the function of reward and punishment in the socialization process (Goslin, 1969, p. 13). The psychologist appears to place greater emphasis upon the effects of reward and punishment in facilitating desired behavioral responses, upon the establishment of the link between the stimulus and the response, and upon the process through which external reward and punishment become internalized over time. The strength of the sanction imposed is important to the psychologist, whether the sanctions are positive or negative; so is the timing of the sanctions with respect to the learner's acts, the frequency and consistency with which the sanctions are imposed, and the form that the sanctions take, i.e., whether they are mediated by verbal and symbolic processes or involve direct physical impact, and whether they are experienced directly or vicariously through observation of outcomes for others (Goslin, 1969, pp. 14–16).

Psychologists have provided experimental evidence that extremely strong negative sanctions result in acquiring response dispositions that are accompanied by high performance motivation and high resistance to extinction. There is further evidence, however, that very strong punishment inhibits the ability of the learner to make necessary subtle discriminations among stimuli, resulting in a decrease in the individual's motivation to perform. Mild sanctions have been found to permit full concentration on the relevant stimuli but may be ineffective in promoting high motivation to perform. It is reported that both positive and negative sanctions can be equally effective in enabling the learner to discriminate appropriate from inappropriate behavioral cues. Further, it has been found that rapid acquisition of desired responses by the learner results from close timing of reward or punishment with respect to the learner's act. More frequent and consistent sanctions are believed to make it easier for the learner to discriminate appropriate from inappropriate role behaviors. For some kinds of learning, however, partial reinforcement results in stronger response acquisition because sanctions are random in probability of occurrence but consistent in nature (Goslin, 1969, pp. 14–16; Parke, 1970, pp. 81–108; 1972, pp. 264–283).

In contrast to the psychologist, the sociologist views rewards and punishments as providing the learner with cues that enable the individual to evaluate consciously the adequacy of his or her role performance and modify behavior accordingly (Goslin, 1969, p. 13). Sanctions are viewed as an integral part of the role negotiation process, with differential outcomes resulting from the distribution and redistribution of sanctioning power (Goslin, 1969, p. 16).

It is generally held that in situations characterized by the imposition of external rewards or punishment for inappropriate role performance, both learning and motivation are likely to be a function of the type of rewards and punishments present. In contrast, when imposition of external sanctions is low, both learning and motivation are likely to be the result of internalized dispositions, i.e., values and motives (Goslin, 1969, p. 14).

Aronfreed (1969, p. 264) defines the concept of internalization as referring "to the child's adoption of social norms or roles as its own, and to the resulting control of its behavior by the most complex mediational functions of cognitive and verbal processes." From Aronfreed's perspective, internalization of values and motives or development of conscience is accomplished through direct training and through observational learning (Aronfreed, 1969, pp. 270–304). Goslin (1969, pp. 16–17) summarizes findings from several studies supporting the notion that internalization is powerfully influenced by the immediacy, availability, and intensity of discriminative cues (rewards and punishments).

The process of acquisition or internalization of values and motives has been studied from several perspectives. The cognitive-developmental perspectives represented by the works of Piaget and Kohlberg trace the acquisition of values through successive stages (Kohlberg, 1969, pp. 347–480; Kohlberg & Kramer, 1972, pp. 336–361; Kohlberg, 1972, 1973, 1975, 1978, 1981; Maccoby, 1968, pp. 229–239; Piaget, 1948). The social learning perspective emanating from the work of Bandura and Walters emphasizes the acquisition of self-control through modeling, direct reinforcement, and reinforcement patterns and disciplinary techniques (Bandura, 1969, pp. 213–262; Bandura & Walters, 1968, pp. 189–191; Bandura, 1977; Maccoby, 1968, pp. 240–262). The psychoanalytic perspective represented by Freud emphasized the mechanisms of defensive and anaclitic identification as underlying the development of an inner conscience (Hoffman, 1963, pp. 295–318).

In contrast, Meadian role theorists emphasize the development of the self as the principal outcome of socialization, which makes internal or self-regulation of behavior possible. This capacity for self-regulation develops as a result of interaction with significant others who present themselves as authoritative role models utilizing positive and negative sanctions to encourage the internalization of appropriate values and norms (Brim, 1966, pp. 11, 15–17; Elkin, 1976, pp. 358–359; Elkin & Handel, 1984, pp. 53–58). It will be recalled that development of the self involves the ability of the individual to take the role of the other, thus enabling the person to act toward him- or herself in much the same way that he or she acts toward other people. "Self-control refers to behavior that is redirected in the light of the manner in which it is imagined to appear from the standpoint of other people who are involved in a cooperative task" (Shibutani, 1968, p. 381). This capacity to form self-images or take the role of the other makes possible the control of the impulsive *I* which is inhibited by the *Me* or the generalized other, making self-criticism and self-control possible. Thus, from a Meadian role perspective, individuals are viewed as internalizing social controls over their own behavior by developing selves (Heiss, 1976, pp. 10–11; Hewitt, 1976, pp. 55–56, 60–61, 82–92; Mead, 1934, pp. 155, 162, 178, 186–192, 210–211, 254–255; Shibutani, 1968, pp. 379–381).

Outcomes of the Socialization Process as Specified by Society

It is the purpose of socialization to assist members of a society to acquire the knowledge, skills, and dispositions that will enable them to function as able members of the society (Brim, 1966, p. 3; Elkin & Handel, 1984, p. 12; Kerckhoff, 1972, pp. 34–35). Thus, a particular society specifies a socialization process wherein certain requirements, demands, and expectations which serve as functional requisites for the continuance of that society are made of its members. The socialized individual is expected to achieve established standards of the society with respect to physical development, skills and capacities, emotional expression, intellectual and conative activity, and patterning of relations with significant others (Brim, 1966, pp. 4–8; Inkeles, 1968, p. 75). Additionally, society is primarily concerned with the acquisition of those characteristics having particular relevance for the performance of adult social roles that the individual will enact with respect to a status position within that society (Brim, 1966, pp. 4–7; Goslin, 1969, p. 10; Inkeles, 1968, p. 77).

The societally expected outcomes of socialization are also determined by society's rules governing access to particular statuses and roles. Roles are either *ascribed* on the basis of such characteristics as social class, ethnic group membership, religion, and gender, or *achieved* on the basis of educational or occupational background (Elkin & Handel, 1984, pp. 38–39; Hewitt, 1976, pp. 93–95; Inkeles, 1968, p. 78). Accordingly, society specifies criteria and procedures that differentiate among children of various social classes, ethnicity, religious affiliation, and sex-role identification, resulting in different sequences of experiences and ultimately different socialization outcomes (Elkin & Handel, 1984, pp. 38–40).

Society makes demands upon the individual member on three levels of generality: those requirements common to any society, those characteristic of a particular society or cultural tradition, and those demanded of individuals belonging to certain subgroups or strata of the society (Inkeles, 1968, p. 78). Inkeles (1968, p. 79–83) summarizes the eight functional requisites for continuance of a particular society as developed by Levy (1952). These requisites for societal functioning include:

(1) provision for an adequate physiologic relationship to the environment through individual acquisition of relevant information, skills, and techniques permitting physical survival and procreation

(2) *role differentiation* and *role assignment*, which facilitate the individual's development of a sense of identity and the similarity or distinctiveness of that identity in relation to others', particularly with respect to gender and age

(3) a "shared, learned, symbolic mode of communication" accomplished through interaction with significant others

(4) "a shared cognitive orientation"

(5) a shared set of goals that have been articulated by the society, including values, needs, and motives

(6) regulations with respect to the means chosen to attain the designated goals, with additional emphasis upon the attainment of the *social self*

(7) regulations with respect to affective modes of expression or functioning and

(8) effective social control of deviant and disruptive forms of behavior through the utilization of sanctions (Inkeles, 1968, pp. 79–83).

Corresponding to these eight functional requisites developed by Levy (1952), Inkeles proposes eight elements of the personal system arising from adequate socialization. These include motor and information skills; a personal identity or development of a self-system; language skills that are accompanied by cognitive content and development; the development of attitudes, opinions, and idea systems; the development of values; the development of the ego accompanying development of the self-system; modes of affective functioning; and finally, moral modes of functioning (Inkeles, 1968, p. 83).

In addition to the functional requisites common to any society, distinctive socialization demands or requirements are specified by particular societies and particular social statuses. These requirements may involve specific demands and personality traits for individuals who would occupy certain statuses in the society. The terms used for stating the requirements may be highly idiosyncratic and variable and they may be applied with varying levels of generality and degrees of precision. It is apparent, however, that there are several recurrent themes in the socialization requirements expected by different societies and of different positions (Inkeles, 1968, p. 87).

In less complex societies, it is expected that individuals will learn through the process of socialization to be reasonably responsive to both the social order and to the requirements of others with whom they have immediate contact, thus demonstrating some degree of social conformity. Also, it is expected that the individual will acquire those skills that will enable him or her to become oriented in space and time, and to his or her physical setting, as well as to perform those requirements specific to particular statuses within the society. The knowledge and skills previously enumerated by Inkeles (1968, p. 83) include motor and mental skills; specialized knowledge appropriate to the individual's status; certain ways of thinking about the world that are organized into distinctive idea systems; development of a set of goals or values that guide the individual's actions; beliefs that are appropriate to attaining the goals; development of a self-concept that serves as the basis of social relations with others; development of a pattern of organizational and psychic functioning that facilitates moral functioning; and the development of a particular "cognitive, conative, and affective style" (Brim, 1966, pp. 8–11; Goslin, 1969, pp. 10–11; Inkeles, 1968, pp. 83–88; Kerckhoff, 1972, pp. 52–59).

Society also expects that the socialization process will develop individuals with characteristics that are common to others within the society, as well as other characteristics that distinguish particular individuals because they are more closely aligned with the social statuses and roles that the individuals occupy (Inkeles, 1968, p. 89).

In more complex societies it is anticipated that individuals will exhibit reasonable conformity to the society's social order, that they will acquire the knowledge and the skills that will permit them to care for themselves physically, and that they will acquire those role prescriptions and role behaviors specific to the particular statuses occupied (Inkeles, 1968, p. 89). It is generally the case that society provides its members with a definition of the goals and means for attaining these goals through either tradition or expert advice (Inkeles, 1968, p. 90). Society is seen to influence the socialization process through direct instruction which may involve formal or written systems of expectations, through explicit training, through the use of sanctions, and through retraining processes (Inkeles, 1968, pp. 93–102).

According to Elkin and Handel (1984, pp. 37–38), the two most basic results sought through the process of socialization are a motivated commitment to continued responsible participation in society and that kind of competence that the society accepts as appropriate. These two anticipated results include the expectation that the individual will recognize and accept the legitimate claims made upon him or her because of the individual's position within the social structure; that the individual will function within the communication and emotional expression limits defined by the society as appropriate for varying situations; that the individual will accept the responsiblities associated with his or her respective roles; and that the individual will develop those competencies appropriate to the statuses and roles assumed (Elkin & Handel, 1984, pp. 35–38). It is anticipated that the socialization process will assist every individual to find an appropriate adult status within the society and to enact a role within the society with the particular type of commitment and competence appropriate to it (Elkin & Handel, 1984, p. 38).

In summary, it is the expectation of Meadian role theorists that the outcomes of socialization will include those acquired skills facilitating role acquisition and role performance, i.e., language acquisition and language facility, development of the capacity to take the role of the other, the development of the self, and the development of interpersonal competence and presentation of self. Equally important are the development of physical and cognitive skills, the learning of role negotiation, and the internalization of motives and values (Brim, 1966, pp. 9–11; Goslin, 1969, pp. 10–11; Heiss, 1976, pp. 6–16; Kerckhoff, 1972, pp. 34–35).

Individual Differences in Socialization Outcomes or Role Performance

Although the general purpose of the socialization process is to prepare its members to perform those adult social roles attached to specific statuses within the society, individual differences in outcomes and role performance may be attributable to the specificity of requirements common to a society, to the particular cultural or subcultural tradition to which the individual belongs, and, finally, to the particular statuses and roles to which the individual, by virtue of position within the society, is allowed access (Elkin & Handel, 1984, pp. 37–38; Hewitt, 1976, pp. 93–95; Inkeles, 1968, p. 78).

The importance of subcultures for socialization is emphasized by Elkin and Handel (1984, pp. 80–82). The child is seen as being socialized into a particular *segment* of the larger society and not into the society as a whole. Through the process of socialization within this subculture the child learns the mores of that particular segment of society and not necessarily the knowledge, skills, dispositions, outlook, or assumptions shared by the larger society. The fact that the child is socialized within a subculture may subsequently limit his or her ability to function in the larger society, where values, beliefs, assumptions, and ways of life may differ significantly from the specific sector of society of which the child is a member. The importance of the subculture to socialization is further emphasized by the fact that the individual's adult status within the society is in part determined by the sector of society of which his family is a member. The child's primary role models come from within the subculture; thus the child's self— which is formed through interaction with significant others within his subculture—may limit his or her language facility, role-taking ability, development of the self, self-presentation and interpersonal competence, and role performance in the larger society.

Brim (1960, pp. 127–128) sets forth a theory of personality in which he attributes interindividual differences in adult social role performance to variation

TABLE 1. TRADITIONAL MODEL OF PERSONALITY THEORIES

Independent Variables	Intervening Variables	Dependent Variables
Socialization practices	Motivation	Interindividual differences in general traits

After Brim, 1960.

in the individual's knowledge, ability, and motivation to meet role demands. These three characteristics are related to the type of social structure in which the individual has been involved, as well as from the cultural and parental idiosyncratic variations in role performance to which the individual has been exposed.

Brim, in order to differentiate the variables important to the study of personality development as role learning, contrasts his theory to traditional clinical and sociopsychologic personality theories. Researchers interested in traditional personality theories seek to discover the antecedent for individuals' high or low scores on various general traits. The dependent variable in these theories is interindividual differences in general traits, i.e., high, medium, or low scores for such characteristics as dependency, achievement, dominance, submissiveness, or aggressiveness. At this general trait level the focus is upon the consistency for the core of personality of an individual in almost every setting. In the traditional model, motivation is the single intervening variable. Behavioral variation is explained post hoc by the high or low strength of one or another of the individual's motives. Socialization processes or practices that determine the individual's prior learning constitute the independent variable (Brim, 1960, pp. 132–133, 144–145; Zigler, Lamb, & Child, 1982, pp. 50–77) (Table 1).

In contrast to traditional personality theories, Brim (1960, pp. 131–143) proposes that the dependent variables are indeed interindividual differences in some characteristics, i.e., motives, ideas, behavior, or effects of action, but occurring within situational or role contexts. Brim's variables include (1) specification of traits within a role context, (2) behavior variation resulting from the person with whom the individual interacts, and (3) the number of episodes in which role behavior is prescribed in ongoing interactions between individuals. Brim defines personality in terms of learned roles and role components, therefore, his focus is upon variation in role performance in response to situational demands rather than upon consistency or conformity of response in different situations. The focus is upon the variation within roles rather than between roles. Socialization is viewed as successful if it prepares individuals to respond to a variety of situational demands with the appropriate amount of a given role characteristic. Socialization accomplishes this end by increasing the individual's repertoire of behavior through extension of the range and complexity of responses that the individual can enact by freeing the individual from a learned series of stereotyped responses, by providing the individual with the ability to discriminate among social situations, and by increasing the number of motives that can be utilized (Brim, 1960, pp. 137–138). Socialization is viewed as unsuccessful if an individual has a consistency of behavioral response in the face of variations in situations.

Whereas personality is viewed in Brim's theory as the learned repertoire of roles, self is viewed as a composite of several selves. Each self consists of a repertoire of self-perceptions specific both to one or another major role and to the expectations of one or another significant other (Brim, 1960, p. 141, 143).

The intervening variables in Brim's model seek to explain individual differences in behavior in specific situations by conceptualizing what is learned through the process of socialization, i.e., roles or role demands (role prescriptions, social norms) which encompass both behaviors and values. While traditional personality theorists have explained variation in behavior by using motivation as the intervening explanatory variable, Brim sees three intervening variables as crucial to the explanation of individual differences in behavioral performance. These variables are awareness and knowledge of the role demands, ability to fulfill the role demands, and motivation to meet the role demands. Thus, major sources of variation between individuals within roles may be the result of (1) ignorance of expectations or role prescriptions or inadequate knowledge, (2) inability on the part of the individual to perform or behave in the expected way because of genetic inadequacies, physical handicaps, or failures in training and learning for specific roles, and (3) lack of or diminished motivation to meet behavioral expectations because of variation in or failure of earlier socialization processes (Brim, 1960, pp. 143–147).

The independent variables in Brim's model seek to explain how differences in role learning occur and identify the variation sources in role learning. Brim identifies specific independent variables: social structural aspects and cultural content and idiosyncratic differences in parental role performance (Table 2). Social structural aspects refer to the network of related statuses in which the individual can be involved, examples of which include the presence or absence of father, of siblings of the same or opposite sex, and of peers. Brim views the social structure as regulating to a large degree those aspects of the culture to which an individual can be exposed and, consequently, those which the individual can learn. If certain statuses are absent or societal rules prohibit access to specific statuses, role learning relative to these respective statuses is deficient. Brim assumes that role learning occurs in rather large response units and through actual interactions with individuals occupying specific statuses within the society. These assumptions raise questions regarding whether roles can be learned vicariously, whether the parent can make up for the absence of important statuses to which the child lacks exposure, and whether deficiencies of early role learning can be remedied through interaction in adulthood with persons in statuses to which the child had no exposure during his earlier years (Brim, 1960, pp. 147–151).

Research relevant to some of the social structural aspects has been done under the rubric of (1) father absence and availability; (2) family size and composition; (3) ordinal position, (4) absence of siblings or peers, (5) working mothers and maternal deprivation, (6) marital disharmony and divorce, (7) traditional family styles including dual career and dual worker families, role-sharing families, role reversal, and single parents; and (8) families in transition.[3]

The second independent variable, cultural content and idiosyncratic differences in parent role performance, has generally been studied under the rubric of child-rearing practices, though genetic and developmental interpretations of social class variations in behavior have been proposed (Zigler, Lamb, & Child, 1982, pp. 105–106). With respect to cultural content, Brim emphasizes that the content

TABLE 2. BRIM'S MODEL OF PERSONALITY DEVELOPMENT

Independent Variables	Intervening Variables	Dependent Variables
Social structural aspects Cultural content and idiosyncratic parental role performance	Role demands: knowledge of, ability to meet, and motivation to meet	Interindividual differences within roles as expressed within situational contexts

After Brim, 1960.

of socialization, i.e., role learning, will vary considerably according to the culture or particular subculture to which the individual belongs. Cultures and subcultures may differ significantly in their conceptions of desirable adult role performance, in the particular ends sought through the socialization process, in the means utilized to attain the desired socialization outcomes, and the idiosyncratic differences resulting from parental variation in role performance to which the child is exposed. Research relevant to cultural content has been reviewed under the topics of (1) the effect of mother-father-infant interactions on subsequent personality and (2) the effects of variations in child-rearing practices in subcultural groups and the effects of between-parent variation in role performance.[4]

Although some findings are contradictory, social class differences in child-rearing practices seem to be of particular significance in accounting for individual differences in socialization outcomes and role performance.[5] There seems to be some consensus, however, that the parent-child relationship in which love-oriented techniques (praise, explanatory techniques, or withdrawal of love) are used rather than power-assertive techniques (physical punishment, expressive responses, or verbal threats) produces different effects on children's behavior in several ways. The use of love-oriented techniques is more likely to result in greater development of moral commitments, higher levels of achievement motivation, clearer and more favorable self-images, greater social sensitivity or role-taking and role-playing abilities, and greater language facility and cognitive development (Becker, 1964, pp. 169–208; 1972, pp. 29–72; Kerckhoff, 1972, pp. 52–57; Kohn & Schooler, 1972, pp. 223–249).

These outcomes are more likely to be observed in middle-class families where love-oriented techniques are typically used; where occupational conditions that emphasize manipulation of interpersonal relations, ideas, and symbols foster self-direction and affirm that "getting ahead" is dependent upon the individual's own actions; where parents value self-direction and freedom of opportunity; where elaborated language and complex cognitive structure result in language facility and cognitive ability; and where the parent-child relationship emphasizes the child's development of motives, self-control, and internal qualities of consideration, curiosity, and initiative (Kerckhoff, 1972, pp. 44–59; Kohn, 1963, pp. 471–480; 1969; Kohn & Schooler, 1972, pp. 223–249; Zigler, Lamb, & Child, 1982, pp. 106–109).

In contrast, the use of power-assertive techniques tends to mediate against the development of moral commitments and fosters low achievement motivation, low self-esteem, and low social sensitivity as a result of a greater emphasis on compliance. These outcomes are more likely to be observed in lower-class families where power-assertive techniques are more frequently used; where occupational conditions emphasize the manipulation of things, emphasize direct supervision, and affirm that getting ahead is achieved through collective action; where parents value conformity to external prescriptions, orderliness, and security; where restricted language and simple cognitive structure result in restricted language facility and cognitive ability; and where the parent–child relationship emphasizes traditional values of order, authority, cleanliness, obedience, and respectfulness (Kerckhoff, 1972, pp. 44–59; Kohn, 1963, pp. 471–480; 1969; Kohn & Schooler, 1972, pp. 223–249; Zigler, Lamb, & Child, 1982, pp. 106–109).

The outcome for the person of lower-class origin is likely to be inadequate early socialization, poor academic performance in elementary school, rejection of academic values in high school, and attainment of a lower level of education. The result is that the individual attains lower adult status within society (Kerckhoff, 1972, p. 102).

SOCIALIZATION AS A CONTINUOUS AND CUMULATIVE PROCESS

Role Learning

It is a basic premise of Meadian role theorists that socialization for roles or role learning is a continuous and cumulative process that corresponds to the sequence of age and sex statuses of the life cycle.[6] It is clear that socialization for roles begins in infancy and early childhood[7] with the acquisition of language or verbal skills, with the development of role taking ability, and with the development of self, interpersonal competence, motivation, and moral values. The learning of specific role demands, however,—the knowledge, abilities, and motivation to enact role behaviors and values—continues as the individual moves through the sequence of age and sex statuses that correspond to the stages of the life cycle: (1) adolescence, (2) adulthood, (3) marriage and parenthood, and (4) middle and old age.[8]

With the exception of old age and, for some theorists, adolescence, each of these important age and sex statuses is distinguished by three important properties of role transitions: rites of passage, social gains, and role continuity (Rosow, 1974, pp. 16–21). Rites of passage, which may be either public or private rituals or ceremonies, such as initiations or graduations, facilitate formal status changes by publicly signaling the individual's change in status, by publicly and socially redefining the individual's role expectations, and by publicly assisting the individual to assume the new status through fostering isolation of the individual from former group memberships and supports (Rosow, 1974, pp. 16, 124).

In addition, for the average individual, movement from a status of lower responsibility and prerogatives to one of a higher status of responsibility is accompanied by an increase in net social gains: increased prerogatives and rewards, larger spheres of decision making, larger numbers of people over whom he or she has authority, smaller numbers of persons who have superior authority, and greater social recognition. Those gains of rewards and prerogatives which are specifically age related, i.e., specifically associated with role transitions from one stage of the life cycle to the next are fundamentally a function of the individual's greater social maturity and competence in meeting increased social responsibilities (Rosow, 1974, pp. 16–19).

Finally, with some exceptions, status succession is accompanied by role continuity, i.e., role demands (prescriptions and expectations relative to behavior and values) of the previous stage and prepares the individual for the responsibilities and prerogatives associated with the next status or position. Thus, the individual experiences no major inconsistencies, reversals, or unlearning of previously learned role demands but rather undergoes a coherent preparation and developmental extension of basic role prescriptions from one age level to the next (Rosow, 1974, pp. 19–21).

Socialization for roles or role learning is further facilitated (Rosow, 1974, pp. 128–137):

1. by minimizing previous status advantages and emphasizing similarities among peer groups
2. by decreasing rewards for conformity to previous role prescriptions and reinforcing expectations associated with the newly assumed statuses
3. by clarifying for the individual those responsibilities accompanying the status change
4. by providing opportunities for rehearsal of future roles and thus cultivating the skills, techniques, and insights of the new status
5. increasing the individual's commitments to the role prescriptions attached to the new status
6. changing the self-image that the individual associates with the new status, and
7. by providing opportunities for successful role performance of the newly adopted status.

In contrast, the transition to old age is marked by occasional rites of passage, such as retirement dinners; social losses rather than gains (declining responsibilities, increasing dependency, alienation from significant social roles through widowhood and retirement, declining income, and increasing illness and physical handicaps); and, finally, sharp role discontinuity involving no anticipatory socialization for such losses and no formal role prescriptions (Riley et al., 1969, pp. 951–982; Rosow, 1974, pp. 22–27, 121–137).

Differences Between Childhood and Adult Socialization

Our previous discussion established the fact that there is need for socialization after childhood into roles not previously learned. From Brim's perspective, childhood and adult socialization differ in three principal ways: (1) adult socialization is limited by the socialization that occurred during childhood, (2) the content of socialization is different, and (3) the relationships between and among socializing agents are different (Brim, 1966, pp. 21–39; 1968a, pp. 555–561).

Adult Socialization. Adult socialization may be limited by both the biologic capacities of the individual and the effects of earlier learning or lack of that learning. Biologic restrictions frequently limit or preclude adequate socialization at an earlier stage of development or at a subsequent time when the individual with limited capacities is unable to meet the role demands of a position or status requiring a higher level of role performance (Brim, 1966, pp. 20–21; 1968a, p. 558; Elkin & Handel, 1984, pp. 15–18).

Because early learning usually occurs under conditions of partial reinforcement within the primary group (the family) it is usually characterized by a particular tenacity and durability. When this learning conflicts with the needs of the adult learner, later learning is much more difficult to achieve. In contrast, when earlier learning provides a strong basis for adult learning it facilitates the process of learning new roles. Where conditions have not fostered the learning of essential content (i.e., language acquisition and facility, role taking ability, development of the self, interpersonal competence, motivation, moral values, and role learning), learning at a subsequent time may be impossible, particularly if learning is found to depend upon the acquisition of particular knowledge, skills, and dispositions during certain critical periods of development (Brim, 1966, pp. 21–24; 1968a, pp. 557–558).

Socialization Content Changes. Brim (1966, 1968a) proposes that there are five major types of socialization content changes that distinguish adult socialization from childhood socialization. These changes include (1) an adult concern with the learning of new overt role behaviors versus a childhood socialization purpose of learning the societal values and motives, (2) a synthesis of material previously learned versus the acquisition of new material, (3) a concern with realism as opposed to a childhood concern with idealism, (4) learning how to mediate conflicts between and among role expectations versus the acquisition of role prescriptions themselves, and finally (5), a concern with the learning of role-specific expectations versus a childhood concern with the learning of the general role demands of the society (Brim, 1966, pp. 24–33; 1968a, pp. 559–561).

Overt Behavior versus Values and Motives. As previously noted in the discussion of Brim's model of personality as a learned repertoire of roles, the intervening variables that Brim used to explain individual differences in behavior in specific situations centered upon the learning of role demands encompassing both behavior and values. With respect to this model, Brim proposed that the individual must have knowledge of the role demands (behavior and values), expectations, and have the ability to carry out these role demands, and, finally, be motivated to fulfill the role demands. Brim used this model to create a paradigm that distinguishes between the content of adult and childhood socialization. As the individual moves through the life cycle the emphasis shifts from concern with motivation to concern with ability and finally to concern with knowledge. Simultaneously, there is a shift from concern with values to a concern with behavior (Brim, 1960, pp. 127–159; 1966, pp. 25–26).

During childhood socialization the highest priority is given to the acquisition of motives and values whereas adult socialization is usually most concerned with the acquisition of knowledge and behavior specific to a particular status. It is assumed that through childhood socialization the individual has been prepared with respect to the knowledge of values to be pursued in different roles and the motivation to pursue these values through socially appropriate means. Thus, adult socialization focuses upon the learning of behaviors appropriate to the acquisition of a specific role rather than upon either acquisition of motives or basic values (Brim, 1966, pp. 25–27; 1968a, p. 559; Kerckhoff, 1972, pp. 34–36).

Society uses at least two major solutions to the problems of the inadequately socialized adult. One solution consists of the anticipatory screening of candidates for a particular position in an adult organization with regard to their possessing the motives and values appropriate to that position and role within the organization. In the second solution, overt concern with the individual's motivation or value system is foregone. Society, which is represented by the organization seeking individuals to fill statuses within its structure, accepts the conformity to the behavioral expectations as evidence of adequate socialization (Brim, 1966, pp. 27–28; 1968a, p. 559; Rosow, 1965, pp. 35–45).

Synthesis of Old Material versus Acquisition of New. As noted previously in this chapter, childhood socialization as viewed by Brim focuses upon developing within the individual a repertoire of behavioral responses that enables the learner to discriminate and utilize appropriate amounts of any given characteristic in response to a variety of situational demands. The focus of adult socialization shifts then, to a synthesizing of previously learned responses into new combinations and forms, rather than to the learning of wholly new complexes of appropriate responses. When necessary, new fragments of behavioral responses may be integrated with previously learned responses so as to meet complex situational demands (Brim, 1966, p. 28; 1968a, p. 559).

Realism versus Idealism. The transformation of childhood idealism into adult realism involves two aspects: learning the informal status structure of the society and learning to distinguish between ideal role expectations and those roles the individual is actually expected to enact. During the period of childhood socialization, emphasis is placed upon the child's learning of the formal status structure of the society and the role prescriptions attached to these various positions. During this period the child is shielded from contact with the informal societal structure or at least is not formally instructed about informal status differentiations. Once the formal status structure has been legitimized for the child, later learning must include the realistic aspects of the informal status structure that facilitate the effective work of the formal system.

While childhood socialization has attempted to inculcate ideal role prescriptions that serve to strengthen and perpetuate the ideals of the society, upon maturation the individual must also learn to differentiate the ideal from the real role expectations of the society. For the individual this means taking part in society according to realistic expectations, rather than conforming to previously learned ideal norms (Brim, 1966, pp. 28–29; 1968a, pp. 559–560).

Intrarole and Interrole Conflict Resolution. Passing through the various stages of the life cycle the individual frequently meets conflicting demands that must be resolved. These may be *intrarole* conflicts, of which there are two types: those in which expectations for role performance differ among two or more individuals and those in which there is a conflict within the individual with respect to different aspects of a role; or there may be *interrole* conflicts, in which conflicts exist between two or more individuals with respect to two different roles or within the individual with respect to the performance of two different roles. Since the child has had little or no exposure to such conflicts during childhood socialization the individual attaining adulthood must learn methods of conflict resolution. Brim, citing Linton and Becker, suggests that conflicts may be resolved by (1) avoiding the conflict situation, (2) withdrawing from the conflict, (3) scheduling conflicting demands in a temporal sequence that results in the disappearance of conflict, or (4) compromising with conflicting demands. Brim suggests a further method of conflict resolution that he designates as learning to employ "meta-prescriptions," which dictate solutions to conflicts that arise from role demands on one's time and loyalties (Brim, 1966, pp. 29–31; 1968a, p. 560).

Specificity versus Generality. The general purpose of the socialization process is to prepare individuals with the general knowledge, skills, and dispositions that will enable them to function as able members of their societies. As the individual matures and assumes particular roles within the status structure of the society, the role prescriptions attached to these positions become much more specific in directing the individual's behavioral responses. It has been previously noted that value systems are associated with particular social classes within a society. With upward social mobility the individual is faced with a legitimate need for resocialization to the role prescriptions of the newly assumed status. There may also be occasion for resocialization that results from movement of an individual from one subculture or culture to another, which necessarily has different role expectations (Brim, 1966, pp. 31–32; 1968a, pp. 560–561).

Changes in Relationships with Socializing Agents

Childhood and adult socialization differ significantly in the relationships of the individual to the socializing agents or agencies. Brim describes three types of changes in relationships during the transition to adult status: changes in (1) the formality of the relationship, (2) the power or support in the relationship, and (3) the group context in which the individual is being socialized (Brim, 1966, pp. 33–39; 1968a, pp. 558–559).

Formality of the Relationship. Brim identifies two ways in which the relationship of the individual to socializing agents may become formalized: (1) the role of learner is clearly specified or (2) the agency or organization in which the individual is being socialized has either a formal or informal organizational structure. These two aspects of formality yield a fourfold classification scheme in which the individual may be socialized. In the first case the organization is formal and the role of the learner is clearly specified. Under this circumstance learning occurs within a well-defined role through formal instruction or training. An example of such a condition might be the on-the-job training or the newly inducted military recruit.

In the second case the organization would be formal, but the role of the learner is not clearly specified. Under these circumstances the outcomes of the learning process depend greatly upon the individual's abilities to observe and obtain needed information through trial-and-error learning. This situation characterizes much of adult socialization.

In the third instance the socialization agency is an informal group, but the role of the learner is clearly specified and prescribed. Under these circumstances the learner's role is well defined; the rights and duties of the socializee are specified and serve to regulate the process through which learning occurs; and the informal group provides opportunities for the learner to be supervised and guided in learning the appropriate responses while at the same time giving occasions for practice in which the individual is protected from punishment because of failure. This situation is characteristic of childhood socialization which occurs within the primary group of the family.

In the fourth instance, the agency is informal and the role of the learner is unspecified. This particular situation is exemplified by such situations as peer group socialization; socialization of a child into a new neighborhood; or socialization of the adult into a new social class, a new community status, or a wider family circle through marriage (Brim, 1966, pp. 34–35).

Power and Support in Relationships. Brim, citing Straus, characterizes relationships along two major dimensions: degree of authority, or power and degree of affectivity. Much of childhood socialization occurs in the context of high affectivity, high power, and high support. It is under these conditions that children acquire deep-seated parental and cultural motives and values. Much of adult socialization by contrast occurs under conditions of low power and low affectivity, and thus is not conducive to the inculcation of motives and values (Brim, 1966, pp. 35–37).

Group Context of the Person Being Socialized. Brim, citing Wheeler (1966, pp. 60–66), describes two further dimensions of group context: (1) where learning occurs on either an individual or collective basis and (2) where learning follows either a serial or disjunctive pattern. These two dimensions result in a four-fold typology descriptive of socialization settings. The individual-disjunctive pattern is characteristic of the first or older child in the family or the first occupant of a newly created job. The collective-disjunctive pattern is characteristic of a group of individuals attending a summer training institute or a group of visiting scholars touring a foreign country. The individual-serial pattern is characteristic of the new occupant of a job previously occupied by another person whereas the collective-serial pattern is characteristic of schools and universities where groups of individuals move together as a collectivity through the system (Brim, 1966, pp. 37–39; Wheeler, 1966, pp. 60–62).

DEVIANCE AND RESOCIALIZATION

Types of Deviance

Deviance is defined by Brim (1968a, p. 561) "as failure to conform to the expectations of other persons." From this perspective what is considered to be deviant behavior or values is determined by both the cultural or subcultural tradition to which the individual belongs and the particular statuses and roles which the individual holds as a member of the particular society. Thus, what may be defined as deviance in one societal group may be seen as conformity in another (Brim, 1966, p. 39; 1968a, p. 561).

As noted in our previous discussion of individual differences in socialization outcomes, Brim (1960, pp. 127–159) identified social structural aspects, cultural content and idiosyncratic parental role performance, ignorance of expectations or role prescriptions, inability of the individual to meet role demands, and lack of motivation to meet role demands as explanatory variables for individual differences in role learning. The three latter variables were also used by Brim (1966, 1968) to delineate six types of deviance. Thus, an individual may be seen by the reference group as being deviant because of: (1) ignorance of the behavior that is expected in a particular situation, (2) ignorance of the values or ends to be sought, (3) inability to meet behavioral expectations because of biologic limitations, (4) inability to internalize particular values because of perceived punishing effects, (5) lack of motivation to fulfill behavioral expectations, or (6) lack of motivation to pursue appropriate values. These six simple types of deviance may also form the basis for more complex deviant actions that involve both values and behavior (Brim, 1966, pp. 40–41; 1968a, p. 561).

Excluding biologic limitations, Brim (1968a, p. 561) identifies two major causes of these deviations. One cause is seen to be ineffective socialization of the individual with respect to particular statuses and roles in a society that is relatively unchanging. The second cause is believed to occur when the adequately socialized individual experiences rapid social changes within the society that leave him relatively unprepared to enact new role demands.

Blake and Davis (1964, pp. 468–482) identified sources of both unintentionally deviant behavior and deviant motivation as outcomes of physical and environmental conditions, intrarole and interrole conflicts, temporal incompatibilities between statuses, restricted access to approved means of reaching societal goals, a state of relative deprivation, the pursuit of illegitimate goals, and failure to pursue legitimate goals. Blake and Davis suggested that internalization of norms, desire for approval, anticipation of formal punishment, anticipation of nonreward, and lack of opportunity for deviant behavior all act as inhibitors of deviance.

Resocialization as a Mode of Control for Deviance

The particular modes of control used to deal with deviance reflect the theories, assumptions, and beliefs about human nature held by a particular society, group, or individual. In some societies and subcultural groups, methods involving isolation from others or severe punishment are used. In other societies or groups resocialization is viewed as the most positive and effective mode of control over deviant behavior and values.

In these latter, deviation of the individual's motivation and values is held to be the most serious form of deviance, for the individual does not share or may even reject the values and the means of the society. Deviance resulting from ignorance or inability to meet role demands is generally more acceptable in our society. There is a tendency, however, to attribute all deviance to the motivation component. This results in placing the blame for deviance, and the burden of proof that motives are pure upon the individual rather than upon the society.

Because the society may mistakenly fail to accept that ignorance or inability to perform may be the causes of deviance, any punishment administered may result in the individual's complete rejection of the values of the society. In this instance the modes of control used by the society do not result in resocialization of the individual but in the individual's alienation (Brim, 1966, pp. 42–44; 1968a, p. 561).

Resocialization would be more effective if modes of control were directed toward correcting the source of the individual's deviance. If the deviance was determined to stem from ignorance of particular role prescriptions and expectations, education would seem the most appropriate method of resocialization. If the deviance was found to result from the individual's inability to meet role demands, resocialization aimed at dealing with the individual's deficiencies would result in more effective resolution of the problem. If the deviance was attributable to deficiencies in motivation, a systematically planned program of reorientation of the individual to appropriate means and goals through the use of reward and punishment might be the most effective mode of resocialization (Brim 1966, pp. 42–44; 1968a, p. 561).

Developmental and Resocialization Settings

Wheeler (1966, pp. 68–69) differentiates developmental socialization and resocialization systems along several dimensions: organizational goals, composition of the recruit population, interaction rates, role differentiation and formation of subcultures, the setting and the external environment, the social climate, and movement through the structure.

Developmental and resocialization agencies differ with respect to the specificity or generality of organization goals. Wheeler, citing Bidwell, distinguishes two types of socialization that may occur within an agency: role socialization, and status socialization. Role socialization is defined as "the training and preparation for performance of specific tasks" and status socialization as "a broader pattern of training designed to prepare the recruit to occupy a generalized status in life with its associated life styles" (Wheeler, 1966, p. 70). In developmental socialization settings, both role and status socialization are sought concurrently. In resocialization settings, vocational or educational programs aimed at teaching the recruit specific skills (role socialization) may be in conflict with the individual's participation in counseling, guidance, or spiritual or moral training sessions (status socialization) (Wheeler, 1966, pp. 69–72).

Developmental and resocialization agencies are also seen as differing significantly in the composition of their recruit population. In the developmental setting—in a school for example—students are usually of similar age and marital status, but they may differ in gender and socioeconomic status. Thus, in this setting gender and social class are seen as broad organizing elements. In contrast, resocialization settings such as prisons are usually single-gender institutions, vary widely in the age of the inmates, have a high proportion of lower social class recruits, and have a large proportion of inmates who are either married or divorced. In this and similar settings, great variations in age and marital status of the recruits are characteristic (Wheeler, 1966, pp. 72–73).

Socialization settings also differ with respect to the opportunity for the recruits to interact with staff. In some developmental and resocialization settings, the individual is isolated and has little contact with the socializing agents. In other settings there is freedom to interact with others. The amount of contact or interaction that does occur between the recruit and socializing agent is often a function of the social ecology of the organization. Thus, in both developmental and resocialization settings, interaction patterns may be determined by the ratio of recruit to socializing agent. The location of recruits within the setting will also determine the access they have to the socializing agents (Wheeler, 1966, pp. 73–75).

Organization goals, variance in group composition, and interaction rates influence the development of subcultures and informal social roles among the recruits in both settings (Wheeler, 1966, pp. 75–79). With respect to the setting's relationship to the external environment, ties may or may not be found between the developmental or resocialization setting and the external community, there may or may not be a transfer of knowledge from the community into the organization, and the organization may or may not have a motivational impact upon its recruits (Wheeler, 1966, pp. 79–81).

Developmental and resocialization agencies are also distinguished by the "social climate" or overall "feeling tone" of the setting. For example, some colleges and universities have developed traditions, values, and norms that clearly differentiate them from other institutions of higher learning. In contrast, resocialization settings such as prisons are seldom distinguished from one another by their distinctive qualities. In great part, the emotional tone of the organization is often the result of the positive or negative relations that exist between the staff and recruits in either developmental or resocialization settings (Wheeler, 1966, pp. 81–83).

Finally, the factor of procession or movement of individuals through the setting is of particular importance in distinguishing between developmental and resocialization settings. Developmental socialization settings are usually significantly different from resocialization settings with respect to several factors: anticipatory socialization, entry procedures, the amount and sources of knowledge about recruits, the fate of role failures, the length of stay, exit procedures, the organization's control over the recruit's later career, and the sequencing of socialization experiences (Wheeler, 1966, pp. 83–99).

SUMMARY

It has been the purpose of this chapter to delineate the nature of childhood and adult socialization and resocialization from a role perspective. Socialization for roles begins in infancy and is a continuous and cumulative process that has significant implications for the development of nursing knowledge across the life span and for the development of individuals entering the various health professions.

NOTES

1. See the following references. Berger & Berger (1979 pp. 12–13, 17–18), Brim (1966, pp. 9–15), Bolton (1981, pp. 245–249), Cooley (1968, pp. 87–91), Cottrell (1969, pp. 543–570), Denzin (1977, pp. 114–169), Elkin & Handel (1984, pp. 18–31, 40–44),

Gergen (1971), Heiss (1976, pp. 8–12), Hewitt (1976, pp. 50–53, 55–56, 59–104), Kerckhoff (1972, pp. 22–31), Lewis (1979, pp. 261–287), Mead (1934, pp. 135–226; 1968, pp. 51–59; 1970, pp. 537–545), Turner (1968b, pp. 93–106; 1976, pp. 989–1016; 1978, pp. 1–23).

2. See the following references: (1) operant learning: Brim (1958, p. 1), Goslin (1969, p. 12), Kerckhoff (1972, pp. 20–24); (2) direct instruction: Elkin (1976, p. 359), Heiss (1976, pp. 6–7, 12–14), Kerckhoff (1972, pp. 20–21); (3) observational learning: Bandura (1977), Damon (1983, pp. 168–172), Elkin & Handel (1984, pp. 54–55), Elkin (1976, p. 360), Heiss (1976, pp. 7, 14); (4) imitation: Bandura (1977), Brim (1966, p. 10), Elkin (1976, p. 360), Flanders (1968, pp. 316–337), Hartup & Coates (1970, pp. 109–142), Heiss (1976, p. 14); (5) role taking: Brim (1966, p. 11), Coutu (1951), Elkin & Handel (1984, p. 57), Heiss (1976, pp. 6–8, 12–14), Hewitt (1976, pp. 53–56, 112–124), Kerckhoff (1972, pp. 32, 57), Mead (1934, pp. 158–173), Turner (1956); (6) role playing: Brim (1966, pp. 11–12), Elkin (1976, pp. 360–361), Elkin & Handel (1984, pp. 54–57), Mead (1934, pp. 160–161); (7) modeling: Bandura (1977), Brim (1966, p. 10), Damon (1983, pp. 170–172, 177–178), Elkin & Handel (1984, pp. 54–55), Heiss (1976, p. 14), Inkeles (1968, pp. 121–123), Kerckhoff (1972, p. 32); (8) trial and error: Brim (1966, p. 11), Elkin & Handel (1984, p. 44), Heiss (1976, p. 7); (9) identification: Damon (1983, pp. 172–179), Elkin (1976, p. 361), Hoffman (1983), Kagan (1958), Kohlberg (1966), Mussen (1967); and (10) role negotiation: Damon (1983, pp. 22–26), Goslin (1969, pp. 7–10).

3. See the following references: (1) father absence and availability: Biller (1971; 1972, pp. 407–433; 1974; 1976; 1981), Blanchard & Biller (1971), Campbell (1964, pp. 289–322), Clausen (1978), Fein (1983, pp. 463–474), Goldstein (1983), Herzog & Sudia (1973), Hetherington (1972), Hetherington & Deur (1971; 1972, pp. 303–319), Kagan (1964, pp. 137–167), Lamb (1976c; 1981), Lamb & Bronson (1980, pp. 339–341), Shinn (1978), Yarrow (1964, pp. 89–136), Zigler, Lamb, & Child (1982, pp, 80–81, 96, 97, 98, 282, 283); (2) family size and composition: Bane (1983, pp. 113–127), Clausen (1966, pp. 1–53), Hareven (1983, pp. 73–91), Laslett (1983, pp. 53–72), Uhlenberg (1983, pp. 92–101); (3) ordinal position: Bragg & Allen (1970, pp. 371–382), Clausen (1966, pp. 1–53), Sampson (1972, pp. 86–122), Steelman & Mercy (1980); (4) absence of siblings or peers: Brim (1958, pp. 1–16), Campbell (1964, pp. 289–322), Zigler, Lamb, & Child (1982, pp. 85–87); (5) working mothers and maternal deprivation: Ainsworth (1972), Hoffman, (1963; 1974; 1979), Hoffman & Nye (1974), Lamb & Bronson (1980), Lamb, Chase-Lansdale, & Owen (1979), Nye & Hoffman (1963), Rutter (1972; 1979), Stolz (1960, pp. 749–782), Yarrow (1964, pp. 116–117); (6) marital disharmony and divorce: Goetting (1983 pp. 367–387), Hetherington, Cox, & Cox (1978) Lamb (1977d) Lamb & Frodi (1979), Pederson (1980), Raschke & Raschke (1979), Rutter (1971; 1979), Wallerstein & Kelly (1983, pp. 438–452); (7) nontraditional family styles: Belsky & Steinberg (1978), Lamb, Chase-Lansdale, & Owen (1979), Lamb, Owen, & Chase-Lansdale (1980), Lein & Blehar (1983, pp. 420–437), Levine (1976), Rapoport & Rapoport (1976), Vaughn et al. (1979); and (8) families in transition: Cairns & Hood (1983, pp. 301–358), Caplow et al. (1982), Elkind (1979, pp. 3–16), Hareven (1983, pp. 73–91), Kagan (1983, pp. 409–420), Laslett (1983, pp. 53–72), Skolnick & Skolnick (1983), and Uhlenberg (1983, pp. 92–101).

4. See the following references: (1) effects of mother–father–infant interactions: Ainsworth (1972, pp. 395–406), Belsky (1979), Caldwell (1964, pp. 9–87), Clarke–Stewart (1978; 1980; 1983), Davis (1976, pp. 297–306), Elkin & Handel (1984, pp. 131–147), Fein (1983, pp. 463–474), Lamb (1976a; 1976b; 1976c; 1977a; 1977b; 1977c; 1978a; 1978b; 1979; 1980; 1982), Lamb & Bronson (1980), Lamb & Campos (1982), Lamb, Owen, & Chase-Lansdale (1979), Lamb & Sherrod (1981), Lamb & Stevenson (1978), Lewis & Rosenblum (1974), Maccoby (1980), Palmer (1969, pp. 25–55), Parke (1979), Pederson (1980), Rheingold (1969, pp. 779–790), Streissguth & Bee (1972, pp. 158–183), Yarrow (1964, pp. 89–136), Zigler, Lamb, & Child (1982, pp. 50–54), and

Zigler & Seitz (1982); (2) effects of varying child-rearing practices: Becker (1964, pp. 169–208), Becker (1972, pp. 29–72), Damon (1983, pp. 189–199), Elder (1972), Elkin & Handel (1984, pp. 77–122), Flacks (1979), Hoffman (1963), Kerckhoff (1972), Kohn (1959; 1963; 1969), Kohn & Schooler (1972, pp. 223–249), Lamb, & Bronson (1980), Lewis (1981), Petersen, Lee, & Ellis (1982), and Staples & Mirande (1983, pp. 496–520).

5. See the following references: Becker (1964, pp. 169–208; 1972, pp. 29–72), Bronfenbrenner (1958, pp. 400–425), Caldwell (1964, pp. 67–75), Damon (1983, pp. 151–168), Elkin & Handel (1984, pp. 82–96), Gecas (1976, pp. 33–59), Kerckhoff (1972), Kohn (1959, pp. 337–351; 1963, pp. 471–480; 1969), Kohn & Schooler (1972, pp. 223–249), Sewell (1961, pp. 340–356; 1970, pp. 572–574), and Zigler, Lamb, & Child (1982, pp. 100–103).

6. See the following references: Brim (1966, pp. 3, 8–12, 18; 1968b, p. 184), Brim & Kagan (1980), Cairns & Hood (1983), Clausen (1968c, pp. 133–138), Damon (1983), Elkin & Handel (1984, p. 253), Emde & Harmon (1984), Gordon (1972, pp. 65–105), Inkeles (1969, pp. 620–623), Kagan (1980), and Rosow (1974, pp. 14–15).

7. See the following references: Brim (1960, pp. 127–159), Clausen (1968c, pp. 130–181), Davis (1976, pp. 297–306), Elkin & Handel (1972, pp. 27–53), Inkeles (1968, pp. 73–129; 1969, pp. 615–624), Kerckhoff (1972, pp. 39–59), McCandless (1969, pp. 791–817), and Rheingold (1969, pp. 779–790).

8. See the following references: adolescence: Berger (1963, pp. 394–408), Cain (1964 pp. 272–309) Campbell (1969, pp. 821–859), Damon (1983, pp. 251–346), Douvan & Gold (1966, pp. 469–528), Dragastin & Elder (1975), Elder (1968), Elkin & Westley (1955, pp. 680–684), Grotevant & Cooper (1983), Matza (1964, pp. 191–216), Parsons (1942, pp. 604–616; 1962, pp. 97–123), Peterson & Peters (1983), Youniss (1983), Westley & Elkin (1957, pp. 243–249); adulthood: Ahammer (1973), Brim (1966, pp. 1–50; 1968a, pp. 552–557; 1968b, pp. 182–226), Dannefer (1984), Elkin & Handel (1984, pp. 259–267), Moore (1969, pp. 861–884), Rosow (1965, pp. 35–45); marriage and parenthood: Barry (1972, pp. 170–179), Christensen (1964), Clarke-Stewart (1983), Elder (1972, pp. 312–335), Fein (1983), Flacks (1979), Goodman (1976, pp. 116–126), Gove (1976, pp. 156–176), Hill & Aldous (1969, pp. 885–950), Hoffman (1976, pp. 177–196), Kiesler & Baral (1976, pp. 105–115), Komarovsky (1976, pp. 129–143), Ladner (1976, pp. 72–89), Lewis (1976, pp. 33–57), Rossi (1976, pp. 129–143; 1979; 1983, pp. 453–463; 1984), Teevan (1976, pp. 90–104), Zigler & Cascione (1982); and middle and old age: Barry & Wingrove (1977), Bennett (1980), George (1980), Hess & Waring (1983), Hoffman (1970), Loether (1967), Mutran & Reitzes (1984), Riley (1979) Riley, Abeles, & Teitelbaum (1982), Riley & Foner (1968), Riley, Foner, Hess, & Toby (1969, pp. 951–982), Rosow (1974), Szinovacz (1980) and Woodruff & Birren (1983).

5

Organizations, Professional Autonomy, and Roles

Mary E. Conway

Organizations can be thought of as social entities that have been fashioned to serve human purposes. While it is evident that organizations differ in terms of goals, decision-making processes, and the bases of their authority, they also have many features in common. For example, all organizations have a discernible administrative hierarchy, a more or less complex division of labor, specified procedures for decision making and a domain within which they market their product or service. In order for individuals to understand how they fit into organizations and how functional roles are developed, it may be helpful to examine in some detail those aspects of organizational life that are particularly salient for understanding the roles of professional workers in contemporary organizations. In keeping with the organizing framework of this book—the roles of health professionals—theoretical concepts are illustrated with appropriate examples drawn from health care settings.

The plan for this chapter is to examine organizations from a systems perspective. The systems perspective offers a unifying concept within which one may examine any number of subsystems; in this particular text it is the subsystem of roles that is of interest. The health professional is trained to perform certain functions that are considered unique; that is, these functions distinguish the sphere of action of health professionals from those of other professionals. Yet, within an organization, the role behaviors of the health professional together with the behaviors of all other persons within the organization form a social system (Katz & Kahn, 1966, p. 37) and a given role can be considered the "set of system states and actions of a subsystem, of an organization, including its interactions with other systems or nonsystem elements" (Kuhn, 1974, p. 298).

Understanding the nature of systems may help the professional cope more adequately with some of the problems that arise as the professional attempts to perform his or her role. For example, Kuhn's (1974) definition of role as a set of system states serves as a reminder that the actions of the individual are not independent but relate to the actions of others and to the state of other subsystems of the organization at any one point in time. Still another way of viewing one's relationship to an organization is to understand that one is involved in a series of *transactions* that are part of the exchange of energy that characterize the system's goal directedness.

ORGANIZATIONS AS SYSTEMS

A formal organization is both a subsystem of a larger system and a composite of additional subsystems that interact toward some goal. The larger system is the institutional system that includes law, government, religion, finance, and education. Subsystems of the organization itself consist of those that deal with maintenance, production, decision making, and technology, to name but a few. For purposes of analysis, organizations can then be viewed as located at one level in a multilevel systems hierarchy. In addition, as systems, organizations are bounded entities having interrelated component parts through which matter, energy, and information are transmitted in the form of inputs, throughputs, outputs, and feedback.

Definitions

- *Input.* Any information, matter, or energy entering the system across its boundary from the environment.
- *Output.* Any information, matter, or energy leaving the system across the boundary of the system to the environment.
- *Feedback.* Return of information as an input when, after a series of interactions the system has deviated from its preset internal state. Feedback is called *negative feedback* when it acts to return the system to a steady state.
- *Equilibrium.* That state in which components of the system continue to interact while at least one variable remains within a specified range (Kuhn, 1974, p. 27).

In the social system model, examples of inputs that relate to hospitals include patients, specialized personnel at both professional and technical levels, knowledge, the sophisticated technologies that are applied in diagnosis and treatment, and the financial resources required to sustain all of these. Examples of throughputs include the activities that facilitate a patient's progress toward well-- ness. Among the outputs of this system are the patients who are treated, improvements in technology, knowledge about disease and its treatment, trained workers, and, in some instances, the provision of technical assistance to other health settings. Examples of this latter output might include the social worker who assists another hospital to organize its social services department, or the director of nursing who offers consultation to his or her counterpart in another setting, or the medical records librarian who helps organize the record keeping system in another hospital so that it can meet accreditation standards.

The following is an example of feedback. A situation might occur in which a number of patients admitted to the hospital for surgery have not fully completed all the necessary preoperative diagnostic tests by the day their surgery is scheduled. The intended operations must be cancelled. This information results in a reordering of work schedules for the radiology and laboratory departments so that all patients admitted with the designation "preoperative" are scheduled to have

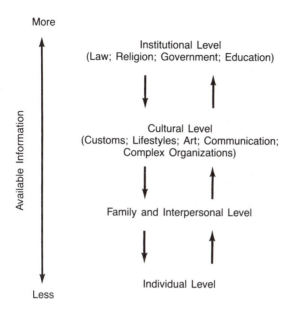

Figure 1. Information as a differential aspect of a sociocultural systems hierarchy.

their tests completed within 12 hours of admission. Nonpreoperative patients, except for emergencies, are given second priority. Thus, the state of the system is "corrected."

While information is considered essential to all living systems, the amount of information available to a system is distributed differentially according to the level of the system. That is, those systems at higher levels within a hierarchy of systems presumably have more information available to them and, further, a small amount of matter or energy at the higher level triggers a large amount of activity of other components in the system, thus making available more energy (Buckley, 1967).

If Buckley's assumption holds with respect to a sociocultural systems hierarchy, we can conclude that less information is available at the level of the individual and more is available at the level of the institution. By the same reasoning we can conclude that a small input of matter or energy at the institutional level should have a considerable impact on individuals. Figure 1 suggests this relationship.

From a systems perspective, organizations are frequently described as relatively open or closed. Those organizations that attempt to exert strong control over their environments are characterized as *closed*; those that do not attempt such stringent control are characterized as *open*. This is much more a theoretical consideration than a pragmatic one; it is doubtful that any organization can exert a significant amount of control over its external environment given the interrelatedness of such factors as fluctuation in market demands, externally imposed controls (e.g., governmental), rapid developments in technology, and the immediate availability of new knowledge. At least one theorist has proposed that organizations aim for *bounded rationality*—a condition of limited rather than total control (Thompson, 1967). Essentially, bounded rationality is the attempt to exert reasonable control over both the task (internal) environment and the external environment in order to achieve the goal of maximizing profit. It assumes the possibility of some unintended events occurring during the course of the organization's progress toward its goals. Further, such controls as the organization does attempt are directed specifically toward protecting the task environment (Thompson, 1967).

PROBLEMS COMMON TO SOCIAL SYSTEMS

There are a number of problems common to social systems. Etzioni (1975, p. 141) conceptualizes four so-called universal functional problems. These include the system's need to: (1) control the environment, (2) secure its goals, (3) maintain solidarity among units of the system, and (4) preserve the system's values. Decisions relating to all of these are of extreme importance to an organization. The better the decision making, the more successful an organization is likely to be in achieving its goals. The ground rules for decision making are generally known to those who are responsible for making decisions at various levels within the organization. For instance, a ground rule might be that decisions are to be made that will yield the greatest profit in the short run; another might be to make decisions that will yield the greatest profit in the long run; still another might be to choose decisions that will sustain the organization's reputation in the market. In the case of a hospital, for instance, decisions that are likely to gain approval of the community will be made—at least they will if the organization wishes to maintain one of its important resources: good will.

Organizations vary in the importance they attach to the participation of subordinates in the decision-making process. There is some evidence that allowing subordinates to participate in decisions which affect their jobs may be "good" for the organization. The "goodness" of decisions made by subordinates, however, is constrained by the amount of information they possess about the organization, particularly its resources, outputs, and market outlook. The extent of participation by subordinates depends upon whether the organization's decision makers believe subordinates have something of importance to contribute (Hall, 1982, p. 182).

At a more abstract level, decision making can be defined as the outcome of a series of transactions engaged in by all relevant role occupants at the various levels of the system (Kuhn, 1974, p. 307). This definition of decision making assumes that all persons involved are in agreement as to the goals of the organization; one person or group may have to "give up" something during the process of arriving at the decision, while others may reciprocate by yielding on some other aspect of the process.

Efficiency

Efficiency is a criterion by which organizations are often assessed. Organizations are characterized as efficient when they make progress toward their goals with a minimum of waste and a maximum of output (Katz & Kahn, 1966; Simon, 1957; Thompson, 1967). In addition, efficiency has been defined as the production of a given effect with the least cost (Rushing, 1976), production of the greatest result given a specific amount of resources (Thompson, 1967), and the ability to exploit resources: that is, obtain the greatest number of positive inputs from the environment (Yuchtman & Seashore, 1967).

Skilled labor is an example of one of the most important of the resources that an organization depends on. If the organization is to be efficient, each worker in the organization must be placed in that job for which he or she is best trained or suited by temperament. Limiting the number of workers employed precisely to that number that will produce the desired number of units of output would also be considered efficient. Another view of efficiency relates the organization's bargaining position relative to its resources. Seashore and Yuchtman (1972, p. 902) state the following proposition: "The highest level of organizational effectiveness is reached when the organization maximizes its bargaining position and optimizes its resource procurement." It is possible for an organization to have more *potential* for efficiency in its operations than is being used. For example, a receptionist in the radiology department of a hospital who while on the job has learned how to process films but who remains employed as a receptionist is operating at less than full potential. The department, therefore, could be considered not to be maximizing its potential for efficiency.

The structure of the organization itself has a bearing on its efficiency. Recent experiments with variations of the traditional bureaucratic structure have been attempted with variable reported degrees of success. Mintzberg (1979), for example, has identified five structural configurations, with *adhocracy* being one of the more recent and, according to him, least competent additions for "accomplishing ordinary things" (p. 463). On the other hand, adhocracy is held to be ideally suited for handling complex, loosely defined, or one-of-a kind problems with which an organization may find itself confronted.

For purposes of assessing efficiency we can characterize organizations in energy terms as having both *energic inputs* and *energic outputs* (Katz & Kahn, 1966). Energic by definition includes both people and materials. Katz and Kahn, using a system's perspective, suggest assessing the efficiency of an organization by examining the ratio of energic output to energic input. Presumably, in their view, if the total cost of people and materials far exceeds the value of net profit of the output, the organization is considered to be nonefficient. There are a number of factors that can cause low efficiency. Among them are inadequate information, a high ratio of production cost to unit output, inadequate supervision, physical location of the organization (i.e., boundaries at too great a distance from its market or the source of its raw materials), and repeated errors in forecasting market conditions. This is by no means an exhaustive list.

An additional condition that can be both a cause and a consequence of lowered efficiency, and one that merits discussion here, is that of *goal displacement*. Goal displacement occurs when the means (bureaucratic symbols or status, for example) for achieving the goals of an organization take on more importance than the goals themselves (Merton, 1968, p. 256) or they are substituted for the ends (Etzioni, 1964). The most serious form of goal displacement—and a potentially destructive one—occurs when the organization actually reverses the priorities given to its goals and its means and commits its resources to the means

(Etzioni, 1964, p. 10). Health care agencies are no exception to the rule in this regard, and examples of goal displacement are common occurrences. One example relates to the problem of the access of clients to the sources of care. For example, the screening procedures of an agency that have been instituted to help ensure that clients applying for assistance receive the services they need sometimes have the effect of excluding from those services the individuals who need them most. The mother whose infant needs an immunization may be denied this service at her neighborhood health center because her income is slightly higher than the income level that agency has set as the qualifying level. At the same time, a mother may not have enough money for transportation to a health center that is some distance from her home. Overly rigid adherence to guidelines in these instances represents extreme cases of goal displacement. A different example of the same phenomenon is the employee who never comes to a decision because of concern with following the rules. Merton (1968) refers to this phenomenon as "trained incapacity." While rules of procedure are necessary for the orderly functioning of an organization and in addition serve to routinize work conditions so that the worker does not have to "think out" the simple actions that are to be performed repeatedly, the rules should serve as "enablers" toward the provision of a service or the processing of a product. While the structure of a large organization in general fosters adherence to rules, there are times when some workers become so involved with application of those rules that this occupies their entire attention. When workers in a service organization such as a health care facility become concerned with rules to this extent, the client becomes "invisible." The client is in effect depersonalized—transformed into the status of an object to be acted upon rather than a person to be assisted (Freidson, 1970).

Rationality

The complex organizations of the postindustrial era are structured according to what is called the *rational* model (Perrow, 1970; Simon, 1955). The term *rational* implies that all of the resources required for accomplishing an organization's goals (i.e., produce its product or service) have been identified and are brought into the production effort in sufficient quantity and at appropriate points in the production process in a way that maximizes goal attainment. Two further assumptions of the rational model are that excessive amounts of input are avoided and that random occurrences are controlled to the extent possible. Those resources needed by all organizations include capital, raw materials, technology, and people. Within health care organizations resources take the form of complex technologies, such as brain and soft-tissue scanners, autoanalyzers, and heart by-pass machines; the specialized technicians who operate these machines; and the professional personnel who make the determinations for the employment of such technologies or evaluate the outcomes of their use. There is disagreement, however, as to how valid the rational model is for use in attempting to study the behavior of organizations. It has been pointed out that the assumptions of the model fail to consider that organizations are subject to environmental influences (Thompson, 1967), that the principles of rationality do not stand the test of empirical research (March & Simon, 1958), and that decision making rests more on the structure of the organization—itself a product of a chain of decisions—than on strict rationality (Sofer, 1972, p. 174).

Of course, random or unanticipated events do occur from time to time in the life of an organization despite attempts on the part of the organization to protect itself from them. A potentially serious disruptive occurrence in a hospital, for example, would be the breakdown of the heart–lung machine on the day that open heart surgery is scheduled. The hospital would presumably have taken precautions against such an event by having a stand-by machine or by having an experienced repair technician available to repair the problem. Similarly, the hospital would very likely have at least two or more experienced technicians to operate the machines so that in the event one became unavailable, the other could take over. Other more general kinds of disruptions to an organization's rational order are such events as fire, theft, strikes of workers, and depression of the market in which the organization's product is sold. While organizations take steps to protect themselves from these sources of disruption, obviously they cannot protect themselves completely. The community health agency operates on the rationality principle when it makes decisions regarding the mix of health professionals it will employ. Such agencies provide a variety of services to their clients, including on-site ambulatory care and, in some instances, care for homebound people. The demographic characteristics of the population served may vary from agency to agency; for example, one agency may serve a relatively lower income, older population while another may serve a younger, middle-income population in which children comprise a large percentage of those receiving health services. In deciding what type of and how many professionals (or paraprofessionals) it will employ, an agency takes these demographic variables into account. In addition it considers such other variables as its specified goals, its commitment to the community, the major health problems of the population to be served, the incomes to be returned via third-party payments such as Medicaid, and the incomes to be realized through direct payment by clients.

Let us take employment of nurses as an example of application of the rationality principle within such an agency. Professional nurses (holders of the B.S. degree) generally comprise the largest share of professional workers in a community health agency. In addition, some agencies employ nurse clinical specialists. These latter are nurses with additional training beyond the baccalaureate degree who specialize in a specified area such as maternal-child health or mental health nursing. If the population to be served by the specified agency is young, highly mobile, and in a middle-income bracket, it might be a rational decision to employ at least one maternal-child health clinical specialist. The specialist, it should be pointed out, will command a higher salary than the generalist nurse. In attempting to make a decision, the agency director considers the additional need of the target population for guidance in nutrition and food purchasing. Given that such a need exists, it would be desirable to employ a nutritionist in addition to the clinical specialist. Rationality, however, demands that the agency attempt to balance—at least in its planning—the possible payoff to be achieved if it employs both of these health specialists, one of them, or neither. Given that each could provide needed services, the agency may have to compromise by hiring one but not both after considering its total anticipated income.

Further complicating the decision process for the agency director is the fact that estimates of income may be imprecise. A large proportion of the community health agency's income is derived from third-party payers such as Medicare (Title XVIII) and Medicaid (Title XIX) and reimbursement rates are subject to change on short notice. In addition, services generally are provided to clients before client eligibility for services is approved by the third party's fiscal intermediary. Those claims that are denied represent income lost. Altogether, absolute rationality in this particular decision process is unattainable.

Inadequacies of the Rational Model

Although the rational model offers insight into how organizations cope with their tasks and achieve their goals, it provides less than an adequate explanation for some aspects of organization behavior. Why, for example, when past experience is evaluated and inputs are known, provided in sufficient amounts, and processed with little untoward interruption do some organizations find the market less than receptive to their product? Or why does a service agency suddenly find that a competitor can provide essentially the same service at a cost so much lower that the first agency is forced into bankruptcy? Has rational planning failed? Part of the answer lies in the fact that knowledge is expanding so rapidly that an organization can comprehend only a limited amount of it at any one time and, further, of knowledge that is comprehended, only a fraction can be integrated into the system's environment within a given period of time. Another part of the answer lies in the fact that over time the external environment becomes increasingly important to the focal organization; and if the analogy to living systems holds, an organization's continued survival depends upon the extent to which it can adapt to the changing contingencies in its environment (Terreberry, 1973). Although the rational model describes the kinds of interchange an organization may have with its external environment and accounts for its dependence upon the environment for both resources and disposal of its product, it gives less attention to the influence on the focal organization of the actions of all other organizations within the same environment.

A reality is that rationality does not govern an organization's decisions at every point in time. Decisions are frequently made by controlling interest groups within an organization whose self-interests may be incongruent with the organization's interest, at least in the short run. Hage (1980, p. 272) has noted, "What is rational in the short run is not [rational] in the long term and vice versa." At times decisions may be made by *coalitions* of interest groups (Bacharach & Lawler, 1980).

An additional explanation as to why rational planning as traditionally practiced may fail in the present unstable, rapidly changing sociotechnologic environment is that reliance on past performance as one variable in forecasting the future—an integral feature of the rational model—is increasingly inappropriate. The past is too unlike the present in terms of significant variables (nuclear energy, for example, being one such variable). In addition to reducing the reliance on the past in predicting the future, there are difficulties inherent in using present conditions as data with which to make future predictions. This difficulty has been identified as the principle of equifinality (Bertalanffy, 1950); that is, systems at the same initial state may reach different end points. Also, the principle of equifinality suggests that systems that are at different initial stages may reach similar end points through a variety of developmental paths. The increasing complexity and rapidly accelerating change of living systems are, perhaps, increasing our awareness of shortcomings of the rational model.

Recognizing the problems of uncertainty embodied in the traditional model, some advocate a *contingency* approach to measuring organizational effectiveness (Khanwalla, 1974; Scott, 1977). Scott proposes a contingency model should predict organizational effectiveness based upon "what an organization is attempting to do and on the conditions under which it is attempting to do it" (p. 90). A central assumption of the structural contingency model is that organizational effectiveness is related to the "goodness of fit" between environmental and structural variables. Tests of the model have provided little support for this assumption. Pennings (1975) found in his study testing this assumption that structural variables and not environmental variables are the strongest predictor of organizational effectiveness.

In summary, although we can anticipate that organizations will continue to plan for the future using all available indicators and relevant data, it is apparent that the achievement of their goals is likely to depend more on their ability to *respond to changing conditions* within their given environments than on the construction of elaborate plans for an uncertain future. Further, it seems a safe assumption that those organizations that are able to apprehend information quickly and to incorporate it while at the same time maintaining sufficient flexibility to respond to unanticipated events within their external environments will be more likely than others to maximize their goals.

THE DIVISION OF LABOR

A functional division of labor is crucial to the goal achievement of an organization whether the goal is a product or a service. Essentially, goal achievement is related to how efficiently workers perform their individual jobs. In turn, worker efficiency is closely related to the degree of order and stability that is maintained within the work environment. Frequent reassignment of work content within jobs or a high rate of worker turnover within an organization are threats to stability of the organization and, in addition, may contribute to such deleterious effects as worker uncertainty and lowered morale. Both types of changes can and often do result in decreased work performance—both qualitatively and quantitatively.

Given that the division of labor is crucial to organization outcomes, it cannot be left to chance. It is deliberately planned (Etzioni, 1964;, Simon, 1976). In role terminology it is appropriate to speak of the division of labor as role differentiation and specialization. That is, roles encompassing specific functions necessary to the accomplishment of the organization's work are identified and persons qualified by training or experience are assigned to these roles. In general, it is fair to say that the requisite skills and responsibilities associated with roles at each level of the system's hierarchy are considered crucial to the goal achievement of an organization (Conway, 1974).

For any number of reasons, it sometimes happens that a worker with the appropriate qualifications for a particular role is unavailable and it becomes necessary to substitute an unqualified individual, either temporarily or for an extended period. In the unlikely event that the substitute individual learns the job requirements quickly and performs capably, all is well. The more likely occurrence, however, is that the work will be performed less than competently and, in the case of the manufacture of a product, the product may be damaged or, at the least, slow in production. The consequences can be equally grave, although of a different order, in the human service sector.

Whereas in the profit sector, the absence of qualified workers can result in a reduced profit margin, in the nonprofit sector—a hospital, for example—absence of qualified workers can be life threatening for patients. Even if not life threatening, either poor performance by hospital personnel or the absence of an essential service is likely to be reflected in lowered quality of care. If such lowered performance persists over an extended time, the hospital's reputation will also suffer. Just as the profit-making corporation depends upon its consumer market for survival, so the hospital depends upon consumer evaluation of its service. To the extent that the hospital's reputation is diminished, it is highly probable that it will lose at least a portion of the financial input necessary to sustain its operation at a cost-effective level. Voluntary community organizations such as social service agencies have even more to lose than the hospital if their reputations are diminished by reason of inadequate or callous rendering of services. Clients generally can avoid use of a social service agency without endangering their lives, but they cannot avoid using the hospital in the event of a grave illness.

Effectiveness is a criterion that has been used in an attempt to assess an organization's total performance. The measurement of effectiveness has eluded the majority of researchers (Campbell, 1977; Scott, 1977) in part because it must be measured in terms of some agreed-upon standard related to output. General agreement upon a standard for assessing effectiveness presents a problem in that a standard that might be set by participants in the organization might or might not be acceptable to informed consumers or external raters of organizational performance (Goodman & Pennings, 1977, p. 8).

Another problem for organizations in their efforts to achieve effectiveness is that they tend to have multiple goals and at times these goals may be in conflict with one another (Hall, 1982, p. 298). Hall (1982) has cited such factors as multiple goals, conflicting internal and external constituencies, and multiple and conflicting time frames as all contributing to what he terms a *contradiction model* for the study of organizational effectiveness (p. 296).

Management of Order

As we have indicated earlier, order is important to organizations and, in recognition of this fact, the management of order is generally a full-time occupation for a specified number of personnel within each organization. Generally speaking, order is enhanced to some extent if the expectations of the occupants of various role positions are congruent with the expectations of other members of their role set (Gross et al., 1966; Merton, 1968, p. 44) and if nearly all subscribe to the organization's goals—at least insofar as they hold similar perceptions of what the goals may be.

Organizations that employ a large number of professionals—as opposed to those composed of a predominately skilled labor force—depend upon the voluntary compliance of their employees to maintain order. This is not to suggest that skilled laborers are more inclined to noncompliance but to emphasize a traditional distinction that is made between the orientation of professionals versus other classes of workers. For professionals the ethic of a service orientation and the salience of the professional organization as a reference group have influenced the means by which professionals have sought to achieve their goals within organizations. Historically, these means have largely been the kind of negotiation that precludes the strike as an acceptable weapon for gaining employee demands. By contrast, technical workers and skilled laborers have sought to win improvements in their working conditions through negotiations in which the strike remains the ultimate weapon for enforcing their demands. The earlier distinction between these two general classes of workers no longer obtains in a strict sense, since all workers have increasingly come to view themselves as professionals. At the same time, professionals such as physicians, nurses, and teachers have turned to the strike as a means of last resort in attempting to achieve their demands. The demands made by professionals in health care institutions tend to deal not only with work conditions per se and monetary issues but also with work conditions that adversely affect the quality of their work and, in turn, the quality of care delivered to clients.

Types of Control

The norms that guide behavior in social situations and the sanctions that are applied to enforce these norms are powerful entities of control. The management officials of organizations recognize the potential that both hold for the behavior of employees and encourage their application.

Order within organizations in terms of employee behavior is the rule rather than the exception. This situation exists partly because it is in the interests of both employers and workers to maintain order, that is, to comply with the rules. Unpredictable work situations and work disruptions are costly for both labor and management in terms of time, energy, and effectiveness. Prudence dictates that organizations take precautions to ensure the maintenance of order among the workers in the event that voluntary compliance is not forthcoming. To this end certain controls are applied—some consistently and others as the need arises. Control may be of two general types: *coercive* and *normative* (Etzioni, 1964). Coercive control is the securing of compliance by force, or the threat of force, where compliance would not occur otherwise. Prisons and mental hospitals, for example, rely on this type of control. Normative control derives from an appeal—implied or explicit—to employees to comply with the organization's rules and policies because that is the reasonable and desirable thing to do.

Normative control is *implicit* when a policy directive from an officer of the organization is published and employees act in accordance with the new policy; it is *explicit* when such a policy directive is formulated and a rationale is appended explaining why it is important that workers conform to the policy. In the latter instance, the explanation is attached as an added inducement to compliance. Normative controls consist of such actions as appeals for cooperation and pep talks; additionally, rewards such as citations for meritorious performance may be given from time to time. Annual award days are a feature of many organizations that employ normative controls. Finally, in the event of occasional failure of a worker to perform at an established standard, punishment is rarely meted out, at least not overtly, where normative control is in effect. Punishment may ensue, however, in the form of failure to grant vacation to an employee who is entitled to such vacation at the specific date he requests.

Legitimacy. As we have noted in the preceding discussion of types of control, a majority of workers apparently comply with the rules and policies of the work setting because they perceive that it is the appropriate thing to do. For professionals the acceptance and adoption of appropriate rules and policies governing behavior occur primarily during socialization into the profession. Employees' acceptance of compliance as appropriate behavior is linked to their perception of the *legitimacy* of management of an organization. In other words, when the authority of those who make the rules is viewed by workers as being properly vested, they are more likely to comply voluntarily with the rules of the work place. Legitimacy is an important attribute of an organization and one that cannot easily be acquired. The value of this attribute is apparent when the owner of a business being sold puts a price on the "good will" that is listed as one of the assets of the firm. The following proposition can be stated with respect to the relationship existing between compliance and legitimacy: compliance on the part of members (employees) of an organization will vary positively with the degree of legitimacy ascribed to the authority structure by the members. It could be argued that while individuals are likely to adhere closely to the rules of their employment setting, they are less likely to be constrained by the rules of those social or religious organizations in which they hold membership. However, on closer inspection it would seem that this proposition needs to be qualified to take into account time and involvement. Those individuals who become increasingly involved in the activities of those affiliate organizations gradually tend to conform more closely to the rules and policies which govern the membership group. Further, it seems likely that this type of conformance takes place without conscious awareness on the part of the individuals concerned (Katz and Kahn, 1966).

Types of Authority. The classic typology of authority is the one developed by the German sociologist Max Weber. Weber described three types of authority: traditional, rational–legal, and charismatic (Parsons, 1951). Only the rational–legal type will be discussed here since it is characteristic of modern organizations. In fact, the bureaucratic structure of complex organizations is viewed by some as the embodiment of the rational–legal authority. In the bureaucractic structure the authority to give orders and force compliance is lodged in the particular office rather than in the incumbent of the office. Thus, the authority is "rational" in that it is impersonally constituted and directed toward the goals of the organization as opposed to those of the individual. Of particular interest within the context of professional roles in organizations is the conclusion of one critique of the Weberian model. Satow (1975) holds that Weber failed to account for yet another type of authority: the *value–rational* type. Value–rational as defined by Satow is obedience given to an ideology or set of ideologic norms rather than to an impersonally constituted set of so-called legal norms. Satow goes on to explain that Weber did not distinguish between those organizations in which the dominant mode of action is based on the *rationally derived purposes* of the organization and those in which the dominant mode of action is based upon *commitment to an ideology*. The assumption is, of course, that professionals are committed first to the goals of their profession and second to the goals of the organization. The notion of a value–rational type of authority does not appear to contradict Weber's essential idea, but it does add to our understanding of the apparent ease with which a majority of professionals are able to function within organizations while maintaining a sense of professional identity.

Motivation. An important problem for the modern organization is how to motivate workers to optimal efforts in the performance of their jobs. The routine nature of many jobs and the workers' distance from the product or service that is the end result of their efforts are often linked to worker apathy. The labor force in general enjoys a high standard of living, with many so-called blue-collar workers owning a recreational dwelling as well as a year-round home. Hence, the higher wages that once provided an incentive for employees are no longer sufficient to encourage greater production; in fact, at least one theorist holds that the "dominance of non-monetary considerations" is more important in motivating workers (Caplow, 1954). A commonly held assumption is that individual workers who are highly motivated will *collectively* produce a high output for the organization. Hage (1980), on the basis of his own research, asserts that such is not the case and that often "ambitious individuals work at cross purposes" (p. 297).

Psychologic growth of the worker and the opportunity to participate in the decision-making of the organization by workers at all levels are widely believed to be at least as important to workers as monetary considerations (Argyris, 1957; McGregor, 1960). The concept of motivation and theories of motivation have captured the attention of researchers in organization, as well as presidents and managers of all kinds of enterprises that depend upon human labor. To the extent that worker motivation is related to the rate of production or output of a profit-making organization—hence profit—even stockholders of corporations have an interest in motivation, theoretically, at least.

Theories of Motivation

Maslow's Theory of Motivation. Motivation has been variously defined. One definition is simply that motivation is the propensity to take action toward a certain goal or goals. For purposes of analysis and comparison when attempting to apply motivation theory to organizations, theories can be categorized as either *content* or *process* oriented (Campbell et al., 1970). Content theories are those that focus on what it is in the individual's environment that sustains or extinguishes his behavior. Process theories are said to be those that explain the *how* of behavior. Nearly all prevailing theories of motivation draw on the work of Maslow, a pioneer in enlarging our understanding of the forces that prompt individuals to act as they do. Maslow has postulated five basic needs a person strives to satisfy: physiologic demands, safety, love, esteem, and self-actualization (Maslow, 1954). These needs are presumed to exist in a hierarchy that puts physiologic needs on the first level. According to Maslow's theory, as lower-order needs are met, the meeting of higher-order needs is attempted. The hierarchical order of these needs is not a constant one; for example, at one time the need for safety may be more important than the need for esteem. It would thus appear that Maslow's theory of motivation fits into the category of content theory.

Motivation is a complex phenomenon. It is a product of many variables including such factors as type of organizational control (Ouchi & Johnson, 1978), individual ability (Locke, Mento, & Katcher, 1978), feedback on performance from others (Hom, DeNisi, Kinicki, & Bannister, 1982) and self-esteem and reward contingencies (Terborg, Richardson, & Pritchard, 1980).

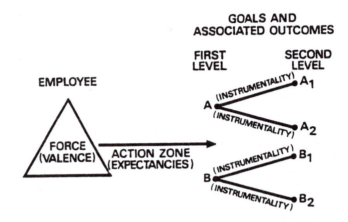

Figure 2. Vroom's theory of motivation. (From Gibson et al. *Organizations.* Courtesy of Business Publications, Inc., 1973).

Expectancy Theory. An additional theoretical model of motivation is expectancy theory (Vroom, 1964). Vroom's explanation of this theory holds that employees are faced with alternative choices for action in the work setting and that they select from among these alternatives on the basis of expected first-and second-level outcomes. The notion of *expectancy* in the theory is that the individual anticipates that a certain action will be followed by some reward that has value—a promotion or a raise in pay, for example. A further assumption of expectancy theory is that workers internalize some order of outcomes that they desire and that a value is attached to each. To the extent expectations of reward are fulfilled, motivation to achieve additional goals is increased. This relationship is demonstrated in Vroom's theory. There is as yet little empirical evidence, if any, to support this theory. There is a problem of intersubjectivity within the model in that the concept Vroom defines as first-level *outcome* appears to be an *action* rather than an outcome. According to Vroom, an employee's increased productivity, for example (which Vroom would term a first-level outcome), is related to what is termed a second-level outcome, i.e., an increase in pay, or a reward for the increased productivity. It would seem that in more generally accepted semantic usage, the employee *acts* to increase his output and in so doing demonstrates an instrumental behavior. Vroom, however, reserves the word *instrumentality* for the link between what he calls first-and second-level outcomes.

Equity Theory. The extent to which individuals are motivated to perform in the employment situation depends at least in part on whether they perceive themselves to be fairly rewarded with respect to their co-workers. Equity theory proposes that individuals assess the outcomes of their interactions with others in terms of the relationship between the contribution each makes to the interaction and the outcomes accruing to each from it. Such interactions can be viewed as exchanges. By definition any situation in which two persons act, communicate with each other, and find the interaction rewarding to both can be called a social exchange (Homans, 1974, p. 53). Each exchange relationship involves both costs and rewards to the participants. Outcomes are the consequences of the interaction and may be either positive or negative. Positive outcomes are defined as rewards and negative outcomes as costs (Walster, et al., 1976, p. 3); the net gain or "reward" to an individual consists of the total outcome minus the cost incurred. Even in instances where one or the other participant in an exchange receives a net gain, he may perceive the gain as not worth the cost involved. It is important to note here that it is not objectively quantifiable outcomes as seen by an observer that determine whether outcomes in an exchange are equal but rather the extent to which the participants perceive themselves rewarded or not rewarded relative to their costs.

An equitable relationship can be said to exist when both participants in an exchange perceive that the outcomes for each are roughly equivalent with respect to the amount each contributed to the exchange (Homans, 1974) or when a participant or an outside observer perceives that the participants are receiving relatively equal rewards from the exchange (Walster et al., 1976, p. 2). Investigations conducted in a variety of work settings have found that individuals tend to behave equitably toward each other (Adams, 1965; Homans, 1961) and, further, that when inequitable situations arise the individuals involved attempt to restore equity (Adams & Jacobsen, 1964; Lawler et al., 1968).

In the work setting, decisions regarding how rewards will be allocated are made on the basis of experience; that is, where the allocator (manager or president of the organization) believes that previous equitable allocations have brought about improved performance, he will tend to continue the practice (Lawler, 1971). Reports of research on the effects of equitable allocations are, however, conflicting. Miller and Hamblin (1963) found that competition for rewards can disrupt a group's task activities, while Goode (1967) and Steiner (1972) noted that those who are less productive tend to become angry when rewards are given on the basis of merit alone.

Exceptions to the norm of equity in employment situations do occur as, for instance, when in an attempt to motivate less-productive workers, such workers are paid more than their inputs merit (Goodman & Friedman, 1968; Greenberg & Leventhal, 1973), or where workers of lesser ability than others produce as much as these others and are accordingly rated as more deserving and rewarded more (Taynor & Deaux, 1973; Weiner & Kukla, 1980).

In one research study that attempted to examine the extent to which worker choice in doing a job and amount of reward (pay) interacted in motivating employees, it was found that both substandard and over-pay reduced *intrinsic* motivation (Folger, Rosenfield, & Hays, 1982). The researchers concluded that when workers believe they must do a job, regardless of the amount of pay they receive their intrinsic motivation toward the job is lowered. Findings from research attempting to establish generalizations about equity and how it is perceived by workers are contradictory (Deci, 1977; Hamner & Foster, 1975; Vecchio, 1981).

While it is obvious that overreward for work is likely to be counterproductive to an organization in the long run, short-run benefits to the organization may justify the practice. And despite the fact that experimental and survey evidence to date suggest that workers tend to be motivated toward greater productivity when they perceive the rewards to be just, much remains unknown about what motivates individuals. An individual's perception of the intrinsic worth of his role or the reward he receives from the knowledge that he has helped a distressed individual by means of his special ability, whatever it may be, are examples of variables which preclude making accurate predictions about behavior where differing types of reward allocation are applied.

Another theory of motivation that draws on Maslow's need-hierarchy is that of Herzberg (1966). In this model a distinction is made between those taken-for-granted aspects of the work situation and the *recognition* aspects. Herzberg labels the former *hygiene* factors and the latter *motivators*. His point is that the so-called hygiene factors are not likely to enhance a worker's loyalty to the organization or stimulate him to improve his performance. A major difference between Herzberg's conceptualization of motivation and Maslow's is that Maslow holds that any unfulfilled need can be a motivator, while Herzberg claims that only the higher-order needs are motivators (Gibson et al., 1973). One can infer, for example, that some individuals derive satisfaction or gratification from the work they perform that is quite apart from the tangible reward of a wage. Further, it can be speculated that the amount of pleasure or gratification an individual derives from his membership in a work group is an influencing factor in determining whether that individual will adhere to the rules and norms governing his work situation. In addition, the greater the amount of gratification an individual derives relative to the amount of deprivation he experiences, the more likely it is that he will adhere to those behaviorial expectations that are normative for the particular group in which he finds himself.

One conception of the relationship between gratification and deprivation is that it represents a *balance* phenomenon. At some time, gratification and deprivation can be said to exist in about equal measure for an individual relative to his own membership in the group, at least theoretically. When this theoretical balance occurs it is presumed that a "total potential return" exists for the individual (Jackson, 1979). That is, the possibility exists for either more gratification or more deprivation. As group interaction continues, feelings of approval or disapproval will be communicated to the individual. And, of course, the individual in turn is conveying those same kinds of feelings to the other members of the group with whom he or she is in contact. A number of organizations exert considerable efforts to enhance the affective "attachment" of their employees to the organization. Presumably this is to increase employee motivation. They encourage employees to participate in activities tangentially related to their work by providing a variety of leisure and educational programs that fall in the category of self-improvement. Etzioni refers to this propensity of organizations to engage their employees' off-the-job time as the attempt to *embrace* the individual (Etzioni, 1975). In those instances where an organization offers a large number of activities in which members participate more with each other than with outsiders, the scope of the organization is said to be broad. By contrast, an organization whose employees share in few non-job-related activities is said to be narrow in its scope (Etzioni, 1975). The trend at the present time is away from broad-scope organizations, large organizations preferring instead to build favorable community relationships where they are located. They do this through their support of those educational, cultural, and recreational activities already existing in the community. The now largely out-dated custom of insisting that medical interns and student nurses live in hospital-attached dormitories is an example of the attempt to embrace.

Organizations continue to encourage positive affective attachment on the part of employees. At the same time, however, they attempt to avoid the appearance of the manifest paternalism of the broad-scope activities of earlier years.

AUTONOMY: A STRUCTURAL ASPECT OF HEALTH CARE

Organized Autonomy

The problems of decision making, division of labor, maintenance of order, control, and motivation are common to organizations in general. Organizations that exist for the purpose of delivering health or welfare services are not exempt from these problems. Such organizations do differ, however, in at least one important respect from other organizations. This difference lies in the exercise—or potential exercise—of professional autonomy by those employees of the organization who occupy the additional status of professional practitioner, e.g., physician, nurse, or social worker. The members of one profession—medicine—exercise what amounts to near absolute autonomy within the health delivery sector. As members of the dominant professional group in health care, physicians have historically exerted effective control of both the activities and scope of practice of all other groups of health workers—professional and nonprofessional alike. The medical profession, as Freidson (1970) points out, represents an outstanding example of *organized autonomy.* That is, it is largely free from external control and, in addition, it controls or delimits the activities of nearly all allied health professionals. This control stems not only from the dominant position of *each* member of the profession within the total hierarchy of health professionals but also from the dominant position of the profession of medicine as an ideal-typical collectivity when measured against the other professions. In the area of legislation, for example, the official voice of the collectivity, the American Medical Association, is regularly heard, if not always followed, when new health legislation is under consideration. It is doubtful whether any other professional collectivity has had as much influence in shaping health legislation as has this one association.

Another important consequence of medical dominance has been the control of access to clients. Once an individual becomes his patient, the physician controls which providers, if any, of a health service shall assist in the care of the patient. In effect, once an individual seeks out a physician and accepts his prescribed treatment he becomes what amounts to the property of that physician. Professionals other than the physician who might be qualified to provide a needed health service can gain access to the patient only by the express permission or invitation of the physician. The physical therapist serves as a case in point. The therapist is well qualified by education and training to assess neuromuscular damage resulting from specific neurologic pathologies in a patient and to institute an appropriate treatment regimen intended to either restore function or retard the loss of function. Yet, in a majority of health care settings such treatment cannot be instituted without the physician's approval or explicit request for the service.

Control of access to clients is closely related to another kind of control: *control of information*. Physician control of the information given to clients was reasonable in an earlier era when the physician was both the sole provider of treatment and certainly the practitioner with the greatest amount of scientifically derived knowledge. However, this control of information is much less appropriate than it once was, given the state of modern health care practice and the knowledge possessed by consumers. Given the increasing professionalization of nursing together with the establishment of schools of allied health professions, there are now many practitioners in a variety of health care settings sufficiently knowledgeable to provide information of a technical nature to clients. Furthermore, clients tend to be well informed on a wide range of matters.

In a study conducted by the author (Conway, 1973) using an attitudinal response instrument, attitudes of a randomly selected sample of an urban population were elicited with respect to readiness to seek medical care. Five items describing conditions symptomatic of illness were used to measure this variable with responses scored on an "agree-disagree" continuum. When controlling for education (years of formal school attendance), an inverse relationship between education and readiness to seek care was found. That is, as expressed by respondents, the higher the level of education the less readiness was there to seek care ($r = -.25$; $p < .05$).

In general, the norm is that information of a technical nature relating to a patient's diagnosis (test results, for example) is not to be communicated to him except by his physician. To the extent that such information could be provided promptly and accurately to patients, that patients or clients could understand it, and that patients do pay for it, it is inappropriate to withhold such information. There are instances, of course, in which it is entirely appropriate and even preferable that the physician be the individual to give information to the patient about diagnosis and treatment. Such instances would be those in which the relevant information is of a highly technical or esoteric nature and the questions the patient is likely to pose would be beyond the scope of knowledge of any other health professional. The reluctance of the physician to relinquish control over the provision of information leads to what has been described by at least one authority as a conspiracy of silence against the patient (Freidson, 1970). Freidson also notes that there are instances when patients *could* be given relevant information but it is withheld even when it is clear that no physician's order or organization policy restricts such provision.

Quint's (1965) findings lend further support to Freidson's observation. In a study of 21 postmastectomy patients (with a diagnosis of cancer), Quint found that patients were not adequately informed about the relative success of their surgery or of its extent. Further, nurses were observed to use avoidance mechanisms such as frequent rotation of assignments to patients in order to limit opportunity for these patients to verbalize their concerns (Quint, 1965).

There are at least two reasons why the matter of control of information will continue to be a problem for some time to come. One is that the line between what is and what is not legitimate medical practice is increasingly difficult to define as more paraprofessionals enter the field of health care and take on responsibilities that once belonged to the physician. The traditional rule of thumb that held that diagnosis and prescribing were functions reserved to physicians can no longer be relied on as an absolute. The term *diagnosis* is periodically submitted to reevaluation and redefinition as, for example, when a state's attorney general promulgates a revised definition of the nursing practice act in that state.

Regardless of statutory definition, it is quite clear that in the coronary care unit of a hospital the registered nurse makes a diagnosis from the electrocardiogram pattern on a cardiac monitor, determines that a patient is defibrillating, and decides to apply electric shock to the heart muscle in an attempt to restore normal sinus rhythm.

A second reason for the control of information remaining a problem is the sheer rapidity of the rate of discovery and transmission of new knowledge. No one professional, regardless of his or her field, can comprehend or apply all the knowledge that is theoretically available, yet the consumer's demand to know—as soon as possible and as much as possible—can be expected to continue unabated.

Recent trends in the health care system may portend alterations in various kinds of control that impact on consumers. The inflationary spiral in the cost of health care, as well as increased response on the part of government to consumer pressures in the making of health care policy, have paved the way for a readiness to experiment with alternatives to the physician as sole provider of care in the delivery system (Brunetto & Birke, 1972; Levine, 1976). Also, there is a heightened awareness among the public that there exists a variety of trained professionals other than the physician who are qualified and able to provide primary care.

As these other professionals (and paraprofessionals) continue to be educated to provide primary care to individuals, restriction of access to clients should lessen. There are, in fact, indications that such restriction has already lessened (Abdellah, 1976; Duncan et al., 1971; Selby, 1984). What seems likely to evolve in place of the present medically dominated system of health delivery is a model in which health care management will be shared by a team of professionals. The physician will retain control of health care when the client requires what is distinctly medical care; other health team members will direct the health team's activities when health prevention or health maintenance is required, or when teaching or counseling are needed. Within the *shared* model of health delivery and policy-making, those practitioners who by their education and training are specialists in a particular area of health will be called upon to advise on the preparation and allocation of practitioners and the development of training programs that will assist the carrying out of federally mandated health policy priorities. For example, it is highly probable that health educators, nurses, social workers, and nutritionists will increasingly be enlisted to help develop programs aimed at combating such persistent social problems as drug abuse and alcoholism in preteen and teenage populations. In addition, continued monitoring and funding by the federal government of health care services, together with consumer representation on Health Systems Agency councils (HSAs), are likely to ensure continued movement toward shared professional control of health policy-making and delivery.

Autonomy: A Professional Attribute

Thus far I have examined some aspects of what can be termed structural autonomy as it relates to the provision of health care. Let us now consider autonomy as it applies to individuals in their exercise of professional roles. Autonomy has been held by some to be a necessary condition for the optimal exercise of one's professional role (Goode, 1957; Moore, 1970). It has been variously defined as freedom on the part of the practitioner to make decisions without external pressure from clients or the members of one's profession (Hall, 1968); as the control over strategic aspects of work (Freidson, 1970); and as the freedom to practice one's profession in accordance with one's training (Engel, 1970). While at one time professionals such as physicians and lawyers commonly exercised what amounted to almost complete autonomy by reason of their relatively small numbers and their monopoly of esoteric knowledge, such is no longer the case. Indeed, it is difficult to find examples of professionals who practice entirely autonomously, at least within the construction of the above definitions.

In actual practice, professional autonomy is relative rather than absolute. That is, the amount of autonomy a given professional possesses is constrained by both the social and professional milieu in which he or she acts. For example, both nurses and physicians possess autonomy by virtue of their being members of learned professions. Yet it is readily apparent that physicians are more autonomous in their professional practice than are nurses. This is explained by a presumption about the physician's comprehensive command of expert knowledge in the diagnosis and treatment of illness as well as by his legally protected right to diagnose—a right denied to other practitioners. Even the physician is not completely autonomous, however. The successful practice of his craft depends upon the cooperation of a number of other professionals as well as upon the support of such services as clinical laboratories and x-ray facilities—all important adjuncts to the physician's diagnosis and treatment of the sick. Peer review acts as yet another limitation on the absolute autonomy of any professional. The consensus of one's peers about what is correct action in a given set of circumstances acts to define a normative structure that circumscribes the individual's actions. The recent imposition of a federal review system (PSRO) further limits the options for individual decision on the part of physicians in the treatment or medical management of patients (P.L., 92–603, 1973).

Autonomy and Commitment to Organizational Norms

The relative strength or weakness of norms in the work setting may influence both the amount of autonomy an individual perceives himself to have and the amount he actualizes in his practice (Goode, 1967). For example, some organizations place a high value on shared decision making. If, for example, the administration of a public elementary school supports the idea of shared decision making relative to curriculum and the decision is made to adopt a given pedagogical style of teaching reading, the individual teacher will have little or no opportunity to experiment with a variety of teaching methods even if there is reason to believe a different method might be more beneficial for the students. Similarly, in group health care settings, such as Health Maintenance Organizations (HMOs), group norms rather than individual professional norms tend to govern medical judgments and treatment. One reason for this is that in general, clients who subscribe to HMOs for their health care are likely to be seen in the course of their treatment by several health care providers. The types of diagnostic tests ordered and even the drugs prescribed for specific illnesses are more likely to be a matter of group consensus among the physicians in that setting than a matter of independent decisions. Within every organization there exist competing sets of norms and in the case of those organizations employing a large number of professionals, the norms of the profession represent one such set. Several studies of organizations have attempted to make the case that the existence of two sets of norms, i.e., the organization's and the profession's, are mutually exclusive and so are inevitably in conflict. In light of available evidence, this may be an overstated position (Kohn, 1971; Wilensky, 1964). It is precisely because organizations have particular goals requiring the expertise of professional workers that professionals tend to find the environment of such settings conducive to using their skills. In fact, the model of bureaucracy upon which organizations are constructed has much in common with the ideal model of the professions. That is, both place a high value on rationality, specialization of skills, and application of knowledge (Kast & Rosenzweig, 1970). While organization and professional norms tend to make mutual accommodation in the majority of settings, there are instances in which the professional's attachment to the norms of his profession may make for conflict. Several studies of organizations have found that some persons tend to act more on their perception of what the profession's ideals call for than what the organization's norms call for (Hall, 1968; Pavalko, 1971). Such persons have been described as *cosmopolitans*, while those who adhere more to the organization's norms have been termed *locals* (Gouldner, 1957).

The organization's need for routine is not readily apparent to the professional who is employed at a large organization, but it remains a constraining force nevertheless (Hage, 1980). The activities of professionals—who, it should be noted, account for only a fraction of the work force—must be meshed with the activities of all other workers in order to accomplish the work of the organization (Blau, 1956; Scott, 1966). The hospital-based nurse, for example, may be unable to give an individual patient the amount of attention she believes the patient's condition warrants if, in the judgment of management, the amount of time involved is too expensive when judged against competing demands for the nurse's expert skills. Nurses require a certain amount of autonomy in the provision of their services and seek to "carve out" autonomy even while conforming to the demands for routine. Both perceived personal control within the work setting and structural factors such as type of assignment have been found to be related to autonomy among staff nurses (Alexander, Weisman, & Chase, 1982) and in one study autonomy was found to be the strongest predictor of job satisfaction (Weisman, Alexander, & Chase, 1981).

In view of present patterns of multidisciplinary approaches to the delivery of health care and evidence that suggests that such patterns will increase, there seems to be a clear implication for health professionals as they develop their roles. One major task facing professionals who seek to maintain their autonomy is that of applying their specialized knowledge in the interest of clients in such a way that the rationality of their professional judgments supports, or at least articulates, the rationality of the organizations in which they find themselves. The decisions that the professional must make for his clients on a day-to-day basis call for his being able to make an accurate assessment of a number of key variables within the specific setting at any given point in time and then base his decision for action on this assessment.

SUMMARY

In this chapter, organizations have been examined using a systems framework to emphasize the fact that efforts to manage order, provide for a functional division of labor, and motivate workers are problems or tasks common to all so-called rational organizations. In addition, some problems unique to those organizations in which professionals form the largest single group of employees have been identified, highlighting autonomy as a key variable in organizations that provide health care. Further, some consequences for health professionals other than physicians who perceive themselves as entitled to autonomy but who have difficulty actualizing it were discussed. Attention was called to the negative impact on consumers that the control exerted by one dominant professional group can have in restricting the access of other health professionals to clients.

6

The Effects of Organizational Structure on Role Behavior

Joy D. Calkin

The thrust of this book is an understanding of the role behavior of health professionals from the perspective of role theory. "Unlike some psychological theories, role theory, with its focus on role enactment, bridges the gap between the individual and the group, between personal history and the social organization" (Sarbin & Allen, 1969, p. 490). According to Heiss (1981, p. 95), the content of role theory, whether from the functional or interactive perspective of social psychology, has as its ultimate dependent variable the understanding of social behavior. It is important to remember, however, that when we view a dependent variable from one perspective, such as role theory, we implicitly or explicitly underattend alternate explanations and understandings. "A way of seeing is a way of not seeing" (Poggi, 1965, p. 283).

The way a person behaves in a role and the prediction of that behavior may be understood from a variety of perspectives. For example, individual predispositions and cognitive functioning may contribute to the way one behaves in the role of nurse. The role making and role taking perspectives of the symbolic interactionists have been discussed in other chapters as a means of gaining insights into social behavior. Notions of the functionalist school of thought about phenomena such as role set and role expectations contribute to the study of social behavior. From another perspective one may view the social behavior of role occupants as a function, in part, of the attributes of the organizations of which they are members. The organizational analytic view is developed in this chapter.

Organizations are simply one form of social structure. They can be viewed as a system of roles. Our interest is in roles occurring in administrative structures and not in kinship or community structures. Wallace notes that an administrative structure, or a formal organization, is always composed of these social groups:

> A group of owners, in whose behalf and under whose auspices certain work is done; a target or clientele population for whom or upon whom the work is done; and the administrative organization proper (or management structure, or enterprise, or service, or locale, or what have you), which is the action group. (1971, p. 1–2)

The student of complex organizations has traditionally focused on the "administrative organization proper." However, it is increasingly the case that owners or boards, clients, the environment of the organization, interorganizational interactions, and sociohistorical contexts have become grist for the mills of organizational theorists (Clegg & Dunkerley, 1980).

One element in the analysis of organizations is the behavior of organizational members. Organizational psychologists are particularly interested in organizational attributes that have an impact on individuals' responses. For example, the exploration of the antecedents and consequences of role conflict has been a focus of this approach (Miles & Perreault, 1976). Organizational sociologists, in contrast, generally explore organizational dimensions, for example, environment and technology, that influence phenomena such as power, innovativeness and coordination which, in turn, affect organizational members. The view presented in this chapter is that organizations and their environments provide a major contingency for the social behavior of organizational members. While one may use anthropomorphic references in discussing organizations (e.g., organizational decision making) it is recognized that persons, and not organizations, departments, and the like, actually act.

COMPLEX ORGANIZATIONAL THEORY

Parallel to the tensions among perspectives of role theorists (Heiss, 1981), organizational theorists have developed multiple ways of understanding what goes on in organizations. In an Hegelian sense, there are a variety of theses, and antitheses among organizational theorists which have not been resolved into a synthesis. The schools of thought regarding organizations each contribute different understandings of organizations and, consequently, of the social behavior of organizational members.

This chapter explores two general views of organizational thought, the rational and the political. The rational school of thought contains such groups as the structural–functionalists and contingency theorists. A major focus on the rational school has been selected because the assumptions of this approach tend to dominate the explicit rationalizations of policymakers and managers in health and illness care organizations. This view of organizational behavior also dominates much of the health care literature about nurses and other providers in organizations. In contrast, the political school of thought is reflected in the focus of Marxists, political economic theorists, and others. The political school is offered as a counterpoint to the culturally dominant view of the rationalists.

It is immediately acknowledged that characterizing organizational theory by only two perspectives is a somewhat simplistic approach. A discussion of the social behavior of role incumbents, however, may be made more evident by means of this reductionism. It will become clear that the rational view presents a perspective of the individual as a role occupant in a system dedicated (ideally) to the efficient achievement of known goals. In an extreme sense, persons are acted upon or react to their organizational context. In contrast, the political view of organizations presents a perspective of role occupants as part of collective groups, or as seeking to achieve their own ends within organizations, or as actors serving the choices of those with power. Although an exploration of these viewpoints may at first take one away from the focus on roles, it is assumed that an enhanced comprehension of organizations will result in a richer understanding of the significance of organizations for health care providers. The majority of health care providers work in complex organizations. The dialectic between the major schools of thought should also enrich one's insights about roles and social behavior.

A RATIONAL PERSPECTIVE OF ORGANIZATIONS

The rational school is not rational in the usual sense of using reason or being sensible. Rather, the term is used to suggest that the goals of the organization come from the top of the organization and are controlled and rationalized from that perspective. The reasons for goals and the decisions made about how they are to be reached are regulated by top-level decision makers. Consequently, the scholars working in this school deal with proposing models for or understanding impediments to administrative control by means of structures and processes found in organizations. This type of thinking continues to predominate among administrators and managers, perhaps because it reduces the ambiguity of the organizational world and because organizational models, such as bureaucracies, have dominated the industrialized world.

A focus of organizational theorists and researchers of the rational school is to determine what forms of organizations (e.g., bureaucratic) are better for certain organizations. This type of thinking continues to predominate among administrators and managers, perhaps because it reduces the ambiguity of the organizational world and because organizational models, such as bureaucracies, have dominated the industrialized world.

Weber's Bureaucracy

Weber's work (English translation by Gerth & Mills, 1946) is considered a genesis of the systematic study of rational organizational structure. Weber's legal-rational authority model of organizations, or bureaucracy, was viewed as a structure that would better accomplish certain functions than earlier forms of organizational authority.

Weber discerned three ways in which power becomes legitimized as authority. Traditional authority arises from a person being part of a group which has "always" had authority. Charismatic authority arises from power gained through an individual's use of sacred symbols or knowledge, or through force of personality. Legal-rational authority, or a system of rules or laws, arises from an overall administrative structure used as the basis of authority.

Structural dimensions, such as hierarchy of authority, division of labor, technical competence of participants, rational discipline, limited authority of office, procedures for work situations, and rules governing the behavior of positional incumbents, all operate in a system to create legal-rational mechanisms to control and discipline participants in a fashion that is functionally efficient. In the Weberian bureaucracy, roles are clearly defined with respect to technical expertise, limitations on how control over others may be exerted, which aspects of organizational work are to be performed, how and what rewards will be used (salary not coercion), and other role expectations. It follows that there are norms and sanctions tied to positions and that incumbents are treated impersonally. That is, they are treated according to rules, procedures and policies rather than idiosyncratically or capriciously.

From a scientific or theory development stance, Weber's work provides a major step in advancing the study of complex organizations in the rational mode. The center of Weber's work is his conceptualization of power-authority relationships, identification of three bases of authority, and the exploration of structural–functional relationships by the description of an ideal type or a model that could be used for purposes of studying and designing organizations. Although Weber perhaps (Gerth & Mills, 1946) overattended structure and underattended functional results of these structures, he did provide definitions of organizational concepts and proposed relationships that continue to be used today.

Health care professionals bring technical and specialized expertise to their roles in health and illness care organizations. A number of writers have implicitly or explicitly identified problems inherent in control by hierarchy of authority in the face of rising expertise (Kramer, 1974) and proposed alternate models, such as self-governance by nurses (Elpern, White, & Donahue, 1984), to create structures that are more functional for professionally prepared role incumbents. The concern with the dysfunctional consequences of the combination of structural elements proposed by Weber has occupied the talents of many students of organization. Gouldner (1954), in his case study of a gypsum plant where a bureaucratic structure was imposed, noted the lowering of morale and ensuing strike behavior which he attributed to the rigidity of the new structure. This study and others contributed to an understanding of the dynamics of structure and their influence on social behavior. In the gypsum plant, new rules were followed by decreases in morale, which led to more rules, which, finally, led to social disruption in the form of a strike by workers. Subsequent large comparative studies of organizations (Blau & Schoenherr, 1971; Pugh, Hickson, Hinings, & Turner, 1968) focused largely on the relationships among structural variables rather than their impact on functioning of organizations and their impact on organizational participants. An understanding of structural variables, however, can assist in developing the context for concepts such as role expectations and stratification and it helps to identify sources of role strain and stress for particular role incumbents. For example, when an administrator uses the hierarchy of authority to refocus social workers on discharge placement of patients to capture prospective reimbursement monies (i.e., diagnostic related grouping-based payment) rather than allowing social workers to use their acknowledged expertise in counseling, it may create role strain. The bureaucratic emphasis on differentiated work and accompanying technical expertise contributes a major element in role conflict arising from differences among technical experts (managers, physicians, nurses), as each group has its own shared ideas, standards, or norms of behavior, and values.

Bureaucracies are structured to deal efficiently with relatively stable, predictable tasks to accomplish overall organizational goals. Power, communication, and much decision making are in the hands of administrative elites. The Weberian worker ideally is clear about his or her tasks, fairly recompensed, equitably treated, and loyal to the organization. Questions about the functional nature of bureaucratic structures for all organizations have, however, led to the movement away from the notion that there is one "best" social structure for organizations.

Mechanistic and Organic Structures

Burns and Stalker (1961) provided an alternate thesis about organizational forms based largely on the structural differentiation needed to deal with markets and technical environments. At the simplest level, the salient environments of organizations can be typified as stable or unstable. Burns and Stalker's observation of the post–World War II environment, with its massive shifts in technology and economics, led them to conclude that survival in turbulent environments requires innovativeness and the capacity for quick internal shifts in goals, technology, structures, and processes. The mechanistic nature of the bureaucratic structure, with its stable structures and processes, simply was not up to the task. They argued that an alternate form, organic in nature, characterized organizations that were able to adapt well to instability. They noted (1961, pp. 125) that the organic system was distinguished by the ability to adjust tasks using lateral communications among participants who had a cosmopolitan orientation and loyalty to their own field of technology and who used a rich context of advice and information to adapt to task redefinition. Control, authority, and communication flowed in a network, both up and down the hierarchy, and laterally, among technical experts and colleagues. Hence, control is not fixed in a position but "moves" on an as needed basis throughout the organization and is determined by consensus about who has the expertise to assume authority regarding a particular task. The organic and mechanistic types of structure were perceived as existing on a continuum with varying degrees of the structural elements in moderate forms.

Burns and Stalker (1961), unlike Weber, noted the tensions created by differing organizational types. For example, they observed that managers were uncomfortable with the situational ambiguity in organic structures and noted the struggle for control over decisions that ensued in such organizations. Their contribution of attention to the immediate organizational environment and descriptions of the organic social structure and decision-making processes resulting from structural differences are important to the rational perspective.

It is probably attractive for the health professional to consider being a role incumbent in the organic organizational structure. The fluidity of decision making, the ability to make an easy transition from one's socialization through education to the organization, the lack of hierarchical control and rules, and the chance to focus on one's professional goals rather than hierarchically determined ends make such a setting appealing. The "loose" and responsive organic structure provides simultaneously an ambiguous environment that is rich in potential for role conflict and high in stress in response to less predictable power bases, decision-making groups and rules, and communication networks both for managers and other role incumbents.

Hage's Axiomatic Theory of Structure and Function

"Structural–functional analysis, in sociology, can be defined as relating structural variables with performance and output variables" (Hage, 1972, p. 197). Hage goes on to note that analysis centers on the study of which functional or dysfunctional performances occur when certain societal structural arrangements are employed. The examples of the rational perspective of organizations presented above appear to be heavy in the consideration of structural characteristics and light in the study of the functional aspects (e.g., efficiency, innovativeness) of organizations. Readers are referred to Chapter 2 for a discussion of the characteristics of structural–functionalism in sociology.

Hage (1980, pp. 34–49) describes his own earlier work, published in the 1960s, as synthesizing the work of Weber and Barnard. His contributions in case studies and comparative studies are numerous, but our attention here is on his axiomatic theory within the structural–functional paradigm. The axiomatic theory was proposed as a means of formulating testable statements from earlier theory to guide future research. The four functions or performances he selected are innovation, efficiency, quantity of production, and morale. Some examples of his seven propositions are:

- The higher the stratification the lower the morale, and vice versa.
- The higher the complexity [i.e. diversity of different specialists], the lower the centralization [of decisions], and vice versa.

From the propositions he derived a set of 21 corollaries, such as:

- The higher the centralization the higher the stratification and vice versa.
- The higher the complexity the lower the morale, and vice versa.
- The lower the morale the lower the innovation, and vice versa.

Hage (1972) has provided a means of clarifying [both] functional and dysfunctional consequences of selected organizational structure variables using an axiomatic approach to theory construction and testing. This approach provides one means for coming to grips with the intricate relationships among structural and functional variables.

On the face of it, this appears to be an arid approach to the rich tapestry within which roles taken and roles made in organizations are interwoven. The threats to roles, such as that to the roles of clinical specialists, may be understood when looked at through Hage's eyes.

> In a similar fashion, the organic model turns out to have dysfunctions as well: The greater the complexity, the less the volume of production; and the greater the complexity, the less the efficiency. Specialists cost money, so that even though they are hired to reduce costs, they actually raise them relative to production volume. Specialists also do not normally emphasize the volume of work, but rather its quality. Conversely, concerns about efficiency and quantity of production lead to a lack of hiring new specialists and a tendency to let them go as concerns about costs mount. (1980, p. 43)

Whereas role making provides a map for the *process* of role modification (Conway, 1978, p. 25), the structural–functional perspective of organizations such as Hage's (1972) provides a *rationale* for the form of role modification. Calkin (1984), for example, used this thinking as an impetus for differentiating advanced nursing practice from basic nursing practice in the face of an unstable environment in the health care field.

Hage's approach to research about organizational structure and function does not appear to be widely read. However, the axioms he has drawn from organizational theory and research are much in need of study. Knowledge of the functional impact of structural variations on morale and innovation, for example, would provide a kind of analysis that might benefit decisions about appropriate structures for organizations.

Technology and Structure

The structural design of an organization is based on a determination of organizational goals and the type of structure that administrative elites think will best fit their goals. The technology "school" within the rational perspective argues that the work to be done by an organization tells us more about structures and processes than do goals alone or the psychological characteristics of its members (Perrow, 1972, p. 176). The work of an organization is to transform inputs, such as a person newly diagnosed with diabetes mellitus, to outputs, such as the person able to manage the disorder. The tasks performed are a better and more direct predictor of elements of structure, including expertise required, how work is divided among workers (specialization), the amount and type of discretion afforded workers, and the need for policies, procedures, and protocols (formalization) than are factors such as the motivation of workers or the goals established by organizational elites.

The germinal insights which Joan Woodward gained from her 10-year study of English industrial firms were an important contribution to this line of thinking.

> While at first sight there seemed to be no link between organization and success, and no one best way of organizing a factory, it subsequently became apparent that there was a particular form of organization most appropriate to each technical situation. (Woodward, 1965, p. 72)

She concluded that a key to understanding organizational effectiveness (a functional outcome) is the study of the fit between the work of an organization and its structure. Similar thinking was developed by other theorists (Lawrence & Lorsch, 1967a; Perrow, 1967). Technology has been found to be different among nursing subunits (Kovner, 1966; Overton, Schneck, & Hazlett, 1977). Woodward's hypothesis that technology and structure jointly account for variances in effectiveness has been supported in an experimental study of nurses providing ambulatory care (Calkin, 1980). The impact of technology or work on structural differences has been demonstrated to be more important than size in a longitudinal panel study of human services organizations (Hage & Aiken, 1964).

A number of insights from studies with this perspective provide a context for the study of roles in health care settings. Students of technology are primarily responsible for clarifying the need for overall organizational and unit level research and conceptualization to be maintained (Van de Ven & Delbecq, 1974). For example, when studying the impact of knowledge and skill to do work or the impact of work itself, it is useful to be aware that structures closest to the core work of the organization are most influenced by technology. The further one moves away from the individual and unit level of work structures toward managerial and board structures, the less the influence of the core work of the organization. Differences in the predictability and analyzability of nurses' work at the individual and unit level have been demonstrated (Comstock & Scott, 1977). Leatt and Schneck (1982) found that the work environment of nursing subunits varied as a function of the technology used for patient care on each type of unit, with intensive care units having the greatest need for environmental interaction. They suggest that structures must differ to provide such interactions and that environmental interaction patterns "may have some direct influence on such behaviors as conflict, stress, satisfaction, and the function and style of leadership" (1982, p. 591). In a national sample of medical units, nurse managers at three levels beyond the staff nurse level were shown to have a different perception of the work of the staff nurse, that is nursing technology, than staff nurses themselves (Armstrong, Krahenbuhl, Muellenbach, & Savage, 1984). These authors conclude that the least congruence in perceptions of staff nurses' work was between middle managers (e.g., clinical directors, evening supervisors) and staff nurses. Because these managers often gain and deploy nursing department resources for nursing units and may create structures for delivery of care (e.g., primary or team nursing assignments), the limited agreement about patient care or unit technology may lead to inappropriate role expectations. In addition, role conflict, role strain, and the misapplication of rewards and sanctions may occur. The researchers suggested additional research was needed to determine whether the lack of consonance in perceptions of nursing technology by different levels in the hierarchy influences morale and satisfaction of staff nurses.

The general theme of the technological perspective leads to the conclusion that the structure of organizations, and especially their subunits, is heavily influenced by the raw materials (e.g., patients) on which they work and by the knowledge and skill required to perform the work. Some work is more routine and programmable than other work. The earlier thinking about mechanistic and organic organizations becomes better understood in light of conceptualizations about technology–structure–effectiveness or functional relationships. As Perrow (1972) pointed out, although a choice of goals (e.g., care of the aged) and products (e.g., rehabilitation) may influence structure, and although an executive may choose to treat nonroutine work as though it were routine, over the long haul it is technology that influences the choice of appropriate structure or "the organization will pay a heavy price in terms of efficiency" (1972, p. 176). The technology-structure group shares with other rationalists an underlying focus on both effectiveness and efficiency—the highest returns of "profit" for resources invested—as functional outcomes sought through structures.

What can we learn from the notion of the *technological imperative* for the structure of health care organizations and persons who have roles in them? The general conclusion is that the work performed in organizations will account for at least a portion of the differences in structural variables, such as levels of expertise, extent of decision making by role occupants, and numbers and types of departments. I do not claim that for any one type of work, such as the treatment of alcoholic persons, that only one type of structural configuration can produce effective care and staff satisfaction. However, I would assert that there is a limited *range* of structural variations that are consonant with alcohol rehabilitation for certain groups of clients. For example, alcohol treatment programs may seek the same outcomes through alternative structures, as shown in Table 1.

The critical issue is that there should be a fit between tasks and structure. The form of the alcoholism treatment program structure would initially be an administrative prerogative often based on who has the ear of the decision maker

TABLE 1. TWO ALTERNATE STRUCTURES FOR DOING THE WORK OF TREATING PERSONS WITH ALCOHOLISM

Unit Structure Variables	Structure A	Structure B
Expertise	Alcohol counselors who are former alcoholics	Physicians (e.g., medical, psychiatric), nurses, social workers
Specialization or division of labor	Generalists in all aspects of treatment program	Relative specialization in aspects of treatment programs
Standardization or formalized rules, policies, procedures for clinical aspects of care	Standardized approach used by all staff (e.g., no medications, use of group sessions)	Few policies and procedures that are universal; most are safety related
Decision making (individual, collegial, supervisory, expert)	Few exceptions to program; exceptions dealt with by collegial discussion and occasional referral to experts	Collegial (team) decisions individual care plans, implementation using individual expertise

and what environmental issues and constraints are operating at the time of the decision. However, the decision maker must face the fact that choices of expertise are finite, that given the choice of expertise certain kinds of specialization (or lack of it) will occur, that standardization will facilitate decision making to varying degrees depending on the care providers, and that decision-making strategies are difficult to force on providers who see them as inappropriate. For example, the providers, in both the A and the B structures in Table 1 are unlikely to go to administrative personnel for clinical decision making. Hence, we conclude from the technologic perspective that where there is a lack of fit between technology and structure the social structure will have dysfunctional effects for role behavior. We can also see that structures A and B, although functional in a treatment sense, are likely to lead to many differences: of expectations for role behavior of other providers, of status levels, and of power within the provider group. Also, others interacting with the group may hold differing behavioral norms. Role conflict and role strain may be the consequences.

Environment and Organizational Structure: Toward Contingency Theory

Until the mid-1960s, the effect of the environment on organizational structures and resulting role behavior lacked the force of a central issue in American sociology (Katz & Kahn, 1966). It is not accurate to state, as some claim, that writers such as Weber ignored the influence of the environment or used a closed system model of organizations. Indeed, we noted earlier that writers such as Burns and Stalker (1961) focused on the need to select structures in light of the technologic environment. The conceptualization of environmental influences, however, did not include a careful exploration of relevant variables and their potential impact on various aspects of structure.

Contingency theory provides the conceptual and empirical notions for much of modern rational administrative science. The thesis of contingency theorists is that functional organizational structure and design are contingent upon or conditioned by interactions between environmental and organizational variables. The selection of appropriate structures and processes, such as coordination and decision making, should be based on a careful analysis of contingencies by decision makers.

An open systems analysis approach (Katz & Kahn, 1966) emphasizes the importance of paying attention to external environments in the study of organizational structures. Two more common environmental attributes considered important are turbulence and complexity (Duncan, 1972). Turbulence is generally defined in terms of the rate of environment shifts, the regularity of such shifts, and the amount of change. Complexity is measured by the number and mix of external events and groups with which the organization must cope in order to carry on with its work. Health care organizations can usually be characterized as dealing with both turbulent and complex environments. Many multimission university hospitals, for example, are forced to respond to rapid shifts in prospective reimbursement formulas. The magnitude of the dollar adjustment depends on the percentage of health maintenance organizations and the percentage of certain federally funded patients in the population they serve. Their environmental complexities are increasing as regulatory bodies, educational programs for health providers, manufacturing organizations, and so on increase in numbers and as demands for alterations in research, education, and service occur. In addition, as competition for scarce patient resources increases, the near monopoly of tertiary referrals enjoyed by many university hospitals is on the decline. These conditions taken together clearly indicate the environment of many university hospitals is uncertain. The question occurs: What actions might organizations take in response to uncertainty?

It has been posited that there *can* be an optimal fit between environment and structure (Galbraith, 1973a). The internal adaptation of the organization to its external environment is one way of creating such a fit. Lawrence and Lorsch (1967a) analyzed 10 competing firms in three industries to determine how different environments were associated with differences in internal environments and how such internal environments influenced coordinating or integrating mechanisms and success of the firms. The firms were functioning in one of three types of industries and thus faced different environmental contingencies. The ways that the firms allocated or divided labor to respond to specific environmental demands were conceptualized in terms of differentiation. As firms became more internally differentiated they required appropriate integration mechanisms, such as hierarchy of command, liaison personnel, and teams and committees to assist the whole organization toward unity of purpose. A study of the integration mechanisms and their use as delineated by Lawrence and Lorsch (1967a, Chaps. 2 and 6) is instructive for health care professionals working in complex, larger health care institutions, as coordination of services continues to be a central issue in these institutions. From a role theory perspective, however, Lawrence and Lorsch's interest in the systemic influence of segmenting organizations into departments and programs on the behavior of managers and subordinates is of greater interest.

Lawrence and Lorsch (1967a) found that managers in different departments and units have different orientations toward particular goals. First, in health-care settings, for example, the goal of high quality patient care as defined by the chief of medicine and the head of housekeeping is likely to be different. Second, managers and subordinates have different time orientations depending on the central function of a department. Third, research-oriented professionals tend to have a much longer time horizon for their work than clinical practice-oriented professionals. Fourth, the interpersonal orientation of managers of departments varies as a function of their work. Social workers are more inclined to maintain relationships in order to achieve departmental goals than is the chief technologist in the laboratory, the latter being more inclined to pay attention to completing laboratory tests according to defined standards. As a consequence of contrasts in inclinations, conflict among role occupants is inevitable. Lawrence and Lorsch (1967b) argued that such conflict is useful as a means of integrating disparate tendencies among departments provided differences in orientation are recognized and dealt with appropriately. That is, they do not agree with writers who view conflict as dysfunctional and the role of structures as being to avoid such conflicts.

Identification of the sources of role conflict, stress, and strain were studied in this research (Lawrence & Lorsch, 1967a, Chaps. 3 and 5). The concepts developed in this research can be extrapolated to the study of health care organizations. The consequences of adapting to environments and to changes in organizational size in health care organizations are to increase the differentiation of work and specialization of workers, with accompanying opportunities for conflict. Such internal differentiation creates a need for integrative mechanisms among departments that may result in the development of new roles (e.g., patient discharge planner) and demands for more integrative ability among occupants of current integrative roles (e.g., head nurse). This study, then, identifies variances in goals, time, and interpersonal orientations as sources of organizational conflict and provides a basis for comprehending the nature of the linkages between external environment, organizational environment, and role behavior. The work was explicitly based on, and extended the thinking of, Woodward (1965), and Burns and Stalker (1961).

Lawrence and Lorsch have been criticized for their failure to identify causes of environmental impacts on organizations (Hall, 1968), also, the reliability of their measures of environmental uncertainty have been questioned (Tosi, Aldag, & Storey, 1973). However, their insights about the firms they studied have made a fundamental contribution to contingency theory of organizations and their effects on member behavior.

One of the seminal works from the rational contingency viewpoint is a slim book by James Thompson (1967). He noted that organizations behave in certain ways because not to do so has such negative consequences. He goes on:

> The concepts of rationality brought to bear on organizations establish limits within which organizational action must take place. We need to explore the meanings of these concepts and how they impinge on organizations. (1967, p. 1)

Thompson argued that technologies and environments are the major sources of organizational uncertainty. Uncertainty is the primary challenge to the ability to rationalize organizational action. He developed a series of propositions about the relationships among environmental and technologic variables and the actions a "rational" organization would take. For example, he noted, "Under norms of rationality, organizations seek to minimize the power of task-environment elements over them by maintaining alternatives." (1967, p. 32)

That is, an organization should not put all its eggs in one basket. A hospital will rationally seek to have a variety of referring physicians and multiple patient sources to avoid being dependent upon and controlled by a narrow sector of its environment.

Thompson attended not only to structure, with its environmental and technological contingencies, but also to the sources of uncertainty arising from organizational members as they exercise discretion and as they interact with others in and outside the organization and with administrative processes. Thompson defended the notion that "the ability and opportunity to exercise discretion is not uniformly distributed throughout the organization" (1967, p. 100). While this observation will come as no surprise to the reader, it is helpful to keep in mind Thompson's position that technology, task environment, design of work (e.g., operating room tasks related to performing surgery require team work) and structure (e.g., allocation of experts) have a distinct impact on discretionary behavior or on the power and dependence of role occupants. Thompson noted that roles provide a sphere of action which "individuals are motivated to protect or enhance" through political processes (1967, p. 106). Also, some positions provide many opportunities to learn and to be visible Assistants to hospital administrators or chief nursing officers have many opportunities to broaden their skills, to observe departmental interactions, and to be quite visible if they perform well or poorly. The chance to see and be seen provides a basis for gaining knowledge that contributes to role making and role taking. Role expectations of organizational members can be better understood and can lend insights about decision making, power, and communication linkages necessary for role shaping when contingencies are understood by the observer.

The writers presented in this section suggest the environmental contingencies and the influence of these conditions on organizational members as they create structures that help the organization cope with environmental uncertainty and also perform the work of the organization. The structures, in turn, provide a set of contingencies within which role incumbents or aspirants live their organizational lives.

Limits to the Norms of Rationality

Thus far in the chapter we have developed a picture of the context of organizational roles as a complex knitting together of the interdependent influences of everything from environment to the time orientations of managers and departmental members. It is as though decision making of role occupants can be made consistent with organizational goals and as if changes in the external environment have a direct, necessary, and predictable impact on all inside the organization—if one can grasp the interacting variables. Observers of the human scene in organizations may well question this picture. What appears to be needed, if one is to retain the rationalist perspective, is a way of thinking about limits to rational norms or to understand whether there are additional processes that affect the complex but rather tidy relationships portrayed above. While still considering the unitary organizational control and direction of the rational perspective, we turn to a brief exploration of organizational decision making and the notion of *loose coupling*.

Much of the focus of functional–structuralists and others discussed above is on the means of controlling behavior through structure (e.g., rules, authority of office). Added to this view have been insights about the influence of professionals, their standards and expectations regarding control of organizations, most especially in organically structured ones. Control, regardless of source, is necessary in organizations for the selection of one decision rather than another and the assurance that decisions will be implemented. The fact that people and not organizations make decisions presents a problem in administrative control of organizations and one that must be dealt with if the rationalist view is to be at all reality based.

Herbert Simon and James March have given a basis for retaining the rationalist perspective while altering our view of rationality or goal-oriented behavior. Simon (1955) recognized that organizational members can make rational decisions with respect to their personal goals with some influence on decisions and goals from their immediate work group. These authors, however, go on to argue later that people are only "intendedly rational" as they simplify alternatives available, select the first acceptable action, and have difficulty establishing preferences when there are several (March & Simon, 1958). Given this model of limited rational behavior it becomes possible to propose that only top administrators must accept organizational goals in a holistic sense. These goals are divided into subgoals structured in such a way that they adequately meet individual goals of many organizational members. These goals and subgoals become quite stable because of the costs of creating the capital and operational assets to carry them out, even though individual role occupants may desire to change them. Essentially, by understanding the limited rationality of human beings we can see that the overall direction of the organization can be maintained because of its sheer complexity. March and Simon (1958) noted that complexities of decision making are simplified by specializing activities and goals so that members direct their attention to a limited set of values; rules, programs and repertoires of behavior limit choices explored in recurrent situations; common channels of communication develop to include some persons and exclude others; recurrent stimuli dominate the behavior within subgroups; education and socialization "cause" individuals to make organization oriented decisions; goals and tasks of one group are kept somewhat independent of those in another group so they are less interdependent, and so on. With this view of the organization,

> . . . the superior has the power or tools to structure the environment and perceptions of the subordinate in such a way that he sees the proper things and in the proper light . . . he sets priorities ("we had better take care of this first," "this is getting out of hand and creating problems, so let's give it more attention until the problems are cleared up") and alters the flow of inputs and stimuli. (Perrow, 1967, p. 152)

Perrow (1967) also points out that March and Simon's model of organizational behavior makes our notions of communication broader and our understanding of organizational control of decision richer. For example, March and Simon note that communication channels become specialized; some are habitually favored over others, vocabularies are developed that underattend some realities (e.g., effective patient care) and overattend others (e.g., cost containment).

Role behavior, then, does not arise from individual decisions and goals, but rather from the premises upon which decisions and goals are based (Simon, 1957). The premises are shaped by such factors as language used by participants, the choice of one type of personnel over another, who communicates with whom about what, how programs are structured, and what activities are standardized and formalized. And these premises can be shaped by superiors through the use of rewards, sanctions, and the stabilizing of norms of behavior over time. Perrow suggests that this neo-Weberian perspective of organizational and individual behavior adds "the muscle and flesh for the Weberian skeleton, giving it more substance, complexity and believability" (Perrow, 1967, p. 146).

Cyert and March (1963) built on this picture of organizational behavior. In one portion of their work they discuss the bargaining process that takes place among the organizational members whose shifting coalitions are needed to gain organizational inputs (e.g., patients) and to produce the work of the organization (e.g., patient care). Organizations are conceived of as coalitions of individuals. For the organization to survive, coalitions must be retained. Cyert and March rejected both the idea that goals are defined as the goals of the top of the managerial hierarchy and the counterproposal that they are consensual or participatory goals (1963, p. 27–28). They suggest that organizational goals are really ambiguous and nonoperational—"high quality patient care at reasonable cost"— and are simply a statement of aspirations. There is no requirement for internal goal consistency. Goals are the result of a bargaining process among coalitions. The continuous shifting of goals suggested by a bargaining model of organizational behavior is limited by agreements and mutual control systems among coalitions, such as budget controls and establishing somewhat stable "territories" through specialization of functions. Organizations also have "memory" in the form of standard operating procedures that lead to semi-permanent behavior (Cyert & March, 1963, Chap. 3). Changes in goals take place slowly and usually in response to a pressing problem such as when a visiting nurse service is suddenly confronted with new home health agencies being established by for-profit companies and community hospitals. New goals (e.g., cost containment) may be developed among coalitions, often in conflict with old goals (e.g., quality of care), conflict which is reduced by attending to one goal at a time unless there are great pressures to deal with both simultaneously. Such goal shifts also give rise to incrementally greater power of one coalition (e.g., fiscal managers) over others (e.g., clinicians) under different environmental and organizational conditions.

Taken together, Simon, March, and Cyert have suggested that organizations are more adequately conceived as being given direction by the views of multiple actors in the organization who have their own definition of situations. Both roles and role incumbents take on a dynamism of their own, albeit within the limits of their own rationality and the constraining structures and processes developed through interacting individuals and coalitions making up the organization. While organizations are still instrumental in carrying out functions, a more action-oriented, volunteer view emerges (Silverman, 1970).

The concept of loose coupling is a second example of the limitations of a purely instrumental, rational view of organizational behavior. If two elements of an organization, or its environments, have little in common, or if the things they have in common are less salient than those they have in common with other elements, they may choose to act independently of each other. Elements within the same organization which act in this manner are said to be loosely coupled (Weick, 1976). If it takes a long time for one element to influence another, they are loosely coupled. If one element makes changes because another element does, they are tightly coupled. Loose coupling among intraorganizational and extraorganizational elements contributes to maintenance of organizational stability. For example, changes in the technologic environment of physicians may influence the medical staff directly and have consequences for the behavior of some elements of the hospital (e.g., purchasing, nursing), not affecting other elements at all (e.g., security, dietary). Aldrich (1971) suggested that group norms may support loose coupling, for example by using "good manners" to quiet and isolate (uncouple) angry members. He also suggested that traditional values may maintain loose coupling between current organizational activities and innovations in the environment. The postulated influences of loose coupling on organizational change, hierarchical structures, and organizational processes are many and complicated.

Writers such as Simon, March, Cyert, and Weick are variously referred to as neo-Weberians, neo-functionalists, and action-theorists of complex organizations. A central issue for action-theorists is attention to the voluntaristic choices that organizational members make, how they make them, and how they shape and are shaped by the goals or intentions of the overall organization. We have moved from the Weberian sense that the behavior of organizational actors is shaped by external, impersonal mechanisms to one in which individuals, especially those with power, may shape their organization and even manipulate their environment (Pfeffer & Salancik, 1978). The ideas of these writers are rational in perspective in the sense of providing a basis for insights about the limits on unitary goal rationality controlled from the top of the organization. They tend to be functionally oriented with an eye to the power of administrative goals and are also arguably political in perspective in the sense that multiple sources of power are analyzed as the bases of organizational decisions. Recently, Astley and Van de Ven (1983) presented what we have combined under the rationalist perspective as two separate views of organizations, the *system-structural* view and the *strategic choice* view.

In sum, the organizational theorists have a predominant focus on organizational goals, structures, and processes, whether deterministically or voluntaristically based (Astley & Van de Ven, 1983). An understanding of the relationships among concepts about environment, goals, technology, structure, and processes is a helpful backdrop for studying roles in administrative social structures. Health care provider roles are largely embedded in social structures of complex organizations. The rationalists contribute to insights about such things as how specialization occurs and why goals are relatively stable even in the face of competing coalitions. These insights can enhance our grasp of notions such as socialization, norms, and role modification as they occur or are constrained from occurring in health care organizations.

A POLITICAL PERSPECTIVE OF ORGANIZATIONS

The action perspective discussed above initiates a loosening of assumptions about the adequacy of a rational view of organizations as *the* means of understanding social structures and role behavior within them. The simple fact is that organizations do not behave in a monolithic and rational fashion. They are not predictably rational even from the viewpoint of the heady heights of the dominant elites. The need for apprehending the behavior of individuals, groups, and coalitions who may not share the goals of administrative or dominant elites is real for theorists and practitioners. The manipulation of international, national, state, and local affairs by some organizations is a problem in need of more study. The rational paradigm, like all paradigms, has provided us with a way of *not seeing* in addition to a way of *seeing* organizational characteristics that affect role behavior.

In this section the unit of organizational analysis is broadened beyond the general, comparative, and static attributes of organizations (e.g., structure, goals) and we note that analyses of organizational participants and larger economic, societal, political, and historical issues deserve attention. The central theme now shifts from goals and how to achieve them to power—its roots and routes. That is, the issue is the politics of organizations rather than the administration of organizations for unitary goals.

The preeminence of the rational or goal paradigm in the study of organizations is evident. The modern organization is fundamentally conceptualized as a goal attainment device (Georgiou, 1973) in this paradigm. The organization is supraordinate to its parts. Individuals and their own needs create some "noise" in the system to which the organization must adapt to retain participants as role players. Yet individuals are not really salient to the basic constructs relevant to organizational analysis. The organization is viewed as adapting *to* its external environment in order to gain and retain resources required for goal attainment, rather than being proactive in manipulating its environments.

First in Europe and more recently in North America, a plethora of implicit and explicit critiques of the rational paradigm have developed. Clegg and Dunkerley (1980) and Zey-Ferrell and Aiken (1981) provide overviews of perspectives critical of the rational paradigm. Both groups of authors see some of the symbolic interactionists, such as Strauss, as contributors to this critical approach. The critics of the goal paradigm have concerns about underlying assumptions of the rational paradigm, with their narrowing influence on a sociology of organizations. Also cited in the critiques are methodological limitations to developing generalizations about organizations.

Zey-Ferrell and Aiken (1981, pp. 1–21) summarize a number of criticisms of the comparative structural–functional and structural–contingency approaches. Several of the criticisms are particularly important to developing theory and research about the relationship between the social structure of organizations and role behavior. Some examples of such critiques include the following. The primacy of the rational paradigm has resulted in an acceptance of the conservative assumptions of administrators and controlling elites regarding the nature and purpose of organizations. (A current example is the assumption that competition in health care leads to efficiency and is good for society in general.) The image of organizations as being overly rational constricts our view of human behavior and of organizations in society. The rational analysts may view organizational members as nonvolitional at one extreme or as developing organizational systems through value consensus at another extreme. Accepting either view forces one to take a reductionist perspective in the study of role behavior. From this perspective static aspects of structure are emphasized, while one ignores shifts in status and roles and a consideration of how such shifts occur. There is serious underattention to analyzing power relationships when one uses the rational paradigm as a point of departure for the study of role behavior, conflict, and change in organizations. Such critiques give rise to the need for antithetical perspectives if we are to adequately understand organizations and their influence on human behavior from virtually any perspective.

Control and the Environment

The rational paradigm tends to create an image of the organization as shaping itself to environmental pressures in order to achieve its instrumental goals. One has the sense that it is reactive or responsive to pressures, demands, and opportunities presented by the environments relevant to the organization (Aldrich, 1979). Analytic concepts, such as the technological environment and measures of the number and types of boundary spanners monitoring important sections of the environment, become part of the study of organizations and environments under the assumptions of the paradigm. These views of the environment are criticized as overly benign characterizations of organizations. They are associated with the ideology of owners and managers and are inattentive to the role of the organizations (read dominant elites) as agents of domination, social change, and social control. Zey-Ferrell and Aiken comment that the study of the societal impact of organizations provides only "few answers to the student seeking clues to better management techniques" (1981, p. 228). That is, owners, managers, and rational theorists have been more concerned, about administrative control than about the influence of organizations on the larger society.

Colignan and Cray (1981) note that criticisms of the rational paradigm have come from individuals holding two perspectives. The first group, the reformists, critique interpretations and methods of studies but do not discard the underlying model of rational organizations. The second group offering critiques, they suggest, includes the Marxists and the political economists who reject the rational paradigm.

The Marxists, bringing their broader societal perspective on issues such as social class, power distribution, social structure, and capitalistic hegemony, have attempted to apply it to organizational analysis (Goldman & Van Houten 1977). Historical–societal studies of the health care environment from a Marxist perspective have emerged with increasing frequency. Waitzkin (1983), for example, studied the interactions of organization such as medical centers, medical technology firms, and insurance companies and the contribution of these groups to the uncontrollability of health costs. These examinations of the health care environment with a focus on the domination and control of the field, brought an additional outlook on the context in which health providers attempt to make operational their professional goals and roles. For example, North American nurses and physicians assume that patients with myocardial infarctions should be cared for in intensive care units in hospitals whereas British studies have provided data suggesting that a lower level of care is adequate. Who profits from the American assumptions?

Drawing from the Marxist and Hegelian perspective, Benson (1977) has criticized the conventional-logical positivist mode of inquiry used in the rational school. The description and analysis of a particular phenomenon as approached by conventional analysis provides only a picture of the current order of organizations or an uncritical acceptance of which organizational goals and structures exist now as a basis for research. The dialectical analysis deals "with processes through which this kind of order is produced and maintained" (Benson, 1977, p. 13). The questions of how the present scheme of things came to be and what social pressures are likely to lead to change are central for a Marxist or Hegelian dialectic inquiry about organizations. Benson suggests that the current work of the symbolic interactionists, political economists, and other students of organizations would benefit from the use of dialectic logic.

The control by organizations of their environments takes on a somewhat less benign posture when viewed by critical analysts. Organizations are theoretically (Gross, 1978) and empirically (Sutherland, 1961) criminal in some of their activities as they seek to control environmental contingencies. In a broader arena, multinational companies use their structures and economic planning power to shape production and markets on an international scale (Hymer & Rowthorn, 1970) and have a major impact on the social-cultural-economic environment of the settings in which they operate. The Marxists draw to our attention that organizations may have a pervasive influence on changes in role behavior on individuals outside of organizational boundaries through seeking to dominate and control the uncertainties of the market place and to gain power or prestige as an end in itself. Critical analyses of organizations are relatively rare among followers of the Weberian legacy; (for an exception see McNeil & Minihan, 1977, on regulation of medical devices and organizational behavior in hospitals).

The political economists, in contrast to Marxists, have traditionally studied the interaction of organizations and society (Karpik, 1978). Much of this writing has developed in Europe. Some American writers (e.g., Galbraith, 1973a,b) have also argued that organizations, especially large ones or cooperating groups of them, exercise their ability to control their environments or to choose in which environment they will operate. Touraine (1971), a political economist, has pointed out that while each level is connected to its social context, members at different levels of the organization are limited in their ability to act by those above that level and likewise limit the actions of those under that level. These connections are especially important in technological capitalism (versus industrial capitalism) as organizations use not only financial and political capital but also intellectual capital to dominate clients, markets, and competitors (Karpik, 1978). Organizational actors and coalitions choose courses of action, Karpik notes, that are consistent with their own economic and social conditioning.

"Efficiency" becomes an integral part of a larger historical and social context in which goal setting especially by dominant coalitions, occurs. Starr's (1982) work, *The Social Transformation of American Medicine*, reflects some of this concern with the historical political–economic context of physicians amid the possible influence of this context on their development of "sovereignty" in the health care field and beyond. As Starr notes, changes in the political economy have prompted many independent, entrepreneurial medical practices to move into corporate settings. A central notion of Karpik's perspective is that individual members' and coalitions' ways of thinking are shaped by their historical political–economic roots and provide the logical basis for their actions. If these members gain power in the organization their logics of action come to dominate corporate strategic decisions. For example, the "logic" of cost-effectiveness has become a dominant view in the health field, probably as a result of cost-effectiveness research by the United States Department of Defense prior to the Vietnam War (Enthoven, 1978).

The methodology of Karpik and others in the political–economic school is to study organizations through analyses of individuals' and coalitions' preferences linked to their historical roots and how they influence and are influenced by organizations and environments through a variety of linkages. Such methods identify the underlying processes of power and influence in and among organizations and their members.

In sum, the reformists, Marxists, political economists, and other groups have shifted from the notion of the benign adaptive organization and the rational perspective of organizations and environments to a perspective that encompasses the dynamic interaction of organization and environment and of the individuals and groups that make up the organization. The latter perspective provides a more historically influenced, action-oriented picture of organization–environment relationships. Concepts such as dominance, control, social class, logics of action, class conflict, and power distribution are added to organization–environment analyses proposed by the rationalists.

Politics Within

The deterministic flavor of the rational perspective creates an image of the organizational member as one acted upon. Rules, norms, and other structural entities shape behavior in the direction of the overriding goals of the organization. Factors such as technology and structure are causally linked to performance and satisfaction of workers.

"Politics within" offers alternate paths to an understanding of role behavior and the contexts in which behavior is embedded. There seem to be two different senses of organizational members reflected in organization literature. First is the sense of the member exploiting the labor class or being exploited for the benefit of capitalist accumulation. A second sense of organizational participants is that they are active negotiators, bargainers, and manipulators. Both views acknowledge social structures, but rarely in the same vein as in the rational paradigm. Both contribute to thinking about power and control in organizations.

Power and control are commonly linked explicitly or implicitly and often sensed as negative forces—especially if the role incumbent feels powerless. Yet in sources such as Plato' s *Republic*, power is clearly linked with providing energy for individual growth and development in the creation of good for society. Some feminist writers refer to this as *empowering*—perhaps to avoid the negative connotation of power. The concept of power is treated from so many perspectives it is not always clear how it has been or should be used in the study of social structures and role behavior. At the simplest level, power may be viewed from a zero-sum perspective: There is only a fixed amount of power and if one person has it then the other does not. At the same basic level, power can be viewed as a resource that can be created and enlarged without taking it away from others—the idea of empowering. The reader will find that much of the following discussion reflects the first view more than the second.

The discussion of Marxist writers about organizational social structures as a context for understanding role behavior admits to some problems. The concern of this school of thought is largely with broad societal issues. Since, however, some of these writers take issue with concepts such as technological determinism of organizational structure and processes (Edwards, 1974), and provide additional notions about social structure (e.g., class), they are referred to here. Their ideology provides an alternative way of understanding role behavior in organizations.

Marx's thesis that the relationship of workers and capitalist employers or managers is necessarily antagonistic is the thesis of a number of works that have implications for the study of intraorganizational behavior (Ehrenreich & Ehrenreich, 1975). Since capitalist employers largely define the work to be done and the means of producing work, they must seek ways of coordinating work and assuming that workers are productive in ways that will produce profit (Edwards, 1979). It should be noted that while many health care institutions are nonprofit in a legal sense, they must frequently produce profits for dominant coalitions in the form of large incomes and prestige not shared by unskilled, and many skilled workers. Thus, while under norms of rationality work flow and work design may be a function of technology (Thompson, 1967), work design and structures may equally well be a function of the best way of controlling the behavior of workers and of achieving the highest return for an investment of resources. To take a familiar example from the industrial world: the building of every car requires the same basic technology; the choice of clustering workers to build much of one Volvo versus building a Ford on an assembly line is a choice with substantially different impacts on role behavior of workers and managers. Similarly, the division of the staff physician's tasks among interns, residents, and fellows in a teaching hospital versus the staff physician's tasks in a nonteaching hospital results in different role expectations of doctors by patients and other staff members. Such task allocation has a distinct influence on what is considered "doctors' work" in each setting and thereby influences who is allowed or expected to do what work.

The control of the proletariat or working class would, in Marx's analysis, lead to the formation of a revolutionary class to overthrow the controlling class through joint worker resistance. Friedman (1977) proposed that Marx did not anticipate how capitalists would co-opt worker groups. Rather than seeing workers as being an homogeneous class, one sees that there are greater and lesser degrees of resistance to management control and divisions among workers. A means of controlling workers and creating divisiveness is by exercising different means of control—direct control and control via responsible autonomy (Friedman, 1977). The former is parallel to bureaucratic control discussed in the rational paradigm. The latter is control via according special status, authority and responsibility and co-opting workers to the ideology of the organization—for example, "good patient care."

Ehrenreich and Ehrenreich (1975) proposed a similar thesis using hospital workers as an example. They suggested that nurses and the new allied health professionals are an advantage to hospital administrators and physicians because they take pride in their craft, identify with members of their own group, and can be trusted "to adhere to the ethics and standards of [their] profession in any situation (1975, p. 50). These authors argued that less-skilled workers may be alienated by their fragmented work, identify with other workers in the institution, unite around grievances, and require close supervision. They pointed out that this creates two classes of workers often reinforced by class differences, income, color, and sex. These differences, they contend, protect the physicians' monopoly over the scientific basis of practice and administrators' control over establishing their own priorities for use of resources. Therefore, divisiveness among the working class enhances the interests of the controlling elite.

The co-opting of professional workers by organizations may be achieved through capitalist control of ends and not the means of production. Derber (1983) considered the possible outcomes of dependent employment for an increasing number of professionals in the post-industrial era. He predicted that professionals in science and science-based technologies may become directly controlled by capital or be replaced by advanced machine technology, causing them to behave in ways and assume roles like those of industrial workers. They may, alternately, interject the values and ideologies of managers and owners, forming a new kind of working class not dealt with in classical Marxist writing. A study of changes in physician role expectations and role modification as physicians move increasingly into corporate structures with predominantly nonphysician boards and well-prepared administrators should provide a rich source of data for Marxist scholars interested in ideological and technical proletarianization.

Marxist writers, then, view most social structures as ways of controlling the means and ends of production and see them as simply mechanisms of capitalist control. In this view, the power of health care providers to control their practice is possible only to the extent that workers comply with the prevailing ideology of the dominant classes in the organization or industry. The role behavior of the skilled, unskilled, and management classes are differentiated from one another, each having its own source of control. The greatest control is held by the managerial (dominant) class because of its increasing control over the means of production. For example, the growth in costly machine technology reduces to some extent physicians' former level of control and results in a greater dependency of physicians on organizations with the capital to afford the machines and personnel to support medical technology. A Marxist perspective may be helpful in suggesting sources of potential role conflict and strain that are attributable to class differences and control by dominant groups. The exclusion of workers from the doing of purposeful, self-controlled work is seen as a major source of class conflict.

Informal Organizations. Another view of organizational members is that of active individuals and coalitions with their own base of power. Although there are many contributors to this line of thinking, only several will be discussed here.

Writers of the Hawthorne studies provided the earlier work on the concept of *informal organization* (Roethlisberger & Dickson, 1939). The impact of the informal group on the behavior of group members is one of the more familiar aspects of group influence in the organizational behavior literature. The status positions of group leader, fringe status, out status, and primary group status have been identified and studied and have contributed to an understanding of the role of informal organization within the organization. The informal group is generally seen as a group affiliated around common interests and friendships (Sayles & Strauss, 1966). However, as can be seen in the original Hawthorne data, these groups develop a self-interest, customs, and so on, that fly in the face of technological or other forms of determinism. The organizational power of such groups is mentioned here because such groups gain power in the organization.

Why and when do some groups or individuals have more power than others? From a rational perspective one might respond in terms of legitimate power (authority) knowledge of work processes, or both, not held by others. There are alternate responses as, for instance, bargaining. Bargaining by role incumbents and collectivities is a subject for both economic (Chamberlain, 1955) and sociologic theorists (Blau, 1964). Bacharach and Lawler (1980) provide a theory of bargaining power based on the notion that dependence is the central concept in an understanding of bargaining relationships. Some degree of dependence is necessary for bargaining to occur. "Bargaining implies a conflict of interest, but more important, it implies a conflict of interest over goals that no party can achieve without taking the other into account" (Bacharach & Lawler, 1981, p. 79). The authors go on to develop a series of propositions about how different types and amounts of dependence affect various aspects of the bargaining process. They point out that the use of punitive tactics, bluffs, and power in bargaining relationships are constrained by certain situational conditions, thus affecting bargaining power. They also argue that bargaining behavior is influenced less by commitment to the objective magnitude of outcomes, such as a salary negotiation of a certain size, than by the importance of the outcome to bargainers. This concept of importance of outcome may explain why under certain conditions a collective bargaining group appears to be heavily committed to a negotiated item that has less objective value than something they are willing to give up. Thus, role behavior under bargaining conditions is likely to be influenced by mutual dependency and importance of outcomes of bargaining.

Bacharach and Lawler assert that their theory of bargaining power is applicable at all levels of organizational and interorganizational interaction. The theory may be useful for considering such issues as role making, role taking, and role conflict under conditions of mutual dependency. To the extent that role modification of a health provider's role can be conceptualized as an outcome to be bargained for, the theory of bargaining power provides a framework for behavioral analysis, and provides the potential for predicting outcomes. For example, the role making and role taking of a nurse practitioner in a rural area unable to recruit physicians may be much easier than in a physician-rich area because of the community dependency on the nurse for care and an absence of territorial issues. Indeed, this is reflected in federal health care reimbursement structures for physician extenders in physician underserved areas.

An extension of the theory of bargaining power has been made with respect to roles and role occupants suggesting that these elements of social structure may be subject to the general propositions of bargaining theory. We now turn to a researcher and theorist who explicitly links bargaining and social structure.

Bargaining and Social Structure. The negotiated order perspective proposed by Strauss (1978) focuses on organizational processes through which organizational arrangements are iteratively altered by organizational members. Using methods of study associated with grounded theory and observational data gathered in two psychiatric hospitals, Strauss and others (1964) identified the concept of negotiated order. This concept was employed to account for changes in social order through the enactment of a key process which has been underattended or ignored by rationalist organizational theorists who focus on such aspects of social order as efficiency, goals, and decision making.

Given his interactionist roots, it is not surprising that Strauss emphasized processes such as negotiation, coercion, manipulation, and persuasion as primary in analyzing social structures between organizations, systems, and nations. He argued that each negotiated order is developed within a negotiation context embedded in a structural context rooted, in turn, in a historical context (Strauss, 1978). Role occupants such as patients, significant others, and providers of care bring to a negotiation preexisting sets of structures that have been developed in earlier interactions or through prior socialization. These structural and historical contexts influence but do not define the present negotiation context. In addition, the products of negotiations such as "contracts, understandings, agreements, rules, and so forth all [have] temporal limits for eventually they [will] be reviewed, reevaluated, revised, revoked or renewed" (1978, p. 5). Thus it is incumbent on the researcher to relate current interactional consequences—for example, the current social structure—to the next round of interactions or structures (Strauss, 1978, p. 259).

Strauss, then, is the first theorist discussed in this chapter who explicitly counters the underlying assumption of the chapter. Until this point we have explicitly and implicitly examined the effects of social structure (independent variable) upon role behavior (dependent variable). The negotiated order perspective suggests, however, that social structure is, in a simplistic sense, a dependent variable. The processes such as negotiation and coercion by those assuming roles in organizational structures are the independent variables. In this view, social structure is the context for the interaction of role incumbents. It affects behavior, but it does not *effect* it.

Strauss's view of negotiated interaction of individuals and groups contributes to our understanding of actors' behavior. Unfortunately, the perspectives of the Marxists, the members of the structural–economic school of bargaining, and others coming from the political perspective (discussed below) have not expressly conceptualized that the *meaning* of symbols and actions to individuals has a (the?) major influence on actors' behavior. While social class, structure, power, and so on may be associated with role-related behavior, it is the meaning attributed to these factors that provides a rich source of variance in the behavior of organizational actors and, accordingly, should be studied.

The final perspective discussed under "politics within" is expressly political in nature. This political perspective of organizations is influenced by the more rational–political tension exemplified by the works of Simon, Cyert, and March discussed earlier in the chapter. However, these writers focused on the individual actor as the unit of analysis for studying power and control. For example, Pettigrew (1973) recognized the limited rationality of actors and the structural, environmental and other constraints affecting them. He emphasized, however, the volitional nature of individuals' behavior in organizations and its expression through groups. Zey-Ferrell and Aiken suggested that Strauss and Pettigrew share the idea that "actors continually negotiat[e] their situation within social settings" (1981, p. 119). Pettigrew (1973) went further to argue that the ability to negotiate one's situation is based upon having the power to impose one's will on other actors even when opposed. He used a broad definition of the sources of organizational power, both formal and informal, and emphasized that all power strategies (e.g., deceit) to attain and retain power must be the subject of an analysis of organizational power. Thus, actors exercise their will in different ways, in different groups, at different levels of the organization, for different purposes. He also assumed, contrary to Strauss, that actors do not consistently act out of self-interest and the wish for rewards, nor with full information about their situation.

The methods of research about power from the political perspective of individuals are consistent with this multidimensional view of actors, decisions, and the intended and unintended consequences of the decisions. An example of such a study can be found in the writing of Allison (1971) regarding the Cuban missile crisis. Allison presented the situation and then asked a series of questions to develop an inductive stance to the data as he focused on power and influence. While the questions raised may be generalizable to other situations, specific analyses and conclusions are clearly bound by a particular situation. For example, if one were to try to determine whether America would launch a nuclear attack, the potential answer would have to be developed in terms of the current actors and their salient issues at a particular time. However, for our purposes it is important only to note the suggestion that political issues and contexts are the major motivating aspects of actors' actions. History, rules, norms, and other elements contribute in varying degrees to actions. Finally, Allison concluded that these actions and decisions are not a result of a solution chosen to fit a problem, but of "compromise, conflict and confusion of officials with diverse interests and unequal influence" (1971, p. 163). Given this image of organizational actions and actors, the need for detailed studies of organizations is clear. Role behavior is thus predictable only in light of such situation-specific data.

In summary, the political perspective of the social structure of organizations adds what appears to be important addition to our understanding of the study of organizations, their environmental interactions, and the relationship of structure and role behavior.

ORGANIZATIONAL ANALYSIS AND ROLE BEHAVIOR

The point of view taken in this chapter is that the study of complex organizations and their environments provides understanding critical for the study of social behavior of organizational members. There are available a number of theories, frameworks, and empirical sources for the analysis of organizations. A variety of prospectives on organizational behavior have been reviewed and reduced here to a rational and a political view of organizations. From the rational perspective, the human actor is perceived to behave in a primarily deterministic fashion. From a political perspective the actor's behavior is primarily volitional or, at a minimum, not a function of benign, unitary goal-directed behavior imposed by the organization.

The development of theoretical concepts and the methods of testing these conceptualizations have moved in somewhat divergent paths. For example, the definition, measurement and testing of technology, goals, and structural characteristics, have tended to move beyond case studies and into comparative studies of organizations. Politically oriented analyses have tended to use organizations that exemplify critical concepts (as contrasted with a sample of organizations), historical explorations, and situational analyses in studying questions. Although it is inaccurate to say that rationalists use only quantitative approaches and politicists use only qualitative approaches, there is some accuracy in that characterization of empirical studies in each area.

Given the dichotomy suggested between the dominant and the critical paradigms of organizational analysis, is there any merit in considering *both* in the study of roles in organizations? I think there is.

First, the intention of research is to develop clearer notions about phenomena of interest and to add to our understandings. One problem with much of our research is that we seek to understand only one perspective through, for instance, testing one or several related hypotheses. An example of a general hypothesis related to nursing is: Differences in selected types of tasks and subunit structural variables effect differences in nurses' work performance and satisfaction with work (Calkin, 1980). A consequence of this researcher's approach was that when some staff in the less structured unit did not "comply" with the experimental manipulation of task and structure, she had to offer alternate explanations for the ensuing social behavior. An alternative approach to research about the behavior of people in organizations is to initially create a Hegelian dialectic between competing hypotheses. This notion was sparked by the work of Mitroff and Bonoma (1978) in their paper on psychological assumptions of decision makers in evaluation studies.

To return to the example, Calkin could have created a dialectic by stating an explicit alternate to her structural–functional hypothesis at the outset of the study, such as: Differences in work performance and satisfaction will be affected by the ability of workers to define and design their work. The study would then have been designed to collect data systematically to address both hypotheses. While such an approach clearly places greater demands on the researcher at the beginning of a study, it may have much greater payoff for organizational analysis. The retention of competing paradigms in research design and analysis is therefore helpful in broadening our understanding of organizational behavior.

A second reason for our consciously retaining competing paradigms is based on the assumption that no group of theorists has a corner on the market of truth. As one reads the rational goal paradigm literature, everyday observations made in ongoing organizations are left partially unexplained. Conversely, the study of negotiated order, bereft of some element of technological or structural determinism, does not seem to account for variances observed in hospitals and clinics.

Third, throughout the chapter it has been suggested that each of a number of perspectives provides the potential for better understanding role behavior in organizational settings. An example of using several views (e.g., cultural, structural) at the individual, professional group, and organizational levels can be found in Temkin-Greener's (1983) paper on teamwork. This able exploration of the reasons teamwork does not seem to work in health care organizations would be enhanced by using some of the perspectives noted above. A Marxist, for instance, would be hard pressed to ignore the dominant elite class of physicians and the nurse worker or perhaps the predominantly male physician class and the predominantly female nurses and the influence of such factors on team behavior. The use of competing paradigms in the study of role behavior in organizations provides, at the very minimum, a set of caveats as one reads single paradigm studies.

Finally, Hardy (see Chap. 1) concludes that neither the symbolic interactionist nor functionalist perspectives of role theory is sufficient to account for observed human behavior. In a similar fashion, no single perspective of the organizational context or single method of research is sufficient for grasping the complexity of organizations and the role behavior in them. More to the point, from a purely pragmatic perspective, the health provider who works in organizations is seriously hampered by assuming either general perspective to be an adequate reflection of reality.

7

Role Stress and Role Strain

Margaret E. Hardy and William L. Hardy

INTRODUCTION

When a social structure creates very difficult, conflicting, or impossible demands for occupants of positions within it, the general condition can be identified as one of role stress. As we shall see, role stress for one individual also results in ambiguous and discordant conditions for occupants of interdependent positions. Social structures form a vital part of the individual's environment; they are a major determinant of social behavior. In this chapter the primary focus is on the structural sources of role stress. Structural role theory is utilized to identify role problems. Merton (1957, 1976, p. 7), a structural theorist, has used a sociologic theory of ambivalence to describe structural stress. The theory does not address personality difficulties but rather refers to incompatible normative expectations, attitudes, beliefs, and behaviors assigned to a social position or set of status. The theory does not describe a feeling state nor is it related to specific types of personalities. Instead, the theory deals with the processes through which social structures generate the circumstances in which the ambivalence is embedded. The theory deals with the specific status or status set together with their associated roles. Merton goes on to propose that one source of stress may be the context of a particular status and another may have to do with the various functions of the status.

Role stress is located in the social structure; the source is primarily external to the individual. It may generate role strain (subjective feelings of frustration, tension, or anxiety) in people in a central role, and in their associated role partners. Not only may high levels of role strain disrupt social interaction, but it may also prevent goal attainment for a role system and its occupants.

Role strain may be managed in several ways. Among the options are redefining the role, redefining what is considered "adequate" role performance, reestablishing priorities within a role and among roles, role bargaining with role partners, and reduced interaction with role partners. Although such actions may minimize the strain for one person, these same actions may interfere with the activities of interdependent role occupants and thus can even jeopardize the goals of the related organization. In crisis-oriented settings such as health care organizations, the effect of role strain may lead to reduced quality of care and may even jeopardize lives. Furthermore, when role strain is prevalent, dissatisfied, tension-ridden health care workers may be drained of both energy and commitment to professional values and patient care.

As role stress and role strain are pervasive and potentially detrimental social conditions, it is important that health professionals have a basic understanding of them.

Because some stress is created by the social structure, it is to the advantage of the individual to be able to identify this type of stress. The potential impact of structural stress may be more easily modified than are other sources of stress, such as stress arising from interpersonal or intrapersonal sources. Different sources of stress dictate different actions to reduce the impact. Also, persons who have difficulty managing their role adequately because of structural stress may mistakenly attribute the problem to their own lack of ability. Their sense of failure may be reinforced by others who mistakenly mislabel them as having "personal problems." The knowledgeable role occupant should be able to identify structural stress and take action to reduce the impact of such stress. Otherwise, the stress-evoking structure could interfere with the role performance of the health professional or it could be primarily detrimental to a client.

Means of preventing or minimizing role stress may be necessary if either the health professional or client is to benefit from a role relationship. Existing research on role stress will be discussed in this chapter, and theory-based descriptions of ways of minimizing the stress will be discussed in the next chapter. A vital need exists, however, for research on specific health care and provider–client systems in which role stress exists. It is only when relevant research is generated from theory and research and findings are integrated into the theory that practitioners may have a sound scientific basis (in contrast to a hypothetical or mythical basis) from which to operate.

In this chapter, minimal use is made of loose descriptive accounts or literary opinion about role stress and role strain. Rather, generalizable research findings have been gleaned for inclusion. The majority of the studies cited have been conducted by social scientists, and the organizational focus is not always on health care systems. The generality and usefulness of the defined concepts and propositions, however, provide the basis for including them in a text for health care providers.

CONCEPTUALIZING STRESS IN A SYSTEMS FRAMEWORK

Our understanding of physical and biologic phenomena has been advanced by conceptualizing phenomena in terms of systems. Stress and strain have been conceptualized using such a framework and have been the basis for scientific progress in physics and engineering (Hook's law), biochemistry, and endocrinology (the work of Selye, 1955). A systems framework with a primarily mechanistic model has been useful in the physical sciences. An organic systems model has been useful in both the medical sciences and the social sciences. The utilization of systems theory as a metaphor may continue to provide insights and be a basis for organizing knowledge about social behavior. Societies, organizations, families and social groups have all been analyzed from a system's framework.

The term *strain* has been used in theoretical discussions of social systems (Bertrand, 1963; Good, 1960; Merton, 1957; Parsons, 1951), and relatively recently strain has been linked to stress in social systems (Hardy, 1978; Miller, 1971).

The systems perspective has been implicit in work on structural role theory. Explicit use of general systems theory makes it possible to identify a role system as a set of interrelated positions; included in this perspective are such ideas as roles, subroles, subsystems, suprasystems, boundary roles, and structural stress. The interactional processes involved include input, output, feedback, strain, and equilibrating mechanisms. The clear identification of stress and strain at the level of social systems moves our view beyond traditional research—which focused on stress at the physiological level within the individual. Role theory, which includes the concepts of stress and strain, may be a useful analytical tool for understanding all types of social relationships, including friends, work groups, family, and organizations. The formulation that role strain is directly related to role stress advances a contention from the system's framework.

The introduction of the construct of role stress utilized to study stress in the social structure follows logically from the stress–strain formulation. In addition, conceptualizing organizations as systems of interrelated positions and roles makes role stress and role strain relevant formulations for analyzing these systems.

The social systems perspective has a strong position in nursing research (Werley et al., 1976) and in some areas of medicine (Engel, 1970) and social work. In addition, it is central to the philosophic foundations of nursing. It is not suprising that the social systems perspective provides direction for curriculums.

Since roles connect individuals to society, it is understandable that from its early beginning role theory has been the subject of interdisciplinary theory and research. In the health sciences it is used as both a descriptive and an analytical tool for evaluating social behavior. Health care professionals interested in organizations, administration, and health care delivery systems use role theory to further understand their own function within the health care system. Others use it in clinical work to gain a fuller understanding of client problems. The theory is sufficiently general to be of use in a variety of contexts and domains. For health care providers such as nurses, the principal domains utilizing role theory include the client, nursing actions, and environment (Kim, 1983). Kim has discussed the importance of understanding the social context of provider–client interactions. Analysis of the role system in which the provider–client interaction takes place contributes to understanding the social context.

A major limitation of systems theory and therefore role theory is that both formulations contain only clusters of concepts and no theoretical statements. This means that systems (of roles) may be described (and this can be very useful), but the other goals of science—explanation and prediction—are not possible. Nevertheless, systems theory has been successful in providing a common vocabulary and a perspective for analyzing what otherwise might appear to be social chaos, and for developing a sense of understanding about social phenomena.

Role Stress Typology

The role stress typology is based on a role stress–role strain framework. The typology was generated by analyzing research on role occupants encountering major difficulties in meeting their role obligations. These role problems were initially analyzed in terms of role expectations—ambiguity, conflict, etc. Then other sources of role problems were considered, including the location of the role in the social structure, the inadequate resources of role occupants, and social context (Hardy, 1978). The classes in this typology are:

1. Role ambiguity—vagueness, lack of clarity of role expectations
2. Role conflict—role expectations are incompatible
3. Role incongruity—self-identity and subjective values grossly incompatible with role expectations (role transition and poor self-role fit)
4. Role overload—too much expected in time available
5. Role underload—role expectations are minimal and underutilize abilities of role occupant
6. Role overqualification—role occupant's motivation, skills, and knowledge far exceed those required
7. Role underqualification (role incompetence)—role occupant lacks the necessary resources (commitment, skill, knowledge)

There is need for sound research on all of these role problems. Although the primary focus in this chapter is on role stress of health care providers, the same sources of role stress need to be examined for clients.

Role stress research requires the development of operational definitions to measure role stress and role strain. The typology of types of role stress systematizes the research but any one of these problems could be quantified. For example, a Likert scale could be developed to measure role ambiguity; a Likert-type scale or a semantic differential scale could also be developed to measure role strain (Banda, 1985; Hardy, 1976).

Guided by the belief that activities of health professionals must be based upon sound knowledge of the phenomena they confront in their roles, an effort has been made to provide metatheoretical discussions along with substantive discussions of theory. We have developed this chapter to provide descriptions of the following topics:

1. Basic concepts, assumptions, and the contributions of symbolic interaction and social exchange theory to structural role theory
2. Conditions contributing to role strain of health care providers
3. The conceptualization of role stress and strain from the symbolic interaction and structural role theory perspectives
4. Further conceptualizing of role stress and role strain
5. Structural locations of role stress
6. Discussion of each type of stress (ambiguity, incongruity, etc.)
7. Analysis of adequate role performance and role competence

The next chapter deals with such means of managing role strain as problem solving, negotiation, and role bargaining.

BASIC CONCEPTS

The general discussion of role theory, scientific theory, the evolving nature of concepts, stages of theory development, and the emergence of systematic research with its empirical generalizations presented in Chapters 1 and 2 are highly relevant to this chapter. Some of the earliest discussions in the social sciences were of "problems between individuals and society."

Focused research on role conflicts initially used no specific, defined concepts; rather, it described conditions that now would be labeled role conflict. Later, specific concepts such as role consensus and lack of clarity in roles were introduced. Role conflict was used to refer to a variety of role problems and remained undefined for some time. Role conflict (inferred) in some of the structural literature identified norms which conflict with each other or with an individual's predispositions. The concepts used often describe role problems which have been constantly evolving.

At the Chicago School, Park, and later Stonequist were interested in the "marginal" man, a person who belongs to two cultures simultaneously and therefore really belongs to neither. The inherent conflicts were presented but not explicitly described. (The concept is still in the literature—see Reid, 1982; Wardwell, 1955). The structural writings focused on the dysfunctional aspects of organizations and social systems (Merton, 1957). Merton, extending Durkheim's (1951) ideas on anomie, focused on the instability of the system and the demoralized responses of persons. Merton saw a breakdown between the normative system and cultural values and goals so that persons could achieve goals only through deviance. This condition of anomie he described as a situation where there is a strain toward normlessness.

Anomie exists in a social system when there is a lack of clear-cut expectations. (Anomie was frequently used in 17th century theology to describe disregard for the law.) Anomie has been described in sociology as a psychological state in which persons feel demoralized; for these persons the norms are weak, ambiguous, and remote (McClosky & Schaar, 1965). Other structuralists developed the idea of alienation, which emphasized the rejection of social norms as a function of faulty socialization. Also, there may be only partial internalization of norms (Parsons & Shils, 1951). Focus is on social structures and the individual. Research has also been done in relation to alienation and work. The concern here is with job dissatisfaction, the extent to which work is meaningful, and whether a person can be self-directed. Powerlessness, a sense that powerlessness is wrong, and meaninglessness are often used as central measures of alienation (Seeman, 1953).

The continued interest in alienation and anomie reflects the ongoing struggle in coming to terms with the relationship of the individual to the social order or society. It may be that alienation is a problem for philosophers to work on whereas anomie is a problem for role theorists and researchers. The theoretical ideas of psychiatrists usually depicted alienation as the state of separation of self from experience. Most of the ideas that have been developed originated with the social theories of Hegel and Marx (see Lutz, 1982). Concern for subjective hostility toward society was implicit in psychoanalytic writings (Freud, 1949). The term has been used by the neopsychoanalytical psychiatrists fairly extensively, and with various referents. Fromm, for example, uses alienation to refer to lack of unity with others, whereas Horney is concerned with alienation from the real self (Erikson, 1956; Fromm, 1955; Horney, 1945.)

In general, the early role theory literature is difficult to analyze, given the diverse terms and definitions. The multidisciplinary nature of research on role compounds the difficulty in identifying relevant literature. This difficulty is perhaps more acute in the area of role stress where role problems have commanded the attention of scientists in both basic and applied fields. Although such diversity increases the complexity of the evolving theory of roles, it also adds to its richness and generalizability.

General Definitions

In this chapter attention is focused on a small *social unit*. A social unit is two or more persons engaged over time in a transaction, a productive social exchange, or a role relationship. The discussion generally focuses on a *dyad* or simple two-person role relationship in which there is an occupant of a focal position and an occupant of a counter position. If the focal person interacts with several persons in counter positions then the persons in these positions are termed the *role partners*.

Norms are rules that either prescribe or proscribe behavior. Norms are expectations, standards, or guidelines that suggest what a person "ought," "should," or "must" do as well as "ought not," "should not," or "must not" do, think, or feel. General social norms are acquired through the process of socialization. Role-specific norms are acquired in a similar manner. Socialization processes are lifelong processes. Change and acquisition of new roles are typical for adults. (See Chapter 4 on socialization and Chapter 9 on socialization into professions). Adherence to norms is positively sanctioned whereas violations are negatively sanctioned. Behavior is not simply compliance with external sanctions; it is strongly influenced by the internalization of norms. This internalization of norms is manifested by moral outrage at the misbehavior of others and by guilt following a personal transgression.

Negative sanctions are punishments for violations of norms. Punishments may include criticism, disapproval, and ostracism; sanctions are delivered either actually or symbolically by the group.

Positive sanctions are rewards or reinforcing acts for adherence to norms. These are social rewards such as social approval, liking, praise, and support; they, too, are delivered either actually or symbolically by the group. Social rewards may be among the most influential of rewards.

Sanctions, both positive and negative, are used in attempts to modify behavior and to maximize adherence to prevailing group norms or prescriptions. Although sanctions are generally external, they may be self-imposed. The degree and type of sanctioning depends upon the visibility of an act and the extent to which it is valued. A nurse, for example, would be more severely sanctioned for narcotic abuse than for unpolished shoes.

Social structures are positions and patterns of behavior woven into systematic and relatively enduring relationships. The structure partially determines the availability of social goals, the means for attaining these goals, and the type and extent of sanctions permissible and employed. One's location in the structure greatly influences the power one has, the access one has to valued resources, and the general respect one receives from others and accordingly gives to one's self. The ideas on self-respect are largely based on the early work of William James (1890) on self-pretensions, which became known as self-esteem.

A *position* (status or office) is a location in a social structure. Occupants of positions are collective categories of persons who differ from the general public in some specific shared attribute or behavior. The basis for the differentiation depends upon the interest of the researcher. For example, individuals may be differentiated on the basis of age, race, occupation, or on some other characteristic such as position (i.e., staff nurse, head nurse, or supervisor). Social systems usually are differentiated into several positions which are often hierarchical. Thus, even a simple triad system (such as nurse, physician, and client) includes different positions. Occupants of these three positions will likely exhibit different behaviors. Also, expectations held by an occupant of one position for the occupants of the other positions depend on what the other position signifies to him or her. A hierarchy is identified in terms of the relative influence that exists between the role occupants. It is a ranking of persons, often in terms of authority and responsibility.

The term *role* has had exceptionally diverse usage. It has been used to indicate expectations (prescriptions, proscriptions, or demands), descriptions, evaluations, behaviors, and actions. *Role* is also used to refer to overt and covert processes, to refer to self, and to refer to other (Thomas & Biddle, 1979, p. 29). The term is commonly used in the literature to refer to both the expected and the actual behaviors associated with a position. In this chapter the more specific referents employed with role, such as role expectations or role behavior, are utilized for the sake of clarity.

A *role occupant* (role incumbent) is a person who holds a position within the social structure.

A *status set* is the complex of distinct positions held by an individual.

Role expectations (obligations, demands) are position-specific norms that identify the attitudes, behaviors, and cognitions required and anticipated for a role occupant.

Role performance (role behavior or role enactment) is differentiated behavior or action relevant to a specific position.

Role identity is the individual's interpretation of role expectations.

A *focal position* is the position under consideration or study, while actor is the occupant of this position.

Subroles refer to the different roles associated with a focal position. Thus, a nurse may be a care giver, a researcher, an administrator, or a teacher. These subroles may be equally important parts of the focal role or one may dominate. For example, the administrative role will be most prevalent for nurse managers.

A *role partner* (counter role occupant) is a person who, while occupying an interdependent position with the occupant of the focal position, holds role expectations for the focal occupant. Role partners may enact the same role as the incumbent (for example, staff nurse with staff nurse) or role partners may enact reciprocal roles (for example, staff nurse with head nurse).

A *role set* is the constellation of relationships with the role partners of a particular position (Merton, 1957, p. 369) (see Figure 1). A role set comprises all of an actor's role partners.

Role stress, external to a role occupant, is a social structural condition in which role obligations are vague, irritating, difficult, conflicting, or impossible to meet. Role stress is a characteristic of the social system, not the person in the system.

In contrast, *role strain* is a subjective state of emotional arousal in response to the external conditions of social stress. It may be experienced by a role

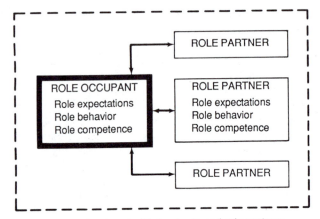

Figure 1. A role set with focal role and role partners.

occupant as an increased level of awareness, general emotional arousal, or such feelings as distress, anxiety, or frustration.

The concepts of structural role theory provide a means of describing a social system in terms of a system of roles, but they do not provide an explanation nor a basis for predicting what is likely to occur. Clearly, prediction beyond what is common sense cannot be provided by a set of concepts alone.

Symbolic interaction adds a different set of concepts and a variety of processes. The latter have provided insightful descriptions of an unusual array of social processes such as identity bargaining, self-presentation, altercasting, strategic interaction, deference, and demeanor. Implicit in the descriptions of many social processes is the notion of social exchange. This orientation is evident from such terms as setting the role price, role bargaining, the norm of reciprocity, negotiation, and a negotiated social order—all of which assume that social behavior involves social exchange processes. The definitions of a social act (symbolic interaction) and an exchange relation are identical (see Chapter 2).

Figure 2 depicts the combination of symbolic interaction and the structural role theory perspective.

The notions of bargaining and barter, inherent in social exchange theory, were described under family theory in the first sociological textbook, which was authored by Thomas and Park. Not surprisingly, the work included concepts and processes that are fundamental in symbolic interaction. Social exchange theory received major development in the 1960s and is now sufficiently well formulated to make explanation and prediction possible. It is sufficiently comprehensive to relate to a wide variety of social phenomena and sufficiently well developed to explain and predict many role-related phenomena. It takes as a minimum unit of analysis the dyad (a synonym for a role relationship).

Symbolic interaction provides a cognitive orientation which complements social exchange theory. Social exchange itself is sufficiently abstract to incorporate both structural and symbolic interaction role concepts. Symbolic interaction adds to the richness of social exchange theory and, in addition, makes it possible to explicate the meaning and further develop some of the central concepts—reward, value, and resources, for example. Use of these concepts increases the

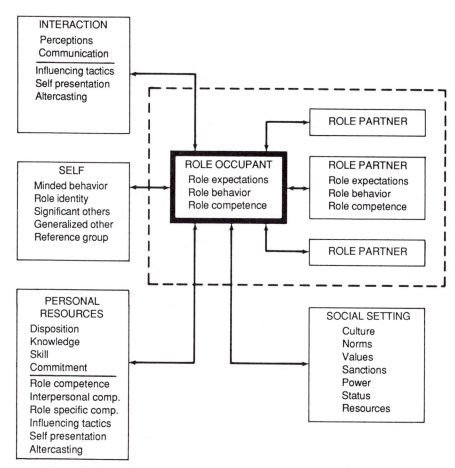

Figure 2. Inter-relating symbolic interaction and structural theories. The broken enclosure represents concepts from structural theory; the remainder enclosures represent symbolic interaction concepts.

predictive power of social exchange theory. Much fuller illustration of social exchange theory (Blau, 1964; Cook, 1987; Emerson, 1962; Homans, 1974) and the related theory of social equity may be found in Walster, Walster, and Berscheid, (1982); Messick and Cook, (1983); and Turner, (1986). Social exchange theory, as a theoretical formulation, has been developed extensively only since 1960.

In this chapter, roles are conceptualized in terms of social exchange theory; that is, they are seen as relationships in which actors provide each other with needed resources. The resources may be acquired or exchanged through negotiation, and the outcome of the negotiation is conditional on interpersonal competence—a concept from symbolic interaction theory. Relationships are initially assessed in terms of the relative costs and rewards, i.e., the fairness of the resources exchanged. The social exchange framework (Blau, 1964; Emerson, 1962, 1976, 1981; Homans, 1974; Thibault & Kelley, 1959) makes use of concepts from economics and operant psychology to analyze social interactions. Interaction is analyzed in terms of rewards and costs (i.e., the positive and negative aspects), equity (sense of fairness), and outcomes. Power, conflict, conflict resolution, cooperation, communication, resources, altruism, and negotiation are some of the relevant concepts of social exchange theory. As in role theory, the unit of analysis is a social unit consisting of two or more persons; the relationship is conceptualized as a social exchange.

The social exchange framework, in addition to introducing some new and useful concepts, provides a basis for evaluating dynamic coping methods, such as bargaining, utilized by persons confronted with role problems. The linking of role theory to the social exchange framework increases the descriptive, explanatory, and predictive capabilities available for the study of social interactions.

Derived Concepts

The following concepts and processes were developed by combining social exchange theory with certain role concepts. These core notions may be extended to other areas of role theory. This combination increases the potential for describing the dynamics of role stress and role strain more fully and accurately than is possible using role theory alone.

A *role exchange* is a type of social exchange in which two or more role occupants contribute specific role resources (knowledge, skills, and behaviors) to generate a final product. This product is different from any product that a single role occupant could create.

Resources are sets of attributes, such as education, experience, and status, as well as particular values, motivation, abilities, knowledge, skills, and behaviors. An important resource is interpersonal competence. Specific role resources are required of occupants of certain positions in a social system. A role occupant's resources are of general value to the role system and of particular value to the role partner(s).

An *output* is the joint product resulting from the transaction of two or more actors.

An *outcome* is the set of rewards an actor receives from a social exchange. The nature of such rewards may be social, such as praise and approval; personal, such as a feeling of pride and self confidence; or material, such as a prize, money, or income.

Role competence, developed through socialization processes, refers to the capacity for adequate role performance. Role performance involves two or more persons who take into account the ongoing nature of the interdependent relationship, their own goals, the goals of the other, and the intended output or joint product of the relationship. Role competence requires interpersonal competence, such as role-taking, communication, relational competence such as skill at role bargaining, an adequate repertoire of lines of action, and a cognitive sensitivity.

ASSUMPTIONS

A basic assumption employed in this chapter is that persons seek out problematic situations on which to use their skills and knowledge. They do not attempt to eliminate all tension and anxiety, but rather may actively seek tension. This idea is in keeping with the literature on symbolic interaction, mastery, competence

(Smith, 1968; Weinstein, 1969) effectance motivation (White, 1959), and self-actualization (Allport, 1955; Maslow, 1954). The approach suggests that persons are predisposed to actualizing their own potential while interacting effectively with the social environment. Socialization is the fundamental process for facilitating the development of interpersonal competence and competence in role relationships. Clearly, the terms mastery and competence imply that role problems or role stress are conditions that will be approached as problems requiring solutions. Mastery has been proposed as an essential concept for the analysis of stress (Howard & Scott, 1965).

Another fundamental assumption based on symbolic interaction theory is that conflict is necessary for progress and developing consensus in society. Similarly, conflict or problematic situations facilitate broadening an individual's perspective. Accordingly, role problems are not necessarily abnormal and undesirable.

Role theorists have investigated conditions that make role enactment difficult and that adversely affect role occupants. The stress–strain analogy and the frameworks of social systems, social exchange, and mastery are utilized in this chapter to aid in the understanding of these conditions.

An underlying assumption made in employing the separate terms of role *stress* and role *strain* is that a stress–strain analogy can be utilized to examine role problems and their consequences. An appraisal of the literature on stress makes it apparent that this term has been used often and in different ways by physicists, biologists, and social scientists.

Stress has been used to describe conditions producing stress reactions, that is, the sequence of events beginning with cause (stressor) and ending with a stress response. It has also been used to describe a general field of study (McGrath, 1972). In the biological sciences, the social sciences, and in the health-related literature, the term stress is used vaguely and inconsistently. It has been used, however, with precision and consistency in the fields of physics and engineering where it originated. In these fields, stress refers to an external force that produces a deformation or strain.

Strain is a temporary or permanent alteration in the structure of the object subjected to stress. Although the use of the engineering analogy has been criticized because it ignores the function of perception and cognition (Kahn, 1970), some writers have conceptualized stress in such a way that the major focus is not on cognitive processes (Kuhn, 1974; Mechanic, 1972; Miller, 1972). One of these theoretical approaches, which in part avoids the question of the importance of individual perception and cognition, is general systems theory. In this interdisciplinary framework (Berrien, 1968; Buckley, 1967; Kuhn, 1974; Miller, 1972), stress (Kuhn, 1974; Miller, 1971, 1972) and strain (Miller, 1971, 1972) have been defined in a manner compatible with the engineering analogy (Kuhn, 1974; Miller, 1972). Drawing upon both the engineering analogy and general systems theory, one may define stress as an external force that disturbs the internal stability or steady state of a system. The resulting disturbance may be termed strain. The use of the engineering and systems theory analogies for the study of disturbances in role relationships is valuable because they make use of well-established relationships and of concepts applicable to many situations.

The general stress–strain formulation is that a problematic social condition (stress) leads to an individual internal response (strain). The subjective response of the individual is termed strain; stress refers to the demands or external pressures. If the problematic condition is one of conflicting, confusing, irritating, or impossible role demands, the condition is one which produces role stress. If the role occupant exposed to these demands experiences tension or frustration, this is a condition of role strain.

CONDITIONS CONTRIBUTING TO ROLE STRAIN OF HEALTH CARE PROVIDERS

Role stress, including role conflict, role ambiguity, role incongruity, and role overload, is probably more prevalent today than ever before. It is reasonable to assume that such prevailing social conditions as rapid social change with concurrent inadequate adult socialization, rapid change in social organizations, and accelerated technology contribute to numerous and extensive role stresses and strains undermining role competence. Communication and social interaction markedly decrease when role stress and role strain are present (Cooper & Payne, 1978; Kasl, 1978). The conditions contributing to role stress are discussed next.

Undermining Role Competence: Socialization Deficits

Socialization (see Chap. 4) is a complex process directed at the acquisition of appropriate attitudes, cognitions, emotions, values, motivations, skills, knowledge, and social patterns necessary to cope with the physical, cultural, and social environment. Socialization is a continuous process occurring from birth to death. Although persons may have basic professional education and socialization, this socialization is not always sufficient to meet the demands of professional careers. Specifically, there is a lack of adequate socialization for roles and status changes for those in the health professions. Medical and nursing students, for example, expend considerable time and energy developing the knowledge, skills, and attitudes deemed necessary for the acquisition of professional roles (Becker et al., 1961; Olesen & Whittaker, 1968). The basic professional socialization, however, has been found inadequate for preparing these students for moving into the work force (Kramer, 1969, 1970). The self-sustaining and self-actualizing process of socialization should be, for health professionals as for all adults, continuous. Career advancement usually requires increasing resources and gaining of expertise.

Within the health professions, explicit anticipatory socialization seldom occurs after the initial professional socialization period. Continuing education programs available for health professionals offer informational updates but rarely address the problems associated with changes in position or status. Movement into a new position, such as from staff nurse to assistant head nurse, is likely to be associated with feelings of uncertainty and role ambiguity. By failing to sufficiently socialize the professional who is moving into a new position, the health care system builds in role stress and thus contributes to role strain. It is uncommon to find nursing supervisors, clinical nurse specialists, members of interdisciplinary health teams, or assistant professors in the health professions, for example, being offered programs that will increase their professional and interprofessional competence prior to their taking occupancy of higher level or new positions within the health care system.

Transitions into new positions or roles would probably be associated with less role strain for these new incumbents, as well as for their co-workers, if the incumbents-to-be were provided with programs designed to facilitate modification and expansion of existing attitudes, knowledge, values, and behaviors appropriate for their new roles. Role transitions might then occur with greater ease and with a greater probability of successful performance. Unfortunately, many individuals moving into new positions in the health care field must rely almost entirely upon their basic education experience, intuition, and on-the-job orientation. Assuming this is the typical pattern, the higher ranking and less traditional positions in the health care system may well be occupied by persons who have received little specific preparation for these positions. These individuals are expected to meet new role obligations in positions with expanded role sets within relatively complicated social networks. To the extent that socialization for roles is deficient, role problems and strain are likely to be prevalent.

Role Differentiation and Specialization: New Roles and Expertise

A social organization such as a hospital may be defined as a system of roles. Organizations are constructed systems designed to achieve special goals. They are subject to relatively rational and purposeful change. Part of the existing social structure may be altered to meet changes in organizational goals or to facilitate achievement of existing goals. Roles in these organizations have become well-established or institutionalized over time. Such roles may be modified through the processes of role differentiation and specialization. Changes in the complementary characteristics of a system of roles are stimulated by technology, increased organizational complexity, and new output or product demands. Role differentiation involves the reallocation of existing role expectations to new positions. Specialization refers to the increased expertise and complexity of activities required of role incumbents to define and fulfill the role requirements of emerging positions. The role expectations associated with these positions and roles are initially unclear and ill-defined. New and emerging roles typically are ambiguous until such roles become well established. In a rapidly changing society, the processes of role differentiation with specialization and the creation of new roles is likely to be an ongoing process—and an ongoing source of role ambiguity.

Changes in Organization and Delivery of Health Care

An important general condition contributing to the proliferation and significance of role problems is the rapidity with which social organizations are changing. In the health care system, for example, rapid changes have occurred since 1980 in the size, structure, and geographic location of subsystems. Decentralization, emergence of new health and wellness centers, holistic clinics, and lay-based organizations have evolved to meet the needs of various consumer groups. Changes have also been occurring within medicine suggesting some limits to its monopoly over health care.

Women's groups have been active in demedicalizing many "normal" bodily processes and teaching women to deal with these themselves. Women's clinics, alternative birthing centers, and family planning and abortion clinics are some of the new care clinics reflecting the trend of women toward looking after their own bodies. They are often run by nontraditional (noncredentialed) personnel, nurses, nurse–midwives, and nurse practitioners (Wilson & Neuhauser, 1982). Other independent health centers have developed which focus on the health and wellness of the whole person. Often clinics in urban health centers and neighborhoods, free standing, and rural family clinics are run by lay persons with or without professional (medical and nursing) consultation.

Self-Care Activities: Redefining Provider–Client Roles

Self-care activities have supplemented and substituted for medical care. (Some would say that medical care has, in the past, attempted to replace self-care with medical care.) Levine and associates (1976) cite various research studies that have identified that 75 percent or more of health care is now undertaken without professional intervention. Self-care is prominent at the primary care level. On the other hand, several research surveys of primary physicians have concluded that approximately 25 percent of visits to the primary medical practitioner could be treated through self-care (Levine et al., 1976). The place that health professionals (other than physicians) have in these activities is unclear.

The economic demands of health care have prompted interest among epidemiologists and health care planners to attempt to assess the economics of self-care. (Assessing the value of medical care itself is very difficult.) An analysis of life expectancy and mortality trends leads one to the conclusion that medical care has had only modest effects (Levine et al., 1976). No useful data base for assessing the economic value of self-care is yet available.

Economic Control: Redefining Patient-Provider Roles

Recent economic controls placed on hospitals are also changing the nature of the health care delivery system. The influence of health insurance on health care is another factor contributing to changes in the delivery of services. For example, surgery is now being done through ambulatory day surgery clinics. In the past, patients having this surgery would have been admitted to the hospital the day before surgery and discharged 3 or 4 days after. The creation of day surgery clinics has been a response of hospital administrations to the controls placed on economic expenditures for health care.

Persons receiving surgery through these centers have minimal contact with nurses and physicians. The influence such centers have had on changing the role expectations and behavior of nurses and physicians is still unclear. Just as the short stay of these patients in hospital has created a new patient population for staff nurses, it has also created a problem (and an opportunity) for community health nurses. These patients are often sicker than the typical patient for whom these nurses previously cared. Changes in role expectations are likely to occur as nurses work with clients whose role behaviors are demanding and different—in hospitals, in day surgeries, and in the community. The creation of a "new" total-care nurse may be a major outcome.

Advances in Technology and Information-Related Sciences

Another important factor, the rapid advancement of technology, contributes to the creation of role problems and introduces its own set of social difficulties. In work settings, for example, the portable computer is being used for recording, thus replacing much handwritten or manually typed work. With professional persons now using computers extensively for monitoring research and clinical activities as well as for developing scholarly ideas, the nature of the work of health providers is changing markedly.

Rather than tending to alienate nurses and physicians, computers are actually beginning to provide increased control over work activities. Personal involvement with computer-based activities requires no technical go-between; thus, the independence of clinicians has been increasing. The instant availability of a working clinical data base and the ability to transmit this information via telephone lines to the office and to others working on the same topic increases the potential for longitudinal collaborative research. The development of computer-resident informational data bases on topics health care providers work on increases ready access to important knowledge. Such information systems, treated as consultant systems, could provide not only factual knowledge but also decision-making capacity. Thus a clinician could determine, for example, how long wound healing in a diabetic patient might take given circulatory complications of an identified type and level. Also, the probabilities of wound infection if the patient were kept in the hospital or at home might be calculated, as well as the relative costs in each instance.

There is an obvious inherent role stress present for those professionals who are not capable of adjusting to such technology for extending their work potential.

In industry and hospitals, self-regulating and self-monitoring equipment is now commonplace. Employee fears that they would be replaced by such technology have been proven largely unfounded. In many instances, employees have had to become more involved and specialized to run and monitor the equipment. Technology in intensive care units, in particular, has changed the roles of nurses, not replaced them. Intensive-care and cardiac-care nurses have become more specialized as the new technology changes their functions.

Another very recent use of computers by nurses has been to try to systematize patient data bases to reflect the nursing care that patients actually receive. Computerized patient data bases using the medical model and medical diagnoses are becoming more common. The current frontier in technology is clinical decision making, with artificial intelligence systems beginning to be developed. Although, presumably, technologic advances contribute to patient health and welfare, it is likely that these very advances also augment role problems for health care workers as expectations expand and the number of role partners increases. Rapid growth in knowledge and the means of acquiring and transmitting knowledge is a particular area of technology that will affect all areas and professions in health care. The development of knowledge and information data bases that can be accessed readily via computer makes scientific knowledge more accessible than it has ever been before. Information from computer-accessed data bases can be used by professionals to make better-informed decisions. The future use of expert systems will be dependent on a willingness of professionals to acquire new values, skills, and knowledge.[1]

A Solution to Maldistribution of Physicians in the 1960s: New Problems of Role Stress in the 1980s

In the late 1960s new role positions were created to complement and supplement physician care. This was to be the solution to the problem of maldistribution of physicians in the country, the problem arising when particular segments—usually rural areas and inner cities—were underserved by physicians. Several federal programs were created to develop practitioners to serve in such areas. One developed nurse practitioners with master's degrees, whereas the other developed physician extenders (physician assistants).

Independent Practitioners in Nursing. The nurse practitioner program was introduced following a very successful pediatric nurse practitioner project in Colorado (1967). Meanwhile, within graduate nursing educational programs, students began enlisting in Clinical Nurse Specialist programs so as to develop an in-depth clinical focus.

Physician Extenders: Physician Assistants. At the about same time, a program was initiated in medicine to extend the work capabilities of physicians by producing assistants. Graduates of these programs were expected to practice routine medical work or to practice in rural areas; travel time to such areas generally made for very inefficient use of physicians' time. The first physician assistant program, started at Duke University in 1966, has served as a model for subsequent programs. It is a 9-month formal and 15-month clinical training regimen. Another program, at the University of Washington, enrolls medical corpsmen into a 3-month university program followed by a 12-month preceptorship (Wilson & Neuhasser, 1982).

The addition of these two clinical specialist practitioner groups has added to the general role stress in the health care system. Both role ambiguity and role conflict arise for the graduates of the two programs—nurse clinicians and physician assistants—as they struggle to define their roles and the boundaries of their work. An added problem is that the two groups are sponsored by different professions.

Now, however, another factor portends further complications for the nurse practitioner and physician assistant roles: there presently is an oversupply of physicians which may be increasing. Eliminating nurse practitioners from the medical realm is one way of making it possible, in fact necessary, to employ more physicians. The high demand of consumers for female practitioners, at least in health maintenance organizations (HMOs), is also a factor that is complicating the provision of health care by male physicians. Thus, role stress appears to have increased recently as medicine deals with the current problems created by the economic system and by the profession itself.

The economic trends starting in the 1980s together with the rapid changes in the health care system in response to tight monetary controls have added to the uncertainty and ambiguity of the newer roles in health care. There has never been so much uncertainty as to the future of nurse practitioners and physician assistants as at present. Studies reviewed by Weinberger, Greene, Mamlin, and Jerin (1981) have identified that nurse practitioners provide safe, high quality, and effective care. Other research they review consistently identifies that patients have favorable attitudes towards nurse practitioners. In a study of nurse practitioners in HMOs, patients were found to prefer care by physician–nurse practitioner teams to total care by one provider or the other (Beiner & Bennett, 1982). Another study of three HMOs (considered to be representative of the 300 in the country) examined the cost effectiveness of nurse practitioners. The authors conclude from their own and other studies that HMOs do and should continue to rely on nurse practitioners to provide significant amounts of care.

The cost effectiveness of nurse practitioner–physician teams over solo physicians has been strongly supported by research (Weiner, Steinwachs, & Williamson, 1986). Physician attitudes towards nurse practitioners are favorable and the nurses' role is seen as complementary to the physician's (Davidson & Lauver, 1984). A recent administrative response to the current difficult economic conditions has been to replace nurse practitioners with physician assistants. Thus, conflict between the two groups—nurse practitioners and physician assistants—seems to have reappeared. This may be primarily a reflection of professional struggles over territory and professional management conflicts.

Changes in Medical Control: Deprofessionalization of Medicine

Recent theorizing on the nature of the professions has included the notion that there is a change underway in the professional status and social control of medicine. The basic thesis is that professions such as medicine are beginning to lose their position of prestige and trust. Haug's work, including subsequent publications on consumerism in medicine and the challenges to physician authority (Haug & Lavin, 1983) is central to this thesis, according to Freidson (1984). Haug has identified the sources of erosion of respect and prestige as being related to the monopoly over a special body of knowledge—a monopoly which is no longer complete. Much of the knowledge is now accessible to the lay public through various publications, but more specifically through the use of computer knowledge bases.

Another factor is that a positive professional image emphasizes the altruistic motive rather than a self-serving motive; nevertheless, medicine demands the power to set its own rules. Haug contends that the prestige and authority of the profession is being undermined by a skeptical and highly knowledgeable clientele. The greater educational level of consumers and the highly specialized work of some require the physician to negotiate where formerly he need not have. In some cases the clientele may be even more informed of the physician's complex body of knowledge than is the physician himself. In addition, physicians more and more depend on other specialists for knowledge and skill that once was found only in their own domain. Thus, with all of these factors, the authority of the physician is being eroded.

Freidson (1984), commenting on this deprofessionalization thesis, notes that it is largely based on the self-help and consumer movement as well as the women's movement of the 1970s. But community groups traditionally are short-lived; thus the reality of a real, long-term deprofessionalization, Freidson concludes, is in doubt. Furthermore, he notes that despite the deprofessionalization thesis, medicine still maintains its prestige and authority as well as its monopoly over a special area of expertise. Freidson reviews how medicine has managed to maintain control and autonomy despite the increased location of physicians within bureaucracies and the formalization of social control through court antitrust decisions that competition cannot be limited and through malpractice suits. An important additional factor, according to Freidson, is medicine's identification with universities and the creation of a knowledge elite. This group influences national policies and serves in an advisory capacity to state and federal governments. Medicine's influence with this elite may forestall major erosion of its role.

With the varied internal sources of turmoil in the medical profession, pressure from consumers for more "relevant" and better care, with qualified practitioners whose roles may be subject to redefinition, and pressures from the economic system to control expenses, the traditionally relatively stable health care system is in a major state of flux. The resulting role stress may produce a major redefinition of roles and functions for several groups of health care providers.

BEGINNING NOTIONS RELATED TO PROBLEMATIC ROLE ENACTMENT

Role stress and role strain are the focus of this section. **Role stress** is used as a general term subsuming role ambiguity, role conflict, role incongruity, role overload or underload, and role under qualification and incompetence (see specific definitions). **Role strain** is defined as felt difficulty in meeting one's role obligations (Goode, 1960). Role strain—one's subjective reaction to impossible role expectations, be they contradictory, incompatible, or excessive—is something to which most people can easily relate. The prevalence of role strain may account for the exceptional interest in the topic. Role stress is generally conceptualized as a source of tension, distress, poor job performance, and reduced involvement in the specific organization. Certainly structural stress takes its toll on individuals and on the efficiency and effectiveness of organizations.

Role stress is important to employees of organizations and to clinical practitioners; however, the literature is difficult to synthesize. The vast body of empirical work on stress tends to be atheoretical. The studies are eclectic and a variety of variables are used—the selection of variables is determined by the experience or interest of the researcher. These studies may provide information on a specific setting and specific stress but do not add to a consistent, growing body of knowledge.

For instance, much of the role stress literature in nursing journals for practitioners and for administrators is anecdotal, descriptive, diffuse, and usually is only based on opinion. This literature cannot be used as a body of scientific knowledge. Similarly, the large number of studies in organizational management literature is of limited value to role theory as a developing body of scientific knowledge. In this case the research designs are basically sound but the measurements of role conflict, overload, and ambiguity are confounded. Furthermore, the many years of research are based on the same set of theoretical and operational definitions.

Applied disciplines usually have a segment of their professionals focus on the generation of knowledge. The knowledge created by this group may be different from the needs and interests of the practice segment of the discipline (see Chapter 1). Special knowledge and abilities are required of those generating knowledge for a practice discipline—those skills that make it possible to conduct research which addresses both practice problems and the task of adding to the knowledge base of the profession.

The notions of role stress and role strain have been studied within the role theory perspective. In this chapter the theoretical aspects of symbolic interaction and the structural role theory perspective are discussed. Symbolic interaction has often been overlooked in discussions of role stress and strain because the concept labels are different from those of structuralism, the dominant theory. Symbolic interaction does, however, include rich descriptive accounts that clearly relate to role strain. This framework therefore has potential for providing understanding and developing interventions at the individual level for minimizing role stress and strain.

Scientific knowledge develops in a relatively systematic fashion if the work is conducted within a theoretical perspective. To organize the scientific knowledge on role stress it is necessary to clearly understand the manner in which role stress and role strain are conceptualized in the two major branches of "role theory".[2]

The focus of structural role theory is on systems of roles and role expectations, whereas the focus of symbolic interaction is on the self in interaction with others. In symbolic interaction the focus is on meaning, interpretation, and dynamic processes developed by individuals. The two branches of role theory complement each other. Structural role theory can be used to identify conditions of structural stress and to specify the *boundaries* of study. The location of role stress is in segments of a set of role systems. The symbolic interaction perspective can then be used to gain understanding of the meaning of the situation for the persons involved and to describe the nature of the interaction as role occupants deal with the problematic situation. Thus the two perspectives can provide complementary insights, explanations, and strategies for intervention and change.[3]

So that the reader may gain a fuller comprehension of role stress and role strain as well as the cumulative nature of knowledge development, the basic ideas are described in the context of an historical overview of the two main branches of role theory.

SYMBOLIC INTERACTION

Early Ideas Relating to Role Strain

Mead (1934), the physiological psychologist and social philosopher, generalized the ideas now called symbolic interaction (see Chapter 2). He saw the emergence of mind, self, and society as being closely connected and interdependent. *Self* was a central concept and he saw it as emerging during the processes of interaction. The transitory self-images developed in interaction with others he saw as contributing to a stabilized self-conception. Mead viewed society as being dependent upon the capacities of the self—where the self was seen from the perspective of the generalized other. A self exists only when it can take itself as object. Mead proposed a variety of stages a person passes through during socialization (see Chapter 4). Two important processes learned in socialization are **role taking** and **imaginative rehearsal**. These processes are central to interaction and are vital for communication. Mead claimed that thinking and symbolic communication make cooperation possible; and cooperation is necessary for survival.

Based on ideas evolving from pragmatism, Mead claimed that persons are active and define things in their environment. These things might be objects, people, or self. Their definitions emerge in interaction. Objects have meaning. Meanings are communicated to oneself and to others. Through the anticipation of one's own responses and the responses of others (the latter notion is called role-taking) persons are able to engage in shared, cooperative activity.

Ideas on Self. Social interaction and meaning are central to symbolic interaction theory. The theory considers that it is through interaction between persons that society is created and the person evolves. Cooley has said succinctly that society and humans are two sides of the same coin. *Meaning* is important for self and *other* and is important in the development of interaction. Interaction and meaning are emergent rather than being like a predetermined script. (The idea of predetermination is often attributed to structural role theory. See Biddle & Thomas, 1966; 1979.)

James (1890) was the first social scientist to develop a clear concept of the self. He recognized the ability of persons to view themselves as objects and to develop attitudes and feelings toward themselves. He identified the existence of multiple selves, with the social self being developed through interaction. He proposed the idea of self-esteem and saw the social order as being maintained out of social habit. James proposed that the self develops in relationship to others and saw habit as being a constraining factor in society.

Cooley proposed that the self is a process by which individuals see themselves and that the self arises out of communication with others in intimate or primary groups. As persons interact they interpret and evaluate each other's gestures and thus are able to see themselves from the viewpoint of the other. They imagine how others evaluate them and derive images and self-feelings from this imagery. This idea has been termed *the looking glass self*. Research on stigma is largely based on Cooley's original ideas and work (Goffman, 1963). Also, discrepancies between the derived self and the perceptions of others' evaluation of self is a source of role incongruity and role strain.

Mead saw the self as developing through interaction with itself and others. It became defined and in turn other selves became defined. The self articulated with society as an organized activity regulated by the generalized other. The entire focus was on the process of interaction, where self and meaning emerged through role taking and reflexive role taking. The self, rather than being a fixed entity as most other theories assumed, was viewed as a process. The process of interaction was described by Mead as a dialectical process. He proposed that self-awareness increased through resolving "problematic situations."

The notion of meaning developing in the process of social interaction has generated additional important concepts. The principal ones include definition of the situation, social construction of self, the problematic situation, and negotiation of reality.

Problematic Situations. The person is seen as an active agent acting in the present. What happened in the past is unimportant; rather, it is the meaning here and now that is important. Growth and self-awareness occur through resolving problematic situations. Successful managing of the environment is possible through the use of awareness, reflexive and flexible thinking, and the cognitive reconstruction of reality. Through dynamic interaction with the environment, multiple selves develop and personal identities change. What makes these changes relevant to this chapter is that they are likely to involve role strain.

These views evolved from the views of the pragmatic philosophers (Dewey and, of course, Mead). Their perspective, with its emphasis on the here and now, is one of the few theoretical orientations that has this positive focus. This perspective may be invaluable to health care professionals. The existence of crisis and role strain are conditions that are viewed as situation specific, and not always negative.

Dewey (1922), a leading pragmatic philosopher, and Mead were fundamental in establishing pragmatism (see Chapter 2). They saw habit as basic to the social order and as necessary for thinking and reflecting. They stressed the uniqueness of mind to human nature and saw thinking as a process leading to adjustment to the environment. Thinking was seen as instrumental, allowing persons to define objects and identify potential lines of action. Choices of "lines of action" are based on imagining what would likely subsequently happen. Mead's theorizing went beyond the basic pragmatism. Mead and Cooley independently developed ideas on self (Cooley, 1902). "Lines of action" are part of the current theorizing on interpersonal competence (Weinstein, 1969) and interpersonal negotiation (see Role Bargaining Responses in the next chapter).

Roles. The work of Mead was further extended by Park and Burgess (1921), who also utilized the notion of roles. Park proposed that persons are connected to society by structural positions and that the self functions within the confines of these roles. Park emphasized, as did Simmel before him, that the self emerges from playing multiple roles which are connected to social positions.

Both Thomas and Park were students of Simmel, a German sociologist whose ideas influenced the thinking of many American sociologists. Simmel saw conflict as being inherent in social relations but he also saw it as contributing to "unity" (Simmel, 1950). Conflict does not necessarily lead to breakdown of the system or to change. It is one of the principal processes operating to preserve the social whole and its subparts (Turner, 1983, 117–136). This is a fundamental assumption in symbolic interaction.[4]

Simmel's ideas included positive connotations of alienation[5] and the dialectic process. Simmel, in turn, derived many of his ideas from Hegel (Hegel, translation 1967). As a result, many of Hegel's ideas of positive alienation are continued in the ideas of symbolic interaction. Hegel used alienation to explain how the self develops. In his use, the term refers to the process whereby the self can become object to itself; it entails the dialectic process of taking this "being different" back into itself and reconciling it with itself. This is similar to some of the notions which Mead later worked on. The notion of being different was further developed by Thomas (1907) and Park (1927). Many of these ideas are in strong contrast to those basic to structural role theory.

Alien: Marginal Man. From the perspective of Simmel, Thomas, and Park, alien meant new and exotic and was seen as an ideal mixture of proximity and distance. Although persons live in a specific time and place, the specific situation or environment is not totally fixed. Persons have mobility. They can acquire qualities from the environment and take their own qualities into the environment. Persons who migrate from one culture to another, then, are in an alien state. This notion is strongly reflected in the concept of **marginal man** used by Thomas (1907) and Park, who were early contributors to symbolic interaction. The idea was used by Park to explain the situation of blacks, immigrants, and others who clearly were members of two cultures but belonged in neither. Their alien view was considered by Parks as an asset, not a hindrance.

The continuation of a positive connotation for alienation and the notion of the dialectic contributed to philosophical underpinnings of the notions of **change and crisis** (Thomas's term). They can be seen as constructive contributions to growth and progress. In addition Darwin's notion of biologic evolution served as a metaphor for developing socially significant ideas relative to change. However, the idea of social evolution was rejected by Mead. The various philosophies contributed to the assumption that the individual is an active rational agent adapting and modifying the social and physical environments.

Symbolic Interaction Ideas Developed in a Social Context. The theoretical notions of the symbolic interactionists were well suited to the social context in which the ideas evolved. Major personal and societal changes were occurring along with concomitant social and personal problems. The symbolic interactionists took an active part in attempting to alleviate some of the more pressing problems. This activity was separate from their scientific work but undoubtedly influenced the direction the theory and research took.

Change and Crisis. Symbolic interaction developed in a period of rapid industrial development, high employment, a significant influx of immigrant families, and rapid economic and social growth. Early theorizing was on the development of self and meaning through interaction. Persons were portrayed as active rather than passive. Other theorizing had to do with trying to understand the problematic situations faced by groups of persons (in particular, immigrants and the unemployed). Symbolic interactionists theorized that social progress was a result of conflict in the social order. Conflict was seen as creating social awareness resulting in a broadening of perspectives. Both personal and social growth were seen to occur through conflict. This focus was central to the work of Thomas, Park, and Mead. Disruption in the social order was seen as the source of progress for the individual and for society. Thomas saw social control and social change as core concepts and the result of reciprocal dependence between social organization and the individual's life; the latter is never static but always in a process of continual evolution (Thomas, 1907).

Thomas and Znaniecki (1918) conducted extensive analytic studies of the social world of the Polish peasants in Chicago to determine the effect that social disorganization had upon adults. From this study came the notion of the *definition of the situation*: "if people believe things are true they are true in their consequences." Thomas believed sociology should study both the objective and subjective aspects of human nature. Through his introduction of this basic concept, the subjective became more readily available for study.

Problematic Situations: Crisis and Change. Thomas, together with other pragmatists and symbolic interactionists, came to the conclusion that behavior was motivated and controlled by social habit. He proposed that disruption of social habit causes an emotional response that increases a person's level of consciousness. He proposed that the resulting state of crisis was a prerequisite for change. With the mind aware of the problem, the problem becomes subject to resolution. The occurrence of a "problem," Thomas claimed, meant that a social habit was inadequate. This notion is compatible with role strain, where role strain is defined as felt difficulty in carrying out role expectations, provided the difficulty has a normative source. The latter condition is termed structural stress in this chapter. Thus, although the terminology of role stress and role strain does not explicitly exist in symbolic interaction, the fundamental ideas certainly do.

Thomas saw personal resources as growing when successful lines of action are taken to solve such "problems." Personal growth occurs, then, through effective interaction with the environment; problems provide an opportunity to learn. The more crises a person has successfully resolved, the greater the social competence and the greater the "intelligence," which evolves through social competence. (The term *intelligence* had for Thomas a somewhat different meaning than our usual definition.)

Mead saw individual behavior as purposeful and rational. He also saw social conflict as generating social awareness and broadening one's perspective. He proposed that persons could be only as complete as their social and intellectual relations allowed; the broader and more diverse persons' social relations, the more highly developed their critical skills and the more fully developed they would be as human beings. Diversity in social relations would increase the social and intellectual perspective of persons. This view has been relatively dormant since the 1940s. Only recently has some of the research on women's roles suggested that role accumulation (a newer term for acquiring multiple roles) can be beneficial (Barnett & Baruch, 1985; Marks, 1977).

In the early 1900s a University of Chicago graduate student took Mead's notion that social conflict generates social awareness as the focus of her thesis. This student, Jessie Taft, like many educated women of her day, found that there was a major conflict in her life. Educated women had been raised by their families to be mothers and wives. As grown women they were expected to be nurturant. Because of their high levels of education, however, they were also expected to be rational and high achievers—just as men were. An awareness of the social bind was a "problematic situation," in Thomas's terminology. Taft conceptualized the problem as a socially generated role conflict.

As a student Taft was strongly influenced by both Thomas and Mead. In her dissertation, "The Women's Movement from the Point of View of Social Consciousness" (Taft, 1916), she attempted to apply Mead's ideas that the limited social relations which would result if women remained in the home as expected would produce a constricted social consciousness. Thus society would inevitably suffer. However, Taft chose not to use her findings at a sociopolitical level to bring about change in society. She believed that change in attitudes toward women had to occur first at the psychological and interpersonal levels, not at the social or political levels. The notion of restricted roles of nonemployed women as being a source of role strain is only now being identified in research (Barnett & Baruch, 1985).

The ideas and research of Mead, Thomas, Park, and their students were the earliest work on role stress and role strain, but they studied them as (societal) crises. A fundamental characteristic of this approach in symbolic interaction was that stress could be a source of growth and increased competence for individuals and for society. Conflict or problems were seen as a challenge and a means for increasing personal competence.

In contrast to views of the early symbolic interactionists, the problematic situation would be identified by structural role theorists as disturbing and undesirable. Fifteen years after Taft's study, Parsons and Komorovsky worked with a similar problem (see Rosenberg, 1983). They called the condition **role strain**, which they used to explain the unhappiness felt by educated women reared to be wives and mothers, but educated to be independent thinkers. Parsons proposed that they ease the role strain by becoming good companions to their husbands. Komarovsky (1946) disagreed; she saw this mode of responding to role strain as eventually destructive to the women and saw abandonment of the traditional female role as the only viable solution. In practice, Parsons's view dominated from the mid-1940s through to the mid-1960s. During that era, women's place was seen to be in the home.

Many subtheories and conceptualizations have been developed within the symbolic interaction perspective and many of these are discussed elsewhere in this text.[6]

STRUCTURAL ROLE THEORY

Structural role theory is to a large extent considered a segment of Parsons's structural theory on society as a social system (Parsons, 1951). The core ideas he proposed are: (1) patterned interactions over time form and maintain the social structure; (2) the social system evolves through interaction among persons pursuing goals; (3) norms emerge to facilitate interaction among these persons; (4) in general actors who occupy statuses enact normatively prescribed roles; (5) general and specific norms are internalized by actors and these ultimately guide and define acceptable role behavior; (6) the importance of the person is primarily in terms of the collective.

A question basic to Parsons's theorizing was, How do societies survive? His theorizing centered on the social system and the notion of social integration. Accordingly, he theorized as to the way in which the personal and culture systems meld with the social system and how they contribute to the emergence of social cohesion through the supportive mechanism of social control. Thus, the stability of the social system is assured through norms and a commitment by persons to conform to these in performing roles. Failure in any of these systems, such as a weakening of the normative system, is seen as a source of structural stress.

Historical Beginnings

The study of society has a long history. It is difficult to summarize the work simply and at the same time provide enough information to make the major theoretical problems associated with structural stress understandable. The initial theorizing in the 1800s proposed that society could be considered a system with interrelated parts. In the late 1800s—after the French Revolution—the first attempts were made to understand society. These attempts often used the biologic organism as an analogy. A risk in using any analogy is assuming that what is true in the analogue model is true in general. The early theorists were very cautious in drawing on concepts from biology. In contrast, Parsons's subsequent theorizing on society assumed that biologic systems and social systems are isomorphic, i.e., the biologic analogy can be taken as a true representation of the social system.

Comte's theoretical work during the period (1798–1857) is particularly significant because he attempted to study society itself as an entity. In addition, he believed that empirical knowledge had to be obtained in order to understand and create a better society. Comte, who advocated the scientific method to study society, is considered the father of positivism. Similarities between biologic organisms and society were identified. These included the idea that social systems have needs and functions which contribute to their survival. This early theorizing lay the groundwork for Parsons's subsequent (1955) theorizing on society.

Herbert Spencer (1820–1903) greatly extended the use of the biologic analogy by adding such concepts as structure, differentiation of function, levels of social systems, and adaptation of the social unit to the environment. The latter included the notion that simple social systems or groups would adapt and progress to become major societies with differentiation of structure and function. Spencer's thinking was heavily influenced by Darwin and, accordingly, his work had as an underlying assumption the idea of social evolution. The assumption of social evolution has since been established as untenable. Spencer's (1864–1867) three-volume work, *Principles of Biology*, contained his efforts at identifying abstract laws which identified parallels in biological and social organization. His work has been virtually ignored by present-day scholars[7] except for Turner (1985), who has proposed that Spencer's work, although not generally acknowledged, has contributed significantly to our current theorizing.

Durkheim's (1858–1917) work included further emphasis on biologic concepts. His analysis of society assumed the biologic analogies of structure, function, need, normality, and pathology. Both Spencer's and Durkheim's ideas lead to the notions of function and needs in societies. Turner (1985) suggests that functionalism might have died with Durkheim except that the anthropologists were attracted to his analysis of society. They saw it as a means for studying simple societies.

The two major anthropologists who utilized Durkheim's work to analyze other cultures were Radcliffe-Brown (1881–1955) and Malinowski (1884–1942). Malinowski (1939) made a significant contribution to structural–functional thinking by introducing the notion that there are levels in a system and that each level has its own set of needs. The levels he identified were biologic, social structural, and symbolic. His approach created renewed interest in studying societies as social systems.

Linton, a University of Chicago anthropologist, made a major contribution to structural anthropology by proposing that societies are composed of patterned relationships which are centered on the reciprocity of rights and obligations (Linton, 1936). The polar relationships which engage in the reciprocal interactions he identified as statuses. The dynamic aspect of statuses, the carrying out of rights and obligations, he termed *roles*. Furthermore he identified that some roles are ascribed and others are achieved.

Thus, several intellectual lines of work influenced Parsons's theorizing. Like the structuralists before him, he viewed integration or social cooperation as the central "need" of society, and existing social arrangements as a reflection of how society could best meet that need. The maintenance of social order through reciprocal role relationships became central to his ideas on societal order.

Parsons's theorizing on society dominated the sociologic literature in this country. His approach floundered in the 1960s, however, as it became apparent that the theory fostered the status quo in society and thus had a strong ideological component. Structural–functional theory assumes that processes and entities exist in society to meet a fundamental need of the system and, because they contribute to its survival, changes will evolve if appropriate. No intervention should occur to purposefully change any societal condition because this would be an unnatural disturbance in the system. Accordingly, this meant that social conditions such as inequity (as experienced by blacks, women, etc.) and conditions of poverty, slavery, illness, and the power of the elite are functional for the system. Thus they contribute to the survival of the system, are therefore necessary and should not be altered, and certainly not eliminated.

Integration of the Personality, Cultural, and Social Systems

Parsons theorized that there are several mechanisms developed in the personalities of individuals that foster the continuity of society. He proposed that personality contributes to social order through:

1. Socialization processes, whereby persons internalize values, attitudes, and behaviors of society
2. Mechanisms in the social structure which serve to ensure individual conformity and eliminate deviant role performance

Socialization. Socialization is a social process vital for sustaining a social system and is the means by which persons acquire the essential knowledge, skills, dispositions, behavior, and motivation to participate effectively in social groups. (See Chapters 4 and 9 for a fuller development of this subject.) The outcome of successful socialization has been identified as social competence (Cottrell, 1969; Smith, 1968). Of particular importance is the acquisition of the motivation to participate in the role system and to conform to its norms. Among the potential sources of role stress are inadequate acquisition of skill and motivation for conformity to enable acceptable role performance. The result is role incompetence.

Social controls via socialization processes, social norms, and sanctions exist to ensure continuity of the social system. The complementary nature of positions, interlocking of roles, and reciprocal role expectations ensure conformity.

The process of anticipatory socialization and the actual prolonged period of professional socialization clarify acceptable and unacceptable behavior and its situation-specific nature. Also learned are the severity of sanctions associated with deviant or nonconforming behaviors and the rewards which accrue for expected role performance. These contribute to clarifying the role expectations for professionals and the extent to which some are more mandatory than others.

Other social control mechanisms that foster acceptable role enactment are the separation in time and space of positions and roles that are contradictory and those that have the potential for producing deviant behavior. Another type of social control comes from the existence of structures for coping with deviants and for bringing the deviant back into line, or rehabilitating him.

Stability of the Social System. Society, or the social system, thus provides mechanisms to foster its own functioning and stability. These mechanisms prevent or reduce the impact of structural stress and also contribute to the survival of the system. Generally reciprocal role relationships, the integration of role behaviors, and conformity to norms are the means of social control and are central to the continuance of society. Relationships are entered into and sustained as a result of shaping personal behavior to "fit" social roles through the internalization of social values and beliefs. Role behavior is sustained as a result of mutual rewards.

Cooperation over time is possible through the development of a common perspective as to values, ways of doing things, knowing what is expected, what is rewarding, what is punishing, and also general goals and the means of achieving them. The existence of a common perspective enables this development without persons needing in each episode of interaction to engage explicitly in prolonged negotiations to reach an agreement on the definition of the situation. Thus, social systems provide structural conditions which prevent or minimize both disagreement and conflict while fostering consensus and interdependent goal-related behavior. Furthermore, the means exist for identifying and reintegrating persons who are in positions that generate deviance.

Although social order and social control are central notions in structural role theory, the study of social control has been limited by a lack of a sound theoretical approach (Gibbs, 1965; Meir, 1982). Some structuralists linked the concept of social control strongly to deviance (LaPierre, 1934; Parsons, 1951). Parsons identified the essence of social control as the ability to react against deviance, since deviance causes strain in the system. A significant area of study that developed in response to this perspective is labeling theory (Lemert, 1967). Another significant line of research is related to the notion of status inconsistency and role conflict (see research review by Stryker & Macke, 1978). Related areas of research were on social conformity and social control. This includes conformity to norms (Deutscher, 1973; Homans, 1964), conformity to authority (Milgram, 1974), conformity in small groups (Bales, 1958; Thibault & Kelley, 1959), and reference groups (Hyman & Singer 1968; Merton & Rossi, 1968; Singer, 1981). The significance of this research tradition is that it identifies to what extent and under what conditions conformity occurs.

Social Change

For the early structuralists, the occurrence of social change was seen as part of the social evolutionary processes, rather than as an abrupt, intermittent, or unpredictable event. Using a similar line of reasoning, Parsons theorized that change in systems occurs in an orderly, slow manner which reflects the system's adaptability and growth. Parsons also drew heavily on the evolutionary model to describe change. He proposed that change results in increasing structural differentiation and the development of new mechanisms of integration. He further suggested that the development of additional mechanisms of integration may become a major problem.

Role Stress and Social Change. Accordingly, change, with increased differentiation in roles, has the potential for creating role problems as new roles emerge and old ones are redefined. The uncertainty in terms of role expectations is likely to increase and generate role ambiguity in relation to the old roles and new roles. As persons move from old roles into newly developing roles, that is, as they engage in the process of role *transition*, role strain is likely to arise. Whether it is seen as desirable and part of a challenge or as undesirable and something to avoid or minimize will be influenced by the social and cultural definition that develops around the new roles.

An example may make this idea clearer. In Massachusetts, rapid entry movement of a professional people into computer-related roles, such as programmer, was for many persons seen as an opportunity and challenge whereas earlier such a move might have been seen by the same people as full of uncertainty. Social and cultural factors supported this redefinition. Funded programs were created for persons to learn the new and different skills necessary for adequate role performance. Furthermore, the influx of people to these roles came largely from the ranks of unemployed teachers, social workers, etc., whose economic future was predicted as bleak. In place of predicted long-term unemployment, these people moved into a sector of the labor market that was anticipating full employment and substantial growth. Thus, the social system fostered a social redefinition of the new computer-related positions and provided the means for acquiring the necessary skills and the incentive for learning them. Teachers who had previously seen computer-related work as being at odds with their own humanistic values, selected, in a state of unemployment, to become computer programmers, and in making this choice cognitively emphasized the intellectual challenge of the job. Thus, role strain in the presence of role ambiguity and during a process of role transition need not be a totally negative experience.

Other role problems would be expected to occur concurrently with role transition and differentiation. As the number and diversity of social positions increases the potential for role conflict and role overload grows. Role differentiation may also reduce communication within a group. The differentiation and certification of various groups of nurses have done just this.[8]

Role stress has been studied intensely since the women's movement began and has produced data indicating that some of the basic assumptions of structural role theory are faulty. In particular, the assumption that role conflict and overload are necessarily detrimental to one's sense of well-being has been thrown into question by recent research on gender.

Thus, there is reason to believe that social change, at least initially, is associated with increased integration problems and role stress. New roles which emerge are usually a source of role stress (ambiguity) until they become well established. Parsons did further theorizing on the factors likely to influence change. He viewed change as a slow, orderly process which facilitates the survival of the social system. Change and associated problems of differentiation may lead to other types of role stress. Lack of clarity of role expectations may be an important problem that decreases individual motivation to perform roles and to conform to norms. This tendency might be countered by control mechanisms in the system, such as negative sanctions, re-educational processes, and the identification of different levels of role performance with associated incremental rewards in the form of increased status and pay. Other mechanisms include the promotion of a sense of belonging through support groups and work-based "retreats."

According to Parsons, the system itself has mechanisms which help to maintain social order. The main mechanisms are the social structure, norms, roles, and other stable, patterned interactions. Additional social control mechanisms may be created, moreover, when these falter. Stability of the system is theorized to be important and necessary. Unanticipated or large changes in the organization, disruption of organizational units, and conflict created by the organization are not expected by the structuralists to occur. If they did, this would be taken by them as an indication that the current social control and equilibrating mechanisms were functioning inadequately.

Structurally generated stress, its cause, conditions, and consequences for individuals and society, has been a major focus of research. Some of this research is identified in this discussion and more is identified in Tables 1 to 5. Many early studies focused on disorganization, role conflict, and deviant behavior. Sources of conflict were studied in terms of membership in multiple groups, in several cultures, and psychologic commitment to multiple groups with or without membership in them (reference groups, for example). Various malintegrations and contradictions in society were studied. Resolution of conflict has been a significant area of research. Underlying most studies is the assumption that role conflict is destructive to the social order, producing deviance and personal disorder.

Illustrations of Structuralist Role Stress Theory and Research

Merton (1957) is a structural theorist whose work stands out, particularly in the area of research on the dysfunctional nature of systems, mainly because of his creative theoretical approaches, his use of middle range theories that could be empirically tested, and for the subsequent research that has been generated from his ideas. He is one of the principal structural theorists who through theory and research analyzed the existence and consequences of dysfunctions, contradictions, and conflicts within the social structure.

He proposed that an important source of contradictions is one's *role set* (Biddle & Thomas, 1979). For every status or position occupied, a person has a role set (set of role partners). Each person is faced with articulating the role expectations of their numerous role partners for their several role sets. Merton proposed that the multiplicity of role expectations and their incompatible or contradictory nature require the role occupant to manage role expectations in such a manner that role conflict is minimized. He further suggested that the conflict generated by one's role set may actually contribute to its articulation. Merton proposed that role articulation in such situations occurs in a more self-conscious manner than if there were no such multiplicity. Rather than directly struggling with conflicting expectations associated with his multiple roles, he suggested that the individual has the option of making conscious and rational choices among roles.

In other theorizing about the social structure, Merton utilized the idea of anomie to describe how people adapt to situations in which the cultural norms and the means for achieving socially accepted goals are not integrated with opportunities for achieving them. Another rich theoretical tradition on the social structure he initiated (together with Rossi) was reference group theory (Merton & Rossi, 1968). (See also Chapter 9.) His work on role set and reference group theory explores contradictory role expectations and mechanisms which individuals may use to reduce the conflict; Merton does not propose that individual options are ready-made but that individuals have to find their own orientation among multiple, incompatible, and contradictory norms. This may be done by identifying more with one group than another.

Structural Location of Role Stress

Structural stress is embedded either in the role or the normative structure. Different types of role stress identified in the research have been categorized on the basis of the nature of the role expectations and the role resources of individuals occupying the roles (see Tables 1 to 5). The resources are primarily a function of the socialization processes. In order to illustrate the impact of the social structure on roles, one source of structural stress—role conflict—has been selected for analysis and discussion. A similar examination could be made with each of the other types of role stress. (For further illustration of single and multiple role conflict see the section on role conflict for women as nurses and researchers on pp. 208–210, 226–228.)

Reference Groups. Conflicting role expectations may come from one's reference group (Becker et al., 1961; Bidwell, 1961; Gross et al., 1958). This has been found to be the case for such professional groups as physicians (Goss, 1961), college professors (Gouldner, 1957), scientists (Kornhauser, 1962), nurses (Kramer, 1968), and social workers (Scott, 1969). Both Olesen and Whittaker (1968) and Simpson (1979) identified student nurses as having to deal with conflicting expectations from their faculty and from their family (Figure 3a). The faculty expected priority and commitment by the students to the nursing role whereas parents emphasized the importance of marriage and child rearing. Thus, the two reference groups expected different interests, involvement, and behaviors of the student nurses.

A third reference group was the student group itself. The norms that develop in this group are those which facilitate passage through the educational system. The scholastic standards set by this group generally scorn high achievement. Thus, the norms of the student group conflict with those of faculty. Olesen and Whittaker note that those students who have a self-established pressure to exceed the norm of mediocrity face the problem of self-management. It is crucial to them that they excel in their course work without offending their classmates. Role conflict for these students is of a slightly different nature than for those who endorse mediocrity, but both sets of students face role conflict between the expectations held by faculty and expectations held by peers. (See Chapter 9.)

Role Set. Another source of conflicting role expectations comes from one's role set (Arndt & Laeger, 1970; Bidwell, 1961; Burchard, 1954; Goss, 1961; Kahn et al., 1964). Various role partners may hold conflicting role expectations for the role occupant (see Figure 1, p. 166). Cross-sectional studies of the stress of critical care nurses (Anderson & Basteyn, 1981; Bailey et al., 1981) suggest that there is conflict in role set between these nurses and physicians and between these nurses and their supervisors. Role stress does not seem to exist between nurses and their peers or between nurses and their patients.

Positions located at the boundary of an organization or positions that link one system to another would be subjected to relatively high role stress. For example, a community health nurse would experience high role stress when she finds that her nursing supervisor, a staff nurse, the agency's physician, the school psychologist, and the patient's family do not agree on how she should work with a particular adolescent.

Multiple Positions. Role conflict may also exist when a person occupies multiple positions (Burchard, 1954; Getzels & Guba, 1954; Gullahorn, 1956; Kahn et al., 1964). Interpositional conflict arises when an actor occupies one position that has one set of role expectations, such as scientist, and a second position that has a completely separate set of role expectations, such as those for a patient. In addition, role conflict may be compounded by the effects of gender roles. This latter type of conflict has only recently been investigated.

An illustration might be helpful: consider a nurse scientist who is also a mother (see Figure 3c). Conflict between her roles is evident when she has a physician consultation because she is losing weight, is unable to keep food down, is tired, and sleeps poorly. She is concerned that she is functioning poorly in the work she once loved—doing research on women's roles and health care in a medical behavioral science department. She knows physicians tend to see women's problem's as psychological and yet, as a nurse, she thinks there is something physically amiss. (Three weeks later she is hospitalized for a ruptured ectopic pregnancy.) She expects to interact with her physician in a cooperative mode of inquiry; an interactional style with which she is familiar with her staff but which is different from the typical female patient–male physician encounter. She expects something akin to a "therapeutic alliance." The physician, however, takes an authoritative role and she is given a prescription for valium. On the basis of her professional role she expected a more egalitarian relationship with the physician. This type of role relationship would have lessened the likelihood of her gender role influencing his perspective and ultimately her diagnosis and treatment (see later section in this chapter on women's roles and role conflict). As a patient she felt too ill to try to influence the nature of his role, and the norms for her as a

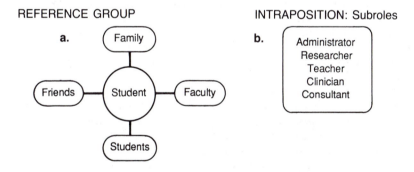

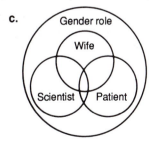

Figure 3. Models of role stress—representing structural stress.

patient dictated that she should not try to unduly influence the physician. As a patient and woman she was expected to comply with the physician's diagnosis and recommendations.

Single Position. Nor is role conflict limited to occupancy of multiple positions. It may exist with occupancy of a single position (Becker et al., 1961; Goss, 1961) (Figure 3b). Here the role expectations the role occupant holds for her subroles may be incompatible. Such intrapositional conflict may be present, for example, for social workers who are expected to be active in professional organizations yet are not permitted to attend professional meetings held during work hours.

Role conflict has been identified as a significant problem in a variety of settings. Although the sources of role conflict may differ, the essential features of role stress are always present: the stress is generated by the social structure and the role occupant is confronted with role expectations that conflict. They are mutually exclusive and thus are impossible to carry out.

ROLE STRESS AND ROLE STRAIN

Although much of the following discussion focuses on one or the other of the two primary concepts, role stress and role strain, it should be kept in mind that both are part of a general theoretical formulation, namely, that *role strain is directly related to role stress*.

Role stress is a general construct which subsumes various types of stress or role-related problems. Seven specific types of role stress are discussed in this chapter. The identification of these types is based on an analysis of the role theory and research literature. It resulted in a typology of role stress (Hardy, 1970 and "Role Stress and Role Strain" in Hardy & Conway: Role Theory, previous edition, 1978).

Four of the role stresses or role-related problems—ambiguity, incongruity, conflict, and overload—have each been investigated in a variety of settings, including dyads, small groups, and organizations. Research on role overload (quantitative and qualitative) is relatively new in the role stress literature, even though overload may be the major role problem that health care professionals face. Its counterpart, role underload, and two other types, role over qualification and role under qualification, have not been examined systematically from a theoretical or empirical viewpoint.

Role strain has been studied as psychological and physiological states related to feelings that role obligations are difficult or impossible to carry out.

The psychological responses have been empirically identified as:

1. Anxiety
2. Tension
3. Irritation
4. Resentment
5. Depression

The measured physiologic responses include:

1. Abnormal levels of adrenalin, triglycerides, cholesterol, and abnormal blood coagulation time

2. Abnormal heart rate and ECG abnormalities
3. Pathologic states of hypertension and coronary heart disease
4. Other physical and psychological symptoms, including headaches, dizziness, shortness of breath, nausea, and fatigue

At a social level, role strain has been related to:

1. Withdrawal from interaction
2. Reduced involvement with colleagues and organizations
3. Job dissatisfaction

The impact at the social level considers how role strain of the focal person influences that person's role set and larger role systems.

Major Theoretical Perspectives for Role Stress Analysis

Two major, but theoretically divergent, approaches are used for the study of role problems. One approach is based on role theory notions that have been developed by the interdisciplinary work of anthropologists, sociologists, and social psychologists in sociology. This is the perspective developed in this book: the combination of structural role theory and symbolic interaction.

The second approach, termed here the *organizational management focus*, looks at the impact of the organization on the individual (Kahn et al., 1964). This approach developed as a consequence of early funded research to apply knowledge in the area of occupational health. The work in this area during the last several years has been primarily conducted by psychologists. Included in this approach is the person–environment fit model developed by French and Kahn (1962). The approach is primarily based on Lewin's field theory (Lewin, 1951). The basic assumptions of this model are almost diametrically opposite to those of role theory, particularly symbolic interaction, and yet for persons in nursing administration this limited model, with its noncumulative research, has unfortunately been identified as the major source of knowledge on organizations. (For more extensive discussion, see "Organization Management Perspective," below.)

Role Theory and Role Stress. In this section the important theoretical work related to the study of role stress and role strain is identified to extend the basic set of concepts. Definitions and specific references are generally not given; the work is so central to the study of role problems that the sources are readily available in the literature.

The analysis of roles and role conflict from the perspective of structural role theory was advanced by Merton's theoretical work and pivotal study on role conflict and resolution of role conflict by Gross et al., (1958). Important theoretical advances have been made through Merton and Barber's notions of structural ambivalence (1963, 1976). Role partners, status articulation, and role articulation are additional concepts Merton introduced to extend the theoretical base. Rose Coser's works on insulation from observability, role distance, structural ambiguity, and role diversity have also extended the theoretical understanding of role stress, as have Goode's theoretical developments on role strain, norm commitment, conformity to role obligations, and the profession as a community (1960, 1973). Lewis Coser (1974) proposed the notion of greedy institutions; shortly afterward, the notion of role accumulation was proposed by Seiber (1977). The latter concept has provided an explanation for a finding of research on women's roles that role overload is not necessarily detrimental but may be associated with health and psychological well being. This idea is discussed later in this chapter.

Role and role-problem concepts and applications tend to be more difficult to identify in the symbolic interaction literature than in the structural literature. Major written contributions have been made by Becker, Davis, Cottrell, Glaser, Goffman, Heiss, Lofland, Psathas, Stone, Strauss, Stryker, Turner, and Weinstein.

Goffman (1959) has introduced into the study of roles various conceptual approaches for investigating factors that may be taken into account in establishing order in interaction, factors which may disrupt the order, and mechanisms that may sustain an established order.

Goffman extended the dramaturgical model by identifying that persons perform to audiences and may stay in role while staging their performance but may break role when there is not a significant audience. For instance, the nurse may take off her shoes and relax once the medical staff and higher ranking nurses have left the ward. Persons may be more involved in some performances of their role than in others, depending upon their audience.

The theoretical importance of structure and social context to role performance has been significantly advanced by Goffman's work. He has attempted to extend our understanding of structural roles by relating them to concrete situations and to individual experiences. The terminology used for this analysis is the dramaturgical model. The position in a system is the person's situation. The analysis involves self-image and image presented to others, tensions, anxieties, and other experiences. Roles, from Goffman's perspective, must be separated into typical responses, normative aspects of role, and the particular individual's role performance.

"In charge of the situation" is a concept Goffman introduces to identify how persons handle a multiplicity of selves. The female nurse, for example, may be a personal friend of a physician on the unit; gender roles may come into play with every new group of interns; and expertise as a nurse may become dominant in the presence of medical students. The nurse's leisure role of financial investor may come into play with new physicians, the woman role may dominate when women patients have major surgery on reproductive organs or when women are "put down" through jokes, the action of physicians, or the response of a husband to his wife's illness. The need to be in charge of the situation and to define to others which of the multiple roles is currently in play informs others of their appropriate behavior.

Goffman uses the idea of situated activity systems to describe role behaviors which occur in a single social setting. Examples might include the actions of a surgeon in the OR or the activities of a physician on a ward. If situated activities occur frequently they become known as the attributes of a situated role. A situated role is a bundle of activities visibly performed for a set of others and meshed into their performance of activities. The idea of situated activity helps make analysis of the complexities of conduct as concrete as possible.

Role distance refers to actions which effectively convey some disdainful detachment of the performer from a given role being performed. Humor, sullenness, irony, and sarcasm are all mechanisms used to distance one's self from certain role obligations. Role distance also relates to the large gap often existing between role obligations and actual performance.

Establishing one's identity is an important notion in the study of roles. Some mechanisms Goffman discusses for establishing identity include the use of the front stage, props, and self-presentation. Interaction is the medium for establishing identities with a potential role partner. If interaction is to continue, negotiation and agreement is necessary and usually a working consensus is developed through influencing strategies that are often subtle.

Failure to have one's identity accepted by the other may be because other factors, such as a spoiled identity, stigma, or contradictory information, undermine the proposed identity.[9] The contradictory information may be found when the other goes backstage. Props and self-presentation may not be convincing to the other or there may be stray pieces of information which contradict the identity. The person may use various verbal explanations to account for the misinformation. Misinterpretation or unwillingness to accept the actor's identity generates tension and strained interaction. This notion of Goffman's could be reconceptualized as role strain. Failure to establish or to sustain a person's self-identity results in role incongruity or role ambiguity.

Role incongruity may exist because the person's self and identity are not congruent with the position occupied. Role ambiguity may be created through uncertainty about the expected role performance In such cases cues and feedback from role partners may be insufficient or nonexistent.

Goffman's study of encounters and the types of rules that are used to establish order and to sustain the definition of reality are closely related to the study of role relationships as negotiated order (Strauss, 1963).

Strauss has contributed to the study of role problems by introducing such notions as negotiated order and trajectories. The ideas he developed in relation to personal change and role incongruity include status forcing to establish identity, turning points and problems of misalignment, shock, anxiety, tension, transformation of identity, status passage, and coaching.

Symbolic interaction utilizes the negotiated order metaphor to describe an organization. This focuses on the experiences of persons in organizations and assumes that conflict is always present. The negotiations are influenced by the membership identities of groups in the organizations. For example, the different ideologies of mental health professionals influence their focus of negotiation when they interact. Those who believe that mental illness is a result of social impairment will want space and time to conduct group work. In contrast, those who see a biochemical imbalance as the central cause of malfunctioning will want money for various pharmaceutical products and possibly research space. The negotiation is further influenced by organizational constraints and the social context. The focus in negotiation may be at the interpersonal level or between groups. Negotiation for roles is learned during the socialization process. Negotiation processes are used by nurses in the work setting (Stelling & Bucher, 1972).

Role Competence. The terms *social competence* and *interpersonal competence* have been well developed and form an important part of symbolic interaction theory. These two attributes are necessary for overall role competence. They are also utilized in an intervention approach utilizing the symbolic interaction perspective. Indeed, the idea of interpersonal competence developed from the perspective of symbolic interaction. The study of interpersonal competence gained support from White's (1959) proposal (from animal and infant research) that persons clearly seek effective interaction with their environment. White suggested that this tendency be termed *effectance motivation*. The sense of personal worth in interacting with others (in the social environment) he termed *competence*. Prior to his extensive review of the existing research, the dominant view had been that animals and humans are basically passive and require stimulation and continuous input from their environment. Following his review, the more prevalent idea is that animals and persons actively seek stimulation. The idea of this active, selective nature of persons has been supported by research on perception, behavior, and interaction.

Interpersonal competence is a vital attribute of persons participating and being successful members of a stable society.[10] *Social competence* is the outcome of role relationships through which individuals are equipped with the appropriate role skills and strategies which enable them to shape the response of others in order to successfully achieve both their own goals and their role-related goals. Strategies are used to influence both the tasks associated with the relationship and the social identities of the actors.

Foote and Cottrell (1955), analyzing the social behavior of adults, introduced the term interpersonal competence to refer to the social skill or ability individuals utilize in attempting to control the outcomes of their interactions. The more skilled individuals typically were intelligent, empathetic, and good problem solvers, and they made good use of information resources.

Weinstein (1969), also studying social interaction, proposed that interpersonal competence involves persons developing and using lines of action which enables them to get others to think, feel, or act as they wanted them to. Success in influencing role partners in this manner is one of the major outcomes of successful socialization.

Lines of action are used to achieve the interpersonal task. This is accomplished through the actions that the focal person uses to elicit desired behavior from role partners. Interpersonal competence is the ability to achieve the interpersonal task. Some of the social skills persons use to manage their social environment have been discussed by McCall and Simmons (1978), studied by Blumstein (1975), and analyzed in terms of agreement on situational identities, projection of identity through self-presentation (Goffman, 1959), and the identity allocated to the other, i.e., altercasting (Weinstein & Deutschberger, 1964).

Persons develop a working consensus as to the definition of the situation. The definition of the situation is the basis for drawing inferences about the desired interpersonal task and about the lines of action which will be used to achieve the set of interpersonal tasks.

In our terms, a *role competance* is as a repertoire of lines of action structured around a specifiable set of interpersonal tasks. From the definition of the situation comes the decision as to which persons will play which roles. Skill at establishing and maintaining desired identities, both for one's self and for others, is what is required to be interpersonally competent. Weinstein suggests that the personal variables which contribute to this competence are role-taking ability and empathy; that is, the ability to predict accurately the impact that various lines of action will have on the others' definition of the situation. Furthermore, it is necessary to have a large and varied repertoire of lines of action and effective and strategic intrapersonal resources.

Fundamental to this notion of competence is the idea that persons are engaged in an interdependent interaction, or role relationship, which exists over time and is influenced by the social context (or third person). The term interpersonal competence is clearly linked to symbolic interaction and therefore incorporates the notions of role identity and definition of the situation. Negotiation over definition of one's role and work in organizations has been proposed to be an important process by symbolic interactionists.

To engage successfully in socially defined roles one needs competent behavior vis-à-vis the interdependent nature of roles, namely the cognitive skills, skill at role bargaining, collaboration, and relationship sensitivity. Role-specific knowledge and skills and knowledge of organizations are also required. In addition, motivation, personal interest, energy, time, and involvement are necessary to engage in a role in a meaningful manner. Role behavior wherever it is enacted does not occur in isolation but in a social context and in relation to one's role set. Persons need to be sensitive to a role occupant's *definition of the situation,* know when it has changed and when it needs to be changed. Important attributes are role-taking ability, reflexive thinking, ability to take distance from others, capacity for innovation, flexibility in thinking, and involvement in the role. Presumably, being able to identify potentially problematic situations and to determine whether a problematic interaction is a result of the definition of the situation or of the individual enacting the role are also important.

In summary, competent role performance requires interpersonal competence. Role competence is the ability of a person in an interdependent or exchange relationship which is ongoing in time (i.e., has both a history and future) to carry out lines of action that are task and interpersonally effective.

Organization Management Perspective. This second important approach to the study of role stress began with Kahn et al., (1964), social psychologists who received major funding to study organizational stress. The theoretical consultants to that project were Gross, Mason, and McEachern, who completed their own study of role conflict in 1958, and Rommetveit (1954), another sociologic role theorist, who contributed the notions of *sent role* and *received role.* The contributions of the sociologic consultants account for much of the appearance of similarity of the Kahn work to traditional role theory.

The study by Kahn et al. (1964) established the basic framework, concepts, and operational definitions for much ensuing research. The original research identified the importance of role conflict, ambiguity, and overload. Unfortunately, the same role problems with the same definitions are still being used to study factors comprising organizational effectiveness without advancing the knowledge base.

The studies of role problems have generally utilized measures identified by Rizzo, House, and Lirtzman (1970). The ensuing research has involved variations of the sample, type of organization, and structural location of the subjects, but has resulted in few new ideas; indeed, there seems to have been little concern with progress in related theory development. The measurement techniques and scales have not substantially advanced beyond the original scales developed by Rizzo et al.

It is difficult to know how to analyze the results of the large number of these studies on role conflict. The scales used do not measure role conflict as it is usually defined outside of the organizational management realm. The scale on "role conflict" contains measures of role incongruity, role under qualification, availability of time and resources, role overload, and conflict in policies and evaluative standards. The scale is supposed to measure role conflict and role ambiguity, but factor analysis by Rizzo et al., shows that the "scales" are not independent. The conceptualizing of all of these role problems as types of role conflict is of questionable usefulness. The role conflict scale is actually a measure of general role stress.

The large number of role conflict studies in the organizational management literature is not further reviewed here. It should be noted, however, that Kasl (1978), in a chapter devoted to identifying the significance of organizational effects on individuals, reviews the research on role problem studies in organizational management and concludes them to be generally trivial work that has not advanced our knowledge appreciably.

Since 1970, more than 50 related studies have been published in organizational management journals. In addition, several major funded research projects have focused on the notion of role problems. These studies have been mainly on job and work stress and on occupational health (Cooper & Payne, 1978, 1980; French, Caplan, & Harrison, 1982).

Person–Environment Model. The basic theory underlying Kahn's work, French's model of person–environment, and the work of the psychologists in organization management is the motivational theory of Lewin, a theory very different from role theory (structuralism and the social psychological theory of symbolic interaction). The theoretical perspective developed by Lewin (1951) attempted to describe the present situation (field) in which persons participate or "behave" in terms of tension, force, and need. The "environment" in the person–environment model represents the "field" in Lewin's approach. Behavior, for example (called locomotion), may be produced by a "need" related to a "tension system." Tension systems are the result of positive and negative forces in any "life space." Psychological forces (needs and motivations) and tension systems provide the basis for change.

Additional variables in the person–environment fit theory are the objective environment and the subjective environment. The subjective environment is the psychological construction of the world the person lives in, including availability of supplies and resources. The objective person refers to the person as he really is, including values, needs, abilities, and attributes. The subjective person represents the individual's perception of the objective self. The theory proposes that a discrepancy between the objective person with needs, values, and attributes (as they relate to the work place) and the subjective person is a source of health strain. Coping in this model consists of actions to change either the person or the objective environment in an attempt to improve the fit between them.

Kasl (1978), in reviewing the organizational stress approaches, has assessed the relative importance of person–environment concepts. By combining results from numerous studies he concluded that environment alone is the most important concept explaining virtually as much variance in the studies as the concepts of person–environment model explain. Accordingly, Kasl questions the value of the model.

Organizational Management Approach to Intervention. Much of the theory from the organizational management approach encourages the view that inadequate individual role performance is a matter of personal incompetence. Organizational theory and managerial programs for employees emphasize the importance of individual motivation and high levels of performance through such mechanisms as time management and goal setting. This focus tends to assume that any resulting poor quality of work is an individual problem.

There has been very little research on role performance as a function of the social structure. Compromised role performance which is due to structural stress cannot be corrected by "shaping up" the individual role occupant. Another managerial program that is intended to increase the efficiency of employees takes the form of group work. Such groups may be assembled for decision making, quality circles, problem solving, etc., or they might entail support groups with an emphasis on working together to foster goal achievement. Such group activities are valuable to lessen the sense that one is alone in experiencing role strain but the source of the problem is usually assumed to be personal or interpersonal, not structural. If the source of the problem is in the social structure then no type of group program will eliminate the role stress. Such programs may only extend how long employees can tolerate the stress.

ROLE AMBIGUITY

Role performance at times is problematic. If little information is available on expected performance or if participants in a role system disagree on the role expectations for a particular role, then the incumbent of that role may experience role strain. The norms for the role may also be vague, ill defined, or unclear. When disagreement on role expectations occur, associated with a lack of clarity in those expectations, the condition is called one of *role ambiguity*. To the extent that ambiguous conditions prevail, the role performance of actors may be idiosyncratic while sanctions may be inconsistent and may be haphazardly applied.

Studies of role ambiguity suggest that the condition is prevalent, that it occurs in many different social positions, that it has a variety of consequences, and is usually more detrimental in its effects than is role conflict (see Table 1). In particular, sociological theory suggests that role ambiguity is a characteristic of professional roles.

Sociologic Ambivalence: Health Care Providers

The factors described above relate role stress and sociologic ambivalence. As noted earlier, professional work with clients is often characterized by structural sources of stress or sociologic ambivalence (Merton & Barber, 1963; 1976). The latter is defined as "incompatible normative expectations . . . assigned to a status" (p.6). Ambivalence refers to the social structure—the incompatible normative expectations, attitudes, beliefs, and behaviors are assigned to the position in the structure—not to the individual. In its most restricted sense, ambivalence refers to the incompatible normative expectations incorporated in a single role of a single position, such as the therapist role of a clinician (Merton & Barber, 1963; 1976). Accordingly the ambivalence is located in the roles and statuses, not the emotions and personality of a role occupant. They point out that there are hostilities toward clinicians that are built into the normative structure of professional work. These include:

TABLE 1. ROLE AMBIGUITY: DEFINITIONS AND SUBJECTS STUDIED BY DIFFERENT INVESTIGATORS

Investigator	Subjects Studied	Definition of Role Ambiguity[a]
Arndt and Laeger (1970)	Directors of nursing service	Vague or unclear role demands
Beehr (1976)	Male wage earners	Uncertainty about role expectations
Bible and McComas (1963)	Teachers	Lack of congruity or consensus on role demands
Ben-David (1958)	Physicians	Disagreement on role expectations
Borgotta (1961)	Military personnel	Lack of congruity or consensus on role expectations
Caplan and Jones (1975)	College professors	Unclear role expectations
Cogswell (1967)	Paraplegics	Vague or unclear role demands
Davis (1954)	Military personnel	Lack of congruity or consensus on role expectations
Hall (1954)	Military personnel	Lack of congruity or consensus on role expectations
Hardy (1976)	Hospital nurses	Lack of clarity in role demands
Johnson and Stinson (1975)	Military and civilian personnel	Lack of clarity about role demands
Kahn et al. (1964)	Male wage earners	Lack of information about position
Komarovsky (1946)	College women	Vague or unclear role demands
Lennard and Bernstein (1966)	Physicians and patients	Dissimilarity in role expectations
Lyons (1971)	Hospital nurses	Role sender's expectations unclear
Miles (1975)	Professional-level employees	Lack of clarity in role expectations and predictability of outcomes
Overall and Aronson (1966)	Physicians and patients	Dissimilarity in expectations for physician
Palola (1962)	College students	Discrepancy between performance and expectations
Snoek (1966)	School superintendents	Lack of information about position
Smith (1957)	College students	Lack of information about position
Wardwell (1955)	Chiropractors	Vague or unclear role demands

[a]The definitions provided by the different authors have been paraphrased here.

1. The expectation that the relationship between the health provider and client will have continuity despite patient dissatisfactions
2. The unquestionable authority of the professional health provider which requires the client to reveal his or her private life and to take advice from the clinician that is distasteful
3. Recognition that the professional services are paid for on a fee-for-service basis and that therefore the professional is dependent on the client for payment
4. The concern of the patient that professional interests of the health provider may be given more weight than the client's needs

The sick role model proposed by Parsons (see Chapter 14) suggests that the normative behavior of patients is well established in the general culture. The notion that the patient should seek competent help and cooperate with the clinician could itself be a source of sociological ambivalence.

Other sources of ambivalence are the client's concern as to the competency of the professional, the relative value of the professional's expertise, and the lack of humanistic care.

The clients' beliefs and general sense of uneasiness contribute to role ambiguity for the physician. Patients are participant observers in "backstage" activities. They see, hear, and make judgments about the quality of their care. They develop a working definition of the situation as they see, hear, and make inferences. The patients' capacity to observe real or imagined errors, their ability to question, complain, and communicate to other patients about what they consider dubious practices or actions by their clinicians also adds to the ambivalent nature of the provider–client relationship.

Clinicians also act to establish for themselves acceptable definitions of the situation. Professional staff often act as if the patient is not in a position to judge professional decisions and actions nor to take part in any decisions related to care.

Goffman (1961) has suggested that the ideal situation for clinicians would be to have patients leave their social selves at home and to send in the physical container to be repaired. Indeed, physicians often act as if this situation actually exists. The individual is treated as an impaired, malfunctioning biological system. The professional staff, through routinized activities, restricted communication, and various evasive and distancing strategies, often define the patient as a nonperson. The working consensus negotiated between the health care providers and patient is often one involving specification of the rules for the patient in the medical workplace.

Patients who are treated as "impaired biological systems" accordingly often have their observations, complaints, and queries of concern thrust aside. Concerns of the client are often justified, however. For instance, Katz (1969) has suggested that nurses help overcome inadequacies in medicine's use of science by preventing knowledge of errors, ambiguities, and uncertainties from reaching patients or their families. Both physicians and nurses effectively and purposefully limit communication with patients to prevent interruption of routines and to mask their shortcomings and failures from the scrutiny of clients (Brown, 1966; Lorber, 1975; Roth, 1963; Skipper, 1965). Limited communication shields doctors and nurses from overt criticism while protecting their stance of detachment and concern (Davis, 1960; Quint-Benoleil, 1965). Studies of surgical patients (Lorber) and cancer patients (Quint-Benoleil) have identified various strategies that professional staff use to maintain distance and convey to patients the notion that lengthy discussions are not appropriate. The preferred patient, however, is not the "good" or passive patient but the patient who lets his medical needs be known yet does not in general require more than routine care. The "problem" patient is the one who is very vocal and generally disruptive of the ward routines.

The Knowledge Base as a Source of Uncertainty and Role Ambiguity

The most important structural dilemma, according to Gross and Etzioni (1985) is created by the use of knowledge. Typically, the specialists or knowledge experts are professionals, those who have had an extended educational period to acquire the complex body of knowledge, skills, and techniques of their profession. These acknowledged specialists usually are located in the middle ranks in their organizations, not in the administrative or hierarchy line positions. The source of structural stress arises from the nature of administrative authority that and professional authority are usually distinct and incompatible. The administrative component of organizations assumes a power hierarchy of coordination and control. Decisions are made on the basis of rules and the approval of the supervisor. The professional component, on the other hand, bases its authority on its specialized knowledge. This knowledge is housed in the profession; the creation and use of knowledge, however, is an individual act. The appropriateness of decisions and actions is based on the professional's best judgment. The professional requires freedom to create, take risks, use knowledge, and in general to work effectively. The two worlds of administrators and of professionals are usually very different, as are their goals.

This idea is discussed later in terms of role conflict; at this point it is important to recognize the implications the "special knowledge" base of professionals has for their role ambiguity problems.

Training for Uncertainty. Another major source of uncertainty for physicians has to do with the clinicians' accurate assessment of the state of the scientific knowledge base used in medicine. Fox (1957), in a discussion of medical education, points out that "training for uncertainty" requires the clinician to recognize the limits of existing knowledge as well as his own limits and to acknowledge that medical work will always have a major component of uncertainty. A primary type of uncertainty is related to the need to make decisions on the basis of limited or incomplete knowledge. There are many gaps in medical knowledge; the number varies among specialities. For example, psychiatric knowledge is much less complete than is knowledge related to obstetrics. A second type of uncertainty is related to incomplete mastery of what currently is known in the medical sciences. A third source of uncertainty identified by Fox is the difficulty in distinguishing between personal ignorance or ineptitude and the true limitations of medical knowledge.

Since the competence of a clinician is dependent on knowing what knowledge is actually known, knowing what information is needed in specific circumstances, and knowing where to find the needed information, it is obvious that inadequate knowledge can be a major source of role ambiguity. Incomplete knowledge and inadequate information relative to one's role have already been identified as major sources of role ambiguity.

Decision-making Strategies. Medicine is not a precise science; medicine as it is practiced is even less precise. For the sake of efficiency, shortcuts are developed and, according to Mechanic (1979), decisions are often made on the basis of limited evaluation and exploration of the patient's problem. The problem of uncertainty is a major component of medical decision making and every clinician learns to live with it.

Scheff (1963) points out that medical decision making is similar in logic to basic statistical decision making. Each step in the decision making process involves probable risks and costs and the clinician needs to weigh whether further costs of diagnostic tests involves a risk to the patient's health.

Physicians have learned search procedures for investigating the rare but dangerous conditions. Since many mild signs and symptoms are similar to serious ones, clinicians need to develop for themselves a means of dealing with this uncertainty. Some physicians do so by making thorough examinations and doing extensive testing; others work more from the probabilities, assuming that most signs and symptoms are trivial and that if a person is "really sick" the problem will eventually be picked up. These latter clinicians claim a thorough workup can do more harm than good.

Role Ambiguity: A Challenge. The members of a profession are usually aware of the uncertainty of their body of knowledge and are comfortable in working with incomplete knowledge. In fact, the risk present in each decision and the potential for becoming a consultant to colleagues as their clinical skills advance may become a source of challenge and reward rather than a source of role stress. The constant nature of uncertainty, rather than being defined as undesirable, is conceptualized as normal and perhaps a challenge as clinicians develop knowledge, skill, and a reputation of clinical expertise. The knowledge base, clinical decision making processes, the artful use of medical science—all are a part of a physician's creative mastery of uncertainty.

Role ambiguity is, by definition, a characteristic of all positions occupied by professionals. Technicians, although highly skilled and able to work out complex phenomena, are likely to be employed in positions where role expectations and outcomes are known and work can often be routinized. Professionals, on the other hand, are much more able to deal with uncertainty and the unexpected. Organizations such as hospitals hire professionals to deal with problematic and unpredictable activities and behavior.

From this discussion of the professional's role in organizations it should be clear that job descriptions for these persons in anything but general terms is difficult. If the organization were able to adequately identify the requisite specific role behaviors needed to deal with the unexpected, then the routine activities might be taught and handled by less costly employees. Furthermore, if a professional person could specify in detail the role expectations (job description) for his position, this could indicate a lack of training for uncertainty. His reluctance to handle uncertainty and greater comfort operating from rules than dealing with undefined situations would confirm this. Role ambiguity is not only a challenge to one's professional skills but provides opportunity for creativity in the role and in role making.

Role Ambiguity and Nurses. There have been some studies that looked at role ambiguity and the nursing role. Role ambiguity has been found to be negatively associated with supervisory support (Randolph & Posner, 1981), to be mediated by supervisory support, associated with job dissatisfaction, propensity to leave the organization, tension, anxiety, and lower levels of productivity (French & Caplan, 1973; see review of this research by Rosse & Rosse, 1981; van Sell, Brief, & Schuller, 1981; Hinshaw & Atwood, 1983). In nursing, role ambiguity has been identified in head nurse positions, clinical nurse specialist positions, and staff nurse positions [Arndt & Laeger, 1970; Banda, 1985; Hardy, 1976 (see Table 1)].

Ambiguity for nurses has been related to their diversity of role partners, the lack of clarity in role expectations, and to an uncertainty as to how to initiate subroles of the nursing role.

Participation in decision making and formalization have both been related to role ambiguity among nurses (Morris, Steers, & Koch, 1979; Szilagyi, Sims, & Keller, 1976). Role ambiguity has been found to be greater at higher levels in the organization (administrators) whereas conflict is stronger for those in the lower levels (professionals). Rosse and Rosse (1981) found that head nurses experience higher levels of role ambiguity relative to aides and LPNs. In these studies of nurses and also in the organizational studies, it has been found that role ambiguity is more detrimental to role performance, satisfaction, and commitment than is role conflict.

Nurses Manage Role Ambiguity. Role ambiguity may be a condition that is particularly detrimental to nurses. Katz (1969), in discussing the harnessing and guarding of knowledge in hospitals, points out that many of the administrative and clerical activities which staff nurses do actually are an effort to eliminate ambiguity in the nurses role. He illustrates this by referring to a tendency of nurses to increasingly formulate their jobs sufficiently clearly so that tasks and subtasks can be written on assignment sheets and checked off when completed. This adds to the clarity and accountability of their role and ensures that the physicians' orders will be accurately carried out. On the other hand, Katz suggests that such devotion to specific detailed task assignments ties nurses up in administrative work with the concomitant boredom [role underload] associated with mechanical activity.

Managing Ambiguity: Nurse Problem or Gender Problem? Ambiguity may not be tolerated well by most nurses. On the other hand the ability to work comfortably with ambiguity may also be gender related. Simpson and Simpson (1969) and Katz (1969), in discussing professions which are primarily composed of women (nursing, librarianship, teaching, social work), note that these groups all work in bureaucratic structures. The type of control found is in marked contrast to control by *autonomous colleagues*, which is what is usually found in the male-dominated professions (law, university professorship, medicine, theology). Furthermore, the type of organizational control found in the bureaucratic organization is evident not only in work settings (in nursing service, schools, libraries, and agencies) but also in group activities such as educational settings and professional organizations. Whether the affinity for bureaucratic organization has to do with controlling ambiguity and uncertainty, the gender of the groups, the stage of professional development of the groups (Simpson and Simpson's explanation) or a function of learning and tradition is not yet clear. In general, research on role ambiguity suggests that the condition is prevalent in health care and general organizations.

Organizations are designed to minimize structurally generated role ambiguity and professional persons are expected to manage ambiguities related to their domain of expertise. In the health care professions, a considerable amount of ambiguity revolves around knowledge. Limits of medical knowledge can be a source of uncertainty to professionals and lack of information can be a source of uncertainty to patients and nurses. Role ambiguity for doctors may be associated with their own limited knowledge (a type of role incompetence). There seem to be more uncertainties associated with the physician role, and possibly with the nurse role, than with the roles of most occupants in business organizations.

Ambiguity may exist in one position in relation to one role partner or in relation to several role partners. It may have more adverse consequences for individuals than any other type of role stress.

ROLE CONFLICT

Role conflict is a condition in which the focal person perceives existing role expectations as being *contradictory* or *mutually exclusive*. In the preceding section we described conditions in which role incumbents have difficulty fulfilling role obligations because the norms are not clear. Even when role expectations are clear, however, there is potential for role stress. This occurs when the role occupant has difficulty fulfilling role obligations because the expectations themselves are contradictory. To meet one set of role obligations precludes meeting the others. Conflict is inevitable in organizations, therefore, role conflict is also inevitable.

A brief overview of why conflict is an inherent characteristic of organizations is discussed next (Table 2), and then we look at specific examples of role conflict.

Conflict: Inevitable in Organizations

The condition of conflict has been consistently identified as being inevitable in organizations and therefore is a constant source of structural stress. The basic conflict, most theorists assume, is in the management–worker relationship (see Calkin, Chapter 6). Efforts by management to motivate workers are basically alienating. There are many ways to make work more pleasant, including allowing participation in decision making, but no way to make it absolutely satisfying. The structuralists accept this view—a combination of analyses by both Marx and Weber (Gross & Etzioni, 1985). Marx proposed that workers are alienated because they control neither the means of production nor the product of their labor. Specialization has broken work into such small segments that there is no concept of the whole effort and the segmented tasks become boring and meaningless. (Team nursing is segmented work; primary care nursing is an attempt to counteract it.) Weber added to the Marxian analysis the idea that the alienation is not only between the worker and the means of production but also between persons who control the means of production (but do not manage it) and those who do "manage."

TABLE 2. ROLE CONFLICT: DEFINITIONS AND SUBJECTS STUDIED BY DIFFERENT INVESTIGATORS

Investigator	Subjects Studied	Definition of Role Conflict[a]
Arndt and Laeger (1970)	Directors of nursing service	Conflicting role demands
Becker et al. (1961)	Medical students and faculty	Different role expectations
Bidwell (1961)	Professionals in army	Inconsistent role demands
Burchard (1954)	Military chaplains	Conflicting role demands
Corwin (1961)	Hospital nurses	Disparity between role norms and behavior
Getzel and Guba (1954)	Military personnel	Contradictory role demands
Gross et al. (1958)	School boards and superintendents	Conflicting role demands
Goss (1961)	Physicians	Lack of congruence in norms
Gullahorn (1954)	Union members	Incompatible role demands
Hardy (1976)	Hospital nurses	Disagreement over role demands
Jacobson (1958)	Family members	Disparity in attitudes
Jacobson et al. (1951)	Union members	Discrepancies in norms
Johnson and Stinson (1976)	Military and civilian personnel	Disagreement over role expectations
Killian (1966)	Families and community	Competing values
Kahn et al. (1964)	Male wage earners	Different role expectations
Kramer (1968, 1969)	Hospital nurses	Disparity between role norms and behavior
Miles (1975)	Professional-level employees	Incongruity in role expectations
Scott (1969)	Social workers	Incompatible role expectations
Simmons (1968)	First-line supervisors	Conflicting role expectations
Smith (1965)	Head nurses and nursing educators	Discrepancies in role expectation
Wilenski (1956)	Labor union members	Conflicting role demands

[a]The definitions provided by the different authors have been paraphrased here.

Gross and Etzioni have summarized this issue:

> To this Marxian analysis, Weber added that the basic estrangement exists not only between worker and the means of production, but also between the soldier and the means of warfare, the scientist and the means of inquiry, and so on. Thus the issue is not really one of legal ownership (e.g., that the gun belongs to the army and not to the soldier) but rather that with ownership goes the right to control, and that those who provide the means also define their use. The worker, soldier, and researcher—and by implication, all employees of organizations—are frustrated and unhappy because they cannot determine what use their efforts will be put to since they do not own the instruments necessary to carry out independently the work that needs to be done. (Gross & Etzioni, 1985, pp. 70–71)

The authors go on to say that probably the most important structural dilemma is the inevitable strain imposed on the organization by the use of knowledge. Administrative authority and professional authority (based on knowledge) are different and often incompatible. The members of professions are responsible for their own decisions and use the peer group of their profession as their source of reference or authority. The professional person is usually structurally outside the administrative hierarchy.

The issue is not one of legal ownership of the means of production but rather the right to control it. This means that organizations which provide the means for doing work determine what use will be made of the resulting product.

Many professions now require costly resources, such as libraries, laboratories, and equipment, so the recent trend has been for professionals to locate in organizations. Accordingly, the management–worker conflict has expanded to management–professional conflict, which also has been studied in terms of role conflict.

Negotiated Order. The inevitability of conflict is a central theme to symbolic interaction. Bucher and Stelling (1969) contend that organizations in which professionals work are not truly bureaucratic. When professionals control an organization such as a hospital, the organization is neither purely bureaucratic nor purely professional. These symbolic interactionists further contend that professionals negotiate their roles with significant others in the organization to create their own roles. They do not fit neatly into established organizational roles. Bucher and Stelling consider that professionals tend to cluster within the organization. This results in spontaneous differentiation rather than differentiation legislated from the top down. The different interests of professionals, these theorists suggest, lead to competition and conflict. Through the political process, individuals attempt to influence the policies and goals of the organization and final power is shifted rather than being located in a particular office.

Benson (1973) has proposed a dialectic approach to the study of professionals in organizations. He suggested that the relationship between professionals in organizations is a negotiated reality. The assumption is that all organizations contain basic contradictions; accordingly, persons negotiate. In order to understand negotiation between parties it is necessary to understand the resources, negotiating rules, strategies, probable lines of action, and desired outcomes. Resources may be experience, expertise, skill, money, prestige, or anything else that is valued by the other person. The negotiation may be modified by other persons or by rules external to the negotiation (norms). There are likely to be a variety of interest groups within occupations or working subunits that influence individual negotiation opportunities.

Most studies of role conflict, although often defining the prevailing problematic conditions in different ways, examine the existence and perception of clear but competing role expectations.

Conflict between Management and New Professionals. The research by Kramer (1968) on newly graduated nurses and by Lortie (1959) on newly graduated lawyers conceptualize the conflict that graduates experience in the workplace as reality shock. Both sets of research also demonstrate the conflict between professional norms idealized by students and management norms.

A study of clinical nurse specialist students at the masters level identified that the role expectations of graduate faculty for these students were different than those of nursing service administrators (Cason & Beck, 1982). The faculties' role expectations for the graduates were autonomy and accountability whereas the nurse-administrators' expectations were collaboration and interdependent care. Thus the role expectations between professional clinicians and administrators differ, reflecting management-professional differences.

Role Conflict of Professionals in Organizations. An area of major theory and research interest is the relationship between professions and bureaucracies. The assumption has been that the two are inherently incompatible and thus are sources of structural stress.

Types of Organizations. The incompatibility of the goals of administration and professionals partly depends on the type of organization. In an organization with the main goal of profit making, the administrative staff are responsible for seeing that this goal is achieved. Professionals in these organizations function primarily as experts or specialists who indirectly may contribute to achievement of the organizational goals. They often are hired into non-line positions. In professional organizations, however, the administrative staff are secondary in that they are responsible for providing the means for professional activity. The final authority rests not with the administration in these settings but with the professional groups, often in the form of boards or committees. In universities, faculty decide on research they will undertake and on the curriculum. Similarly, physicians decide on the proper treatment (and, therefore, necessary equipment) and special clinical focus. Administrative staff may advise professional staff in terms of costs and economics relative to the organization but generally do not make the important decisions.

Semi-Professionals. These are the other major groups that work in organizations. Semi-professionals typically have a shorter educational program than the professionals, communicate rather than generate knowledge, and are part of an administrative hierarchy—often their own. Gross and Etzioni (1985) suggest that persons in these groups have skills and personality traits more compatible with administration than those required for creation of knowledge. Indeed, the semi-professional is likely to run the organization.

Nurses in hospitals are in the semi-professional sector rather than the administrative. Their work is typically less autonomous and more controlled by those higher in the hierarchy. Those in nursing who do research and practice relatively independently—nurse practitioners and clinical nurse specialists, midwives, and nurses working with complex technology, such as in intensive care units—are at the professional end of a semi-professional–professional continuum. Katz (1969) has noted that nurses generally have more autonomy where medical knowledge stops, such as with the senile and incurables where provisions of comfort, nurturance, and easing of pain may be all the help that is left.

Another way in which semi-professionals are different from professionals is that not only do they work in hierarchies but they are often supervised and evaluated by superiors. Staff nurses often are evaluated by and responsible to both physicians and nursing supervision. This norm of evaluation by others in the organization is not part of the professional's world.

Professionals have a strong identity with their profession, usually as a result of their extensive socialization periods. A study by Gouldner (1957) examined the orientation and source of identity among university faculty members. Essentially, he asked them for their reference group. There were two main identifiable groups among them, those who identified more with their profession (their specialty) than the university (their organization) and those who identified more with the organization. The former group Gouldner labeled cosmopolitans and the latter the locals. The physiologists who were cosmopolitan adhered to standards of other physiologists in doing research. The university setting was seen as interchangeable. With advancement in their careers these persons readily moved on to other universities. The locals saw themselves as employees of the organization, committed to the needs of the teaching department and doing little research. Their standards and authority resided in the university, to which there was a strong loyalty. Gouldner proposed that role conflict would likely be greater for the cosmopolitan group and subsequent research has supported this view.

Research on Role Conflict. Gross, Mason, & McEachern (1958), in a sound theoretical study, analyzed the conflicting expectations held by school superintendents and their school boards; of particular interest was the legitimacy of role expectations and the resolution of conflict. Haas (1964) identified conflicting role expectations held among the staff in hospital nursing stations as a predictor of friction. Role conflict was the major variable in a study of a state police organization (Preiss & Ehrlich, 1966). Here conflict between work demands and home demands was a major source of conflict. Kahn et al., (1964) studied the effect of organizational stress; both a national survey and in-depth interviews of persons at different levels in the organization were conducted. In each of these studies, role conflict on workers was found to make a significant impact.

Interrole Conflict: Multiple Position Occupancy. Interrole conflict exists when position incumbents are required to enact many roles simultaneously. An illustration of this type of conflict was identified in a study of a community disaster. Local officials were obligated to deal with the community disaster and at the same time their position in the family required that they locate and assist their family members (Killian, 1952).

Identifying Vulnerable Groups: Disposition. Persons respond in different ways to role stress. Personality disposition has been investigated to account for some of the differences.

A personal flexibility inventory has been used to classify persons into highly flexible and less flexible or rigid categories. McMichael (1978) reports that academicians, physicians, scientists, and others who live in a world of uncertainty scored as highly flexible on this scale whereas blue collar workers, such as train dispatchers, tended to scored lower in flexibility. Kahn et al., (1964) found that anxiety-prone individuals faced with conditions of high role conflict were likely to experience the greatest tension. Similarly, introverts (as compared to extroverts), when confronted with role conflict, experienced more tension and their interpersonal relations deteriorated more. The personality dimension of flexibility–rigidity mediated even more strongly the relationship between role conflict and tension. In a high-conflict situation flexible persons experienced high levels of tension whereas less flexible or rigid people experienced virtually no tension.

Role Conflict in Nursing. Role conflict may be a much more important problem for nurses than is ambiguity. Research on staff nurses has identified conflicts for nurses between their roles relative to service, the hospital bureaucracy, and their profession (Corwin, 1961). Those who scored low in bureaucratic and high in professional orientation had the lowest alienation score whereas those with both high bureaucratic and high professional score had the highest alienation score.

Two major pieces of research have been concerned with turnover of nurses; one was a stress audit for intensive care nurses by Bailey and the other is a model of turnover by Hinshaw and Atwood (1977).

Bailey, Steffen, and Grout (1980) surveyed the perceived stressors of 1800 intensive care nurses. They found the most stressful areas for nurses in the three samples reviewed (regional, national, and Stanford Hospital nurses) were:

1. Management of the intensive care unit
2. Interpersonal relations
3. Patient care

These three areas were identified by each group but not in the same order. For example, the Stanford Hospital nurses ordered the sources of stress (from most to least stressful) as:

1. Interpersonal relations (personality conflicts with staff, physicians, administration, and residents)
2. Inadequate staffing
3. Patient care (critical, unstable patient, and lack of work space)

Additional sources of stress for all three intensive care groups were:

4. Knowledge and skills
5. Physical work environment
6. Life events and administrative reward

Staffing creates major overload problems for critical care nurses. The areas that critical care nurses found most rewarding were patient care, knowledge and skills, and interpersonal environment. Bailey points out the striking similarity in the areas nurses find stressful and those they find satisfying. The major intervening variable is, according to Bailey, the "perception" of the individual in identifying stressors.

A smaller study of stress by Anderson and Basteyns (1981) of critical care nurses identified that among 182 full-time intensive care nurses, the major sources of stress were staffing problems, heavy workload, and communication difficulties with physicians. They note that all of these factors are externally controllable.

Both these researchers and Bailey et al., emphasize the important function that nursing administrators can play in reducing role stress for critical care nurses.

Hinshaw and Atwood (1983) analyzed a number of studies on organizational stress, nursing staff turnover, and job satisfaction. These authors identified individual characteristics, such as expectation of tenure and mobility, age, and education, as important factors in the initial stage of turnover. The important midstage factors were performance rewards and incentives, job stress, role expectations and conflict, job satisfaction, and "intent to leave." The midstage factors tended to reflect individual staff responses and perceptions. Job stress, a major variable, was identified as being cognitively mediated and related through job dissatisfaction to turnover and productivity. The types of stressors (or causes of stress) were physical work environment, professional–bureaucratic role conflict, management and communication patterns, leadership style, staffing and work load patterns, and inadequate knowledge and skill. The authors identify individual strategies, such as stress reduction programs, and organizational efforts, such as support groups, changes in staffing patterns and shifts in workload, as possible ways of handling the job stress.

Banda (1985), in her research on master's-prepared clinical nurse specialists (CNS) in acute care hospitals (*tall* structure) and community health agencies (*flat* structure), utilized structural role theory and Hardy's role strain and role stress scales. She found that almost 90 percent of the CNSs perceived that their major function was consultation and teaching; 68 percent saw administration and 57 percent saw research as part of their role expectations. The research and administrative subroles were cited as the greatest source of role strain. Of the role problems, ambiguity was most strongly correlated with role strain; however, role overload was identified as the major role stress for the CNS. This was the case for nurses working in both the tall and flat organizations. Within the hospital, however, it was a major problem only for nurses in line positions.

The strong correlation between administrative role activities and role strain may reflect the individual's annoyance and frustration at not functioning in the clinical role which the nurses were prepared to enact. It may also be that their role strain reflects the problem that professional persons often experience in relation to the administrative part of an organization. The conflict between administrative authority and professional authority has been a major source of stress for nurses.

Role Conflict Independent of Administrative–Professional Conflict.
Some sources of role conflict may have to do with structural sources of stress other than the management–worker relationship. The role conflict of nurses who do field research is an example of role conflict that exists independent of management–worker conflict. Symbolic interaction provides a way of analyzing such role conflicts in terms of the actors involved.

An example of both conflicting role expectations associated with a single position and the conflicts arising for a single individual in multiple positions is illustrated using a nursing field study of patients' experiences with cancer (Quint-Benoleil, 1965).

The study illustrates the two main types of role conflict. They arose for the researchers who were conducting a field study in which participant observation and open-ended interviews were utilized for data collection. The particular focus of the 18-month study was to examine the effect that having a mastectomy had on the patient as a woman and on her family. Part of the study involved examining the social setting of the hospital ward and outpatient department where the women received treatment.

Role Conflict in a Single Position. Role conflict in a single or focal position (intrarole conflict) is exemplified by the nurse who was doing the patient research. In the Quint study the nurse was confronted by contradictory expectations while exploring postsurgical cancer patients' needs. Patients were found to require a great deal of emotional support and, at the same time, honest information about their malignancy. The overwhelming need for emotional support was an unanticipated condition. The researchers identified that the problem arose because of the controlled and minimal communication in the hospital setting between these patients and the usual professional staff. The field workers presented the patients with a major opportunity to discuss their multiple worries (see Figure 3b).

As a nurse, the researcher usually had read the pathology report and had a full understanding of its implications for the patient. At the same time she experienced a conflicting expectation coming from her understanding that as a professional person she would support the physician and not discuss privileged information with the patient, "since physicians are the legitimate definers of the patient's diagnostic identity" (Quint-Benoleil, 1965).

Role Conflict in Multiple Positions. The second type of role conflict is associated with multiple role occupancy. This conflict is also illustrated by drawing from the Quint-Benoleil article. In the study, each nurse researcher had multiple roles: field researcher, nurse, and woman. Role conflict arose because of different expectations held for each of these multiple roles:

1. A role expectation associated with the position of "nurse" was sensitivity to the needs of oncology patients and competence to discuss emotionally laden topics of concern. However, this ability, which is clearly appropriate for the nurse role, conflicts with the expectations associated with the researcher role. It is impossible to carry out adequately the role functions of the researcher unless one maintains the impartial, uninvolved observer status (Quint-Benoleil, 1965).

2. A role expectation associated with the position of field researcher is that systematic data collection will be uninfluenced by the personal feelings and thoughts of the researcher. However, Quint-Benoleil notes that the field researchers often provided the only outlet for the women patients to talk about their real worries. "Sometimes our feeling of outrage and helplessness interfered with our effectiveness as field workers." Furthermore, the field workers became significant others to the patients. Thus the researchers had a role conflict between their researcher role and their compassionate human role.

3. The gender role (woman) became one of the researchers' multiple positions by virtue of the female subjects in the study. The subjects talked of personal and stressful experiences with which the researchers, as women, could not help but identify. "Not only were we vulnerable as women, identifying with a frightening event which could happen to any woman but we had to struggle [as researchers] without identities as nurses who are supposed to be impersonal and uninvolved."

The Quint-Benoleil study contains many other illustrations of role conflict. Of interest here is that when the field researchers began their research they viewed themselves as occupying a single position with clear, nonconflictual expectations. The problems of entanglement with the personal lives of interviewees is a problem experienced by others doing field work (Olesen & Whittaker, 1968).

Role Conflict in Systems Outside Work Organizations. Role conflict has been studied in the family, small groups, and communities. Some of the studies on role conflict also include an analysis of role overload. This has been the nature of much recent research on women's roles. An initial assumption in the early 1980s was that multiple roles (wife, mother, career woman) would create role conflict and role strain. Measurement of role-strain, however, indicated that role conflict and role overload are not major problems. The research then refocused on the effects of multiple roles. Some of that research is reviewed in this section.

Other work examines preparation and entry into careers and various educational systems at midlife and the effects of taking careers in nontraditional fields. The research focuses on changes in life styles, self-concept, and roles. Peer and colleague groups facilitate career entry and transitions, as we shall see.

Women's Roles and Role Conflict

Research on women has focused on their experiences and conflicts as they move into the labor force and create new careers. Sources of role stress such as role conflict and role overload have been studied in families as they alter their roles to accommodate this change. Role stress and role strain have been conceptualized as conditions to be expected for those advancing their careers.

Generally, the persons studied were working parents. There has been a marked change in life styles and the definition of "family" as the typical family becomes a dual-career family. Women who had been devoting full time to sustaining a family have refocused their efforts and begun to establish themselves in careers. For these women, life styles must change, so must their ways of meeting the role expectations associated with their traditional positions of "mother" and "wife."

Women moving into careers have been exposed to major types of role stress, primarily **role overload** and **role conflict** (Barnett & Baruch, 1985; Hall, 1972; Holmstrom, 1972; Stryker & Statham, 1985). While experiencing the associated role strain they must learn the necessary skills for moving into the job market and a new career. Role conflict and role overload are major obstacles for women in the dual-career family.

In some cases, role conflict and role overload for working women have been associated with a sense of well being and better mental health than has the role overload of women who are primarily in the home (Barnett & Baruch, 1985). This research has been interpreted to mean that role strain may be cognitively defined as being associated with role competence and success or it may be associated only with frustration and predictable inadequate role performance. The latter is the more traditional viewpoint and most of the studies of role conflict and role overload support this view (see Role Overload below). Much of the research with the new and anomalous finding has been research on nontraditional roles and in organizations. Thus, gender and the particular setting may influence the nature of role strain. It is too early to say whether the woman's multiple roles and the diversity of her role set will continue to foster a sense of well being. It may be that the association of role overload and sense of well-being may be a phenomenon found only in women with nontraditional professional careers.

Analysis of the achievement motive has traditionally been developed in a male context. Horner (1972) has hypothesized that females expect achievement to be associated with social rejection and has proposed that women might therefore act to avoid success. This notion has since been replaced by one relating to an "expectation of negative consequences: succeed and be punished."

It is clear that women were virtually excluded from the achievement literature until 1960 (Laws, 1975). This author further notes that there are complexities in women's achievement behavior rooted in sex-typing of occupations. Women aspiring to male-dominated professions tend to threaten the masculinity of the job and those holding such jobs. Gender role conflict results as these women face challenges to their femininity in roles traditionally male. On the other hand, women experiencing overload often display competent behavior (Bremer & Wittig, 1960). Vaughn and Wittig (1980) found that others assessed the intelligence and competence of women in traditional and nontraditional careers differently.

Other research has identified role conflict as the primary source of frustration for the career woman. The conflict of having to choose from among several options is stressful. The choice forced on the professional woman is between the coordination of her career, work, and vital home responsibilities (Coleman, 1976). There is also pressure to achieve and behave in certain ways. This is particularly the case where sex role stereotypes are central to the family and the woman is expected to behave consistent with those stereotypes. A conflict may arise between "career achievement" and social acceptance of a "female." Powell and Rezinkoff (1976), in their measurement of attitudes on sex roles, found women who maintained more contemporary sex role values experienced a greater incidence of psychologic distress. The serious conflict women face, whether in traditional or nontraditional work roles is, according to Lemaku (1980), between femininity, competence, and motherhood. For women in nontraditional career roles the dilemma is to maintain "femininity" while meeting the requirements for achievement in the "masculine role."

Some of the stress comes from having to make forced choices between the options of coordinating the household activities and being goal directed at work (Coleman, 1976; Hall 1972; Lemkau, 1980). These stresses, which are usually associated with juggling two roles, are often compounded by the sex stereotyping of jobs—whereas the women often hold more contemporary sex role values (Laws, 1975; Horner, 1972; Powell & Rezinkoff, 1976).

ROLE INCONGRUITY

The term **role incongruity** is not clearly developed in the literature, yet it is a major type of role stress that is very different from role conflict and role ambiguity (Table 3).

There are several sources of role incongruity: (1) *Person–role fit is problematic*. This is the result of incompatibility between one's skills and abilities and one's role obligations. The study of this incongruity has been of particular interest to those studying occupations, the work role, and organizational management (see discussion on person–environment model in preceding section). (2) *Personal values and self concept are incompatible* with expected role behaviors. This role incongruity is more pervasive and comprehensive than person–role fit because basic values and self-concept are at odds with role expectations. The incongruity in this case is not time limited as it generally is with person–role fit (the latter being usually limited to working hours). The incompatibility may be between a woman's self-concept and her expectations of, for instance, the mother role. It may be between a woman's self-concept and her role in a new culture (the cultural difference in gender roles may preclude a women from functioning autonomously and independently). Or it may be between an individual's self-concept and the expectations of her professional position (as might occur for the nurse who, because of economic reasons, does primarily managerial functions when she more deeply values providing patient care).

TABLE 3. ROLE INCONGRUITY: DEFINITIONS AND SUBJECTS STUDIED BY DIFFERENT INVESTIGATORS

Investigator	Subjects Studied	Definition of Role Incongruity[a]
Backman and Secord (1968)	College students	Demands of role incompatible with self-concept
Beckhouse (1969)	College students	Role expectations run counter to individual disposition, attitudes, and values
Borgotta (1955)	Military personnel	Lack of congruence between role demands and personality
Davis and Olesen (1963)	Student nurses	Norms in new role conflict with occupant's values
Hardy (1976)	Hospital nurses	Personal values conflict with role demands
Johnson and Stinson (1975)	Military and civilian personnel	Need for achievement and independence and their effects on role conflict and ambiguity
Lyons (1971)	Hospital nurses	Need for clarity and its effect on role ambiguity
Martin and Katz (1961)	Novices	Norms in new role conflict with occupant's values

[a]The definitions provided by the different authors have been paraphrased here.

Role Transition: Incompatibility Between Self and New Role

In role transition, the self and self-perceptions are incompatible with the expectations associated with a new role. The central criteria are a *change in position* and the necessary *time* to bring about changes in self so that the self and role expectations become compatible. For instance, the change in position may occur through socialization into one of the professions. The socialization process that enables an individual to make a significant role transition has been found to create conflict between the individual's values and those of the profession.

Changes in position have also been examined as role discontinuity.

Role Incongruity and Role Transition

The role incongruity that generates the most role strain is **role transition**, in which there is an extensive incompatibility between the self concept the self identity, and the social roles (see Figure 4). The incompatibility will last until the self-identity and values fall into line with those expected by the social environment (or the environment changes). Because role transition is such a good example of role incongruity and is an extensive process which can be illustrated by research and theory on professional socialization, it will be discussed in some detail. Included in the discussion are factors that contribute to role strain and factors that act to ease role transitions. Gender is explored as a factor that adds to the role stress of nurses and physicians.

The conceptualization of **professional socialization** in terms of role transition clearly bring this process into the domain of role theory. Furthermore, it identifies important concepts that are common to all role transitions. Analysis of the professionalization processes typically draw upon symbolic interaction theory to describe the process, whereas structural role theory provides the direction, constraints, and outcomes expected from the process.[11]

Role transition occurs as a person moves from one major position to another. The role transition usually involves social processes that bring one's self-perception and behavior into line with the role expectations associated with the new social position. The social processes foster major changes in social identity, self-concept, values, and role behaviors. It is only when these changes have been successfully made that an actor is considered to have moved from one position to another. The process usually occurs over a prolonged period of time and is associated with varying degrees of role strain as the new role behaviors are learned (Figure 4 a & b).

Some position changes do not require a prolonged period of preparation for the new role. Such changes may be acknowledged formally through a certificate or by informal celebrations. A move from student status to employee, or from being single to married, are changes of this type.

Characteristics of Role Transition

Role transitions are usually made **voluntarily**; they involve a process of personal change which makes it possible to move from one position to another. For some groups, role transition may be the primary means for upward mobility; individuals

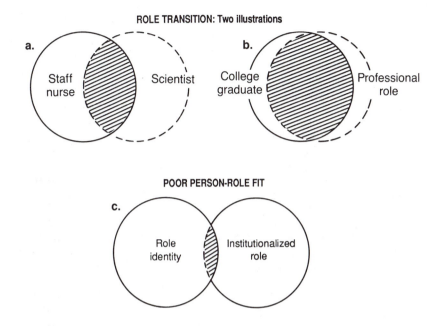

Figure 4. Role incongruity. Hatched areas represent compatibility between self concept and role expectations and unhatched areas indicate degree of compatibility.

advance through sequential positions. Common role transitions for students involve moving from the role of ordinary student to the specialized education or training for a profession. Some of the professions require an extended period to make the transition to becoming a professional. The process of becoming a nurse, physician, engineer, librarian, or physiotherapist all involve a transition from college student to professional over a span of 4 to 8 years. In addition, specialization and graduate study of 1 to 8 years is a common extension of the role transition process.

Role transition usually involves **stages of progress** as the neophyte assimilates the appropriate values, language, skills, and knowledge. For instance, graduate level nursing students require two years of professional socialization processes before becoming full-fledged liaison mental health nurses. In acquiring their master's level degree these students progress through five identifiable stages (Garey, 1985).

Completion of a recognized period of education in which new behaviors and values are acquired is a usual requisite of educational institutions. Whether the learning of new adult roles occurs in a vocational school, a college, a seminary, or in a specific type of occupational, career, or professional school, the process and outcomes acquired through long hours of education usually end with a credential certifying the accomplishment, and the graduate moves into the workforce or continues the educational process—a move into specialization.

The transition from the educational setting to the work setting may be problematic, with its own sources of role strain.

The difficulty nurses encounter in their role transition from the educational setting to the worksite has been the subject of much systematic research by Kramer and associates (Kramer, 1968, p. 69; Kramer & Schmalenberg, 1977). The introduction of an educational program to ease this transition has also been a recent occurrence (Hollaran et al., 1980).

This transition has been termed **role conflict** or **role shock**. It has also been identified as resulting from **inadequate socialization** (Braito & Caston, 1983; Kramer & Schmalenberg, 1977). The meaning of role shock has been explicated by Minkler and Biller (1979). The term is used to refer to the tension associated with discrepancies between the *anticipated* nature of an unfamiliar role and the *actual* role encounter (or on discovering that a major role change had occurred where no such change was anticipated). The tension arises from the disruptive role transitions for which changes in the self and role conceptions are required. Minkler and Biller (1979) make conceptual distinctions between role shock and role loss. Other terms used include **role discontinuity**, nonscheduled **status passage** (Glaser & Strauss, 1965), and **identity crisis** (Erikson, 1968). Lortie (1959) has used **role shock** to refer to the transition of law students to the role of lawyer and Kramer has used it to describe the transition of student nurses into the role of nurses.[12]

Role Strain Associated with Role Transition. Role strain will invariably accompany major efforts at role transition. Indeed, role strain may be a prerequisite to learning a new role. The heightened awareness of one's skills relative to what they should be may facilitate the learning. Role strain, if managed successfully—that is, if it facilitates changes in role behavior—will then dissipate. As pointed out by Howard and Scott (1965), it is when the strain is prolonged and no means nor sign of progress is identified that the ensuing anxiety and frustration can inhibit the learning process. Initially, however, role strain may engage the cognitive and emotional processes to facilitate adult socialization. A student will quickly gain awareness of the complexities of a new role. Special skills, knowledge, appropriate attitudes, and complex sets of behaviors may be seen as separate aspects of the educational process. Eventually these complex factors become integrated as the student progresses through a program.

For instance, third-year student nurses or third-year medical students are still recognized as learners, but their ability to try on the professional role is more believable than during their first year.

Alteration in Self-Identity. Also associated with role transition and acting as an additional source of strain is the alteration in one's **self-identity** and ultimately one's **self-concept**. Social identities are socially learned and are altered primarily as a result of social interaction. The "others" may be "significant others" or numerous role partners (such as patients, other nurses, physicians, aides, physiotherapists, and teachers). Changes in one's perception of one's self results from the influence of others; they are socially situated and largely based on how one is defined and regarded by others in social interaction.

It is the long-term commitment to a new network that makes possible a major change in one's self-concept, social identity, behavior, and values. Such changes are generally entered into on a voluntary basis, whether one is entering a profession, a marriage, a major religious commitment, emigrating to another culture, or attempting to establish one's self in another social system.

Biddle's (1966) description of life in the army illustrates the major role transition that occurs when a civilian role is replaced by one in the armed services. Studies on professional socialization into medicine and into nursing illustrate how totally time-consuming and all-consuming the educational process actually is. Olesen and Whittaker (1968), in their study of nurses and Coombs (1978), in his study of medical students, show how much time students spend together above and beyond normal classroom time. Eating and leisure time become informal learning time. Students spend less and less time with their friends and family and more and more time with their classmates and instructors. This isolation from reality adds to the intensity of the learning period.

Changes in position have been particularly well described by Goffman (1959) in terms of the characteristics of the setting that bring about role transitions. He vividly describes the "processing" that occurs in "total" institutions where the spheres of work, play, and sleep occur with the same persons and under a constant authority. Such is the case for a novice, a recruit in the army, a student in a boarding school, a mental patient, or a criminal in an institution. Probably diploma schools of nursing and some medical schools come close to being total institutions and consequently have an immense impact and influence in bringing about desired changes in social identities, self-concept, and desired role behaviors of their students.

Nonvoluntary changes, such as those associated with alterations in health status, may be best understood as taking place initially in a total institution setting.[13]

Role Transition and Professional Socialization

Role transition is a useful way to analyze the **position change** and associated **social processes** which occur between the time a college student enters a professional school and when the student graduates. Professional socialization has many of the characteristics of role transition. Professional education, whether it is in nursing or medicine, is designed to shape attitudes, values, self-identity, role skills, role knowledge, and role behavior. The faculty in a profession are responsible for establishing the best curriculum for achieving this and for selecting recruits who are most likely to acquire the desired knowledge, skills, and values with the least difficulty.

The selection of students with desirable characteristics and good potential for becoming a dentist, a pharmacist, or a physician implies that there are certain characteristics which differentiate the applicants to professions. Studies have supported this. The social characteristics of recruits do differ on the basis of the profession chosen. This differentiation is one mechanism for reducing the amount of change that has to be made by the recruit and hence the amount of role strain.

A second variable that the professions differ on is their decision-making processes and factors influencing decision making.

In the following section the nature of role transitions is discussed, then illustrations are drawn from professional socialization research.

Role Transition: Changes in Self-Concept

Role transition is a prolonged process in which the social environment is influential in bringing about changes in the self-concept (Allen & van de Vliert, 1984; Glaser & Strauss, 1971; Hormuth, 1982; Olesen & Whittaker, 1968; Secord & Backman, 1964). The change in self-concept and the learning of new role behaviors occurs in interaction with multiple role partners. Many of these role partners will become significant others over time, part of a reference group, and subsequently a membership group for the individual. The learning of new role behaviors and development of a new social identity are associated with on-going role enactment of behaviors associated with the new positions. For instance, clinical practicums in the educational programs of student nurses are safe environments for neophytes to enact in public their role of the student nurse.

Factors That Limit Role Stress during Role Transition. Research on the characteristics of recruits to various professions has made it possible to identify some factors which differentiate the recruits. The new students' personal attributes, style, and general traits have been found to be specifically compatible with their particular chosen profession (Hanson & Chater, 1983; Preiss, 1968; Secord & Backman, 1964). Some differentiating characteristics may actually reduce role strain for the neophyte. For example, values and personal characteristics of medical students are more compatible with medical education than with dentistry or engineering. Dental students emphasize mobility, status, and economic rewards (Denzin & Mettlin, 1968) whereas medical students emphasize the humanitarian aspect of their work.

Career Choices: Influence on Time for Values to Develop

Analyses of professional careers have identified medical students as making their career decisions at a relatively young age. Typically several family members are physicians (Coombs, 1978). Nurses, on the other hand, do not make their career decision until relatively late. The decision to become a nurse on the surface seems to lack rationality but when family needs and economic contingencies are taken into account the process is rational (Katz & Martin, 1972; Psathas, 1968; Simpson, 1979). (See the discussion in the next section.) Typically, reality is introduced into their decision by family members who are nurses (Olesen & Whittaker, 1968). Both physicians and nurses cite humanitarian reasons for their choice and a desire to work with people as strong motivating factors influencing the career decision.

Another group that works with sick persons are chiropractors. Chiropractic recruits typically come from "humble" origins. Some wish to become physicians but lack money or the ability to meet admission standards (Wardwell & Pavalko, 1972). Their motivation seems to be a combination of humanitarianism, economics, and status (Denzin & Mettlin, 1968).

Dental students usually claim dentistry is their first career choice. These recruits choose dentistry because it is neither overly difficult to gain entry into nor to graduate from dental school. These students are committed to making money and to achieving status. They generally come from upwardly mobile families in which the father is a successful businessman. Thus, status and money are valued in the family (Sherlock & Cohen, 1972).

Pharmacy recruits also subscribe to the self-rewarding and economic security aspects associated with their profession. Humanitarian motives are less strong. The orientation of pharmacy students is mixed; no dominant orientation is apparent among pharmacy students as there is among medical students.

Women in Professions May Not Endorse the Relevant Professional Values

Davis and Olesen (1963) point out that structural and cultural attributes, such as maleness, middle-class membership, achievement orientation, and professional status, are all normal attributes of persons planning to enter the professions. These authors also raise the question of what happens when the bulk of recruits to a profession lack one or more of the major motivating factors.

The studies of professional socialization of nurses in college settings by Olesen and Whittaker (1968) and by Simpson (1979) illustrate the cross pressures students are exposed to as they struggle with the goals of marriage, family, and career. The partial commitment to typical career goals and to their profession and the role conflict generated by outside social pressures add to their role strain. The students in these two studies came from the middle class and had strong parental support for their decision to enter nursing. Simpson found that students valued helping persons and being with people; Olesen and Whittaker found that demonstrating care and concern for others and service to humanity were values held by most of the incoming nursing students. Family and marriage were more important to both sets of incoming students than was their career. Katz and Martin conclude from their study that a nursing career is less a deliberate choice than the cumulative result of a series of specific acts or solutions (to live near family, to be with a friend) unrelated to the career of nursing. They found that the majority of students made their decision to enter nursing at between 16 and 20 years of age.

Psathas (1968) has proposed that a variety of social, family, and economic factors are likely to influence the career decisions of women. Of central importance is the relationship between the sex role and the occupational role. Marriage right after high school limits the option of a career; on the other hand, education may be seen as a means for making a daughter more "marketable" in marriage.

Psathas goes on to note that nurses typically come from the upper-lower to lower-middle classes and are likely to marry above their originating social class. This is particularly the case for nurses in college programs. Their family finances are usually restricted and the allocation of funds for education will likely depend on there being few financial crises. Also the number of siblings and the birth order of the male siblings will influence the allocation. Vocational or occupational training for sons is generally seen as more important than for daughters (Simpson, 1979). Thus, Psathas's proposal is congruent with Katz and Martin's conclusion that the decision to enter nursing may be the result of situational-specific decisions relatively unrelated to a specific career decision.

The decision made by the majority of women would appear to be ambivalent and, on the basis of the two longitudinal studies of nurses, the career choice is not given priority over marriage and family. Thus the mixed commitment of nurses to the general achievement goals of careers and to the career itself. The external pressures, many of which are internalized, stressing marriage over career for women add to the normal role stress and role strain associated with their role transition.

Outcomes of Professional Socialization of Nurses. Simpson (1979), in her study of professional socialization of nurses (class of 1965), found that the values endorsed consistently by the students in their first year were the desire to be with people, work with people, help people, and be of service. By graduation these values had been replaced by a bureaucratic orientation and a stronger commitment to family than to themselves or nursing. Olesen and Whittaker's study (a West Coast nursing class of 1963) asked students on entry and at graduation to rate themes, both traditional and contemporary, generally attributed to nursing and to indicate how much they themselves endorsed each. There was little congruence in the themes and the ratings by freshman and even less congruence for the ratings by the graduating class. If the nursing educational process had been successful, one would have expected a high level of congruence between the nursing themes and the ratings of the graduating class. The graduating students, however, had become less authoritarian, more emotionally expressive, and had an increased capacity for complex thinking and dealing with novel situations.

Compatibility between Social Orientation and Career. Coombs's (1978) longitudinal study of professional socialization of 68 medical students presents comparative data over time and highlights the processes students go through in making a transition from college student to physician. The Olesen and Whittaker (1968) study in nursing is an excellent descriptive study utilizing the symbolic interaction perspective. Coombs combines the same theoretical perspective with quantitative measures obtained across the socialization period and, therefore, the role transition process can be more readily summarized.

The compatibility of the orientation of medical students with their role expectation goes deep. About half the students came from families which already had a physician member. They generally came from well-to-do homes, were primarily Protestant, and 50 percent had made the decision to be a physician before entering high school. The compatibility of orientation is illustrated in Coombs's comparison of freshman and senior values which showed a remarkable stability or congruence between the two sets of measures. He summarizes the class of students he studied as being well suited for the stressful competitive demands of medical school—they were intelligent, resourceful, serious minded, self-assured, and they thought well under pressure. Likewise, early career decisions, which is typical of medical students, provided time for preparation and their activities related well to their chosen career. This process of anticipatory socialization, personal commitment, and motivation to become a physician eases the role transition processes.

Besides a change in self-concept, professional socialization brings about a change in social identity. Only 2 percent of the freshmen Coombs studied identified themselves as doctors whereas 45 percent of the seniors identified themselves that way.

Coombs provides sound additional information relevant to the socialization process. One aspect of medical socialization has to do with attitudes that develop around the patient. Coombs found that initially students were aware of the need to portray confidence in their interaction with patients. Thirty-five percent of the freshmen tried to impress with self-assurance and confidence; the percentage peaked in the junior year (53 percent) then fell to about 40 percent in the final year.

Some of the techniques described by the students for portraying self-confidence include:

1. Look squarely at patients, keep them busy answering questions so they won't have time to ask questions, and don't talk too much (which might reveal student's lack of knowledge)
2. Never hesitate, keep busy; just keep moving a step at a time
3. Assume an air of authority
4. When stuck, give a plausible answer, leave, reorganize and return

The students preferred to work with middle-class adult male patients with an acute organic illness. The majority of students identified interpersonal skills as essential for being a successful doctor; these skills were mentioned more often than technical competence.

The interaction of medical students with nursing staff is another important aspect of professional socialization. It is complicated by the ambiguous status of medical students. At first they are inferior to nurses in terms of experience and knowledge, but they know that when they graduate nurses will follow their orders. Their ambiguous status is a source of confusion and strain. However, as students gain competence their status relationship with nurses changes. Twenty-five percent of the freshman medical students saw themselves with higher status than nurses; by their senior year this increased to 52 percent. Working relationships with nurses began to improve in the junior year and were much better by the senior year. One senior student said nurses now respect them; another pointed out that nurses had reached a status plateau while the career potential of the medical students was just beginning.

The difficulties that status differences create for nurses and medical students have been noted by others (Coser, 1962; Rushing, 1962). Coombs concludes by noting that there is little doubt in the eyes of the students as to the status and role of the physician. Freshmen and seniors have similar ideas of what makes for a good and a bad doctor and there were few changes in what was seen as rewarding and a liability. Among valued items were interaction, feeling of personal accomplishment, interesting and challenging work, opportunity for independence and responsibility, sizable financial income, status, and prestige. The liabilities included the demanding nature of the work, the potential of work intruding on personal lives, and difficulties dealing with problem patients.

Coombs's longitudinal study made it possible to trace the development of an identity with the role transition from student to physician. After an initial dip in self-confidence, students began to fulfill their responsibilities, wear the physician regalia, and be called physicians by faculty, patients, and their peers. By graduation their self-confidence was high.

Coombs concludes that medical students are propelled by a need to achieve career prominence; their aspirations get them through the tough spots, and their personal qualities make them well able to handle competition and the demands of medical school.

On the basis of the professional socialization literature reviewed here—and, as most was published prior to the women's movement, it is distinctly biased toward "typically" female and male careers—the socioeconomic levels, aspirations, and values of those entering their chosen field seem wise. The chiropractic student from humble beginnings does not compete with the well-financed, academically proficient students entering medicine and law. The socialization of medical students as reported by Coombs illustrates successful role transition over a four-year period with minimal alteration in basic values and attitudes; only additional values are added. The role transitions which occurred during the socialization processes of the two nursing classes were less successful from a faculty perspective. Students did not acquire faculty career values, and initial values for a marriage and family rather than a career remained unchanged. The dual commitment of entering nursing students to the profession and to family life creates dilemmas and role stress not experienced by males in professions.

There are no comparable longitudinal studies of professional socialization in nursing since the major changes of cultural and social values in 1968. There is, however, a longitudinal study of 241 female students at an Ivy League college in 1979, Komarovsky (1985). The two previously mentioned studies of nurses were conducted between 1963 and 1965; thus, the two groups of women would have developed very different expectations for themselves and for women and men in general. The social class differences between the nurses and the Ivy League women would also add to differences in their orientation. One obvious difference is that the student nurses were already on the road to a career and economic independence whereas the college students had not yet made such a commitment. Even given these limitations, the homogeneity of gender of these two groups may make them more alike than different in terms of the relative importance of a career or family.

Komarovsky's (1985) longitudinal study of Ivy League college women led her to conclude that the majority of incoming students wanted a career, marriage, and children (76 percent) while the next choice (14 percent) was for marriage and a career (no children). Over the four-year period of college, the group that had wanted only marriage and a career decreased to 7 percent while those preferring a career, marriage, and children increased from 76 to 85 percent. Those planning to go to a professional school increased over the four years from 27 to 36 percent. Thus, this group of contemporary women were struggling with the relative importance of career and family, with most deciding they wanted both.

From Komarovsky's study it seems that women still face more role stress as they enter college than do men. Not one of the studies of professional socialization of men identify family as an important goal. Career activities were the males' total reported focus. The question still of concern is the extent to which a professional's gender influences the direction and nature of his or her career.

Current professional socialization of women in medicine provides some insights as to changes in socialization of women since medical schools became legally bound to increase their female and minority enrollments. In 1968, only 8 to 9 percent of all entering medical students were female; by 1977 the number had risen to more than 25 percent (Coombs, 1978). Lorber (1972) provides some information on women in medicine. She notes that even though women in medicine tend to come from the upper middle class, be married to professionals, and do very well academically, upon graduation their incomes are considerably lower, they have fewer hospital appointments, and have fewer appointments in professional organizations than do their male counterparts.

Furthermore, female physicians are overrepresented in the less prestigious specialties such as pediatrics, psychiatry, and public health. Lorber doubts that this greater representation in the lower status positions is due to attempts to minimize conflict between sex and professional roles. She notes that Linn (1971) found in a study of 800 dentists that women tend to choose to work alone because they like the independence. The gravitation of women physicians to public health positions (with its much lower general level of competitiveness) may be for a similar reason. Lorber does consider that structural reasons such as educational tracking may be a partial explanation. Until recently women were not readily admitted to the more prestigious medical schools. Also, as Mumford (1970) has reported in the one longitudinal study of medical education which does include women, women interns preferred to locate at a nonaffiliated community hospital where the experience, training, and envisioned future careers for interns are in marked contrast to the university hospital, where the chiefs are university professors. The male interns who overwhelmingly predominate at the university hospitals were expected and encouraged to go into research or a prestigious specialty. In an unrelated study of 146 female interns by Campbell (1973) (also cited by Lorber), it was noted that the "boys club" ambience was strong, with the resulting educational opportunities and awarding of scholarships still discriminatory against females. However it could also be inferred that women turn to the less prestigious 9-to-5 jobs so they can more readily manage their family responsibilities. Lorber does note that Dykman and Stalnaker (1958) found that 45 percent of the female physicians curtailed their full employment after graduation. Those women who did limit their employment did so because of marriage, not children.

In summary, the role transition of college and career-oriented women is unduly fraught with additional role stress and role strain. This may be a result of gender still being a major (but often invisible) wall requiring additional vigilance and energy by women who are trying to prepare themselves for challenging careers. Gender for nurses and college students is a major source of ambivalence. Career, marriage, and motherhood are the identified goals, with nurses choosing family life first and a career to fall back on. The ambivalent endorsement of career goals and the uncertainty as to whether marriage will occur adds to the normal role strain associated with their role transition. Loneliness and uncertainty were common emotions cited by Komarovsky's student college sample. Women medical students may experience loneliness, but they also experience anger and frustration at blatant inequities they perceive in the system. The process of role transition for women—whether in college, medical school, or in nursing programs—appears to have more structurally generated stress than males experi-

ence making similiar transitions into professions. In summary, professional socialization for women is related to two types of structural stress. One, role ambiguity,
is related to role transition, whereas the other, role conflict, is related to gender.

ROLE OVERLOAD

Another major form of role stress is *role overload* (Table 4). In the presence of
overload, a role occupant experiences difficulty in fulfilling *role obligations* which
are excessive relative to the limited time available. Although able to perform each
individual role obligation competently, the actor is unable to carry out all role
obligations in the time available. Furthermore, the excessive obligations and the
time restrictions do not change over time. Roles which are characterized by
cyclical overload, such as those of nurses working in emergency rooms and
professors and secretarial persons in the academic settings, permit the incumbents
to plan and create temporary priorities in their role obligations and responsibilities
and thereby modify their allocation of energy, time, and attention depending on
the cycle of their work periods.

Role overload is a major source of role stress. Insufficient time, not inability
to perform all the components of the role obligations, has been found in earlier
studies to be the primary necessary condition for the existence of role overload
(Hardy, 1971; Miller, 1968; Sales, 1969). Subsequent research has primarily
examined effects of variations in the excessive role obligation and time restrictions.

Conditions Necessary for Role Overload

Available Time. Research by Sales (1969), following up on Kahn's study of role
overload, found time to be the important central factor. Time has been investigated in terms of both its objective and subjective aspects. The latter refers to a

**TABLE 4. ROLE OVERLOAD: DEFINITIONS AND SUBJECTS STUDIED BY DIFFERENT
INVESTIGATORS**

Investigator	Subjects Studied	Definition of Role Overload[a]
Arndt and Laeger (1970)	Directors of nursing	Workload too heavy.
Hardy (1971)	Male college students	Lack of time to meet role demands
Hardy (1976)	Hospital nurses	Lack of time to carry out role obligations
Caplan and Jones (1975)	University professors	The amount of work to be completed in a given amount of time. Too much
Kahn et al. (1964)	Male wage earners	Impossible to meet role demands within given time
Sales (1969)	Chartered accountants	Incapable of meeting role obliga-tions in allotted time
Snoek (1966)	School superintendents	Role demands exceed worker's capacity

[a]The definitions provided by the different authors have been paraphrased here.

person's perception of time, which may be different from the actual or objective time (Caplan & Jones, 1975; Rosenman & Friedman, 1974; Friedman & Rosenman, 1959; Sales, 1969). These investigators found that subjective time for certain personality types, such as high achievers and persons with type A dispositions (Friedman & Rosenman, 1959), is markedly different from objective time. Type A personalities have a greater sense of "time urgency" compared to type B personalities and are more responsive to the pressures of deadlines. Thus, time is a major source of strain for these "types" of persons. (See also Persons Who Seek Role Overload later in this chapter.)

Excessive Role Expectations or Demands. A central characteristic of role overload is excessive expectations or role demands. Some authors have concluded that excessive demands, all of which are appropriate to a role, produce a problem of conflict between priorities (Arndt & Laeger, 1970; Snoek, 1966). This perspective, however, overlooks the core nature of role overload. By definition, even given that a role occupant can prioritize the important obligations and responsibilities, it still would be impossible to carry out *all* of them.

Frankenhauser and Gardell (1976) have reported relevant research on the impact of technology on health and satisfaction. The research of these authors represents the approach of social psychologists and psychophysiologists. Control over one's work and the ability to assess that work role relative to a meaningful whole and the opportunity for cooperation and fellowship were found to be important factors. These factors are severely affected in overload conditions in which work is mechanically controlled, involves repetitive cycles, and permits only limited opportunity for interaction.

These investigators have looked specifically at the effects of overload and underload. They define **quantitative load** relative to the amount of work to be done per unit of available time. **Qualitative load** they use to refer to the complexity of the tasks to be performed, irrespective of time. The two parameters can be used to describe and study both overload and underload conditions. The investigators utilized two related groups of workers who differed in the nature of their work. One group (the at-risk workers) had jobs entailing work with significant physical strain, extreme repetitiveness, restricted social interaction, and mechanical pacing of their work. The control group were workers able to control their pace and place of work.

The high-risk group was found to have high levels of catecholamines, psychosomatic illness, and signs of maladjustment. The major sources of strain were monotony of the job and lack of personal control. Data analysis from the study showed that degree of repetitiveness coupled with duration of the work cycle were the major contributors to the stress condition and created the highest incidence of pathophysiologic conditions. Quantitative overload, characterized by monotonous, repetitive work, was found related to a low sense of well being and undesirable changes in physiologic parameters. The authors identified the crucial work stress as the demand on the worker to make skilled decisions in an extremely short time when the work is paced by machine. The skill and experience which the workers had available for decision-making could not be utilized because of the fast pace of the machines. A concomitant sense of not living up to one's potential was a major threat to the workers' self-esteem. The work system prevented them from doing a good job and from utilizing their expertise.

The major finding is that their work was characterized by both quantitative overload and qualitative underload. Frankenhauser and Gardell (1976) point out that in both quantitative overload and in qualitative underload a worker's skill is underutilized.

Qualitative overload seems also to be a stress source for managers. French et al., (1982) looked at the qualitative and quantitative overload conditions of 122 university administrators and professors. They found that low self-esteem was related to qualitative overload for the professors but not for administrators. Qualitative and quantitative overload consistently was associated with job dissatisfaction, tension, smoking, sense of threat, embarrassment, high cholesterol levels, and increased heart rate (Cooper & Marshall, 1978; French & Caplan, 1973). Many managers react to overload by working overtime. In a study of executives, 45 percent reported working all day, in the evening, and all weekend (Cooper & Payne, 1978).

One study reported several types of role stress including overload were more aversive for managers in low-enriched jobs than those in highly enriched jobs (Abdel-Halim, 1978). The low-enriched jobs could be interpreted as jobs in which the conditions limit the utilization of the manager's abilities.

Role Overload Compared to Role Underload

Role overload refers to inadequate resources (relative to possibly excessive demands) whereas **role underload** refers to insufficiently challenging demands. Inadequate resources in the form of knowledge, experience, values, and motivation, along with the necessary basic skills can make meeting the demands of adequate role performance difficult. This is the condition of **qualitative role overload**—too few resources to meet the normal demands of the role. In contrast, the condition of **qualitative role underload** is one in which whatever demands actually exist are essentially too easy to perform—in essence, they produce boredom. A role with qualitative underload would be characterized as demanding too little responsibility and permitting too little participation in decision-making.

Having too few personal resources while having to keep up with increasing standards of performance while managing new technological challenges are common sources of role stress, generally classified as qualitative overload. However, by their lack of adequate response, those experiencing this stress might also be moved into a standstill condition (i.e., not be able to do anything) and, hence, a condition of underload. There seems to be little current research on this anomalous condition (Cooper & Marshall, 1978). One study by Kay (1974) has identified middle managers' verbal response to this stress as "what am I here for?" These persons start feeling salary compression, job insecurity, vulnerability to redundancy, and a sense of no available options as new recruits move into their organizations.

Cooper and Payne (1978) also suggest that role underload occurs in the same jobs which have overload. These would be jobs with periods of work overload and periods of underload—such jobs as nursing, police work, air traffic control, emergency room attendance, international airline piloting. The difficulty is one of maintaining vigilance while "waiting for something to happen." The wait is often boring and the employee loses efficiency. Shift work often has peak periods and then slack periods and conditions are often compounded by insufficient sleep so efficiency is even further jeopardized.

Whether or not the level of workload is related to job satisfaction depends upon the occupation. Scientists and administrators who undertake work that is intrinsically satisfying find underload stressful; people in jobs such as police or assembly line work are relatively unaffected by underload.

Sources of Role Overload

Role-Set Diversity. The existence of a form of role overload characterized by multiple compatible role demands within one's role set has been identified by Katz and Kahn (1966). In this form of overload the demands are individually compatible, but there are too many of them. Snoek (1966) found that role strain was greater for those persons who interacted with a more diversified role set. In their structural analysis of the circumstances of this strain, the interests and loyalties present in a role set were identified as being more important than the actual number of persons with whom the focal person interacted. The concept of a class of role senders was used to take into account all the role relationships involving subordinates.

In a study of head nurses, role overload was found to be associated with role strain (Arndt & Laeger, 1970). The overload related to the diversity of the nurses' role set and was interpreted as being a function of role conflict and frequency of interaction. In a study of tax accountants, physiological indicators of stress were found to disappear after April 15th (Friedman et al., 1957; Sales, 1969). The stress was found to be related to a constant interaction with their pressured clientele rather than it being a problem related to meeting the deadline.

Opportunity for Autonomy. Coser (1983), reporting on recent theoretical work, continues her interest in health care structures and health care providers and their functioning in conditions of structural ambivalence. She considers that the various forms of role stress can be interpreted as providing an opportunity for role occupants to acquire a sense of autonomy. Coser discusses her earlier research findings to illustrate this hypotheses.

In the study she compared two types of hospital wards. One type (Sunnydale) was characterized as dealing with terminal illness. Nurses more or less ran the ward and they seldom saw a physician. The other type (Center), was characterized as a rehabilitation ward; it had four active physicians along with two psychologists and several physiotherapists and psychiatrists, all of whom prescribed different regimens for their patients. At Center the nurses had to make decisions in light of the different perceptions and conflicting expectations of members of their role set. Coser measured autonomy in terms of the nurses perception of their work, the centrality of the patient to their work, and the extent to which the nurses held their work to be part of their identity.

Nurses at Center and Sunnydale had quite different social identities in relation to their work. Center nurses saw themselves as organizers, teachers, and politicians. Nine of the 10 nurses referred favorably to their professional role and included the patient as part of their role set. This was in contrast with Sunnydale nurses, who described their most important task as routine activities such as "keeping the patient clean." Sunnydale nurses were much less likely to identify themselves as professionals (only two of the 17 nurses did so) or include patients in their role set (three nurses perceived patients in this way). The professional nurses at Center, who were involved in a complexity of roles, continually had to articulate their role in face of inconsistent, incompatible, and conflicting expectations. As a consequence of their continuous interaction and negotiation with members of their role sets, the nurses made decisions and functioned autonomously.

Coser proposes that individuals who are in complex role sets are required to distance themselves, reflect upon the appropriate course of action, decide, reinterpret or defy directions, and to weigh each of their decisions in relation to their own purposes of action and the purposes of others. This, Coser suggests, requires innovation and often results in violation of custom and standard hierarchical modes of functioning. It also requires some degree of self-direction and flexibility as differences are "ironed out" through negotiation and compromise utilizing a careful recognition of the viewpoints of others. The existing complexity of one's role set (having role partners differentially located in the social structure) is associated in Coser's view with internal decision making and intellectual flexibility. She theorizes that in complex role sets individuals are encouraged to take distance and to articulate their roles and their thoughts, and that such persons are able to develop a degree of individuation that goes together with rationality and flexibility. Referring to the seminal work of Merton on social structure, Coser reemphasizes Merton's belief that modern society is not disastrous and restrictive but a source of opportunity. Coser's research on role sets helps support this view. Her research is interesting from several perspectives. Given the two wards, it would not seem unlikely that if nurses were asked about functioning autonomously and professionally that nurses at Sunnydale ("run by the nursing staff") would claim they were both professional and autonomous. A second point of interest is that past theorizing has proposed that holding multiple roles (called role segmentation) can be a source of anomie (Seeman, 1959) or alienation (see discussion near the beginning of the Role Conflict section on the inevitability of conflict in organizations). Coser's view, which is complementary to Merton's work, is unusually optimistic.

Multiple Roles. Some studies have looked at role overload in terms of the total number of roles a person has. Research has, in general, identified that the greater the number of roles one has, the greater the overload. As women accumulate additional roles such as wife, mother, and career women, they may acquire too many tasks to perform in the time available (Vaughn & Wittig, 1980; Vriend, 1977).

Role Accumulation. The symbolic interaction perspective proposes that a diversity in social relations increases the social and intellectual capacity of persons, while structural role theory identifies multiple roles as undesirable in that persons have only so much energy and time; the more roles one has the less energy and time there is available per role.[15]

Recent theory and research emphasize the benefits of multiple role involvement. Gove and Tudor (1973) proposed that multiple role involvement of males enhances their sense of well being through their simultaneous commitment to work and family; this may account for the fewer psychiatric symptoms reported by men relative to women. Marks (1977) and Seiber (1974) have proposed that commitment to multiple roles may be energy generating. Spreitzer et al. (1979)

have tested the notion that multiple roles are not necessarily stressful. They found that the accumulation of roles can actually be enriching because of cumulative rewards. Differential allocation of energy to different roles may also be important. Studies of work, marriage, and family roles support the view that persons allocate and generate energy according to the value of a particular role. Any investment of emotional energy may be viewed as a result of negotiation and trade-off. This idea has been supported by a study of multiple role occupancy by women in which the multiple roles of work and family were not found related to symptoms of poor mental health (Woods, 1985).

Additional research on working wives and mothers, conceptualized as multiple roles, supports the role accumulation hypothesis. In an important series of studies, Barnett and Baruch (1981, 1982, 1983, 1985) found that role strain was a relatively weak variable and that role overload and role conflict were related to variables of psychological well being, pleasure, and mastery. Also, role overload, role conflict, and role strain (anxiety) were not found to depend on employment status. Mothers, however, experienced higher levels of role overload. Only for nonemployed wives and mothers was role strain strongly related to role *overload*.

Initial and subsequent research by these authors suggests that role overload was only a characteristic of the mother role and was not predictable from the number of roles the women held. For instance, it was not found to be a consequence of juggling role obligations associated with multiple role occupancy but rather it was a function of occupying one role: mother.

The authors propose that nonemployed women may respond to lack of structure and legitimacy in their commitments, which would provide a basis for establishing priorities for some roles and eliminating others.

Stress and the Benefits of Multiple Roles. Role conflict has been conceptualized as a problem associated with multiple roles. Role conflict generally increases with higher levels of education and higher education is itself related to the acquisition of additional roles.

The recent research approach to role-stress studies emphasizes role commitment and the rewarding outcomes associated with multiple roles. Combining this approach with knowledge of role strain from the structural approach, one can make a dynamic analysis of roles using the social exchange framework. A significant body of research now identifies multiple roles as a source of role overload and as being associated with role strain. Another body of research is accumulating which identifies the benefits associated with multiple role occupancy. The next step is to begin to use social exchange theory and examine the benefits relative to the costs. The prediction would be that if the benefits outweigh the costs, then multiple role occupancy would likely be associated with a sense of well-being. If the net costs are greater than the benefits role strain would be the expected dominant experience. Other dysfunctional states are also possible.

Conditions Modifying the Responses to Role Expectations

Individuals do not respond in a uniform manner to role overload. Research by psychologists has focused on identifying groups of persons vulnerable to role overload. They have found that persons with type A personality are particularly vulnerable to role overload conditions. (See also Conditions Necessary for Role Overload on p. 224 of this section.)

Persons Who Seek Role Overload. Some persons seem to be constantly in situations of role overload. Some of these persons have been identified by Rosenman and Friedman (1974) as displaying type A behavior, which is more common in men than in women. For both men and women, type A coronary prone behavioral disposition is correlated with cardiac disease (Chesney & Rosenman, 1980; citing Blumenthal et al., 1978; Rosenman et al., 1975; Waldron, 1978). These predictions were also found true for women in an eight-year prospective study known as the Framingham study (Chesney & Rosenman citing Haynes, et al., 1978).

The behavioral dispositions of type A persons automatically places them in a high-risk category for role overload and role strain. The dispositions include ambition, competitiveness, aggressiveness, being hard driving, and having a strong sense of time urgency (French, Caplan, & Van Harrison 1982). Persons with type A personality (Sales 1969; French & Caplan, 1973) experience relatively high levels of role overload (Orphen, 1982). Sales (1969) has proposed that type A persons self-select challenging jobs with greater exposure to role overload. This generalization is consistent with the idea noted earlier that persons actively seek activities in which they can utilize their skills.

ROLE UNDERQUALIFICATION

Work demands have been identified as having both qualitative and quantitative aspects (see previous discussion in Role Overload). The qualitative aspect refers to the complexity and difficulty of the tasks. Qualitative overload refers to work that is too difficult to do (it is beyond the person's capabilities) (Caplan, 1975; Frankenhauser & Gardell, 1976; French & Caplan, 1972; Sales, 1969). Qualitative overload thus introduces the idea of lack of personal and environmental resources. The underqualified role occupant lacks role competence and the resulting role performance is not adequate. Role underqualification should be distinguished from another condition in which the focal person may have more than the necessary expertise but may lack the opportunity to perform due to other factors, such as restricted available time. This latter condition can be described as quantitative overload and possibly simultaneously qualitative underload if their qualifications are greater than those needed. For instance, severe time restraints may result in underutilization of a focal person's full expertise. Someone with less expertise might find such a situation less frustrating (although this person also would have quantitative overload—but not the qualitative underload).

Reality Shock[15]

The gap between what one is taught to expect in the work setting prior to entry and what actually is encountered in the early phases of work has been called reality or culture shock in anthropology. The phenomenon has been identified for lawyers (Lortie, 1959), nurses (Kramer, 1968), teachers (Eddy, 1971; Wright & Turner, 1971), and social workers (Ehrlich & McClure, 1974; Practice & Academia, 1973). The numerous studies by Kramer and a recent study by Ahmadi et al. (1987) are based on scales developed by Corwin (1961). A major problem of validity has been identified in the scales (Minehan, 1977).

Inadequate General Resources and Gender Differences

Differences based on gender in the socialization of children have in many respects limited the general resources of women for entering the professions, science, academia, and general leadership positions. Recent research on gender differences has identified the style of communication, approaches to thinking, preferred interactional patterns, and general beliefs and attitudes of the traditional female as being variables acting to limit their available role resources. In addition, the problem of role conflict for the majority of female health professionals (in terms of their having a preference for family life over professional involvement) is strong on their completion of their professional education and entry into the work force (Davis & Olesen, 1963; Olesen & Whittaker, 1968; Simpson, 1979). This role conflict and the associated role strain is present throughout the initial period of professional socialization of nurses and is maintained as they enter the workforce. It should be noted, however, that the traditional female role orientation may be changing (see Chapter 12). Such traditional female role qualities as avoidance of competition and conflict, preference for social communication and personal relationships, rather than the thinking style required for scientific research (Gilligan, 1982), may make advancement in that male-dominated context difficult.

The ability to function as an equal with other professional persons is a major problem for women. For instance, nurses with better than adequate credentials may encounter role stress associated with role underqualification as a result of their acquired (female) beliefs, attitudes, and role behaviors, which are at odds with the normative expectations of the dominant group. For example, the competition for research grants, on-going publications in refereed (and therefore competitive) journals, the tolerance of uncertainty, and the value of general scientific knowledge over applied knowledge all require values and role skills which many females lack, including many who have earned a doctoral degree.

It may be that many female health professionals initiate their careers with some role underqualification unrelated to the special knowledge required for their profession. However, the necessary skills, techniques, values, belief systems, and behaviors are aspects of role that can be learned.

Occupational Obsolescence

Health professionals, once well motivated and qualified for their work, may find their professional knowledge and skills have become inadequate. Their minimal commitment to their role (a common condition in women's roles—see Women in Professions May Not Endorse the Relevant Professional Values on p. 219 in this chapter) and limited knowledge and skills may be a result of disuse. Minimal role commitment is likely to be associated with a decline in intellectual pursuits and decreased propensity to advance one's professional knowledge base. Persons in clinical situations are somewhat less vulnerable to sanctions for knowledge obsolescence than are those who are in administrative positions because their work is less visible.

Obsolescence is a problem in all occupations. Rapid growth of knowledge and technology not only devalues the knowledge base a professional has acquired but creates a sense of career vulnerability. Since upward mobility in most of the health professions is severely restricted, the career pattern of successful health professionals may be in moving out of traditional roles and into new and more challenging settings and positions.

The professional with limited role competence also has the option of interorganizational mobility. Even though this option exists, however, the professional may have a major commitment to the position he or she presently occupies. Commitment in the form of "side bets" (Becker, 1960) does not mean that the current employment is continued because the work is valued. Rather, it is a recognition that role occupancy over time is associated with various types of social investments. These include time, energy, and personal involvement in committees, friends, and colleagues, resulting in specialization of the investment. The security of a position, not only monetarily but in terms of social and economic factors, may be identified as an asset. Other actions or "side bets" tend to be cumulative over the years. There may be investments of various types made in a spouse's career, children's college career, the community, and friends. These may all limit a nurse who has developed role incompetence from freely seeking employment in another organization.

Those who no longer are functioning effectively are in a difficult situation, and so are their role partners. The members of the individual's role set may become aware of the role incompetence and attempt to compensate for reduced inputs from that person by increasing their own inputs. It is not clear in the literature what events or series of events precipitate an administrative decision to move this now underqualified professional to a "safe" position in the organization. Movement will likely be horizontal to another department. For example, the physician who loses surgical privileges may move from the cardio-thoracic surgery department to become a consultant or "talking doctor" in an out-patient department. Demotion in terms of status, pay, and other rewards is an option organizations often prefer to use over directly firing such persons. Goode (1973) has proposed that these underqualified persons serve a function of "protection of the inept." They identify for the rest of the employees the "floor" of what is acceptable. In this respect they protect the mediocre, who would be threatened if the inept person were fired, for this would then raise the overall level of expected performance.

The problem of determining what is acceptable or adequate performance is seldom openly addressed among persons in the professions. Indeed, professionals implicitly believe that their work can be assessed only by their peers. Adequate role performance is expected to come from their commitment to the work of the profession. In addition, persons engaged in scientific work are used to delayed gratification and slow results. It may not be possible to assess the immediate value of some activities, such as theorizing, research resulting in contradictory findings, etc. Who is going to evaluate the relative "usefulness" of noncomparable types of work? The question is: Useful to whom? Assessment of productivity in terms of the quality of publications is supposedly a judgment which can be made only by one's colleagues and peers.

Graduate Education: A Mixed Option

For dealing with role incompetence the option of going back to school is a respectable alternative for the nurse. Learning the most up-to-date formal and clinical knowledge may not be easy, but in the end there is a credential attesting to one's competence. In addition, a stronger identity and a transition into a role of greater complexity is likely to occur. There are also costs associated with this legitimate credentialing. The economics of not having a salary and of giving up one's identity and associated safeguarded status in the organization only to move into a low-status position of student is costly.

Indeed, the graduate student role is also certainly one of substantial role stress. It is typified by role ambiguity and incongruity. Role overload is cyclic; some find that the quantitative overload is a minor problem relative to that part of the workload typified by qualitative overload. These stresses are understandable and are predictable from the professional socialization perspective but are often unanticipated by individuals entering graduate programs.

These role stresses are at least potentially greater for the health professional who has a problem with role competence compared to the motivated health professional who returns to the university to specialize or to obtain advanced preparation in an area of interest.

ADEQUATE ROLE PERFORMANCE

The theoretical perspectives of Goode and Merton are based on the idea that an organization is a system of interrelated positions and role relationships. They propose that at times, possibly most of the time, role enactment is problematic. Goode suggests this may be the case for one entire set of roles, whereas Merton identifies some specific roles as being typically conflictual. The writing of both authors supports the ideas basic to this chapter, namely that role stress and role strain are omnipresent conditions. Goode theorizes that it is normal to find that roles are overdemanding, conflictual, and ambiguous, and he suggests that the construct of role strain is an intervening variable between role expectations on the one hand and role behavior and the social structure on the other. Goode proposes that role relations consist of a sequence of role bargains; individuals continuously make selections between alternative role behaviors in order to reduce their role strain. He observes that one's roles may be onerous and a frequent source of role strain. This observation raises the question as to what is a reasonable "role price" for adequate role performance.

Merton's theoretical work on the social structure is rich and extensive. He proposed that strain, tension, contradiction, and discrepancies between the cultural and social structure exist in any social system. They are likely to be not only dysfunctional to the social system but they also can be a source of conforming, innovative, or even deviant behavior for the individuals involved. In his work with Barber on sociologic ambivalence, Merton emphasizes that the ambivalence is in the social definition of roles and statuses and not in the feeling state of an individual.

Sociologic ambivalence is discussed relative to a single status, a status set, and a role set. Merton (1976) discusses sociologic ambivalence inherent in the scientific role, the physician role, and the leader or administrator role. The works of Merton and Merton and Barber identify problematic role enactment. Merton also suggests ways individuals cope, sometimes deviantly, when faced with a problematic role.

The perspective that socially generated conflict, disjunction, and ambiguity are all normal conditions has also been proposed by Merton (1957). In addition, Goode (1960) suggests one's total role obligations are often overdemanding. Therefore, conformity to one set of role obligations is a viable option only if other roles and role obligations are ignored. Adequate role performance for any one role in a system typified by conflict is likely to require skill in role negotiation.

Goode uses the term *role price* to refer to the level of role performance which the individual settles upon for an entire set of roles (that is, what the individual is willing to put into the role, such as time and energy). Factors likely to have an impact on this choice are commitment to the system or role, interpersonal and economic costs, rewards associated with the relationship, available time and energy, required effort, personal interest, and relative priorities among the roles. Competence is needed in negotiating one's role and in determining the role price. It is important to recognize when the situation is one of structural stress. If it is, then no matter how hard an individual tries, the structural stress will remain; the stress may be managed differently by individuals but it will always be present unless a change is made in the social structure.

Role Stress and Resources

Inadequate role performance may result from malintegration in the social structure or resource excesses or deficits of role occupants. A sense of inadequacy or frustration rather than being rightfully attributed to the nature of the social structure often is attributed to personal resource deficits or to the limited capabilities of role occupants. The experience of role strain may be associated with a sense that the role expectations are beyond one's capabilities. Unfortunately, the next step—determining whether the problem is an individual one of role incompetence or one generated by the social structure—may never be taken. Sometimes it is difficult to differentiate the part that the social structure plays from the part the actors play in creating role strain. Often the important part played by the social structure is overlooked.

From the structural role theory perspective, a lack of resources for appropriate role performance is seen as either a result of inadequate socialization or as a failure of the social system or organization to select individuals with the appropriate and necessary resources. It is, however, often easier to blame the role occupant than deal with abstractions about the social structure.

Certain positions, such as those of researcher or staff nurse, are inherently influenced by structured ambivalence. Others, such as director of nurses, general practitioner, and administrative secretary, are structurally linked to a large number of social positions. These positions are all likely to be conflictual and overdemanding. They may also be very rewarding.

ROLE COMPETENCE

For structural theorists, competence is a matter of capacity for role performance (Inkles, 1968; Smith, 1968). The focus for these theorists is on society and its manpower needs whereas the focus for symbolic interactionists is on the individual's communication and interactional skills.

Role competence means that a person has interpersonal competence as well as the necessary specialized knowledge, skills, abilities and motivation to perform successfully. It refers to the overall capacity and commitment for adequate role performance. Persons will usually use their interpersonal competence skills to have their role partners accept the role price which they propose. For the focal role occupant to be successful in this negotiation, role partners must feel that the individual has role-specific competence.

Role partners who work together for a time and have complementary role-specific resources and interpersonal competence can create a very productive unit. Health professionals often develop their own cognitive orientation in the process of complementary role performances. However, the complex individual sets of tasks and perspectives of different members of the health professions need to be coordinated with an eye toward the larger organizational goals.

Both structural theorists and symbolic interactionists agree on several points concerning role competence:

1. Competence is learned through the socialization processes
2. Competence is necesary for adequate role performance
3. Competence makes for individual and social progress

Fundamental to the notion of competence is the belief that persons are engaged in interdependent role relationships which exist over time and are influenced by the social context (presence of a "third person").

To engage successfully in roles, persons need role-specific skills but they also need interpersonal competence to guide the ongoing role behaviors of the role set. Inherent in the building of interpersonal competence are such personal attributes as cognitive skill, skill at role bargaining and collaboration, relationship sensitivity, knowledge of organizations, and role-specific knowledge and skill. In addition, motivation, personal interest, energy, time, and involvement are all necessary for engaging in a role in a meaningful way.

Role behavior does not occur in isolation but in a social context. Persons engaged in role relations need to be sensitive to the existing "definition of the situation" and know when it has changed, when it needs to be changed, and how to change it. Both Coser's and Goffman's work would lead one to identify reflexive thinking, ability to take distance from others, capacity for innovation, flexibility, and involvement in the role as the necessary attributes for accomplishing this. Presumably, being able to identify potentially problematic situations and determine whether the problematic interaction is a result of the definition of the situation or of the individual enacting the role would also be important.

In summary, competent role performance requires interpersonal competence and role-specific competence. Role competence is the ability of a person in an interdependent relationship that is on-going in time to carry out lines of action which result in adequate role performance. A summary of the types of roles is presented in Table 5.

TABLE 5. ROLE STRESS: ILLUSTRATION OF DIVERSITY OF SUBJECTS AND VARIABLES

Author	Subjects and Variables	Type of Role Stress
Banda	Clinical nurse specialists (social structure: tall (hospitals); flat (community agency)	Ambiguity Overload Conflict Incongruity
Barnett Baruch	Women (paid worker, wife, mother)	Overload (multiple roles) Conflict
Bibace and Walsh	Psychologists (scientist and practioner)	Conflict
Braito and Caston	Newly graduated nurses	Underqualification
Fain	Academicians (nurses)	Ambiguity
Fogarty, Rapport, and Rapport	Working women (spouse, friend, career)	Conflict (multiple roles)
Gray	Married professional women	Conflict
Gupta and Beehr	Employees of 5 organizations including hospital and research organization	Ambiguity Overload Qualitative overload
Huckaby and Jagula	Nurses (coronary care unit)	Overload (qualitative) specialized knowledge; lack adequate resources. Overload (quantitative): time
Komarovsky	Female college students (career, family roles)	Ambiguity
Luukkomen-Gronow and Stolte-Heiskanen	Women scientists	Conflict
Reid	Physicians (academics, practitioners)	Conflict
Rosse and Rosse	Nurses (4 levels)	Ambiguity Conflict
Szilagy, Sims and Keller	Nurses, engineers (3 levels)	Ambiguity
Vaughn and Wittig	Working women traditional and nontraditional perceived competence	Overload
Woods	Working mothers	Conflict

NOTES

The ideas in this chapter have been developed from a variety of sources.

Textbooks: Charon, 1985; Goslin, 1969; Heiss, 1981; Lauer & Handel, 1977; Lindesmith & Strauss, 1968; McCall & Simmons, 1978; Rock, 1979; Secord & Backman, 1974; Turner, 1985.

Collections of readings: Gordon, 1968; Manis & Meltzer, 1978; Rose, 1962; Rosenberg & Turner, 1981; Stone & Faberman, 1981.

1. Nurses and other health professionals now have immediate access to information that used to require innumerable hours of library research. Accessing relevant information related to a patient's diagnosis regardless of whether the diagnosis is nursing or medical can greatly influence the scope of care provided. Data bases on nursing and medicine can be accessed with a computer terminal to determine current relevant information on the probable progress of an illness. For example, if caring for a patient with a diagnosis of acquired immune deficiency syndrome (AIDS), the clinician can determine the likely accuracy of the medical diagnosis (all diagnoses have some probability of error), the means of transmission, the likely body system responses, and the probable subjective responses of the patient and family. A local data base may also provide information on services available from health and religious agencies and individual professionals working with persons diagnosed as having AIDS.

2. Although a theory is a set of interrelated concepts and statements that can be (and have been) empirically tested, we use the term *theory* in this section to refer to theoretical formulations that are not as rigorous as true scientific theory. Symbolic interaction theory and structural role theory are both rather loose collections of empirically tested ideas and therefore are more perspectives or frameworks than theories. They are typical of "theories" in the social sciences. In the discussion that follows we use perspective and theory interchangeably, recognizing that both formulations are rather loose.

3. The paradigm of role theory includes two distinct research traditions because the theoretical formulation of symbolic interaction and structural role theory both have some different assumptions about human nature, and a different set of concepts and subtheories. [See Hardy, Chapter 2, for an explanation of the preference (not mandated by Mead's theoretical work) for a research tradition of descriptive research.] Each of these approaches contains a variety of conceptions, subtheories, and core theoretical notions. They have in common the assumption that social life has structure and structure is important for the development of persons. They both emphasize analyzing social phenomena from the perspective of the individual. They both see socialization processes as important for role effectiveness. Neither formulation includes physiologic parameters, although symbolic interaction theory has the capacity to include them. Both are concerned with social order: how it is developed and sustained through interaction and how disruption and disorganization occur. However, they conceptualize all of these notions of social disruption and conflict differently.

The value of the two different but complementary theories for those in applied fields is a theme throughout this book. Structural role theory and symbolic interaction have generated significant but different knowledge and utilize different research methods. In order to understand the complementary nature of the theories and their different approaches to role stress they need to be viewed as subsets of an overriding theory/research set termed a Research Tradition Based On Theory (see Chapter 2). A description of the historical development of each theory may be the clearest way to present this as well as make it possible for the reader to identify each theory's boundaries. Commonalities and difference in the two theories are also identified.

First the identifying characteristics of nonscientific research, so common in the area of stress, is presented. Both theories use the theater as a metaphor to study social life, but they differ in their focus, i.e., the location of the stage, the types and number of roles on the stage, and the nature of the script. Symbolic interaction theory has as an underlying theme the adaptation of persons to their environment as they interact over time. The core concepts are mind, self, and meaning as they develop through interaction. Stress is referred to as a *problematic situation*. On the other hand the focus for structural role theory is on the interrelatedness of positions, roles, norms, role behavior, and expectation that person-role fit is snug. Conformity to role expectations over the history of the social system is typical; role strain is uncommon. The most frequently studied structure has been organizations. The most common type of role stress studied has been role conflict, i.e., conflict between role expectations. Usually studies of role stress have used one or the other theory as a framework, but some recent research has used both. The two theories provide significant but very different ideas for attempting to understand and relate research on role stress.

4. Simmel (1950) was the first sociologist seriously to study interaction or what he termed *sociability*. He was concerned with the causes and consequences of different types of interaction. He and Hegel were among the first to introduce the term *dialectic*. Simmel used this idea to explain the potential for order and disorder and for stasis and change in human relations. His essay on the web of affiliations points out how the personality emerges and is developed by the various groups with which the individual associates. This notion and his basic ideas on conflict can be seen in many of the writings of the symbolic interactionists.

5. The negative meaning of alienation is used in structural role theory. This type of alienation is seen as a response or adaptation to role stress. The positive meaning in symbolic interaction has been used to identify groups of persons who are likely "to see the world differently." We assume that these groups may have had a high level of role stress but were able to minimize role strain.

6. Some of these include definition of the situation, reference group, socialization processes over the life course, self-theory, self-concept changes, self-esteem, self-person merger, role transitions, identity, situated identities, and role competence. Interaction has been conceptualized in terms of emergent exchange processes, encounters, episodes of interaction, reciprocal behaviors, bargaining, and negotiation processes. These are altered by mutual influence strategies such as self-presentation and altercasting. Stigma, ambiguity, marginality, negative identity, and social distance are other conditions which influence interactions. Deviant behavior and mental illness have also been explained in terms of labeling theory.

7. Miller (1971, 1972) has attempted to identify similar abstract "principles" which hold true for all systems' levels. His work is based on an inductive strategy of summarizing empirical work rather than on abstract theorizing. From his work it is clear that the biologic systems are much more thoroughly studied than are the social systems.

8. Nursing has become specialized with additional credentialing in the areas of psychiatry, intensive care, cardiac care, emergency room care, community health, midwifery, etc. The introduction of such specialties actually prevents nurses from communicating as nurses; their communication tends to be kept primarily within their own specialty units. Structural theorists would see this differentiation as a means of augmenting the stability of the system.

9. Goffman's insightful work on stigma (1962) builds on similar ideas initially proposed by Cooley.

10. Interpersonal competence is a measure of how skilled individuals are at influencing others so they "get what they want." This skill in achieving cooperation and desired outcome is gained through socialization processes. Role relationships require interpersonal competence. Some, such as the nurse-physician relationship, require a skillful interaction (see Rushing, 1962; Stein, 1967), while others, such as the nurse-dietician relationship, are usually relatively routine. Systematic study of the methods and means by which individuals influence others in interaction has been undertaken either by observation of behavior (Goffman's work) or by experimental studies with observation (Weinstein, Blumstein). Generalization about the strategies individuals use to influence others should be based on research.

It would be erroneous to say that people always consciously do what is necessary to manipulate the persons with whom they interact. Unfortunately, there is a tendency to conclude that such manipulation is always at a conscious level. (I [MEH] have found this to be a consistent theme from students reading in this area.) Persons' awareness of their efforts to influence others will probably vary with their situation. For instance, the white lab coat worn by health professionals is part of the culture. Most people putting their lab coat on as they begin to work would not be thinking about the influence this "sign" has on others. On the other hand, persons going for job interviews consciously consider how their appearance will be interpreted. The same occurs in dating. Efforts are made to have one's apparel and personal appearance convey the best image possible.

A striving for interpersonal competence actually may be a source of conflict for some health professions. Interpersonal competence is a desirable resource. The influence of psychiatry in the health professions, however, has resulted in labeling manipulation as undesirable. The culture of some of the professions, particularly nursing and social work, may actually negatively sanction efforts at interpersonal competence.

11. Three major longitudinal studies of professional socialization have been undertaken from the structural role theory perspective: *Student Physician* (Merton, 1957); *Interne: from student to physician* (Mumford, E., 1970); and *From Student to Nurse* (Simpson, I., 1979). Two have been undertaken from the symbolic interaction perspective: *Boys in White* (Becker et al., 1961) and *Silent Dialogue* (Olesen & Whittaker 1968). Coombs (1978) appears to combine both perspectives.

12. Elsewhere in this chapter (p. 230) reference is made to the difficulty encountered in moving from the "ideal" of the student role to the "reality" associated with the work-place.

13. Role transition may be a useful frame of reference for studying transitions from normal health to ill health or vice versa. Such role transitions, however, are not voluntary.

14. Goode's theorizing on role strain (1960) illustrates this perspective.

15. The recent literature on stress and burnout among people-oriented professions could be conceptualized as an extension of reality shock. The literature is not reviewed because of the lack of definitional clarity and loose descriptive studies.

8

Managing Role Strain

Margaret E. Hardy and William L. Hardy

The general formulation in this chapter is that problematic situations such as role stress induce an internal response, role strain. The individual subjected to stress will attempt to utilize personal resources and problem solving processes to manage the environment and reduce role strain. If the negative experience—strain—is not reduced, there is reason to assume that other adaptive responses may be employed. Since the role theory literature per se does not fully explicate techniques for strain reduction, additional processes derived from the social exchange literature are described so as to demonstrate the broad range of strain reducing strategies available. The strain reducing strategies may range from simple problem solving methods, through various bargaining techniques, to symbolic interaction strategies. These adaptive processes will be explored next and related to the role theory concepts with which they are entwined.[1]

PROBLEM SOLVING RESPONSE

An actor or role occupant, faced with an ambiguous situation, may proceed to deal with the "problem," but not necessarily at a fully conscious level. First, the individual might appraise the situation in order to identify the various facets and the lines of action available and their probable consequences. On the basis of the alternatives available, probable outcomes, and personal values and motivation, the actor would select a line of action, then mobilize the resources necessary to act.

As a consequence of this role enactment and from subsequent information or feedback, the actor would then evaluate the behavior. If found to be unfavorable, the actor might then take steps to modify the decision–performance sequence. Modification might involve reformulation of the problem, identification of additional or different lines of action, or mobilization of other resources. It should be noted that even when a problem solving attempt is successful, a time gap may exist between the identification of the problem and its acceptance as being solved.

During the period when resources are being mobilized, subjective tension is experienced. This tension may be dissipated when it becomes apparent that the problem is or can be successfully managed. It should also be noted that the entire problem solving response may be experienced symbolically; that is, an anticipation of failure or success in coping can respectively induce or reduce the strain. If the problem is not solved or if it becomes apparent that no solution is available, tension will remain high and must itself be handled. Unresolved tension may be managed by intrapersonal adaptive techniques or by role bargaining and symbolic interaction strategies.

ROLE BARGAINING RESPONSES

Role bargaining has been identified as an actor's allocation of some bearable portion of his total available resources (Goode, 1960). Role bargaining is defined here as a process of negotiation, involving two or more actors, on acceptable role behaviors to be enacted by the parties involved. There is a considerable range in the explicitness of the bargaining process. In some situations role bargaining involves open communication to reach agreement, whereas in other cases the process is less explicit, with one role occupant as the prime decider and the counter role occupants indicating acceptance or rejection of the solution only by their ensuing behavior.

The resolution of role strain is a complicated process that, it is hoped, will be clarified by future studies. A promising new direction in the social sciences is the examination of social behavior in terms of transactions or exchanges. This approach leads to a consideration of the relative costs and rewards associated with actors' social structure, resources, and outcomes. It further leads to a consideration of role relationships as dynamic processes in which actors engage with varying degrees of awareness in role bargaining.

Social Exchanges and Bargaining

Role relationships may be examined as transactions or *social exchanges* in which role occupants are aware of the resources (skill, experience, education) they contribute to the transaction, the costs (role strain, anxiety, frustration, tension) they bear in the transaction, and the outcomes or rewards (social approval, feeling of self-worth, monetary gains) they gain from the transaction.

The social psychologic research literature suggests that people prefer to maintain a sense of equity or fairness in their social relationships (Adams, 1965; Blau, 1964; Homans, 1974). Role incumbents would thus not be expected to endure excessively costly role relationships nor sustain relationships where the rewards far outweigh the costs. Rather, they would be expected to bargain for equitable relationships or to eliminate from the various positions they occupy those in which they experience a strong sense of inequity. Furthermore, persons might be expected to develop a hierarchy of positions ranging from the most to the least equitable and rewarding. The least equitable and rewarding positions would receive the least commitment and presumably they would be the most expendable. Thus, role occupants would aim to achieve a set of positions that, taken together, are relatively equitable and rewarding.

Selecting Positions

All actors have a degree of freedom in selecting or rejecting some positions they could occupy. However, some positions, particularly those associated with gender, age, and race, cannot be discarded. Other positions, such as parent and wage earner, once occupied, are relatively obligatory positions and cannot easily be abandoned. A factor that significantly influences the decision to eliminate a position is the degree of dependence upon that position. Positions representing considerable commitment on the part of an actor are also less readily eliminated, whereas positions with relatively low commitment, such as those in voluntary organizations, can be more easily dismissed. For example, a nurse who accumulates 10 years of college education and 15 years of experience in nursing has made a major career commitment. Developing a career in an unrelated field would involve a major position change and concomitantly a significant degree of role strain. The same nurse might easily give up her involvement in a local choral group if a conflict arises.

Resource Allocation

Actors can decide to what degree they will allocate their resources to the social positions they do hold. One person wishing to excel in a particular career may expend far more time and energy in career-related enterprises than in family-related enterprises; another person, who gives priority to the family, may make the opposite choice. In each position they occupy, role occupants can overtly or covertly negotiate with their role partners concerning the allocation of their available resources. This negotiation over inputs into a role relationship centers around the issues of *whether* a relationship will occur, *when* it will occur, and *what* it will entail. The negotiation over deployment of resources may involve a variety of strategies. If an actor decides a relationship is feasible he may modify his role through the processes of role taking and role making. In addition he may determine his performance in a role relationship by controlling his availability, accessibility, and visibility. An actor may further influence the nature of his relationships through self-presentation (Goffman, 1959), altercasting (Weinstein & Deutschberger, 1964), and ingratiation (Jones, 1964).

Role Taking and Role Making. These two techniques, described in symbolic interaction theory, may be utilized in the process of role bargaining. Role taking and role making are discussed by Turner (1956) as means of creating and modifying one's concept of one's own role and one's concept of the role of other. Role taking is the process of imputing purpose and motive to the other. This projection of oneself into the situation of another, including imagining how one would feel in the other person's position, will reflect, with varying degrees of accuracy, the motives and feelings of the other. The process of role taking, which may be viewed as being synonymous with empathy, is necessary for skillful interaction and successful role bargaining. Having imputed a purpose to other's behavior, the actor modifies his or her own behavior to sustain or to alter other's behavior.

Role making emphasizes the interpretation of one's own role prescriptions and emphasizes the positive process of creating and modifying one's own role. Role prescriptions are generally not rigidly defined but rather are loosely outlined. To some degree they are open to individual interpretation, with selective emphasis and selective lines of action. The development of an acceptable role enactment occurs through a process of interaction. In this process both actor and other present behaviors that are interpreted by each as appropriate for their own position in a subtle and complex process of role bargaining (see Chapter 3 for more detail).

In one example a social worker may negotiate her role by deemphasizing some behaviors and emphasizing others. She may find individual counseling relatively unrewarding and take the option of spending relatively less time directly with clients and more time arranging for client placement or performing other tasks involving interacting with staff and other health care givers. She will meticulously carry out these activities. Her role performance may be positively sanctioned by members of her role set even though it involves relatively little care to clients. If she receives such sanctioning, then her role bargain is settled; the social worker will likely have redefined her role so that she perceives client placement as a more important part of his/her role expectations.

In another example, a physician may negotiate his/her role obligations to delegate some of the less desirable activities and simply omit others. For instance, talking with patients' families may be delegated to nurses and specific patient teaching and counseling may be entirely omitted. These delegated and omitted role behaviors may be defined by the physician as not being essential to the primary role.

The processes of role taking and role making are influenced by an actor's definition of role. Redefining or cognitive restructuring of one's role is a method of resolving conflict. This technique has not been specifically investigated for occupants of a single position, but it has been examined for occupants of multiple positions. Role restructuring may be a typical response in multiple position occupancy (Bidwell, 1961; Getzels & Guba, 1954; Gross et al., 1958) or in roles characterized by strong cross pressures (Bar-Yosef & Schild, 1966). In health care organizations, the nature of the compromises and the degree of role restructuring would affect the health care given to clients.

Controlling the Availability of Resources. A role occupant may influence role relationships by controlling availability, accessibility, and visibility to role senders. One health care worker, a director, may manage his role obligations by presenting himself as a busy individual occupying many positions and appearing to be highly involved in each. By presenting himself as a scarce resource in high demand, this actor may convey the message to his counter role occupants that he should not be expected to carry out all normal role obligations. Thus, it may be acceptable that the busy director miss or be late for meetings while other staff members do not have this freedom. A physician may establish a tradition of being difficult for staff nurses to locate. A nursing director may utilize her secretary to judiciously schedule contacts with members of her role set and a professor may maintain low visibility by being absent from the office or building when not lecturing. By attempting to control one's accessibility, availability, and visibility, an actor attempts to influence the nature of role relationships. In essence, an actor negotiates the availability of his or her resources.

If one limits the extent to which one is available to role senders, one is partially withdrawing from role relationships. Partial withdrawal and avoidance are adaptive techniques often found in association with the presence of role stress (Bidwell, 1961; Kahn et al., 1964; Weitz, 1956). These two responses may be detrimental to both the actor's role performance and to the role performance of members of the role set. Partial withdrawal from interaction with role senders creates difficulty in coordinating activity and in performance. The conditions of partial withdrawal have been discussed in terms of role distance (Coser, 1966;

Merton, 1957) and partial withdrawal has been viewed as one way of resolving ambivalence (Coser, 1966, p. 175) and avoiding role conflict (Kahn et al., 1964; Wolfe & Snoek, 1962). Coser makes a distinction between withdrawing from a status one plans eventually to abandon and withdrawing in order to better maintain status (Coser, 1966, p. 184). This latter type of withdrawal may facilitate carrying out role obligations, but there do not seem to be empirical studies suggesting that the mechanism is successful. In fact, several studies (Kahn et al., 1964; Overall & Aronson, 1966; Wardwell, 1955; Weitz, 1956) indicate that partial withdrawal reduces the actor's level of performance. Thus, the use of this mechanism in health care organizations would probably adversely influence the health care given to clients.

Selective Presentation of Self. In selective presentation of self (Goffman, 1959), the actor conveys to others an image or identity he or she wishes to assume in a situation. In assuming the identity, the actor also indicates the resources he or she possesses. If the performance is skillful, others will not question the presented identity nor its associated resources. The actor's performance both presents and sustains the claim; if it succeeds, others interact with the actor accordingly. This self-presentation involves proficient use of dress, demeanor, and conduct. For example, a person in a white lab coat with a concerned expression walking purposefully down the corridor of a hospital and carrying a stethoscope will probably be perceived by others as a physician. This same person, attired in a white dress and cap and walking down the same hallway, would probably be perceived as a nurse. By the act of selective presentation to others, an individual makes a claim to a certain identity and to the resources associated with that identity. An individual's presentation exerts a social pressure on others to support his or her identity claim.

Altercasting. Another interactional tactic similar to presentation of self is altercasting (Weinstein & Deutschberger, 1964). The focus here is on influencing the behavior of a counter role occupant rather than on portraying and thereby establishing an identity by the actor. The compliant behavior produced by successful altercasting advances the actor's preferences and goals by influencing the resource allocation of other. For example, when a physician interacts with a nurse as if the nurse were a handmaiden, the physician is engaged in altercasting. The nurse may or may not act in a manner to support the physician's conception. If the altercasting is successful, the nurse will indeed behave toward the physician as a handmaiden rather than as a co-worker.

Ingratiation. Ingratiation strategies are employed to increase one's attractiveness in the eyes of others in the hope of augmenting one's own rewards (Jones, 1964). This strategy may be employed in role bargaining to enhance the value of one's own resources. An occupant of a focal position may complement and conform to opinions of a role partner in the hope of appearing similar, likeable, and intelligent. Being liked by one's role partner increases the significance of an actor's resources and the probability that the role partner will provide help and rewards.

Coalition. Bargainers may combine their resources or form a coalition to achieve a common outcome against a competing party. (Caplow, 1968; Gamson, 1964; Tedeschi, Schlenker & Bonoma, 1973). Likewise, role incumbents experiencing similar problems may pool their resources to eliminate or neutralize role strain.

The study of group resolution of role strain has received only brief attention (Bar-Yosef & Schild, 1966; Becker et al., 1961; Blau & Scott, 1962). These studies have shown that when confronted with cross pressures, role occupants reduce the impact of pressure by creating mechanisms for collective decision making or altered divisions of labor.

Two studies indicate that group responses can reduce the effect of external pressures (Becker et al., 1961; Blau & Scott, 1962). Other studies indicate that role strain experienced within one position may be responded to by the group (Davis & Olesen, 1963; Olesen & Whittaker, 1968). These and other studies (Goldman, 1966; Kahn, et al., 1964; Perry & Wynne, 1959) suggest that conflict may be resolved by restructuring roles or by joint action within the group. The conditions that increase or decrease the likelihood of utilizing such methods of resolution have not yet been identified, nor have the subsequent effects on group performance been analyzed.

Conditions Influencing Role Bargaining Response

As a dynamic and flexible feature of role relationships, role bargaining may occur in the initial phase of a relationship and may be repeated as circumstances change. When two people interact with each other they will probably both engage in role taking, role making, and selective presentation of self; both may altercast and both may use some form of ingratiation. The extent to which lines of action, resources, roles, and the identities presented by each and imputed to the other are agreed upon or found acceptable is negotiable. In order to continue a role relationship, the two parties must come to some form of agreement on each other's claims. Furthermore, they must agree on when the relationship will occur and on acceptable role behaviors and resources. This bargaining process may be influenced by a variety of conditions. These conditions, discussed in the following sections, have been identified in social psychologic studies of bargaining and negotiation—and they appear to be highly relevant to role bargaining.

The Presence of Others. It is not equally mandatory that all role expectations be met. Personal and internalized professional values, as well as the type, strength, and availability of sanctions within a system, are major determinants of which role behaviors are negotiable. The presence of other individuals, audiences, and reference groups plays a major part in defining the values, norms, and sanctions to be taken into account by a role occupant. If the other is a reference group, the additional social influences of loyalty and commitment to the group would be expected to operate. If the third party is nonsignificant or neutral, the social influence of this audience on the actor may be much less strong.

The presence of groups important to an actor brings into play the actor's self-esteem and need for social approval and, therefore, may significantly influence bargaining. It has been found that concessions in a bargaining situation may be associated with loss of self-esteem and loss of face (Deutsch & Krauss, 1962; Stevens, 1963). In summarizing a variety of experimental bargaining studies, Rubin and Brown (1975) concluded that audiences of significant others are likely to generate strong feelings of loyalty, commitment, and advocacy of the preferred position of bargainers; at the same time such audiences are likely to reduce the number of perceived alternatives. This would suggest that an actor confronted with conflicting bureaucratic and professional expectations will, if professional ties are dominant, resist the bureaucratic demands and remain strongly committed to professional norms. Special note should be made of the possibility that, even though reference groups may be present only symbolically, their impact on an actor may be very strong. This would be the case, for example, when a nurse representative negotiates with an administrator for improved working conditions. Although she is only one person engaged in a transaction with an administrator, the wishes and values of the group she represents will significantly influence her actions.

Effect of a Neutral Party. Intervention by a neutral third party can facilitate the reduction of conflict in bargaining situations (Krauss & Deutsch, 1966; Meeker & Shure, 1969; Pruitt & Johnson, 1970). The third party may facilitate agreement by minimizing both irrationality and costs to each party and aid in the identification of additional resources and alternative solutions. In addition, the presence of the third party may legitimize the removal of negotiations from public scrutiny, thus saving face for both negotiating parties while still enforcing social norms.

Communication Patterns. Communication patterns have been identified as important for the perception and resolution of role stress (Kahn et al., 1964; Wolfe & Snoek, 1962). The degree of openness in communication may depend on the issue at stake, the intensity of the conflict, and the behavior of the involved parties. For bargainers to reach agreement, not only must channels of communication be available, but the parties must use these channels and demonstrate a sense of openness and trust. Deutsch and Krauss (1960) found that the higher the intensity of a conflict, the less effective was the bargaining, regardless of the communication channels available. Several other studies of bargaining indicate that a relative increase in bargaining effectiveness occurs when open and free communication exists (Bixenstine & Douglas, 1967; Deutsch, 1958; Martin, 1966; Terhune, 1968). These findings suggest that, for role bargaining to be successful, role incumbents must be readily available to each other, be able to freely communicate, and actually communicate. Thus, two health care professionals who respect each other and work in the same neighborhood clinic may more readily resolve their role conflicts than would two professionals located in different agencies.

Among the communications that bargainers may exchange are threats and promises associated with compliance. An actor must assess the credibility of the other bargainer's stance, as well as the projected costs and rewards. In general, bargainers comply more frequently when greater cost is associated with noncompliance (Tedeschi, Banoma, & Brown, 1971). Also, bargainers are more compliant to an accommodative than to an exploitative stance, because the accomodative bargainer provides positive incentive for compliance (Schlenker, Banoma, Tedeschi, & Pivnick, 1970).

Rank and Power of Bargainer. A variety of factors, including social structure, environmental conditions, and personal characteristics, has been considered to affect the outcome of bargaining. One factor that may be particularly relevant is the degree of legitimate power or rank held by a bargainer. Faley and Tedeschi (1971) found that low-ranking bargainers are more compliant than high-ranking bargainers and that the latter are more resistant to threats from their low-ranking adversaries. In their review of bargaining studies and power, Rubin and Brown (1975, p. 199) found that a common level of power among bargainers facilitates bargaining. They also reported that conditions of unequal power result in a tendency to exploit the less powerful bargainers. In applying these findings to a health care setting, one would expect that relatively low ranking health care workers would bargain more effectively with each other than with those of higher rank. Thus, a staff nurse may role bargain effectively with other staff nurses or with nurses aides, but in negotiating with a nursing supervisor or staff physician her bargaining might be less effective and she would tend to be more compliant and more open to exploitation.

Behavioral Disposition of Bargainer. Individual differences in values, beliefs, and behavioral dispositions would be expected to influence both the extent to which an actor engages in bargaining and the effectiveness of the bargaining efforts. The literature examining the effects of individual differences in bargainers is extensive and will not be reviewed in detail here; however, some general characteristics will be noted.

Persons who think abstractly or demonstrate cognitive complexity as opposed to those who think in more concrete terms or demonstrate less cognitive complexity have been found to be relatively more cooperative in bargaining situations (Leff, 1969; Phelan & Richardson, 1969).

The need for achievement affiliation and power has been found to affect the conditions of bargaining. Persons with a high need to achieve and a high need for power tend to behave competitively, while those with a high need for affiliation tend to behave cooperatively when bargaining (Terhune, 1968). In summarizing studies in this field, Rubin and Brown (1975, p. 181) suggest that persons with a high need to achieve behave competitively, while persons with a high need for affiliation and power respond to the expected or actual behavior of their opponent: if the opponent is cooperative, they are cooperative; but if the opponent is competitive, they are competitive. Further, those with a high need for affiliation and power are sensitive to the behavior of opponents, but only those with a high need for power use this behavior as a source of information about their opponent; this information, in turn, is used for the purposes of exploitation.

Other studies of behavioral dispositions and studies of such attributes as age, race, gender, intelligence, and social rank all suggest that differences in backgrounds of individual bargainers are important determinants of both the approach to bargaining and the bargaining outcome.

In some of the literature on social interaction including social exchange theory, symbolic interaction theory, role theory, and theory derived from studies of bargaining in conflict situations, interaction is conceptualized as a dynamic process. This literature depicts interaction as a process in which lines of action are open to interpretation and modification. The bargaining model implicit in both the social exchange and the symbolic interaction formulations assumes that behavior is goal directed and that individuals selectively engage in lines of actions that will further these goals. The theory and research relevant to role bargaining and the growing body of bargaining research suggest that roles may be perceived as opportunity structures in which actors actively negotiate by utilizing resources to their advantage.

CONDITIONS INFLUENCING THE GENERAL RESPONSE TO ROLE STRAIN

In addition to the implications for role bargaining derived from bargaining studies, a number of factors that have been found that alter the manner in which individuals respond to role strain. The major factors to be considered are the actor's resources, the structural location of the target of stress, and the characteristics of the structure.

Resources of the Role Occupant

A role incumbent's resources are not only valued by role partners, but they influence role strain and the role incumbent's response to strain. A review of studies of role stress and strain indicates that personality variables (Mishler, 1953; Stouffer & Toby, 1951), educational level (Bar-Yosef & Schild, 1966), status incongruity (Grief & MacDonald, 1973), race (Rich, 1975), age, aspiration level, and length of employment (Kahn et al., 1964), values (Martin & Katz, 1961), and behavioral dispostion (Kahn et al., 1964; Lyons, 1971) are factors influencing both the perception of role strain and the response to it. It should be noted that many of these factors were identified earlier as influencing the *process* of bargaining.

Actors who occupy similar positions within a social system may experience different degrees of strain if their resource levels are dissimilar. For example, a nurse with a master's degree and five years of teaching experience is likely to perceive fewer environmental stressors in a new teaching position than a nurse with a bachelors degree and no teaching experience. A speech therapist who has a high need to achieve may be more vulnerable to an increased workload than a co-worker who has a relatively low need to achieve.

Structural Location of the Target of Stress. An additional important factor bearing on the response to stress is the structural location of the target of the stress. The response will be significantly affected by whether the target of the stress occupies a single position or several positions. If role strain arises from the incompatible demands of several positions occupied by a single actor, the actor may be able to manipulate his or her role structure to manage the stress. There is evidence that role strain arising from multiple-position occupancy is resolved by subordinating one or more roles (Burchard, 1954; Getzels & Guba, 1954). By making some roles subordinate to others a person decreases the relative significance of the associated role expectations. If, on the other hand, the strain arises from incompatible demands associated with a single position, the role occupant has less freedom to manage stress. The difference between intrapositional and interpositional role stress is illustrated in the following. A nurse researcher may have difficulty resolving demands for sufficient research that is also at a high level of quality, as these demands may be mutually exclusive. She may, however, experience less difficulty reducing the strain associated with the competing demands for her time in the positions of mother and researcher. A subordination of one of the positions—the position of mother through the use of day care facilities, for instance—reduces the strain experienced with those positions. In order to resolve intrapositional role strain an actor may attempt to establish a priority in the role demands within one role, although this technique is likely to be less satisfactory than when it is used by the occupant of multiple positions. Conflict associated with a single position can result in a very high tension level (Gross et al., 1958; Kahn et al., 1964).

Characteristics of the Social Structure. The social structure plays a major part in producing and sustaining conditions of role strain. The communication network, affective network, normative structure, power structure, and interaction network all modify the impact of role stress and the response to role strain. The social structure may influence the extent to which the environment is identified as stressful. In addition, the nature of the subjective experience, the availability of responses, the consequences of such responses, and the feedback available to evaluate performance are all factors influencing strain. Furthermore, the social structure may itself create stressful positions. Some research has been conducted on this important area. For instance, it has been found that the presence of others is an important factor in defining an ambiguous situation as threatening or non-threatening (Schacter & Singer, 1962) and that the presence of friends may reduce the perception of environmental events as threatening (Gerard & Rabbie, 1961). Other research suggests that existing norms may define which resources are available (Roy, 1952) and what adaptive responses may be used.

The choice of adaptive response may be influenced by the perceived legitimacy of norms and by perceived sanctions and values (Ehrlich et al., 1962; Getzels & Guba, 1954; Gross et al., 1958; Snoek, 1966). Other social factors that can influence the response to stress are visibility of the role occupant in an organization (Coser, 1966; Kahn et al., 1964; Wolf & Snoek, 1962), dependence on a role (Kahn et al., 1964), rank or social status of both role occupant and role senders (Kahn et al., 1964; Simmons, 1968; Wolfe & Snoek, 1962), patterns of interaction and communication in a group (Kahn et al., 1964), group cohesion (Blau & Scott, 1962), and an actor's reference groups (Bidwell, 1961; Goss, 1961; Gullahorn, 1956).

EFFECT OF ROLE STRESS AND ROLE STRAIN ON WORK PERFORMANCE

Of major concern is the impact that role strain in a focal position has on the output or productivity of role relationships. In discussing this question, first, possible effects are considered and then pertinent research findings will be reviewed. Since few studies of role strain consider output or level of productivity as dependent variables, these must often be inferred from the available data.

If the role occupant experiences difficulty in meeting role obligations, then the person's input and output levels will probably change. For instance, inputs (energy level or concentration) may increase. As a result, the level of performance (also an input) may then be adequate or it may still be less than adequate in terms of the relative outputs and outcomes of the relationship. In any case, the continued presence of role strain for the actor is likely to impact on the counter role occupant and result in an increased use of resources by one or both actors. Thus, role strain generally will impact on the relationship.

Consider a situation of two interdependent actors, a community health nurse and a social worker working in the home of a family with an alcoholic member. If the nurse observes that her input in the form of home visits and counseling is increasing, although not necessarily observable to the social worker, the nurse may face role ambiguity and role overload and may consider the escalating cost of the associated role strain excessive. In subsequent interactions the nurse might seek less costly roles and transfer a greater proportion of her efforts to roles where the outcomes are more in accord with her input. Such a response would become evident in terms of decreased level of performance in the role relationship with the social worker. The alteration in the role performance by the nurse will in the long run have an effect on the inputs required by the social worker, who would be required to invest greater inputs to maintain the relationship. The social worker may decide that such an increased input would be undesirable and she might even reduce her inputs—perhaps expending more of her resources on other role activities with higher outcomes. The net result would be a decline in productivity (output) of the nurse–social worker relationship. Since this relationship is focused on client care, the client would ultimately receive a reduced level of health care.

Studies of the Effects of Role Stress and Strain: Productivity

There are only a few studies that have directly examined the effects of role stress and role strain on the productivity of social relationships. These studies examine the effects of role stress; it is assumed that role strain is the intervening variable. Role incongruity (Borgotta, 1961; Smelser, 1961), role ambiguity (Greene & Organ, 1973; Smith, 1957), role conflict (Greene & Organ 1973), and role overload (Hardy, 1971) have all been found to be associated with relatively low levels of productivity or job performance. Results from other studies indicate indirectly that role performance is adversely affected by the presence of role strain. Teachers perform with greater efficiency when role consensus exists among their role senders (Bible & McComas, 1963). Also, for individuals in the military, conflicts between a teacher role and officer role result in a reduction in the efficiency of performance of at least one of these positions (Getzels & Guba, 1954). These studies clearly indicate that certain types of role stress can be detrimental to role enactment.

Studies of Indirect Effects
of Role Stress and Strain: Partial Withdrawal

Partial withdrawal is one response to role strain. It has been found, for example, that resolution of role conflict in multiple-position occupancy occurs by establishing one role as dominant (Bidwell, 1961; Burchard, 1954; Gouldner, 1957; Gross et al., 1958). A resolution of this type implies that some subordinate roles will be performed less adequately, if at all. In the example discussed earlier, both the nurse and social worker were providing less than optimal care in the specific transaction involving the two of them, but each could have redirected her energies into transactions involving other role partners. Partial withdrawal from a role relationship presumably would adversely affect the quality of work.

The impact of partial withdrawal is likely to be strongest where there is high interdependency between role partners. Kahn et al. (1964, p. 222) noted that a strong interdependency is conducive to the development of intense inner conflicts, low satisfaction, and a sense of futility. As a result, occupants of focal positions having strong interdependency might exhibit psychologic withdrawal that would be reflected in a weakening of interpersonal bonds. Furthermore, it was noted that partial withdrawal from interaction does not necessarily eliminate strain. These investigators found that a relatively low degree of communication (i.e., a partial withdrawal) is associated with a high probability of conflict. Thus, attempts to avoid stress in role relationships by withdrawal can create the very conditions the role occupant is trying to avoid, i.e., further role conflict. In highly interdependent relationships, resolution by partial withdrawal may not be permitted by role partners (Kahn et al., 1964, p. 222). For example, partial withdrawal of an assistant head nurse from interaction with the head nurse may ultimately increase role strain because of the inherent strong interdependency of these two positions. Because of this interdependency the head nurse may insist on resolving the conflict in ways other than by partial withdrawal.

Decreased Conformity to Norms

Decreased conformity to norms may occur in response to role strain. It has been reported that persons who identify strongly with groups outside of the work situation exhibit more limited conformity to their work organization (Gouldner, 1957). Role strain has been found to be associated with a reduction in conformity (Beckhouse, 1969; Kahn & Wolfe, 1964) and a decrease in risk taking (Beckhouse, 1969; Mitchell, 1958). Information from these studies makes it apparent that role strain is associated with decreased conformity to organizational norms. Kahn and Wolfe (1962, p. 120) suggest this is expensive to organizations. From the perspective of the organization, conformity is desirable since it is associated with predictability of performance and dependable output.

Nonconformity to role demands could, however, be a successful means of coping with role strain. Role occupants either individually or in concert develop successful methods that both reduce role strain and facilitate the functioning of the organization. These methods may not conform with the normative structure but may produce an effective alteration of the role structure; the development of new roles can decrease both the presence and effects of strain. For instance, the development of such roles as clinical nurse specialist, intensive care unit nurse, and nurse practitioner was contrary to prevailing norms; such developments, however, may have been a means of reducing strain associated with the existing traditional nursing positions. Although role strain is usually considered to be undesirable, it can ultimately lead to higher levels of functioning. This perspective, however, has not yet been explored in detail.

SUMMARY

In this chapter the theories of symbolic interaction, structural role theory, and social exchange have been integrated in order to more fully describe the dynamics of the role stress–role strain relationship. The integration of these perspectives makes it possible to develop testable hypotheses for the purposes of *explanation* and *prediction*. In contrast, structural role theory, which has traditionally been the perspective utilized in the study of organizations, can be used only to provide descriptive, nontestable statements. The validity of descriptive statements cannot be evaluated on the basis of empiric criteria; rather, they can be judged only in terms of their relative usefulness in conveying a sense of understanding. Therefore, structural theory alone cannot advance our scientific knowledge of role stress and role strain.

Fortunately, symbolic interaction, the other main branch of role theory, does provide both a useful and insightful perspective for studying social behavior and makes available testable statements. Some areas of the theory consist of particularly strong scientific bodies of knowledge (for the behavioral sciences). Other areas have developed only descriptive statements, sensitizing concepts, and a grounded theory approach. The descriptive approach is used to accurately represent the perspective of subjects, the social context, the social processes, and the interrelationships of these three. Some of the theorizing in symbolic interaction has been very insightful, providing both description and prediction. The development of scientific knowledge in symbolic interaction has been furthered by empirical testing. The theory contains concepts describing subjective (inferred or cognitive) states and processes and externally observable social behavior along with the mutual interaction of these two. The need to study two levels scientifically (both the psychologic and the social) has been a basic commitment among symbolic interactionists since the initial development of the subject in the early 1900s. This work requires skill and time; not surprisingly, the systematic development of empirically grounded knowledge has been slow. However the scientific work has resulted in identifying important characteristics of participants who engage in social interaction. These include skill in role taking, perception, and communication, and a common perspective that makes it possible for persons to agree on a working definition of their situation. This agreement includes accepting the role identities of the participants and agreeing on rules of interaction and outcomes. If any of these characteristics are problematic they may provide a source of role strain. Illustrations are given in the chapter of situations in which limitations or variations in these characteristics do lead to strain.

The characteristics of social interaction have been identified in terms of the processes of exchange, reciprocity, mutual influence, and social differentiation processes. Conditions such as power imbalance, disagreement in expected outcomes, and perception of inequity are sources of strain that can jeopardize the continuation of social relationships. Strain may develop when norms governing interaction are violated or if actors believe that the norm of reciprocity or the norm of fairness has been violated. The conditions that may modify the process of interaction have been identified.

Symbolic interaction theory has inherent in it the assumption that change and conflict are desirable conditions for individuals and social systems. These conditions provide opportunities for individuals to develop broader social perspectives and to increase their social competence. For the symbolic interactionists, conflict is regarded as necessary for change and is seen as the basis for progress and social unity. The more problematic the situations an individual encounters, according to the early symbolic interactionists, the greater the individual's ensuing social competence and maturity. Any importance of the social structure for behavior or the contintuity of positions, roles, role expectations and performance over time is deemphasized in symbolic interaction theory. Much of the research on interaction utilizes the assumption that persons engage in the process of social exchange. The theory clearly links persons to the larger social units of organizations and society but the effect of the social structure on persons and on social interaction is ill-defined.

The integration of social exchange theory with symbolic interaction provides a collection of necessary and clearly defined concepts which depict the basic characteristics of social exchange processes. In addition the concepts are interrelated into sets of propositions which are amenable to testing. Resources, a concept arising with social exchange, is used in defining the two components of role competence, namely, social competence and role specific competence. It was only following the integration of social exchange theory with symbolic interaction that the notions of both symbolic interaction and structural role theory could be explicated, interrelated, and meaningfully utilized.

Social exchange theory provides a clear set of core concepts—cost, reward, resources, values, and perception. Conditions which create dynamic interactional processes are derived from this set of concepts. The set of conditions—power, conflict, and inequity—have a strong impact on interaction and its outcomes. Structural role theory assumes that a person's behavior is based on compliance to role expectations and societal norms. The emergence of the ideas of power, conflict, and inequalities among role incumbents signficantly alters the evaluation of interaction. In addition, stratification processes influence the nature of the social structure. The core and derived concepts of social exchange theory are sufficiently abstract, yet clearly defined, to be useful for analysis of social processes at both micro and macro levels.

The last third of the chapter focuses on methods for reducing role strain. These methods include independent problem solving and negotiation processes. The latter involves processes of influencing the members of one's role set so they will agree to accept the proposed alteration in the allocation of resources. A variety of influencing strategies are identified as well as structural and contextual conditions which may modify the value of resources and the bargaining processes.

Unsuccessful role bargaining may result in a role occupant establishing role distance. The impact this has on communication, interaction, and productivity of the role set is discussed. There is strong empirical evidence that role stress influences a wide variety of positions in the health care community. The importance of developing a knowledge base which health care providers can utilize to prevent or eliminate detrimental effects of role strain will make it possible for providers to devote their energies to constructive aspects of their role.

NOTES

1. The theoretical foundations for this chapter were developed in Chapter 7. The reader is encouraged to review the basic theoretical foundation developed for the study of role stress and role strain. Of particular value are the basic concepts and their definitions the discussion of the theoretical perspectives on roles which are central to the two branches of role theory. That is review—symbolic interaction and structural role theory. Of equal importance is the explication of social exchange and the discussion which identifies the different views the two branches of role theory propose relative to role stress.

The latter discussion is fundamental to the initial development of this chapter. Symbolic interaction and its view of role stress has been selected by the authors to explain role strain and its management. Structural theory is introduced later to augment this explanation. In Chapter 7 we emphasized the importance of recognizing the very different notions of stress and strain found in symbolic the interaction perspective relative to the structural branch of role theory. The ideas are almost opposing. In symbolic interaction the term stress does not exist. The conditions of role stress are analyzed in terms of "*problematic situations.*" These situation are unusual or difficult and interfere with normal activities. The theory holds that the unusual nature of situations increases the level of awareness of persons. This energy is directed towards the normal process of problems solving as a means for success-fully dealing with the unexpected situation. Such "problematic situations" are conceptual-ized as challenges and providing a basis for advancing the intelligence of persons. In general, the view is that the more "problematic situations" persons successfully contend or cope with the more adept they become in re-defining unusual situations and in identifying successful courses of action and hence are more able to function in changing social situations and therefore more intelligent. The notion of *crisis* developed by W.I. Thomas is similar to its usage today. He proposed the idea in relation to the process of coping with "problematic situations" when normal problem solving efforts are unsuccessful other means of managing the "situation" are used. These crises may be the source of creative action. Unresolved situations (there may be no adequate solution) are associated relatively high levels of tension and less than optimal actions. At this point, the tension would be considered strain. The person at this point would try other methods of resolving the problematic situation.

Structural role theory does not propose role stress as a challenge, but rather as a detrimental or undesirable condition which exists in the social system as a result of the malintegration of role systems or a malfunction of the system in general. From the structural perspective role stress is tied to a position in the role structure. No matter how able and skilled the role occupant, he will not eliminate the role stress or the associated subjective state of role strain. The role stress is assessed as a detrimental condition because it interferes with the efficient operation of the system and ultimately compromises the role performance of the role occupant.

9

Reference Groups and Professional Socialization

Jean L.J. Lum

The concepts of reference group and socialization have always been central to role theory and the symbolic interactionist tradition. Reference groups provide one with the sources of values that one selects in guiding behavior, especially in situations where a choice has to be made. In other words, reference groups are those groups whose perspectives constitute the frame of reference for the individual. When viewed as a perspective (Shibutani, 1955), the concept of reference group points more to a psychologic phenomenon than to an objectively existing group and may therefore refer to a cognitive organization of an individual's experience. A reference group thus becomes any collectivity, real or imagined, envied or despised, whose perspective is assumed by the individual.

Reference groups may be groups to which an individual belongs, but not necessarily. In any case, they provide direction for the behavior of the individual concerned. In the enactment of their professional roles, the actions of health care professionals are strongly influenced by their perception of the norms and values of those groups in which they hold membership or those groups to which they aspire.

Reference groups play a significant part in the socialization process. In this chapter these and related concepts are presented as a fruitful and useful perspective for understanding the process by which neophytes become health professionals.

REFERENCE GROUPS

The term *reference group* was first proposed by Herbert Hyman (1942) and was used to increase the understanding of how an individual forms a conception of his status or position in society. Hyman suggested that, since one's position in society is defined relative to that of others, a person's view of his or her status depends upon the particular group of people one compares oneself with, i.e., the reference group. Reference groups were thus originally viewed as points of comparison in evaluating one's own status.

The concept of reference group did not come into general usage until Merton and Kitt (1950) published their widely known work on the utilization of the reference group idea as developed by Stouffer and associates (1949) to account for the attitudes and feelings about willingness to go into combat of American soldiers during World War II. Three groups of soldiers were studied: (1) inexperienced soldiers in units composed wholly of their own kind, (2) inexperienced soldiers who were replacements in units otherwise composed of combat veterans, and (3) veteran soldiers. Combat veterans had a strong group code against any tendencies to glamorize combat or to express eagerness for combat. Comparisons of attitudes indicated that while 45 percent of the inexperienced men were ready to go into an actual battle zone, only 15 percent of the veterans felt that same way. In units otherwise composed of combat veterans, 28 percent of the inexperienced replacements expressed readiness for combat. Merton and Kitt interpreted these results as indicating some degree of assimilation by these soldiers of the attitudes held by the veterans. As the inexperienced replacements sought affiliation with the authoritative and prestigious group of veterans, they moved from civilian–like values toward the more tough-minded values of the veterans.

With the passage of time, the concept of reference group has acquired an increasingly broader meaning. It is now commonly used to refer to any group to which a person relates his or her attitudes or to any group that influences the person's attitudes. It denotes any group, collectivity, or person that an individual takes into account in some manner in the course of selecting a behavior from a set of alternatives, or in making a judgment about a problematic issue.

Based upon the above usage, Newcomb (1965), Sherif (1948), and Siegel and Siegel (1957) have developed a general theory of reference groups designed to take account of attitudes anchored in both membership and nonmembership groups. It is important to note that reference groups and membership groups are not necessarily identical: a reference group may be a membership or a nonmembership group. They are identical when an individual aspires to *maintain* membership in a group and they are disparate when the group in which a person aspires to *attain* membership is one in which the person is not a member. Thus, both membership groups and reference groups affect the attitudes held by the individual.

A reference group to which an individual does not yet belong can serve as a powerful influencing factor, provided the person perceives that group to be one from which to seek acceptance and approval. Such a group is said to have a positive influence on the individual. In other instances, an individual may be influenced by a group he or she dislikes. In this case one is motivated to adopt attitudes and behaviors contrary to those of the group. In this situation, the group is a negative reference group. Individuals generally have multiple reference groups. However, their impact varies according to given situations. The effect of a reference group depends on its salience at a given moment with regard to a particular problem at hand and with respect to the degree of attractiveness of the group to the individual.

In an experimental study on positive and negative referent others as sources of influence on helping behavior, Schwartz and Amos (1977) noted that observers of positive referents tend to behave in congruence with the information provided by the referents while observers of negative referents tend to behave in opposition to the information the referents provided. Observers helped most when positive referents expressed favorable feelings and negative referents expressed unfavorable feelings.

Type and Functions of Reference Groups

Several types of reference groups are identified in the literature. These include normative groups, comparison groups, and audience groups. As will be seen, each of these groups serves different functions.

Normative Groups. Kelley (1965) describes normative groups as those groups, collectivities, or persons that provide a person with a guide to action by explicitly setting norms and values. The normative group makes its expectations known and assumes that the person will comply with these norms and values. For example, one's family, one's religious community, and one's nation may each constitute a person's normative group. The major characteristic of a normative group is that the person acts relative to norms and values that the group has espoused and brought to the person's attention. The group functions as a normative reference group for a person to the extent that one's evaluation of oneself and the group's evaluation are based upon the degree of one's conformity to certain standards of behavior or attitude and to the extent that the delivery of rewards or punishments is determined by the results of these evaluations. Normative reference groups then become the sources and enforcers of standards. The normative functions are a part of a general reference group theory of goal setting and motivation.

Comparison Groups. Another type of reference group identified by Kelley (1965) is that of comparison groups. These are groups, collectivities, or persons that provide a person with standards or comparison points that one can use to make judgments and evaluations. Comparison groups in this instance set the standards themselves against which a person can evaluate self and others. A group serves as a comparison reference group only when it is so perceived by an individual.

Kemper (1968) has elaborated on the concept of comparison groups and proposed four types. The first type is called the *equity group* and is used as a frame of reference for judging whether or not a person's situation or fate is fair or equitable. As an example, Merton's (1957) "married men in the army" employed as equity groups both married men not in the army and unmarried men in the army. According to culturally traditional standards of equity, the married men in the army perceived unfairness in the fact that not all married men were enduring the same fate and that they were forced to be in the same situation as unmarried men. An even more drastic comparison could have been made had the married soldiers employed as their equity group unmarried men not in the army.

Kemper's second type of comparison group is referred to as the *legitimator group*. This is a group that an individual uses when a question arises as to the validity of behaviors or opinions. For example, opinion leaders who set the tone for their social circles act as legitimators of attitudes and behaviors. In like manner, the Kinsey study sample can be assumed to have been a legitimator group for persons who previously considered their own sexual behavior as deviant. The knowledge that other people are doing the same thing as oneself serves to legitimate behaviors.

The *role model* is proposed as the third type of comparison group. The role model is generally viewed as an individual (rather than as a group) who possesses certain skills and displays techniques that the individual lacks and from whom, by observation and comparison with one's own performance, the individual can learn. For example, a student may adopt his professor as a role model or a son may adopt a father as his role model.

The fourth type of comparison group is the *accommodator group*. As Kemper explains, this refers to a group or person that provides cues for a person's responses in cooperative or competitive situations. Behavior is accommodated or adjusted to the perceived behavior of the other. For example, in a cooperative situation there is a normative overtone to the behavior of the other. In competitive situations, on the other hand, the other's behavior serves as a trigger for greater exertion for the individual. In both cases, however, the other is a referent and guide to the individual's behavior.

Audience Groups. An additional type of reference group cited in the literature is that of audience groups. In the ideal case, audience groups are said to demand neither normative nor value-validating behavior of the person for whom they serve as referents. With respect to this type of group, the individual is believed to attribute certain values to an audience group and to attempt to behave in accordance with those values. The individual is guided by an understanding of the values of the audience. To this extent the audience is like the normative group, but it differs in that an audience group does not even take notice of the individual whereas a normative group demands conformity to its norms and values. On the contrary, according to this theory, an individual must attract the attention of the audience.

Goffman (1958) has identified the audience as a group whose presumed interests guide the actor in special ways. In his introductory remarks in *The Presentation of Self in Everyday Life*, Goffman describes how Preedy, a vacationing Englishman, makes his appearance on the beach and calculates his performance to evoke a positive impression on the people on the beach who constitute his audience.

While the above discussion presents an analysis of the "ideal" types of reference groups, it does not presume that the types and functions are mutually exclusive within a given group. In other words, normative, comparison, and audience groups can coincide and often do. In addition, there may also be an overlap between these functions in the same group or person. This introductory discussion has been primarily analytical and has highlighted the richness of the reference group concept. The various conceptualizations are useful in accounting for the choices individuals make among apparent alternatives, in summarizing differential associations and loyalties, and in understanding the mechanism by which the socialization process is enhanced and facilitated.

REFERENCE GROUPS AND SOCIALIZATION

The preceding discussion about reference groups illustrates their value in guiding the opinion or action of the individual. In like manner, reference groups also serve to articulate individuals with significant social processes in society, especially that of socialization. Socialization refers to the "process by which individuals acquire the knowledge, skills, and dispositions that enable them to participate as more or less effective members of groups and the society" (Brim, 1966). It is primarily in interactional processes that a person's behaviors and attitudes are modified to conform to expectations of the group to which the individual belongs or aspires to belong. Additionally, it is primarily by virtue of the normative function of reference groups that the norms and values are prescribed and espoused for a given group. Normative reference groups therefore play a significant part in the socialization process by providing an individual with a set of norms and values and a standard for the proper level of performance in a given role.

The comparison reference group, particularly a role model, is likewise relevant to the socialization process by providing assistance on the way a role is to be performed. The availability of a role model facilitates the acquisition of an adequate level of role performance. Finally, it is Kemper's (1968) contention that it is the audience reference group, with its stated or imputed values, that encourages and motivates an individual to exert himself to bring his or her performance to an achievement level in the socialization process.

By definition, socialization entails social learning. In this sense learning is contrasted with maturation, which is the unfolding of the potentialities of the organism occurring more or less automatically except in situations of marked deprivation. Social learning includes learning to behave, feel, and see the world in a similar manner as other persons occupying the same role position as oneself. Social or role learning also includes acquiring an understanding of the attitudes of occupants of counter positions and learning certain skills and techniques associated with the role.

An inherent aspect of the socialization process is that of social control. According to Janowitz (1975), social control refers to the capacity of a social group to regulate itself through conformity and adherence to group norms to maintain the social order or organization within a group. Norms are enforced by means of sanctions. Sanctions refer to those actions of others or of an individual that have the effect of rewarding conformity or punishing nonconformity to norms. Positive sanctions are rewarding to the individual while negative sanctions have the effect of punishing the individual.

Furthermore, where the source of the reward or punishment rests in the behavior of others, external sanction is employed. An example of an external negative sanctioning is that of a mother punishing her child for an inappropriate behavior. Internal sanction is employed where the source of the reward or punishment lies within the individual. An example of internal positive sanctioning is that of an individual rewarding himself for a job well done. Both role learning and adequate role performance during the socialization process depend, in part, on the effectiveness of these internal sanctions.

From a sociologic perspective, reward and punishment may also be viewed as a means of providing the learner with cues that enable one consciously to evaluate the adequacy of one's performance and modify behavior where necessary. Expectations on the part of individuals that reward and punishment for specified acts will be forthcoming serve as important energizers or inhibitors of behavior. Socialization implies that the individual is induced to conform willingly to the ways of the particular groups to which the individual belongs. Norms therefore become internalized standards. More emphasis is likely to be focused on internal as opposed to external sanctions (Shibutani, 1962, pp. 128–147). The group's values become the individual's values and are hopefully recognized as having legitimacy or validity.

Various factors that either facilitate or interfere with the socialization process have been identified in the social system. One important condition is the clarity and consensus with which roles and positions are perceived by occupants, aspirants, and counterposition occupants. Another important condition is the degree of compatibility of expectations within role sectors and within role sets. To some degree, role learning may be facilitated by learning that occurs before entry to a position. Socialization agents, such as teachers, also differ in both their capacity and their efforts to manage the socialization process. There is variation in a faculty's ability to select recruits, in the amount of advance preparation they require of the recruit, and in the amount of time that intervenes between selection for an organization and actual participation in it. In addition, socialization agents differ in their capacity to control the sources and extent of prior knowledge the learner acquires about the profession he is to enter.

Anticipatory Socialization

Many elements of a role are learned prior to the time a person occupies a given position. This premature taking on of the behaviors and attitudes of an aspired-to reference group is termed *anticipatory socialization* (Wheeler, 1966). It is by virtue of a person's capacity for reflective thought through the manipulation of symbols that social situations and social roles can be acted out in the imagination. By adopting a role in play and in fantasy, persons can rehearse in advance the roles they will play in the future.

For example, small children "playing house" are not merely imitating their parents; they are also rehearsing in advance the roles that they will play in the future. Their portrayal of their role is based on their perceptions of the routines and interactions of family life. Often they are given feedback from their playmates as to how they are performing. By means of reflective thinking a medical student envisions himself as a doctor confronted with difficult clinical decisions and imagines what demands will be placed on him and what expectations he will be asked to fulfill. Anticipatory socialization thus entails a variety of mental activities that include daydreaming, forecasting future situations, and role rehearsing (Clausen, 1968a). In essence, it requires of the individual some degree of self-socialization and role rehearsal, wherein he learns a new self-identity. The individual has the ability to see himself in many different situations and to predict his action in them. However, the individual can only rehearse those roles or social situations that have been made known to him. Furthermore, the individual will tend to rehearse those roles that seem most desirable.

Additionally, learning a new role can also be facilitated by learning roles of a similar type. For example, first-aid techniques learned in Boy Scout or Girl Scout groups can later be part of a nursing student's repertory of skills. Similarly, occupying a position that relates to another position provides a person with additional opportunities to gain acquaintance with the roles associated with that counterposition. For example, a nursing student who has occupied the position of patient may have learned certain elements of the counterposition, nurse. Many students find numerous opportunities for role rehearsal by working in related jobs prior to entering school for formal professional education. Olesen and Whittaker (1968) found that almost one half (44 percent) of the nursing class they studied had prior experiences in hospital jobs such as aides, ward clerks, or volunteers. Another 23 percent had worked in blood banks, medical libraries, doctors' offices, or had nursed sick relatives at home.

Such prior experiences are common among young adults since formal education of the student professional occurs in late adolescence or early adulthood. Some socialization to a professional role frequently occurs for the individual prior to entry into a professional school. Accordingly, most persons are introduced to a new institution or organization only after they have had time to think about and to tentatively develop their own perspective on the profession.

SOCIALIZATION IN THE HEALTH PROFESSIONS

The process of becoming a health professional is a process of both adult and occupational socialization. As in any other role or position, social forces and trends move the individual toward or away from particular life goals. The decision to become a health professional is influenced by the individual's perceptions of positive and negative consequences that the individual weighs in some manner. People are differentially attracted to occupations by factors such as income, accessibility, and the fit of the job to their skills and their personalities. Unlike providing training for an occupation in general, the goal of professional training institutions is to inculcate into their aspirants the norms, values, and behaviors deemed imperative for survival of the occupation.

The Origin and Nature of Professions

In its early simplicity, society existed with few special services and therefore with few professional groups. By contrast, recent decades have seen an increase in the numbers of professionals that, as a proportion of the labor force, has exceeded that of all other categories of workers except clerical workers (Kerr, 1973). There has been tremendous growth in new and emerging health professions and a consequent growth in professional education. Each profession struggles with competing occupations and crafts; each tries to secure greater legitimacy for itself in society; and each seeks to define professional territories and to bring about uniformity in practice among practitioners. Finally, each attempts to define and meet the needs of new and changing clientele. Examples include the role and function of the psychiatrist as contrasted with those of the psychologist, psychiatric social worker, and psychiatric nurse.

The professions have developed as outgrowths of society's needs or desires for special services. Historically, professions arose when a group of persons was recognized as having unusual abilities to assuage the hurts and calm the fears of others by mediating among and between them and the powers of the universe. Only those with special preparation and skills, such as the medicine man, could deal with these forces, for no lay person could command the power. Since the time of the medicine man, the professional person has been recognized as an individual possessing unusual but needed gifts. Because of these special competencies and society's need for them, society allows the professional person to have a monopoly in that particular occupation. Only those with the necessary skills and knowledge are permitted to practice. Over the years, more detailed descriptions and criteria have evolved to distinguish professions from other occupations. Briefly stated, professions are intellectual, learned, and practical; they have techniques that can be taught; their members are organized into associations; they are guided by altruism; and they deal with matters of great human urgency and significance (McGlothlin, 1964). In consideration of these special conditions, society continues to allow professions to have a monopoly over their specialized services. Under this monopoly, the profession controls the body of knowledge on which its practice rests; it controls the number and kind of persons who are allowed to practice; it regulates the number and kind of persons entering the profession, and it guides the education of these neophytes.

Characteristics of Professional Socialization

Formal and Informal Educational Process. Of the many roles that the adult is called upon to perform, few exceed in importance the acquisition of the requisite skills, norms, values, and attitudes for occupations. All occupations that are called professions are entered in a similar way and require a long period of formal schooling. The number of years of schooling varies, but the sequence is fixed and follows the general pattern of high school (standard four years), college (varying from none to four years), and professional study (varying from one to four years). The medical and legal professional models illustrate the pattern of study most clearly. During or after completing the standard sequence required for admission to the profession, the candidate may either be required or may choose to engage in supervised practice. An internship program in a particular discipline illustrates this characteristic. In addition, the candidate may study in a particular area for certification as a specialist, such as is required during a surgical residency. Hughes (1973) has described this sequence as the fixed nature of American professional education.

The processes by which persons become professional are similar regardless of the specific profession. A profession requires not only formal education but also an informal, internalized system of ethics that guide the practice of the professional role. Therefore, while the knowledge acquisition necessary for achieving professional status varies, the process is common for all professions. These socialization procedures result in new images, expectations, skills, values, and norms related to how the person defines himself or herself and to how others view the person. There are both internal and external changes within the individual, in the individual's role set, and in the interactions among all of these.

Students undergoing professional socialization are placed in subordinate role arrangements in relation to their teachers. This is not surprising since it is, after all, the faculty in whom the institution and the profession have invested the authority and responsibility to pace, order, and sanction the progress of neophytes in the profession. Faculty therefore establish entry criteria, develop curricula, structure learning experiences, and evaluate students as they progress through the program. However, at the same time it is apparent that students do take an active part in shaping their own education and roles and even in influencing the faculty. Students in any professional school participate in their own education by making those choices necessary to meet faculty demands, to handle noninstitutional pressures, and to handle situations of their own creation.

Exposure to Multiple Agents of Socialization. At the same time, students are exposed to multiple agents of socialization. Some of the agents whom students encounter include clients, professional colleagues, other health professionals, and family and friends who occupy roles both within and outside the formal institutional structure. Students therefore have access to many sources of information about the profession in addition to the faculty. Information thus obtained is sometimes congruent with and sometimes discrepant from what students think of themselves or what the faculty want students to think of themselves. For example, Olesen and Whittaker (1968, p. 98) found that students with nurse relatives have a more negative image of nursing than the faculty would have preferred. The ability to place in perspective the views of those in other roles as sources of information and as ratifiers of a professional self is an important aspect of students' separation from the world of laymen. As indicated earlier, these multiple others influence students not only during their formal schooling but also before and after formal schooling. Socialization into the professional role may therefore be either facilitated or hindered depending upon the degree of congruity between the role expectations of these multiple agents, those of the faculty, and those held by the neophyte aspiring to the profession.

Transition from Adolescence to Adulthood. An additional facet of professional socialization merits attention here. A large segment of professional education occurs for many students while they are making the transition from adolescence to adulthood and from layperson to professional. For this reason these years of professional socialization may take on the additional dimensions of developmental socialization related to acquiring an adult role and a conception of self during resocialization from layperson to professional. While these socialization procedures occur simultaneously, they do not necessarily proceed smoothly or harmoniously (Marini & Greenberger, 1978). The roles that an individual assumes in other spheres of life may not blend comfortably with the roles in professional education. For example, a medical student who finds himself in the new roles of husband and father may discover that he does not have the time to devote to his wife and family because of his busy clinical schedule. Socialization during this period of an individual's life is thus multidimensional in that students simultaneously acquire new views of self along with new role behaviors (Hogan, 1980).

Heterogeneity of Students and Socializing Agents. Although the process of socialization is similar for all aspirants to a profession, students cannot be viewed as entirely homogeneous upon entry into professional schools. Not every student starts from the same baseline with respect to his qualifications or the awareness he has of the profession and of the self as a professional. Furthermore, instructors may also differ on this. For example, there are differences for both students and instructors with respect to age, lifestyle, social class, marital status, and in outlook, all of which impact differently on the individual. The socialization process involves taking a heterogeneous group of students and changing them into a more homogeneous group with respect to the knowledge, values, attitudes, behaviors, and skills that they will have following socialization.

Hazing, Ritualism, and Monopoly of Students' Time. Moore (1969) contends that in order to achieve maximum socialization, some professional schools virtually sequester their trainees in situations that amount almost to "total institutions," setting them apart from normal social activity. Still other professional schools approximate such isolation by the sheer burden of work demanded of students through extended class, laboratory, study, and practice hours. Moore further contends, as support for his punishment-centered theory of socialization, that the initiate is often required to perform unpleasant and even hazardous tasks and duties in order to remain in good standing. It is his thesis that practices such as hazing or suffering have a definite function in the socialization into all occupations, and particularly into the professions. These practices are intended to emphasize strong attention to standards of competence and performance and to identify with the occupation as a collectivity. Some of these difficult tasks are commonly ritualized and to that extent are arbitrary. Marks of success are likewise ritualized. Punishment is prolonged, however, for neophytes in occupations high in the scale of professionalism. The neophyte professional in medicine, for example, is usually required to do the "dirty work" or the "scut work" of the profession until such time as he or she has proven worthy to enter into the professional community by demonstrating knowledge, competence, and adherence to appropriate norms. While greater freedom follows successful survival of trials, the persistent possibility of failure is a characteristic of most professional occupations. Moore (1969) suggests this is an important ingredient of continuing professional occupational commitment.

Learning a Technical Language. Another feature of professional socialization is the learning of a technical language. Aside from facilitating precise technical communication, an esoteric vocabulary serves to identify those who belong in the group and to exclude those who do not. Thus it confirms occupational identity. Those who successfully learn the language and skills and survive the ordeals of punishment will emerge with an internalized professional commitment and identification with the collectivity. As long as the socializing system endures, the shared experiences of past suffering and success serve as a powerful bond for continued commitment and identification among and between the young and the elders within the professional collectivity.

Professions in a State of Flux. It has been observed that professional socialization proceeds at a more uneven pace and results in a less integrated professional self-image in those institutions that are in a state of flux and in those professions undergoing a transition in role definition. Olesen and Whittaker (1968) illustrate some of the problems faced by students confronted with such dilemmas. They found that the institutional climate impacted upon students. For example, the introduction of advanced ideas and avant-garde themes into a nursing program served to heighten previously existing strains among various faculty factions. In turn, faculty factionalism posed problems for the students in their relationships with their instructors. The differing nursing ideologies not only resulted in differential emphasis within the faculty culture and curriculum but also became the foci around which students could interact with faculty and around which the students gradually came to see different styles of nursing and different models of the nurse in contrast to an initially undifferentiated picture of nursing.

The impact of changing role definitions on socialization has received little study. Nursing, however, provides a classic example of a profession undergoing dynamic reconsideration of itself and its social role. Conflicts in definition of and

preparation for the nursing role are brought sharply into focus with the proliferation of such new categories as the expanded and extended roles of the nurse. The
less-established and emerging health professions may be confronted with similar
situations in their development. Unless there is consensus and clarity of the
norms, values, and behaviors expected within the given profession, it will be
increasingly difficult to socialize the neophyte into its ranks.

Student Culture. Socialization in professional schools does not take place in
formal classroom and clinical situations alone nor solely with professors. Without
question, one of the most powerful mechanisms of professional socialization is
informal interaction with fellow students. The peer group therefore serves as a
potent reference group for the student in the development and acquisition of
values and norms. Studies of medical and nursing schools in particular have
pointed to the existence of student cultures. These cultures represent a rich life of
interaction and shared understanding that develops among cohorts of students.
Students collectively set the level and direction of their efforts to learn and hence
exercise social control over the extent and direction of socialization. Students tend
to develop perspectives incorporating such crucial elements as a definition of the
situation in which they are involved, a statement of the goals they are trying to
achieve, a set of ideas specifying the kinds of activities that are expedient and
proper, and a set of activities or practices congruent with all of these (Flach,
Smith, Smith, & Glasser, 1982). The following discussion of student cultures
revolves around significant case studies of professional socialization in medicine
and nursing.

In their classic study *Boys in White,* Becker et al. (1961) found that freshmen
medical students at the Kansas University Medical School evolved their own set
of goals, working agreements, and solutions that were sometimes in conflict with
official definitions of the student role, e.g., when they were confronted with a
common problem such as having to do more work than they could possibly
handle. During the clinical years of medical education, students defined their
situation as one in which the goal of learning what was necessary for the practice
of medicine might be interfered with by the structure of the hospital and by the
necessity of making a good impression on the faculty. These students developed
new goals that were more specific than prior ones as they came in contact with
clinical medicine. They learned to want clinical experience and to want the
opportunity of exercising medical responsibility. They developed ideas about how
they must deal with the faculty, with patients, and with each other. And they
developed ways of cooperating among themselves to handle their work load, to
deal with the problem of making a good impression on the faculty, and to get as
much clinical experience and medical responsibility as possible. Under these
existing circumstances, students tried out various solutions to problems encountered and those solutions that worked best were then used by all the students,
provided it was possible for them to communicate their thoughts and discoveries
to one another (Bloom, 1973, p. 77). As a result of shared goals and exposure to
a body of crucial experiences and adversities, these medical students became a
community of fate and of suffering, bound together by feelings of mutual cooperation, support, and solidarity.

Similarly, Olesen and Whittaker (1968) observed the existence of a student
culture in their study of professional socialization among undergraduate nursing

students at the University of California School of Nursing in San Francisco. *Studentmanship* describes a form of underground student behavior that played a prominent part in shaping interactional styles, operational values, and staunchly held attitudes among students. The term studentmanship closely approximates the *student culture* concept of Becker et al. By practicing the art of studentmanship, these undergraduates managed to exercise some control over the process of becoming a nurse and found solutions to the perpetual problems of how to get through school with the greatest comfort and least effort and how to preserve themselves as persons, while at the same time being a success and attaining the necessities for their future life. Students were found to develop norms on a wide range of activities with regard to scholastic achievement, methods of bargaining, fronting (how to make a good impression on the faculty), how to bolster a classmate in the eyes of the faculty, how to "psych out" the faculty, how best to look attentive in a classroom, and how to behave appropriately "nursely" on a ward.

Olesen and Whittaker found that for some students, however, there was a self-established pressure to defy the norms of the student culture. For this group of students the problem became how to excel without offending their classmates. The front they chose to present was designed to soothe the anxieties of classmates and leave them with the impression that they had not been betrayed. The student culture did open a few avenues for excelling by occasionally providing the fleeting reference person who suggested something beyond the norm. The student culture on the whole, however, outwardly discouraged the education for excellence that the faculty desired for students and it suggested rather an education for mediocrity. Yet, while competition was muffled in public, it flourished rather lustily in private and in less obvious ways in the subtle rivalry revealed in fronting. On one hand, the authors observed that this student culture was a hindrance to socialization by its leveling influences and its perpetuation of the unsocialized self. On the other hand student culture enhanced the socialization process by disseminating knowledge, by sustaining and assisting fellow students, and by promoting the competition that it overtly attempted to squelch.

The preceding two studies of student culture were based on a symbolic interaction approach to socialization. A contrasting perspective on student culture reported in the literature is that described by Merton et al. (1957). Their study *The Student-physician* was based on a structural–functional approach to socialization. The authors identified a student culture at Cornell which, compared with the Kansas case, was more integrated with the formal educational system. It functioned to maintain the communications network of the school, to clarify standards, and to control behavior based on norms that were mutually held by students and faculty. The Cornell students are portrayed as "physicians-in-training," whereas the Kansas students are viewed as "boys in white." The Cornell study reflects a context in which students are already accepted as colleagues, proceeding more or less smoothly to full membership in the profession. In contrast, the Kansas study illustrates a situation in which students and faculty are set apart, with distinctive and even conflicting interests, and with students in a position that is both isolated and subordinate, making it clear that they are not yet professionals (Arnold, Willoughby, & Calkins, 1985).

These two studies began with different conceptions of the socialization process and of the medical school and its relation to the profession. Also, the studies were conducted in different types of educational settings, Kansas being traditional, state supported, and Midwestern whereas Cornell is experimental in curriculum and philosophy, private, and Ivy League.

Development of a Professional Self-Image

By what interactional processes occurring throughout the socialization experience do neophytes develop a professional self-image and come to regard themselves as bona fide health professionals? Olesen and Whittaker (1968) propose two related processes, *legitimation* and *adjudication,* as a framework for analyzing and understanding the experiential transactions through which students develop their professional identities. Although Olesen and Whittaker studied the socialization of student nurses, their suggestions have potential utility in studying other health professional neophytes.

Legitimation as used by Olesen and Whittaker refers to the process by which others sanction the student's claim to the role of health professional. (Legitimation, then, consists of a series of sanctions applied to the student's claim on the general role of that health profession to which the student aspires; the concept subsumes those sanctioning interactions encountered by the student as being generally accepted or rejected.) Adjudication as used by these authors refers to the continual refereeing and negotiating of the minute, face-to-face transactions between students and faculty relative to the technical, refined aspects of role performance. During the adjudication process the student's claim on a role is met with a variety of instructor styles that acknowledge it to be accurate or inaccurate. If the role is inaccurate, suggestions for corrections are made by instructors. The cycle comes full circle when the student has the opportunity to demonstrate awareness of appropriate altered behavior in the future. The adjudication process leads to legitimation, for it is through the vivid presence and interaction of the other that students come to incorporate the role of the other in developing their own professional identities. Legitimation of the physician role occurs at a different pace for women than for men. The professional careers of men as physicians tend to build in a more sustained manner than do those of women (Lorber & Ecker, 1983).

Olesen and Whittaker (1968) enumerated a variety of legitimation sources relevant to the role of nurse. They noted that students received legitimation in encounters with various persons in their role set. These legitimations included (1) nonofficial legitimation from parents, friends, strangers, or former college friends; (2) legitimation from fellow students; (3) formal modes of legitimation derived from grades and evaluations given by the faculty; (4) legitimation from staff nurses, doctors, and supporting personnel such as aides, orderlies, and licensed practical nurses; and (5) legitimation from patients or clients.

The nonofficial legitimators included all those persons in the role set who gave only the most general acknowledgment of the student's claim on his or her role. Students derived great reassurance from these nonofficial legitimators, particularly in the early phases of their education. However, in the long run, faculty won out over these nonofficial legitimators as those who could most meaningfully legitimate and adjudicate students' achievements and claims. Student legitimation resulted from an assessment of the manner and style in which students presented themselves to one another. Paradoxically, student judgment was influenced by the very same fronting that would earn the desired legitimation from faculty. The instructor's periodic evaluation of students and their grades served as reference points against which students could compare and legitimate themselves and, in passing, could assess their fellow classmates. In addition, Olesen and Whittaker noted that the student nurses' early contact with others practicing the profession to which they aspired resulted in legitimation from staff nurses. At times, legitimation from the staff was earned at the cost of that of the instructors, since the staff's ideas about techniques were frequently divergent from those of the instructors. Students frequently encountered radical differences in emphasis between the advanced notions of the faculty and the more conservative views of the hospital or agency practitioners. Where role conflict was high, students faced a problematic dilemma in obtaining legitimation from two divergent sources. Not surprisingly, physicians remained significant legitimators throughout the socialization period. Legitimation from supporting persons such as aides, orderlies, and licensed practical nurses was paramount during the summers when many students found employment in hospitals. Finally, patients constituted a particularly significant group of legitimators for students at the onset of their careers but diminished as the students became more able to evaluate and legitimate themselves.

While legitimation of the role of nurse comes from patients, staff and others in the hospital setting, there are circumstances in which this legitimation is withheld. In those practicum settings where faculty retain control and direction of the students' assignments and performance, other nursing personnel may consider the students to be outsiders and not accept them fully. As a consequence, identification with the nursing role as well as attraction to the occupation may be diminished (Simpson, 1979).

Huntington's (1957) study of how medical students come to view themselves as doctors also draws upon an analysis of the students' self-images and role set. Huntington contends that students typically think of themselves primarily as students at the beginning of their medical training and come progressively to think of themselves as doctors as they advance through medical school. However, it is vis-à-vis patients more than with any other group in their role set that medical students tend to see themselves as physicians. Legitimation of a professional self-image can thus be seen as resulting from multidimensional transactions taking place with persons in their role set during the formal and informal encounters that occur throughout the professional socialization experience.

Ongoing Professional Socialization

Socialization that takes place during the formal years of education plays an important part in the development of a professional self-identity. However, students progress at different rates through the program and this has implications for role assimilation. Thus, while students in general assimilate a central core of values emphasized by the faculty and the profession, within a collection of graduating students there can be found wide divergence in types of professional role assimilation, varying degrees of self-awareness, and differences in professional behavior and knowledge. Furthermore, the process of socialization does not terminate with graduation from a program of study, but continues as the neophyte commences a professional career. In reality, regardless of the outcome of the initial socialization, the process of professional socialization continues throughout life.

It has been noted that the greater the congruence of the norms, values, and behavioral expectations between the educational organization of the profession and the realities of the work setting, the smoother the transition will be from neophyte to full-fledged professional. Kramer (1974) proposes the concept of *reality shock* to highlight the discrepancies between the norms, values, and behavioral expectations existing in the educational setting of nursing and those of the work situation. She believes shock results from an inadequate socialization of the neophyte during formal schooling. Kramer contends that because of these discrepancies the neophyte is unprepared to function effectively in the world of reality. Reality shock is a term Kramer used to describe the phenomenon of shocklike reactions of new workers when they find.themselves in the work situation for which they have spent several years preparing and for which they thought they were ready, only to suddenly find that they are not. Kramer has suggested an anticipatory socialization program as a means for transmitting role-specific behaviors intended to meet the exigencies of the work world and to acquaint nursing students with the realities of the "Positive Now" (Kramer's term) without losing their vision and ability to function in the "Relative When."

The fact is, the initial work experience must be viewed as a continuation of professional socialization because it is in this situation, as the neophyte begins his professional career, that role-specific behaviors are learned. A major portion of professional socialization thus occurs after completion of the formal years of schooling. In the field of medicine, Olmstead and Paget (1969) and Bloom (1971) document the important contributions made by the internship and residency experiences. Initial work experiences in the other health professions likewise provide ongoing socialization in their respective disciplines. It is during this crucial period that the values, norms, and behaviors to which the individual has been exposed during his formal education are most likely to become internalized.

SOCIAL CONTROL WITHIN AND BETWEEN PROFESSIONS

Society accords a monopoly to a profession with respect to its practice and standard setting on the premise that no layperson understands esoteric knowledge on which the profession rests, and therefore no layperson can judge what should be done. Society allows a profession to hold a monopoly because it is convinced that the profession is dedicated to an ethical or altruistic ideal in serving society. Society continues to allow this monopoly as long as it is convinced that a profession is exercising its privileges responsibly and aids and serves its clientele without exploitation.

Under its monopoly, a profession has the purpose of protecting not only the society it serves but also its members, making it possible for them to practice effectively. Its protection, which occurs through methods passed on by socialization, takes different form as the profession confronts internal as well as external dangers.

Internally, a profession must protect society and its members against the incompetent or dishonest member whose actions may damage trust in the profession. A profession controls the number and kinds of persons who are allowed to enter and to study through the establishment of admission criteria and determining the length and types of programs allowed. These controls are imposed to prevent incompetent persons from entering the profession and to avoid an oversupply of practitioners as well. In addition, a profession controls the body of knowledge on which its practice rests and maintains the quality and standards of its education through a process of external accreditation. It further controls admission to the profession through licensing procedures as well as through various certification and credential procedures. It opposes efforts to establish conditions that would make its practice difficult or impossible. Each profession has an obligation to police its own ranks and to make certain that those who wear the name and display the license are in fact ethical and competent practitioners. From this obligation stem efforts to enforce the code of ethics of the profession even to the extent of expelling members who flagrantly violate provisions of its code. Thus, a physician's license can be revoked or a lawyer can be disbarred. Professional associations aid practitioners in obtaining legal sanction for their monopoly. Once a profession is awarded legal status and is given the exclusive right to practice in the field of its competence, it can inhibit the practice of imposters by taking action in the courts to bring them to trial and punishment.

Each profession defines an area of practice in which it has a monopoly and it fights hard to preserve that unique area. A profession thus protects its members against nonlegitimate individuals and groups who may try to encroach on the area of practice reserved to the profession. In summary, a profession engages in a variety of activities that are designed to monitor and control itself while maintaining its claim as an autonomous body among other professional disciplines.

SUMMARY

Professional socialization is a process that continues throughout an individual's adult and occupational life. Concepts from role theory and reference group theory have been discussed and proposed as a framework for analyzing and understanding the mechanisms through which neophytes acquire norms, values, knowledge, and skills appropriate to a given occupation. Means of inducing compliance with normative expectations have been elaborated. Factors contributing to differential assimilation of a new professional self-image have been cited. Additionally, social control measures have been presented to illustrate the methods by which professions monitor themselves and legitimize their claims as autonomous disciplines within society.

10

A Reevaluation of the Queen Bee Syndrome

Magaret M. McGrath

The predominance of females in the nursing profession has profoundly influenced the nature of that profession (Meleis & Dagenais, 1981). Several authors have identified nonsupportive patterns of behavior in relationships between and among women; these patterns are found in female nurses' relationships (Bush & Kjervik, 1979; Fromm, 1977; Grissum & Spengler, 1976). Nonsupportive behavior patterns suggest that nurses have not developed a sense of sisterhood and relatedness. Spengler (1976) claims that competition, lack of group cohesiveness, and conformity are as apparent among groups of nurses as they are in other groups of women. Nursing cannot escape the labels placed upon its members both as women and nurses. Spitzer (1986) has asserted that nursing history has worked against the socialization of women and nurses in a competing modality.

Other authors argue that women are not such a monolithic group that they can be characterized by similar patterns of behavior (Epstein, 1980; Riger & Galligan, 1980). Epstein (1980) cautions that we should consider the social contexts in which women's attitudes toward other women are labeled. Stereotypes are usually framed when women step out of traditional roles. Epstein (1980) asserts that both men and women share a cultural ambivalence about women's work outside traditional roles. When women do not support other women and demonstrate their nonsupport behaviorally, the underlying reason may be women's relative lack of power in the structure of which they are a part or personality differences that are not gender specific. In light of these alternatives it is important to reevaluate the circumstances leading to nonsupport. This may be done through an investigation of one stereotype labeled the Queen Bee syndrome.

THE QUEEN BEE SYNDROME

The metaphor of the Queen Bee was originally coined by Staines, Tavris, and Jayratne (1974) to describe antifeminist behaviors employed by certain women.

Acknowledgment is given to Suzanne Halsey-Levy for the original empirical investigation of the Queen Bee Syndrome. The reevaluation of the Queen Bee Syndrome is based on the data presented in the first edition of this volume.

Queen Bee women have been identified as having secured positions in management or other traditionally male-dominated careers. Staines et al. (1974) describe the Queen Bee as an unusual antifeminist because she is successful in the traditional sphere of marriage and family, as well as in her professional role. These authors present the behavior of the Queen Bee as being the outgrowth of a role dispute between professional career women and traditional women.

As an "honorary man," the Queen Bee's countermilitancy has its roots in her personal success within the system; both her professional success and her social success. Staines et al. (1974) maintain that the Queen Bee's professional behavior is entrenched in self-centered motivation. The Queen Bee shuns her protegees, quells potential competition, and co-opts membership in the dominant group.

To validate the existence of the Queen Bee syndrome, Staines et al. (1974) analyzed data that had been collected by one of the authors in an earlier *Psychology Today* questionnaire titled, "Woman and Man" (Athansiou, Shaver, & Tavris, 1970). The first *Psychology Today* questionnaire, which yielded 20,000 replies from both sexes, did not claim to be a representative sample of the American public. For purposes of convenience, Staines et al. (1974) labeled all professional women in the sample as Queen Bees. The Queen Bee group was compared to two other groups of female respondents. One group comprised traditional, nonorganizational women, and the other group was composed of women who belonged to three different types of feminist organizations.

The authors compared the data responses of the three groups to a set of statements designed to elicit the attitude of women toward their role status. The Queen Bees in Staines' (1974) sample were more likely than feminist or traditionalist women to be individualists, deny discrimination, and to reject the assumptions and goals of the women's movement. Staines et al. (1974) did not present statistical analyses, nor did they state whether the three categories of women were mutually exclusive. Despite the logical limitations of the first description of the Queen Bee syndrome, social scientists have been quick to adopt the label "Queen Bee" (Berry & Kushner, 1975; Bush & Kjervik, 1979; Schaef, 1981).

Bern (1987) devoted an entire chapter to stories of Queen Bee bosses who intimidate subordinates. Men and women alike relate anecdotal descriptions of the Queen Bee. Epstein (1980) highlights this tendency when she states, "When speakers discuss the Queen Bee Syndrome, eyes light up. Many women seem to agree it exists, and offer anecdotes showing successful women are not helpful to subordinates" (p. 326).

In another anecdotal description, Spengler (1976), a nurse-author, adopted Staines' metaphor of the Queen Bee and concluded the syndrome does exist in nursing. Spengler emphasizes that in nursing, Queen Bees are characterized by a number of behaviors. They are talented women who excel in their chosen area of interest and view themselves as successful. They also view themselves as special and different from other nurses. Consequently, they do not want to associate closely with other nurses, preferring to identify with people outside nursing. Queen Bee nurses maintain allegiance to men and to the system. Compared with other nurses, Queen Bees are usually found to hold higher-paying, more prestigious positions. (They do not, however, hold positions that are as well paying and prestigious as men in the same system.) Because Queen Bees enjoy a privileged position they are not necessarily concerned about making changes in the system (Spengler, 1976).

Both Spengler (1976) and, ten years later, Spitzer (1986) describe the difficult task of working with a Queen Bee nurse, who typically demands allegiance to her rather than loyalty to an ideal. Special skills are not shared and if referrals are warranted they are channeled to outside resources, not to nursing colleagues. A Queen Bee's conditions for working with other nurses include special treatment or recognition and a demand to be in charge. Again, the decision to be involved with colleagues is based on the Queen Bee's self-serving interest and not to the benefit to her colleagues' expertise.

A Queen Bee Study

Halsey (1977) conducted an exploratory study to determine if the Queen Bee syndrome existed in nursing and, if so, to establish if Queen Bees become more prevalent in progressively higher levels of nursing management. Halsey designed a 44-item Likert-type questionnaire designed to measure Queen Bee characteristics in nurse managers. The statements chosen to elicit Queen Beeness were based on seven distinct conceptual categories from the literature (Halsey, 1977). The first category related to the Queen Bee's relationship to her reference group. The second category dealt with the Queen Bee's alignment with the establishment and her resistance to change. Closely related to this status quo tendency is the third category: the Queen Bee holds antifeminist beliefs that she projects onto other women. The fourth category deals with the Queen Bee's desire to be in control at the expense of other competent women. Fifth, the Queen Bee, as a decision maker, works independently of others and avoids group work or group solutions. Sixth, because she feels that she is appropriately rewarded for her expertise and "specialness," she views the system in which she works positively. The final conceptual category, which is specific to nurse Queen Bees, relates to the degree of perceived nurse-doctor conflicts (Spengler, 1976). Figure 1 illustrates the theoretical development of the Queen Bee continuum (Halsey, 1978).

Halsey's Queen Bee questionnaire yielded a summary score for the noted dimensions which reflected qualities of high Queen Beeness and low Queen Beeness. On a 1- to 7-point Queen Bee scale, 4 was selected as the cut-off point for Queen Bee behavior; those achieving a score greater than 4 were labeled Queen Bees (Halsey, 1977). Validity was obtained by administering the questionnaire to persons who had previously been identified by their peers as high or low in Queen Beeness.

Halsey (1977) distributed her questionnaire to a convenience sample of 140 nurses in management positions: 50 head nurses, 43 supervisors, and 47 directors of nursing. Of the 140 respondents, 40 persons or 28 percent were determined to be Queen Bees. To test her second hypothesis, the author asked if Queen Bees were more prevalent in increasingly higher levels of nursing management. She found support for this hypothesis. Halsey determined that only 2 percent of the head nurses and 16 percent of the supervisors, but 70 percent of the nursing directors, qualified as Queen Bees. This hypothesis was accepted using three different statistical analyses, all with significant findings at the $p = 0.05$ confidence level.

Halsey's (1977) results indicate that reference group affiliation changes as nurses move up the career ladder, with directors and supervisors tending to identify with people outside nursing. In addition, the maintenance of the status quo was more predominant in directors of nursing than in head nurses. Directors

Queen Bee Continuum	
Low Queen Bee	**High Queen Bee**
Subordinate Career Development	
facilitates development shares skills and knowledge delegates	*"runs the show"* *"uneasy with knowledgeable subordinates"*
Decision-Making Method	
participative management *"group participation"* *"group work"*	authoritarian, individual strategies *"I make decisions on my own"*
Perspective of Existing System	
many inequities *"salaries and benefits not commensurate"*	fair, just *"fair hirings and promotions"*
Women's Movement	
feminist *"collective assertiveness"* *"self awareness"*	anti-feminist *"household obligations"* *"husband's career"*
Perspective Toward Change	
initiates change *"troublemaker, gets things done"* *"unconventional solutions"*	maintains status quo *"problems handled as before"* *"vacancies filled by cooperative nurses"*
Doctor-Nurse Relations	
acknowledges conflict *"more comfortable with nurses"*	denies conflict *"conflict imagined"*
Reference Group	
nurses *"good job nurse approval"* *"lunch with nurses"*	other professionals *"aim to please medical staff"* *"administrator likes my work"*

Figure 1. The theoretical development of the Queen Bee continuum *(with paraphrased questionnaire statements).*

also denied conflict or tension when dealing with the medical profession.

Post-hoc factor analysis identified two important factors related to the Queen Bee syndrome. The primary factor was identified through statements relating to the Queen Bee's orientation to society, adherence to the status quo, and to traditional and conservative beliefs. The statements that positively correlated with this factor were those that were antifeminist, those that supported maintenance of the status quo, and those that acknowledged a need for endorsement from hospital administrators and medical staff (Halsey, 1977). The secondary factor isolated identified the respondent's relationship with their nurse constituency and with the organization. Statements related to this factor concerned nurse reference groups, perceptions of the organizations, and the individual's methods of making changes. Halsey (1977) determined that the factor analysis empirically verified the seven conceptual categories of Queen Beeness developed from the literature. The seven conceptual categories, however, were reduced to two general conceptual areas; the first factor is identified as orientation with society, and the second is orientation with the nurses and the organization.

Replication Study

Story (1986) conducted a replication of Halsey's (1977) study to determine if the Queen Bee syndrome existed in nursing education and, secondly, if Queen Bee behavior was increasingly more prominent in progressive levels of nursing education. The sample included 150 nurse educators, stratified on the basis of educational program: baccalaureate, associate, and diploma. The sample was randomly selected from the National League for Nursing publication, *State Approved Schools of Nursing, R.N. #1981* (Story, 1986). Associate degree nursing educators comprised 36.7 percent of the sample, baccalaureate nurse educators 32.7 percent, and diploma educators 30.6 percent of the total sample. Story (1986) altered the wording of the Queen Bee questionnaire to reflect the population under investigation. This modification indicated role positions in nursing education rather than nursing administration. Instead of Halsey's (1977) hospital titles of Head Nurse, Supervisor, and Director of Nursing, Story substituted Instructor, Assistant Professor, and Chair or Head. In addition, questions that referred to the hospital were changed to read institution. Reliability and validity measures for the modifications in the Queen Bee questionnaire were not reported.

In revising the Queen Bee questionnaire, Story was assuming that the role requirements of the nurse educators are equivalent to Halsey's sample of nurse managers. The job description and level of responsibility may be significantly different for nurse educators who are department chairs within a group of faculty versus directors of nursing who are department heads of an institution.[1] Story (1986) identified 60 percent of her sample as chairs or heads of educational programs. It is not clear whether these women held an equivalent amount of responsibility similar to Halsey's (1977) 47 nursing directors. This potential sample difference between the two studies may confound the results of the investigation in relation to the Queen Bee syndrome.

Story's (1986) method of data analysis for the revised Queen Bee questionnaire corresponded to Halsey's (1977) original scoring method. Responses to the Queen Bee statements were measured on a 7-point Likert scale ranging from strongly disagree to strongly agree. A composite score was determined from the Queen Bee statements, with 1 being the lowest possible score and 7 being the highest possible score. Using Halsey's scoring method individuals were labeled Queen Bees if their score was greater than 4. Seven of the 98 respondents or 7 percent were identified as Queen Bees (Story, 1986). This is in marked contrast to the 28 percent identified in the nurse administrator sample (Halsey, 1977). Tables 1 and 2 present Queen Bee scores for nurse managers and nurse educators according to job level.

Story proposed, as did Halsey in her second hypothesis, that the Queen Bee syndrome was more prevalent in progressive levels of nursing education. This hypothesis was partially supported. Of the seven Queen Bee nurse educators in Story's sample, one Queen Bee held a faculty position, indicating 3 percent of the faculty group were Queen Bees. This in contrast to the six Queen Bees who were chairpersons, indicating 10 percent of the chairperson group were Queen Bees. The Queen Bee in the faculty position was employed in a diploma education program. Of the six Queen Bees found in chairperson positions, three were employed in baccalaureate nursing programs, two in associate degree programs, and one in a diploma education program. The rank of these Queen Bees was not reported in Story's findings. Based on these data, Story concluded that Queen Bees were more prevalent in increasing levels of nursing education.

Unlike Halsey, who noted a significant increase in Queen Bee scores with each level of nursing education ($F = 102.37$, $p < 0.001$) Story did not find a significant difference in Queen Bee scores with each level of nursing education. Story also did not find a significant correlation between Queen Bee scores of nurse educators and job level. Thus, unlike Halsey, who found that there was an increase in Queen Bee scores with each higher level of nursing management and a significant correlation between job level and Queen Bee scores, Story noted only an increase in the number of Queen Bees from faculty to chairperson positions.

Halsey's and Story's demographic characteristics were remarkably similar for gender, age, and experience. The respondents were all women. Mean age for nurse managers was 40 years and for nurse educators 42.2 years. Mean years of nursing experience was 18 for both samples, whereas in Halsey's study, nursing directors had 26 years of experience and nursing educators had 25 years of experience. As Halsey's study was completed in the Northeast, Story controlled for demographic location in her sample. Thirty percent were from the Northeast, 29 percent from the Southeast, 25 percent from the Midwest, and 11 percent from the Western part of the United States. Story concluded that the occurrence of respondents who scored on the high end of the Queen Bee continuum was not related to area of residence.

The most striking difference between Halsey's sample of nurse managers and Story's sample of nurse educators is their difference in educational preparation as illustrated in Table 3. Fifty-two percent more of the educators than the managers had master's degrees or higher. Also, most of Halsey's sample of nurses and supervisors had less than a baccalaureate education, whereas 31 percent of her sample of directors possessed master's degrees.

The educational level of Halsey's sample of nurse administrators is in marked contrast to Story's sample of nurse educators. Eighty-three percent of Story's sample earned a master's degree or higher contrasted with Halsey's 31 percent in

TABLE 1. QUEEN BEE SCORES FOR HALSEY'S (1977) NURSE MANAGERS ACCORDING TO JOB LEVEL

Job Level	Mean Queen Bee Scores	SD	No. of QBs[a]	No. in Group
Head Nurse	2.75	0.55	1	50
Supervisor	3.69	0.42	6	43
Directors	4.47	0.75	33	47
Total	3.61	0.93	40	140

[a]Those identified as Queen Bees had to score greater than 4 on the Queen Bee questionnaire.

TABLE 2. QUEEN BEE SCORES FOR STORY'S (1986) NURSE EDUCATORS ACCORDING TO JOB LEVEL

Job Level	Mean Queen Bee Scores	SD	No. of QBs[a]	No. in Group
Faculty	3.21	0.40	I	39
Chair	3.39	0.46	6	59
Total	3.30	0.43	7	98

[a]Those identified as Queen Bees had to score greater than 4 on Queen Bee questionnaire. Rank of Queen Bee educators was not provided.

her sample. Eighty-two percent of the faculty and 85 percent of chairpersons in the nurse educator sample possessed master's degrees or higher.

Noting this significant difference in education and also the marked difference in the number of Queen Bees found in managers versus educators, Story speculated that the difference between the education in the samples provided data for one of Halsey's research implications. Halsey (1977) concluded from her study that Queen Bee behavior is learned either on the job or through the socialization process of nursing education. Halsey based this conclusion on the strong correlation found in her sample between age, education, and job level of nurse managers ($r = .67, p = < .001$). Story concurred with Halsey that Queen Bee behavior is a learned behavior; however, she speculated that this is more the product of on-the-job socialization than of the socialization process of nursing education. Yet, it is also noteworthy that only 7 percent of Story's sample "learned" the Queen Bee behavior. Story does not speculate whether these Queen Bee women differed in educational level, were self-selected, or were previously employed in managerial or administrative positions outside of education.

Both Halsey's and Story's implications are open to further discussion. It may be that both samples of nurses have self-selected characteristics that influenced their responses to the Queen Bee questionnaire.[2] Additional data is needed to correlate educational levels, rank, and position with the responses from the Queen Bee questionnaire before conclusions can be drawn.

TABLE 3. EDUCATIONAL PREPARATION FOR THE TOTAL RESPONDENTS OF HALSEY'S (1977) NURSE MANAGERS AND STORY'S (1986) NURSE EDUCATORS

Highest Degree	Nurse Managers N = 140 (%)	Nurse Educators N = 98 (%)
Doctorate	0	7
Master's	31	76
Baccalaureate	27	14
Diploma	40	3
Associate	2	0
Total	100	100

Queen Bee Questionnaire. The purpose of Story's (1986) replication study was to obtain psychometric data on Halsey's (1977) questionnaire. Halsey did not report formal reliability measures on the Queen Bee questionnaire. Story established the reliability of the Queen Bee questionnaire on nurse educators through the method of internal consistency. She noted that the alpha coefficient was low (alpha = 0.47). The stability of the questionnaire was another reliability measure secured by Story. Test–retest procedures, using 20 faculty retested for two weeks following the first test, yielded a Pearson Product Moment Correlation Coefficient of $r = 0.67$.

In an attempt to establish construct validity, Story determined her sample of nurse educators was not large enough for a factor analysis for reliability or validity and therefore she completed a Guttman scalogram for unidimensionality.[3] The coefficient of reproducibility was 0.76. Story reported a coefficient of reproducibility of 90 percent is needed to define a scale as unidimensional (Gorden, 1977). This finding may be misleading as Halsey (1977) did not attempt to devise a unidimensional scale. Seven conceptual domains were identified which were consistent with Queen Bee behavior (Halsey, 1977). A factor analysis further reduced these conceptual categories into two factors.

In addition to the factor analysis for construct validity, Halsey (1977) established content validity from the literature by using graduate students and faculty to sort statements into high and low Queen Bee categories. Construct validity for the categories was obtained from nurses identified as having high or low Queen Bee behavior. Of the 23 to whom a questionnaire was sent, 13 of the designated Queen Bees responded, 10 in the direction consistent with their Queen Bee labels. Although these findings were not treated statistically, the differences were assumed to provide some validity for the tool (Halsey, 1978).

Story (1986) further explored the validity of the Queen Bee scale in her sample of nurse educators. Content validity was assessed through completion of a Content Validity Index (CVI). Two unspecified judges were given the list of domains and items and were asked to rate independently the relevance of each item to the domains using a 4-point rating scale. The CVI is the proportion of items given a rating of 3 or 4 by both raters. The CVI for the Queen Bee's questionnaire was 0.48. A CVI of 0.50 indicates an unacceptable level of content validity (Waltz, Strickland, & Lenz, 1984).

Based on the above data, Story (1986) concluded that further refinement of the Queen Bee questionnaire was indicated. She suggested it be used as a peer evaluation tool rather than a self-report measurement because of the response bias inherent in admitting to negative evaluations of self.[4] The two empirical investigations thus far suggest that Queen Bee characteristics differ for the two separate samples of nurses. Methodological limitations inherent in existing studies warrant that further investigation be pursued concerning Queen Bee behaviors in nursing and other populations. Personal and multiple institutional variables may also influence nursing managers' or academicians' viewpoints as to behaviors that are essential to their respective roles.

An additional explanation for the discrepancy in the number of Queen Bees between the two samples is also possible. The general contexts which support or hinder Queen Bee behavior may be different for nurse educators than for nurse managers. A collegiate environment, in which nurse educators function, may be qualitatively different from hospital settings where head nurses and directors work. The differing environments in these samples raise issues regarding the situational contexts which facilitate or hinder Queen Bee behavior. Educators, for example, may have more opportunity to work independently in research or scholarship activities. Thus, a profitable course for reevaluating the Queen Bee label may be to examine the contexts in which the stereotype is applied.

Support is found in the literature for consideration of situational versus personal explanations of Queen Bee behavior. Yoder, Adams, Grove, and Priest (1985) refuted the Queen Bee label in an analysis of a sample of exit interviews from the first women cadets to graduate from West Point. The analysis revealed that the failure of upperclass cadet women to sponsor incoming women was the logical outcome of situational pressures exerted on these women. An examination of various perspectives in the literature related to the Queen Bee phenomenon will clarify the social contexts in the reevaluation of the Queen Bee metaphor.

THEORETICAL APPROACHES

Staines et al. (1974) approached the Queen Bee metaphor as an adaptation of their countermovement theory. The women's movement is the initial social movement and its proponents are termed feminists. Staines et al. (1974) contended that, as occurs with all social revolutions, countermilitants emerge (i.e., antifeminists) who organize and fight for the status quo. Queen Bee behavior is a product of this countermilitancy.

A different perspective has been suggested by Ward (1979), who asserts that the overwhelming attitudinal conservatism evinced by professional Queen Bee women is a product of what Allport (1954) in his book, *The Nature of Prejudice*, terms "exploitative advantage." This phenomenon occurs in select groups who have gained a secure economic standing, social snobbery, and a feeling of moral superiority. The maintenance of these exploitative advantages is largely dependent upon the acceptance of sex role stereotypes.

Epstein (1980) explores the myth of "minority group self-hatred," coined by Lewin (1948) to describe a process in which the out group shares the poor opinion of itself that the in group expresses (i.e., women who wish to associate only with men because women are inferior). Again, the maintenance of this explanation is dependent on accepting the sex role stereotypes fostered by in groupers.

Spitzer (1986) proposes that women's lack of the military tradition in their socialization process promotes the Queen Bee syndrome. She refers to Harrigan's (1977) book, *Games Mother Never Taught You*, to cite women's ignorance of the rules of the team network. As noted previously, acceptance of this explanation depends on accepting traditional sex role stereotypes.

Such explanations of development of Queen Bee behavior depend upon acceptance of gender-specific notions applied to women in professional roles. By definition the characteristics attributed to the Queen Bee are person-centered or trait-oriented. Thus, the characteristics are ascribed to the Queen Bee herself (Riger & Galligan, 1980).

To examine this difference between person-centered and trait-oriented characteristics, Kanter (1977) explored both person-centered and situation-centered explanation for gender differences related to promotion within the corporation. Person-centered approaches explained the paucity of top ranking women executives by pointing to the lower aspirations of women. Women were also said to be insensitive to cues from managers as to promotion behavior, therefore, fewer women were promoted. Because these inadequate aspirations resided within women themselves, it was suggested that women be changed to bring about more equal promotional rates. In contrast, Kanter (1977) argued from a situation-centered perspective, pointing to the differences in opportunities available to women and to men within the structure of the corporation.

In summary, by endorsing a trait explanation for the Queen Bee syndrome it may be assumed that many women who become successful, regardless of the circumstances of their success, will naturally exhibit the Queen Bee syndrome (Berry & Kushner, 1975). Situation-centered explanations focus on the characteristics of social context. Specifically, the focus is on the role position the Queen Bee occupies in interaction with others rather than on the individual personal characteristics of the Queen Bee.

Halsey, in her published study (1978), viewed the Queen Bee role performance as one way of diminishing role conflict. The Queen Bee develops the behaviors inherent in the syndrome through role making and role taking. Halsey (1978) states:

> For her, the Queen Bee behavior offers a way of coping with the conflicting demands of the contemporary professional role model and the traditional family role model. It permits her to operate on a double standard; what is right for her is not always right for the other women. Due to this double standard, the nurse Queen Bee may frequently be haunted by decisions that she has made from these two conflicting frames of reference. (p. 247)

Symbolic Interaction View

Here, Halsey is hinting at the dynamic processes inherent in the Queen Bee's role-taking and role-making actions. Recently, symbolic interaction has offered a valuable insight into the dynamic nature of role relationships (Hardy, 1988). This theoretical approach emphasizes the emergent quality of role relationships derived from social interactions. In conjunction with structural role theory, symbolic interaction provides an organized perspective of viewing the Queen Bee's behavior.

Symbolic interactionists assert that the actions of individuals occur in relation to other individuals (Charon, 1985). Lines of action are negotiated with role partners who also have desired lines of action (Mead, 1934). Role partners evaluate the attitude and intentions of others and then act within the context of any given situation; role partners have their own intentions and also the intentions they attribute to others (Mead, 1934). An important aspect of this perspective is the ability of the actor to interpret the intention of the acts of others. This ability is defined as role taking (Mead, 1934). Role taking is a process of anticipating another's behavior by viewing it in the context of a role imputed to that other (Turner, 1956). Thus, the situational context which permits the Queen Bee to negotiate her lines of action to quell potential competition and shun her protegees is predicated on her viewing the role of her protegees as irrelevant or even a hindrance to her own career goals and her position.

Role making, like role taking, involves taking the attitudes of others who are involved in an interaction, but includes the element of modifying the interaction to make explicit certain aspects of the roles (Turner, 1956). Halsey (1978) contends that the Queen Bee structures her role in such a way as to control and limit the power of her subordinates. The Queen Bee uses particular lines of action when working with her subordinates (e.g., referring clients only to colleagues outside of nursing). Because such referrals are likely to be reciprocated, the Queen Bee will see more "valuable" clients and maintain her status among her male colleagues.

Weinstein and Deutschberger (1964) proposed that lines of action are used to enable the focal person to elicit desired behaviors from their role partners. Therefore, when a Queen Bee utilizes a line of action to maximize her outcomes while at the same time maintaining control of scarce resources, the status quo is maintained. Nurses who are subordinate to the Queen Bee see themselves as less powerful because they lack access to resources important for career advancement (e.g., referrals, network connections, information). Weinstein and Deutschberger (1964) would interpret the Queen Bee's particular line of action as successful altercasting. The compliant behavior produced by the successful altercasting advances the Queen Bee's goals by impacting the resource allocation of the other (Hardy, 1988).

Thus, any particular line of action is formed in the light of the situation in which it takes place. Situations are contexts in which individuals construct their behavior (Stone & Faberman, 1970). Prior to any self-determined action, an individual engages in examination and deliberation referred to as the "definition of the situation" (Thomas in Manis & Meltzer, 1978). In essence, "our realities are our definition of the situation" (Charon, 1985, p. 139). One can appreciate the importance of an individual's selective perception in Thomas' pronouncement: "If men define situations as real, they are real in their consequence" (p. 154). Therefore, from the point of view of the actor, in this instance the Queen Bee, the definition of the situation is the sum total of all recognized information which is relevant for her to engage in self-determined lines of action and interaction. In the Queen Bee's selective perception the traditional family role model is prescribed exclusively for other women (Halsey, 1978). Lines of action employed to maintain this perception win the favor of men in her work setting and minimize the competition from other talented women who also wish to succeed.

Structural Role Stress

Another way to view the Queen Bee phenomenon is to identify the structural sources of role stress experienced by the Queen Bee. Hardy (1978) notes,

> Structural stress is embedded either in the role or the normative structure. The different types of role stress have been categorized on the basis of the nature of the role expectations and role resources of individuals occupying the roles. (p. 32)

The Queen Bee's role set is a potential area for conflicting role expectations. Role set is the complement of role relationships which the Queen Bee has by virtue of occupying her leadership position (Merton, 1968). Behavioral specifications for the Queen Bee are established both by the functional needs of the role and the role expectations that members of her role set have of each other. The Queen Bee's enactment of her role is affected by the individuals within her role set as they, in turn, are affected by her.

Merton (1968) argues that structural configurations are the source of instability in the focal person's role set. Due to the differences in social structure location, it is not surprising that role partners are motivated by different values and expectations than the Queen Bee. Arndt and Lager (1970) established that nurse managers receive conflicting role expectations from their role sets. However, the number of nurse managers who demonstrate Queen Bee behaviors when faced with role set conflicts is not known. Kahn, Wolfe, and Quinn (1964) noted the status of role-set members influenced the focal person's response to conflicting demands. Thus, it may be less conflicting for a Queen Bee to comply with role expectations of a male physician than those of the staff nurse.

Reference Groups. A second area of structural role stress, related to role set, noted by Hardy (1988), is the location of the reference group. Halsey (1978) found that the reference group was different for nursing directors and for supervisors than for head nurses. In the first group hospital administrators were the reference point, whereas the head nurses in her sample seemed relatively unconcerned about the administrator's opinions. Corresponding to this finding, head nurses in Halsey's (1978) sample indicated that staff nurses' opinions serve to them as indicators of a "job well done," which was not true of the supervisors or directors. These findings support Merton's (1968) and Coser's (1983) contentions that individuals may identify more with one group than another in the face of conflicting norms.

The Queen Bee's choice of a reference group appears to be a powerful influence on her behavior (Halsey, 1978). Originally, reference groups were viewed as points of comparison in forming judgments about one's self, especially about one's status (Lum, 1978). Currently, the concept has been broadened to mean "any collectivity, real or imagined, envied or despised, whose perspective is assumed by the actor" (Shibutani, 1978, p. 109). A perspective denotes a world view held by the focal person. A reference group provides the matrix through which the actor perceives events and also her role in these events by selecting behavior from a set of alternatives (Lum, 1978). To the extent that the focal person develops an organized perspective which she brings to bear on all new situations, her behavior will have a degree of consistency. In a complex society, however, individuals internalize several perspectives; that is, they have several reference groups (Murphy, 1985).

Lum (1978) has noted that several writers have described various types of reference groups. She also notes that both positive and negative reference groups can influence an individual's behavior. One type of reference group may have particular relevance to the Queen Bee's behavior. Goffman (1959) refers to this group as an audience. Within this reference group the individual is believed to attribute certain values to an audience group and to attempt to behave in accordance with the values of her audience. To this extent the audience is like a normative group, although it differs from a normative group in not being aware the person is utilizing them as a reference. Thus when a Queen Bee attributes the label "traditional woman" to her subordinate or the value of omnipotence to her administration colleagues and behaves accordingly, she is deferring to the values attributed to her audience. When the Queen Bee devalues her nurse subordinates she is exercising role distance between herself and her subordinates (Goffman, 1959).

Role Conflict. By virtue of occupying role positions in both the social and professional spheres, the Queen Bee may experience stress via her multiple positions (Halsey, 1978). Recent work indicates that multiple positions generate stress within family and work; what is important is how the career woman handles them (Gray, 1983; Johnson & Johnson, 1977). Research findings suggest that specific aspects of organizational and personal realities may serve either to enhance or diminish gender differences that already exist (Deaux, 1984; Epstein, 1970; Hearn & Parkin, 1983; Horner, 1972).
   Epstein (1970) states:

> Most fundamentally, the woman professional must face a conflict in the hierarchy of status priorities in Western society. For women, the obligations attached to family statuses are first in priority, while for men the role demands deriving from the occupational status ordinarily override all others. (p. 98)

Hardy (1988) claims this interpersonal conflict arises when an actor occupies one position that has two sets of role expectations for the role occupant. The role conflict experienced by the focal person may be compounded by the effects of gender roles (Hardy, 1988).
   An example of this role conflict might be when the hospital administrator asks the nurse leader to make a budget cut in her department to facilitate financing equipment for another department. The nursing staff might object because a budget cut would severely compromise patient safety and the quality of nursing care. The nurse leader must make a decision for or against the budget cut based on either her personal or professional values, each of which may be in conflict with the other.
   In a theory of role conflict resolution, Gross, Mason, and McEachern (1957) identify a process intended to overcome both intrarole and interrole conflict. Three factors are considered before resolving a conflict: "(1) the relative legitimacy of the expectations, (2) the sanctions incumbent upon the non-fulfillment of each of the expectations, and (3) the moral orientation of the actor" (Shaw & Costanzo, 1982, p. 309). Thus, the nurse leader must formulate her position on the basis of the legitimacy of the administrator's request, the reasonableness of the nursing staff's objections, and the potential rewards and punishments, including loss of personal job security, diminishing respect from one's reference group, and the possibility of professional ostracism. Her professional values and standards will be the key determinants in her decision making. This active process is called role conflict resolution (Goode, 1960).
   In her professional role the Queen Bee may function in one of two ways. She may be very hardworking and productive in her career, in which case the organization will benefit from the short-term gain of her personal endeavors. In the long run, however, the organization will suffer because her subordinates are not trained or developed and her expertise is hoarded rather than shared. The role distance maintained by the Queen Bee decreases communication between her and her

subordinates. Kahn et al. (1964) found that role partners faced with continued conflict and stress decreased their communication and soon lacked the necessary information and feedback on their role performance.

On the other hand, the Queen Bee may be ineffective because, with her strong orientation toward maintaining the status-quo, she is reluctant to initiate changes. As the Queen Bee is unwilling to take risks, her organization remains static and immobilized. This results in poor staff morale, little interest in work, poor motivation, and poor performance. Regardless of her personal level of productivity, Queen Bee behaviors in nurse leaders have a negative effect on the institution, other nurses, the nursing profession, and on the quality of nursing care (Halsey, 1978).

GENDER-SPECIFIC LABELS VERSUS "MENTOR"

Gender-specific explanations for Queen Bee behaviors suggest that female socialization practices encourage the development of behavior patterns which are contrary to leadership behavior (Spengler, 1976). An alternative paradigm emphasizes the normative structure of the social context which facilitates Queen Bee behavior (Riger & Galligan, 1980). A reevaluation of the Queen Bee label suggests this latter explanation is more plausible in attempting to understand the Queen Bee phenomenon (Riger & Galligan, 1980; Yoder et al., 1985).

In support of this explanation, Yoder et al. (1985) attributed the tendency of the first West Point women graduates to mimic Queen Beeness by not sponsoring plebe cadets to the structural context in their role as token women. Extensive exit interviews with these women revealed that the competitive context of their perceived role exaggerated pressures to perform, encapsulated the women into feminine roles, and threatened their persistent marginal peer acceptance by the dominant group (Yoder et al., 1985). Furthermore, these first women graduates perceived that the addition of greater numbers of women would dilute the "specialness" they cherished in the dominant group.

The Queen Bee, by definition, is successful in both professional and social spheres. Yet, her antifeminist tendencies and "specialness status" within the dominant group ensures her continuing marginality (Laws, 1975). The irony of this situation is that the continuing and permanent marginality of a token group empowers the dominant group to remain powerful (Laws, 1975).

In diminishing the gender-specific aspects which promote Queen Bee behavior, several additional questions are raised. What is the label applied to men who thwart competition, maintain allegiance to the system, hinder subordinates' growth, and identify with those in higher hierarchical positions? General opinion acknowledges the behavior exists, yet the gender label is missing. There is also consensus that a "neuter" label prevails which describes behavior that is the antithesis of Queen Beeness. This label is mentor. Hamilton (1986) discusses the dichotomy between Queen Bee behavior and mentoring. She states:

> Many women have learned to be successful in a painful sacrificing way and in turn cannot help younger women in a mentor relationship. Queen Bee behavior is for these women a way of coping with demands of being a contemporary professional whose history is one of being a traditional female (p. 149).

By definition, a mentor shares knowledge, understanding, and competency (Hamilton, 1986; Pillette, 1986; Roche, 1979). The leadership of the mentor aims directly toward the determining emergence of the mentor's professional actualization (Pillette, 1986). Unfortunately, the same social context which fosters Queen Bee behavior may hinder mentorship behavior. The situational contexts of many professional women do not allow them to be a supportive sponsor or to support regular professional contacts (Hamilton, 1986).

Conditions may be improving, however, as nurses recognize the need to share skills and promote colleagueship. In a survey of nursing leaders, a significant proportion (83 percent) reported having mentors during their professional development, and 93 percent were consciously aware of being mentors to others (Vance, 1979). Thus nursing, as a predominantly female profession, should not commiserate over the fact that it cannot escape the labels placed upon it as women and nurses, but rather emphasize that there are alternatives to nonsupportive patterns of behavior. Nurses are not such a homogeneous group that they can be stereotyped by similar characteristics of behavior. If similiarities are noted in patterns of nonsupportive behavior it usually is not gender specific and most often is compounded by the social context in which the nurse is found.

NOTES

1. Models of nursing education vary across the country in relation to administrative and management responsibilities. Comparable data are necessary to establish the equivalency of the samples in relation to job descriptions. This potential sample difference raises the issue that Story's study may be an extension rather than a replication study. Polit and Hungler (1983) define replication as the "duplication of research procedures in a second investigation for the purpose of determining if earlier results can be repeated" (p. 621).

2. Kerlinger (1973) notes that "self-selection occurs when members of the group being studied are in the groups in part because they differentially possess traits or characteristics extraneous to the research problem, characteristics that possibly influence or otherwise are related to the variables of the research problem" (p. 381).

3. Personal communications with author, Donna Story (1986), followed the rule-of-thumb convention for factor analysis, which specifies a minimum of 10 subjects per item on a questionnaire. Story consulted with Waltz, Strickland, and Lenz (1984) for the methodology in her study (see reference).

4. Personal communication with author, Donna Story, February 27, 1987.

11

Stratification

Bonnie Bullough

Any study of the roles and interaction patterns within the health care delivery system would be incomplete without an examination of the impact of social stratification upon those roles. The health care delivery system is a highly stratified industry and although to a large extent the stratification of the industry reflects the stratification patterns of the total society, there are special characteristics of the system which are addressed in this chapter.

At the present time the health care delivery system is experiencing tension and unrest. Consumers are seeking more power over their own health care; unions are striving to upgrade salaries of the lower level workers; women in the system are demanding more distributive justice; podiatrists, optometrists, and others are attempting to break down the monopoly power of medicine, and nurses are claiming more decision-making power. This unrest suggests that a conflict model may be the most useful current stratification theory for understanding the system and its impact on the social roles of its members.

STRATIFICATION THEORY

Definitions

The concept of stratification means the hierarchical ranking of people according to their wealth, power, or social class. Power is ordinarily defined as influence or the authority to make decisions for others. Wealth is usually defined and measured in terms of income, property, or other possessions. Social class, which is the stratification system most studied by American sociologists, refers to groups of people identified by their relationship to the other two major variables (wealth and power) as well as their prestige and life-styles. Social class is currently measured by such indicators as reputation, occupational level, education, and the details of one's life-style (Bendix & Lipset, 1966; Davis & Moore, 1945; Lenski, 1966; Light & Keller, 1975; McCord & McCord, 1977; Mills, 1956).

Differentiation is a term that subsumes stratification, since it covers a wider variety of distinctions that are made between people. Stratification involves a ranking system, but people are often differentiated by such factors as gender differences or ethnic characteristics which do not always include a ranking system (McGee et al., 1977). Role differentiation divides people by the set of expectations for performance that are associated with a social role. Roles can be differentiated into a stratified pattern when one role is superordinate and the other subordinate—as is the case between the registered and the practical nurse—or they can be differentiated into separate specialty functions—as is the case between the coronary care nurse and the public health nurse. The concept of role differentiation that is used in this chapter refers to a process in which a single work role is divided or differentiated into two or more new work roles.

The empirical questions asked about stratification, the explanations given, and the conclusions drawn all tend to be influenced by the theoretical framework with which one starts. Thus an intelligent reading of the stratification literature involves at least some acquaintance with the major alternative theoretical schools of thought. William and Arline McCord enumerate the five dominant schools in stratification research as follows: Marxism, Weberianism, status analysis, functionalism, and conflict theory (1977, pp. xxvi–xxvii, 87–152). The following explanation of each of these five approaches is drawn from the McCord book on stratification as well as a variety of other sources.

Marxism. Social class was a central concept in the writings of the nineteenth century social philosopher, Karl Marx. He and his co-author, Friedrich Engels, saw social class as derived from a relationship of the individual to the means of production. The owners formed one major social class and the workers, who were exploited to produce a profit for the owner, were the other class. Thus the basic dichotomy in modern industrial societies is based upon economic power. They argued that although all class societies have been characterized by this basic dichotomy, the capitalistic society accentuates the division (Bendix & Lipset, 1966; Marx & Engels, 1932, 1959).

Marxist theory is very much alive today. Modern Marxists have built upon the concepts of Marx and Engels to produce full-scale analytical theory and social stratification. This is the focus of much of their current research. For example, Albert Szymanski, in a recently published work on social class argues that modern capitalistic societies include three basic classes: the capitalistic class (the bourgeoisie), the middle class (the petty bourgeoisie), and the working class (the proletariat). He suggests that contemporary capitalistic societies also include a fourth group (the lumpen proletariat) who have no relationship to production, and are therefore not a social class. The capitalist class owns the means of production and exchange. Members of the middle class may control their own labor power but do not to any significant degree control the work of others. The working class does the labor. The excluded sector includes all the unemployed who do not belong to a nuclear family of a class member, the disabled, people who have given up and remain unemployed, as well as the various kinds of illegal or semi-legal hustlers (1983, pp. 229–279).

Citing a variety of studies of social mobility, Szymanski points out that the United States is far from being a land of opportunity. Rather, social class tends to be passed on from one generation to another by means of the inheritance of property and the differential ability of parents to buy education for their children (1983, pp. 280–296). Both of these factors limit social mobility.

Weberianism. Sociologists who build upon the work of Max Weber, another important 19th century theorist, view social stratification as a consequence of other forces as well as the economy. Weber described three different stratification systems: (1) the "class order," which is stratified by the production and acquisition of goods and so carries an essentially economic meaning; (2) the "social order," which is differentiated by the consumption of goods as represented by life style, and (3) the "party," which is the ideologic or political arena of power (Weber in Gerth & Mills, 1946, pp. 180–184; Weber, 1947, p. 152).

The Weberian approach broadens the basis for analysis. It permits an examination of the congruence between the three systems and the consequence of status inconsistency. Probably most modern sociologists, with the possible exception of the pure Marxists, derive at least part of their theoretical generalizations concerning stratification from Weberian concepts.

Status Analysis. In the twentieth century social inquiry passed into an empirical phase, as opposed to the social philosophy of Weber and Marx. A series of stratification studies was undertaken in small American towns using a reputational approach. W. Lloyd Warner, a leader in this effort, worked through the third and fourth decades of the twentieth century. "Yankee City" and "Jonesville" were his major field research settings, although his students carried out similar projects in many other localities. These researchers could ordinarily identify and rank five or six distinct social classes in the towns they studied (Warner & Lunt, 1941; Warner, et al., 1944). Using data from these studies, Warner constructed an index of social class which employs four factors to rank subjects: (1) occupation, (2) income, (3) source of income, and (4) dwelling area (Warner, et al., 1949). Similarly, August Hollingshead classified the families in "Elmtown" using four criteria: (1) life-style, (2) income and possessions, (3) participation in community affairs, and (4) prestige (Hollingshead, 1949). While the basis of these scales of social class are still appropriate for some types of research, their small-town roots and emphasis on reputation limit their applicability to structures in which the distributive systems are more complex.

Functionalism. The twentieth century also saw the development of a major sociologic theory called structural functionalism, or simply functionalism. Davis (1942) and Davis and Moore (1945) published two key papers in the 1940s using this approach to stratification. They noted that stratification systems were found in all societies and argued that such systems exist because they fill an important function, namely that of motivating people to fill important jobs that are difficult, unpleasant, or require long training periods. Davis and Moore gave the following illustrative example:

> Modern medicine, for example, is within the mental capacity of most individuals, but a medical education is so burdensome and expensive that virtually none would undertake it if the position of the M.D. did not carry a reward commensurate with the sacrifice. (Davis & Moore in Bendix & Lipset, 1966, p. 49)

Melvin Tumin wrote a critique of the Davis and Moore papers a decade after they were written (1953). He pointed out that two major factors blocked mobility: patterns and advantages that were passed on from one generation to another and prevented talented people from entering the highly rewarded occupations. Tumin noted, in addition, that the financial sacrifices involved in securing a college degree are seldom borne by the student-professional—who enjoys the rewards,—but rather, by the parents.

Talcott Parsons, considered by many the major theorist of functionalism, brought a conservative point of view and positive perception of the value of inequality in the social system to his analysis of social roles. This view of inequality can be noted clearly in Parsons's treatment of the roles of doctors and patients as they interact. Physicians, as high status professional persons, are pictured as knowledgeable, objective, and in possession of most of the power in the interaction. Patients who enter the sick role are excused from their normal work responsibilities, but their obligations are many. They are supposed to admit they are ill, seek expert technical advice, follow it, and try to get well. Arguments about treatment modalities or the right to shop around for advice are frowned upon. Thus, the interaction is seen as a stratified one with the high status health care provider rightfully in charge (Parsons, 1951, pp. 428–479).

Conflict Theory. The fifth category of theorists listed by the McCords are the conflict theorists who read Marx but have deviated from the original Marxist positions. These theorists also trace their origins to another nineteenth century writer, Georg Simmel (1908), who viewed conflict as inevitable but believed that the private ownership of property was not its only cause. Conflict theorists also differ with functionalists because they view broad inequalities in the stratification system as dysfunctional for society because they limit opportunities. Functional theorists would view inequalities as contributing to the stability of the system and therefore being necessary. Current conflict theorists include Ralf Dahrendorff, Dennis Wrong, and others who view conflict as an ever present social force (McCord & McCord, 1977, p. xxvii). Dahrendorff, Collins, and Coser have been identified as analytical conflict theorists who see conflict and its roots as permanent and conflict of interests inevitable. They believe it is possible to develop a body of objective scientific knowledge from a study of the omnipresent condition. These analytic conflict theorists do not see society segmented along a single dimension as do the Marxist theorists and C. Wright Mills, with the ruling group at the top opposing the masses. Rather, they believe that many societies are far more complex in the way power and status are distributed; they believe there are interlocking patterns of stratification rather than a single dimension of stratification.

All the theories introduced in this chapter offer insights about stratification as it relates to the health care delivery system. As indicated in the introduction, however, conflict theory is used here because of the current unrest in the system and the increasing theoretical interest in conflict theory by sociologists. The primacy of conflict theory was also decided by elimination. Weberian thought has been updated and so well integrated into sociological thought that it has become part of the fabric of the work of sociologists and modern theorists, including the conflict theorists; it is used as it is needed without identifying the historical source of the concepts. Similarly, the work of the status analysts has been integrated. Their contributions were partly methodological and, as a result, sociological knowledge became more empirically based. They also produced some theoretical insights using an inductive process rather than the deductive approach of earlier theorists. Studies of stratification now incorporate empirical testing as well as the use of the inductive approach, so contributions of the status analysts are also well integrated into the knowledge base of stratification. Most of their specific findings about stratification are, however, too bound to the small community to apply directly to the health care delivery system.

Marxism poses a difficulty because the pure Marxists do not allow the master's words to be updated or modified. They call such updating revisionism. They disallow modern historical scholarship that shows there was significant repression of the masses, including women, before the advent of capitalism. Their analysis of the class system has not been updated to include the changes of the postindustrial era, changes that are very evident in the health care delivery system.

Functionalism has limitations even though it offers many insights about the health care delivery system. For example, it is possible to outline carefully the structure of the system to note how the various parts of the system function and to analyze those elements that keep it viable. Observations about the structure of the system and how it functions are made throughout the remaining portion of the chapter. Functionalism does, however, tend to be a static analytic framework that ignores the dynamics of change.

The discussion that follows looks at the static aspects of the system, point out where changes are taking place, and examines some of the more problematic inequalities in the system that are creating conflict or that suggest conflict is on the horizon.

THE STRATIFICATION OF HEALTH CARE OCCUPATIONS

The single variable that is probably most often used as a measure of stratification is occupation (Blau & Duncan, 1967). Occupational prestige seems to be a fairly stable phenomenon. In two separate studies done in 1947 and 1963, researchers connected with the National Opinion Research Center (NORC) asked a nationwide sample of respondents to rank the occupational prestige of 100 major occupations. The ratings tended to be consistent over time; although a few scientific occupations gained prestige, most occupations remained virtually the same, with street sweepers and shoe shiners at the bottom, and supreme court justices and physicians at the top of the list. With few notable exceptions, such as nightclub singers and bartenders, the ratings tended also to correlate with both education and income (Hodge, Seigel, & Rossi, 1964).

To facilitate the use of occupations as an index of social class, Bogue (1963) prepared a more detailed rating system of occupations and keyed it to the list of occupations used by the Department of Labor. These rating scores range from 184 for physicians to 44 for personal service laborers. Bootblacks, who were the baseline occupation in the 100 NORC occupations, score 47 on the Bogue scale. Nurses, who are not one of the NORC sample members, score 107, which is slightly above the midpoint on the scale. Table 1 lists the health occupations in the order they were listed in the 1980 census with the Bogue prestige rating beside each occupation. As can be noted, the system spans a broad range of prestige levels. The spread of the system becomes more evident when the health occupations are compared with workers in the educational complex. Using the same ranking system as is shown in Table 1, college professors and administrators are rated 145; grade school teachers, 132; and school office employees, 102. The power, prestige, and income of the physician is significantly higher than that of the college professor, and the nursing aide enjoys less power, prestige, and income than the person who works in the local grammar school office.

There are several reasons why the stratification system within the health care industry is so broad. Some of these factors seem legitimate, while others are more problematic and suggest that the system is in need of reform. First, the industry is large and growing rapidly; it now includes more than five million workers (National Center for Health Statistics, 1976–77, p. 5). Although size and complexity do not always go together, they often do. Certainly the rapid growth in the number of health workers has paralleled the increased complexity of the system, and the simple doctor–nurse team of the early twentieth century has given way to the array of workers shown in Table 1.

A second factor in the development of the elaborate stratification system of the health occupations has been the emergence of the professionalization process as a significant factor in stratification. In earlier agrarian societies, wealth and property were more crucial variables in stratification. Recent trends have given primacy to knowledge as the basis of stratification and the learned professions have emerged as the most powerful occupations.

In 1956, when C. Wright Mills described the power elite, he included three types of professionals in this category: the military, high government officials, and an emerging managerial class. These professionals had joined the owners to form the power elite in society (Mills, 1956). Daniel Bell argues that the increase in the number of professionals is the hallmark of a new era which he calls the postindustrial society. This society brings with it a change in the class structure. The structure of industrial societies as described by Marx, was characterized by a dichotomy between owners and nonowners. In the postindustrial society, technological developments have lessened the need for workers in production so the labor force has shifted to service workers who now hold more than 60 percent of the jobs in service occupations. The most well educated of the service workers are

TABLE 1. SOCIOECONOMIC INDEX OF THE MAJOR HEALTH OCCUPATIONS

Occupation	Socioeconomic Index
Physicians	184
Dentists	177
Optometrists	144
Veterinarians	142
Pharmacists	140
Chiropractors	132
Health administrators	130
Therapists	120
Clinical laboratory technicians	117
Health records technicians	112
Registered nurses	107
Radiologic technicians	106
Dental hygienists	106
Dieticians	96
Practical nurses	80
Health aides (nonnursing)	74
Dental assistants	74
Nursing aides and orderlies	74

From U.S. Bureau of the Census, 1980; Bogue, 1963, pp. 516–521.

the professionals, the scientists, and the technicians. These *Technocrats* as Bell terms them, have become a new power elite (Bell, 1973; McCord & McCord, 1977, pp. 87–106).

The professionals are particularly important in the health care delivery system and it is the continued professionalization of the upper ranks of the system that has widened the gap between the upper and lower ranks.

Although a variety of definitions of professionalization are in use, professionalization is basically a process whereby an occupation gains in power and prestige because it gains a unique body of knowledge that is not shared by its clients. In part because of this protected knowledge, the public is forced to allow professions significant control over their own affairs (Daniels, 1971; Freidson, 1970a, 1970b). The learned occupations in turn have furthered the professionalization process by lengthening training programs, organizing into collectivities, seeking support from the state through licensure or similar devices, and by taking pains to enhance the charismatic mystique that surrounds their expertise (Carr-Saunders & Wilson, 1933; Freidson, 1971; Greenwood, 1957; Vollmer & Mills, 1966) . Thus, professionalization has increasingly separated the high status health occupations from the untrained or minimally trained health workers and has even increased the social distance between them and their patients. For example, the social distance between the modern specialty physician and his or her patients is greater than that between the old family doctor and his or her patients.

A third basis for the broad span of the stratification system is the fact that the health care industry is labor intensive. As the cost of labor has risen, health care costs have escalated. Moreover, the work is often of an emergency nature and so staffing needs cannot be totally predicted; this in turn leads to overstaffing on the "quiet" days (Georgopoulos, 1972, p. 17). Technologic advances in health care in the last few decades, including automation and the development of elaborate diagnostic and monitoring devices, have tended to broaden the spectrum of patients who can be treated effectively rather than cutting down the amount of labor needed to diagnose and treat patients. Some of the machines have in fact increased the requirements for personnel by necessitating a new class of technicians to monitor or utilize them. Consequently, the health care industry has not reaped the cost-saving benefits of the industrial revolution that have accrued in other industries.

In an effort to deal with the problem of escalating labor costs, hospital administrators and clinical managers have sought to rationalize the system by breaking down work roles into component parts and assigning the simpler tasks to workers with less formal training. This has led to the development of a whole army of medical technicians. While a few of these roles, such as those of the physiotherapist, x-ray technician, dietician, health records technician, and the inhalation therapist, grew out of the nursing role, most of the laboratory and engineering specialties had their origins in the traditional job description of the physician.

The major differentiation of the nursing role occurred in the decade following World War II. During the war the Office of Civilian Defense and the Red Cross experimented with trained nurses' aides to augment the wartime shortage of nurses. At first these aides were allowed to perform only those tasks that were not directly related to patient care, but as the shortage of help continued, they also took on some of the less complicated patient care tasks. This development, which was begun as a temporary expedient, marked the beginning of team nursing. It demonstrated that much of the work role of the nurse could be safely delegated to less expensive workers. What previously had been a single occupational role broke down into at least three levels: nursing aide, licensed practical nurse, and registered nurse (Bullough & Bullough, 1978, pp. 186–189).

Although contemporary nurses often decry this breakup of the nursing role as a source of fragmentation of patient care, there was little opposition from the profession when this division began. Indeed, the American Nurses' Association sponsored a series of studies and reports that recommended that the nursing role be differentiated. The most influential of these was done by Esther Lucile Brown, who surveyed the work nurses were doing in various settings and recommended the development of a "nonprofessional trained nurse" who could carry out the routine procedures and allow registered nurses more time to concentrate on complex procedures (Brown, 1948). Following this recommendation, schools for practical nurses proliferated rapidly and by 1952, 39 states had established provisions for licensing practical nurses. The next year, Lambertson published a landmark book that described the stratified arrangement of nursing roles and called it team nursing (Lambertson, 1953). By 1960 all states had passed laws licensing practical nurses or vocational nurses, as they are called in two states (Roberts, 1961, p. 514). The hierarchical nursing team has remained the dominant staffing pattern, although the current experimental trend toward providing primary nursing by a single nurse who has full responsibility for his or her patients over a 24-hour period may be the beginning of a new countertrend.

The role of the physician has been more resistant to differentiation than that of the nurse. Although it is true that myriad technical specialties have developed from the basic discipline, this represents a slightly different process from that which took place when nursing split into the practical, registered, and aide levels. A similar differentiation of the medical role may, however, actually be occurring at the present time with the development of nurse practitioners and physicians' assistants (Bullough & Bullough, 1978). Again, the basic driving force behind this differentiation is probably an economic one.

Starting in 1910 with the Flexner report, medical education went through a period of significant upgrading. Many substandard schools were closed and others limited their enrollment. These reforms helped keep the physician-to-population ratio stable for the next half century at the level of approximately 150 doctors per 100,000 persons (Fein, 1967). While the demands for physicians increased, medical science and technology were expanding the range of services that a physician could perform; and, concomitantly, consumer demand for services increased. These factors inflated the fees and salaries charged by physicians. The number of physicians has now risen to a level of approximately 181 physicians and osteopaths per 100,000 persons (U.S. Bureau of the Census, 1981, p.106). However, the specialty trend has complicated the situation. In 1910 most physicians were general practitioners; now, however, specialists outnumber general practitioners by five-to-one (U.S. Department of Labor, 1983).

This means there are fewer physicians available for the first level or primary care. Of course, general practitioners are not the only ones who give primary care; osteopaths, internists, and pediatricians are also engaged in this type of practice, at least part of the time. Osteopaths remain few in number, and both internists and pediatricians have gone through lengthy specialty training that is reflected in their fees. One approach to filling the primary care gap has been to replace the dwindling numbers of general practitioners with family practice physicians. It is unlikely that this effort will completely solve the problem because the family practice training programs are as lengthy as those of many specialties; thus, another specialty is being created. Graduates of family practice residencies feel entitled to the same income as specialists in other fields and although this argument is undoubtedly valid, it means that family practitioners do not replace the general practitioners who were willing to accept lower incomes than did specialists. It seems, therefore, that the problem is not so much one of a shortage of physicians, or even a shortage of physicians who can give primary care, but a shortage of people who can deliver safe, efficient primary care at a reasonable cost. Consequently, nurse practitioners, and to a lesser extent physicians' assistants moved to fill this gap.

Three major explanations for the broad stratification pattern of the health occupations have been offered: (1) the size and complexity of the industry, (2) the professionalization of the high level occupations in the health field, and (3) the economic realities that stimulate role differentiation. Although these three factors appear to be legitimate causes of the many levels of power, income, and prestige within the industry, there are two additional factors that are more problematic: gender and race, both of which contribute to the allocation of power and prerequisites within the system. Although these discriminatory elements of the system are currently under attack, it would be naive to think they are no longer operative.

GENDER AND RACE IN STRATIFICATION OF HEALTH OCCUPATIONS

One of the most obvious characteristics of the health occupations is their marked sex segregation. Most jobs can be classified both statistically and in terms of their public image as being either male or female. Table 2 shows the percentage of female and black workers in each of the major health occupations. It can be noted that the high status, predominantly male occupations tend to represent a much smaller population than the predominantly female ones. Moreover, the distribution

TABLE 2. HEALTH OCCUPATIONS IN ORDER OF PRESTIGE

Occupation	Number (1000s)	Percent Female workers	Percent Black workers
Physicians	486	14.8	2.3
Dentists	121	3.3	2.5
Pharmacists	168	23.8	3.6
Health administrators	228	50.9	3.5
Technicians	657	72.9	9.7
Therapists	252	70.6	7.9
Registered nurses	1415	95.6	8.2
Dieticians	70	90.0	24.3
Practical nurses	400	97.0	16.3
Health aides	333	86.2	15.9
Nursing aides and orderlies	1136	87.1	29.0

From U.S. Bureau of the Census, *Statistical Abstract of the United States 1984*, ed 105. Washington, DC: GOP, p. 109.

of women is a pyramidal one, with only a few women in the high status health professions and heavy representation of women in the low status health occupations.

While the causal factors in this pattern are many and undoubtedly include all of the usual prejudices against women in the work force, these prejudices are mediated through the professional schools. In spite of the efforts of Elizabeth Blackwell (1895) and the other nineteenth century pioneers, medical colleges and the other high status professional schools remained resistant to admitting women throughout most of the twentieth century or (and this was especially true of medical schools), felt it sufficient to admit a few "token" women. The situation started to change in the 1960s so that by 1970, 10 percent of the admissions to medical schools and almost 5 percent of the admissions to dental school were women. By the 1981–1982 academic year, 31 percent of the admissions to medical school and 20 percent of the admissions to dental school were women (Datagram, 1982; Solomon, 1982).

Schools of nursing were also a significant factor in creating the sex segregation pattern. According to the 1910 census figures, approximately 7 percent of the student and trained nurses were men. Most of these came from schools connected with mental hospitals or from one of the few all-male schools, such as those run by the Alexian Brothers in Chicago and St. Louis, and the Mills School, which was affiliated with Bellevue Hospital. The twentieth century efforts of nursing to upgrade its educational programs forced the mental hospitals to close. This effectively cut out nursing opportunities for men except in the all-male schools, because the general hospital schools excluded men. This was done for an interesting reason. The hospital schools required student nurses to live on the hospital grounds in nurses' homes so that the institution could maintain surveillance over their behavior and to keep them available for night work. The norms of that period would allow men to live neither in these quarters nor in the higher status male interns' quarters. Consequently, men were simply excluded from hospital schools. By 1950 only one percent of the practicing nurses were men (Bullough & Bullough, 1978, pp. 215–217). The current changeover to collegiate nursing has again opened opportunities for men to enter nursing, although there is still room for improvement. Approximately 5 percent of the registered nurse students are now men (Facts About Nursing, 1982–83, p. 145).

The problem of breaking down the sex barriers in nursing is different from the sex-discrimination problem in medicine and dentistry, where opening the doors was sufficient. In nursing, low salaries and lack of autonomy make it less attractive than other occupations at the same educational level, so there is a shortage of male applicants. It becomes a circular problem: sex segregation helps to keep the profession suppressed and its low status helps to keep it segregated.

The educational system has also been a significant force for excluding blacks and other minorities, as well as women, from the high status health professions—although economic deprivation is certainly a factor. Table 2 shows similar percentages for black workers as for women, although the gender differences are not as great. The education problem for minority students, particularly black students, starts in elementary school with segregated eductional patterns; and dcspite anti-busing rhetoric, the fact remains that segregated education is inferior education (Bullough, 1972; Coleman, Campbell, Hobson, et al., 1966; Myrdal, 1944). Consequently, few minority members were prepared for admission to professional schools. Even those who managed to acquire a good basic education faced both overt and covert discriminatory patterns when they applied to high status professional schools. Until the 1960s, when federal legislation outlawed discrimination in publicly supported educational programs, many American medical schools had never accepted a black applicant, and even those with reputations for open admissions had accepted only a handful throughout their entire history. The only significant opportunity available for black students to enter medicine was through the segregated schools (Cogan, 1968; Morais, 1968; Norman, 1969). The situation was similar in dentistry, which remains the health occupation with the lowest minority representation (Dummet, 1952).

The pattern in nursing was also segregated throughout most of the early part of the twentieth century. It changed somewhat during World War II because of the Bolton Act, which created the Cadet Nurse Corps and included nondiscriminatory provisions. After the war some of the nursing schools retained their nondiscriminatory practices, so the minority exclusion in nursing was less oppressive than in the higher-status health professions (U.S. Public Health Service, 1950). In 1963 there were 22 segregated black schools; most of them were underfinanced and only nine were accredited (Carnegie, 1964). A study of one segregated nursing school published in 1971 documented the negative mental health and attitudinal consequences of this pattern and encouraged integrated nursing education (Gunter, Crecraft, & Kennedy, 1974). Since that time, the level of integration in nursing has improved: 14 percent of the students admitted in 1981 were minority group members (Facts About Nursing, 1983, p. 142). Nonetheless, the consequences of the past discriminatory pattern is evident in the present work force. The overall pattern remains one in which minorities are overrepresented in the low level jobs and underrepresented in the high status jobs.

STRATIFICATION PATTERNS OF HEALTH CARE INSTITUTIONS

Our focus has been on the total health care industry, but if the individual institution rather than the total health care delivery system is taken as the unit of analysis, it is again possible to note complex stratification systems and to see the impact of the stratification on the roles of its members. Since hospitals have been the subject of a significant body of sociologic inquiry, they will be the focus of this discussion; it should be noted, however, that many of the generalizations that have been made about hospitals could be applied equally to ambulatory care settings or nursing homes.

Evolution of Hospitals

Hospitals were an early medieval development, traceable to the development of the concept of Christian charity, and to parallel developments in the medieval Moslem world. Hospitals were originally generalized institutions, furnishing sanctuary for the poor, orphans, widows, and the aged, as well as the sick. In the postmedieval period hospitals gradually became more specifically, lodging places for the sick poor and the victims of contagious illnesses or pestilences; hence the name pesthouse is, somewhat paradoxically, a relatively recent term (Clay, 1909; Rosen, 1963).

The bacteriologic revolution that occurred in the nineteenth century and the advent of the trained nurse revolutionized hospitals in the twentieth century. Hospitals were cleaned to prevent cross infections and nursing care was markedly improved. The hospital became a place where one might recover rather than die—in contrast to earlier history. Consequently, physicians moved their primary locus of practice from office and patients' homes to the hospital. Physicians had been almost unknown in the generalized medieval institutions and even as hospitals became institutions for care of the sick, the physicians who entered them tended to be of lower status. Those university-trained physicians, who were teachers with doctoral degrees, treated affluent patients in their homes. The physician's entry into the hospital in the twentieth century has been further stimulated by insurance company reimbursement policies that pay for hospital but not office procedures. While physician care is certainly a major factor in the improved recovery rates in hospitals, the presence of physicians has complicated the formal organization pattern of such institutions. Physicians are high status, powerful professionals who are essentially outside the bureaucratic structure of the hospital. Bureaucracies tend to be built upon clear lines of authority, written rules, and a hierarchical structure in which lower level persons report to those at higher levels. Physicians complicate this structure because they are neither part of the hospital structure nor clients of the hospital. In viewing this structural problem, one authority has described the hospital as "an organization at cross purposes with itself" (Smith, 1958). Nurses have tried to mediate this confusion but have never been completely successful (Croog & VerSteeg, 1972).

Implications for Patient Care

This bureaucratic structure clearly creates problems in communication. After studying one community hospital in depth, Duff and Hollingshead (1968) concluded that a lack of effective communication between members of the health team, particularly between nurses and physicians, was a significant factor in explaining the poor patient care they found. The communication gap that exists between nurses and physicians is not the normal one that occurs in complex organizations with multiple levels of workers; rather, it is an exaggerated one resulting from sex segregation with a peculiar, stylized pattern that has been termed the *doctor–nurse game*. The classic description of the doctor-nurse game was written by a psychiatrist, Leonard Stein. He was fascinated by the strange way nurses made recommendations to physicians; they pretended they had not done so. Physicians, in turn, pretended the nurses never made recommendations, yet Stein noted that the more highly regarded physicians were careful to follow nurses' recommendations. Stein called the pattern a "transactional neuroses" (Stein, 1967). It appears to be an exaggerated version of the traditional male–female game in which relatively powerless females gain power over men by manipulation. It is supported by reciprocal systems of reward and punishment, as well as by tradition. Most nurses are apparently unconscious of the game, yet they play it well and have been conditioned to do so throughout their professional lives. Unfortunately for patients, however, the tortured communication pattern of the game is not efficient. Crucial information is lost or its transmission slowed. Patient care suffers and the dignity of both the nurse and physician roles is lessened. This is another aspect of the system that needs reform.

ROLE THEORY

Both the differentiation of the nursing role and the development of multiple medical technician roles have resulted in fragmented and depersonalized hospital care. It is not unusual for a hospitalized patient to have contact with as many as 30 people in one day and yet feel lonely because the encounters are brief and impersonal. For example, consider the following hypothetical day of Mr. J.D., recovering postoperative patient with lung cancer:

> Before breakfast, an aide checked Mr. D's vital signs, a technician drew blood, and a registered nurse checked his chest tube and discontinued his intravenous fluid. An aide brought breakfast. The registered nurse returned with oral medication and a hypodermic for pain. The inhalation therapist helped him with intermittent positive pressure breathing (IPPB). A practical nurse helped him to dangle his feet over the side of the bed. A messenger came to transport him to the x-ray department where a technician took chest x-rays.
>
> His surgeon stopped by (wearing his hospital greens, and a mask around his neck); he checked the chest tube and said everything was fine. An aide brought him water; a young woman from the diet kitchen asked him to select tomorrow's meals from a mimeographed menu; the inhalation therapist returned; a clerk from the business office brought insurance forms for him to sign, and the maintenance man replaced the television set on the wall with another one. Another aide brought him lunch. After lunch the head nurse came in carrying a clip board and asked Mr. J.D. how he felt, but she looked so busy he told her "fine." Another technician did an electrocardiogram. The practical nurse checked his vital signs and the janitor mopped the floor. He rang the bell once that afternoon to ask to have his urinal emptied. The ward clerk responded through the speaker (using her "announcement" voice) and told him he would have to repeat the request; she then sent an aide. By three o'clock, when the shift changed, Mr. J.D. had experienced 23 encounters with 18 different people. None of them stayed long enough for him to learn their names (he already knew the surgeon's name). He was unable to ask any of them the dreadful question that plagued him; he wanted to know if he was going to die.

ECONOMIC IMPLICATIONS OF THE STRATIFICATION SYSTEM

Differences in income are a part of the stratification system and the difference between those at the top of the system and those at the bottom is wide. Current estimates of physicians' salaries place them over $80,000 for incorporated physicians and over $60,000 for unincorporated (Statistical Abstract, 1984 p. 107). The average starting salary for a hospital nurse in 1982 was $17,600; head nurses started at $21,800; and clinical specialists at $21,500 (Facts About Nursing, 1983, p. 192). Median annual salary for practical nurses working in hospitals was $12,500, but they earned about 20 percent less if they worked in nursing homes (Facts About Nursing, 1983, p. 287). Hospital aides' salaries varied widely from city to city ($4.50 an hour in Houston to $7.80 an hour in San Francisco) but most earned about $11,000 annually (Facts About Nursing 1983, p. 294).

The difference between $11,000 and $80,000 is wide and the salaries at the bottom level are too low to support a family at anything but a poverty level. Yet there are more than one million workers at that level; 87.5 percent of them are women and 28.8 percent of them belong to a minority group. The salaries of registered nurses, one third of whom are now graduating with baccalaureate degrees (Facts About Nursing, 1983, p. 129) and clinical specialists who graduate with master's degrees, do not compare equitably with physicians and dentists who graduate with professional doctorates. The salary system lacks distributive justice.

Collective Bargaining

Yet nurses have been slow to take steps to deal with their low salaries and poor working conditions, a reluctance that has helped keep their status low because income is a key variable in status. This is partly because many nurses have felt that showing concerns about either money or power is undignified or unprofessional. The American Nurses' Association first adopted a position paper on economic security in 1946. The statement called for a 40-hour week and minimum wage, and indicated that state and district nursing associations could participate in collective bargaining. The impact of the position paper was, however, blunted by a statement that ". . . under no circumstances would a strike or similar coercive device be countenanced" (The Biennial, 1946).

At the time the paper was issued hospitals were covered by the 1935 Wagner Labor Relations Act, which obliged them to bargain in good faith with their employees. The 1947 Taft-Hartley Labor Management Relations Act, however, specifically exempted nonprofit hospitals from the necessity of bargaining with their employees; given their no-strike pledge, nurses had no way of forcing hospitals to the bargaining table. The no-strike pledge was finally repealed in 1968 and in 1974 the labor relations act was extended to employees of nonprofit health care institutions (Bullough & Bullough, 1978, pp. 208–212). Since that time the state nurses' associations have moved to organize nurses and significant gains in salaries and working conditions have been made. The move came at least a half century after the major industries were unionized. Most state nurses' associations still suffer from a lack of experience in collective bargaining. That experience is being developed, but it is a difficult, uphill road.

Job Worth

The second approach to reform of the disparities in income is coming through the courts using either the Equal Pay Act of 1963 or Title VII of the Civil Rights Act of 1964. At first these two nondiscriminatory laws were narrowly construed to mean that female nurses should be paid as much as male nurses. Unfortunately, the sex segregation of nursing was such a damper on the pay scale that correcting this inequity had little practical effect. More recently, however, nurses and other women have realized that the laws might be applied at the occupational rather than individual level.

To accomplish this the theoretical concept of job worth was applied. This concept was borrowed from business administration and economics. Administrators had used it to establish equitable pay systems for complex organizations by evaluating objective factors, such as the knowledge required by the position, supervisory span of control, complexity of the job, physical demands, interpersonal demands, and the work environment. Sometimes all of these factors are used; sometimes just one or two. Economists have also used the job worth concept as a research and analytical tool.

Nursing's first use of the concept of job worth was in 1977, when the nurses of the city and county of Denver started to prepare their case for wage equity. They had noted that the entry level salary for registered nurses was lower than that of city and county tree trimmers, sign painters, plumbers, and parking meter repair men. They studied their key classification system and noted that it incorporated sex as a variable in setting wages. On the basis of these observations the nurses and their lawyer hired an economist, Richard Beatty, to perform a job worth analysis. He found that the lower level nursing jobs were at a 55-percent disadvantage when compared to male-dominated jobs with similar levels of education and responsibility. At the middle range, head nurses were at a 40-percent disadvantage, while directors of nursing in a hospital and a community health agency were at an 80 percent disadvantage when compared to male administrators with similar spans of control and similar education requirements (Barnes, 1980).

In addition to these data, the trial brief included a historical and sociological analysis of nursing, documenting its sex segregation. The plaintiffs held that the community standards that were used in the existing wage classification system should not be used as the norm because they were contaminated by the sex segregation of nursing and outdated beliefs that nurses, being predominantly women, should earn less than men with comparable jobs (*Lemons et al.* v. *City and County of Denver*, Bullough, 1978).

The judge of the Tenth Federal District Court ruled against the nurses. He acknowledged that the evidence presented showed that comparable occupations in which men predominated were salaried at a higher level than nursing but he held that this type of differential payment was not covered by Title VII of the 1964 Civil Rights Act or any other law. He also indicated that it was necessary to rule against the nurses because a favorable ruling would have the potential of "disrupting the entire economic system of the United States of America" (Bullough, 1978). An appeal of this case was lost and the Supreme Court refused to hear it.

In her analysis of the case in a comprehensive paper on comparable job worth, Roslyn Feldberg points out that there was a basic contradiction in the judge's ruling.

> On one hand women are not acknowledged to be working for subsistence and therefore cannot claim fair wages. On the other hand, the economy rests on paying women low wages. This paradox reveals how important women are as low wage workers subsidizing the economy and how difficult it is for at least some men in positions of power to take seriously the idea that wage discrimination on the basis of sex is wrong. (Feldberg, 1984)

The findings in *Christensen* v. *the State of Iowa* were similar. The University of Iowa was paying its secretaries less than its physical plant employees even though they were ranked at the same grade level. The judge ruled that the differences were due to market forces rather than discrimination (Feldberg, 1984).

The breakthrough came in 1981 in the case of the *County of Washington (Oregon)* v. *Gunther*. The United States Supreme Court acknowledged the doctrine of comparable worth as a valid legal theory and indicated that the Equal Pay Statutes Act of 1963 and Title VII of the 1964 Civil Rights Act covered not only people in the same jobs but also people in jobs requiring comparable skills, effort, and responsibility (Hershey, 1983).

Using this decision as a basis, a judge in the State of Washington ruled in 1983 that the state had illegally maintained a system of compensation that discriminated on the basis of sex and ordered the state to pay women at a rate reflecting the "full evaluated worth" of their jobs (Hershey, 1983). In 1984, the Reagan Administration announced it was considering challenging the decision. Officials of the Justice Department indicated that although such a move would be politically unpopular, they would not be deterred from preventing what they saw as a dangerous precedent. They listed three objections to the ruling: (1) Women have an equal opportunity to seek higher-paying jobs so the fact they have not done so cannot be thought of as discrimination; (2) it is difficult to assess comparable worth; and (3) it would be difficult to equalize salaries; it might even require lowering men's salaries.

California has passed a job-worth bill for state employees and nurses in San Jose and San Francisco, focusing their collective bargaining efforts on the concept of comparable worth in an effort to extend the coverage to the private sector. Thus, efforts to use the concept of job worth are escalating, although the outcome cannot be predicted.

RATIONALIZING THE SYSTEM

The process of dividing a role into its component parts and allocating the parts to individual workers to maximize efficiency is sometimes called rationalizing the system. Mr. J.D.'s hospital experience in the previous example suggests that the nursing role has been rationalized to an irrational level. To a large extent, nurses are aware of the negative consequences of role differentiation on patient care. In addition, many nurses feel personally deprived because the resultant fragmented roles are less satisfying (Kramer, 1974). Some nurses also decry the fact that the role of the registered nurse has changed from one of direct patient care provider to one of coordinator, administrator, or technician. The nursing literature includes several papers addressing this role fragmentation and urging nurses to "come back to the bedside" to preserve the essence of nursing (Norris, 1970; Reiter, 1966; Rogers, 1970).

To put this suggestion into operation, two related movements have emerged: in the mid-1960s the role of the clinical nurse specialist developed; more recently there has been an experimental restructuring of hospital wards or units emphasizing primary nursing. Clinical specialists are nurses who have obtained educational preparation at the master's degree level to enable them to give expert care to seriously ill patients, act as role models, and spend time with patients who need emotional support (Riehl & McVay, 1973). Unfortunately, because the movement started in the educational system with nurse educators trying to reform the practice setting by preparing graduates to fill a new role, rather than in the service system itself, there have been problems institutionalizing the clinical specialist role. Because hospital and nurse administrators were the authors of the original differentiation of the nursing role, its reformation by educators—outsiders—has not been entirely successful. Some administrators indicate they are willing to accept clinical specialists if these nurses will also take on administrative roles, while others suggest that clinical specialists should be willing to work for the same wages as basic registered nurses. Despite these obstacles to change, progress is being made in the acceptance of the specialists, at least in the more up-to-date centers.

A second and more recent effort to combat the fragmentation of care has been the development of primary nursing units. In these units the nursing team is replaced with registered or practical nurses who give total care on their shift to a group of patients and plan for the patient's care on the other shifts. This gives the patient one person to relate to (Marram, Schlegel, & Bevis, 1974).

Actually, these two movements are related. An early successful trial of clinical specialists used an administrative structure similar to the primary nursing model (Georgopoulos & Christman, 1973). Although the primary nursing approach sounds in many ways like a return to nursing care as it was delivered before the role was differentiated, it has some different elements. Probably the key element in its success is in the power given to nurses when they are made accountable for small groups of patients, rather than simply using them in place of aides. In one California study two models of primary care were compared: one in which primary nurses were held accountable for their patient load and one in which they were not. The nurses with the higher level of nursing responsibilities were found to produce the most favorable patient outcomes (Brault, 1977).

Despite these countermovements aimed at reducing the fragmentation of patient care, it seems safe to assume the overall picture will remain substantially unchanged relative to status differentials, and the health team will remain stratified. Once an occupational role has been created, it is unlikely that anyone will consider eliminating that role or category. For example, there are nurses who believe that the role of oxygen therapist should not have developed because it is a narrow, dead-end job that could have been handled by a nurse. This argument comes too late; oxygen therapists now exist and they want and need their jobs. Moreover, the teachers who prepare oxygen therapists want and need their jobs. As the need for intermittent positive pressure breathing lessens with new treatment modalities, oxygen therapists are finding new roles. Thus, the role has a momentum of its own. The same can be said for registered nurses, practical nurses, or any other category of health worker. As long as the occupation is cost effective and delivers a wanted service it will continue to exist.

IMPLICATIONS FOR THE PHYSICIAN'S ROLE

The differentiation of the nurse's role that is currently occurring with the development of the nursing specialties, including nurse practitioners, nurse midwives, and clinical nurse specialists, has implications for the role of the physician. Using the differentiation of nursing as a model, it seems safe to say that medical care will become increasingly stratified. This will cause discontent among patients who wish to have a warm, personal relationship with their doctor rather than be treated by a nurse specialist. The new nursing roles may well improve patient care, however, because physicians have already left the field of primary care underserved. Many physicians are being drawn away from the more emotionally satisfying role of primary care giver into teaching, supervisory, and coordinating roles. In the future, those who want to focus entirely on patient care will probably gravitate to the more complex specialties because at the primary care level they will have to compete with the lower salaried and lower status nurse specialists.

Thus, the trend towards specialization in medicine can be thought of as both a cause and a consequence of the differentiation of the physician's role. While recent figures suggest that family practice is growing in popularity, specialists still outnumber general practitioners by more than five to one.

STRATIFICATION AND THE CONSUMER ROLE

The professionalization of the high status health occupations and the increasing stratification of the health care delivery system are significant factors in the current wave of consumer discontent. Consumers are expressing their discontent, not only in print, but more significantly in malpractice suits (Holder, 1975; Noble, 1976).

From the sociologic point of view, this growing social distance between professionals and their clients has interesting implications. In this climate of consumer suspicion, the old concept of the sick role may well be out of date. The concept of the sick role as described by Talcott Parsons is a state in which patients are excused from their normal role responsibilities; in return, they are presumably obliged to comply with the medical regimen in order to get well. Physicians as described in this system were benevolent, knowledgeable authority figures not unlike fathers; patients were viewed as dependent, obedient, and childlike, although as they recovered they became less childlike (Parsons, 1951; Parsons & Fox, 1952). Conflict or even a legitimate difference of opinion is not a part of this conceptualization, although a failure to comply is possible and there is a growing body of sociologic literature that addresses the phenomenon of noncompliance with the medical regimen.

A more appropriate model of the patient role in light of the current state of affairs is a conflict model proposed by Eliot Freidson (1960). He saw patients and providers as occupying different positions in the social system and indicated that a clash in perspectives is not unexpected. According to Freidson, physicians are not just benevolent authority figures, they are members of a powerful monopoly who, by virtue of their position in the system, have the power not only to recognize illness but to define and even create it as a social role. In this respect physicians are similar to judges and priests who, by their power to define, can actually create crime and sin (Freidson, 1961, 1970). In *Professional Dominance*, Freidson extends his consideration of the medical monopoly to look at the power of physicians over other members of the health care team and the virtual inaccessibility of the health care industry to any effective consumer or quality control (Freidson, 1970). This approach necessarily modifies the sick role concept to include people who are ill but do not accept the childlike obedient stance, nor accept the physician and other health professionals as benevolent authority figures. These consumers want to be treated as adults and participate in decisions that are made about their health care.

SUMMARY

In this chapter the concept of stratification was reviewed. It was argued that the health care delivery system is highly stratified and several factors were advanced to explain this situation. The health care delivery system is a large and complex system marked by professionalization at the high status levels and low salaries at the lower levels. It is a labor-intensive system that has tried to cope with its economic problems by dividing the medical role and differentiating the nursing role. Race and sex discrimination have entered into the system as irrational stratification variables.

Individual health care institutions are also stratified and at this level the situation is made more complex by the emergence of physicians as high status professionals who have complicated the functioning of the bureaucratic institutions.

The implications of this stratification system were traced. The steep gradient of the system is in many ways dysfunctional—blocking opportunities, making communication difficult, and fragmenting care. Reform of the system began with collective bargaining and court cases to improve lower level salaries. Patient care reform through primary nursing and the increased use of clinical specialists has started. However, the problems are major and reform efforts bring conflict into the system.

The steep power gradient of the system has consequences for the roles of the workers and their interaction patterns. Status makes those roles more superordinate and subordinate than collegial.

12

Gender Roles and the Health Professional

Phyllis Beck Kritek

The concept of sex roles, placed within the larger context of role theory, is a subset of the generic concept of role, a subset linked to the human attribute of gender. Thus one's sex role is but one of several roles one may assume and alter. It is unique, however, not only in the centrality assigned to it by diverse societies but also in its introduction at a very early point in the human life cycle. The latter is perhaps best exemplified in the United States by the emphasis parents place on the gender of their newborns and their early instruction to toddlers clarifying personal gender. Roles learned and reinforced at such an early stage of development generally are considered not readily altered.

This early introduction of sex roles emerges, quite understandably, from the centrality given gender by human groups. Whereas many roles are optional, the roles assigned to individuals by reason of their gender are hardly optional. Gender is a central physical attribute of all persons, an attribute associated with species' procreation functions. One cannot be gender free. This is further confounded by the dichotomous nature of gender, i.e., one is either a female or a male. Persons born with an unclear gender designation are viewed as anomalies and are surgically "corrected." Dichotomous distinctions, such as "yes" and "no" or "true" and "false," give an appearance of extreme mutual exclusivity. The choice between black and white does not accommodate gradients of gray. Such mutual exclusivity can, and has been, applied to gender-linked norms.

Holter (1970), defining role as a set of norms directed toward an individual in a given position, views sex roles as "those norms which are applied to a man because he is a man, or to a woman because she is a woman" (p. 54). She observes that such sex differentiating norms are, however, understood and experienced at the individual level. She further asserts that the differential ordering of norms for women and men refers not so much to two different sets of norms as to the "different intensities with which given norms are applied to each sex" (p. 55). These intensities vary within and among groups. Thus the basic substrata of human attributes, attitudes, and activities receive differential societal emphases which are gender-linked.

Roles of great centrality, such as sex roles, affect all human enterprise. This has special implications for health professionals for several reasons. Clients assume and alter sex roles. Health care professions in the United States have been highly sex role structured. Health care has been sex role structured as have the organizations where health care is provided. Sex role structuring is a pervasive, often unexamined component of the health care professional's daily experiences.

I believe that the nature, impact, and future of sex roles is therefore an issue of concern to health professionals. In this chapter I delineate the nature of sex roles, demonstrate their impact, and explore their future implications for health professionals in this country.

HISTORICAL CONTEXT

Human inquiry is the struggle to move beyond the obvious, culturally inculcated explanation of events and experiences to ask questions that challenge accepted prejudices. Each unseating of such accepted biases is a benchmark of scientific growth, the precursor to new paradigms of discovery. Galileo, Darwin, and Einstein personify this truism.

Such occurrences also exemplify the inherent risks the scientist takes in challenging the status quo. Old, familiar explanations are not readily abandoned, in part because of the familiar explanation that they "seem so true" it is difficult to envision life without them. New explanations are often disruptive, confusing, even threatening; old beliefs are shaken.

Sex Role Research

The gradual increase of systematic inquiry into sex roles reflects this process. The development of the social sciences in the late nineteenth and twentieth centuries provided tools to explore sex roles. Gould (1981) traces the uses of statistical tools by social scientists to perpetuate common cultural beliefs. Craniology, recapitulation, criminal anthropology, and innate IQ were all theoretical constructions developed to explain the inferiority of undesirables, selected minority races, and women. Such explanations were efforts to utilize emerging paradigms of social science to perpetuate popular role norms. As social science developed, these explanations were discarded for theoretical constructs that better approximated the observable. Minorities and women increasingly challenged the culturally embedded explanations of their status.

In the United States, the social movements of the sixties initiated public scrutiny of many cultural realities which impinged on the experience of its citizens (Reich, 1970). Among these movements, the women's movement, with its heightened visibility and activity, increased public awareness of the relationship between sex roles and a wide range of social and psychological phenomena (Bird, 1968; de Beauvoir, 1961; Friedan, 1963; Millet, 1969). More specifically, the conceptualization of one's sex role identity as partitioned into orthogonal, gender linked bipolar constructs of masculinity and femininity was questioned (Bem, 1974; Holter, 1970; Maccoby, 1966). The cultural inculcation and perpetuation of stereotypic sex roles persisted, but their inevitability and utility were increasingly disputed through both theoretical and empirical investigation (Astin, 1969). New paradigms of inquiry uniquely sensitive to the sex role experiences of women emerged. These focused on women's sex role identity and their sex role self-perceptions in terms of attitudes, values, beliefs, and behaviors. In time, male sex role identity received more deliberate scrutiny and a body of literature emerged explicating this newer understanding of gender-linked phenomena.

While initial explorations focused on general sex role phenomena experienced by the individual, some investigators of sex role identity became interested more specifically in the individual's organizational experiences (Acker & Van Houten, 1977; Garland & Price, 1977). Concurrently, some organizational theorists began to analyze the fact that existing organizational models flow out of exclusively male models, focus primarily on male organizational participants, and tend to evaluate female organizational participants on their degree of deviance from male models (Henning & Jardim, 1977; Kanter, 1977; Stewart, 1978). Arguing from the historical, institutionalized dichotomization of sex role identities, they believed that heuristic attention to the gender of participants would alter existing organizational models.

This "new" insight into male dominance in the conceptualization of reality has gradually altered all academic disciplines over the past 50 years, primarily through women's studies curricula and research programs (Coughlin, 1984). The subsequent paradigm shift has resulted in uneven change patterns within society. As a result, sex role research results are characterized by population-specific variance and rapid obsolescence.

The literature of the current decade gives evidence of heightened consciousness about sex role ideology on the part of social scientists, male and female alike. This has resulted in an increasingly diversified and expansive body of literature that not only manifests increased sensitivity to the gender of subjects, but incorporates the exploration of gender comparisons as the actual focus of the study. This focus tends to be predicated on clearly articulated assumptions about gender. These studies range from explorations of gender differences in graffiti styles (Loewenstine, Ponticos, & Pauldi, 1982) to portrait posing (Mills, 1984, Ragan, 1982) to assertive acts in toddlers (Fagot, Hagan, Leinbach, & Kronsberg, 1985). Such studies, however, continue to reflect limited population variance and replication. The problem of rapid obsolescence of findings because of intensive social change also persists.

Sex Roles and the Health Professional

As noted earlier, recent developments in sex role ideology have particular relevance for health professionals. The reasons are many.

Health care occupations are virtually caricatures of sex structuring. As Greenleaf (1980) observes in her careful analysis of this phenomenon, "occupational segregation by sex predates the industrial revolution and is rooted in predominantly patriarchal cultural patterns" (p. 23). Occupational sex structuring or sex segregation occurs when 70 percent of the work force in a given job category is one sex. In 1970, just as the impact of women's rights upheavals were being experienced, the Federal Bureau of Labor Statistics listed the worker category of registered nurses as having the highest rate of women as a percent of total (99 percent), with dieticians and occupational therapists tying for second rank at 90 percent (U.S. Department of Labor, 1973). More recent estimates indicate that 93 percent of physicians are men and 98 percent of nurses are women (Spiker & Gadow, 1980, p. 61). Dental health care occupations reflect a comparable sex segregation. This finding recently evoked more deliberate occupational sex structuring investigations in this field (Hamby, 1982a, 1982b).

In addition to occupational sex structuring, health care itself is sex structured, embedded as it is in a cultural context and reinforced by the diverse role players in a given health care transaction. Both clients and health care providers share in the diverse sex role ideologies evident in society today. Hubbard (1983) and Keller (1983) have amply documented and analyzed the androcentric perspective of the physical and behavioral sciences that inform the practice of medicine. Keller does a particularly effective job of sketching a picture of the scientific masculine *self*, which strives to retain separation from and control over others in order to sustain its identity.

More recently, feminist philosophers such as Daly (1984), Harding (1986), and Grimshaw (1986) have introduced seminal explorations of an alternative to these masculinist perspectives. While clearly these are freshly minted ideas, they do give promise of introducing a more balanced approach to knowledge generation about humans. Harding, in particular, provides a comprehensive and articulate discussion of these issues. Concurrently, feminist scientists such as Bleier (1984, 1986) and more mainstream scholars such as Schur (1984) and Shaver and Hendrick (1987) are developing explorations of the persisting impact of sexism embedded in science. Perhaps the most intriguing of these developments is the work of Belenky, Clinchy, Goldberger, and Tarule (1986), who have confronted the underlying epistemic dilemmas by contrasting women's ways of knowing with the dominant world view of the scientific community. Their findings elicit a nagging question: do women in health care utilize their own unique ways of knowing or do they accommodate a masculinist paradigm?

The impact of this dominant world view has been explored by numerous feminist authors. Ashley's (1976) powerful synthesis of the effects of structured misogyny on the politics of care brought the discussion of sexism in health care to a new level of frankness in nursing literature. It has subsequently become common to find commentaries on the implications of sexism in such literature, exemplified in the work of Hull (1982), Pinch (1981), and Wilson, Rainey, and Norton (1982). Concurrently, this viewpoint has become more visible in nursing literature in countries such as Australia (McCullock, 1982), New Zealand (Millikan, 1981), and Great Britain (Bowman, 1983). Authors such as Ashley draw heavily on the radical feminism of women like Daly (1978) and Rich (1976), who have described the destructive effects of male dominance in health care provided to women, particularly by gynecologists.

Franks and Rothblum's (1983) collection of readings focuses on the stereotyping of women and its negative effects on mental health. While their work primarily focuses on women, it indirectly touches on effects on males, such as rapists and wife abusers. This view is presently receiving more attention, for instance, in the work of Skord and Schumacher (1982), rehabilitation counselors troubled by the difficulties experienced by disabled men who are forced to abandon masculine stereotypes of behavior. They express concern not only about the clients but also about the health care providers who may engage in sex discrimination against such men.

Indeed, recent studies that confront this issue yield results that substantiate their concern. A study by Biggs and Fiebert (1984) found strains in contemporary male values caused by the emergent changes in sex role expectations in four functional areas: relationships with women, children, work, and other men.

Veenendall (1982) found that, contrary to his prediction, wives of sex-typed males perceived their husbands as more confirming of them than the wives of males who were not sex-typed. Maier and Lavrakas (1984) found that men with traditional delimiting attitudes toward women were also more personally rigid and preferred an idealized male physique. The diverse foci of these studies are useful not only in demonstrating the numerous approaches evident in current sex role research, but also in demonstrating converging outcomes. The former study substantiates the strain created by shifting sex roles; the latter gives evidence of the resistance to these shifts.

The literature cited in this section indicates a heightened awareness on the part of both clients and providers of the impact of sex roles on health care practices and professions. Such literature demonstrates that an uninformed approach to sex roles in health care can leave the client at risk and define the practitioner as irresponsible. Professional and societal sanctions on the unexamined perpetuation and imposition of sex roles in health care do not yet exist, however.

This introduction provides an overview of various scholarly efforts to address the phenomena related to sex roles. The remaining portions of the chapter provide a more detailed review of the theoretical and empirical bases of sex role study and their implications. Particular attention is given to the discipline of nursing.

THEORETICAL PERSPECTIVES

Sex Role Ideology

Sex role ideology refers to the beliefs, theories, or philosophies used to explain and understand sex roles. Ideology is used here because of its connotation of belief system, giving the implicit message that these theoretical bases are simply alternate constructions of reality to be tested and challenged. As Leshan and Margenau (1982) observe:

> Science today, both in physics and in the social sciences, has brought us to the point where we must face the fact that if we wish to proceed on the scientific path and attempt to make our data lawful, we simply cannot have only one set of principles about how reality works. We need to allow for a number of alternate realities. (p. 21)

Arguing that what we can know of reality is not reality itself but our own organization of it, Leshan and Margenau note that "different methods of organizing reality will work best for different purposes" (p. 24). Thus, the ideologies described here do not make a claim to status as truth but only to being ways of viewing reality that have a coherent fit with my purposes. They tend to focus on women's sex roles, but this delineation highlights the traits of male sex roles as well. Two theoretical formulations will be given specific attention: those of Jean Baker Miller (1976) and Sandra Lipsitz Bem (1974).

Jean Baker Miller. Miller, who initially had limited visibility in the literature on feminine ego psychology, was selected because of her skillful synthesis of traditional feminine sex role attitudes with emergent feminist attitudes. In her analysis of the societal status of women, Miller differentiates between the destructive aspects of the subordination of women and the positive traits in women that subordination has diminished. Thus, she sees authenticity and subordination as incompatible. This is not due exclusively to the consequences of subordination, some of which may have creative potential, but partially to the inherent potential for destructiveness in subordination. Miller is able to distill positive consequences from the subordinate status of women and explicates how these consequences could profit both men and women if subordination were to cease.

Miller initiates her discussion with a distinction between temporary inequality (as in the case of children or apprentices) and permanent inequality (as in the case of some minority groups and women). Both are structured and perpetuated through social relationships. Permanent inequality is due to ascription and leads to the structuring of dominant and subordinate groups in a society. Miller describes these groups in some detail. Dominants define subordinates as inferior and then make this definition operational. They define subordinates' roles as those that provide services no dominant wants to perform. The functions of the dominant group are highly valued and guarded, keeping subordinates out; the subordinates' activities are undervalued and demeaned. Subordinates are said to be innately unable to perform preferred roles and are described as having—and encouraged to develop—personal psychological characteristics such as submissiveness, passivity, docility, lack of initiative, dependence, inability to act, think, decide. Subordinates who demonstrate developing initiative or intelligence are viewed as unusual or abnormal.

Dominants, possessing both power and authority, determine and perpetuate society's outlook on philosophy, morals, science, and social theory. They avoid conflict that would create changes in this, especially where their hold on dominance appears tenuous. "Normalcy" is defined as holding another group as inferior, therefore destructiveness, derogation, impeding development and freedom, and opposing equality are also normalized. It is in this sense that one can identify war as a "dominant" masculine problem-solving mechanism in our society, or capitalism as a "dominant" masculine economic system.

The behaviors and negotiations of the subordinates, because they tend to focus on basic survival won from dominants, tend to be more complex and less overt. Subordinates avoid direct, honest reaction to destructive treatment or open self-initiated action in their own self-interest due to fear of reprisal. They resort to disguised, indirect modes of action and reaction which are designed to please and accommodate dominants. Such accommodation is contingent on substantial amounts of accurate information about dominants which subordinates acquire for survival negotiations, but do not share with dominants. Thus, subordinates know dominants better then dominants know themselves.

Further, subordinates, while having extensive information about dominants, have little behavioral information about themselves; there is no reason to acquire such knowledge. Subordinates tend to internalize the dominants' belief structure, including untruths about themselves. This, however, creates inner tension, as subordinates sense some conflict with truth. To resolve this some subordinates identify with and imitate dominants, others resist societal norms and are viewed as deviants or troublemakers, and many simply exist within a status quo of inner tension.

Having completed this brief dominant-versus-subordinate sketch, which is highly compatible with numerous descriptions of the black American experience (Allport, 1958; Carmichael & Hamilton, 1967; Silberman, 1964), Miller moves on to a more detailed description of how the subordinate role of women is structured and institutionalized in our society. Although Miller labels her theory a "psychology of women," the weight she gives to the society-person interplay makes it more appropriately a "social psychology of women."

Based on her discussion of subordinates and dominants, Miller notes that subordinates, assigned less valued tasks, are usually involved in providing personal needs and comforts, both physical and psychological, to others. Miller observes that some of the most critical areas of concern expressed by feminists today reflect this involvement in human needs and comforts: the push for increased physical, sexual, and emotional frankness, an emphasis on the demands of human development, a redistribution of responsibilities for service functions, an emphasis on personal creativity and private and public equality, and an overall thrust toward humanizing society.

Miller contends that this list of concerns demonstrates that dominants (men) may have relegated to their subordinates (women) not only the areas they experience as most problematic and troublesome but also areas that are involved in the species' greatest necessities: intense, emotionally connected cooperation and creativity. Women, in filling these needs for centuries, have developed many extremely valuable psychological qualities. The current changes in the status of women may be seen by women as the time for these qualities of cooperation and creativity to be acknowledged and addressed. Thus, Miller sees women not only as subordinate but, within that role, as sustaining a special, total dynamic of humanity. "Women's psychological characteristics are closer to certain psychological essentials and are, therefore, both sources of strength and the bases of a more advanced form of living" (p. 27).

Miller identifies some of these strengths. The first involves human feelings of vulnerability, weakness, and helplessness, feelings women are in touch with as central to the human condition. She argues that they thus defend less, deny less, and understand and work with weakness better—abilities which constitute a strength in women although women often, she acknowledges, deny this strength. A second strength involves participating in the development of others, a task generally relegated to women with little cultural support. Miller notes, however, that women realize intuitively and experientially the opportunities for self growth inherent in assisting the growth of others.

Miller also explores the strength of cooperation, exemplified in the balance of needs managed by women in families, and creativity, focusing not on artistic or enterprising creativity but on the intensely personal creating of oneself in terms of one's immediate life. Miller contends that women, to deal with the inner tension created by a subordinate role, have generated a basis for worthiness different from the dominant culture. Women's worthiness is based on caring for others and participating in the development of others, activities viewed as enhancing women's self-esteem. Miller argues that these attributes reflect a sophisticated level of creativity. In addition, she notes, women as subordinates have less to lose societally by cooperating and are thus capable of a high degree of cooperation, for example, in shared child rearing with friends and neighbors. Miller also discusses giving, passivity, and adaptation to changes as strengths of women.

She then discusses how these strengths are made to look like weaknesses and the effect this has on women in terms of limited ego development or self-integration. She concludes by exploring the fact that the division of human nature into male and female roles creates serious psychological and sociological problems for women and men. She sees the special psychological skills developed by women as giving promise of a solution to this problem, given that women will deliberately use the skills and men will be receptive.

Miller's theoretical position accommodates what few female ego psychology theories ever address: the possibility that women, while cherishing emergent feminist values of self-actualization and equality for women, may concomitantly value such traditional feminine values as caring, giving, cooperation, and passivity. Miller does not take an either/or stance but provides a way of integrating both positions. This stance seems most suited to the historical and present-day position of women in the health professions.

Sandra Lipsitz Bem. Miller's theoretical formulations provide a logical introduction to the the second part of this theoretical discussion of the sex role identity of women. This section focuses on Bem's (1974, 1975a, 1975b) theoretical discussions of psychological androgyny. Miller concludes her analysis of the subordination of women with a contention that the special psychological skills of women could provide the species with a more positive level of existence. She argues that women must retain these skills and make them available to men; that women must concurrently cease to be subordinated, but rather discover and integrate the positive skills of the dominant (male) group. Bem's conception of psychological androgyny describes that process.

Bem's (1972) starting point is a critique of two related phenomena: psychology's unconscious assumptions about sex role ideology and psychology's assumptions about the nature of personality.

Psychology, Bem observes, has engaged in extensive research about sex roles and the process of sex typing. These studies, however, are predicated on relatively unconscious assumptions: (1) that sex typing is a desirable process, (2) that sex-typed persons are healthier, and (3) that adjusting to society's sex role ideology is desirable. Bem argues that these assumptions, which unconsciously perpetuate society's sex role stereotyping, must be empirically questioned. Both her own studies (1975a, 1977), those by Bem and Lenney (1976), Bem, Martyna, and Watson (1976), and many others substantiate the need to question these assumptions. A high femininity level in women has consistently been correlated with low self-esteem, low social acceptance, and high anxiety (Gall, 1969; Gray, 1957; Sears, 1970; Webb, 1963). Although a high masculinity level in males has been correlated during adolescence with more positive psychological adjustment (Mussen, 1961), it has been correlated during adulthood with high neuroticism, high anxiety, and low self-acceptance (Hartford, Willis, & Deable, 1967; Mussen, 1962). Sex-typed boys and girls have been found to have lower overall intelligence, spatial perception ability, and creativity (Maccoby, 1966). In addition, cross sex typing (masculinity in girls and femininity in boys) has consistently been correlated with greater intellectual development (Maccoby, 1966).

These findings, Bem (1977) argues, demonstrate that rigid sex typing may have limited utility and may indeed be destructive. She further contends that successful adult existence in our society requires an ability to blend both domains, to express both feminine and masculine modalities. This integrated, balanced personality, she posits, is the androgynous personality.

Bem also explores psychology's assumptions about the nature of personality. The problematic assumption Bem highlights is that human personality shows a high degree of cross situational consistency. Mischel (1968), she contends, has aptly demonstrated the inaccuracy of this assumption, showing that behavior is situation-specific and inconsistency is the norm. The inaccurate assumption of consistency, internalized as a societal value, can lead individuals to be taught and to behave in a narrow, sex-typed manner, whether situations warrant such behavior or not. Thus this assumption, while reinforcing sex typing, can lead to constricted individual behaviors which are situationally inappropriate.

Bem posits that if the reality of inconsistency were recognized by personality theorists, the androgynous person would clearly emerge as the individual best equipped to contend with diverse life situations. Because both masculinity and femininity can be viewed as complementary domains of positive behaviors (Erickson, 1964), the androgynous person utilizes each as situations demand. Bem concludes that the domains rest not in specific genders, individuals, or roles, but are complementary modalities available to all persons to aid them in contending with different situations. It is in this sense that she argues "behavior should have no gender" (1975b, p. 15).

Finally, Bem argues for a distinction between sex role identity and gender identity. Given the diminishment of sex role norms and the societal acceptance of androgynous norms, one could more clearly view gender objectively as a set of biological givens. Thus gender identity involves being comfortable with one's body. It need not, however, have a marked influence on one's behavior or lifestyle. Indeed, when gender no longer implicitly connotes a set of lifestyle and behavioral constructs, that is, when sex role norms are no longer rigid expectations, one can finally accept gender simply as a given in the same matter-of-fact way one accepts the reality that we are human. As Bem observes, once we can accept gender in this objective sense we will no longer need "to think about it, to assert that it is true, to fear that it might be in jeopardy, or to wish that it were otherwise" (1975b, p. 17).

Bem's theoretical stance relative to sex typing of individuals has relevance for a sex-typed occupation. If sex typing limits the individual it can also collectively limit the sex-typed occupational group. The androgynous life-style as an alternative to sex typing has great utility for health professionals. This fact has recently received attention in nursing literature (Dean, 1978; Minnegerode, Kayser-Jones, & Garcia, 1978; Ziel, 1983). Finally, the use of masculine or feminine traits according to specific situations, a potentially valuable concept, is largely unexplored. We do not yet know what situational factors evoke masculine, feminine, or combined responses. This question increases in complexity when the situation involves a predominantly feminine-normed person interfacing with a predominantly masculine-normed environment. It is such an interface that characterizes women's involvement in health care delivery systems.

ALTERNATE SEX ROLE PERSPECTIVES

In summary, Miller's theory of the social psychology of women demonstrates that a woman's sex role identity can accommodate both the caring, productive, nurturing components of traditional, socially valued personality and behavior norms, as well as the more assertive, self-actualizing, independent, and achieving personality norms historically associated with masculine behavior and personality norms. Indeed, such a merger of behaviors and traits may, as Bem posits, be a more positive state in terms of the individual person's coping and negotiating repertoire. Thus, in situations where both masculine and feminine modalities are expected, the individual with an androgynous personality and androgynous attitudes concerning sex roles presumably would be well equipped to negotiate the situations.

These two theoretical perspectives provide constructions of reality that may appear relevant to health professionals grappling with sex role issues. Given both the sex structuring of health care occcupations and the gender-linked health care concerns of clients, Bem and Miller enable one to rethink the concepts of masculine and feminine from a new perspective.

Historically, the terms feminine and masculine referred to sets of fairly well defined traits and behaviors believed to be inherent in and appropriate to women and men, respectively. These traits and behaviors were thus viewed as gender-linked and to some degree gender-induced. Masculine trait clusters were more positively valued.

These stereotypic trait clusters, which exist more as the attitudes of society than the gender-linked self-descriptions of specific men and women, persist. They can predominate as the attitude set guiding various human enterprises, including health care provision. Bem and Miller provide an alternate construction of these realities.

Occupational Sex Structuring in Health Care

Health occupations in the United States persistently manifest clear evidence of sex typing, with males assuming largely high status, leadership positions and females occupying lower status, auxiliary occupations (Carpenter, 1977). Although the women's movement and subsequent legislation supportive to their aims have enhanced women's health career options, most women continue to select and pursue traditionally female occupations and roles (Lebowitz, 1977). These trends and patterns have particular relevance to the status of nursing as a predominantly female occupation.

NURSING AS A WOMAN'S OCCUPATION

Nursing's viability as a profession has been historically interlocked with the status of women (Flanagan, 1976). An assumption is frequently made that the predominance of women in nursing is a significant factor. This significance is rarely explored or explained. Feminist literature and texts that explore the experience of being a woman often do not even index nursing (Epstein, 1970b; Gornick & Moran, 1971). Those that do often refer to nursing in the context of the typical sex role-linked career choice for women or actually refer to breast feeding (Rich, 1976). People who write about women's movements thus either ignore nursing altogether or discuss it as a field to which women with limited aspirations are attracted. Both treatments do little to shed light on the historical implications of nursing as a woman's occupation.

Nurses have given some attention to this historical fact. Goren (1976) links the traditional powerlessness of nurses with the traditional powerlessness of women, stating that nursing "remains, at least for the present, a women-dominated profession beset by the problems of being female in our society" (p. 25). A comparative study of the history of nursing and the history of women in the United States demonstrates that the gains and losses of these two groups are remarkably parallel (Brand & Glass, 1975). A relatively formal research effort to explore these patterns, among others, was conducted by the profession in the late 1960s. The results of this study, edited primarily by Jerome Lysaught, were published in a primary report, "An Abstract for Action" (1970), followed by a series of supplemental reports (Lysaught, 1971, 1973a, 1973b).

Lysaught repeatedly identifies female predominance as an important factor in understanding the status of nurses and nursing. In his analysis of motivation in nursing as related to salaries, he observes that "nursing salaries are depressed in comparison with certain female occupations, even more depressed in comparison with other female professional workers, and severely depressed in the health field" (1973a, p. 194). Lysaught attributes this pattern to the economic depriva-tion of women in our society and the fact that men control these salaries. Elsewhere he observes that nursing has been subjected to a set of cultural con-straints that have doomed nurses to organizational failure. "We have placed nursing in a subordinate position and then accused it of lack of independence" (1973b, p. 182).

Another facet of the female predominance in nursing is attrition. In 1972 the American Nurses' Association (ANA) conducted a national inventory of regis-tered nurses and found about 28 percent of all registered nurses were unemployed. Of the total unemployed group, 91 percent were not seeking employment in nursing at that time (American Nurses' Association, 1977). The 1979 ANA national survey revealed an unemployment rate of slightly over 30 percent, with married and widowed nurses showing lower employment rates. Married nurses were also more likely to work part time (Moses & Roth, 1979). A 1974 survey indicated that the overwhelming reason given by over one-third of the unem-ployed RNs was "young children at home." The second most frequent reason was "husband against working," the third, "prefer homemaking" (ANA, 1977, p. 18). Lysaught (1970) also explored the problems confronting the nursing profession in terms of retention of active participants. He observed once more that this is a factor related to nursing as "a woman's profession." In considering possible solutions, Lysaught did not focus on the option of altering the status of women, but raises the question: "Should nursing overtly attempt to discard its feminine image and seek to attract a dramatically larger proportion of men into its ranks?" (pp. 6–7). Lysaught asserts that men could hasten the economic and role changes needed by the profession, drawing an analogy to elementary and secondary teachers. While noting the improved salaries and conditions subsequent to in-creased male participation in these fields, he fails to mention the rapid decrease in decision-making power of and administrative control by women that consequently occurred in the field of education. The Lysaught report essentially suggests that since the status of women cannot be altered, the profession of nursing requires increased numbers of males to provide it with an improved, i.e., more masculine, image. Nursing as predominantly female is recognized as a critical variable, but the implications are never explored. Solutions involve changing the status of female dominance, not the status of women or nurses as women.

Reflecting a viewpoint comparable to Lysaught's, Glaser (1966) commented that "the leaders of nursing have wanted their followers to become successful professionals, but instead American nurses seem to have become successful and satisfied American women" (pp. 25–26). One is left with the impression in Glaser's analysis that successful professionals and successful American women are mutually exclusive roles.

These authors reflect a recurring recognition of the problems associated with nursing as a predominantly female profession, coupled with solutions which essentially reflect an acceptance of existing stereotypic sex role norms. It is only recently that the nursing profession's literature has begun to reflect a response to these problems from a more feminist posture, a viewpoint that explores nursing's future in the light of changing societal sex role norms (Christy 1971; Cleland 1974; Grissum & Spengler, 1975; Kennedy & Garvin, 1981; Lieb, 1976; McInernay, 1974; Vance, 1979).

Brown (1948), in her in-depth study of the profession of nursing conducted more than 30 years ago, took a singularly prescient stance comparable to that of contemporary feminists. She documented the frustrations experienced by nurses from unresponsive health care organizations and an unsympathetic public. She noted that this creates decreased self-confidence in nurses which further erodes public confidence. Her prescription to nurses was to develop an abiding conviction of the social worth of nursing. She argued that nursing "must take a positive position concerning itself and the significance of its function" (p. 198).

NURSING EDUCATION

Although Brown's insight was valuable to nursing, it was not a new insight in nursing. Perhaps no effort in nursing better reflects the struggle to move beyond constrictive feminine sex role norms than the effort to enhance nursing education.

In 1900, efforts were alive in the United States to set professional standards for nursing education. These efforts were coupled with an active attempt by nurses to improve the quality of faculty and, subsequently, nursing education practices. Nursing leaders struggled to enhance educational standards, often against great opposition. As one physician observed, the education of nurses was giving to them "a power and importance never originally contemplated by the medical profession" (Thompson, 1906, p. 744).

Ashley's (1976) historical analysis, *Hospitals, Paternalism and the Role of the Nurse*, has more than adequately documented the exploitation of nurses in this country, an exploitation perpetrated by physicians and hospital administrators, but condoned by society at large. Like most women of their era, nurses were clearly burdened with responsibilities and devoid of rights.

The profession's leaders persisted, developing increasingly educationally sound training schools. At the same time, counterforces escalated their efforts. Short courses and attendant programs were initiated by physicians and hospital administrators to counteract the efforts to improve nursing education through competition for jobs. As Isabel Maitland Stewart (1949) recounted:

A continuous campaign of publicity was organized at a time of unprecedented

prosperity, to prejudice the public against professional nurses and higher standards of nursing education and to create a reaction in favor of semitrained or
untrained workers, thousands of whom were foisted on the public without any
sort of training to distinguish them from well trained nurses. (p. 194)

The relatively powerless and subservient status of nursing in the early part of the
twentieth century is a theme in nursing's early efforts at educational attainment.
Both nursing leaders and those who opposed nursing's continued development
recognized education as a means to gain a voice in political arenas (Grace, 1978).
This move toward political viability became most visibly manifest during the
midcentury as the profession moved toward baccalaureate education.

Despite the persistent obstructionism experienced by professional nursing in
the first half of this century, nursing education began to take root in the early
1900s in university settings, gradually increasing until it expanded rapidly after
1950. Throughout this period of professional development several major studies
of the profession were published and had an impact on subsequent development.
The Goldmark Report (Committee for the Study of Nursing Education, 1923)
noted the incompatible goals of service and education within training schools and
documented the inadequacies of nearly half of such existing schools. Twenty-five
years later Brown (1948) found a wide range of levels of quality and recommended nursing's increased involvement in education in institutions of higher
learning.

In 1965, the American Nurses' Association published a position paper addressing the education of those who work in nursing. One of the assumptions of
the position paper was that "education for those in the health professions must
increase in depth and breadth as scientific knowledge expands" (p. 4). Among
other subsequent positions taken was one which held that "the education for all
those who are licensed to practice nursing should take place in institutions of
higher education" (p. 5) and that the "minimum preparation for beginning professional nursing practice at the present time should be baccalaureate degree education in nursing" (p. 60).

Lysaught (1970) reinforced the importance of the shift of nursing education
to collegiate institutions. Pellegrino (1968) argued that the future of nursing as a
profession and its ultimate effectiveness as a social instrument were contingent
upon the degree to which nursing established contact with the many university
disciplines requisite to its growth.

The American Nurses' Association's statistical reports indicate that diploma
(DIP) programs are experiencing a long-term downward trend in admission; associate degree (AD) programs are experiencing a slowing of their trend of long-term
growth, and baccalaureate (BS) programs continue their long-term upward trend
in admissions. Of the employed registered nurses surveyed in 1964, 88.8 percent
were DIP or AD graduates, 8.9 percent were BS graduates. A decade later, the
distribution was 81.5 percent for DIP or AD graduates and 15.2 percent for BS
graduates. The following year, 1975, the distribution was 80.7 percent and 15.9
percent (ANA, 1977). More recent statistics indicate that this distribution now
shows 78.2 percent DIP or AD graduates and 17.5 percent BS graduates. In
addition, 11.8 percent of practicing registered nurses are enrolled in a formal
educational program (Moses & Roth, 1979).

Thus, although the move to the collegiate institution is occurring, it tends to
be a slow process. Other factors also impinge on the process. As the 1965

American Nurses' Association position paper notes, opportunities for women in traditionally male-dominated professions and business fields will have a growing impact on nursing student recruitment (p. 13).

Bullough (1972) observed that "as a low-status feminine occupation already tied to an apprenticeship training program, nursing faced real obstacles in being accepted in the collegiate setting" (p. 6). She discussed the impact of "having to prove oneself repeatedly to a skeptical audience" that nursing experienced in its effort to gain entry into academia and noted that nursing responded with diffidence or overcompensation.

In summary, early nursing education was characterized as a constricted, hospital-based apprenticeship system which was exploitative and paternalistic in character. It was influenced by the rigid sex role norms of the era. In the second half of the twentieth century, despite persistent obstructionism and opposition, nursing intensified its gradual move to collegiate institutions for education. The transition continues today, but involves multiple obstacles. Sex role norms continue to shape nursing's educational experiences.

HEALTH CARE ORGANIZATIONS

As open systems, organizations comprise the cyclic patterned activities of a number of individuals. These activities are complementary or interdependent and are related to energic input into the system, the transformation of energies, and the resulting product or energic output. All activities are carried on within a specific external environment with which the organization continuously interfaces and interacts. Katz and Kahn (1978) give significant weight to environmental factors, observing that an open systems theory of organizations can attempt to make long-range predictions about such structures only when environmental factors are included. "In an uncertain and constantly changing environment, such predictions take the form of contingent statements" (pp. 5–6).

Relative to this environmental emphasis, a more recent trend in organizational theory involves the use of a political economy perspective developed in conjunction with an open systems view of organizations. This perspective emphasizes resource dependencies within organizations, between organizations and environments, and within interorganizational networks.

Pfeffer and Salancik (1978), who have made contributions to this perspective at both a theoretical and an empirical level, argue that the organization is controlled by, and one can better predict its behavior from, a knowledge of resources rather than a knowledge of management strategies. Organizational behavior involves the evaluation of available resources and acquisition of resources crucial to survival and adequate functioning.

These organizational perspectives have relevance for health care. Health care organizations, particularly in current times of changing demands and supply patterns, experience unique vulnerabilities in regard to available resources. Energic inputs are markedly controlled by environmental forces—societal views concerning professionals are one such energic input. More specific to this discussion, societal views about *nurses* and *nursing* constitute a powerful environmental force. As the status of women in our society experiences fluctuations, such shifts affect health care organizations where large numbers of women are employed.

As a resources model of organization demonstrates, the theoretic picture of an organization tends to focus more concretely on competence, action, instrumentality, goal achievement, and acquisition than on nurturance, passivity, warmth, expressiveness, receptivity, or emotionality. It is in this sense one can argue that organizational theories are essentially masculine paradigms.

Most health care is provided in organizations influenced by these models and constructs. The vast majority of nurses are employed in hospitals or health care agencies where they are viewed as workers with maintenance functions, that is, they keep the organization afloat both by housekeeping types of activities and "around-the-clock" patient maintenance. These functions are carried out in organizations where physicians are viewed as professionals and all other health care professionals are viewed as quasi-professional employees. Physicians are predominantly male, nurses and other health professionals are primarily female. This in effect creates an institutionalization of gender dominance and sex role linked behavior patterns at the organizational level. It is within this context that health professionals must examine the realities of sex roles.

EMPIRICAL EXPLORATIONS

Most empirical exploration of sex roles was initiated during the 1960s, with a few notable exceptions. It has been documented that most research in the social sciences involves the use of male subjects (Holmes & Jorgensen, 1971); however, where male-female comparisons have been made, significantly different findings are often evident (Carlson & Carlson, 1960). Perhaps in part in response to this state of affairs, most recent sex role research focuses on women. Housewives and female college students and professional workers have been primary populations for sample selection, placing constraints on generalizability (Hochschild, 1973).

Most sex role research has used a survey method. Hochschild (1973) has categorized the research that focuses on women into four main perspectives: (1) sex differences, (2) sex roles, (3) women as a minority group, and (4) politics of caste. Utilizing this taxonomy, this discussion focuses primarily on the first and second types and to a lesser extent on the third category in terms of women in organizations.

Most sex *difference* research has focused on emotive and cognitive personality traits whereas sex *role* research focuses on roles and their proscribed activities, role conflict, and role models. The third perspective, which focuses on women as a minority group, utilizes constructs such as prejudice, deviance, assimilation, and marginality. Recent research on women as health care clients or women as workers often uses this perspective.

Research on Sex Differences

One perspective on sex role research, conducted primarily by psychologists, has a lengthy history and thus a vast accumulation of literature. Much of the early research focused on the nature-nurture controversy or on diverse socialization theories. Often it served primarily to highlight the social embeddedness of science where researchers, starting from a premise of superiority of a given gender, set out to demonstrate that "fact."

One of the earliest comprehensive studies on sex-linked trait differences (Terman & Miles, 1936) related sex-difference correlations to specific occupations. Because their work related more to that aspect of research, it will be discussed under research on women in organizations. Terman and Miles's work is relevant, however, because it constitutes foundational research in this area. It is the first serious attempt to establish scientifically valid and reliable measures for differentiating between the sexes. As was noted earlier, it also exemplifies research that not only demonstrates differences but also interjects value positions concerning these differences (Gould, 1980, 1981).

Eleanor Maccoby, who may be the foremost contemporary expert in the field of sex differences (Lee & Stewart, 1976), has published, with Jacklin, a two-stage comprehensive analysis of the psychology of sex differences (1974). Her first volume provided a survey of viewpoints on the development of sex differences (1966). The second volume (1974) is a collection and assessment of all empirical work to date on the topic of sex differences. Although much extant research focuses on children and their development rather than on adults, Maccoby's conclusions are relevant to this discussion.

Maccoby and Jacklin (1974) set out to analyze existing empirical data in an effort "to discover which of the widely held beliefs about sex differences are myth, which are supported by evidence, and which are still untested" (p. 349). They found that generally speaking there is more variance *within* gender groups than variance *between* gender groups in terms of stereotypic sex-normed traits and behaviors. They found only four sex differences empirically well established: (1) girls have greater verbal ability than boys, (2) boys excel in visual-spatial ability in adolescence and adulthood, (3) boys excel in math ability beginning at about 12 to 13 years of age, although different populations show wide variance, and (4) males are more aggressive, at least through the college years.

The myths about sex differences that Maccoby and Jacklin label as unfounded are also discussed. Contrary to popularly held myths, they found girls are not more social or suggestible than boys, girls do not have lower self-esteem or lack achievement motivation, and boys are not more analytic. Neither sex is more visual or auditory; more affected by heredity or environment; better at rote learning, simple repetitive tasks, higher level cognitive processing, or the inhibition of previously learned responses.

Finally, Maccoby identifies those issues for which she believes existing research has yielded ambiguous or contradictory results. She identifies the following traits or characteristics as open questions in terms of sex differences: tactile sensitivity; fear, timidity, and anxiety; activity level; competitiveness; dominance; compliance and nurturance; and maternal behavior.

These issues are particularly relevant. With the exception of tactile sensitivity, all are popular stereotypes held by society about women—either in terms of pronounced presence or absence of the trait. These issues remain unresolved because adult differences have not been adequately assessed.

Some recent studies point to increased exploration in these areas. Research by Hochschild (1973) indicates that women are inclined not only to analyze their feelings more than men but also to shape, manage, and direct their feelings more than men. Safilios-Rothschild (1977) terms this *other-directedness* and the need to be liked, and notes that women will achieve "if they are willing to conform to what others went them to do" (p. 39).

Attempting to focus more specifically on the feminist personality (women who report a commitment to feminist goals), Fowler and Van de Riet (1972) examined personality norms or traits. They compared the adjective checklist scores of feminists with other groups of women. They found that the feminist women did not differ significantly on any dimension from university women. Feminist women were, however, found to be significantly more autonomous, aggressive, dominant, self-confident, and less deferent and affiliative than a normative group of women. The feminist woman's ideal self significantly exceeded her real self in nurturance, endurance, self-confidence, self-control, and personal adjustment. Women's real selves significantly exceeded their ideal selves in aggression. These findings reflect not only the changes feminists may report in their own personality traits but also their possible ambivalence in viewing their feminist selves as their real and ideal selves. This ambivalence is reflective of Miller's (1972) theoretical stance.

Indeed, Epstein (1975), in introducing the collected papers reporting a 1975 national conference on the status of women in higher education and the professions, states unequivocally that enough data have been generated and collected to demonstrate that inequality continued to exist between men's and women's status in society in the mid-1970s. To create new options in personality traits while maintaining women's status within existing societal norms may, at the least, create ambivalence.

Such studies indicate the complexity of sex-difference research. Meeker and Weitzel-O'Neill (1977), in assessing research on sex roles and interpersonal behavior in task-oriented groups, analyze the theoretical roots of sex difference explanations. They, as have others, find the male-instrumental/female-expressive distinction of limited explanatory utility and view more positively the potential of status processes explanations. Lenney (1977), assessing women's self-confidence in achievement settings, finds that situational factors such as specific ability and availability of feedback explain more variance around self-confidence scores than does the gender of the subject.

Maccoby and Jacklin (1974) document this situation-specific factor and also note that "sex differences may be greater among certain sub-groups of men and women than among others" (p. 359). Gender as central to self-concept may thus also be an unmeasured source of variance in selected samples. If one seeks population-wide generalizability, this is an issue of some import.

These perspectives set the stage for the intensive research activity of the current decade, which has tended to involve discrete studies on numerous aspects of sex role differences. While differences continue to be explored—often in a fragmented and reductionistic fashion—current practice increasingly reflects a cautious effort to avoid frank sex role assumptions on the part of the researchers. Thus, explanatory notes explicating study results are generally focused far less on assumed intrinsic gender differences and far more on the impact of social processes.

Research on Sex Role Stereotypes

A subset of the body of research on sex differences deals specifically with sex role stereotypes—persisting consensual beliefs about the differing characteristics of men and women in a society. The presence of such stereotypes in our society is extensively demonstrated in existing literature (Fernberger, 1948; Komarovsky, 1950; McKee & Sherriffs, 1957; Wylie, 1961). The tendency of sex role stereotypes to ascribe greater social value to masculine than to feminine behaviors is also well established (Kitay, 1940; Lynn, 1959; McKee & Sherriffs, 1957; Sherriffs & Jarrett, 1953; White, 1950).

More recently, the implications of the factors associated with sex role stereotyping have been further explored (Broverman, Broverman, Clarkson, et al., 1970; Clarkson, Vogel, Broverman, et al., 1970; Rosenkrantz, Vogel, Bee, et al., 1968; Vogel, Broverman, Broverman, et al., 1970). This group of researchers developed and used a sex role stereotype questionnaire to explore this concept.

In 1972, this group reviewed its work and noted and explored some of its important findings, including: (1) sex role stereotypes are held by large and varied samples within the United States population, (2) sex role stereotypes are incorporated into the self-concepts of both men and women, (3) sex role stereotypes are deeply ingrained attitudes in our society, (4) antecedent conditions are associated with individual differences in stereotypic sex role perceptions, and (5) stereotypic sex role self-concepts correlate with actual and desired family size (Broverman, Vogel, Broverman, et al., 1972).

More specifically, this group's research indicates that "women are perceived as relatively less competent, less independent, less objective, and less logical than men . . . men are perceived as lacking interpersonal sensitivity, warmth, and expressiveness in comparison to women" (p. 75). Stereotypically, male traits are more often perceived as desirable and mental health professionals see mature healthy women as differing from mature healthy men and mature healthy adults, sex unspecified, in these stereotypic parameters. Both men and women incorporate these stereotypes, positive and negative, into their self-concepts. Since negatively valued traits are feminine traits, women tend to have more negative self-concepts than men.

The researchers, exploring the implications these findings have for women, commented that:

> Women are clearly put in a double bind by the fact that different standards exist for women than for adults. If women adopt the behaviors specified as desirable for adults, they risk censure for their failure to be appropriately feminine; but if they adopt the behaviors that are designated as feminine, they are necessarily deficient with respect to the general standards of adult behavior. (p. 75)

In examining behavioral correlates of sex role stereotypes, the researchers found that mothers who scored low on negatively valued female traits and high on positively valued masculine traits had relatively fewer children than women who scored high on negatively valued female traits and low on positively valued male traits. The scores on positively valued feminine traits showed no relationship with family size (Clarkson, et al., 1970).

In exploring the relationship between mother's employment status and sex role perceptions of college students, they found that students' perceptions of differences between men and women were smaller for daughters and sons of employed mothers than for those of homemaker mothers. Daughters of employed mothers perceived women as more competent (Vogel et al., 1970). The work of this group has provided an expanded insight into the persisting phenomena of sex role stereotyping, a critical factor in gender-dominated occupational groups.

Bem (1974), taking the self-report method of sex role personality trait measurement a step further, developed and implemented a new sex role inventory that measured not only masculinity and femininity but added the conceptual distinction of androgyny. This tool moved past the bipolar continuum view of sex differences to a third, androgynous conceptualization.

Bem's theoretic formulations of androgyny were discussed previously. To test these formulations, Bem hypothesized that psychologically androgynous individuals would be more likely than either feminine or masculine individuals to demonstrate sex role adaptability across situations (1975b). Androgynous subjects were able to display situationally effective behavior. All nonandrogynous subjects showed behavioral deficits, with feminine females demonstrating the most pronounced deficits.

A subsequent study (Bem & Lenney, 1976) indicated that sex-typed subjects were more likely than androgynous or sex-reversed subjects to prefer sex-appropriate activity and resist sex-inappropriate activity, even when it cost them money. The sex-typed subjects reported greater psychological discomfort and more negative feelings about themselves when engaging in cross-sex behavior.

Bem also explored differences between androgynous subjects who score high on both masculine and feminine traits and those who score low on both. Though her results are not completely conclusive, Bem found adequate differentiation to warrant a distinction between two groups, labeling the former androgynous and the latter undifferentiated (1977). Specifically, undifferentiated subjects were significantly lower in self-esteem. Studies utilizing Bem's instrument have begun to provide support for the hypothesis that sex-typed individuals will differentiate along a gender-related dimension significantly more than will androgynous individuals (Deaux & Major, 1977; Lippa, 1977).

Kelly (1983) observed that the sex role stereotype research of the 1970s successfully challenged the traditional bipolar conceptualizations of masculinity and femininity; the "new" conceptualizations, however, are less clear. Noting that while research does demonstrate that rigid, stereotypically feminine sex roles are not associated with psychological wellness, "masculinity in both females and males primarily contributes to positive adjustment indices, leaving unclear the manner in which stereotypic femininity independently contributes to enhanced adjustment" (p. 17).

In contrast to this feminist dialogue, numerous sex role studies have emerged that build on the work of the 1970s but include, at least implicitly, the assumption of social change and its impact in sex role phenomena. An excellent example of this is a series of studies reported by Heilbrun and Schwartz (1982). They conducted two different sets of secondary analyses on various measures of androgyny (as they defined it) from data collected between 1958 and 1978. They also conducted a laboratory study following these studies. In all studies, men were reported as more androgynous than women. However, androgyny in men declined in the sixties, and increased in the seventies; the reverse pattern occurred with women.

In 1983 Ruble reported on a study focused on sex stereotypes as they appear to have changed in the 1970s. In rating the typical and ideal man or woman, subjects reported rating differences by gender in 53 of 54 items for the *typical* man or woman, and 12 of 54 for the *ideal* man or woman. The investigator suggests that sex stereotypes appear to remain strong, but sex-biased attitudes appear to have become less polarized. In a somewhat comparable study, McPherson and Spetrino (1983), using the Short Bem Sex Role Inventory, selected 20 subjects in four categories: androgynous females, sex-typed females, androgynous males, and sex-typed males. These 80 subjects then rated ideal males and females. The two female groups demonstrated no differences; the male groups differed. They suggest, therefore, that gender rather than sex role beliefs and expectations may explicate differences in beliefs about gender polarity, i.e., that women have a single vision of an ideal.

Research on Sex, Family Orientation, and Work Roles

This area of research, which deals specifically with the roles women assume in their activities and the norms governing them, is the most extensively explored area of feminine sex role attitudes. Most of these studies focus on the roles of women in the family or in the economy and, in particular, the personal and societal consequences of assuming roles in both. These studies demonstrate a wide diversity of interests, value orientations, and perspectives.

Although women's movements and their perspectives have doubtless stimulated much interest in this research, persisting myths about employed women are perpetuated alongside these feminist views. In a publication dealing with advice on "managing women in business," Ellman (1967) discusses the changing roles of women and their expanding opportunities and notes that some problems persist. He quotes a study conducted in the 1920s (U. S. Public Health Service, 1927) to demonstrate the persisting problem of absenteeism. Much of what Ellman has to say is worth noting as it exemplifies many of the assumptions frequently made about women who are employed:

> Women's dual responsibility in the home and on the job can create problems for the manager or supervisor, particularly in a work situation which requires steady and systematic attendance (p. 10). . . . Women display less desire for advancement than men. Furthermore, they are limited in advancement potentiality (p. 11). Occasionally you may 'bend' the age specification, but in such cases you may be interested in considering whether the woman appears younger than or older than her age. . . . Woman are prone to lie about their age (p. 36). . . . Woman's different emotional make-up, their lack of permanence and stability in the work force, their split loyalty to the family and the job, and their limited aspirations for advancement—all must be considered as challenges or obstacles for management to overcome (p. 120). . . . Woman's normal ambition is marriage, her normal destiny is biological. This reality may always conflict with her ultimate acceptance as an equal in the world of jobs and industry. (p. 147)

These views present a useful backdrop for empirical work dealing with the dual role aspects of working women's lives. They also demonstrate an underlying premise of much of the work in this area. This premise holds that women's career patterns and motivation must be the same as men's, and if they are not they create constraints on excellence and commitment. This premise again demonstrates the influence of male paradigms in social science research.

Lebowitz (1977), summarizing her results of a study of women in the health care industry, observes that most employed women, whatever their occupation, continue to struggle with conflicts between "family obligations, personal desires and ambitions, and the demands and limitations of their work" (p. i). She also concludes that social norms and psychological theories disapproving of working mothers have engendered feelings of doubt and anxiety, particularly among middle-class professional women.

Angrist (1969) analyzed these issues in terms of sex role learning and sex role flexibility. She observed that changing sex role norms are vague and shifting. In her study (1967) of single and married women's home-versus-career preferences she found that to some degree women did perceive themselves as having options in their adult roles, but that these options were considered around several contingencies central to women's sex role learning. The primary contingency is marriage, but several secondary contingencies impinge on women and their later role behavior. Among these contingencies are the number and age of children, widowhood, divorce, and the eventual departure of children from the home. She found that women explicitly planned around the contingency of marriage, but only vaguely around work options. This was, however, less true for single women, a finding supported by Havens (1973), who found a direct relation between economic attainment and unmarried status in women workers. Havens argues that such women may choose not to be married because they are career committed and wish to avoid the constraints of marriage as a contingency. Feldman (1973) presents essentially the same argument in terms of marital status and graduate student attainment. His study indicates that graduate students' success is linked to marital status. "It appears that divorce becomes a force for liberation for women students, while it becomes a source of strain for men. Men lose a supportive relationship, while women lose a source of severe role conflict" (p. 231).

Returning to Angrist's discussion of contingency factors, it becomes evident that a portion of the dual role issue is tied to marriage as a central contingency in female socialization. Marriage can create a sense of limited options in terms of occupation, a factor that makes standard (male modeled) occupational choice theories inappropriate to women's contingency orientations (Psathas, 1968; Psathas & Plapp, 1968). As Ginzberg, Ginzberg, Axelrod, et al., (1963) note "major adjustments must be made in the general [occupational] theory before it can be applied to girls" (p. 176).

None of this research confronts the question of whether such adaptation is viewed negatively or positively, that is, whether such proposed adaptations demonstrate women's contingency planning as positive, negative, or neutral as viewed by society or employers. Value choices are clearly present in women's contingency planning.

While women's contingency planning around marriage is evident, it does not of necessity indicate more limited productivity. Ferber and Loeb (1971, 1972) found that female faculty members, married and single, are as productive as their male colleagues, although not always similarly well rewarded. A study of female PhD.'s conducted by Simon, Clark, and Galeway (1967) indicated that despite this equal productivity, both married and single academic women earned less than their male colleagues. They also found that single women tended to receive higher salaries and attain higher ranks than married women.

Ferber and Loeb (1973), expanding on their initial studies, assessed marital and parental status of male and female faculty members in relation to productivity, salary, rank, and specialty. They summarized their results as follows:

> Married women with or without children are no less productive than single ones, yet appear to experience less success in academic life. Marital and, for men, parental status may enter reward decisions as a possible indicator or perceived financial need. Men and women in fields with relatively high concentrations of women appear to experience no deficit in productivity or reward: so-called upgrading of fields by increasing male participation is unlikely to affect individual rewards. . . . Perception of sex discrimination appears to be more accurate among women than men; for example, considerably more women than men seem to be aware of salary and rank inequities which have been documented elsewhere. Among women, married women seem more aware than single women of discriminations, possibly because they have, as suggested earlier, experienced more of it. (p. 239)

What these studies consistently demonstrate is the presence of a persistent although imprecisely defined relationship between women's family or marital roles and their work roles.

Dual-Role Interactions. Steinmann (1963), in an attempt to explore the ambiguities that such dual role interactions create for society, investigated the concept of the feminine role held by college-age women and their parents. She differentiated between the "traditional" feminine role which she called "other-oriented" and which is linked with a familial focus, and the "liberal" feminine role which she called "self-oriented" and which is linked with a career or self-fulfillment focus (p. 341).

In reviewing her extensive findings, Steinmann observes that college-age subjects consider the feminine role to be made up of approximately equal amounts of other-oriented and self-oriented elements, and that this is true for both their real and ideal selves. However, the subjects' concept of the average woman, of men's ideal woman, and of their fathers' expectations of them are all significantly more other-oriented than their own self-concept. The most pronounced discrepancy was reported to exist with men's ideal woman. These findings highlight women's perceptions of societal expectations. In subsequent exploration of these issues, Steinmann and Fox (1966) compared how women viewed themselves, how women think men would like them to be, and how men viewed their ideal woman. They found comparability between the first and last measures and discrepancies between these and the middle measure. Women saw themselves as balanced between other-oriented and self-oriented, but believed men's ideal was an other-oriented woman. Men stated that their ideal woman was a balance of the two emphases. In analyzing responses by item, however, the researchers found that although men were quite "liberal" on global items such as "women should use their talents," on more specific items they were far less liberal: for example, when men were asked if a woman's own work and self-realization might be the most important aspect of her life, their answer was no.

Based on these results, Steinmann and Fox concluded women face ambiguous role expectations. American women are what they like to be, but do not believe it is what men want them to be. In the eyes of American women,

American men seem to desire a type of woman that women have no wish to be. American men are sending American women contradictory clues about the kind of women they prefer. This frank ambiguity further confounds the complexity of women's dual role concerns. The ambiguity of men's message to women about preferences can confound the experience of female organization members interacting with male-dominant organizations.

Subsequent research has focused on specific aspects of the dual role issue. Gump (1972) studied the sex role concept of 162 senior college women in relation to ego strength, happiness, and achievement plans. She found that the majority of her subjects believed it possible to assume the roles of wife and mother while concomitantly pursuing extrafamilial interests. Neither happiness nor the establishing of relationships with men were related to differences between traditional sex role orientation and an orientation directed more at self-realization. Differences in ego strength were found to be associated with plans for a combination of marriage and career. Subjects with the highest ego strength scores were actively pursuing both goals. Gump suggests that this finding may indicate a negative relationship between adoption of the traditional female sex role and ego strength.

Joesting (1971) compared a group of college women associated with formal women's movement groups with matched peers. She found that women's movement subjects scored significantly higher on risk-taking, creativity, and originality, and had earned more honors and higher grade point averages. It is noteworthy however, that both of these studies utilized college student samples.

Looking at studies focusing on adult women, Lipman-Blumen (1972) surveyed 1012 married women and found a strong interaction between the concept a woman held of the feminine role and her educational aspirations. More than 50 percent of the women who held the traditional view of the female role did not plan to seek a degree beyond the bachelor's level, whereas a majority of the women with a more contemporary viewpoint aspired to graduate studies, with 58 percent possessing medium aspirations and 11 percent possessing high aspirations. In a somewhat related study, Waite and Stolzenberg (1976) found that a woman's plans to participate in the labor force when she is 35 have a substantial effect on the total number of children she plans to bear in her lifetime.

Studies such as these indicate that women moving away from a traditional perception of feminine sex roles are electing dual role options. The decisions they make may increasingly include the dual role as an option. Social systems such as the family may simply be in transition in response to these changes. In addition, these studies indicate that to some degree, the dual role option is associated for many women with a positive sense of self; a desire to balance traditional roles of women with emergent roles of women. There is little evidence that women with career aspirations continue to view these as one of two mutually exclusive options. The dual role trend will almost certainly have an impact on male-dominated organizations. It already has had an impact on family social structure.

Aronoff and Crano (1975) specifically focused their research on this female dual-role feature of family social structure. Approaching a reexamination of the instrumental/expressive distinction from a cross-cultural perspective, they studied 862 societies to explore the degree to which men, to the exclusion of women, assume the role of task specialist in subsistence economy. Their analyses reveal that overall, women contribute appreciably to subsistence economy, an average of 44 percent, demonstrating that males are not instrumental specialists. Rather than role *segregation* they saw role *sharing* occurring, with a continuous distribution of the instrumental role across sexes within a culture. While this incursion into male's instrumental role has been scrutinized, empirical findings on men's incursion into female expressive roles is at present indirect and sketchy (Biggs & Fiebert, 1984). Haavio-Mannila (1967) did, however, find that in Helsinki, where sex role ideology shifts are somewhat "ahead" of the universal average, employed women are more dissatisfied with the division of household tasks at home than with their occupational positions. She contends that the norms demanding equality of the sexes may be better followed in public life than in private life.

What the studies previously discussed presage, and allude to, is the potential for women of role conflict. Hall (1974) observes that while much popular debate has focused on the issue of whether women should have careers outside the home, academicians have tended to focus more on how, rather than on whether. In his study relative to the how question, Hall focuses on the types of conflicts faced by married women as the result of multiple role performance, strategies used for coping with these conflicts, and the varying degrees of satisfaction to be gained from different strategies.

Hall identifies three possible strategies: (1) structural role redefinition which involves altering external, structurally imposed expectations relative to roles, (2) personal role redefinition which involves changing one's own behavioral expectations and perceptions, and (3) reactive role behavior, which involves finding ways to meet all role expectations. His results indicate that the simple act of coping (as opposed to not coping) may have a stronger relationship to satisfaction in women than the particular type of coping strategy. Type 3 coping has been identified elsewhere as the most common coping mode for working women (Wilensky, 1968).

Carrying this role tension theme further, Yogev (1981) studied the marital dynamics of 106 faculty women at Northwestern University. The study focused on the division of housework and childcare. Professional married women in the sample reported two contradictory patterns regarding this division of labor. While they perceived their relationship with their husbands as egalitarian, they assumed most of the responsibilities for housework and child care and neither expected nor wanted their husbands to assume an equal share. Yogev argues that these women had expanded their roles rather than redefined them, and observes that such role expansion in the professional woman of today will give way to a more truly egalitarian role redefinition process in professional women of the future. She proposes that the traditional sex role socialization experienced by both partners in these marriages may impede more extensive role redefinition, given the inherent cultural lag between recognition of a new possibility and real behavioral change. In terms of the impact of dual roles on marriage happiness, Orden and Bradburn (1969) found that both partners score lower in marriage happiness if the wife participates in the labor market out of economic necessity rather than by choice. They found that "a woman's choice of the labor market over the home market strains the marriage only when there are preschool children in the family" (p. 392). Other factors did not reveal a pattern; however, the labor market choice was generally associated with a higher balance between tensions and satisfactions for both partners. This last finding is worthy of emphasis in that it notes not only the increased tensions created by dual-role women, but also the increased satisfactions. To date, exploration has focused more heavily on the former.

Dual-role research tends to focus on the cultural contradictions in these roles, as evidenced by the emphasis on tension. It is predicated on an ascriptive familial role for women that is obsolete in modern industrial society (Marwell, 1975). Horner's (1969, 1970, 1972) work perhaps best exemplifies this focus: she concludes that woman's "will to fail" is based on her fear of success outside of ascriptive feminine roles.

Problems with Research. The key difficulty with work such as Horner's is that it may have oversimplified and overstated the problem; what is *now* may have become viewed increasingly as what is *forever*. The study is dated, involves a college-age sample, and when it had its impact was unreplicated. Indeed, a subsequent replication found no significant fear of success related to sex differences (Levine & Crumrine, 1975).

Anderson (1978) dissected the construct further and discovered ambivalence was more prevalent than fear (motive to avoid success) and that clusters of women students with various patterns of ambivalence toward success related to diverse personality traits. She noted further that this ambivalence might be a temporary developmental phenomenon. Perhaps of greater interest is the work of Feather (1975), Feather and Simon (1975), and Janda, O'Grady, and Capps (1978) replicating Horner's work, but changing the sex typing of the occupations used in the study (Horner used medical school vignettes). These studies found a relationship between the sex of subject and the sex typing of the occupation; that is, the reaction to success of both males and females was related to the sex-typed appropriateness of the occupation. Interestingly, these studies used nursing as the female sex-typed occupation.

These authors argue for more caution and replication prior to the wholesale adoption of a single study's findings. They note a comparable situation in a second study by Goldberg (1968). Goldberg had reported results that indicate that women are biased against professional women. Ferber and Huber (1973) unsuccessfully attempted to replicate his findings; in fact, their findings contradicted Goldberg's. They found that "while women students have some prejudice against women teachers when confronted by a hypothetical choice, they tend to like women teachers when actually exposed to them" (p. 962). They further found contact diminished the effects of stereotypes. They argue that sex bias on the part of the researcher can be an important source of bias in sex bias research.

Sex of researcher may in part explain the mixed results of studies in these areas. Other factors may include the year of the study, region, sample age, socioeconomic level, and educational achievement of subjects, as Pheterson's (1969) work indicates.

All of the studies examined thus far do reflect changes in earlier sex role stereotypes; changes that continue and may alter the findings of replications in a few short years. Karen Oppenheim Mason (1975) has been prominent in conducting comprehensive work that has documented change. Her work focuses specifically on changes occurring between 1964 and 1974. She utilized data from five previously conducted surveys to·explore her interest in changes in women's sex role ideology during that time. Her analyses indicate that during those 10 years women from across the United States, representing fairly wide variance on all demographic variables, moved toward a more egalitarian definition of the mutual responsibilities and rights of men and women. Currently employed women usually were found to be more egalitarian. By 1974, a large majority of American women reported that they endorsed men sharing housework, they believed working mothers could have successful relationships with their children, and equal rights with men in employment were important to them. Much reported sex role research undoubtedly was conducted at various intervals while these changes were taking place. As Komarovsky (1973) commented in analyzing data collected in 1970:

> Attitudes toward working wives abounded in ambivalences and inconsistencies. The ideological supports for the traditional sex role differentiation in marriage are weakening, but the emotional allegiance to the modified traditional pattern is still strong. These inconsistencies did not generate a high degree of stress, partly, no doubt, because future roles do not require an immediate realistic confrontation. In addition, there is no gainsaying the conclusion that human beings can tolerate a high degree of inconsistency as long as it does not conflict with their self-interest. (p. 122)

Research on Women in Organizations

In 1973, Hochschild observed that recent research on women at work "has yet to filter into the traditional preserve of family theory" (p. 255). Thus, while dual-role research occurs, it tends to be taken from one perspective with little recognition of implications for the other. In addition, most research on women at work tends to focus on professionals, especially women in male-dominated professions or organizational situations (Astin, 1969; Bernard, 1964; Epstein, 1970b; Henning & Jardim, 1977; White, 1967). Yet most women workers, approximately 70 percent, are clerical and service workers. Occasionally studies of these groups are based on an organizational perspective, with results weighed in terms of utility to the organization. In this sense they can be viewed as the imposition of the male paradigm on female groups.

Marrett (1972), for instance, reviewed evidence for the argument that female predominance in complex organizations encourages centralization. Because of the attitudes and values as well as the nonwork commitments of women in the organizations in which they participate, staff are allowed only limited involvement in the decision-making process. Marrett concluded that extant studies show mixed results, some indicating that sex has no significant influence on centralization, thus suggesting that further systematic study is warranted.

Status and migration as familial factors have also been explored in terms of wives' employment. Ritter and Hargens (1975) explored the class identifications of married working women in an effort to examine the traditional assumption that wives derive their class positions and identifications exclusively or predominantly from the occupational positions of their husbands. They found that this assumption no longer holds for working wives. Traditional sociologic assumptions about the American nuclear family have included the idea that the overwhelmingly predominant status resource of a married woman is the occupational position of her husband (Acker, 1973, p. 938). Ritter and Hargen's results suggest that studies of status ranking of families as units will show that the occupational statuses of working wives have an impact on family status just as do those of their spouses.

In comparable research, Duncan and Perruci (1976) studied dual-occupation families and migration and found that while a husband's prestige or income increment opportunities increased with migration, the same was not reflected in the wife's pattern. They contend that a lack of pattern exists to explain what happens to employed wives when couples migrate. This may be due partly to complex interactions of moderator variables such as type of occupation or reason for migration. Federico, Federico, and Lundquist (1976) studied women's employment turnover from another perspective, treating it as a function of "extent of met salary expectations." They found a significant relationship between the two factors.

Some research has focused on male responses to women in organizations, particularly in higher status positions. Garland and Price (1977) studied male subjects' attitudes toward women in management. They found subjects' attitudes toward these women unaffected by the descriptions of successful or failing managers. When success descriptions were read, subjects with positive attitudes attributed success to ability and effort whereas subjects with negative attitudes attributed success to luck and easy job. No "failure description" relationships were found.

Naastrom (1976) explored the male attitude toward affirmative action for women in education. He found that affirmative action programs do not elicit widespread enthusiasm among males. Subjects' attitudes stemmed from assertions that women are unprepared to assume a wider role, perceived differences in leadership behavior on the part of men and women, and job holders' fear for their employment security.

Perhaps more problematic is the simple fact that men have fewer opportunities or reasons for attitudinal change. As Irvine and Robinson (1982) observe, "women have experienced attitude changes in a relatively short time through consciousness-raising and other techniques. Men have had both fewer opportunities and less encouragement than women to examine their attitudes toward their own and the other sex" (p. 203). They found that supportive attitudes toward women and women in managerial roles were dependent on an individual's own sex role orientation, with persons who perceived themselves as highly androgynous and with high sex role flexibility being more supportive. Women were significantly more liberal in their attitudes than men. This general issue of the lag in male attitude change is a persisting theme in more recent sex role literature, including that of health professionals (Faunce, 1977; Lieb, 1978; Schein, 1978; Symonds, 1983).

Epstein's (1970a) analysis of sex-status limits on women's careers in the professions identifies several processes male-dominated professions use to limit women's participation. She observes that institutionalized channels of recruitment and advancement, such as the protege system, are not easily available to women. She also identifies womens' behaviors that reinforce career limits, behaviors that flow out of women's minority status.

In those studies which focused on male responses to women in organizations, some light was shed on one characteristic of the interface between the female employee and the male-dominated organization. The receptivity of the males in an organization to some degree functions as a mediator in male–female interaction.

More recently, empirical exploration of female-dominated work cultures and organizations has emerged. Petty and Miles (1976) found that sex role stereotypes exist for the leadership role, even in female-dominated work cultures, and that these stereotypes are shared by subordinates of both sexes. They raise the interesting point, based on conflicting results from a related study by Moses and Boehm (1975), that affirmative action responses in male-dominated work cultures will perhaps lead to the promotion of women with behaviors similar to those of males in management.

Rosen and Jerdee (1973, 1974a, 1974b, 1974c, 1975) have done extensive organizational research on sex role stereotyping utilizing a laboratory methodology. Their results indicate that sex role stereotyping may exist in real organizational situations involving employee selection, placement, and disciplinary decisions, as well as preferences for supervisory behaviors.

Within the overall category of female-dominated work cultures, some studies have focused specifically on nursing. Lebowitz (1977), reporting on an exploratory study of women's labor force participation in the health care industry, notes that "while dental hygienists, dentists, and health care administrators are struggling for gains within the existing male-dominated structure of health occupations, registered nurses are trying to generate a system of health care delivery parallel to and competitive with the physician-dominated system" (p. 7). In this same study, registered nurses, discussing career options, indicated that they believe they suffered less from sexual discrimination than from limited options available in a female-stereotyped occupation (p. 9).

The author of this study comments that "the traditional male-female relationship between physicians and nurses is firmly entrenched not only in the structure of the health care system, but also in the education and socialization of nurses" (p. 12). She observes that registered nurses stated that other nurses often "oppose or subvert their efforts to assert themselves and to enhance the power and position of nursing within the health care system" (p. 12).

More recently, Bauder (1982) used a more qualitative sociologic approach to analyze a serendipitous discovery she made as a consultant to schools of nursing. Schools of nursing, contrary to her expectations, consistently emphasized organizational demands over human needs. She saw this manifested in three ways:

> Each school of nursing evidenced three key findings: (1) heavy workloads were expected of the faculty and expected by the faculty, though sometimes reluctantly; (2) the discontents that faculty felt were dealt with individually rather than collectively; and (3) those discontents which did surface did so as crises that were managed rather than as structural issues that systematically could be debated and resolved. (pp. 156–157)

Bauder identifies a number of factors which she believes explains these findings. She notes that as members of female schools in male universities, faculty must work exceptionally hard to establish their credibility and earn prestige, a subset of the truism that "women must work harder for the same recognition"—a phenomenon documented elsewhere (e.g, Quell & Pfeiffer, 1982). She further observes that nurse educators accommodate these organizational demands at some personal cost both because nurses, as women, are other-oriented, in this case oriented to the school, and also because they wish to earn recognition from a reluctant academic community, even if it requires excessive work and professional demands. Thus the effort to bootstrap oneself upward, characteristic of women's efforts, may in this case occur at the organizational as well as the individual level.

As was indicated earlier, one final empirical base of this discussion involves research that focuses on nursing although it was designed ostensibly to focus on sex differences. A discussion of this work concludes this section.

Sex Roles in Nursing

One of the earliest attempts to explore sex differences was conducted by Terman and Miles (1936). This investigation involved more than 11 years of research with diverse samples. Their work continues to be a classic in the field of sex-difference research, despite valid criticisms subsequently generated.

Terman and Miles reported some findings not fully explored by them or by subsequent researchers. They noted "special groups selected with respect to occupation or other characteristics do not always conform to the expectations based on the findings for the general population" (p. 156). The examples of this cited for women in their studies are "the relatively masculine professional female nurses and the extremely masculine intellectual groups" (p. 156). Interestingly, in contrast they found that student nurses are less masculine than any of the college groups of equal age, but less feminine than younger, high school juniors. Terman and Miles noted that older, practicing nurses, "score more masculine than any of the general population groups of adult women of any educational level" (p. 154). Unfortunately they elected to limit analysis of their data about nurses (p. 185) although they analyzed some other occupational groups in greater detail. They briefly commented that in the higher masculinity scores of nurses "age is apparently without influence; some other factor or factors, perhaps occupational interests and habits, are evidently dominant" (p. 154). The nature of these "other factors" is left unexplored.

Other generalizations they presented appear important in relationship to their overall conclusions, however. These are: (1) that women's occupations requiring the most training and intelligence rate most masculine; (2) this trend is also increased in occupations requiring leadership, the direction of other people, or implementing a program; and (3) working outside the home appears to be related to increased masculine scores. All of these trends are important to nurses in general and, in fact, Terman and Miles identified nurses specifically as representative of the second trend (p. 181).

Terman and Miles (1936) noted in their conclusions that

> . . . as long as the child is faced by two relatively distinct patterns of personality, each attracting him by its unique features, and is yet required by social pressures to accept the one and reject the other, a healthy integration of personality may often be difficult to achieve. (p. 451)

One other finding of Terman and Miles is noteworthy in light of the focus of this discussion. They generalized that marriage has a feminizing influence. They noted, but did not further analyze, one exception to this pattern. In discussing their subsample of professional women (64 nurses, 20 librarians, and 153 teachers who rated on masculinity scores in that order) they observed:

> The subgroups of the three constituents do not follow the same order: married nurses, married librarians, and single teachers are more masculine; single nurses, housewives formerly librarians, and housewives formerly teachers rate most feminine. But as married and single women occupationally active outside their homes score normally at about the same point, and more masculine than housewives formerly so engaged, the only divergence from the norm is the position of the unmarried nurses. (p. 185)

The possible basis for this divergence was left unexplored, although smallness of sample size is noted. Thus, while the study is dated, the scores of nurses and their variability raise the possibility of some unanswered questions about nurses and their sex role identities.

Very recently there has been evidence of an increased interest on the part of nurse researchers in questions related to sex role attitudes. Glass (1977) observes that "the history of nursing, its problems, and practices, can be seen in a feminist perspective; research in nursing is no exception" (p. 230). Moore, Decker, and Dowd (1978) attempted to determine if nursing and nonnursing students changed their attitudes about themselves and the "typical nurse" in relation to feminist movement goals. Female nursing students showed significantly more feminist leanings, both in terms of self and "typical" nurse. Male nurses, nonnurses, and females in typical and atypical female majors rated themselves lower than female nurses on the feminist scale.

Simpson and Green (1975), using Bem's (1974) Sex Role Inventory scale, found only 38 percent of their sample of nurses described themselves as androgynous. Simpson and Green argue that it is very important for nurses to be psychologically androgynous, basing their argument on the findings of Spence et al., (1975) that androgynous individuals score high on self-esteem and on Bem's (1975a) finding that androgynous persons show higher sex role adaptability.

Minnigrode, Kayser-Jones, and Garcia (1978) followed the same line of reasoning as Simpson and Green to generate notably different results. Undergraduate and graduate student nurses rated their ideal nurse as highly masculine and highly feminine, i.e., androgynous. Three factors may shed light on these discrepancies. Simpson and Green conducted their research at an earlier time, perhaps prior to more general acceptance of feminist thinking. In addition, their study was conducted on practicing nurses rather than students. Finally, they used a sample of Canadian nurses. These factors are relevant, as year and geographical region of study are critical variables, as are sample characteristics.

The work of Meleis and Dagenais (1980) further supports this observation. They compared feminine characteristics of nursing students in programs at three levels (associate degree, diploma, and baccalaureate degree) with national normative female college student data. Nursing students' scores on sex role items were similar to national norms in their sex role identity and ratings did not differ significantly by program. Increased masculinity in sex role identity was associated with professional values and was more characteristic of associate degree and baccalaureate degree students, who scored higher on professionalism. They conclude that their results dispel "the popular myth that nursing students manifest more feminine characteristics than other women in college and points to the need to differentiate the outcomes expected from education in nursing at the technical and the professional levels" (p. 162).

In a study conducted by the author (Kritek, 1980), 109 school of nursing faculty from three different schools were measured on the Bem Sex Role Inventory. Using Bem's (1977) median split methods and standardized medians to differentiate among masculine, feminine, androgynous, and undifferentiated subjects, 49 percent of the study sample were androgynous, compared to the 29 percent found in Bem's sample. Only 13 percent of the study sample was undifferentiated. Such findings futher substantiate the need to empirically challenge stereotypic assumptions about nurses' sex role identity.

EMPIRICAL BASES: A SUMMARY

This far-ranging review of sex role research demonstrates several realities. Although the studies reported here make an important contribution to a better understanding of sex roles, the literature can hardly be described as an organized body of research. Tools are relatively new and untested. Sample groups often have been nonrepresentative, limiting generalizability. Almost all researchers have used traditionally male research paradigms to investigate women's realities, an increasingly suspect conceptual base. Most studies lack replication; many reflect the bias they meant to challenge. Feminists, eager to balance the male dominance of centuries, have conducted research equally lopsided in its approach. It is no more realistic to study women out of context, as if laboratory animals in a sterile (and male-free) environment, than it is to study men in this fashion. Sex roles are dichotomous and interactive, and the research about them must accommodate this fact. More recently sex role researchers have begun to do this, but the imbalance is still apparent.

The social embeddedness of research is a given. The distortions introduced by men studying men using male paradigms will not be solved by women studying women using only female (or male) paradigms. A creative and integrated "middle ground" has yet to be discovered.

Implications

The world of sex roles is a rapidly changing one: cognitively, emotionally, and behaviorally at the individual, group, and national levels. Each of us takes some position of the many available on the myriad issues engendered by shifts in public opinion and resistance to changes in sex roles. For most of us, most of the time, the position is not so much an ideal one as feasible. The centrality of sex role identity makes comfort an essential to continued human adaptation to changes in sex role ideology.

What is apparent, however, is that ignorance or indifference to sex role phenomena is increasingly untenable, and that reasoned sex role ideologies are difficult to structure and maintain. Rapid social change and knowledge generation have tended to create more quandaries than solutions. Health care professionals participate in all these currents and quandaries, whether by conscious choice or not.

Future Directions

Several immediate developments around sex role phenomena deserve special attention. They may serve as indicators of future developments during a period of rapid social change.

There is no doubt that during the last 20 years significant societal shifts have occurred in sex role values, beliefs, and activities. An objective assessment of these changes, however, demonstrates some uncertainty about outcomes. New problems emerge and scholars must address these problems.

When entire societies attempt to shift old, established attitudinal and behavioral norms, the results can evoke significant disorganization. Individuals socialized into a fairly rigid sex role ideology find that old beliefs and behaviors are not readily altered. Many women eager to challenge extant male dominance structures find themselves co-opted by these structures, utilizing male values to perpetuate male norms. They suddenly find themselves denigrating and debasing women and women's activities. Feminists who depict nurses as inferiors do this, but so also do nurse practitioners who practice medicine to achieve power and status, and so do nurse administrators who reward assertiveness more than nurturance. Masson (1981) and Newton (1981) have both reported their alarm at this trend, the implicit "masculinization" of nursing, with a concomitant abandonment of nursings' valuable feminine qualities.

When the obstacles to membership in a sex-structured group are removed, persons of either sex may become members. But new problems emerge. This is apparent in the sex-structured health professions. Although women are increasingly enrolling in medical schools (about 25 percent of medical students are women), they continue to cluster in specific specialties and avoid others (Beil, Sisk, & Miller, 1980; Harris & Conley-Muth, 1981). They tend to have values and operational styles not always compatible with the medical system and its supporting ideologies (Hammond, 1981). Conversely, men who enter nursing schools may find that they are viewed as uniquely problematic (Tumminia, 1981). They may find that their female nurse colleagues value their presence primarily for strength-related characteristics such as physically lifting clients (Cowan, 1981). Because some persons alter their sex role ideologies does not assure that others will. Nor will this be done at a uniform rate within groups or by gender groups. To date, men have changed more slowly than women.

As societal shifts occur, generational differences in sex role ideologies become more pronounced (e.g., Cox & Lewis, 1981; Moore, Conine, & Laster, 1980). Health professionals may find themselves struggling not so much with conflicting sex role ideologies between professional groups as much as conflicts within groups and between generations. Such conflicts prohibit internal professional cohesivness.

Finally, the difficult question of the changing and emerging relationships between men and women require scrutiny, since they too will influence the work and work environment of the health professional. A virtual deluge of contemporary popular press works evidences a serious societal uncertainty about this issue. Much of the current sex role research literature concerning relationships between men and women shows the scope of this preoccupation, with reports of explorations of partner intimacy (Levenson, 1984; Tesch, 1984; Waring & Reddon, 1983), communication and understanding between partners (Linder & Bauer, 1984; Litterst, 1983; Shamberg, 1985), and violence between partners (Richardson, Leonard, Taylor, & Hammock, 1985).

This sampling of new sex role problems may appear pessimistic in tone. There is also, however, reason for hope. New efforts to solve these quandaries emerge. The fact that sex role problems are readily identified and discussed is itself positive, and scholars are struggling for a more reasoned approach to the concerns outlined.

Two recent books exemplify this recent effort at a more balanced approach to sex role ideologies. Gilligan (1983) has developed a thoughtful, empirically grounded description of women's moral development, blending the work of Piaget, Freud, Erikson, and Kohlberg with her own insights and her investigations into women's moral decision processes. This effort to create bridges between male and female paradigms gives promise of generating new creative syntheses of utility for men and women. Her conclusion reflects this vision. She argues for a recognition of women's experiences.

> Through this expansion in perspectives, we can begin to envision how a marriage between adult development as it is currently portrayed and women's development as it begins to be seen could lead to a changed understanding of human development and a more generative view of life. (p. 174).

Edwin Schur (1984) utilizes extant sociological theories on labeling and deviance to analyze and explicate this perspective as it relates to women. He effectively weaves a picture of the uses of labeling of deviance as a backdrop for explicating women's societal experiences such as sexual harassment and prostitution. His starting point is that being a woman means being a deviant, i.e., one lacking status and identity, one who can be dealt with in depersonalized, categorical terms, and one who can be victimzed. He traces this back to prevailing gender norms and notes that they affect both men and women. He also argues for a more qualitative analysis of such phenomena, noting the masculine proclivity for quantification to assure apparent objectivity. His merger of existing male paradigms with emergent female paradigms demonstrates again the promise of more balanced syntheses which are human in character.

The work of both Gilligan and Schur, a woman and a man concerned about human issues, is but one example of a larger struggle toward a more balanced sense of human wholeness occurring in the latter half of the twentieth century (Capra, 1982). Changing sex roles are merely one symptom among several of a declining patriarchal structure, doubts about reductionistic scientific thought, and a renewed sensitivity to the fragility of the human environment and the planetary ecosystem. In that larger context one can anticipate continued change and adaptation. Health care providers in the aggregate will be one of several players in these changes. They may not initiate change but they inevitably will be called upon to change.

13

Role Attitudes and Opinions: A Measurement Alternative

Ada Sue Hinshaw

Role attitudes and opinions are subjective phenomena learned from social and cultural experiences. Such attitudes and opinions include preset ideas of what to expect from the performance or enactment of roles as well as evaluative judgments of completed role performance. In all cases the role attitudes and opinions represent subjective phenomena that are difficult to make operational or measure in the real world. Two questions are important: Why are social attitudes and opinions related to health care roles and role performance important to study? What are the problems in making operational such health care role phenomena?

At times the expectations of providers of health care and those of their clients may differ. This incongruency in the expectations can create conflict among health care providers and even negatively influence consumer satisfaction with care. In order to counteract the negative consequences arising from incongruency in role phenomena, it is necessary to understand and predict the various sets of expectations from different role perspectives. Understanding and prediction can be gained from studying the attitudes and opinions of individuals who occupy the various health care roles. A crucial problem, however, is the ability to measure and put into operation various attitudes and opinions concerning the expectations and performance of different health care roles in the real world. A major problem is measurement error. The traditional techniques for measuring subjective phenomena, such as attitudes and opinions about roles and role performance, result in a sizeable degree of measurement error. The error problem results from several conditions of the basic scaling strategies: i.e., the production of primarily ordinal level scales and the use of the scales in designs that do not control for intersubject or intrasubject variation on extraneous variables or factors.

In nursing science the measurement problem is of major concern in the generation and testing of nursing theories. The ability to test nursing practice theories as they are constructed depends on the availability and use of accurate measurement strategies and indices for making operational the nursing phenomena under study. The measurement strategies must provide valid, reliable, and sensitive instruments which result in minimal measurement error (Hinshaw, 1984). As long as measurement error remains high as a result of moderate reliability, questionable validity, and gross levels of measurement in terms of sensitivity, it is not possible to distinguish conceptual or specification error in the practice theory from measurement error in the instrument. Thus the building of nursing knowledge is impaired.

Magnitude scaling, a set of measurement strategies adapted to the social sciences and nursing from psychophysics, shows promise for handling the problem of measurement error with subjective phenomena such as role attitudes and opinions. Innovators of the technique suggest that measurement error is reduced by producing ratio level scales for subjective responses, such as attitudes and opinions, and by making operational the techniques within mathemetical designs. Correlational and experimental mathematical designs reduce error by holding conditions statistically constant, averaging out random measurement error arising from nonsystematic intersubject variation, and specifically testing for the function best fitting the data rather than assuming a linear function. In addition, magnitude scaling is put into operation through multiple modalities, such as giving numbers (magnitude estimation), drawing lines (line production), gripping a hand dynamometer (muscle force), or adjusting sound on an audiometer (sound pressure). Each of these modalities can be used to reflect the intensity of a subject's response in terms of attitudes and opinions. The type of modality can be matched to the capability of the subject population. For example, health care professionals use magnitude estimation easily while elderly, ill clients respond well using line production (Hinshaw & Oakes, 1977; Hinshaw & Schepp, 1983).

This chapter reviews the concept of role, summarizes the traditional scaling models and measurement methods for subjective phenomena such as role attitudes and opinions, delineates the theoretical paradigm and general measurement strategies for magnitude scaling, and discusses the sources of error and issues to consider when using magnitude scaling.

ROLE DEFINITIONS AND ORIGINS

Role, as a construct, has been consistently difficult to define and analyze systematically because of its multidimensional nature. As Neiman and Hughes (1951) noted in their classic survey of the use of the term *role*, it may be defined in terms of the personal dimension that deals with the dynamics of personality development or in terms of a structural dimension that speaks of social roles that are the functional units of systems, such as formal and informal groups of society in general.

A variety of perspectives has been adopted in relationship to roles, role performance, and role socialization. Conway (see Chapter 3) identifies two prominent perspectives, the functionalist and the interactionist approach. Hurley-Wilson (see Chapter 4) acknowledges the legitimacy of both approaches. As Conway states, "Social action [role expectation and performance] is constructed not simply as learned responses but as an organizing and interpreting of cues in one's environment" (1978, p. 18). Thus, several commonalities in the two orientations to role are evident: role always involves either an individual's definition of a specific situation or an individual's acceptance of a group's definition of a specific situation. In addition, both perspectives assume a process of interaction and communication (socialization) as a prerequisite to preparing the individual for enacting a specific role. It is the merged role theory perspective that is basic to this chapter on the measurement of role characteristics such as attitudes and opinions.

When considering health care roles, Scott's (1970) conceptualization is useful. He defines role as a "set of shared expectations focused upon a particular position; these expectations include beliefs about what goals the position incumbent is to pursue and the norms that will govern his behavior" (Scott, 1970, p. 58). The set of shared expectations evolve from the incumbent's socialization experiences and the values and attitudes internalized while taking and shaping the position as well as adapting to the expectations socially defined for the position.

A role consists of several components which include: values, attitudes, and behaviors (Linton, 1945). Values are defined as ideas held in common by members of a social structure, such as a group, that guide the identification and prioritizing of goals or objectives (Scott, 1970). Attitude is considered a tendency, a set, or a readiness to respond to social objects or events in the real world in terms of a favorable or unfavorable evaluation; opinion is defined as expressed attitude (Katz, 1960). According to Anderson et al. (1975), values generally refer to abstract but stable aspects of an individual's overall belief system, whereas attitudes are more specific and usually are indicative of the values held. Attitudes are assumed to guide role judgments and behaviors (although assumption of a relationship between role attitude and behavior is controversial). Behavior is defined as observable social acts performed by an individual. This chapter focuses on the more subjective components involved with roles such as values, attitudes, and opinions. Nunnally (1978) labels such phenomena *sentiments*.

Socialization Processes

Socialization for both child and adult is the process by which roles are defined by their occupants and by which occupants are able to learn and shape roles as well as accept society's definitions of a role. Hurley suggests there are several common characteristics of all socialization processes; i.e., "what is to be learned, how it is learned, why it is learned and what are the expected outcomes" (1978, p. 31). In addition, the process can be assumed to be either an active or a passive role for the socializee. The most current view, however, suggests an individual is active in the socialization process and both learns the role and shapes the role by responding to selective cues. The active view is consistent with the interactionist and integrated perspective of roles and role performance.

The learning of roles—socialization—is a two-pronged process. It involves (1) the internalization and shaping of specific values and attitudes and (2) the acquisition of skills for the enactment of appropriate behaviors. Operationally, the concept of socialization refers to individuals acquiring the necessary knowledge and skills, as well as internalizing and shaping the values and attitudes of a particular social system, in preparation for fulfilling a specific role in that system.

Thus, life roles that are to be enacted in society are learned. Early informal socialization prepares individuals to function in personal roles, such as woman or mother. In addition, formal educational processes and experiences provide the basic knowledge and skills that individuals require as prerequisite to adult socialization.

Individuals enact multiple roles in society in a variety of social systems. For example, a woman may be a daughter to her parent, a mother to her immediate family, and a professor to her students. These roles are interactive and an individual moves between them. Internalized values, attitudes, and learned behaviors accompany each of the roles. The interaction of such roles brings the values, attitudes, and behaviors into juxtaposition, continually forcing integration or generating conflict (Hurley, 1978; Kramer, 1974).

In attempting to study human behavior as exemplified in life roles, it is necessary to deal with how individuals define and subjectively judge their roles. Specifically, understanding and predicting the role behaviors of individuals occupying health care roles, such as patient, nurse, or other professionals, requires isolating certain identifiable aspects of each one's internalized role values as well as understanding one's attitudes and opinions. In addition, methods must be developed that will allow valid and reliable measurement of these role dimensions. As Biddle and Thomas (1979) note, in the field of role theory and research there is a strong reliance on the subjective self-reports of individuals occupying roles and being socialized into roles. Questionnaires of survey-type design dominate the reported research. Measurement of role values and attitudes is a complex process requiring a knowledge of scaling models, measurement strategies, and the issues of validity, reliability, and sensitivity.

Role attitudes and opinions, which are subjective social phenomena, have been extensively studied. The study of such role phenomena requires clear conceptual and operational statements of definition. The conceptual definition of a role attitude or opinion refers to the meaning the term or phrase has within an abstract theoretical system. An operational definition is specified for a concept by defining it in terms of a measurement instrument. In attempting to measure attitude, many studies use some form of self-report questionnaire or measurement scale to describe role attitudes or attitude formation and change. The purpose of such scales is to identify and quantify an individual's present attitudes and his or her possible change regarding a specific role object or event. Several methods or techniques have been developed for empirically quantifying role attitudes and opinions (Guttman, 1956; Likert, 1932; Thurstone & Chave, 1929). These methods are discussed after the general principles of attitude measurement are examined. An additional measurement method, magnitude scaling, is explored as a potentially useful scaling alternative for studying subjective phenomena such as role attitudes and opinions.

GENERAL PRINCIPLES OF ATTITUDE MEASUREMENT

The purpose of attitude measurement is twofold: to establish the existence of an attitude, and to establish its relative strength. Construction of a scale allows numerical quantification of an attitude. Such quantification leads to indexing attitude variables for the purpose of identifying the central patterns evident among many individual respondents. It is the central pattern from which researchers are able to explain and predict. For example, patients' attitudes toward the technical care they receive can be assessed by requesting a number of them to choose a single response from a set of terms which represent felt satisfaction states, ranging from strongly satisfied to strongly dissatisfied, related to a specific aspect of nursing care. The strongly satisfied to strongly dissatisfied categories can be converted to numbers. Then, by averaging or summarizing across the quantitative scale for all the respondents, the general attitude toward technical nursing care could be estimated.

Both the attitudinal phenomena and the process of measurement require further consideration. In measurement theory, attitude is defined as an " implicit cue-drive-producing response" to socially relevant characteristics that is basically evaluative in nature (Anderson et al., 1975, p. 32). The word *implicit* suggests an attitude or opinion inherent within an individual and the phrase *drive-producing* means that the attitude will tend to predispose an individual to form or hold certain expectations and act in a selective manner. The term *response* suggests that a behavior or judgment reflecting an attitude or opinion can be elicited by providing appropriate stimuli. *Appropriate stimuli* refers to socially relevant situations with which individuals have had experience. Lastly, the word *evaluative* in the definition of *attitude* suggests that such opinions are based on values held by individuals and will vary from positive to negative (Anderson et al., 1975).

The definition of *attitudes* in measurement terms does not conflict with the definition generally used in role theory literature. Both definitions speak of attitudes as predisposing individuals to certain expectations and behaviors, which in role theory can be understood in terms of expectations and behavior involved with role performance. In addition, both definitions emphasize the evaluative nature of attitudes. For example, Himmelfarb and Eagly (1974) suggest that operational measures of role attitudes scale the intensity of the opinions toward social (role) objects or events on a favorable to unfavorable dimension.

"In its broadest sense, measurement is the assignment of numerals to objects and events according to rules" (Stevens, 1952). The term *numerals* refers to the use of numbers (1,2,3, . . .) to describe a variable response. *Assignment* involves mapping the numerical response from one set of objects onto the response of another set. In attitudinal measurement, numerals representing the intensity of response to socially relevant stimuli are assigned to individuals according to their attitudinal responses on a measurement scale. The rules are the set of guidelines, that is, explicit instructions for assigning the intensity of attitudinal response to the social stimuli presented (Kerlinger, 1973). For example a rule might say:

> Assign the numerals 1 through 5 to nurses who have worked with you according to how satisfied you are with their care. If a nurse gives very good care, assign the number 5. If a nurse give very bad care, give the number 1.

In summary, the measurement definition of attitudinal phenomena dictates two key properties that are necessary in constructing a measurement scale. First, a measurement tool or scale must present the subject with a series of socially relevant stimuli so as to provoke an attitudinal response. Second, in order to assess the evaluation component, the scale must allow the individual to give the intensity of his response on a positive to negative dimension according to specific rules.

Accuracy of Measurement Scales

Several major conditions must be considered in constructing and using attitudinal measurement scales. These are validity, reliability, and sensitivity. The accuracy of the scales depends on these characteristics meeting certain criteria, which indicate measurement error has been minimized. Recall, high accuracy, and the minimization of measurement error are critical if theoretical model testing is to occur.

Validity. Validity is defined as the extent to which the scale measures the theoretical dimension it is constructed to measure. In other words, does the scale measure what it is intended to measure? For example, while a scale may be constructed to measure a client's perception of or satisfaction with the amount of teaching a nurse included in her care, *does* the scale measure that perception or satisfaction level? Among the kinds of validity generally considered with measurement scales are: face validity, content validity, criterion validity, predictive validity, and construct validity (American Psychological Association, 1974). Face validity, the weakest form of validity, consists of "eyeballing" or reviewing the scale in relation to the theoretical dimension it is constructed to measure and deciding that validity seems to exist. Content validity is the extent to which the scale represents the generally held consensus about the concept under measurement. This type of validity reflects primarily the degree to which the measurement tool contains the elements of the attitude that are agreed upon in the literature and by known experts in the field to make up the domain of the concept. Content validity can also be referred to as consensus validity, for the process involved with estimating content validity is often to determine the consensus of the literature or of a set of expert judges on the validity of the scale content. Criterion validity is the degree to which the scale under consideration correlates with other scales constructed and tested to measure the same attitude or concept.

Predictive and construct validities are relatively powerful and quite similar types of validity testing. As Kerlinger (1973) notes, the power of these forms of validity comes from their unification of "psychometric notions with theoretical notions." Predictive validity, a type of construct validity, is estimated by studying the degree to which defined theoretical concepts and predicted relationships are empirically substantiated (Cronbach & Meehl, 1955). It requires first, a clear definition of the concepts or variables under study and a prediction of their relationships and second, it is necessary to identify clearly the scales that will measure each concept. If the study data substantiate the predicted relationships, then the scale can be estimated to yield a valid measure of the concept (for an example see Hinshaw, Gerber, Atwood & Allen, 1982). In addition, construct validity may specify two types of relationships: (1) among constructs that should converge or be correlated positively and (2) among constructs that would be different or divergent. In the latter the construct measurements would correlate negatively or have no correlation. Initially, the constructs are defined and the convergent and discriminant relationships are specified. Multiple measurement scales may then be selected or created for each construct. Construct validity can be estimated to the degree that the study data substantiate the specified converging and diverging relationships among the theoretical variables and among the multiple indicators of each construct (Campbell & Fiske, 1959). Corroboration of predictive and construct validity can be obtained only through replication (Kerlinger, 1973).

Reliability. Reliability refers to the consistency with which individuals are ordered or scored on a measurement scale. "If no true change occurs in a given attitude an individual holds, does the attitude scale consistently yield the same ordering (or score) for him(her) relative to others?" (Bohrenstedt, 1970). Reliability is a matter of degree and generally can be defined and tested since "the greater the correlation between two parallel forms the greater the equivalence is presumed to be" (Bohrenstedt, 1970). Essentially, three types of reliability are estimated: stability, equivalence, and internal consistency (Mehrens & Lehmann, 1973). Stability refers to the degree to which an individual's score on an attitude scale varies from one measurement to another. The technique generally used to estimate stability is test–retest; that is, the testing is repeated. Equivalence refers to the degree to which several items in an attitude scale appear to measure the same theoretical underlying attitude. Equivalence is generally measured by using a two-form technique. Two forms of a test with equal content are given to individuals and the results are correlated (Mehrens & Lehmann, 1973). The focus of internal consistency tests is to estimate the degree of homogeneity of the items within the scale as well as the degree to which the item responses correlate with the total test score. (See Bohrenstedt, 1970; Kerlinger, 1973; and Mehrens & Lehmann, 1973, for detailed discussion of the conditions of validity and reliability and for the techniques used in their estimation.) A variety of techniques is used to estimate internal consistency; e.g., Kuder-Richardson estimates, coefficient alpha, and theta coefficients.

Sensitivity. Sensitivity is the level of measurement that can be assumed about the scale and the finiteness with which opinions can be given or recorded. Four levels of measurement are described by Stevens (1952): nominal, ordinal, interval, and ratio. For nominal scale measurement, attitudes can be determined to be in only one of several exhaustive, mutually exclusive categories. With ordinal data, in addition to being categorized an individual's attitudinal response can be ranked or ordered relative to other possible responses; i.e., to be greater than or less than a contrasting response. The interval level of measurement encompasses the categorical and ordering properties of the responses and also suggests there are equal intervals between the categories, each of which has an arbitrary beginning or zero point. The fourth level of measurement is a ratio scale, which includes all the properties of the nominal, ordinal, and interval levels in addition to possessing a zero point (Hamblin, 1971). Attitude measurement scales generally attain an ordinal level of measurement, although several techniques—the Thurstone scale, for example (Thurstone & Chave, 1929)—profess to have characteristics of interval scales as well.

If quantification of data is desired, then the highest possible level of measurement is preferable. The higher the level of measurement, the more information is available about the attitude under study and the more sensitively the attitude will be scaled. For example, an interval scale yields information about the type or category of attitude response, where it ranks relative to other possible responses, and asserts that there are equal intervals between the categories of possible responses. With greater amounts of information available about the attitudinal response, more precise and powerful statistical procedures can be utilized, e.g., correlation and regression statistics rather than lambda or gamma techniques.

In addition to level of measurement, the sensitivity characteristic refers to the finiteness with which the response can be scored on the attitudinal dimension. For example, a number of Likert scales are constructed on a one to five response continuum. Is this finite enough? One subject might feel moderately strong to strong about an item and respond with a five since a choice must be made between four and five. Another individual may feel very strongly about an item but still must answer five because that's the extreme end of the response range. Thus the same number is selected by the subjects to reflect opinions of differing intensity because of a lack of an adequate number of options and an inability to set their own upper range on the response continuum. In addition, the one to five response format forces subjects to choose one option when their true feelings about the item might be more sensitively reflected by using a fractional number in between one of the five options. Thus, the sensitivity of a measurement scale can provide a rather gross view of a subject's actual response.

The accuracy of information gained from attitude measurement depends on the assurance of validity, reliability, and sensitivity. With respect to validity and reliability, evidence of the degree to which these conditions are fulfilled in the scale needs to be reported. In terms of sensitivity, the goal is to use the highest level of measurement possible.

Traditional Methodologies for Role Attitude Measurement

Measurement of attitudes about roles is a measurement of subjective phenomena and therefore has been difficult to make operational. Two factors have contributed to the problem: the amount of measurement error involved in the scales for measuring attitudes about roles and the use of scales in designs that do not allow control over a number of extraneous variables. For example, the measurement of patient satisfaction with nursing care may be made by a Likert-type scale within the context of a quasi-experimental or descriptive design. The Likert scale at best can be assumed to yield interval data, although the researcher may question whether the data are only ordinal. In addition, validity and reliability estimates are necessary for the satisfaction scale for one to judge the degree of measurement error from those sources. The use of these scales in descriptive or quasi-experimental designs introduces another source of error that, when compounded with the measurement error from the scales, makes it very difficult to operationalize or tap the "real world" attitude that is of theoretical interest.

A number of scaling models and measurement methods have been used to index attitudes about roles and opinions. Three of the most popular are the models and methods of Thurstone and Chave (1929), Guttman (1956), and Likert (1932). The important issue to consider in selecting a scaling model is whether its characteristics will match the type of response the subject is being asked to give. For example, measuring the intensity of a subject's response is different from measuring his or her categorization of a phenomenon. Measuring the *intensity* of a response is defined as indexing a *prothetic* continuum whereas placing a response in a qualitative category is termed *metathetic* measurement (Hinshaw & Murdaugh, 1985; Perloe, 1963). If a prothetic or intensity measurement is indexed on an inappropriate scaling model, the measurement is gross rather than sensitive. Metathetic measures can be indexed on most scaling models without a loss of sensitivity for the index. Prothetic or intensity measures need to be instrumented using more sensitivity scaling models such as magnitude scaling (Perloe, 1963). All of the scaling models and measurement methods discussed can be used to construct self-report instruments for indexing verbalized attitudes or opinions.

Thurstone. Thurstone's method of equal-appearing intervals (Thurstone & Chave, 1929) is a technique for achieving interval-level scales. The scale items are constructed to measure an attitude on a positive-to-negative dimension, which assumes that the underlying theoretical attitude is continuous (Nunnally, 1978).

Thurstone's technique involves scaling predetermined attitudinal statements. Initially, a set of judges ranks a series of attitudinal statements from 1 (strongly negative) to 5 (strongly positive). The mean or median of the set of judgments is assigned to each attitudinal statement. These judgments locate each item on the positive-to-negative attitude continuum. Individuals whose attitudes are to be measured are asked to agree or disagree with the prejudged statements. Scores for each individual are obtained by adding the scale values preassigned to the statements from the judgment procedure (Anderson et al., 1975).

Guttman. The cumulative scale model suggested by Guttman (1956) approaches the measurement of attitudes differently. It is based on a deterministic characteristic that assumes there is no variation in the response to an attitudinal statement or set of statements. Statements for this scale are constructed as either highly positive, positive, negative, or highly negative, but any one statement presumably reflects only one predetermined attitude position. In a series of statements, if a respondent answers one statement as positive, he or she can then be predicted to answer the others in a similar manner (Nunnally, 1978).

Initially, attitudinal statements varying on a conceptual dimension are formulated. Subjects are asked to respond to the statements, after which the statements are analyzed to determine if they form a deterministic scale and can be arranged as theoretically constructed. In essence, the attitudinal statements are arranged in a hierarchical order such that an individual responding positively to one statement also responds positively to all other items ranking lower on the single conceptual dimension (Shaw & Wright, 1967).

Likert. Likert's method of summated rating (1932) directly scales individual attitudinal responses to social objects. This summative technique constitutes a linear model for scaling; i.e., the sum of the attitude statement scores has a linear relationship to the attitude under study and the model leads to a linear combination of items. These characteristics and their underlying assumptions are basic to the argument that scales based on this model can be assumed to produce an interval level of measurement. There is a lack of consensus, however, as to whether the scaling technique produces ordinal- or interval-level data.

Initially, a set of positive and negative attitudinal statements is formulated. The individuals whose attitudes are to be measured respond to each statement by using a multiple-point scale such as: 5, strongly agree; 4, agree; 3, not certain; 2, disagree; and 1, strongly disagree. Each statement is assigned a score of 1 to 5 depending on the response selected and the scores are then summed. The total scale score for an individual on the attitude is the sum of the statement scores (Anderson et al., 1975). Research suggests the Likert technique can provide data on attitudes equally as valid and reliable as can the Thurstone technique and with greater economy in terms of the time required for instruction and grouping of subjects and judgments (Barclay & Weaver, 1962; Nunnally, 1978).

According to Shaw and Wright (1967), each of these major techniques for attitude measurement yields satisfactory scales; however, controversy exists as to whether they include equality of intervals. Thus, all of these techniques may produce ordinal-level rather than interval-level measurement scales.

Magnitude scaling is a scaling model and measurement method developed in the field of psychophysics (Stevens, 1957). The method purports to yield a ratio level of measurement which is sensitive to small changes in prothetic or intensity responses of subjects. In addition, it is used within the context of mathematical correlational or experimental designs that allow the researcher increased control over extraneous variables. Because of these two features which decrease operational error, magnitude scaling has been adopted for use in the social sciences for the measurement of subjective phenomena such as attitudes about roles. The remainder of this chapter focuses on magnitude scaling as an alternative measurement method for subjective phenomena in nursing when the investigator wishes to index the intensity of a subject's responses. Two types of measurement strategies or modalities are discussed: magnitude estimation and line production.

PSYCHOPHYSICAL PARADIGM AND MAGNITUDE SCALING

The psychophysical scaling model and methods were developed to study the relation between physical properties of objects or stimuli and the sensory response they produce (Stevens, 1975). *Physical stimuli* refers to presenting respondents with varying levels of events or objects—such as degrees of sound, tactile stimulation, light—and asking them to judge the sensory response that is evoked. One basic characteristic of the physical stimuli used for each of these examples is that they are scaled on a ratio scale, e.g., degree of loudness is delivered to the respondent in terms of decibels of sound. The magnitude of the sensory sensation that is evoked has been measured in a variety of ways, including assigning a number to various degrees of response, drawing lines proportional to the sensation evoked, and squeezing a hand dynamometer to describe the intensity of response. These magnitude-judging techniques are among the best known and simplest techniques for constructing magnitude scales.

Developed in the field of psychophysics, the purpose of the magnitude scaling technique is to form a ratio scale mapping the magnitude of a sensory sensation to the magnitude of a physical stimulus for each individual subject. In the social sciences and in nursing, magnitude scaling has been used to produce scales describing subjective or attitudinal responses to socially relevant stimuli (Hamblin, 1974). The work with magnitude measurement techniques has evolved concurrently with study of the function of the relationship between sensory or subjective responses and physical or social stimuli.

Adaptation to Nursing and Role Phenomena

The social science adaptation of Stevens's research with the psychophysical law and the accompanying measurement strategies have been used by several nurse researchers in an attempt to index nursing staff and client subjective responses (Atwood & Hinshaw, 1977; Field & Hinshaw, 1977; Hinshaw & Field, 1974; Hinshaw & Oakes, 1977; Hinshaw & Schepp, 1983; Murdaugh, 1981; Murdaugh & Hinshaw, in press; Sennott, 1980). Hinshaw and Field (1974) indexed nursing staff's opinions on factors which influence their assignment of professional status to colleagues. Hinshaw, with various other investigators, has measured nursing staff and patients' opinions on definitions of quality care, intrusiveness of nursing care actions, and such behaviors needed to implement nursing care tasks. Murdaugh (1981) and Sennott (1980) have indexed factors which motivate and influence preventive health behaviors by using magnitude scaling strategies. Volicer (1973) has used magnitude measurement methods to develop scale values for the intensity of stress experienced with various hospitalization activities.

Subjective responses given by nurse and clients are often indicative of role attitudes and opinions. The definition of attitude as an implicit cue-drive-producing response qualifies the phenomena as a subjective response to certain socially relevant stimuli. This suggests that the relationship of role attitudes to social stimuli can (1) be described with the psychophysical paradigm as adapted to the social sciences and nursing and thus (2) be measured through the use of magnitude scaling devices, e.g., magnitude estimation. For example, studies determining subjective responses of nurses, doctors, or other health care workers to certain professionally (socially) relevant stimuli, such as their opinions of what defines quality health care, are tapping role attitudes and opinions reflecting professional socialization processes based on education and experience. Investigations focused on client attitudes and responses, such as their opinions of health care, tap cultural socialization processes and experiences of the patients. In such investigations, the psychophysical paradigm allows the researcher to identify the general attitude pattern of the collective group that reflects the values and norms of prior types of socialization.

Psychophysical Paradigm: Form of the Stimulus-Response Relationship

Since the 1930s, psychophysicist S. S. Stevens and his colleagues have conducted a number of experiments to determine the form of the relationship between sensory responses and physical stimuli (Stevens, 1957; Stevens & Mack, 1959). Their results consistently have indicated that a power function best describes the relationship:

$$\psi = \phi c^n$$

where the magnitude of the sensory response (ψ) increases as a power function of the magnitude of the physical stimuli (ϕ), with c and n as parameters that can be empirically estimated. By 1960, Stevens had documented the existence of this function between at least 22 sensory responses and their physical stimuli (Stevens, 1975). These studies used magnitude scaling techniques for producing ratio level data. From this base of research, Stevens postulated the power law of psychophysics, i.e., the magnitude of sensory responses increases as a power function of the magnitude of the physical stimuli (Stevens, 1957). Stevens suggests the power function is a necessary consequence of the ratio invariance: "Equal stimulus ratios produce equal perceptual or sensation ratios" (Stevens, 1966).

Psychophysical Paradigm Adapted to Social Sciences

One of the first generalizations of Stevens's psychophysical methods and theory to the relationship between social stimuli and subjective attitudinal responses was by Hamblin, Bridger, Day, and Yancy (1963), who were investigating the influence of interference on aggressive behaviors and produced measureable amounts of interference and frustration in the subjects. The subjective aggression responses were scaled using magnitude scaling techniques. The form of the relationship between interference and frustration and aggression was best described by the power function. Using magnitude scaling techniques for the variables under study, Hamblin (1974), Hamblin and Smith (1966), Rainwater (1972), and Shinn (1969) have further substantiated the generalization of Stevens's psychophysical law to social stimuli and subjective responses. In addition, a series of studies indirectly substantiating the power law phenomenon between social stimuli and attitudinal responses were summarized by Stevens (1966). These studies examined subjective preferences for wristwatches, aesthetic value of music, seriousness of criminal offenses, and levels of punishment.

From these earlier studies, Hamblin and Smith (1966) suggested a general form of the power relationship or power law:

$$R = cS^n$$

where the magnitude of any conditioned response (R) increases as a power function of the eliciting stimulus (S), with c and n as parameters that can be empirically estimated. In addition, Hamblin and Smith (1966) suggested that the power law phenomenon governing behavioral stimulus response relationships could be logically extended to the multivariate form:

$$R = cS_1{}^n1 \times S_2{}^n2 \ldots S_k{}^nk$$

where the magnitude of the response (R) will be a multivariate power function of the magnitudes of the eliciting stimuli ($S_1, S_2 \ldots S_k$).

Their hypothesis concerning the multivariate power relationship was subsequently supported in several studies on values, status, and professors (Hamblin & Smith, 1966), and components of national power (Shinn, 1969). Shinn (1969) contends the power law phenomenon can be expected to describe relationships in at least two classes of response variables: (1) those reflecting cultural conditioning and (2) those reflecting technical expertise or educational conditioning. Like Stevens (1966), Shinn labels these "consensus" variables, for they reflect group values and norms, not merely individual perceptions and standards. The components of general status are examples of the cultural conditioning category of consensus variables. The subjective responses to social stimuli, such as amount of income, types of occupations, and levels of education, can be generated by a variety of subjects because such responses are based on cultural conditioning (e.g. college students and navy seamen, Hamblin, 1974; and adults in metropolitan Boston, Rainwater, 1972). Shinn's (1969) "Components of National Power" study serves to illustrate the second type of consensus relationship because educational expertise was necessary for an individual to give opinions on the political stimuli.

Magnitude Estimation and Line Production Strategies

Magnitude estimation and line production are two of the most useful of the magnitude scaling methods for producing ratio scales because of their relative simplicity. Essentially, the scaling methods ask subjects to estimate the apparent strength of the intensity of their sensory responses relative to a set of stimuli (Stevens, 1960). The magnitude estimation strategy requires the subjects to give numbers to describe the intensity of their responses, whereas line production asks subjects to draw lines, with the length of line matching the intensity of response.

Hamblin (1974) and Stevens (1975) suggest magnitude scaling strategies should be used in conjunction with mathematical experimental or correlational designs. Hamblin suggests that it is generally recognized that ratio measurement is in many ways superior to lower levels of measurement; however, such power is limited in anything less than the mathematical experiment (1971). The conditions necessary for a mathematical experiment are summarized as: (1) manipulation of one or many independent variables, (2) control by constancy (all subjects respond to all research treatments or independent variables), (3) simultaneous ratio measurements of all independent and dependent variables (magnitude scaling), (4) averaging out of random measurement error, and (5) summarization of the relationship(s) between variables with the best-fitting algebraic equation(s). If condition (1) cannot be fulfilled, then the design is one of mathematical correlation.

Constructing instruments through magnitude scaling requires the identification of (1) a set of social stimuli, (2) a population of appropriate respondents or subjects, (3) identifying operational definitions for the attitudinal variables under study, (4) training the respondents to give proportional judgments, and (5) having all subjects on all the attitudinal variables give numbers or draw lines to describe their subjective reactions to the set of stimuli.

Set of Social Stimuli. Two models have been used to provide the set of social stimuli; i.e., either a list of objects or events or a list of people to be judged on the attitudinal variables. Several basic principles must be observed in constructing the social stimuli set. As in general attitude measurement, the stimuli must be clearly and concisely stated so as to decrease the "noise" in the stimulus. Social stimuli tend to be quite noisy; they contain multiple cues including cues the researcher does not intend. The stimuli need to be precisely stated in order not to be confusing to the respondents. Another principle needs to be considered; the set of stimuli must vary on at least one major attitudinal dimension under study. If all the stimuli in the set evoke neutral responses or all evoke extreme responses, there will be no variation in attitudinal responses. The magnitude judgments assume the sets of stimuli vary and can be scaled on an empirical range. A series of pretests is necessary to clarify the social stimuli and insure their variation.

Appropriate Respondents. Not everyone is an appropriate subject for magnitude scaling strategies. The crucial criterion to be satisfied in selecting a group of respondents or subjects is that they possess the knowledge or experience needed to give the required judgments and that the subjects have a common socialization experience. As was noted earlier, magnitude scaling depends on prior conditioning—cultural, educational, or both. For example, if patients are to judge nurses on the quality of care the nurses give, they must have experience in the patient role as well as knowledge of the nurses to be judged. If nurses are to judge a set of patient care tasks in terms of the tasks' professional complexity, they must have experienced prior professional nursing socialization.

Another question to consider in adapting psychophysical measurement is: What size sample or population of respondents is desirable? Essentially, the focus is on identifying the central or general pattern of responses across a group. The researcher is confronted with the problem of how large a sample is necessary to identify such a pattern. Hamblin and Smith (1966) suggest that samples should include 20 to 30 respondents. A smaller sample is permissible if the socialization process underlying the responses is strong, i.e., includes cultural and educational socialization. If the socialization base is relatively weak, then the sample size needs to be larger (Hinshaw & Murdaugh, 1985). Prior research suggests that samples numbering 60 or more are solid with more heterogeneous groups.

Operational Definitions. Broad definitions are constructed for each attitudinal variable to be measured. Although the definitions contain only one theoretical dimension to be measured or scaled, they are developed broadly so as to stimulate subjective valuing or attitudinal processes from prior conditioning. For example, a definitional cue used by Hinshaw and Murdaugh (1985) when doing magnitude scaling reads:

> Task Complexity: Some patient care tasks are more complex and require more professional knowledge, skill, and experience than others—others are relatively simple.

Note that the definitional cue is deliberately broad but contains only one conceptual dimension to be judged or scaled. One of the major problems with magnitude estimation and line production as used in the social sciences is the difficulty of defining precisely attitudinal variables so as to insure that there is a single conceptual dimension to be scaled and, simultaneously, being able to leave the operational definitions fairly broad. Several pretests are usually necessary before the definitions are clearly defined so as to contain only one dimension.

Training Session. Magnitude scaling requires that respondents or subjects be able to give judgments of proportional degrees on the set of social stimuli. In order to insure that subjects are prepared to give this type of judgment, a training session should be conducted. The judgments elicited in the training sessions are given in response to a physical metric so they can be confirmed by the investigator. Several methods have been used for training purposes (Hinshaw & Field, 1974). The following protocol has been used in several studies to train subjects:

> Let's work first on the method by which I'd like you to give your responses. For these responses, I'd like you to be thinking in proportional terms. Now, this may sound simple and rather silly, but to be sure we are together in our thinking, let's practice with a few numbers, OK?
> Given the number 10, I'd like you to give me a number:
> Twice as large (20)
> Half as large (5)
> One-third as large (3.3)
> Five times as large (50)

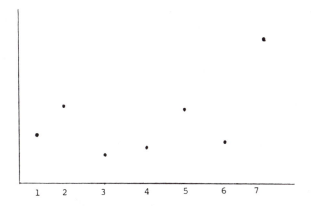

Figure 1. Seven-point graph used in training subjects to make proportional judgments. No scale on the y axis was presented to subjects. The investigator judged respondent's estimate against centimeter markings on the y axis. From Hinshaw, *Professional Decisions: A Technological Perspective.* Unpublished doctoral dissertation, University of Arizona, 1975.

Now, note what you have done. You have given all these numbers in proportion or in relationship to the first number, 10; i.e., 20 is twice as large as the first number and five is one half as large, etc.

Let's practice for a few more minutes, thinking in proportional terms. Take a look at Figure 1. There are seven points on this graph. Point 1 is 10 units above the base line. If point 1 is 10 units above the base line, then how many units above is each of points 2 through 7?

The graph was presented to the subjects on a five-by-eight card. The correct responses were: 1 = 10; 2 = 16; 3 = 6; 4 = 7.5; 5 = 15; 6 = 9; 7 = 30.

The subjects gave numerical estimates, that were plotted on log–log coordinates in relationship to the actual physical measurement from the baseline, which is consistent with work by Hamblin (1974). If the estimates given by a subject varied markedly from a straight line on the log–log coordinates, then an additional training session was conducted. Thus, the training session had the advantage of allowing the subject to visualize his or her progress through the use of the graph.

The training session is crucial because the ability to produce magnitude scales depends on the use of the proportional judgment technique. If the researcher suspects later in the measurement protocol that proportional judgments are not being given, the training session can be repeated.

Lodge (1981) recommends another type of training session. He suggests the training judgments be reversed between two modalities based on a known physical metric scale. For example, have the subjects judge a series of lines of known length as stimuli and give numerical or magnitude estimation responses. Then reverse the procedure with a set of numbers serving as the stimuli and the subject drawing lines (line production) to describe the intensity of the number. Lodge suggests the data from the training session can serve a second purpose: i.e., estimating the degree of regression bias in the judgments of subjects. This idea is considered further in the section on sources of error.

Attitudinal Variable Scaling. All subjects should judge the set of social stimuli on all independent, dependent, and control variables in random order (control by constancy principle). Magnitude scaling or proportional judgments are given on the set of social stimuli for each variable. The numbers assigned to each stimulus or length of the line drawn form the respondent's scale for the variable. The ratio or proportional concept requires the respondent to select a standard or average stimulus for each variable, such as professional complexity. That standard stimulus is assigned an arbitrary number of units that is easily treated in calculating proportions or ratios, e.g., 10, 60, 100, etc. If line production is used, then a standard line of 10 mm or 60 mm is given instead of the numerical estimate. Then all the remaining stimuli are judged (give numbers or draw lines) in relation to the standard; twice as much equals 20, 120, 200, respectively, and one half as much equals 5, 30, or 50. The attitudinal variables and the set of social stimuli are presented to each respondent or subject in a random order. This is done in order to counter any systematic initial excitement, fatigue, or ordering bias (Poulton, 1977).

A set of instructions is given to the respondents to direct their magnitude scaling efforts. For example, Hinshaw and Murdaugh (1985) gave the following set of instructions to their subjects as they judged 13 patient care tasks on the basis of several professional variables using magnitude estimation.

> I would like for you to use the same technique in judging the placement of a set of care activities on two characteristics. I will present you with a set of 13 cards, each one containing the description of an activity. You will be asked to judge these activities according to two characteristics. You are to take a professional orientation to the activities and consider both the techniques involved and the judgments required for their implementation and modification.
>
> Here is a list of the care activities; take a minute to read through it before we start. (pause) With each characteristic, you will be asked to select one of these activities as an average task. It will be assigned 60 units, just like in the training session. Then, you will be asked to judge the other 12 tasks in proportion to the average activity. For example, if you think an activity has more of the characteristic than the average activity, then assign more units. If you think it has less of the characteristic, give it fewer units. In other words, assign higher or lower numbers to the tasks to reflect your judgment of the characteristic in relation to the average. If the activity has none of the characteristic, give it a 0.
>
> *Complexity*: Some patient care activities are more complex and require more professional knowledge, skill and experience than others—others are relatively simple.
>
> *Control*: You have more control over some care activities than others—with some you have less control.
>
> Select one activity which has an average amount of complexity/control in your judgment. Investigator has subject select the standard stimulus. (Place activity card for stimulus in front of subject.) This activity has an average or standard of the number 60. I want you to judge each of the remaining activities against the standard. One-by-one, tell me each of the numbers you choose to represent the activities.

The magnitude scaling method described using the magnitude estimation and line production strategies encompasses the original dicta used by Stevens in psychophysics. Field and Hinshaw (1977) summarize these as adapted for the social sciences.

1. Start the measurement series by asking the subject to select a standard stimulus condition whose level of magnitude is in the middle of the stimulus range
2. Present other variable stimuli that are both above and below the standard
3. Call the standard by a number, such as 10, 60, or 100, or a standard line of 6 or 10 mm, that is easily multiplied and divided
4. Assign a number or line to the standard only and leave the subject completely free to decide what to call the rest of the stimuli
5. Use only one standard in any experiment (an arbitrary number)
6. Randomize the order of presentation of the stimuli
7. Keep the experimental session as short as possible or give breaks periodically
8. Allow the subject to present the stimuli to him- or herself
9. Use a group of subjects large enough to produce a stable median

These instructions and the magnitude scaling methods can be used either with individuals in private interviews or in a group. In a group, the most difficult aspect of the protocol is the random ordering of both variables and sets of stimuli for all subjects.

Validity and Reliability

When using magnitude scales, two types of validity checks have been conducted: (1) the validity of the ratio properties of the instruments produced and (2) construct validity in terms of the instrument's indexing the concept it was assumed to measure. Several types of reliability strategies have been used with magnitude scaling.

Validity. The issue of validity of the ratio scales has been questioned because the use of magnitude scaling in nursing and the social sciences often violates the basic premise under the power law. The premise is: Equal stimulus ratios produce equal sensory ratios. In psychophysics, the stimuli are usually scaled on a physical metric: e.g., sound pressure is measured in decibels. In nursing and the social sciences, however, the stimuli are more complex, often consisting of words and phrases that can have multiple meanings. In addition, the stimuli may lend themselves to an ordinal level of measurement. Thus, the question has been raised: Will response scales with ratio properties be produced under the condition of violating the "equal stimuli ratios" premise?

To test the production of ratio scales with magnitude scaling in the social sciences and nursing, Hinshaw and Murdaugh (1985), and Lodge, Cross, Turskey, et al., (1976), have replicated the original research in psychophysics. Using a cross modality model adapted to the social sciences, subjects were asked to use several modalities to judge social stimuli. If the response scales created on the modalities possessed ratio properties, then three criteria would be met: (1) the response scales produced on the several modalities would correlate highly, $r = 0.95$ or higher, (2) the correlation plots would be linear in logarithmic space, and (3) the empirical exponents generated from data could be predicted via a mathematical formula using the characteristic psychophysical exponents for each modality. If ratio scales do not exist, then the mathematical predictions would not correspond to those generated empirically from the data.

In the Hinshaw and Murdaugh (1985) cross modality study, 90 registered nurses were asked to judge 13 nursing care activities (social stimuli) on the concept of professional complexity. These judgments were made on three modalities: magnitude estimation, line production, and static muscle force (hand grip). In terms of the ratio scale criteria, the correlations among the modalities were $r = 0.94$ to 0.99. The plotted correlations were linear in log–log space for all modalities. In addition, for six matches of the empirical to predicted exponents, all six were alike. Thus the use of magnitude scaling with nursing stimuli and concepts was substantiated as producing instruments with ratio properties.

When considering the validity of the concept/instrument relationship, validity is usually estimated with such traditional strategies as face, content, criterion, and construct techniques. Face and content techniques have been used primarily to clarify and estimate the content of social stimuli sets when objects or events make up the set. Validity of the operational definitions is estimated usually through predictive modeling and other construct validity techniques, as magnitude estimation and line production are generally used in a mathematical design to test theoretical models with predicted relationships.

Reliability. Reliability is not addressed explicitly by either Lodge (1981) or Hamblin (1974). Nursing investigators have experimented with strategies for estimating reliability. Reliability is generally approached through the use of test–retest techniques. A major disadvantage of the test–retest technique is memory bias: i.e., the respondent remembers what he or she answered in the initial test and deliberately repeats that decision, thus giving a biased, inflated reliability score. When using magnitude scaling methods, however, this source of bias is minimized because the respondents are making approximately 100 judgments (judging 10 to 16 stimuli on 6 to 10 variables) in a random order in both the test and retest period. Under these conditions, the likelihood of recalling the judgment on any one stimulus with any one variable is minimized. In Hinshaw and Schepp's (1983) study of the effect of intrusion on the recovery patterns of elderly clients, the test–retest coefficients on seven variables ranged from $r = 0.90$ to 0.99. Retesting 45 registered nurses on their judgments of the professional complexity of 13 nursing care activities provided a coefficient of $r = 0.96$. Thus, the test–retest reliability on magnitude scaling tends to be quite strong; approximately $r = 0.90$ or higher.

Analysis Protocol for Magnitude Scaling Data

The general protocol for analyzing data using magnitude scaling methods consists of standardizing the data methodologically, averaging out random measurement error, logarithmically transforming the averaged data, and then using apropriate statistics—statistics that require assuming linearity of the data. The production of data is standardized through the instructions given to the respondents. They are asked to select an average stimulus from the set of social stimuli that is assigned an arbitrary number (e.g., 10, 60, 100). This average becomes the standard against which all other stimuli are proportionally judged.

The data from individual respondents are usually averaged because the researcher is primarily interested in identifying the general attitudinal or consensus pattern based on the respondent's socialization and conditioning background. This requires averaging or obtaining a "central tendency" statistic: i.e., the geometric mean or the median. In attempting to identify a central pattern, nonsystematic individual variations and preferences can be considered random error that needs to be eliminated in order to reveal the general pattern. Thus, all subjects' responses to each stimulus on each attitudinal variable are averaged to a set of geometric means or medians. The set of geometric means or medians becomes the basic data base with which further analysis is conducted.

One characteristic of data obtained by magnitude scaling and described by a power function is that it is linear in log–log space (Stevens, 1966). Thus, the basic set of data needs to be logarithmically transformed before linear statistical techniques can be utilized.

This section has reviewed the procedures involved in using magnitude scaling methods. In summary, several procedural elements are required for the use of magnitude estimation and line production; i.e., a set of social stimuli, a population of appropriate respondents as subjects, a set of broad operational definitions for the study variables, a structured training plan, and a procedure that allows all subjects to respond to all the variables in relation to the social stimuli. These elements are operationalized in correlational or experimental mathematical designs. The sensitivity of the scales produced by magnitude scaling is maximized (ratio-level scales) and variation from intrasubject variation is decreased by averaging the data obtained from individual respondents.

Sources of Error: Magnitude Scaling

A number of issues evident with magnitude scaling need to be acknowledged, as these can become sources of error. The issues to be considered are: (1) prothetic versus metathetic continuum, (2) ambiguity of social stimuli, (3) regression bias, and (4) fixed versus open range (Lodge, 1981; Poulton, 1977). Each issue will be discussed in terms of the problems that can be created and strategies for handling the difficulties posed.

Prothetic versus Metathetic Continua. Sensory and subjective responses to stimuli vary in terms of kind. A major distinction must be made between continua that deal with quantitative versus qualitative judgments or responses. Another way of phrasing the distinction is magnitude versus kind. According to Stevens, "the prototypes of the two kinds of perceptual continua are exemplified by loudness and pitch" (1975, p. 13). In sound, degree of loudness illustrates the concept of magnitude or intensity, whereas pitch references a "kind" of position or a qualitative point on a continuum. The intensity type of continuum is labeled prothetic; the qualitative one is termed metathetic. Sensory or subjective responses given on a prothetic continuum are described as a "degree of" concept and responses on a metathetic continuum are a "kind of" and measure concepts that deal with "what" and "where" (Ekman, 1961).

One strategy that can be used to estimate whether a prothetic or a metathetic continuum exists is to plot the subject responses to the stimuli on two scaling models, such as Likert and magnitude estimation on semi-log coordinates. If the prothetic continuum exists then the Likert arithmetic means and magnitude estimated medians will form a linear line or "fit" to the data. A metathetic continuum exists under the data when a curvilinear plot is evident between Likert means and magnitude medians.

Either of the two types of continua can be described using magnitude scaling, however, a less sensitive scale will result if nonmagnitude scaling is used with prothetic continua, such as Likert or Guttman. Conversely, magnitude scaling does not need to be used with metathetic continua. One can choose among several scaling models. Knowing whether a response is based on a prothetic or a metathetic continuum assists the investigator in choosing which type of scaling model to use under the different conditions.

Ambiguity of Social Stimuli. One problem to consider in magnitude scaling is the ambiguity of social stimuli. Social stimuli must fit the characteristics outlined for any scale item (Nunnally, 1978). As such, each stimulus should contain only one cue for the subject to respond to and be clear in its wording. On the other hand, the psychophysical paradigm requires that social stimuli be broad enough to elicit a subject's socialization background and thus give a socialized response. Lodge (1981) and Hinshaw (1978) comment that social stimuli are clearly more ambiguous than physical stimuli.

To decrease ambiguity requires clarifying the social stimuli as much as possible. This clarification process involves pretesting the stimuli in one or several pilot studies before proceeding with the major investigation (Lodge, 1981). This process provides the opportunity for interviewing subjects on the clarity of the stimuli and assessing whether subjects with homogeneous characteristics respond essentially alike (Hinshaw, 1978).

Regression Bias. In making subjective responses with magnitude estimation and other ratio scaling methods, subjects tend to show regression bias. Regression bias is defined as a "tendency of a respondent to drift toward a set of mean responses" (Lodge et al., 1976, p. 161). In essence, the empirical values tend to underestimate higher subjective values and overestimate lower values. This bias is evident in category scaling as well but introduces a special problem with ratio scaling. With a less refined type of measurement system regression bias can be tolerated, but with the stronger measurement systems it must often be corrected.

Correction of the regression bias can be made under certain specified conditions: (1) the two response modality scales correlate at $r = \geq 0.95$, (2) response modalities are linearly related in log–log coordinates and thus fit a power function, and (3) the direction of bias is the same for the two response modalities. Thus, if the data can be assumed to be best described by the power function, the correction for regression is appropriate. Such correction will bring the empirical scale values into a closer fit with what can be assumed to be the true values (Lodge, 1981, p. 55).

A calibration procedure suggested by Lodge (1981, p. 44) can be used to provide the data needed to correct for regression bias. Essentially, the calibration procedure requires that magnitude estimation or the assigning of numbers be conducted with a series of line length stimuli. The process is then reversed with lines drawn (line production) to express a subject's responses to a series of stimuli numbers. These lines provide data to judge the degree to which greater stimuli are underestimated and lesser stimuli are overestimated. Correction procedures can then be utilized (Lodge, 1981, p. 54). Lodge also uses this procedure for training subjects to give proportional judgments.

Limited versus Open Range with Stimuli. Perloe (1963), in his comparison of category scaling to magnitude scaling, investigated the effect of subjects setting a limit on the upper and lower ranges of the magnitude scales. The two scales (category and ratio) behaved as expected for the "open range" subjects but not as predicted for subjects who limited the range. Thus, it is important to designate those subjects who "fix" or "limit" the range when using ratio scaling. According to Perloe (1963), "fixing" the range is a violation of the ratio method; thus, the technique is not really made operational. Both Hamblin (1971) and Lodge (1981) discuss training procedures for obtaining ratio-scaled responses and for countering a possible subject tendency to limit the subjective response range. In addition, confirmation can be requested of subjects post interview as to whether they had a "top" in mind for their range of judgments. The existence of a power function for the data can then be examined for all subjects with an upper range versus an open range.

SUMMARY

Nursing investigations often involve the measurement of subjective attitudes and opinions related to health care roles. Frequently, subjective and attitudinal questions are asked, as for example: What attitudes basically guide the delivery of health care? or, for a client: What constitutes quality health care? Understanding and predicting answers to these questions is hindered by the inherent difficulty of putting into operation or measuring role attitudes and opinions in the empirical or real world. The measurement of role attitudes is likely to be biased because of several basic sources of error, i.e., measurement error due to level of scale measurement and design problems from intersubject error. This chapter has presented the general strategies of magnitude scaling and mathematical designs used in the study of subjective phenomena. Magnitude scaling strategies have been compared to other traditional measurement techniques.

Magnitude scaling, a measurement method adapted to the social sciences from psychophysics, shows promise for coping with several of the traditional sources of error in attitude measurement. This technique can increase the sensitivity of measurement by producing ratio level scales. Further, the technique is used in the context of mathematical design, which can decrease error caused by intersubject variation.

14

The Sick Role

Afaf Ibrahim Meleis

INTRODUCTION

Health and illness status of an individual can be measured from a variety of theoretical perspectives. The medical model is one such perspective; it focuses on biological and physiological structure and function of the organism. When we wish to take into consideration the entire gamut of experiences associated with illness and health, e.g., patterns of recognizing and labeling symptoms, patterns of help-seeking behavior and social functioning, then a different framework is required—one that makes it feasible for us to describe, explain, or predict variations in the illness experience. Role theory could be such a framework. It is useful in generating propositions which, when subjected to empirical testing, may help increase our understanding of the health and illness experiences.

Nurse–client interactions in the context of social structure can be conceptually organized into roles. Such organization permits description, explanation, and a certain degree of predictability. Nurse–client interactions within the context of health and illness include two central roles, the sick role and the at-risk-role. Both these roles are enacted in relationship to a number of counter roles enacted by members of the health team as well as by significant others. When clients master the performance or enactment of either of the roles, they are considered to be complying with or adhering to the clinical prescription that is designed to treat illness or maintain or promote health (Dracup & Meleis, 1982).

When clients are not able to enact either of the roles, role insufficiency is the result. Role supplementation, a nurse therapeutic strategy, is proposed to help clients and significant others in their role transitions toward enacting the sick and at-risk roles. Each of these concepts is discussed in this chapter using symbolic interaction as the guiding framework.

THE SICK ROLE

Although the "special position" of the sick person was first considered in 1929 by Henry Seigrist (1960), the concept of sick role was coined by Talcott Parsons

365

(1951), who has been given credit for developing the concept. To Parsons, sick role evolves out of role theory and is defined in terms of rights and obligations. Illness is considered a form of deviance, the nature of which is different from that inherent in criminal roles in several ways. Unlike the latter, becoming sick is not instigated by a person's motivation, nor should the person be responsible for his or her sick actions. Also, unlike with criminal roles, society is expected to accept the sick role as long as the person continues to accept four conditions. The ill person is:

1. Obligated to seek help and cooperate with the help being given
2. Obligated to want to get well and admit that sickness is undesirable
3. Exempted from usual tasks and from moral responsibilities for becoming sick (providing that the ill person accepts patient status)
4. Entitled to competent technical help

Most significant in these conditions is the obligation of the person to abdicate all responsibilities while taking the responsibility to seek competent help, to want to get well, and to try to do so by following the prescribed clinical regimen. It is important to note, however, that Parsons's definition releases the person from any responsibility for having gotten sick as well as from any ability to self-heal.

Validation of the sick role is twofold. Society must validate the relinquishment of usual responsibilities and the health care system must validate the status of illness. When those two conditions are present, then the sick role is legitimate and can be assumed by an individual. "Provisional validation" may be granted by a person's lay referral system until legitimation occurs by competent professionals—the physician, according to Parsons (Suchman, 1965a, b). Parsons's view of the sick role is a structural–functional one representing a sociological school of thought that adheres to expectations and actions that are primarily dictated by the norms of the social structure. There are problems with this school that may have limited the utility of Parsons's sick role concept. Critics of Parsons and the sick role have identified several problematic empirical and conceptual issues.

One such issue is that enactment of a new role is dynamic and developmental in nature, yet Parsons's conceptualization of the sick role lacks a temporal dimension and suggests it is possible only to enact or not enact a sick role (Hover & Inglsgood, 1978). Another issue is that people may identify and enact sick roles in a variety of ways (Twaddle, 1969). Yet, Parsons's conceptualization indicates there is only one type of sick role (Coser, 1962; Suchman, 1965a). A third issue is the difficulty in demonstrating the sick role empirically (Idler, 1979; Twaddle, 1969), and existent research has been done in a noncumulative or unsystematic way (Becker, 1979b). A further issue is that Parsons's conceptualization incorporates a dimension of seeking professional care and legitimization of the role of the sick by a professional as conditional to one's assuming and enacting the sick role. Mechanic (1972, 1978) questioned these prerequisite conditions and demonstrated that individuals vary in their perceptions and interpretations of symptoms and, although taking differing actions that may or may not include medical treatment, they still may enact a sick role.

Parsons appears to view patients as helpless victims of illness who have to take responsibility only for seeking care, while remaining the subordinate member of the patient–physician dyad. With changing health care values, the declining of physicians' authority, and an increase in consumerism and patient advocacy in the

United States, patient responsibility and legitimation of sick roles may have acquired a different meaning. The extreme gap between the competent professional's authority and the client's subordination that appears to permeate the early definition of the sick role may not apply under more contemporary values. Prevailing values about health care, therefore, may not require illness validation by physicians in order for an individual legitimately to assume the sick role; indeed, the role may be validated once the individual decides to seek such legitimation.

Empirical data support the shift away from this notion of validation (Haug & Lavin, 1979; Wolinsky & Wolinsky, 1981). Two patterns of sick role legitimization have been demonstrated by Wolinsky and Wolinsky (1981). Persons who expect sick role legitimization by a professional tend "to be older, less educated, poorer and are less likely to be white or to have health insurance coverage" (p. 239). The other pattern is related to the differences between those who expect legitimation and get it (winners), and those who expect it but do not get it (losers). The winners are more likely to maintain contact with a regular physician than are the losers; they apparently visit a physician fairly regularly and have shorter intervals between appointments than do the losers.

Acquiring the sick role, from a structuralist's view, makes it appear to be a one-step process. Once the four conditions—abdication of responsibilities, seeking competent help, being motivated to get well, and receiving validation for illness—are met, a person acquires a sick role. Although this view includes some form of dynamic interaction, i.e., the need for validation and legitimization, it is nevertheless, a static and one-dimensional view of reality, closer to the traditional sociological view that considered position, status, and role as synonymous (Linton, 1936). It has become evident that role learning, role acquisition, and role relinquishment are not static processes; rather, that they are dynamic, complex, multidimensional, and continuous (Blumer, 1962; Hadley, 1967; Thornton & Nardi, 1975; Turner, 1978). Some roles are integrated with oneself, others are compartmentalized, and still others are never adopted. The latter may occur even when a person has been occupying a position for some time. Changing societal values also may have influenced conceptions of the sick role. Competent professionals include more practitioners than physicians; validation may not be limited to the physician and choosing a mode of treatment may encompass self-healing or alternative treatment modalities to those dictated by western medicine. Even relinquishment of one's responsibilities is dynamic, fluid, and contingent upon many conditions; it may be advisable in some situations and not advisable in others.

INTERACTIONIST SICK ROLE

Some of the conceptual limitations of the sick role may be ameliorated when role is considered from an interactionist perspective. Whereas Parsons provided the link between roles and health, the interactionist perspective provides a framework more congruent with the assumptions that guide nursing practice, as is discussed below.

The interactionist perspective maintains that the sick role evolves from the interactions of a person with the social system of which he or she is a part, and those interactions are important in the acquisition, modification, and enactment of roles. Role evolves out of every designated reciprocity in which an interaction or an exchange takes place (Stryker, 1980). Roles are not viewed or interpreted in isolation; they are viewed in relation to other roles. Roles in an interaction perspective are not culturally determined nor structurally prescribed but derive from the voluntary actions of an individual in interaction with others (Blumer, 1962; Honig-Parnass, 1981; Turner, 1962). Such actions are motivated by the expected returns from others. A role assumed by a person has to have a reciprocal or counter role in the environment before it is totally assumed. Relevant counter roles take on a more profound meaning when enacted by significant others. These others could be the patient's family or the members of the health care system who are working with the patient.

A role, in this view, is discovered, created, modified, defined, and played within a given interaction (Conway, 1978; Stryker, 1980, p. 54; Turner, 1962). It is more than the tasks performed by nurses, more than the patient's expectations of the role, and more than a set of responsibilities and obligations. Role incorporates all of these as well as *perceptions* of the role, *validation* of the role, *reciprocation, motivation, communication,* and *social circumstances.* The self–other interactions impact on the development of the roles and counter roles that are enacted and on the meanings attributed to behaviors (Turner & Shosid, 1976).

An interactionist view of sick role presupposes a diversity of sick role behaviors and a diversity in central conditions that affect the enactment of sick role behaviors. The definition of the sick role from an interactionist perspective thus presupposes that roles emerge from the interaction of self and others' roles with the environment and on the basis of goals related to health and illness. While occupying the position of the sick role may be a voluntary or involuntary action, enactment of the sick role is skewed more to the voluntary end on a continuum of voluntarianism–involuntarianism. Actors elect to enact one or the other form of the sick role motivated by the returns expected and received from counter roles. Roles assumed by self in a given situation, therefore, are validated when others (health care members or significant others) reciprocate in some way and thus are reinforced (either negatively or positively).

Once a role evolves, the need to reciprocate in role behaviors actually becomes a need for benefits received in order to continue receiving them. Perception of the exchange process, the rewards, the losses, and the ratio between them continue to influence the role that is being enacted (Blau, 1964; Homans, 1974). Therefore, interactionist sick roles are tentative and fluid and evolve in the process of interaction between a person perceiving self-as-sick and others in the environment responding to such perception. Sick roles are continuously changing and are manifested in different patterns of behavior as well as through expressed feeling —internal or external. Essential components for describing, explaining, and predicting interactional sick roles are:

1. Expectations of self in health and illness
2. Meaning ascribed to situation by self and others
3. Significant other roles enacted in relationship to self-roles
4. Expectations of sick role by others in the health care situation
5. Congruency or incongruency between self and others' expectations and meaning
6. Patterns of communication regarding expectations and meaning attached to them

7. Behaviors and expressed feelings of self and others in health-illness situations (and unexpressed feelings to the extent they can be accurately inferred)

Therefore, the sick role cannot be understood, explained, or predicted on the basis of acceptance of help and legitimization of condition of illness only. Nor does sick role performance depend on societal norms or cultural expectations alone. Rather it encompasses and is mediated through norms, expectations, feelings, and meaning to the role incumbent;, modified in interactions with significant others and the environment, and expressed in behaviors and feelings. Furthermore, sick role from this perspective can become a more useful concept when viewed both situationally and contextually—that is, in terms of other well roles or helping roles.

Situational conditions are those occurring at the time of interactions. These include interactions of person roles with others' roles in the health care system or alternative care systems. Contextual conditions incorporate expectations of self in health and illness and meaning of situation to self and significant others that may be influenced by such variables as culture and gender.

Interactional sick roles evolve out of a synthesis of situational and contextual conditions. Changes in any of these conditions therefore will be manifested in one or more of the essential components of the interactionist's sick role. Hence, a person may enact a diverse array of sick roles evolving from a variety of interactions and a nearly unlimited number of variables.

To recapitulate, the sick role is defined as patterns of behaviors and actions manifested in an interaction with significant others by a person perceiving self as sick and in reciprocation with other counter roles. The enactment of the sick role encompasses a perception, an awareness, interaction, reciprocation, feelings, behaviors, and patterns of action and reaction.

Support for the multiplicity and interactional nature of sick roles is ample. Gender and illness behavior is one example. There is much documentation that women manifest more illness behavior, assume the sick role more readily, and utilize health services more often than do men (Nathanson, 1975), but they have lower mortality rates and demonstrate more resistance to both infectious and degenerative diseases (Nathanson, 1977). Biological theories alone have not been able to explain such differential illness status. The concept sick role was used to explore sex differences in these reported studies.

Enactment of sick role by males and females was studied by Brown, Buchanan, and Hsu (1978). They compared the recovery of 50 male and 50 female patients following open heart surgery by considering (1) day of transfer from the recovery room, (2) day of discharge from the hospital, (3) achievement of independence in self-care and ambulation, and (4) amount of pain medication and tranquilizers received. They found that the significance of sex as a variable in these sick role behaviors was minimal for this sample of seriously ill patients. In an earlier study, however, Brown and Rawlinson (1975) concluded that sex of the patient related to the rapidity with which the patient relinquished the sick role. Males tended to relinquish the sick role more quickly than females. While there is no empirical evidence for differences in the enactment of sick roles on the part of males and females, results of this study indicate that differential perceptions of sex role enactment by health professionals may contribute to a lingering enactment of sick role.

Relinquishment of the sick role is quicker for males than for females (Brown & Rawlinson, 1975). This fact poses significant research questions and hypotheses. Is it possible that the relinquishment rate differs because of the roles imputed by significant others during the operating cycle transitions? Hadley (1966) demonstrated that children's relinquishment of sick roles after corrective heart surgery was directly related to their mothers' perceptions and expectations. An interactionist's view of sick roles permits further exploration of these hypotheses.

Two processes are necessary for enacting the sick role. The first is clarity of what the role entails as perceived by both role incumbent and significant other, and a certain degree of congruency between both perceptions. Congruency helps continuity of role interactions. The second process is role taking, i.e., the ability to assume imaginatively the point of view of each other in sick and counter roles, and therefore be able to make predictions about each other (Turner, 1962). Processes of clarification and role taking help in explanation, description of perceptions, degree of awareness of behaviors, feelings and meanings, and provide a certain degree of prediction for sick role patterns. The same processes could be utilized in the enactment of at-risk roles.

AT-RISK ROLES

The conceptualization of sick role is more useful in understanding the behavior of a patient's acute short-term illness and far less useful for chronic, long-term illness and rehabilitation types of conditions (Levine & Kozloff, 1971; Segal, 1976). A more useful concept for describing behavior enacted during these situations is the at-risk role (Baric, 1969). The development of this concept is another indication of the diversity in patterns of sick role behaviors. When an individual agrees to enact the behaviors inherent in the sick status, it is said that the person has more or less accepted the sick role. On the other hand, when an individual becomes aware of potential hazards to his or her health and chooses to enact certain prescribed health care behavior with the goal of maintaining health, averting a certain hazard or preventing a potential illness, then a person is enacting an *at-risk role*.

An at-risk role incorporates a sense of acceptance by a person that he or she may become sick if certain variables exist and interact in such a way to change the at-risk role to a sick role. An at-risk status may be designated by health care professionals and ascribed to a person or a community; however, unless the person or the community demonstrates behaviors congruent with the status, it remains an academic label. To wear seat belts for the goal of protecting oneself against major injuries in auto accidents is to have assumed an at-risk role for a motorist or a car passenger. To exercise regularly, eat a low cholesterol diet, modify type A behavior, avoid stress, omit cigarettes, and keep blood pressure under control for the purpose of preventing cardiovascular diseases or recurrence is to enact an at-risk role of cardiovascular diseases or accidents. "The individual recognizes his risk for developing or experiencing a recurrence of a certain disease to decrease that risk" of whatever condition for which he or she is at risk (Dracup & Meleis, 1982, p. 33).

The differences between the sick role and at-risk roles are apparent in the emphasis on certain conditions (Baric, 1969). For example, whereas institutional affiliation may not be essential for the sick role, it definitely is not inherent in the at-risk role. The at-risk role has obligations and responsibilities (a certain regimen, a diet, etc.), but permits the individual far less reduction in other social responsibilities and obligations. An at-risk role depends less on a regular enforcement by health professionals and more on other counter roles; also, it lacks the feedback in symptoms, signs, and treatment that tend to accompany sick roles.

Finally, time boundaries are not readily apparent for the at-risk role. There is more indefiniteness surrounding the enactment of the at-risk role than the sick role.

ROLE INSUFFICIENCY

Although a sick role or an at-risk role performance may be expected from a certain person or population, such roles may be enacted partially or totally in ways that are not effective in achieving the individual's goals for maintaining, promoting, or achieving well being. Such disparity in fulfilling role expectations, obligations, or goals as perceived by self or significant others is labeled role insufficiency.

Inadequate role enactment may occur voluntarily or involuntarily. Voluntary inadequacy in role enactment may be demonstrated in persons who have accepted the ascribed status but have made a deliberate decision not to enact either the sick role or the at-risk role. A noncompliant person in an illness situation, therefore, may not abdicate other role responsibilities, that is, responsibilities that would appropriately be expected by significant others to be abdicated. Or, a noncompliant person may not seek health care. For example, a patient with a breast lump may refuse to have the lump appropriately evaluated, therefore voluntarily refusing to enact the sick role or at-risk roles. Or a cardiovascular patient may refuse bed rest and continue to carry on regular role responsibilities in a type A manner. Role insufficiency in this case is, therefore, in the performance of a sick role. On the other hand, a rehabilitating cardiovascular patient may not follow an exercise, nutrition, and work schedule regimen that has been prescribed by members of the health care system; or alternative healing approaches, for that matter. Role insufficiency in this case is related to the at-risk role.

Voluntary role insufficiency may be a function of a person's knowingly weighing the rewards to be derived, the costs the role taken will incur, and the balance between the rewards and costs. When the person perceives that the costs of the sick or at-risk roles outweigh the gains, a voluntary role insufficiency ensues. In the process of perceiving such a balance, reinforcement by others plays a significant role. Whether the insufficiency in role enactment persists will depend on the extent of reinforcement by significant others in or out of the health care system.

Role insufficiency in either the sick or the at-risk roles may ". . . also result from poor role definition, the inner dynamics of role relationships, or simply from lack of knowledge of role behaviors, sentiments and goals. It may also be generated when perceptions or interpretations of role behavior cues are impaired or absent" (Meleis, 1975, p. 266) and this role insufficiency may be involuntary (Kaas & Rousseau, 1983). The consequences of voluntary or involuntary role insufficiency may be a temporary or permanent delay in assuming a well role.

ROLE SUPPLEMENTATION

Role supplementation is defined as the process of interaction through which sick roles, at-risk roles, and counter roles are clarified by use of such strategies as role taking, role modeling, and role rehearsal. It is the conveying of information or experience necessary to bring the role incumbent and counter role incumbent to full awareness of role expectations, anticipated behavior patterns, feelings, and sensations involved in each role and its counter role. It includes relevant knowledge, experience, and expression of feelings with emphasis on understanding one's own roles and others' roles and the reciprocity inherit in the role relationship. Role supplementation may be both preventive and therapeutic. When role supplementation is used as a way of clarifying the sick role or at-risk role for persons anticipating a transition to each of these roles, then it is used for prevention (Meleis & Swendsen, 1978; Swendsen, Meleis, & Jones, 1978). Therapeutic supplementation on the other hand is resorted to when role insufficiency has become manifest (Dracup, 1982; Dracup, et al., 1984).

Role Clarification

The process by which the knowledge, skills, and boundaries of either the sick or the at-risk roles are identified, shared, and defined is called role clarification (Burr, 1972; Cottrell, 1942; Meleis & Swendsen, 1978). It includes making explicit the following: expectations of self and significant others in health-illness situations; and the meaning of the situations, behaviors, and expressed or unexpressed feelings. It incorporates the development of mutual awareness by self roles and others' roles in health and illness situations (Thornton & Nardi, 1975). Role clarification includes delineating what the particular role entails in terms of behaviors of self and others, what the role entails in terms of feelings, what the goals of role enactment are, together with costs and rewards entailed in enacting the role. It also incorporates the extent to which significant others reinforce or validate the role behavior with counter roles.

Role Taking

Role taking is another essential component in role supplementation. It incorporates the empathetic abilities of the self, both cognitively and affectively. Lindesmith and Strauss (1968) defined role taking as "imaginatively assuring the position or point of view of another person" (p. 282). Smooth transition into acquiring a new role is enhanced by role taking since the self enacts a role by vicariously assuring the role of the other. This is based on the assumption that individuals enact roles in pairs and not singularly (Turner, 1962, 1980). (Role taking is explored more extensively in Chapter 3.)

Strategies for Role Clarification and Role Taking

When a role is observed being enacted so that an individual is able to understand and emulate it, role modeling occurs (Bandura, 1963). Role modeling could occur through incidental encounters with others who have enacted the sick role or the at-risk role. In a mobile, highly developed, technical society, incidental role modeling is reduced to a minimum. Because sick roles and at-risk roles are seldom modeled on others, it is possible that a person may not know how to enact a sick role or an at-risk role, or what to expect from counter roles. Also, the media may have portrayed glamorized or unattractive models of patients, nurses, physicians, and so forth, with the result of a singular, stereotyped conception of the sick or at-risk roles. Another person may have been exposed to a sick role or at-risk role model from another culture. In any of these situations, clarification of roles and counter roles will reveal different models and perceptions and, perhaps, project a new, more effective model.

Role clarification is further realized when the patient successfully rehearses some of the behaviors expected of each role. When the person fantasizes, imagines, and mentally enacts a certain role and a counter role, it is said that a person is *rehearsing a role* (Biddle, 1979, pp. 328–331; Blumer, 1969; Meleis, Swendsen, & Jones, 1980). Role rehearsal involves both these internal activities as well as external activities. The external enactment occurs when the person is prompted to enact significant behaviors that will be expected in a specified role. An example is rehearsal of coughing before surgery (Lindeman & Aernam, 1971).

Role rehearsal serves the crucial function of anticipating and planning the course of future role enactment and is an important antecedent to role taking. How the sick or at-risk roles actually are enacted may be quite different from the way they are rehearsed in fantasy because in reality they are modified and recreated by interactions with other roles and influenced by other situational and contextual variables (Shibutani, 1955; Turner, 1968). Role rehearsal enables the person and the significant others to anticipate behaviors and feelings associated with the roles being rehearsed. Role rehearsal is a strategy to enhance the clarification of the sick, the at-risk, and the counter roles. The strategy of role rehearsal also enhances the empathetic abilities of a person enacting a counter role in response to sick or at-risk roles. A viable clarification of roles and counter roles occurs only when a person's significant others' roles are identified and included in the clarification. Their expectations, the meaning they attribute to behavior and feelings, and their goals together shape the emergent sick and at-risk roles. Role-specific behaviors are enacted if the role receives validation from all significant others involved. Consistency in expectations, in rewards, in reinforcements, and in clarification are important ingredients influencing the way in which a role will be enacted (Turner, 1968, 1979–80). Such consistency has more potential for occurring if there is clear communication and interaction of behaviors, expectations, feelings, and meanings. Mutually agreed upon roles evolve in the presence of these conditions—all of which in turn make the process of transition into enacting specified roles less problematic and more effective.

CONCLUSION

Behavior is meaningful when regarded within a context of other behaviors, sentiments surrounding it, and the rationale for that behavior. The attribution of certain meanings to behavior are not possible without considering counter behavior. It is such a context that creates the notion of a role. To consider behavior within roles permits the consideration of expectations surrounding the role, competency in enacting a role, mastery of role, and the relationship between roles and the self.

Nursing has claimed a domain that considers the relationship between person and environment. The self as conceptualized within symbolic interactionist role theory is defined in terms of the quality and quantity of roles as perceived by a person and significant others. Such a definition is congruent with assumptions and phenomena of the domain of nursing.

The sick role and at-risk roles are constellations of behaviors organized around a theme, a set of goals and objectives, a set of normative behaviors and expectations of how one behaves in health or illness. They are tentative, fluid, and changeable, and their enactment is influenced by a host of situational and contextual variables. To consider such roles allows for understanding behaviors of health care clients, for evaluation of competency and mastery in role enactment, and provides a framework to plan congruent nursing care. Inability to enact either of these roles is manifested in role insufficiency. Role supplementation, a nursing intervention, is the process through which role insufficiency is prevented or therapeutically treated.

Each of the concepts provides the nurse clinician with a framework for care, and provides the nurse scientist with the potential for developing propositions for further theorizing or for empirical testing.

15

The Use of Knowledge

Mary-'Vesta Marston-Scott

During the past 10 years, health psychology has come into its own as a substantive field of theory, research, and practice. Depending upon the disciplinary affiliations of professionals working in this area it is sometimes called behavioral medicine, although there are subtle distinctions between the two. *Health psychology* is concerned with applying knowledge from psychology to health promotion, health maintenance, prevention of illness, illness detection, and coping with illness. *Behavioral medicine* incorporates the contributions of many disciplines and brings them to bear at all levels of health promotion and disease prevention (Weiss, 1982). Behavioral scientists have discovered that health is a fertile field for applied research and nurses with advanced graduate preparation are utilizing and adapting models and theories from the behavioral and biological sciences as well as developing their own theories and models for health promotion and disease prevention.

Since the late 1960s there has been growing awareness of the need for individuals to assume more responsibility for maintaining their health and for following treatment regimens when ill. Today, noncompliance is considered one of the most significant problems facing medical practice (Eraker, Kirscht, & Becker, 1984) and patient care generally. Estimates of the extent of noncompliance vary and depend in large part on (1) the type of medical regimen being considered; for example, the taking of medications, the prescription of exercise routines, and the proscription of harmful substances such as tobacco and alcohol; (2) the criteria used to classify patients as compliant or noncompliant; and (3) factors related to diagnosis. According to Becker (1979b), among all patients approximately one third fail to follow their regimens; when the regimen involved is a preventive one, or there are no symptoms, or the illness is a chronic one, approximately one half of patients are noncompliant; and finally, among low income populations approximately two thirds of patients fail to comply.

The importance of health promotion was highlighted by publication of the Lalonde report, *A New perspective on the Health of Canadians* (1974), which set forth directions for health promotion and disease prevention programs in Canada. In the United States, the *Forward Plan for Health* (1975, 1976) served a similar function. Conferences were held addressing the importance of understanding the behavioral aspects of nutrition (Tillotson, 1976), control of cardiovascular disease (Dembroski, 1978; Enelow & Henderson, 1975; Weiss, 1975), aspects of diabetes management (Hamburg, et al., 1980), management of patients with rheumatoid arthritis (de Blecourt, 1980), detection and treatment of cancer (Cullen, Fox, & Isom, 1976), determinants of compliance with treatment regimens (Barofsky, 1977; Cohen, 1979; Haynes, Taylor & Sackett, 1979; Sackett & Haynes, 1976), and the relationship between behavior and health (Hamburg, Elliott, & Parron, 1982). In 1979, *Healthy People: The Surgeon General's Report on Health Promotion and Disease Prevention* (1979a, b) was issued. This document set forth health goals to be reached by specific segments of the population by 1990. Subsequent official government publications such as *Promoting Health, Preventing Disease: Objectives for the Nation* (1981), and *Health, USA* (1980, 1981) spelled out even more explicitly how various health goals could be met.

The United States' official publications as well as the Lalonde report were based, in large part, on the Alameda County study (Berkman & Breslow, 1983). Subjects were a random, stratified sample of the residents of Alameda County, California. Between 6000 and 7000 people were a part of the original sample and they have now been followed for approximately 15 years. This study identified seven important lifestyle practices associated with increased longevity and reduced morbidity and mortality: These [are] (1) eating breakfast regularly; (2) eating three meals a day and avoidance of snacking; (3) exercising regularly; (4) sleeping 7 to 8 hours a night; (5) not smoking; (6) keeping weight within normal limits; and (7) drinking not at all, or in moderation. One widely publicized finding of the Alameda County study was that, on average, adherence to 6 out of 7 lifestyle practices resulted in an 11-year greater life expectancy for a 45-year-old man. The increase in life expectancy for women who adhered to a similar number of lifestyle practices was eight years. *Healthy People* added three other lifestyle practices to the list: (1) adhering to the 55-mile an hour speed limit; (2) wearing seat belts; and (3) participation in screening procedures, especially for hypertension and cancer.

The Lalonde report (1974) suggests that the following four factors make a major contribution to the causes of death and disease: (1) behavioral factors or unhealthy lifestyles, (2) inadequacies in the health care system, (3) environmental hazards, and (4) human biological factors. The leading causes of morbidity and mortality are cardiovascular disease, stroke, cancer, and accidents. The Lalonde report estimates that unhealthy lifestyles are responsible for half of this morbidity. Therefore, a greater impact may be made on the major causes of morbidity and mortality by making simple changes in lifestyle, rather than by relying on sophisticated medical technology and pharmaceutical agents to halt or reverse morbid processes once they have begun. Many years of unhealthy lifestyle practices are required before some of the conditions mentioned here appear.

There is a danger that too much emphasis on the pathogenic influence of unhealthy lifestyles could lead to holding people responsible for their illnesses, that is, "blaming the victim." We need not only to promote more healthy lifestyle practices, but also the best medical wisdom available, along with a working knowledge of how to help those clients who want our help in improving their lifestyles or to follow prudent treatment regimens so as to regain health. Also needed are legal and collective efforts—for example, industrial and governmental—aimed at reducing and controlling exposure to hazardous substances in the workplace, and cleaning up and reducing sources of environmental pollution.

Any discussion of health promotion, disease prevention, and compliance with treatment regimens requires understanding the meanings and usage of these terms. *Health behavior* is defined as "any activity undertaken by a person believing himself to be healthy, for the purpose of preventing disease or detecting it in an asymptomatic stage" (Kasl & Cobb, 1966, p. 246). *Health promotion* is similarly defined. *Illness behavior* is any activity undertaken by an individual who thinks he or she may have a symptom of illness, and should this be confirmed, any activity to learn what remedy he or she should take. *Sick role behavior* is any activity undertaken to facilitate recovery from illness. In this chapter, *compliance* is defined as "the extent to which a person's behavior (in terms of taking medications, following diets, or executing lifestyle changes) coincides with medical or health advice" (Haynes, Taylor, & Sackett, 1979, p. xv). The term compliance is usually used with patients who have treatment regimens associated with specific diagnoses and is not intended to imply coercion.

Kasl and Cobb's definition of sick role behavior (1966) is compatible with that of Parsons's (1951). Parsons spelled out what he called the "rights" and "obligations" of the sick role as follows: The person who enters the sick role has a right to be exempted from the usual obligations at home and at work and a right to be taken care of; at the same time, the person has an obligation to follow whatever treatment is prescribed. Illness is assumed to be an undesirable and temporary state of affairs to be ended as soon as possible. There is the implication that if a patient follows a treatment regimen he or she will recover. The sick role is much more appropriate for patients with short-term self-limiting illnesses and injuries than for patients with chronic diseases, where the treatment regimen may be for the rest of the patient's life and there are likely to be complications or progressive deterioration. The concept of the sick role is useful primarily when the patient has a realistic hope of complete recovery.

Recently there has been a change in the way the terms health promotion and disease prevention are used. For example, in *Promoting Health, Preventing Disease: Objectives for the Nation* (1981), chronic illnesses, such as hypertension, are presented as posing problems of both health promotion and disease prevention. First, emphasis is placed on promotion of health through educational programs targeted to the population at risk as well as to the general population. In the case of hypertension which is potentially controllable by drugs, diet, and lifestyle, emphasis is placed on prevention of the complications of the disease, which may occur as a consequence of failing to follow treatment regimens.

The concept of the *at-risk role* (Baric, 1969) has been introduced to describe a role that includes both healthy people who wish to change lifestyle practices (e.g., stopping smoking, losing weight) to enhance their health even further and patients who have nonobvious diagnoses (e.g., for hypertension, diabetes) which necessitate the following of specific treatment regimens. The sick role, as described by Parsons, imputes institutionalized rights and obligations; the at-risk role does not. One important characteristic of the at-risk role is that the person must be aware that the risk is for a particular illness, hazard, or complication. The availability of social supports is particularly important for encouraging persons in at-risk roles to remain on treatment regimens or take special precautions to protect their health, as there are relatively few immediate and obvious advantages to doing so.

This chapter examines those theories, models, and constructs that have been found to be predictive of health behavior and compliance with recognized treatment regimens. Emphasis is placed on those theories that have been researched thoroughly. Those for which we now have the most support are the *health belief model*, the *locus of control construct*, *social support*, and *behavior modification*, including contingency contracting. Sufficient research has been generated by these theories on which to base nursing intervention research and nursing interventions. It is important that knowledge related to these models and constructs become a part of the role preparation of practicing nurses. There are several other concepts, such as the patient–provider relationship, and theories, such as Fishbein's theory of reasoned action and attribution theory, on which health-related research is beginning to be based. At this time, however, there is insufficient research based on these latter frameworks to serve as a foundation for developing sound nursing interventions, although this probably will not be the case within a few years.

HEALTH BELIEF MODEL

The health belief model is probably the most extensively developed model presently available, and the one which thus far has been most useful in predicting health-related behaviors and compliance with treatment regimens (Becker, 1974a, 1979a; Becker, Haefner, Kasl, et al., 1977; Mikhail, 1981). The model was first proposed in the late 1950s and early 1960s by Hochbaum (1958) and Rosenstock (1966, 1974), and their colleagues (Kegeles, 1963; Leventhal, Rosenstock, Hochbaum, & Carriger, 1960) for the purpose of explaining preventive health behavior. In the mid-1970s Becker and his colleagues expanded the model for use with patients with acute and chronic illnesses (Becker, 1974b; Kasl, 1974; Kirscht, 1974), and as a basis for intervention studies (e.g., Innui, Yourtee, & Williamson, 1976; Kirscht & Haefner, 1973; Kirscht, Haefner, & Eveland, 1975; Kirscht, Becker, Haefner, & Maiman, 1978).

Both Hochbaum and Rosenstock were influenced by the phenomenologic orientation of Kurt Lewin (1951). Two assumptions underlying the health belief model have their roots in Lewin's field theory. First is the assumption that people behave on the basis of their perceptions of situations in which they find themselves. A frequently quoted statement of Rosenstock is, "It is the world of the perceiver that determines what [an individual] will do and not the physical environment except as the physical environment comes to be represented in the mind of the behaving individual" (Rosenstock, 1974, p. 329). Secondly, the life space, described by Lewin as comprising an interdependent unit of the individual and the individual's meaningful environment, comprises areas of positive, negative, and neutral valence or value; people are attracted to areas of positive value and repelled by areas of negative value. Health is assumed to have a positive value and illness to have a negative value.

Level of aspiration studies, which were based on Lewin's field theory, suggest that behavior is determined by the value that an individual places on a particular outcome and his estimate that a particular behavior will bring about that outcome (Lewin, Dembo, Festinger, & Sears, 1944). The health belief model is often referred to as a "value expectancy theory," which postulates that the value associated with the desire of the individual to avoid illness and achieve health coupled with a subjective estimate that a particular course of action will bring about that which is of value to the individual, will result in a reduction in the threat of illness.

The five major variables or concepts of the health belief model that are considered important in explaining and predicting health related behavior and compliance with treatment regimens are:

1. *Perceived susceptibility or vulnerability.* Does the individual believe that he or she might be susceptible to a particular illness? Does the individual believe that he or she might be susceptible to future problems if illness already exists where complications are likely, as is the case with hypertension, diabetes, and glaucoma? Does he or she feel vulnerable to another attack, as might be likely with untreated epilepsy, rheumatic heart disease, or tuberculosis?

2. *Perceived seriousness or severity.* Does the individual believe that if he or she contracted a particular illness or complications thereof, the outcome could be dangerous, i.e., pose a threat to health, or interfere with his or her usual life-style?

    Sometimes perceived susceptibility and perceived seriousness are combined and termed *psychological readiness.* The implication is that relatively high degrees of both perceived susceptibility and perceived seriousness combined are more predictive of health-related behavior and compliance than is a relatively high degree of perception of susceptibility *or* severity. Combining perceived susceptibility and perceived severity would reduce the number of variables when using this model. Depending upon the patient population, however, combining the two may not increase the predictive capacity; too high a level of perceived severity may hinder some health-related behaviors and, indeed, exert the opposite effect of that which is desired. For example, Becker and his colleagues (Becker, Kaback, Rosenstock, & Ruth, 1975) reported that a combination of *high* perceived susceptibility and *low* perceived severity was predictive of participation in a Tay-Sachs screening program in the Baltimore area. Given the large population presumably at risk for Tay-Sachs and the relatively small sample in this study, one can only speculate about the larger population. It is possible that potential carriers may be so threatened by the possibility of having their fears confirmed that they avoid being screened.

3. *Perceived effectiveness or benefits of treatment.* Does the individual believe that whatever course of action has been recommended will be efficacious in preventing illness, treating diagnosed illness, or preventing the complications of chronic illness?

4. *Perceived relative absence of barriers or impediments to taking action.* Does the individual perceive a relative absence of barriers to taking action, such as expense, inconvenience, and side effects of drugs? Sometimes this variable is termed "costs" and is weighed against the perceived effectiveness of treatment as "benefits minus costs."

5. *Perceived cues to action.* Cues to action may be internal, as for example, symptoms; or external, such as becoming aware of health education messages from the mass media, or post card reminders. Both cues to action and barriers are important, but they are difficult to research because people differ in what they consider barriers and what to them are cues.

Becker and colleagues (Becker, 1974a, 1979b) have added a large number of "modifying and enabling" variables to the health belief model. These include demographic factors, attitudes toward visits to a clinic or physician's office, attitudes toward the health facility, attitudes toward the physician, quality of the patient–provider relationship and aspects of the interaction, health motivation, locus of control, intention to comply, belief in personal control, and the role of social support. The modifying and enabling variables are postulated to interact with the main variables of the health belief model. However, the ways in which they are thought to interact have never been spelled out or tested. Most research based on the health belief model measures some or all of the five major variables described above. To date there has been no research testing the health belief model as modified by Becker and it is probably not possible to test the model in its entirety in any one study. The research findings discussed below utilize primarily the variables of perceived susceptibility, severity, and benefits.

There are several reasons why it is difficult to arrive at firm conclusions concerning the usefulness of the health belief model:

1. Most studies have utilized cross sectional designs with convenience samples, which do not permit time ordering of the variables. Some studies with longitudinal designs (Taylor, 1979) investigated whether relevant beliefs existed at the time of diagnosis or whether patients developed their health beliefs as they gained experience with their illness—in this case, hypertension. Taylor found that pretreatment beliefs are not predictive of compliance at 6 months; however, health beliefs concerning the seriousness of hypertension assessed after 6 months of treatment were significantly associated with compliance measured at the same time as well as at 12 months after treatment was begun. Perceived benefits of treatment measured after six months was predictive of compliance after 12 months of treatment. There are even fewer studies in which the knowledge we now have has been used as a basis for interventions designed to enhance health related behaviors or compliance with treatment regimens.

2. Among the very few reliable and valid measures of major variables of the health belief model are the scales for diabetic patients (Given, Given, Galin, & Condon, 1983), for hypertensive patients (Hamilton, 1982), and for obese children (Maiman et al., 1977). It is probably impossible to develop scales which could be used with every patient population because most diagnoses have particular hazards associated with them, and treatment for some illnesses is more effective than for others. It is a disadvantage not to have reliable and valid measures of health beliefs which could be used for any patient population, but the fact is that health beliefs, used differently for different patient populations, do predict relevant health-related behaviors and, therefore, compliance with treatment regimens can be seen as a strength of the model.

3. Health beliefs concerning susceptibility, severity, and benefits may be different for different levels of health promotion. For example, at the level of disease detection the variables that predict whether clients will participate in genetic screening, as for example, Tay-Sachs, may not be the same as those that predict participation in blood pressure screening, obtaining Pap tests, having an amniocentesis, or engaging in breast self-examination. At the

tertiary level, the variables that predict compliance with a treatment regimen in hypertension may not necessarily be the same as those that predict compliance in diabetes, arthritis, asthma, end stage kidney disease, and mental illness. Not enough research of any type—cross sectional, prospective, or intervention—has been done with any one diagnostic group or preventive behavior, such as screening, for us to know whether the results of studies done with diverse diagnostic groups can be examined as a whole. For example, the largest number of studies of any one diagnostic group is 13, using hypertensive patients (Andreoli, 1981; Cummings, Kirscht, Binder, & Godley, 1982; DeVon & Powers, 1984; Given, Given, & Simoni 1978; Glanz, Kirscht, & Rosenstock, 1981; Hamilton, 1982; Hershey, Morton, Davis, & Reichgott, 1980; Johnson, 1979; Kirscht, Kirscht, & Rosenstock, 1981; Kirscht & Rosenstock, 1977; Nelson et al., 1978; Taylor, 1979; Watts, 1982). In the screening area, four studies each have been done on Tay-Sachs screening (Beck, Blaichman, Schriver, & Clow, 1974; Ben-Sira, 1978; Kaback, Becker, & Ruth, 1974; Vertinsky, Yang, MacLeod, & Hardwick, 1976) and on breast self-examination practices (Fink, Shapiro, & Roester, 1972; Hallal, 1982; Schlueter, 1982; Stillman, 1977). In the area of health promotion there are five studies on immunization practices (Cummings, Jette, Brock, & Haefner, 1979; Larson, Olsen, Cole, & Shortell, 1979; Leventhal, Rosenstock, Hochbaum, & Carriger, 1960; Levine & Trent, 1978; Rundall & Wheeler, 1979), and four studies on smoking cessation (Croog & Richards, 1977; Sutton & Eiser, 1984; Weinberger, Greene, Mamlin, & Jerin, 1981; Windsor, et al., 1984).

4. Some variables may be more predictive of health-related behavior and compliance with treatment regimens early in the course of an illness and others may be more predictive after patients have had considerable experience with their illness. The evidence for this statement is scattered through many studies. Not all studies provide clear information concerning how long patients have had their illness because convenience samples still predominate.

In spite of the limitations of existing research, the most serious of which are outlined above, and the position of some colleagues who believe more correlational and prospective studies need to be done before intervention studies are attempted, this author takes the position that we now have sufficient knowledge concerning the predictive capacity of the health belief model so that intervention studies and nursing interventions are in order. It is important that nurses acquire a working knowledge of ways in which the health belief model can be used in practice; listed below are some of the more clear-cut ways this can be done.

Sensitization of Care Givers to Influence of Health Beliefs on Compliance with Treatment Regimens. Innui, Yourtee, and Williamson (1976) reported a study in which physicians staffing hypertension clinics were given a one-to two-hour tutorial to sensitize them to both the magnitude of the noncompliance problem and also to strategies for influencing patients' beliefs concerning the seriousness of their condition, susceptibility to complications, and efficacy of treatment. Experimental patients were those whose physicians had received the tutorial; control patients attended a hypertension clinic on different days than the experimental patients. Their physicians were given a written communication informing them of the existence of the study and telling them there would be chart reviews of their patients. Experimental patients took significantly more of their antihypertension medications (as measured by pill count) and the proportion of experimental patients with blood pressure under control was significantly greater over a 5-month period. This study raises unanswered questions concerning the Hawthorne effect, and the effect of changes in how experimental physicians used the time spent with their patients. The results are convincing, and are complemented by other research findings identifying the quality of the patient–provider relationship as also being important in facilitating compliance. Increasingly, nurses are assuming primary responsibility for the supervision of patients with stable chronic illnesses such as hypertension. Sensitization of nurses to the potential influence of health beliefs on compliance behavior would also be expected to result in greater compliance. As primary care givers, nurses could incorporate as a part of their role the giving of systematic attention to finding out about patients' health beliefs and the tailoring of health education interventions to take these beliefs into account.

Need for Reducing Danger Associated with Illness as Well as Coping With Feelings of Vulnerability.

People must be engaged by an issue if they are to take action. People who are not aroused about political candidates and issues are not as likely to vote as those who are; in a similar fashion, people who are not aroused or sensitized to health issues are less likely to undertake appropriate health-related actions. Health beliefs concerning personal susceptibility and seriousness can be roughly equated with being aroused or sensitized to specific health issues. Leventhal, who was one of the original architects of the health belief model, made health beliefs concerning susceptibility and seriousness operational by communications designed to motivate college students to obtain tetanus immunizations (Leventhal, Singer, & Jones, 1965). Subjects were exposed to high, medium, or low fear communications concerning the prevalence and seriousness of tetanus. Half of each group was provided specific information concerning hours and whereabouts of clinic facilities. The fear communications were designed to increase subjects' perceptions of both their personal susceptibility to tetanus and the seriousness of the disease; specific information concerning how and where the subjects could procure tetanus immunizations was aimed at reducing feelings of personal threat and vulnerability. In this study, high fear communications accompanied by specific information as to how and where subjects could obtain tetanus immunizations resulted in significantly more students actually obtaining their immunizations. Later, Leventhal further developed this parallel response model, specifically intended to explain the processes involved in danger control and fear control (Leventhal, 1970).

Health professionals should hesitate to use fear communications as motivators of health-related behavior and compliance with treatment regimens, for too high a level of threat may cause a patient to deny the communication and become more fixed in noncompliance. Furthermore, threat has a rapid decrement in effect, and therefore little usefulness for behaviors which must be repeated for an indefinite time, as in many chronic illnesses. There is probably little to be gained from the deliberate use of fearful or threatening communications that could not be accomplished better with another approach, one example being an emphasis on the benefits of treatment.

Leventhal's parallel response model has many important implications for nursing practice when patients are already fearful, as, for example, when facing a surgical procedure. Based on Leventhal's model, Fortin (1983) taught experimental presurgical patients to use the relaxation response (Benson, 1975) to help control pain postoperatively; control patients received the usual preoperative instructions, which included deep breathing and turning (Fortin, 1983). As predicted, experimental patients experienced significantly less postoperative pain and anxiety than did the control patients. With little difficulty nurses could incorporate techniques such as the one used by Fortin into their usual presurgical nursing care.

Patients need not be presented with frightening information in a deliberate manner; sometimes this occurs when it is unintended, as, for example, when a patient is asked to give informed consent for a procedure or is told of a particular diagnosis. Leventhal's parallel response model is useful in planning interventions to alleviate the fear that has been aroused; at the same time the patient is assisted to take appropriate actions to cope with the health danger.

The Question of When Perceived Susceptibility and Seriousness or Perceived Benefits are More Predictive. An important question yet to be answered definitively is whether health beliefs concerning susceptibility and seriousness can be counted upon to prompt people to take health-related actions regardless of the health issue. In spite of cautions about combining results addressing different health promotion issues presented earlier in this chapter, preliminary data suggest that perceived susceptibility or perceived seriousness may be a somewhat better predictor of a variety of preventive measures, such as stopping smoking (Aho, 1979), obtaining immunizations (Larson, Olsen, Cole, & Shortell, 1979), and use of a protective glove (Suchman, 1967) than they are predictors of compliance behaviors by patients with diagnosed illnesses. Furthermore, the literature on compliance with treatment regimens by patients with chronic illnesses raises the question of whether perceptions concerning susceptibility and severity may not be more effective when patients are first diagnosed, becoming less important with increasing experience with the illness. After patients have gained some experience with their illness and its treatment, perceived benefit may become a more important predictor of compliance. Much more research will be needed before we know whether the presently observed trends in the data hold up and are both statistically significant and practically meaningful. However, there is still enough evidence on which to base sound nursing interventions. Nurses can safely emphasize in their health teaching of patients what the benefits are offered of well recommended treatments and medications. The discussion in the previous section provides guidelines for interventions which address the importance of fear and danger reduction.

THE LOCUS OF CONTROL CONSTRUCT

The locus of control construct has produced nearly as much research with direct implications for nursing practice as has the health belief model. Like the health belief model, the locus of control construct is considered to be a value expectancy construct, in that Rotter's social learning theory (Rotter, 1966; Rotter, Chance, & Phares, 1972), from which the locus of control construct is derived, is based in part on Lewin's field theory and in part on Skinnerian learning theory. Rotter's theory proposes that the likelihood of a behavior occurring in a particular situation is dependent upon the expectancy that a particular outcome or reward will follow, and the value this outcome has for the individual.

According to Rotter, in the course of everyday living people develop expectations concerning the amount of control they believe they have over their reinforcements, that is, those things that are of value to them. People are assumed to be distributed on a continuum from thinking they have complete control over their own rewards to thinking they have no control whatsoever over what happens to them. People who think that what happens to them is primarily due to their own efforts and abilities are labeled "internals," that is, as having a *belief in internal control;* people who think that what happens to them is primarily due to chance, luck, and the influence of powerful others are labeled "externals," that is, as having a *belief in external control.* No one is ever all one or all the other, but people usually have a predilection in one direction or the other. Because expectancies for control are developed on the basis of one's experiences, an individual can come to have expectancies for control in some kinds of situations, but not in others.

The concepts described have appealed to health workers. Much research has been done with patient and quasi-patient populations and there are excellent reviews of this research (Arakelian, 1980; Strickland, 1978; Wallston & Wallston, 1978). These reviews demonstrate that belief in internal control more often than not is associated with health-related behavior and with compliance with treatment regimens. In a few papers, however, belief in *external* control has been found to be associated with compliance behavior (e.g., Battle, Halliburton, & Wallston, 1982; Lowery & DuCette, 1976). Lowery and DuCette reported that patients who had a diagnosis of diabetes for several years were more external in their control beliefs than were those who were newly diagnosed. Battle et al., found that belief in external control among psychiatric patients was associated with compliance behavior. In both of these studies, experience may have demonstrated to patients that, with respect to their illness, at least, they were really not in control. Also, it is possible that research papers which fail to report an association between belief in internal control, which is more socially desirable, and compliance behavior are less likely to be published.

Various instruments have been developed for measuring belief in personal control. The discussion is limited to those most relevant for the health field. The most frequently used measure has been the 29-item forced-choice measure of generalized expectancies for internal–external control (Rotter, 1966). When an individual has had little or no experience with a particular situation, the generalized measure is considered the most appropriate one to use because expectancies developed over a variety of situations will be brought to the new situation. When the individual has had considerable experience with a particular situation, however, specific expectancies for control in that situation may have already developed and specific measures may be more appropriate. For this reason, Rotter suggested that to increase predictive capacity investigators might develop instruments with items specific to the problem being investigated or specific to the subject group (Rotter, 1975).

In the health field, the Wallstons (Wallston, Wallston, Kaplan, & Maides, 1976) developed first a health locus of control scale and later a multidimensional health locus of control scale (Wallston, Wallston, & DeVellis, 1978). The reliability of these scales has not held up well in subsequent studies (Wallston & Wallston, 1981). Several even more specific measures have been developed in the health field: Saltzer (1978) developed a four-item weight locus of control measure. This was adapted for a four-item hypertension locus of control scale (Hamilton, 1982). Hamilton's scale successfully predicted blood pressure control in newly diagnosed hypertensive patients over a 3-month period at p 0.02. Saltzer's scale was also adapted, for a four-item diabetes locus of control scale for use with juvenile diabetics (Gelfand, 1984). Over a 1-year period Gelfand found that juvenile diabetics who did not admit any feelings of not being in control of their diabetes were in significantly better diabetic control, as measured by glycohemoglobin levels, than were patients who admitted some feelings of external control. Mikhail (1984) developed a pregnancy locus of control scale, but this was less predictive of health related behavior (appointment keeping behavior) than were the other specific scales. Work with all of these scales, although in the beginning stages, appears to be promising.

People's beliefs about their perceived control are considered to be relatively enduring personality characteristics. Since individuals' expectations are determined by their experiences of control over outcomes, learning experiences can be structured to change expectations and associated behaviors. People with a belief in internal control have been found to be resistant to influence attempts unless they perceive that the person attempting to influence them has "legitimate expertise." They are likely to seek information on which to base their actions and to make better use of information available to them. On the other hand, people with a belief in external control are more easily persuaded by authority figures. In sociological terms, people with a belief in external control would be considered to be alienated. In most situations a belief in internal control is more socially desirable and more likely to be associated with attempts to cope actively with problems, including health and illness problems.

Several interventions have been developed for changing people's locus of control orientations in the more desirable internal direction (Dua, 1970; Masters, 1970; Reimanis, 1974;). Dua described and demonstrated that a behaviorally oriented action approach is more useful in helping students improve their interpersonal relationship skills and increasing their beliefs in internal control than is a psychoanalytically oriented approach aimed at increasing self-insight. The counseling approach developed by Reimanis involves encouraging people to express feelings of internal control. In the reconstrual of stimuli approach of Masters, clients are encouraged to entertain how different sequences between events which could be under their control can result in (for them) rewarding outcomes.

Psychologists may be actively concerned about the possibility of changing basic personality orientations. The three approaches described briefly were developed by psychologists to help clients become more internally oriented so they could cope more effectively with situations they found overwhelming. Nursing's focus is primarily on helping clients cope with health and illness issues; the approaches used *may* result in more internal orientations. A change to a more internal orientation, as measured by a paper and pencil test, is an indication that the patient may be better able to engage in effective self-care practices.

The reasons it is difficult to arrive at firm conclusions concerning the usefulness of the locus of control construct are similar to those described for the health belief model:

1. Although a great deal of research has been done utilizing various locus of control scales, all kinds of designs exist—the problem of time ordering of variables is a major one. Unanswered are questions of when generalized or specific locus of control measures are more useful and with which samples and situations. As with the health belief model, it appears that locus of control orientation may develop in relation to experience with a particular diagnosis.

2. Reliable and valid scales for measuring generalized locus of control orientation are available. The best known is the scale developed by Rotter (1966). Scales for use with specific patient populations are beginning to be developed, but much more research needs to be done in this area. Our understanding of the need to consider the appropriateness of generalized versus specific locus of control measures for specific purposes and samples has developed slowly and apparently is not widely understood, which makes interpretation and comparison of findings from different studies difficult. With the locus of control construct, as with the health belief model, the need for diagnosis-specific scales can be regarded as a disadvantage as well as a strength. It would be desirable to have one reliable and valid scale which could be used with different subject groups, but if researchers or practitioners are working with patients who have had considerable experience with their diagnosis, prediction is increased by the use of diagnosis-specific scales. Therefore, different ways of using locus of control which are consistent with the theoretical definitions of internal and external control and successfully predict relevant behaviors are seen as a strength.

3. There is an assumption that an internal locus of control is more desirable than an external locus of control because it is indicative of better adjustment and compliance with medical regimens. With increasing use of diagnosis-specific scales with a variety of chronic illnesses, however, we may find that when patients are not in control of their illness, an external orientation may be an accurate appraisal of their situation; then the most appropriate interaction may be not to attempt to increase orientation toward internality.

The following are some implications for use of the locus of control construct as a basis for nursing interventions.

Assessment of Patient Locus of Control as Part of Total Patient Assessment. The research literature demonstrates that usually an internal locus of control orientation is associated with several treatment regimens. Some of the newly developed brief, specific measures of locus of control (Gelfand, 1984; Hamilton, 1982; Mikhail, 1984; Saltzer, 1978) could provide practicing nurses with approaches most likely to be successful in helping their clients manage self-care. For example, as mentioned earlier, the person with an internal orientation is more likely to be influenced by a care giver perceived as having expertise—one who makes good use of educational materials; whereas the person with an external orientation responds better to an authoritarian approach. In the same way that

Innui et al. (1976), succeeded in sensitizing physicians to the importance of taking patients' health beliefs into consideration, practicing nurses could be sensitized to the importance of the the control orientations of their patients when planning care. The use of these and other instruments should not, however, be a basis for a prescriptive approach, but used together with other data obtained from the patients concerned.

Use of Intervention Approaches Developed by Psychologists. Although the three intervention approaches described earlier—Dua's action oriented approach (1970), Reimanis's counseling approach (1974), and Masters's reconstrual of stimuli (1970)—were developed by psychologists, they are equally appropriate for nursing situations.

Arakelian (1984) has completed dissertation research based on Reimanis's counseling approach (1974). Using a prospective design, diabetic patients with an external orientation (experimental subjects) received two sessions of counseling intervention designed to help them manage their diabetic treatment regimens; control subjects received a teaching intervention. Experimental subjects became significantly more internal in their orientation and their self-management scores improved significantly. Changes in glycohemoglobin levels were in the direction of better diabetic control, although the change was not statistically significant. Arakelian concluded that the counseling approach developed by Reimanis is a viable nursing strategy that could be adopted by nurses working with patients who have external orientations. Arakelian's interventions were intentionally designed to be fairly brief so that if successful, nurses could incorporate them into their practice.

The study by Dua (1970) demonstrates that a behaviorally oriented action approach is more useful in helping students improve their interpersonal relationship skills and increasing their beliefs in internal control than is a psychoanalytically oriented approach focusing on self-insight. In the action oriented approach students were presented with alternative behaviors from which they choose to improve their interpersonal relationships. A similar approach could be used with patients to help them sort out how they could cope with treatment regimens that are inconvenient, unpleasant, and expensive in terms of time and money. This approach could also be used to reduce anxiety as well as avoid some of the potential dangers of noncompliance.

Bigbee (1983) based an educational intervention with obese adolescents on Masters's reconstrual of stimuli technique. No statistically significant changes were found in either locus of control or weight loss, probably because eating patterns are among the most difficult behaviors to change and subjects were followed for only a 2-month period. Nurses interested in using the reconstrual of stimuli approach should not necessarily be deterred from trying this technique with other target behaviors.

SOCIAL SUPPORT

Since 1978 there has been increasing interest in the relevance of social support in health and illness care (Gottlieb, 1981, 1983). Cobb (1979) pointed out that for centuries the major religions of the world have advocated loving thy neighbor as thyself, but it is only recently that behavioral scientists and health professionals have begun to pay serious attention to the importance of social support. Recently, findings from the Alameda County study (Berkman & Breslow, 1983; Berkman & Syme, 1979) provided an additional impetus for interest in this concept. The Alameda County study demonstrated that even when defined by rather crude indicators such as membership in trade unions and churches and frequency of visits with relatives, social support predicted morbidity, longevity, and health status prospectively over a 15-year period. These findings were independent of whether people were following desirable life-style practices which also significantly influenced morbidity, longevity, and health status. As yet there is no clear-cut theory, with the possible exceptions of the stress buffering hypothesis and social comparison theory, which purports to explain how and why social support makes a significant difference with respect to health-related behaviors, compliance with treatment regimens, and health outcomes. But there is a large amount of empirical research to show that social support *does* significantly influence all of these. In this section the stress buffering hypothesis is discussed, some major ways in which social support has been defined are outlined, the major instruments developed by nurses for measuring social support are reviewed, and tentative suggestions are made concerning how knowledge in this area can be utilized in nursing practice.

The stress buffering hypothesis proposes that for people in crisis, the presence of social supports buffers, or ameliorates, the effects of stress (Cobb, 1976, 1979; Kaplan, Cassel, & Gore, 1977). According to Cobb, "Social support can protect people in crisis from a wide variety of pathological states: from low birth weight to death, from arthitis through tuberculosis to depression, alcoholism, and the social breakdown syndrome. Furthermore, social support may reduce the amount of medication required, accelerate recovery, and facilitate compliance with prescribed medical regimens" (Cobb, 1976, p. 300). Nuckolls's research, which demonstrated that prenatal patients who had experienced many life changes and who lacked social support developed significantly more complications of pregnancy than did those who had adequate social supports, is often cited in support of the stress buffering hypothesis (Nuckolls, Cassel, & Kaplan, 1972). Gore (1981) and Thoits (1982) have criticized the stress buffering hypothesis and pointed out that sometimes life events that cause stress, such as the loss of significant others, are confounded by social supports. But it does not appear that even more careful research designs with clearer definitions and measures of social support and stressful life events will indicate a reduced importance of social support. In many cases social support appears to exert robust effects with or without the presence of stress. The accumulation of additional research findings will permit us to draw more precise conclusions concerning what kinds of social support are most helpful in specific kinds of situations.

Other important examples of the influence of social support on health and illness behavior and health outcomes follow:

1. The presence of social supports has been reported predictive of seeing a doctor when symptoms are present (Berkanovic & Telesky, 1982),
2. Asthma patients with a high level of social supports required significantly smaller doses of steroids to control their symptoms than did patients without social supports; this relationship held regardless of the number of

life changes that occurred (de Araujo, van Arsdale, Holmes, & Dudley, 1973),

3. When mastectomy patients had few physical complications, those with a high level of social supports had a low number of symptoms, although this relationship did not hold when the number of physical complications was high (Woods & Earp, 1978),

4. A positive association has been reported between presence of social support and morale among patients undergoing hemodialysis (Dimond, 1979),

5. Persons exposed to a high number of stressful life events, but who had more social supports, experienced less psychological distress than did those with fewer social supports (Wilcox, 1979).

One of the problems inherent in attempting to summarize the research findings on social support is attributable to differing definitions of social support. Cobb (1979) defined four types of social support: (1) Emotional support, which conveys the message to the individual that he or she is loved, cared for, esteemed, valued, and that he or she is a member of a community of mutual obligation, (2) instrumental support, or counseling, (3) active support, or mothering, and (4) material support. Dimond and Jones (1983) presented a set of definitions from a nursing point of view. These include support as relational provisions, as information, as structure, and as interaction. Cobb's definition of emotional support, which expresses man's concern for fellow human beings, probably cannot be surpassed in the depth of meaning it conveys; Dimond and Jones define this as informational support. Relational provisions include attachment, social integration, opportunity for nurturance, reassurance of worth, sense of reliable alliance, and the obtaining of guidance. Social support as structure is defined by characteristics of social networks, such as size and density. Social support as interaction includes the content of interactions, the amount of mutual sharing, and the intensity of the bonds between people.

Because our definitions of what is meant by social support are less than clear, development of instruments to measure social support has been slow. In the nursing literature, Norbeck's instrument has received the most careful attention with respect to instrument construction and testing (Norbeck, 1981; Norbeck, Lindsey, & Carrieri, 1981, 1983). Other instruments measuring social support have been developed by Dimond (1979), and by Brandt and Weinert (1981). Because all three of these instruments were developed recently, there is little or no published research based upon them. Mikhail (1984) used Dimond's instrument to predict appointment keeping behavior among prenatal patients, and Hamilton (1982) used the same instrument to predict compliance with a hypertension treatment regimen. In neither case, however, did Dimond's measure predict compliance behavior.

Assessment of Patients at Risk Because of Lack of Social Supports. It is essential that data concerning social support be obtained as part of the nursing assessment, since such data will provide information concerning those patients at greatest risk of failing to follow their treatment regimens and of developing complications. There are no clear-cut guidelines as to what kinds of interventions will be most effective in preventing noncompliance and the development of complications, but there are a few clues as to what may be helpful. Research has shown that as long as public health nurses made home visits hypertensive patients' blood pressures remained under control, but when visits were discontinued their blood pressures went out of control (Wilbur & Barrow, 1969). It is impossible to say whether the public health nurses provided social support or whether their professional services and the professional relationship with their patients accounted for their apparent influence over patients' blood pressures (and, presumably their medication taking behavior). Elderly patients with chronic illness who are discharged from a health service after recovery from an acute episode or after completion of self-care teaching are at risk for noncompliance. In an attempt to meet this problem, an agency in the Boston area has instituted a Warm Line where friendly nonprofessionals make periodic telephone calls to inquire how former clients are getting along. We do rot know yet whether a telephone call is as effective as a home visit by a nurse in encouraging continued self-care.

Two research projects have attempted to introduce social support in the form of a buddy system to encourage compliance among hypertensive patients (Caplan, Robinson, French, et al., 1976; Caplan, Harrison, Wellons, & French, 1980), but the results are disappointing. Social comparison theory (Festinger, 1954) proposes that people seek out others similar to themselves to determine whether they are better or worse off, and whether others have a better way of coping with a given problem than they themselves have. Theoretically, if people who have specific health problems could be encouraged to seek support from others with similar health problems, they would be more likely to give and receive social support. This is one of the bases for mutual help groups, such as Alcoholics Anonymous. If patients could be encouraged to seek such support on their own, rather than having the system set up for them, as the two Caplan et al., studies attempted, the results might be better.

BEHAVIOR MODIFICATION AND
CONTINGENCY CONTRACTING

Behavior modification and contingency contracting are based on Skinnerian learning theory. A major underlying assumption is that behavior is under the control of consequences. This approach has sometimes been unjustifiably attacked because, under some circumstances, people's behavior can be shaped or changed without their permission. These techniques need not be used in a surreptitious manner, however; there is no reason why patients cannot be consulted about their participation in these types of treatments. Indeed, in some of the more successful applications of learning theory, such as losing weight, patients decide how often and in what ways they will reward themselves for changes they have decided to make in their behavior. Berni and Fordyce (1977) have spelled out specific nursing applications of major concepts of behavior modification and these techniques have found their way into the practice of many nurses.

Steckel has probably done the most work to clarify and publicize the usefulness of contingency contracting by nurses (Steckel, 1982; Steckel & Swain, 1977; Swain & Steckel, 1981), and Janz, Becker, and Hartman (1984) reviewed the research utilizing contingency contracting to enhance compliance. Steckel's approach to contingency contracting is one way of doing something tangible about the patient–provider relationship. By contingency contracting Steckel means that patient and provider (in this case, the nurse) negotiate an agreement whereby the patient will follow certain aspects of the treatment regimen in return for a reward of the patient's choice, such as an uninterrupted period with the nurse to discuss topics of concern, assistance with insurance forms, tickets to baseball games, paperback books—all items of very small monetary value. Both nurse and patient sign the agreement, which is appropriately changed and renewed on each clinic visit. Of course, a potential disadvantage of this intervention is that if the contracting, along with accompanying rewards, is discontinued, the desired behavior may be extinguished. Use of this technique requires that the care giver be in a position to make a sustained commitment over time.

In one study, Swain and Steckel (1981) randomly assigned hypertensive patients to one of three groups: (1) regular clinic care, (2) patient education (concerning hypertension and its treatment), and (3) contingency contracting. At the end of 2 years, patients who were treated with contingency contracting had blood pressures that were under the best control; second best were those patients who received customary clinic care; and poorest of all were patients who received the education treatment, many of whom had dropped out of care. The investigators interpreted their results to mean that patients in the education treatment group received information they did not know how to use and were not given help to use. As a result they felt guilty and many dropped out of care. This interpretation is in keeping with Leventhal's parallel response model (1970), described earlier in this chapter, which holds that specific instructions must be given as to how threats and danger can be reduced to manageable proportions if patients are to be expected to comply.

SUMMARY

This chapter has reviewed some of the more important social psychological theories, models, and concepts which explain and predict health-related behaviors and compliance with treatment regimens. Attention has been focused on those models for which there is adequate research for use as a basis to design sound nursing interventions. No attempt has been made to review all the research based on each of these models because the numbers of studies involved make this prohibitive. Instead, research of particular relevance to nursing has been used for illustrative purposes.

There have been some major omissions in this discussion. Health education was intentionally omitted because by itself, patient knowledge is not a reliable predictor of health-related behaviors and compliance with treatment regimens. Patient education should be an integral part of the suggested nursing interventions outlined for the four major models. Conspicuous by its absence is discussion of the patient–provider relationship. Like their physician counterparts, nurses in practice are also concerned with the influence that aspects of the patient–nurse relationship may have on patient behavior and health outcomes. The patient–provider relationship is one of the fastest growing research areas within health psychology and behavioral medicine. However, no two studies agree on a definition of what is meant by quality in the patient–provider relationship. Interpretation of some of the research findings is problematic and specific implications for professional nursing roles in intervention are, as yet, unclear. Two other promising models, Fishbein's theory of reasoned action and attribution theories, were also omitted, for the same reason.

This author takes the position that sound empirical data based on the health belief model, the locus of control construct, social support, and behavior modification and contingency contracting now exist. The following is a summary of some of the nursing interventions which can be based on these models. With respect to the health belief model; first, orientation of practicing nurses to the importance of their patients' health beliefs and the tailoring of health education interventions designed to take these beliefs into account, should result in more desirable health behaviors and compliance with treatment regimens. Second, there is a need to help patients cope with their fears as well as the threat their illness may pose. Fears and anxieties associated with learning of a particular diagnosis or that one must follow a specified treatment regimen must be controlled if patients are to take constructive action to reduce the actual threat associated with their illness. Specific advice on actions the patient can take—and how to take such actions—are extremely important. Third, on the basis of data now available it appears that attention to perceived susceptibility and severity may increase compliance when patients are first diagnosed as having a chronic illness, whereas emphasis on the benefits of treatment may be more effective later. Nurses should assess their patients' locus of control and either take this information into consideration when planning nursing interventions or utilize one of the intervention approaches outlined in this chapter with patients found to have external beliefs. When nurses ascertain that particular patients are at risk of noncompliance because of lack of social supports, strenuous efforts should be made to provide periodic and on-going support or supervision. Contingency contracting has been identified as an effective technique for enhancing compliance among patients with long-term treatment regimens who are seen at regular intervals by the same care giver.

There is often a lag between the discovery of knowledge and its implementation in practice. Nursing does not differ from the other behavioral and biological sciences in this respect, unless perhaps it is that nurses are less willing to try interventions for which there is not a great deal of research support. There is considerable research support for the approaches suggested in this chapter, and this author believes it is important that the knowledge presented here become a part of the role preparation of practicing professional nurses.

References

Abdel-Halim, A. A. Employee affective responses to organizational stress: Moderating effects of job characteristics. *Personnel Psychology*, 1978, *31*, 561–579.

Abdellah, F. Nurse practitioners and nursing practice. *American Journal of Public Health*, 1976, *66*, 245.

Abramson, J. *The Invisible Woman*. San Francisco: Jossey-Bass, 1975.

Acker, J. Women and social stratification: A case of intellectual sexism. *American Journal of Sociology*, 1973, *78*, 936–945.

Acker, J., & VanHouten, D. R. Differential recruitment and control: The sex structuring of organizations. *Administrative Science Quarterly*, 1977, *22*, 152.

Adams, J. S. Inequity in social exchange. *Advances in Experimental Social Psychology*, 1965, *2*, 267.

Adams, J. S., & Jacobsen, P. R. Effects of wage inequities on work quality. *Journal of Abnormal and Social Psychology*, 1964, *69*, 19.

Ahammer, I. M. Social-learning theory as a framework for the study of adult personality development. In P. B. Baltes & K. W. Schaie (Eds.), *Life-span Developmental Psychology: Personality and Socialization*. New York: Academic Press, 1973, pp. 253–284.

Aho, W. R. Smoking, dieting and exercise: Age differences in attitudes and behavior relevant to selected Health Belief Model variables. *Rhode Island Medical Journal*, 1979, *62*(3), 85–92.

Ainsworth, M. D. The effects of maternal deprivation: A review of findings and controversy in the context of research strategy. In D. R. Heise (Ed.), *Personality and Socialization*. Chicago: Rand McNally, 1972, pp. 395–406.

Alexander, C., Weisman, C., & Chase, G. Determinants of staff nurses' perceptions of autonomy within different clinical contexts. *Nursing Research*, 1982, *31*, 48.

Aldrich, H. E. *Organizations and Environments*. Englewood Cliffs, NJ: Prentice-Hall, 1979.

Aldrich, H. E. Organizational boundaries and interorganizational conflict. *Human Relations*, 1971, *24*, 279.

Allen, V., & van de Vliert, E. R. (Eds.) *Role Transitions: Explorations and Explanations*. New York: Plenum, 1984.

Allison, G. T. *Essence of Decision: Explaining the Cuban Missile Crisis*. Boston: Little, Brown, 1971.

Allport, F. H. *Theories of Perception and the Concept of Structure*. Wiley, 1955, p. 131.

Allport, G. *The Nature of Prejudice*. Boston: Beacon Press, 1954.

Allport, G. W. *The Nature of Prejudice*. Garden City, NY: Doubleday, 1958.

Alonzo, A. An illness behavior paradigm: A conceptual exploration of a situational-adaptation perspective. *Social Science and Medicine*, 1984, *19*, 499.

Alonzo, A. An analytic typology of disclaimers, excuses, and justifications surrounding illness: A situational approach to health and illness. *Social Science and Medicine*, 1985, *21*, 153.

American Nurses' Association. *Educational preparation for nurse practitioners and assistants to nurses: A position paper.* New York: American Nurses' Association, 1965.

American Nurses' Association. *Facts about nursing 76–77.* Kansas City: American Nurses' Association, 1977.

American Nurses' Association. *Facts about nursing 82–83.* Kansas City: American Nurses' Association, 1983.

American Psychological Association. *Standards for educational and psychological tests.* Washington, DC: Author, 1974.

Anderson, R. Motive to avoid success: A profile. *Sex Roles*, 1978, *4*, 239–248.

Anderson, S. B., Ball, E., & Murphy, R. *Enclyclopedia of Education Evaluation.* San Francisco: Jossey-Bass, 1975.

Anderson, C. A., & Basteyns, M. Stress and the critical care nurse reaffirmed. *Journal of Nursing Administration*, 1981, *11*(1) 31.

Andreoli, K. G. Self-concept and health beliefs in compliant and noncompliant hypertensive patients. *Nursing Research*, 1981, *30*, 323.

Andrews, P., & Yankauer, A. The pediatric nurse practitioner: Growth of the concept. *American Journal of Nursing*, 1971, *71*, 503.

Angrist, S. S. Role constellation as a variable in women's leisure activities. *Social Forces*, 1967, *45*, 423.

Angrist, S. S. The study of sex roles. *Journal of Social Issues*, 1969, *25*, 215.

Arakelian, M. An assessment and nursing application of the concept of locus of control and the I-E scale. *Advances in Nursing Science*, 1980, *3*(1), 25.

Arakelian, M. *An investigation of the effects of an internalization intervention on compliance in adult diabetics.* Unpublished doctoral dissertation, Boston University, 1984.

Argyris, C. *Management and Organizational Development.* New York: McGraw-Hill, 1957.

Armstrong, S., Krahenbuhl, C., Muellenbach, R., & Savage, J. *Effects of hierarchical position on perceptions of nursing technology.* Unpublished master's thesis, University of Wisconsin-Madison, 1984.

Arndt, C., & Laeger, E. Role strain in a diversified role set: The director of nursing service, (Part 2), 1970, 19(*3*), 253.

Arndt, C., & Laeger, E. Role strain in a diversified role set: The director of nursing service. Part II: Sources of stress. *Nursing Research*, 1970, *19*(6), 445.

Arnold, L., Willougloby, T. L., & Calkins, V. Self evaluation in undergraduate medical education: A longitudinal perspective. *Journal of Medical Education*, 1985, *60*, 21.

Aronfreed, J. The concept of internalization. In D. A. Goslin (Ed.), *Handbook of Socialization Theory and Research.* Chicago: Rand McNally, 1969, pp. 263–323.

Aronoff, J., & Crano, W. D. A re-examination of the cross-cultural principles of task segregation and sex role differentiation in the family. *American Sociological Review*, 1975, *40*, 12.

Ashley, J. A. *Hospitals, Paternalism and the Role of the Nurse.* New York: Teacher's College, 1976.

Astin, H. *The Woman Doctorate in America.* New York: Russell Sage Foundation, 1969.

Astley, W. G., & Van de Ven, A. H. Central perspectives and debates in organization theory. *Administrative Science Quarterly*, 1983, *28*, 245.

Athansiou, R., Shaver, P., & Tavris, C. Woman and man. *Psychology Today*, 1970, *4*, 37–52.

Atwood, J. R. The phenomena of selective neglect. In E. Bauwens (Ed.), *The Anthropology of Health.* St. Louis: Mosby, 1977, pp. 192–200.

Atwood, J. R., & Hinshaw, A. S. Multiple indicators of nurse patient outcomes as a method for evaluating a change in staffing patterns. *Communicating Nursing Research*, 1977, *10*, 235.

Bacharach, S. B., & Lawler, E. *Power and Politics in Organizations*. San Francisco: Jossey Bass, 1980.

Bacharach, S. B., & Van de Ven, A. H. *Bargaining: Power, Tactics, Outcomes*. San Francisco: Jossey-Bass, 1983.

Backman, C., & Secord, P. The self and role selection. In C. Gordon & K. J. Gergen (Eds.), *The Self in Social Interaction*. New York: Wiley, 1968.

Bailey, J., Steffen, S., & Grout, J. The stress audit: Identifying the stresses of ICU nursing. *Journal of Nursing Education*, 1980, *19*(6), 15.

Baldwin, J. D. *George Herbert Mead*. San Francisco: Sage, 1986.

Bales, R. F. Task roles and social roles in problem-solving groups. In E. E. Maccoby, T. M. Newcomb, & E. L. Hartley (Eds.), (3rd ed.), *Readings in Social Psychology*. New York: Holt, Rinehart, & Winston, 1958, pp. 437–447.

Banda, E. E. Role problems, role strain: Perception and experience of the clinical nurse specialist. Unpublished master's thesis, Boston University School of Nursing, 1985.

Bandura, A. The role of imitation in a personality development. *Journal of Nursing Education*, April, 1963, *18*, 207.

Bandura, A. The role of modeling processes in personality development. In W. W. Hartup & N. L. Smothergill (Eds.), *The Young Child: Review of Research*. Washington, DC: National Association for the Education of Young Children, 1969a, pp. 42–58.

Bandura, A. Social learning theory of identificatory processes. In D. A. Goslin (Ed.), *Handbook of Socialization Theory and Research*. Chicago: Rand McNally, 1969b, pp. 213–262.

Bandura, A. *Social Learning Theory*. Englewood Cliffs, NJ: Prentice-Hall, 1977.

Bandura, A., & Walters, R. *Social Learning and Personality Development*. New York: Holt, Rinehart, & Winston, 1963.

Bandura, A., & Walters, R. H. The development of self-control. In C. Gordon & K. J. Gergen (Eds.), *The Self in Social Interaction*. New York: Wiley, 1968, pp. 186–196.

Bane, M. J. Here to stay: Parents and children. In A. S. Skolnick & J. H. Skolnick, *Family in Transition*, (4th ed.). Boston: Little, Brown, 1983, pp. 113–127.

Barber, B. *Science and the Social Order*. New York: Free Press, 1952.

Barclay, J. E., & Weaver, H. B. Comparative reliabilities and ease of construction of Thurstone and Likert attitude scales. *Journal of Social Psychology*, 1962, *58*, 109.

Baric, L. Recognition of the "at-risk" role: A means to influence health behavior. *International Journal of Health Education*, 1969, *12*, 24.

Barnes, C. S. Denver: A case study. In B. Bullough (Ed.), *The Law and the Expanding Nursing Role*. New York: Appleton-Century-Crofts, 1980, pp. 125–137.

Barnett, R. C., & Baruch, G. K. *Multiple role strain, number of roles and psychological well-being*. Unpublished manuscript, Wellesley College, Center for Research on Women. Wellesley, 1981.

Barnett, R. C., & Baruch, G. K. *On the psychological well-being of women in the mid-years*. Unpublished manuscript, Wellesley College, Center for Research on Women. Wellesley, 1982.

Barnett, R. C., & Baruch, G. K. *Women's involvement in multiple roles, role strain and psychological distress*. Unpublished manuscript, Wellesley College, Center for Research on Women. Wellesley, 1983.

Barnett, R. C., & Baruch, G. K. Women's involvement in multiple roles and psychological stress. *Journal of Personality and Social Psychology*, 1985, *49*, 135.

Barofsky, I. (Ed.). *Medication Compliance: A Behavioral Management Approach*. Thorofare, NJ: Slack, 1977.

Barry, J. R., & Wingrove, C. R. (Eds.). *Let's Learn about Aging: A Book of Readings*. New York: Wiley, 1977.

Barry, W. A. Marriage research and conflict: An integrative review. In D. R. Heise (Ed.), *Personality and Socialization*. Chicago: Rand McNally, 1972, pp. 170–179.

Bar-Yosef, R., & Schild, E. O. Pressures and defenses in bureaucratic roles. *American Journal of Sociology*, 1966, *71*, 663.

Battle, E. H., Halliburton, A., & Wallston, K. A. Self-medication among psychiatric patients and adherence after discharge. *Journal of Psychiatric Nursing and Mental Health Services*, 1982, *20*(5), 21.

Bauder, L. Balancing organizational demands with human needs: The ironic emphasis in schools of nursing. *Western Journal of Nursing Research*, 1982, *4*, 153.

Beck, E., Blaichman, S., Schriver, C. R., & Clow, C. L. Advocacy and compliance in genetic screening. *New Engl J Med*, 1974, *291*, 1166.

Becker, H. *The Outsiders*. New York: Free Press, 1963.

Becker, H. S., Geer, B., Hughes, E. C., & Strauss, A. L. *Boys in White: Student Culture in Medical School*. Chicago: University of Chicago Press, 1961.

Becker, H. S. Notes on the concept of commitment, *American Journal of Sociology*, 1960, *66*, 32.

Becker, M. H. (Ed.). *The Health Belief Model and Personal Health Behavior*. Thorofare, NJ: Slack, 1974a.

Becker, M. H. The health belief model and sick role behavior. In M. H. Becker (Ed.), *The Health Belief Model and Personal Health Behavior*. Thorofare, NJ: Slack, 1974b, pp. 82–92.

Becker, M. H. Understanding patient compliance: The contribution of attitudes and other psychosocial factors. In S. J. Cohen (Ed.), *New Directions in Patient Compliance*. Lexington, Mass: Health, 1979a, pp. 1–31.

Becker, M. H. Patient perceptions and compliance: Recent studies of the health belief model. In R. B. Hayes, et al., (Eds.), *Compliance in Health Care*. Baltimore: Johns Hopkins University Press, 1979b, pp. 78–109.

Becker, M. H., Haefner, D. P., Kasl, S. V., et al.: Selected psychosocial models and correlates of individual health-related behaviors. *Medical Care*, 1977, *15*(suppl), 27.

Becker, M. H., Kaback, M. M., Rosenstock, I. M., & Ruth, M. V. Some influences on public participation in a genetic screening program. *Journal of Community Health*, 1975, *1*, 3.

Becker, W. C. Consequences of different kinds of parental discipline. In M. L. Hoffman & L. W. Hoffman (Eds.), *Review of Child Development Research* (Vol. 1). New York: Russell Sage, 1964, pp. 169–208.

Becker, W. C. Consequences of different kinds of parental discipline. In D. R. Heise (Ed.), *Personality and Socialization*. Chicago: Rand McNally, 1972, pp. 29–72.

Beckhouse, L. S. *Behavioral resolution of role incongruity: An interactional approach*. Unpublished dissertation, Vanderbilt University, 1969.

Been, P. *How to Work for a Woman Boss*, New York: Dodd Mead, 1987.

Beehr, T. *Role ambiguity as a role stress: Some moderating and intervening variables*. Unpublished dissertation, University of Michigan, 1974.

Beil, C., Sisk, D. R., & Miller, W. E. A comparison of specialty choices among senior medical students using Bem Sex-Role Inventory Scale. *Journal of the American Medical Women's Association*, 1980, *35*(7), 178.

Belenky, M. F., Clinchy, B., Goldberger, N. R., & Tarule, J. M. *Women's Ways of Knowing*. New York: Basic, 1986.

Bell, D. *The Coming of Post-Industrial Society*. New York: Basic Books, 1973.

Belsky, J. Mother-father-infant interaction: A naturalistic observational study. *Developmental Psychology*, 1979, *15*, 601.

Belsky, J., & Steinberg, L. The effects of day care: A critical review. *Child Development*, 1978, *49*, 929.

Bem, S. L. Psychology looks at sex roles: Where have all the androgynous people gone?

Paper presented at the UCLA Symposium on Women, Los Angeles, May 1972.

Bem, S. L. The measurement of psychological androgyny. *Journal of Consulting and Clinical Psychology*, 1974, *42*, 155.

Bem, S. L. Sex role adaptability: One consequence of psychological androgyny. *Journal of Personality and Social Psychology*, 1975a, *31*, 634.

Bem, S. L. Beyond androgyny: Some presumptuous prescriptions for a liberated sexual identity. Keynote address for APA-NIMH conference on The Research Needs of Women, Madison, Wisc, 1975b.

Bem, S. L. On the utility of alternative procedures for assessing psychological androgyny. *Journal of Consulting and Clinical Psychology*, 1977, *45*, 196.

Bem, S. L., & Lenney, E. Sex typing and the avoidance of cross-sex behavior. *Journal of Personality and Social Psychology*, 1976, *33*, 48.

Bem, S. L., Martyna, W., & Watson, C. Sex typing and androgyny: Further explorations of the expressive domain. *Journal of Personality and Social Psychology*, 1976, *34*, 1016.

Ben-David, J. The professional role of the physician in bureaucratized medicine: A study in role conflict. *Human Relations*, 1963, *11*, 255.

Bendix, R., & Lipset, S. M. Karl Marx' theory of social class. In R. Bendix & S. M. Lipset (Eds.), *Class, Status, and Power: Social Stratification in Comparative Perspective* (2nd ed.). New York: Free Press, 1966, pp. 6–11.

Bendix, R., & Lipset, S. M. *Class, Status, and Power: Social Stratification in Comparative Perspective* (2nd ed.). New York: Free Press, 1966.

Bennett, R. (Ed.). *Aging, Isolation and Resocialization*. New York: Van Nostrand, Reinhold, 1980.

Benoleil. J. Q. Institutionalized practices of information control. *Psychiatry*, 1965, *28*, 119.

Benoleil, J. Q. Grounded theory and qualitative data: The socializing influences of life-threatening disease on identity development. In P. J. Woolridge, J. K. Skipper, R. C. Leonard, & M. H. Schmitt (Eds.), *Behavioral Science and Nursing Theory*. St. Louis: Mosby, 1983, 141.

Benson, H. *The Relaxation Response*. New York: Avon Books, 1975.

Benson, J. K. The analysis of bureaucratic-professional conflict: Functional versus dialectical approaches. *Sociological Quarterly*, 1973, *14*, 376.

Benson, J. K. Organizations: A dialectic view. *Administrative Science Quarterly*, 1977, *22*, 1.

Ben-Sira, Z. "Instrumental coping" and "affective defense": An additional perspective in health promoting behavior. *Social Science and Medicine*, 1978, *12*, 163.

Benton, T. *Philosophical Foundations of the Three Sociologies*. Boston: Routledge & Kegan Paul, 1977.

Berger, B. M. Adolescence and beyond: An essay review of three books on the problems of growing up. *Social Problems*, 1963, *10*, 394.

Berger, P., & Luckman, T. *The Social Construction of Reality*. New York: Free Press, 1966.

Berger, P. L., & Berger, B. Becoming a member of society. In P. I. Rose (Ed.), *Socialization and the Life Cycle*. New York: St. Martin's Press, 1979, pp. 4–20.

Berkanovic, E., & Telesky, L. Social networks, beliefs, and the congruent and incongruent patterns. *Medical Care*, 1982, *29*, 1018.

Berkman, L. F., & Breslow, L. *Health and Ways of Living: The Alameda County Study*. New York: Oxford University Press, 1983.

Berkman, L. F., & Syme, S. L. Social networks, host resistance, and mortality: A nine-year follow-up study of Alameda County residents. *American Journal of Epidemiology*, 1979, *109*, 186.

Bernard, J. *Academic Women*. University Park: Pennsylvania State University Press, 1964.

Berne, P. *How to Work for a Woman Boss: Even if You Would Rather Not*. New York: Dodd Mead, 1987.

Berni, R., & Fordyce, W. E. *Behavior Modification and the Nursing Process* (2nd ed.). St. Louis, Mo: Mosby, 1977.

Berrien, K. F. *General Social Systems*. New Brunswick, NJ: Rutgers University Press, 1968.

Berry, J., & Kushner, R. A critical look at the Queen Been syndrome. *Journal of the National Assocation for Women Deans, Administrators, and Counselors*, 1975, *38*, 173.

Bertrand, A. L. The stress-strain element of social systems: A micro theory of conflict and change. *Social Forces*, 1963, *42*(1), 1.

Bibace, R., & Walsh, M. E. Conflict of roles: On the difficulties of being both scientist and practitioner in one life. *Professional Psychology*, 1982, *13*(3), 389.

Bible, B. L., & McComas, J. D. Role consensus and teacher effectiveness. *Social Forces*, 1963, *42*, 225.

Biddle, B. *Role Theory: Expectations, Identities, and Behaviors*, New York: Academic Press, 1979.

Biddle, B., & Thomas, E. (Eds.). *Role Theory: Concepts and Research*. New York: Wiley, 1966.

Biddle, B., & Thomas, E. *Role Theory: Concepts and Research*. Huntington, NY: Robert Krieger Publishing Co., 1979.

Bidwell, C. The young professional in the army: A study of occupational identity. *American Social Res*, 1961, *26*, 360.

Biener, L., & Bennett, S. Doctors and nurse practitioners: Styles of team relationship and their impact on team effectiveness. Unpublished manuscript, Wellesley College, Center for Research on Women, Wellesley, 1982.

Bigbee, J. L. Locus of control and the obese adolescent: A pilot study. In P. L. Chinn (Ed.), *Advances in nursing theory development*. Rockville, Md: Aspen Systems, 1983, pp. 153–172.

Biggs, P., & Fiebert, M. S. A factor-analytic study of American male attitudes. *Journal of Psychology*, 1984, *116*, 113.

Biller, H. B. *Father, Child, and Sex-role*. Lexington, Mass: Heath, 1971.

Biller, H. B. Father dominance and sex-role development in kindergarten-age boys. In D. R. Heise (Ed.), *Personality and Socialization*. Chicago: Rand McNally, 1972, pp. 73–85.

Biller, H. B. *Paternal Deprivation*. Lexington, Mass: Heath, 1974.

Biller, H. B. The father and personality development: Paternal deprivation and sex-role development. In M. E. Lamb (Ed.), *The Role of the Father in Child Development*. New York: Wiley, 1976.

Biller, H. B. Father absence, divorce, and personality development. In M. E. Lamb (Ed.), *The Role of the Father in Child Development* (2nd ed.). New York: Wiley, 1981.

Bird, C. *Born Female: The High Cost of Keeping Women Down*. New York: McKay, 1968.

Bixenstine, V. E., & Douglas, J. Effect of psychopathology on group consensus and cooperative choice in a six-person game. *Journal of Personality and Social Psychology*, 1967, *5*, 32.

Blackwell, E. *Pioneer Work in Opening the Medical Profession to Women*. London: Longmans, Green, 1895.

Blake, J., & Davis, D. Norms, values, and sanctions. In R. E. Faris (Ed.), *Handbook of Modern Sociology*. Chicago: Rand McNally, 1964, pp. 456–484.

Blalock, H. M. *Theory Construction*. Englewood Cliffs, NJ: Prentice-Hall, 1969.

Blalock, H. M. *An Introduction to Social Research*. Englewood Cliffs, NJ: Prentice-Hall, 1970.

Blanchard, R. W., & Biller, H. B. Father availability and academic performance among third grade boys. *Developmental Psychology*, 1971, *4*, 301.

Blau, P. *Bureaucracy in Modern Society*. New York: Random House, 1956.

Blau, P. M. *The Dynamics of Bureaucracy*, (2nd ed.). Chicago: University of Chicago Press, 1963.

Blau, P. M. *Exchange and Power in Social Life.* New York: Wiley, 1964.

Blau, P. M., & Duncan, O. D. *The American Occupational Structure.* New York: Wiley, 1967.

Blau, P. M., & Schoenherr, R. A. *The Structure of Organizations.* New York: Basic Books, 1971.

Blau, P., & Scott, W. R. *Formal Organizations.* San Francisco: Chandler, 1962.

Bleier, R. (Ed.). *Feminist Approaches to Science.* New York: Pergamon, 1986.

Bleier, R. *Science and Gender.* New York: Pergamon, 1984.

Bloom, S. W. Power and Dissent in the Medical School. New York: Free Press, 1973.

Bloom, S. W. The medical school as a social system: A case study of faculty-student relations. *Milband Memorial Fund Quarterly,* 1971, *49,* 1.

Blumenthal, J. A., Williams, R., Kong, Y., et al. Type A behavior and angiographically documented coronary disease. *Circulation,* 1979, *58,* 634.

Blumer, H. The problem of the concept in social psychology. *American Journal of Sociology,* 1940, pp. 515–523.

Blumer, H. Society as symbolic interaction. In A. Rose (Ed.), *Human Behavior and Social Processes.* Boston: Houghton, Mifflin, 1962, pp. 179–192.

Blumer, H. *Symbolic Interactions: Perspective and Method.* Englewood Cliffs, NJ: Prentice-Hall, 1969.

Blumer, H. Comment: Mead & Blumer: the convergent methodological perspectives of social behaviorism and symbolic interactionism. *American Sociological Review,* 1980, *45,* 409.

Blumer, H. Response to McPhail and Rexroat. *American Sociological Review,* 1980, *45,* 409.

Blumstein, P. W. Identity bargaining and self-conception. *Social Forces,* 1973, *53,* 476.

Bogue, D. V. *Skid Row in American Cities.* Chicago: University of Chicago Press, 1963.

Bohrenstedt, G. W. Reliability and validity assessment. In G. F. Summers (Ed.), *Attitude Measurement.* Chicago: Rand McNally, 1970, pp. 80–99.

Bolton, C. D. Some consequences of the Meadian self. *Symbolic Interaction,* 1981, *4*(2), 245.

Bolton, C. D. Is sociology a behavioral science? In Munis & Meltzer (Eds.), *Symbolic Interaction.* Boston: Allyn & Bacon, 1967.

Borgotta, E. Role playing specification, personality and performance. *Sociometry,* 1961, *24,* 218.

Bowman, M. Female chauvinists. *Nursing Mirror,* 1983, *156*(14), 34.

Bragg, B. W., & Allen, V. I. Ordinal position and conformity: A role theory analysis. *Sociometry,* 1970, *33*(4), 371.

Braito, R., & Caston, R. Factors influencing job satisfaction in nursing practice. In N Chaska (Ed.), *A Time to Speak.* New York: McGraw-Hill, 1983, pp. 346.

Brand, K. L., & Glass, L. K. Perils and parallels of women and nursing. *Nursing Forum,* 1975, *14*(2), 160.

Brandt, P. A., & Weinert, C. The PRQ—A social support system. *Nursing Research,* 1981, *30,* 277.

Brault, L. *Primary nursing: the variable of accountability.* Unpublished thesis, California State University, 1977.

Bremer, T., & Wittig, M. Fear of success: A personality trait or a response to occupational deviance and role overload? *Sex Roles,* 1980, *6*(1), 27.

Brim, O. G., Jr. The parent-child relation as a social system: I. Parent and child roles. *Child Development,* 1957, *28*(3), 345.

Brim, O. G., Jr. Family structure and sex-role learning by children: A further analysis of Helen Koch's data. *Sociometry,* 1958, *21,* 1.

Brim, O. G., Jr. Personality development as role-learning. In Iscoe, & H. W. Stevenson (Eds.), *Personality Development in Children.* Austin: University of Texas Press, 1960.

Brim, O. G., Jr. Socialization through the life cycle. In O. G. Brim, Jr. & S. Wheeler (Eds.), *Socialization after Childhood: Two Essays.* New York: Wiley, 1966, pp. 1–50.

Brim, O. G., Jr. Adult socialization. In D. L. Sills (Ed.), *International Encyclopedia of the Social Sciences*. Boston: Little, Brown, 1968a, pp. 555–562.

Brim, O. G., Jr. Adult socialization. In J. A. Clausen (Ed.), *Socialization and Society*. Boston: Little, Brown, 1968b, pp. 182–226.

Brim, O. G., Jr. Glass, D. C., Lanvin, D. E., & Goodman, N. *Personality and Decision Processes: Studies in the Social Psychology of Thinking*. Stanford: Stanford University Press, 1962.

Brim, O. G., Jr., & Kagan, J. Constancy and change: A view of the issues. In O. G. Brim, Jr. & J. Kagan (Eds.), *Constancy and Change in Human Development*. Cambridge, Mass: Harvard University Press, 1980, pp. 1–25.

Bronfenbrenner, U. Socialization and social class through time and space. In E. E. Maccoby, T. M. Newcomb, & E. L. Hartley (Eds.), *Readings in Social Psychology*. New York: Holt, Rinehart, & Winston, 1958.

Broverman, I. K., Broverman, D. M., Clarkson, F. E., et al. Sex-role stereotypes and clinical judgements of mental health. *Journal of Consulting and Clinical Psychology*, 1970, *34*, 1.

Broverman, I. K., Vogel, S. R., Broverman, D. M., et al. Sex-role stereotypes: A current appraisal. *Journal of Social Issues*, 1972, *28*, 59.

Brown, E. L. *Nursing for the Future*. New York: Russell Sage Foundation, 1948.

Brown, E. L. Nursing and patient care. In F. Davis (Ed.), *The Nursing Profession*. New York: Wiley, 1966, pp. 176–203.

Brown, J. S., Buchanan, D., & Hsu, L. N. Sex differences in sick role behavior during hospitalization after open heart surgery. *Research in Nursing and Health*, 1978, *1*(1), 37.

Brown, J. S., & Rawlinson, M. Relinquishing the sick role following open-heart surgery. *Journal of Health and Social Behavior*, March, 1975, *1*, 12.

Brunetto, E., & Birke, P. The primary care nurse: the generalist in a structured health team. *American Journal of Public Health*, 1972, *62*, 785.

Buban, S. L. Studying social processes: The Chicago & Iowa schools revisited. In N. Denzin. (Ed.), *Studies in Symbolic Interaction*, Supplement 2, (Part A). 1986, pp. 25–38.

Bucher, R., & Stelling, J. Characteristics of professional organizations, *Journal of Health and Social Behavior*, 1969, *10*, 3.

Buckley, W. *Sociology and Modern Systems Theory*. Englewood Cliffs, NJ: Prentice-Hall, 1967, p 42.

Bullough, B. You can't get there from here: Articulation in nursing education. *The Journal of Nursing Education*, 1972, *11*(4), 4.

Bullough, B. Alienation and school segregation. *Integrated Education*, 29, March–April, 1972.

Bullough, B. The struggle for women's rights in Denver: A personal account. *Nursing Outlook*, 566, September, 1978.

Bullough, V. L., & Bullough, B. *The Care of the Sick: The Emergence of Modern Nursing*. New York: Prodist, 1978.

Bulmer, M. *The Chicago School of Sociology*. Chicago: University of Chicago Press, 1984.

Burchard, W. Role conflict of military chaplains. *Am Social Rev.*, 1954, 19, 228.

Burns, T., & Stalker, G. M. *The Management of Innovation*. London: Tavistock, 1961.

Burr, W. *Theory Construction and the Sociology of the Family*. New York: Wiley, 1974.

Burr, W. Role transitions: A reformulation of theory. *Journal of Marriage and the Family*, August 1972, 407.

Burr, W. R., Hill, R., Nye, I. F., & Reiss, I. L. (Eds.). *Contemporary Theories about the Family*. Nw York: Free Press, 1979.

Bush, M. A., & Kjervik, D. K. The nurse's self-image. In D. K. Kjervik & I. M. Martison (Eds.), *Women in Stress: A Nursing Perspective*. New York: Appleton-Century-Crofts, 1979.

Cahill, S. E. Directions for an interactionist study of gender development. *Symbolic*

Interaction, 1980, *3*(1), 123.

Cain, L. D., Jr. Life course and social structure. In R. E. L. Faris (Ed.), *Handbook of Modern Sociology*. Chicago: Rand McNally, 1964, pp. 272–309.

Cairns, R. B., & Hood, K. E. Continuity in social develpment: A comparative perspective on individual difference prediction. In P. B. Baltes & O. G. Brim, Jr. (Eds.), *Life-span Development and Behavior* (Vol. 5). New York: Academic Press, 1983, pp. 301–358.

Caldwell, B. M. the effects of infant care. In M. L. Hoffman & L. W. Hoffman (Eds.), *Review of Child Development Research* (Vol. 1). New York: Sage, 1964, pp. 9–87.

California Decrees Comparable Worth of Women's Work. *American Journal of Nursing*, 1981, *81*.

Calkin, J. D. *Effect of task and structure on nurse performance and satisfaction: A part-replica experiment*. Unpublished doctoral dissertation, University of Wisconsin-Madison, 1980.

Calkin, J. D. A model for advanced nursing practice. *Journal of Nursing Administration*, 1984, *14*, 24.

Campbell, D. T., & Fiske, D. W. Convergent and discriminant validation by the multitait-multimethod matrix. *Psychological Bulletin*, 1959, 81.

Campbell, E. Adolescent socialization. In D. A. Goslin (Ed.), *Handbook of Socialization Theory and Research*. Chicago: Rand McNally, 1969, pp. 821–859.

Campbell, J. D. Peer relations in childhood. In M. L. Hoffman & L. W. Hoffman (Eds.), *Review of Child Development Research* (Vol. 1). New York: Sage, 1964, pp. 289–322.

Campbell, J. P., Dunnette, M., Lawler, E., & Weick, K. E., Jr. *Managerial Behavior, Performance, and Effectiveness*. New York: McGraw-Hill, 1970.

Campbell, J. P. On the nature of organizational effectiveness. In P. Goodman & J. Pennings (Eds.), *New Perspectives on Organizational Effectiveness*. San Francisco: Jossey Bass, 1977.

Caplan, R. D., & Jones, K. W. Effects of work load, role ambiguity, and type A personality on anxiety, depression and heart rate. *Journal of Applied Psychology*, 1975, *60*, 713.

Caplan, R. D., Harrison, R. V., Wellons, R. V., & French, J. R. P. *Social Support and Patient Adherence: Experimental and Survey Findings*. Ann Arbor: Institute for Social Research: University of Michigan Press, 1980.

Caplan, R. D., Robinson, E. A. R, French, J. R. P, et al. *Adhering to Medical Regimens: Pilot Experiments in Patient Education and Social Support*. Ann Arbor: University of Michigan Press, 1976.

Caplow, T. *The Sociology of Work*. New York: McGraw-Hill, 1954.

Caplow, T., Bahr, H. M., Chadwick, B. A., et al. New York: Bantam, 1982. *Middletown Families: Fifty Years of Change and Continuity*.

Capra, F. *The Turning Point: Science, Society, and the Rising Culture*. New York: Simon & Schuster, 1982.

Carlson, E., & Carlson, R. Male and female subjects in personality research. *Journal of Abnormal and Social Psychology*, 1960, *61*, 482.

Carmichael, S., & Hamilton, C. V. *Black Power: The Politics of Liberation in America*. New York: Vintage, 1967.

Carnegie, M. E. Are Negro schools of nursing needed today? *Nursing Outlook*, 1964, *12*, 52.

Carpenter, E. S. Women in male-dominated health professions. *International Journal of Health Sciences*, 1977, 7(2), 191.

Carr-Saunders, A. M., & Wilson, P. A. *The Professions*. Oxford: Clarendon Press, 1933.

Cason, C. L., & Beck, C. M. Clinical nurse specialist role development. *Nursing and Health Care*, 1982, 25, 35.

Cermak, A. Community based learning in occupational therapy. *American Journal of Occupational Therapy*, 1976, *30*, 157.

Chamberlain, N. W. *A General Theory of Economic Process*. New York: Harper, Row, 1955.

Charon, J. *Symbolic Interactionism: Introduction, an Interpretation, an Integration.* Englewood Cliffs, NJ: Prentice-Hall, 1979.

Charon, J. M. *Symbolic Interactionism: An Introduction, an Interpretation, and Integration* (2nd ed.). Englewood Cliffs, NJ: Prentice-Hall, 1985.

Chauncey, R. L. Comment of "The labeling theory of mental illness." *American Sociological Review,* 1975, *40,* 248.

Chesler, P. Are we a threat to each other? *Ms.* 1972, *1*(8), 88.

Chesney, M. A., & Rosenman, R. H. Type A behavior in the work setting. In C. L. Cooper & R. Payne (Eds.), *Current Concerns in Occupational Stress,* New York: Wiley, 1980, pp. 187–212.

Chomsky, N. *The Logical Structure of Linguistic Theory.* Cambridge, Mass: MIT Press, 1975.

Christensen, H. T. (Ed.). *Handbook of Marriage and the Family.* Chicago: Rand McNally, 1964.

Christenson v. the State of Iowa

Christy, E. Equal rights for women: Voices from the past. *American Journal of Nursing,* 1971, *71,* 288.

Churchman, C. W. *The Design of Inquiring Systems.* New York: Basic Books, 1971.

Clark, E. V. Language change during language acquisition. In M. E. Lamb & A. L. Brown (Eds.), *Advances in Developmental Psychology* (Vol. 2). Hillsdale, NJ: Erlbaum, 1982, pp. 125–170.

Clarke-Stewart, K. A. And Daddy makes three: The father's impact on mother and young child. *Child Development,* 1978, *49,* 466.

Clarke-Stewart, K. A. The father's contribution to children's cognitive and social development in early childhood. In F. A. Pederson (Ed.), *The Father-Infant Relationship.* New York: Praeger, 1980.

Clarke-Stewart, K. A. The family as a child-care environment. In A. S. Skolnick & J. H. Skolnick, *Family in Transition,* (4th ed.). Boston: Little, Brown, 1983, pp. 563–575.

Clarkson, F. E., Vogel, S. R., Broverman, I. K., et al. Family size and sex-role stereotypes. *Science,* 1970, *167,* 390.

Clausen, J. A. Family structure, socialization, and personality. In L. W. Hoffman & M. L. Hoffman (Eds.), *Review of Child Development Research* (Vol. 2). New York: Sage, 1966, pp. 1–53.

Clausen, J. A. A historical and comparative view of socialization theory and research. In J. A. Clausen (Ed.), *Socialization and Society.* Boston: Little, Brown, 1968, pp. 18–72.

Clausen, J. A. Introduction. In J. A. Clausen (Ed.), *Socialization and Society.* Boston: Little, Brown, 1968b, pp. 1–17.

Clausen, J. A. Perspectives on childhood socialization. In J. A. Clausen (Ed.), *Socialization and Society.* Boston: Little, Brown, 1968c, pp. 130–181.

Clausen, J. A. American research on the family and socialization. *Children Today, 46,* (March-April) 1978, 7.

Clay, R. N. *The Medieval Hospitals of England.* London: Methuen, 1909.

Cleary, P. D., & Mechanic, D. Sex differences in psychological distress among married people. *Journal of Health and Social Behavior,* 1983, 24, 111.

Clegg, S., & Dunkerley, D. *Organization, Class and Control.* Boston: Routledge, Kegan Paul, 1980.

Cleland, V. S. Symposium on current legal and professional problems: To end sex discrimination. *Nursing Clinics of North America,* 1974, *9,* 563.

Cobb, S. Social support as a moderator of life stress. *Psychosomatic Medicine,* 1976, *38,* 300.

Cobb, S. Social support and health through the life course. In M. W. Riley (Ed.), *Aging from Birth to Death: Interdisciplinary Perspectives.* Boulder, Colo: Westview Press, 1979, pp. 93–106.

Cogan, I. *Negroes for Medicine: Report of a Macy Conference.* Baltimore: Johns Hopkins

University Press, 1968.

Cogswell, B. Rehabilitation of paraplegics: Processes of socialization. *Social Inquiry*, 1967, *37*, 3.

Cohen, A. R. Attitudinal consequences of induced discrepancies between cognitions and behavior. *Public Opinion Quarterly*, 1960, *24*, 297.

Cohen, S. J. (Ed.). *New Directions in Patient Compliance.* Lexington, Mass: Health, 1979.

Coleman, J. S. *Abnormal Psychology in Modern Life.* Ill: Scott, 1976.

Coleman, J. S., Campbell, E. Q., Hobson, C., et al. *Equality of Educational Opportunity.* Washington, DC: Office of Education, Department of Health, Education, and Welfare, 1966.

Colignan, R., & Cray, R. New organizational perspectives: Critiques and critical organizations. In M. Zey-Ferrell & M. Aiken (Eds.), *Complex Organizations: Critical Perspectives.* Glenview, Ill: Scott, Foresman, 1981, pp. 100–117.

Colomy, P., & Rhoades, G. Role performance and person perception: Toward an interactionist approach. *Symbolic Interaction*, 1983, *6*(2), 207.

Colton, M. R. Nursing's leadership vacuum. *Supervisor Nurse*, 1976, *6*, 29.

Comaroff, J., & Maguire, P. Ambiguity and the search for meaning: Childhood leukemia in the modern clinical context. In P. Conrad & R. Kern (Eds.), *The Sociology of Health and Illness* (2nd ed.). New York: St. Martin's Press, 1986, pp. 100–109.

Committee for the Study of Nursing Education. *Nursing and Nursing Education in the United States.* New York: Macmillan, 1923.

Comstock, D. R., & Scott, W. R. Technology and the structure of subunits: Distinguishing individual and work unit effects. *Administrative Science Quarterly*, 1977, *22*, 177.

Conway, M. Are attitudes toward work related to attitudes toward seeking medical care? *Nursing Research*, 22, (March-April) 1973, 123.

Conway, M. E. Management effectiveness and the role making process. *Journal of Nursing Administration*, *4*, (November-December) 1974, 25.

Conway, M. E. Management effectiveness and the role making process. *Journal of Nursing Administration*, 1974, *66*, 604.

Conway, M. Theoretical approaches to the study of roles. In M. Hardy & M. Conway (Eds.), *Role Theory: Perspectives for Health Professionals.* New York: Appleton-Century-Crofts, 1978.

Cook, K. *Social Exchange Theory* San Francisco: Sage, 1987.

Cooley, C. H. Primary groups. In C. H. Cooley, (Ed.). *Social Organization.* New York: Schocken Books, 1962, pp. 23–31.

Cooley, C. H. *Human Nature and the Social Order.* New York: Schocken Books, 1964.

Cooley, C. H. The social self: On the meanings of "I". In C. Gordon & K. J. Gergen (Eds.), *The Self in Social Interaction.* New York: Wiley, 1968, pp. 87–91.

Coombs, R. H. *Mastering medicine: Professional socialization in medical school.* New York: Free Press, 1978.

Cooper, C. L., & Marshall, J. Sources of managerial and white collar stress. In C. L. Cooper & R. Payne (Eds.), *Stress at Work.* New York: Wiley, 1978, pp. 81–105.

Cooper, C. L. & Payne, R. (Eds.), *Stress at Work*, New York: Wiley, 1978.

Cooper, C. L. & Payne, R. (Eds.), *Current Concerns in Occupational Health.* New York: Wiley, 1980.

Cooper, C. R., Grotevant, H. D., & Condon, S. M. Individuality and connectedness in the family as a context for adolescent identity formation and role-taking skill. In H. D. Grotevant & C. R. Cooper (Eds.), *Adolescent Development in the Family.* San Francisco: Jossey-Bass, 1983, pp. 43–59.

Corti, W. R. (Ed.). *The philosophy of George Herbert Mead.* Amriswiler Bucherei, 1973.

Corwin, R. The professional employee: A study of conflict in nursing roles. *American Journal of Sociology*, 1961, *66*, 604.

Coser, L. A., (with R. Coser). *Greedy Institutions.* New York: Free Press, 1974.

Coser, L. A. Sociological theory from the Chicago dominance to 1965. In A. Inkeles, J. Coleman, & N. Smelser (Eds.), *Annual Review of Sociology* (Vol. 6). Palo Alto, Cal: Annual Review, Inc., 1976, pp. 145–160.

Coser, R. Commentary and debate: A note on the Concept of Role distance. *The American Journal of Sociology*, 1962, 247.

Coser, R. Role distance, sociological ambivalence, and transitional status systems. *American Journal of Sociology*, 1966, *72*, 173.

Coser, R. The complexity of roles as a seed bed of individual autonomy. In L. A. Coser (Ed.), *The Idea of Social Structure: Papers in Honor of Robert K. Merton*. New York: Harcourt, Brace, 1983, pp. 237–264.

Coser, R. L. *Life in the Ward*. East Lansing, Mich: Michigan State University Press, 1962.

Costner, H. L., & Leik, R. K. Deductions from Axiomatic theory. *American Sociological Review*, 1964, *29*, 819–835.

Cottrell, L. S. The adjustment of the individual to his age and sex-roles. *American Sociological Review*, 1942, *5*, 617.

Cottrell, L. S., Jr. Interpersonal interaction and the development of the self. In D. A. Goslin (Ed.), *Handbook of Socialization Theory and Research*. Chicago: Rand McNally, 1969, pp. 543–570.

Cottrell, N. Interpersonal interaction and the development of the self. In D. Goslin (Ed.), *Handbook of Socialization Theory and Research*. Chicago: Rand McNally, 1969, pp. 543–570.

Coughlin, E. K. Women's studies: Changing the landscape of the traditional academic disciplines. *The Chronicle of Higher Education*, August 1, 1984, pp. 5–6.

County of Washington (Oregon) v. Gunther

Coutu, W. Role-playing vs. role-taking: An appeal for clarification. *American Sociological Review*, 1951, *16*, 180.

Cowan, C. E. Sexism by nurses. *The Lamb*, 1981, *38*(8), 5.

Cox, B. G. & Lewis, L. A. Responses of medical women to a survey on sexist language in medical publication. *Journal of the American Medical Women's Association*, 1981, *36*(1), 15.

Crocker, L., & Brodie, B. Development of a scale to assess student nurses' views of the professional nursing role. *Journal of Applied Psychology*, 1974, *59*, 233.

Cronbach, L. J., & Meehl, P. E. Construct validity in psychological tests. *Psychological Bulletin*, 1955, *52*, 281.

Croog, S., & Ver Steeg, D. The hospital as a social system. In H. E. Freeman, S. Levine, & L. G. Reeder (Eds.), *Handbook of Medical Sociology*. Englewood Cliffs, NJ: Prentice-Hall, 1972, pp. 274–314.

Croog, S. H., & Richards, N. P. Health beliefs and smoking patterns in heart patients and their wives: A longitudinal study. *American Journal of Public Health*, 1977, *67*, 921.

Cullen, J. W., Fox, B. H., & Isom, R. N. (Eds.). *Cancer: The Hidden Dimensions*. New York: Raven Press, 1976.

Cummings, K. M., Jette, A. M., Brock, B. M., & Haefner, D. P. Psychosocial determinants of immunization behavior in a swine fluenza campaign. *Medical Care*, 1979, *17*, 639.

Cummings, K. M., Kirscht, J. P., Binder, L. R., & Godley, A. J. Determinants of drug treatment maintenance among hypertensive persons in inner city Detroit. *Public Health Reports*, 1982, *97*, 99.

Cyert, R. M., & March, J. G. *Behavioral Theory of the Firm*. Englewood Cliffs, NJ: Prentice-Hall, 1963.

Daly, M. *Gynecology: The Metaethics of Radical Feminism*. Boston: Beacon Press, 1978.

Daly, M. *Pure Lust: Elemental Feminist Philosophy*. Boston, Mass: Beacon Press, 1978.

Damon, W. *Social and Personality Development*. New York: Norton, 1983.

D'Andrade, R. G. Sex differences and cultural institutions. In E. E. Maccoby (Ed.), *The*

Development of Sex Differences. Stanford, Cal: Stanford University Press, 1966, pp. 173–204.

Daniels, A. K. How free should professions be? In E. Freidson (Ed.), *The Professions and Their Prospects.* Beverly Hills, Cal: Sage, 1971, pp. 39–57.

Dannefer, D. Adult development and social theory. *American Sociological Review,* 1984, *49,* 100.

Datagram: Applicants to U.S. Medical Schools 1977–78 to 1981–82. *Journal of Medical Education,* 1982, *57,* 882.

Davidson, R. A., & Lauver, D. Nurse practitioner and physician roles: Delineation and complementarity of practice. *Research in Nursing and Health,* 1984, *7,* 3.

Davis, F. Definitions of time and recovery in paralytic polio convalescence. *American Journal of Sociology,* 1965, *61,* 582.

Davis, F. Deviance disavowal: The management of strained interaction by the visibly handicapped. *Social Problems,* 1961, *9,* 120.

Davis, F. Uncertainty in medical prognosis: Clinical and functional. *American Journal of Sociology,* 1960, *66,* 41. In A. R. Lindesmith, & A. L. Strauss (Eds.), *Readings in Social Psychology.* New York: Holt, Rinehart, & Winston, 1969, pp. 153–160.

Davis, F., & Olesen, V. Initiation into a women's profession: Identity problems in the status transition of coed to student nurse. *Sociometry,* 1963, *26,* 89.

Davis, J. Conceptions of official leader roles in the air force. *Social Forces,* 1954, *32,* 253.

Davis, K. A conceptual analysis of stratification. *American Society Review,* June 1942, *7,* 309.

Davis, K. Final note on a case of extreme isolation. In J. Heiss (Ed.), *Family Roles and Interaction: An Anthology* (2nd ed.). Chicago: Rand McNally, 1976, pp. 297–306.

Davis, K., & Moore, W. E. Some principles of stratification. *American Sociological Review,* February 1945, *5,* 242.

Davis, K., & Moore, W. E. Some principles of stratification. In R. Bendix, & S. M. Lipset (Eds.), *Class, Status, and Power: Social Stratification in Comparative Perspective* (2nd ed.). New York: Free Press, 1966, pp. 47–53.

Dean, P. G. Toward androgyny. *Image,* 1978, *10*(1), 10.

de Araujo, G., van Arsdale, P. V., Holmes, T. H., & Dudley, D. L. Life change, coping ability, and chronic intrinsic asthma. *Journal of Psychosomatic Research,* 1973, *17,* 359.

Deaux, K. From individual differences to social categories: Analysis of a decade's research on gender. American Psychologist, 1984, *39,* 105.

Deaux, K. U., & Major, B. Sex-related patterns in the unit of perception. *Personality and Social Psychology Bulletin,* 1977, *3,* 297.

Deaux, K., & Hanna, R. Courtship in the personals column: The influence of gender and sexual orientation. *Sex Roles,* 1984, *11*(5/6), pp. 363.

de Beauvoir, S. *The Second Sex.* New York: Bantam, 1961.

de Blecourt, J. J. (Ed.). *Patient compliance: Proceedings of an international symposium held during the 9th European Congress of Rheumatology,* Wiesbaden, September, 1979. Bern, Switzerland: Hans Huber, 1980.

Deci, E., Reis, H., Johnston, E., & Smith, R. Toward reconciling equity theory and insufficent justifications. *Personality and Social Psychology Bulletin,* 1977, *3,* 224.

Dembroski, T. M. (Ed.). *Proceedings of the forum on coronary-prone behavior.* (DHEW Publication No. (NIH) 78-1451). Washington, DC: U.S. Government Printing Office, 1978.

Denzin, N. K. *Childhood Socialization.* San Francisco: Jossey-Bass, 1977.

Denzin, N. K., & Mettlin, C. J. Incomplete Professionalization: A Case of Pharmacy, *Social Forces,* 1968, *46,* 376.

Derber, C. Managing professionals: Ideological proletarianization and postindustrial labor. *Theory and Society,* 1983, *12,* 309.

Deutsch, M. Trust and suspicion. *Journal of Conflict Resolution,* 1958, *2,* 265.

Deutsch, M., & Krauss, R. M. The effect of threat upon interpersonal bargaining. *Journal of Abnormal Social Psychology*, 1960, *61*, 181.

Deutsch, M., & Krauss, R. M. Studies of interpersonal bargaining. *Journal of Conflict Resolution*, 1962, *6*, 52.

Deutscher, I. *What We Say/What We do*. Glenview, III: Scott, Foresman, 1973.

DeVon, H. A. & Powers, M. J. Health beliefs, adjustment to illness, and control of hypertension. *Research in Nursing and Health*, 1984, *7*, 10.

Dewey, J. *Human Nature and Conduct: An Introduction to Social Psychology*. New York: Carlton House, 1922.

Dewey, J. Prefatory remarks. In A. E. Murphy (Ed.), *George Herbert Mead: The philosophy of the present*. Chicago: University of Chicago Press, 1932 and 1980.

Dimond, M. Social support and adaptation to chronic illness: The case for maintenance dialysis. *Research in Nursing and Health*, 1979, *2*, 101.

Dollard, J., Doob, L., Miller, N., et al. *Frustration and Aggression*. New Haven, Conn: Yale University Press, 1939.

Douvan, E., & Gold, M. Modal patterns in American adolescence. In L. W. Hoffman, & M. L. Hoffman (Eds.), *Review of Child Development Research* (Vol. 2). New York: Sage, 1966, pp. 469–528.

Dracup, K. A. Influence of a role supplementation program on the psychological adaptation of cardiac patients and spouses. 1982.

Dracup, K. A., & Meleis, A. J. Compliance: An interactionist approach. *Nursing Research*, 1982, *31*(1), 31.

Dracup, K. A., Meleis, A. J., Baker, K., & Edlefsen, P. Family-focused cardiac rehabilitation: A role supplementation program for cardiac patients and spouses. *Nursing Clinics of North America*, 1984, *19*(1), 113.

Dragastin, S. E., & Elder, G. R., Jr. (Eds.). *Adolescence in the Life Cycle: Psychological Change and Social Context*. New York: Wiley, 1975.

Dreitzel, H. P. Introduction: Childhood and socialization. In H. P. Dreitzel (Ed.), *Childhood and Socialization* (Recent Sociology No. 5), New York: Macmillan, 1973, pp. 5–24.

Dua, P. S. Comparison of the effects of behaviorally oriented action and psychotherapy reeducation on intraversion-extraversion, emotionality, and internal control. *Journal of Counseling Psychology*, 1970, *17*, 567.

Duff, R. S., & Hollingshead, A. B. *Sickness and Society*. New York: Harper, Row, 1968.

Dummet, C. O. *The Growth and Development of the Negro in Dentistry*. Chicago: Stanek Press, 1952.

Duncan, B., Smith, A. N., & Silver, H. K. Comparison of the physical assessment of children by pediatric nurse practitioners and pediatricians. *American Journal of Public Health*, 1971, *67*, 1170.

Duncan, R. B. Characteristics of organizational environments and perceived environmental uncertainty. *Administrative Science Quarterly*, 1972, *17*, 313.

Duncan, R. P., & Perrucci, C. C. Dual occupation families and migration. *American Sociological Review*, 1976, *41*, 252.

Durkheim, E. A study of suicide trends. In J. A. Spaulding & G. Simpson. *Editor* J. Simpson, Glencoe, Ill: The Free Press, 1951.

Durkheim, E. *The Division of Labor in Society*. New York: Free Press, 1964.

Dykman, R. A., & Stalnaker, J. M. Survey of women physicians graduating from medical school, 1925–1940. *Journal of Medical Education*. 32:part 2, 1958, 3–25.

Eddy, E. M. *Becoming a Teacher: The Passage to Professional Status*, New York: Columbia University Teachers College Press, 1971.

Edwards, R. C. The social relations of production at the point of production. *The Insurgent Sociologist*, 1978, *8*, 109.

Edwards, R. C. *Contested Terrain: The Transformation of the Workplace in 20th Century America*. New York: Basic Books, 1979.

Ehrenreich, B., & Ehrenreich, J. H. Hospital workers: Class conflicts in the making. *International Journal of Health Services*, 1975, *5*(1), 43.

Ehrlich, J. L., & McClure, J. F., The grassroots and the ivory tower. *Social Work*, 1974, *19*, 653.

Ehrlich, H. J., Rinehart, J. W., & Howell, J. C. The study of role conflict: Explorations in methodology. *Sociometry*, 1962, *25*, 85.

Eisenstein, H. *Contemporary Feminist Thought*. Boston, Mass: Hall, 1984.

Ekman, G. A simple method for fitting psychophysical power functions. *Journal of Psychology*, 1961, *51*, 343.

Elder, G. H., Jr. *Adolescent socialization and Personality Development*. Chicago: Rand McNally, 1968.

Elder, G. H., Jr. Role relations, sociocultural environments, and autocratic family ideology. In D. R. Heise, *Personality and Socializatoin*. Chicago: Rand McNally, 1972, pp. 312–335.

Elkin, F. Socialization and the presentation of self. In J. Heiss (Ed.), *Family Roles and Interaction: An Anthology* (2nd ed.). Chicago: Rand McNally, 1976, pp. 354–362.

Elkin, F., & Handel, G. *The Child and Society: The Process of Socialization* (4th ed.). New York: Random House, 1984.

Elkin, F., & Westley, W. A. The myth of adolescent culture. *American Sociological Review*, 1955, *20*, 680.

Elkind, D. *The Child and Society*. New York: Oxford University Press, 1979.

Ellis, G. J., Streeter, S. K., & Engelbrecht, J. D. Television characters as significant others and the process of vicarious role taking. *Journal of Family Issues*, 1983, *4*, 367.

Ellman, E. S. *Managing Women in Business*. Waterford, Conn: Prentice-Hall, 1967.

Elpern, E., White, P. M., & Donahue, M. F. Self-governance: The experience of the nursing unit. *Journal of Nursing Administration*, 1984, *14*, 9.

Emde, R., & Harmon, R. (Eds.). *Continuities and Discontinuities in Development*. New York: Plenum, 1984.

Emerson, R. *Contemporary Field Research*. Boston: Little, Brown, 1983.

Emerson, R. M. Power-dependence relations. *American Sociological Review*, 1962, *27*, 31–41.

Emerson, R. M., Turner, R., & Short, J. (Eds.). Social Exchange Theory, *Annual Review of Sociology*, 1976, *2*, 335.

Emerson, R. M. Social exchange theory. In M. Rosenberg & R. Turner (Eds.). *Social Psychology: Sociological Perspectives*. New York: Basic Books, 1981, pp. 30–65.

Emmerich, W. Socialization and sex-role development. In P. B. Baltes & K. W. Schaie (Eds.), *Life-span Developmental Psychology: Personality and Socialization*. New York: Academic Press, 1973, pp. 123–144.

Enelow, A. J., & Henderson, J. B. (Eds.). *Applying Behavioral Science to Cardiovascular Risk*. American Heart Association, 1975.

Engel, G. Professional autonomy and bureaucratic organization. *Administrative Science Quarterly*, 1970, *30*, 12.

Ehthoven, A. C. Consumer-choice health plan. *N Engl J Med*. 1978, *298*, 650, 709.

Epstein, C. F. Women's attitudes toward other women: Myths and their consequences. *American Journal of Psychotherapy*, 1980, *34*, 322.

Epstein, C. F. *Woman's Place: Options and Limits in Professional Careers*. Berkeley: University of California Press, 1970a.

Epstein, C. F. Encountering the male establishment: Sex status limits on women's careers in the professions. American Journal of Sociology, 1970b, *75*, 965.

Epstein, L. K. (Ed.). *Women in the Professions*. Lexington, Mass: Lexington Books, D. C. Heath, 1975.

Eraker, S. A., Kirscht, J. P., & Becker, M. H. Understanding and improving patient compliance. *Annals of Internal Medicine*, 1984, *100*, 258.

Erikson, E. Inner and outer space: Reflections on womanhood. In R. J. Lifton (Ed.), *The

Woman in America. Boston: Houghton Mifflin, 1964.

Erikson, E. H. The problem of ego identity, *Journal of American Psychoanal. Assn*, 1956, *4*, 56.

Erikson, E. H. *Identity, Youth and Crises.* New York: Norton, 1968.

Etzioni, A. *Modern Organization.* Englewood Cliffs, NJ: Prentice-Hall, 1964.

Etzioni, A. *A Comparative Analysis of Complex Organization.* New York: Free Press, 1975.

Fagerhaugh, S. Y., & Strauss, A. *Politics of Pain Management: Staff-Patient Interaction.* Menlo Park: Addison-Wesley, 1977.

Fagot, B. I., Hagan, R., Leinbach, M. D., & Kronsberg, S. Differential reactions to assertive and communicative acts of toddler boys and girls. *Child Development*, 1985, *56*, 1499.

Fain, J. A. *A Study of the Relationship Between Role Conflict, Role Ambiguity, and Job Satisfaction Among Nurse Educators.* New Haven: Yale University School of Nursing, 1985.

Faley, T., & Tedeschi, J. T. Status and reactions to threats. *Journal of Personality and Social Psychology*, 1971, *17*, 192.

Faris, R. *Chicago Sociology 1920–1952.* San Francisco: Chandler Pub, 1967.

Faunce, P. S. Psychological barriers to occupational success for women. *Journal of the National Association for Women Deans, Administrators, and Counselors*, 1977, *40*(4), 140.

Feather, N. T. Positive and negative reactions to male and female success and failure in relation to perceived status and sex-typed appropriateness of occupations. *Journal of Personality and Social Psychology*, 1975, *31*, 536–538.

Feather, N. T., & Simon, J. G. Reactions to male and female success and failure in sex-linked occupations: Impressions of personality, causal attributions, and perceived likelihood of different consequences. *Journal of Personality and Social Psychology*, 1975, *31*, 20.

Federico, S. M., Federico, P. A., & Lundquist, G. W. Predicting women's turnover as a function of extent of net salary expectations and biodemographic data. *Personnel Psychology*, 1976, *29*, 559.

Feffer, M., & Gourevitch, V. Cognitive aspects of role-taking in children. *Journal of Personality*, 1960, *28*, 383.

Fein, R. *The Doctor Shortage: An Economic Diagnosis, Studies in Social Economics.* Washington, DC: Brookings Institute, 1967.

Fein, R. A. Research on fathering: Social policy and an emergent perspective. In A. S. Skolnick, & J. H. Skolnick, *Family in Transition* (4th ed.). Boston: Little, Brown, 1983, pp. 463–474.

Feldberg, R. L. Comparable worth: Toward theory and practice in the United States. *Signs: Journal of Women in Culture and Society*, 1984, *10*, 311.

Feldman, S. D. Impediment or stimulant? Martial status and graduate education. In J. Huber (Ed.), *Changing Women in a Changing Society.* Chicago: University of Chicago Press, 1973.

Ferber, M. A., & Huber, J. A. Sex of student and instructor: A study of student bias. *American Journal of Sociology*, 1973, *80*, 949.

Ferber, M. A., & Loeb, J. W. Performance, rewards and perceptions of sex discrimination among male and female faculty. In J. Huber (Ed.), *Changing Women in a Changing Society.* Chicago: University of Chicago Press, 1973.

Ferguson, L. R. Dependency motivation in socialization. In R. A. Hoppe, G. A. Milton, & E. C. Simmel (Eds.), *Early Experiences and the Processes of Socialization.* New York: Academic Press, 1970, pp. 59–79.

Fernberger, S. W. Persistence of stereotypes concerning sex differences. *Journal of Abnormal and Social Psychology*, 1948, *43*, 97.

Festinger, L. A theory of social comparison processes. *Human Relations*, 1954, 7, 117.

Field, M. A., & Hinshaw, A. S. Magnitude estimation: A method for measuring subjective phenomena. *Communicating Nursing Research*, Boulder, Colo: WICHE, 1977.

Fink, R., Shapiro, S., & Roester, R. Impact of efforts to increase participation in repetitive screening for early breast cancer detection. *American Journal of Public Health*, 1972, 62, 328.

Fisher, B. M., & Strauss, A. L. George Herbert Mead and the Chicago tradition of sociology. *Symbolic Interaction*, 1979, 2, 9.

Flach, D. H., Smith, M., Smith, W., & Glasser, M. Faculty Mentors for Medical Students. *Journal of Medical Education*, 1982, 57, 5147.

Flacks, R. Growing up confused. In P. I. Rose (Ed.), *Socialization and the Life Cycle*. New York: St. Martin's Press, 1979, pp. 21–32.

Flanagan, L. (Ed.). *One Strong Voice: The Story of the American Nurses' Association*. Kansas City, Mo: American Nurses' Association, 1976.

Flanders, J. P. A review of research on imitative behavior. *Psychological Bulletin*, 1968, 69(5), 316.

Flavell, J. H., et al. *The Development of Role-taking and Communication Skills in Children*. New York: Wiley, 1968.

Fleishman, E. G. Sex-role acquisition, parental behavior, and sexual orientation: Some tentative hypotheses. *Sex Roles*, 1983a, 9, 1051.

Fleishman, E. G. Sex-role acquisition, parental behavior, and sexual orientation: Some tenative hypotheses—a rejoinder. *Sex Roles*, 1983b, 9, 1063.

Fogarty, M. Rapoport, R., & Rapoport, R. *Sex, Career, and Family*. London: George Allen & Unwin, 1971.

Folger, R., Rosenfield, D., & Hays, R. Equity and intrinsic motivation: The role of choice. In Katz, Kahn, & Adams (Eds.), *The Study of Organizations*. San Francisco. Jossey Bass, 1982, pp. 265–274.

Foote, F., & Cottrell, N. *Identity and Interpersonal Competence*. Chicago: University of Chicago Press, 1955.

Fortin, J. D. *An investigation of the effects of a selected coping intervention on pain and anxiety in adult surgical patients*. Unpublished doctoral dissertation, Boston University, 1983.

Forward plan for health FY 1977-81. (DHEW Publication No. OS 76-50024). Washington, DC: U. S. Government Printing Office, 1975.

Forward plan for health FY 1978-82. (DHEW Publication No. OS 76-50046). Washington, DC: U. S. Government Printing Office, 1976.

Fowler, M. G., & Van de Riet, H. K. Women, today and yesterday: An examination of the feminist personality. *Journal of Psychology*, 1972, 82, 269.

Fox Keller, E. *A Feeling for the Organism*. New York: Wit Freeman & Co., 1983.

Fox Keller, E. *Gender and Science*. New Haven, Conn: Yale University Press, 1985.

Fox, R. Training for uncertainty. In Merton, Reader, & Kendall. *Student Physician*, 1957, pp. 207–244.

Frankenhaeuser, M., & Gardell, B. Underload and overload in working life: Outline of a multidisciplinary approach. *Journal of Human Stress*, 1976, 2, 35.

Franks, V., & Rothblum, E. D. (Eds.). *The Stereotyping of Women: Its Effects on Mental Health*. New York: Springer, 1983.

Freeman, J. Growing up girlish. *Transaction*, 1970, 8, 36.

Freidan, B. *The Feminine Mystique*. New York: Dell, 1963.

Freidman, A. *Industry and Labor: Struggle at Work and Monopoly Capitalism*. London: Macmillan Press, 1977.

Freidman, M., Rosenham, R. H., & Carroll, V. Changes in the Serum cholesterol and clotting time of men subject to cyclic variation of occupational stress. *Circulation*, 1957, 17, 852.

Freidman, M., & Rosenman, R. H. Association of specific overt patterns with blood and cardiovascular findings. *Journal of the American Medical Association*, 1959, *169*, 1286.

Freidson, E. *Patient Views of Medical Practice*. New York: Russell Sage Foundation, 1961.

Freidson, E. Dominant professions, bureaucracy and client services. In W. Rosengren & M. Lifton (Eds.), *Organizations and Clients*. Columbus, Ohio: Merrill, 1970a.

Freidson, E. *Professional Dominance: The Social Structure of Medical Care*. New York: Atherton, 1970b.

Freidson, E. *Profession of Medicine*. New York: Harper and Row, Pub., 1970.

Freidson, E. (Ed.). *The Professions and Their Prospects*. Beverly Hills, Cal: Sage, 1971.

Freidson, E. The changing nature of professional control. In R. Turner & J. Short (Eds.), *Annual Review of Sociology*, 1984, *10*, 1.

French, J. R., & Kahn, R. A. A programmatic approach to studying the industrial environment and mental health. *Journal of Social Issues*, 1962, *18*, 1.

French, R. P., & Caplan, R. D. Organizational stress and individual strain, In A. J. Marrow (Ed.), *The Failure of Success*. New York: Macom, 1973, pp. 30–65.

French, R. P., Caplan, R. D., & Van Harrison, R. V. *The Mechanisms of Job Stress and Strain*. New York: Wiley, 1982.

French, R. P., et al. *Workload of university professors*. Unpublished research report, Ann Arbor, Mich: The University of Michigan, 1965.

Fromm, E. *The Sane Society*. New York: Holt, Rinehart, & Winston, 1955.

Fromm, L. The problem in nursing: Nurses. *Supervisor Nurse*, 1977, *8*, 5.

Galbraith, J. K. *Designing Complex Organizations*. Reading, Mass: Addison-Wesley, 1973a.

Galbraith, J. K. *Economics and the Public Purpose*. New York: Signet, 1973b.

Gall, M. D. The relationship between masculinity-feminity and manifest anxiety. *Journal of Clinical Psychology*, 1969, *25*, 294.

Gamson, W. A. Experimental studies of coalition formation. *Advances in Experimental Social Psychology*, 1964, *1*, 82.

Garey, M. *Professional socialization: The experience of the graduate psychiatric nursing student in the consultation/liaison role*. Unpublished dissertation. Boston University, 1985.

Garland, H., & Price, K. H. Attitudes toward women in management and attributions for their success and failure in a managerial position. *Journal of Applied Psychology*, 1977, *62*, 29.

Gecas, V. The socialization and child care roles. In F. I. Nye, *Role Structure and Analysis of the Family*. Beverly Hills: Sage, 1976, pp. 33–59.

Gelfand, E. B. *Psychological perspectives on diabetes: The impact of locus of control orientation on information, psychosocial adjustment, and metabolic control*. Unpublished doctoral dissertation, Boston University, 1984.

George, L. *Role Transitions in Later Life*. Monterey, Cal: Brooks/Cole, 1980.

Georgiou, P. The goal paradigm and notes toward a counter paradigm. *Administrative Science Quarterly*, 1973, *18*, 291.

Georgopoulos, B. S. (Ed.). *Organization Research on Health Institutions*. Ann Arbor, Mich: Institute for Social Research, 1972.

Georgopoulos, B. S., & Christian, L. The clinical nurse specialist: A role model. In P. O. Riehl & J. W. McVay (Eds.), *The Clinical Nurse Specialist: Interpretations*. New York: Appleton-Century-Crofts, 1973, pp. 335–353.

Gerard, H. B., & Rabbie, J. M. Fear and social comparison. *Journal of Abnormal Social Psychology*, 1961, *63*, 586.

Gergen, K. J. *The Concept of Self*. New York: Holt, Rinehart, & Winston, 1971.

Gerth, H. H., & Mills, C. W. *From Max Weber: Essays in Sociology*. London: Routledge, Kegan Paul, 1946.

Getzels, J. W., & Guba, E. G. Role, role conflict and effectiveness: An empirical study. *Am Social Rev*, 1954, *19*, 164.

Gewirtz, J. L. Mechanisms of social learning: Some roles of stimulation and behavior in early human development. In D. A. Goslin (Ed.), *Handbook of Socialization Theory and Research*. Chicago: Rand McNally, 1969, pp. 57–212.

Gibbs, J. P. Norms: The problem of definition and classification. *American Journal of Sociology*, 1965, *70*, 586.

Gibson, J. L. Ivancevich, J., & Donnelly, J. H., Jr. *Organizations*. Dallas: Business, 1973.

Gilligan, C. *In a Different Voice: Psychological Theory and Women's Development*. Cambridge, Mass: Harvard University Press, 1982.

Ginzberg, E., Ginsberg, S. W., Axelrod, S., & Herma, J. L. *Occupational Choice: An Approach To a General Theory*. New York: Columbia University Press, 1963.

Given, C. W., Given, B. A., & Simoni, L. E. The association of knowledge and perception and medications with compliance and health states among hypertensive patients: A prospective study. *Research in Nursing and Health*, 1978, *1*, 76.

Given, C. W., Given, B. A., Galin, R. S., & Condon, J. W. Development of scales to measure beliefs of diabetic patients. *Research in Nursing and Health*, 1983, *6*, 127.

Glanz, K., Kirscht, J. P., & Rosenstock, I. M. Linking research and practice in patient education for hypertension: Patient responses to four educational interventions. *Medical Care*, 1981, *19*, 141.

Glaser, B. G., & Strauss, A. M. *Awareness of Dying*. Chicago: Aldine Press, 1965.

Glaser, B. G., & Strauss, A. L. *The Discovery of Grounded Theory*. Chicago: Aldine, 1967.

Glaser, W. A. Nursing leadership and policy: Some cross-national comparisons. In F. Davis (Ed.), *The Nursing Profession: Five Sociological Essays*. New York, 1966.

Glaser, B. G., & Strauss, A. M. *Status Passages*. Chicago: Aldine Press, 1971.

Glass, H. P. Research: An international perspective. *Nursing Research*, 1977, *26*, 230.

Goetting, A. Divorce outcome research: Issues and perspectives. In A. S. Skolnick, & J. H. Skolnick, *Family in Transition* (4th ed.), Boston: Little, Brown, 1983, pp. 367–387.

Goff, T. W. *Marx and Mead*. Boston: Routledge & Kegan Paul, 1980.

Goffman, E. *The Presentation of Self in Everyday Life*. New York: Doubleday, 1959.

Goffman, E. *Asylums*. New York: Anchor Books, 1961.

Goffman, E. *Stigma: Notes on the Management of Spoiled Identity*. Englewood Cliffs, NJ: Prentice-Hall, 1963.

Goldberg, P. Are women prejudiced against women? *Transaction*, 1968, *5*, 28.

Goldman, P. A theory of conflict processes and organizational offices. *Journal of Conflict Resolution*, 1966, *10*, 328.

Goldman, P., & Van Houten, D. R. Managerial strategies and the worker: A Marxist analysis of bureaucracy. In J. K. Benson (Ed.), *Organizational Analysis: Critique and Innovation*. Beverly Hills, Cal: Sage, 1977, pp. 291–310.

Goldstein, H. S. Father's absence and cognitive development of children over a 3- to 5-year period. *Psychological Reports*, 1983, *52*, 971.

Goode, J. The protection of the inept. *American Sociological Review*, 1967, *32*, 5.

Goode, W. Community within a community: The professions. *American Sociological Review*, 1957, *22*, 194.

Goode, W. J. A theory of role strain. *American Sociological Review*, 1960, *25*, 483.

Goode, W. J. The protection of the inept. In J. W. Goode (Ed.), *Explorations in Social Theory*. New York: Oxford University Press, 1973, pp. 121–144.

Goodman, M. Expressed self-acceptance and interpersonal needs: A basis for mate selection. In J. Heiss (Ed.), *Family Roles and Interaction: An Anthology* (2nd ed.). Chicago: Rand McNally, 1976, pp. 116–126.

Goodman, P., & Friedman, A. An examination of the effect of wage inequity in the hourly condition. *Organizational Behavior*, 1968, *3*, 340.

Goodman, P., & Pennings, J. (Eds.). *New Perspectives on Organizational Effectiveness*. San Francisco: Jossey Bass, 1977.

Gordon, C. Self-conceptions: Configurations of content. *In Self in Social Interaction*. In C. Gordon & K. J. Gergen (Eds.), New York: Wiley, 1968, pp. 115–136.

Gordon, C. Role and value development across the life-cycle. In J. A. Jackson (Ed.), *Role*. Cambridge: Cambridge University Press, 1972.

Gordon, R. *Unidimensional Scaling and Social Variables*. New York: Free Press, 1977.

Gore, S. Stress-buffering functions of social supports: An appraisal and clarification of research methods. In B. S. Dohrenwend, & B. P. Dohrenwend (Eds.), *Stressful Life Events and Their Contexts*. New York: Prodist, 1981, pp. 202–222.

Goren, S. Innocence as an impediment to power. In *People, Power, Politics for Health Care*, Conference of the Northeast Regional Assembly of Constitutent Leagues for Nursing. Washington, DC, April 8–9, 1976. New York: National League for Nursing, 1976, pp. 25–31.

Gornick, V., & Moran, B. K. (Eds.). *Woman in a Sexist Society: Studies in Power and Powerlessness*. New York: Basic, 1971.

Goslin, D. A. Introduction. In D. A. Goslin (Ed.), *Handbook of Socialization Theory and Research*. Chicago: Rand McNally, 1969, pp. 1–21.

Goslin, D. A. (Ed.). *Handbook of Socialization Theory and Research*. Chicago: Rand McNally, 1969.

Goss, M. Influences and authority among physicians. *Am Social Rev.*, 1961, *26*, 39.

Gottlieb, B. H. (Ed.). *Social Networks and Social Support*. Beverly Hills, Cal: Sage, 1981.

Gottlieb, B. H. (Ed.). *Social Support Strategies: Guidelines for Mental Health Practice*. Beverly Hills, Cal: Sage, 1983.

Gould, S. *The Panda's Thumb: More Reflections in Natural History*. New York: W. W. Norton & Co., Inc., 1980.

Gould, S. *The Mismeasure of Man*. New York: W. W. Norton & Co., Inc., 1981.

Gouldner, A. *Patterns of Industrial Bureaucracy*. New York: Free Press, 1954.

Gouldner, A. Toward an analysis of latent social rules. *Administrative Science Quarterly*, 1957, *2*, 281.

Gouldner, A. W. Cosmopolitans and locals: Towards an analysis of latent social roles—I. *Administrative Science Quarterly*, 1957, *2*, 281.

Gouldner, A. W. The norm of reciprocity: A preliminary statement, *American Sociological Review*, 1960, *25*, 161.

Gove, N., McEachorn, A., & Mason, W. S. Role conflict and its resolution. In B. Biddle, & E. Thomas (Eds.), *Role Theory: Concepts and Research*. New York: Wiley, 1979.

Gove, W. R. The labeling theory of mental illness: A reply to Scheff. *American Sociological Review*, 1975, *40*, 242.

Gove, W. R., & Tudor, J. F. Adult sex roles and mental illness. *American Journal of Sociology*, 1973a, *78*, 812.

Grace, H. The development of doctoral education in nursing: In historical perspective. *Journal of Nursing Education*, 1978, *17*(4), 17.

Gray, J. D. The married professional woman: An examination of her role conflicts and coping strategies. *Psychology of Women Quarterly*, 1983, *7*(3), 235.

Gray, S. W. Masculinity-feminity in relation to anxiety and social aceptance. *Child Development*, 1957, *28*, 203.

Greenberg, J., & Leventhal, G. Violating equity to prevent group failure. Proceedings of the 81st Annual Convention of the American Psychological Association. City Publisher, 1973, pp. 215–216.

Greene, C., & Organ, D. An evaluation of casual models linking the received role and job satisfaction. *Administrative Science Quarterly*, 1973, *18*, 95.

Greenleaf, N. P. Sex-segregated occupations: Relevance for nursing. *Advances in Nursing Science*, 1980, *2*(3), 23.

Greenwood, E. Attributes of profession. *Social Work*. July 1957, *2*, 44.

Grief, S., & MacDonald, R. Role relationships between nonphysicians and treatment team leaders and team psychiatrists. *Community Mental Health Journal*, 1973, *9*, 378–387.

Grimshaw, J. *Philosophy and Feminist Thinking*. Minneapolis: University of Minnesota Press, 1986.

Grissum, M., & Spengler, C. *Womenpower & Health Care*. Boston: Little, Brown, 1976.

Gross, E. Organizations as criminal actors. In P. R. Wilson & J. Braithwaite (Eds.), *The Two Faces of Deviance: Crimes of the Powerful and Powerless*. St. Lucia: University of Queensland Press, 1978, pp. 119–213.

Gross, E., & Etzioni, A. *Organizations in Society*. Englewood Cliffs, NJ: Prentice-Hall, 1985.

Gross, N., Mason, W., & McEachern, A. *Explorations in Role Analysis: Studies of the School Superintendency Role*. New York: Wiley, 1958.

Gross, N., McEachern, A., & Mason, W. Role conflict and its resolution. In B. Biddle & E. Thomas (Eds.), *Role Theory: Concepts and Research*. New York: Wiley, 1966.

Grotevant, H. D., & Cooper, C. R. (Eds.). *Adolescent Development in the Family*. San Francisco: Jossey-Bass, 1983.

Gullahorn, J. Measuring role conflict. American Journal of Sociology, 1956, *61*, 299.

Gump, J. P. Sex-role attitudes and psychological well-being. *Journal of Social Issues*, 1972, *28*, 79–92.

Gunter, L., Crecraft, H. J., & Kennedy, E. J. Mental health in a segregated setting. In B. Bullough & V. Bullough (Eds.), *New Directions for Nurses*. New York: Springer, 1974, pp. 303–310.

Gupta, N., & Beehr, T. A. Job stress and employee behaviors. *Organizational Behavior and Human Performance*, 1979, *23*, 373.

Guttman, L. Best possible systematic estimates at commonalities. *Psychometrics*, 1956, *21*, 273.

Haas, J. E. *Role Conception and Group Consensus*. Columbus, Ohio: Bureau of Business Research, Ohio State University, 1964.

Haavio-Mannila, E. Sex differentiation in role expectations and performance. *Journal of Marriage and the Family*, 1967, *29*, 568.

Hadley, B. J. *Becoming well: A study of role change*. Unpublished doctoral dissertation, University of California, Los Angeles, 1966.

Hadley, J. The dynamic interactionist concept of role. *The Journal of Nursing Education*, 1967, *24*, 5.

Hage, J., & Aiken, M. Routine technology, social structure and organization goals. *Administrative Science Quarterly*, 1964, *14*, 366.

Hage, J. *Techniques and Problems of Theory Construction in Sociology*. New York: John Wiley & Sons, 1972.

Hage, J. *Theories of Organizations*. New York: John Wiley & Sons, 1980.

Hagstrom, W. O. *The Scientific Community*. New York: Basic Books, 1965.

Hall, D. T. A model of coping with role conflict: The role behavior of college educated women. *Administrative Science Quarterly*, 1974, *19*, 471.

Hall, R. Professionalization and bureaucratization. *American Sociological Review*, 1968, *33*, 92.

Hall, R. Organizations: *Structure and Process* (3rd ed.). Englewood Cliffs, NJ: Prentice-Hall, 1982.

Hallal, J. C. The relationship of health beliefs, health locus of control, and self-concept to the practice of breast self-examination in adult women. *Nursing Research*, 1982, *31*, 137.

Halsey, S. The Queen Bee Syndrome: One solution to role conflict for nurse managers. In M. E. Hardy & M. Conway (Eds.), *Role Theory: Perspectives for Health Professionals.* New York: Appleton-Century-Crofts, 1978.

Halsey, S. The Queen Bee Syndrome in Progressive levels of nursing management. Unpublished master's thesis, Boston University, Boston, 1977.

Hamblin, R. L. Ratio measurement for the social sciences. *Social Forces*, 1971, *50*(2), 191.

Hamblin, R. L. Social attitudes: Magnitude measurement and theory. In H. M. Blalock, Jr. (Ed.), *Measurement in the Social Sciences.* Chicago: Aldine, 1974, pp. 61–120.

Hamblin, R. L., Bridger, D. A., Day, R. C., & Yancy, W. The interference aggression law? *Sociometry*, 1963, *26*, 190.

Hamblin, R. L., & Smith, C. R. Values, status and professors. *Sociometry*, 1966, *29*, 183.

Hamburg, B. A., Lipsett, L. F., Inoff, G. E., & Drash, A. L. (Eds.). *Behavioral and Psychosocial Issues in Diabetes: Proceedings of the National Conference.* Madison, Wisc. (DHHS PHS Publication No. (NIH) 80-1993). Washington, DC: U. S. Government Printing Office, 1980.

Hamburg, D. A., Elliott, G. R., & Parron, D. L. (Eds.). *Health and Behavior: Frontiers of Research in the Biobehavioral Sciences.* Washington, DC: National Academy Press, 1982.

Hamby, C. L. Dental hygiene students: Stereotypically feminine. *Psychological Reports*, 1982a, *50*, 1237.

Hamby, C. L. The role of psychological androgyny in female students' dental career choices. *Journal of Dental Education*, 1982b, *46*, 537.

Hamilton, M. Mentorship: A key to nursing leadership. In E. J. Nicholson (Ed.), *Contemporary Leadership Behavior: Selected Readings*, 1986, pp. 143–154.

Hamilton, G. A. *A multivariate approach to compliance in hypertension.* Unpublished doctoral dissertation, Boston University, Boston, 1982.

Hammond, J. M. Social support groups, women's programs, and research on gender differences: The bad press for women in medical education literature. *Journal of the American Medical Women's Association*, 1981, *36*(5), 162.

Hamner, W., & Foster, L. Are intrinsic and extrinsic rewards additive: A test of Deal's cognitive evaluation theory of task motivation. *Organizational Behavior and Human Performance*, 1975, *14*, 398.

Handel, W. Normative expectations and the emergence of meaning as solutions to problems: Convergence of structural and interactionist views. *American Journal of Sociology*, 1979, *84*, 855.

Hanson, H. A., & Chater, S. Role selection by nurses: Managerial interests and personal attributes. *Nursing Research*, 1983, *32*(1), 48.

Harding, S., & Hintika, M. B. (Eds.). *Discovering Reality: Feminist Perspectives on Epistomology, Metaphysics, Methodology, and Philosophy of Science.* Dorrecht, Holland: D. Reidel, 1983.

Harding, S. *The Science Question in Feminism.* Ithaca: Cornell University Press, 1986.

Hardy, M. E. *Role strain: an Analytical Concept.* Unpublished manuscript, No. 12. Institute for Social Research, University of Washington, 1970.

Hardy, M. E. *Role overload and inequity: Their consequences for social exchange.* Dissertation, University of Washington, Seattle. Dissertation *33*, 16-0468020, (University Micro-film No. 72–20, 870, 1971).

Hardy, M. E. Role problems, role strain, job satisfaction and nursing care. Paper presented at the annual meeting of the American Sociological Association, New York, 1976.

Hardy, M. E. Role stress and role strain. In M. E. Hardy & M. E. Conway (Eds.), *Role Theory: Perspectives for Health Professionals.* Norwalk, Conn: Appleton-Century-Crofts, 1978.

Hardy, M., & Conway, M. *Role Theory: Perspectives for Health Professionals* (2nd ed.). Norwalk, Conn: Appleton & Lange, 1988.

Hardy, M. E., & Conway, M. E. *Role Theory: Perspectives for Health Professionals*. New York: Appleton-Century-Crofts, 1978.

Hardy, M. E. Stages of theory development. In Proceedings of Boston University nursing second annual Nursing Science Colloquium Stategies for Theory Development in Nursing—II. Boston University, 1985.

Hardy, M. E. Theories: components, development, evaluation. *Nursing Research*, 1974, *23*, pp. 100–107.

Hareven, T. K. American families in transition: Historical perspectives on change. In A. S. Skolnick & J. H. Skolnick, *Family in Transition* (4th ed.). Boston: Little, Brown, 1983, pp. 73–91.

Harrigan, B. L. *Games Mothers Never Taught You*. New York: Ross & Associates, 1977.

Harrington, H. A. & Theis, E. C. Institutional factors perceived by BS graduates as influencing their performance as staff nurses. *Nursing Research*, 1968, *17*, 228.

Harris, M. B., & Conely-Muth, M. A. Sex role stereotypes and medical specialty choice. *Journal of the American Medical Women's Association*, 1981, *36*(8), 245.

Hartford, T. C., Willis, C. H., & Deabler, H. L. Personality correlates of masculinity-femininity. *Psychological Reports*, 1967, *21*, 881.

Hartup, W. W., & Coates, B. The role of imitation in childhood socialization. In R. A. Hoppe, G. A. Milton, & E. C. Simmel (Eds.), *Early Experiences and the Processes of Socialization* New York: Academic Press, 1970, pp. 109–142.

Haug, M., & Lavin, B. *Consumerism in Medicine: Challenging Physician Authority*. Sage Publications, 1983.

Haug, M. R. The deprofessionalization of everyone? *Social Forces*, *3*, 197.

Haug, M. R., & Lavin, B. Public challenge of physician authority. *Medical Care*, 1979, *17*, 844.

Havens, F. Women, work, and wedlock: A note on female marital patterns in the United States. In J. Huber (Ed.), *Changing Women in a Changing Society*. Chicago: University of Chicago Press, 1973.

Haynes, R. B., Taylor, D. W., & Sackett, D. L. (Eds.). *Compliance in Health Care*. Baltimore, MD: Johns Hopkins University Press, 1979.

Haynes, S., et al. The relationship of psychosocial factors to coronary heart disease in the Framingham Study: II. Prevalence of coronary heart disease. *American Journal of Epidemiol.*, 1978, *107*, 384.

Health, United States. (DHHS Publication No. PHS 82-1232). Washington, DC: U. S. Government Printing Office, 1981.

Healthy people: The surgeon general's report on health promotion and disease prevention. Background papers. (DHEW Publication No. 79-55071A). Washington, DC: U. S. Government Printing Office, 1979.

Hearn, J., & Parkin, P. W. Gender and organization. *Organization Studies*, 1983, *4*, 219.

Hegel, G. H. Phenomenology of spirit. In J. B. Baillies (Ed.), *Introduction and Notes*. New York: Macmillan, 1967.

Heidbreder, E. *Seven Psychologies*. Englewood Cliffs, NJ: Prentice-Hall, 1933.

Heilbrun, A. B., Jr., & Schwartz, H. L. Sex-gender differences in level of androgyny. *Sex Roles*, 1982, *8*(2), 201.

Heiss, J. An introduction to the elements of role theory. In J. Heiss (Ed.), *Family roles and interaction: An anthology* (2nd ed.). Chicago: Rand McNally, 1976, pp. 3–30.

Heiss, J. Social roles. In M. Rosenberg & R. Turner (Eds.), *Social Psychology: Sociological Perspectives* New York: Basic Books, 1981, pp. 94–129.

Heiss, J. *The Social Psychology of Interaction*. Englewood Cliffs, NJ: Prentice-Hall, 1981.

Hempel, C. G. *Philosophy of Natural Science*. Englewood Cliffs, NJ: Prentice-Hall, 1966.

Hennig, M., & Jardim, A. *The Managerial Woman*. Garden City: Anchor Press, 1977.

Hershey, J. C., Morton, B. G., Davis, J. B., & Reichgott, M. J. Patient compliance with antihypertensive medication. *American Journal of Public Health*, 1980, *70*, 1081.

Hershey, R. D., Jr. Women's pay fight shifts to comparable worth. *New York Times*, A15, November 1, 1983.

Herzberg, F. *Work and the Nature of Man*. Cleveland: World, 1966.

Herzog, E., & Sudia, C. Children in fatherless families. In B. M. Caldwell & H. N. Ricciuti (Eds.), *Review of Child Development Research* (Vol. 3). Chicago: University of Chicago Press, 1973.

Hess, B. B., & Waring, J. M. Changing patterns of aging and family bonds in later life. In A. S. Skolnick, & J. H. Skolnick, (Eds.) *Family in Transition* (4th ed.). Boston: Little, Brown, 1983, pp. 521–537.

Hetherington, E. M. Effects of father-absence on personality development in adolescent daughters. *Developmental Psychology*, 1972, *7*, 313.

Hetherington, E. M., Cox, M., & Cox, R. The aftermath of divorce. In J. P. Stevens & M. Matthews (Eds.), *Mother/Child, Father/Child Relationships*. Washington, DC: National Association for the Education of Young Children, 1978.

Hetherington, E. M., & Deur, J. L. The effects of father absence on child development. *Young Children*, 1971, *26*, 233.

Hetherington, E. M., & Deur, J. L. The effects of father absence on child development. In W. W. Hartup (Ed.), *The Young Child: Reviews of Research* (Vol. 2). Washington, DC: National Association for the Education of Young Children, 1972, p. 303.

Hewitt, J. P. *Self and Society: A Symbolic Interactionist Social Psychology*. Boston: Allyn & Bacon, 1976.

Hilbert, R. A. The acultural dimensions of chronic pain: Flawed reality construction and the problem of meaning. *Social Problems*, 1984, *31*, 365.

Hill, R., & Aldous, J. Socialization for marriage and parenthood. In D. A. Goslin (Ed.), *Handbook of Socialization Theory and Research* Chicago: Rand McNally, 1969, pp. 885–950.

Himmelfarb, S., & Eagly, A. H. Orientations to the study of attitudes and their change. In S. Himmelfarb & A. H. Eagly (Eds.), *Readings in Attitude Change*. New York: Wiley, 1974.

Hinshaw, A. S. Role attitudes: A measurement problem. In M. Hardy & M. Conway (Eds.), *Role Theory: Perspectives for Health Professionals* New York: Appleton-Century-Crofts, 1978, pp. 273–304.

Hinshaw, A. S. *Socialization and Resocialization of Nurses for Professional Nursing Care* (Publication No. 16-1569). New York: NLN, 1982.

Hinshaw, A. S. Theoretical model testing: Full utilization of data. *Western Journal of Nursing Research*, 1984, *6*(1), 5.

Hinshaw, A. S., & Atwood, J. R. Nursing staff turnover, stress, and satisfaction: Models, measures, and management. *Annual Review of Nursing Research*, 1983, *1*, 133.

Hinshaw, A. S., & Atwood, J. R. Anticipated turnover: A preventive approach. *Western Journal of Nursing Research*, 1982, *4*, 54.

Hinshaw, A. S., & Field, M. A. An investigation of variables that underlie collegial evaluation: Peer review. *Nursing Research*, 1974, *23*(4), 292.

Hinshaw, A. S., Gerber, R. M., Atwood, J. R., & Allen, J. The use of predictive modeling to test practice outcomes. *Nursing Research*, 1982.

Hinshaw, A. S., & Murdaugh, C. Validity of Ratio Measurement of Nursing Concepts: A Cross Modality Study. Tuscon: University of Arizona College of Nursing, 1985.

Hinshaw, A. S., & Oakes, D. Theoretical model testing: Patients', nurses' and physicians' expectations of quality nursing care. *Communicating Nursing Research*, 1977, *10*, 163.

Hinshaw, A. S., & Schepp, K. Territorial intrusion and client outcomes: The use of magnitude estimation. *Communicating Nursing Research*, 1983, *16*, 77.

Hochbaum, G. M. *Public Participation in Medical Screening Programs: A Sociopsychological Study.* (PHS Publication No. 572). Washington, DC: U. S. Government Printing Office, 1958.

Hochschild, A. R. A review of sex role research. In J. Huber (Ed.), *Changing Women in a Changing Society.* Chicago: University of Chicago Press, 1973, pp. 249–267.

Hodge, R. W., Seigel, P. M., & Rossi, P. H. Occupational prestige in the United States. *American Journal of Sociology,* 1964, *70,* 286.

Hoffman, A. M. *The Daily Needs and Interests of Older People.* Springfield, Ill: Thomas, 1970.

Hoffman, M. L. Parent practices and moral development: Generalizations from empirical research. *Child Development,* 1963, *34,* 295.

Hoffman, M. Affective and cognitive processes in moral internalization. In E. T. Higgins, D. N. Ruble, & W. W. Hartup (Eds.), *Social Cognition and Social Behavior: Developmental Perspectives.* New York: Cambridge University Press, 1983.

Hoffman, L. W. Effects on children: Summary and discussion. In F. I. Nye & L. W. Hoffman, *The Employed Mother in America.* Chicago: Rand McNally, 1963.

Hoffman, L. W. Effects of maternal employment on the child: A review of the research. *Developmental Psychology,* 1974, *10,* 204.

Hoffman, L. W. The decision to become a working wife. In J. Heiss (Ed.), *Family Roles and Interaction: An Anthology* (2nd ed.). Chicago: Rand McNally, 1976, pp. 177–196.

Hoffman, L. W. Changes in family, sex roles, socialization, and sex differences. *American Psychologist,* 1977, *32,* 644.

Hoffman, L. W. Maternal employment. *American Psychologist,* 1979, *34,* pp. 859–865.

Hofman, L. W., & Nye, F. I. *Working Mothers: An Evaluative Review of the Consequences for Wife, Husband, and Child.* San Francisco: Jossey-Bass, 1974.

Hogan, D. P. The transition to adulthood as a career contingency. *American Sociological Review,* 1980, *45,* 261.

Holder, A. R. *Medical Malpractice Law.* New York: Wiley, 1975.

Hollander, E. P., & Hunt, R. G. (Eds.). *Classic Contributions to Social Psychology.* New York: Oxford University Press, 1972.

Hollaran, S. D., Mishkin, B. H., & Hanson, B. L. Bicultural-training for new graduates. *Journal of Nursing Administration,* 1980, *5,* 17.

Hollingshead, A. B. *Elmtown's Youth.* New York: Wiley, 1949.

Holmes, D. S. & Jorgensen, B. W. *Do personality and social psychologists study men more than women?* Washington, DC: Government Reports Announcements, December 25, 1971.

Holmstrom, L. L. *The Two-career Family.* Cambridge, Mass: Schenkman, 1972.

Holter, H. *Sex Roles and Social Structure.* Oslo, Norway: Universitetsforlaget, 1970.

Hom, P., DeNisi, A., Kinicki, A., & Bannister, B. Effectiveness of performance feedback from behaviorally anchored rating scales. *Journal of Applied Psychology,* 1982, *65,* 574.

Homans, G. C. *Social Behavior: Its Elementary Forms* (rev. ed.). New York: Harcourt, Brace, & World, 1974.

Homans, G. C. *Social Behavior: Its Elementary Forms.* New York: Harcourt, Brace, & World, 1961.

Honig, A. S. Sex role socialization in early childhood. *Young Children,* 1983, *39*(6), 57.

Honig-Parnass, T. Lay concepts for the sick role: An examination of the professionalist bias in Parson's model. *Social Science and Medicine,* 1981, *15A,* 615.

Hormuth, S. E. Transitions in commitments to roles and self concept change: Relocation as a paradigm. In V. Allen & E. R. van de Vliert (Eds.), *Role Transitions: Explorations and Explanations.* New York: Plenum, 1982.

Horner, M. Fail: Bright women. *Psychology Today,* 1969, *3,* 36, 38, 62.

Horner, M. Femininity and successful achievement: A basic inconsistency. In J. Bardwick, et al., (Eds.), *Feminine Personality and Conflict*. Belmont, Cal: Brooks, Cole, 1970, pp. 45–47.

Horner, M. The motive to avoid success and changing aspirations of college women. In J. M. Bardwick (Ed.), *Readings on the Psychology of Women*. New York: Harper & Row, 1972.

Horner, M. Toward an understanding of achievement-related conflict in women. *Journal of Social Issues*, 1972, *28*, 157.

Horney, K. *Our Inner Conflicts*. New York: W. W. Norton and Co., Inc., 1945.

Hoschild, A. R. A review of sex role research. In J. Huber (Ed.), *Changing Women in a Changing Society*. Chicago: University of Chicago Press, 1973, pp. 249–267.

Hover, J., & Inglsgood, N. The sick role reconceptualized. *Nursing Forum*, 1978, *17*(4).

Howard, A., & Scott, R. A proposed framework for analysis of stress in the human organism. *Behavioral Science*, 1965, *10*, 141.

Hubbard, R. Have only men evolved? In S. Harding, & M. B. Hintikka (Eds.), *Discovering Reality: Feminist Perspectives on Epistemology, Metaphysics, Methodology, and Philosophy of Science*. Dorrecht, Holland: D. Reidel, 1983, pp. 45–69.

Huber, J. Symbolic interaction as a pragmatic perspective: The bias of emergent theory. *American Sociological Review*, 1973, *38*, 274.

Hughes, E. C. Introduction. In E. C. Hughes, B. Thorne, A. M. DeBaggis, & D. Williams (Eds.), *Education for the Professions of Medicine, Law, Theology, and Social Welfare*. New York: McGraw-Hill, 1973.

Hull, R. T. Dealing with sexism in nursing and medicine. *Nursing Outlook*, 1982, *30*, 89.

Hunt, R. G. Role and role conflict. In J. H. Hartley, & G. F. Holloway (Eds.), *Focus on Change and the Social Administration*. Buffalo: State University of New York, School of Education, 1965.

Huntington, M. J. The development of a professional self-image. In R. K. Merton, G. G. Reader, & P. L. Kendal (Eds.), *The Student Physician*. Cambridge, Mass: Harvard University Press, 1957.

Hurley, B. A. Socialization for roles. In M. E. Hardy, & M. E. Conway (Eds.), *Role Theory, Perspectives for Health Professionals*. New York: Appleton-Century-Crofts, 1978, pp. 29–72.

Hyman, H. H. The psychology of status. *Archives of Psychology*, 1942, *38*(267), 6.

Hyman, H. H., & Singer, E. (Eds.), *Readings, in Reference Group Theory and Research*. Glencoe, Ill: Free Press, 1968.

Hymer, S., & Rowthorn, R. Multinational corporations and international oligoply: The non-American challenge. In C. P. Kindleberger (Ed.), *The International Corporation*. Boston: MIT Press, 1970.

Idler, E. Definitions of health, illness and medical sociology. *Social Science and Medicine*, 1979, *13A*, 723.

Inkeles, A. Society, social structure, and child socialization. In J. A. Clausen (Ed.), *Socialization and Society*. Boston: Little, Brown, 1968, pp. 73–129.

Inkeles, A. Social structure and socialization. In D. A. Goslin (Ed.), *Handbook of Socialization Theory and Research*. Chicago: Rand McNally, 1969, pp. 615–632.

Innui, T. S., Yourtee, E. L., & Williamson, J. W. Improved outcomes in hypertension after physician tutorials: A controlled trial. *Annals of Internal Medicine*, 1976, *84*, 646.

Irvine, J. J., & Robinson, C. The relationships among sex role orientations, general attitudes toward women, and specific attitudes toward women in managerial roles. *Journal of Educational Equity and Leadership*, 1982, *2*, 196.

Jackson, J. Structural characteristics of norms. In B. Biddle & E. Thomas (Eds.), *Role Theory*. New York: Wiley, 1979.

Jacobson, E., Chambers, W., & Lieberman, S. The use of the role concept in the study of complex organizations. *Journal of Social Issues*, 1951, *7*, 18.

James, W. *The Principles of Psychology*. New York: Henry Holt, 1890, 1, 292.

Janda, L. H., O'Grady, K. E., & Capps, C. F. Fear of success in males and females in sex-linked occupations. *Sex Roles*, 1978, *4*, 43.

Janowitz, M. Sociological theory and social control. *American Journal of Sociology*, 1975, *81*, 82.

Janz, N. K., Becker, M. H., & Hartman, P. E. Contingency contracting to enhance patient compliance: A review. *Patient Education and Counseling*, 1984, *5*, 165.

Jenkins, J. J. The acquisition of language. In D. A. Goslin (Ed.), *Handbook of Socialization Theory and Research*. Chicago: Rand McNally, 1969, pp. 661–686.

Joas, H. George Herbert Mead and the "division of labor": Microsociological implications of Mead's social psychology. *Symbol Interaction*, 1981, *4*, 177.

Joas, H. *G. H. Mead*. Cambridge: Cambridge University Press, 1985.

Joesting, J. Comparison of women's liberation members with their non-press peers. *Psychological Reports*, 1971, *29*, 1291.

Johnson, C. L., & Johnson, F. A. Attitudes toward parenting in dual career families. *American Journal of Psychiatry*, 1977, *134*, 391.

Johnson, S. S. Health beliefs of hypertensive patients in a family medicine residency program. *Journal of Family Practice*, 1979, *9*, 877.

Johnson, T. W., & Stinson, J. E. Role ambiguity, role conflict, and satisfaction: Moderating effects of individual difference. *Journal of Applied Psychology*, 1975, *60*, 329.

Jones. E. E. *Ingratiation: A Social Psychological Analysis*. New York: Wiley, 1964.

Kaas, M. J., & Rousseau, G. K. Geriatric sexual conformity: Assessment and intervention. *Clinical Geronotologist*, 1983, *2*(1), 31.

Kaback, M. M., Becker, M. H., & Ruth, M. V. Sociologic studies in human genetics. I. compliance in a voluntary heterozygote screening program. *Birth Defects*, 1974, *10*(6), 145. (Original article series).

Kagan, J. The concept of identification. *Psychological Review*, 1958, *65*, 296.

Kagan, J. Acquisition and significance of sex typing and sex role identity. In M. L. Hoffman, & L. W. Hoffman (Eds.), *Review of Child Development Research* (Vol. 1). New York: Sage, 1964, pp. 137–167.

Kagan, J. Perspectives on continuity. In O. G. Brim & J. Kagan (Eds.), *Constancy and Change in Human Development*. Cambridge, Mass: Harvard University Press, 1980, pp. 26–74.

Kagan, J. The child and the family. In A. S. Skolnick & J. H. Skolnick, *Family in Transition* (4th ed.). Boston: Little, Brown, 1983, pp. 409–420.

Kahn, R., & Wolfe, D. Role conflict in organizations. In R. Kahn & E. Boulding (Eds.), *Power and Conflict in Organizations*. New York: Basic Books, 1964.

Kahn, R. L., Wolfe, D. M., Quinn, R. P. et al. *Organizational Stress: Studies in Role Conflict and Ambiguity*. New York: Wiley, 1964, pp. 18–21.

Kahn, R. L. Some propositions toward researchable conceptualization of stress. In J. McGrath (Ed.), *Social and Psychological Factors in Stress*. New York: Holt, Rinehart, & Winston, 1970.

Kalish, B. J., & Kalish, P. A. A discourse on the politics of nursing. *Journal of Nursing Administration*, 1976, *6*, 29.

Kang, W. *G. H. Mead's Concept of Rationality: A study in the use of symbols and other implements*. The Hague: Mouton, 1976.

Kanter, R. M. *Men and Women of the Corporation*. New York: Basic, 1977.

Kaplan, B. H., Cassel, J., & Gore, S. Social support and health. *Medical Care*, 1977, *15*(Suppl), 48.

Karpik, L. *Organizations and Environment: Theory, Issues and Reality*. Beverly Hills, Cal: Sage, 1978.

Kasl, S. V. The Health Belief Model and behavior related to chronic illness. In M. H. Becker (Ed.), *The Health Belief Model and Personal Health Behavior*. Thorofare, NJ: Slack, 1974, pp. 106–127.

Kasl, S. V. Epidemiological contributions to the study of work stress. In C. L. Cooper, & R. Payne (Eds.), *Stress at Work*. New York: Wiley, 1978.

Kasl, S. V., & Cobb, S. Health behavior, illness behavior, and sick role behavior. *Archives of Environemntal Health*, 1966, *12*, 246.

Kast, F., & Rosenzweig, J. *Organization and Management*. New York: McGraw-Hill, 1970.

Katz, D. The functional approach to the study of attitudes. *Public Opinion Quarterly*, 1960, *24*, 163.

Katz, D., & Kahn, R. *The Social Psychology of Organizations*. New York: Wiley, 1966.

Katz, D., & Kahn, R. *The Social Psychology of Organizations*. New York: Wiley, 1978.

Katz, F. E. Nurses. In A. Etzioni (Ed.), *The Semi-professions and Their Organization*. New York: Free Press, 1969, pp. 54–81.

Katz, F. E., & Martin, H. W. Career choice processes. In R. M. Pavalko (Ed.), *Sociological Perspectives on Occupations*. Itasca, Ill: Peacock Publishers, 1972, pp. 96–104.

Kay, E. Middle management. In J O'Toole (Ed.), *Work and the Quality of Life*. Cambridge, Mass: MIT Press, 1974.

Kegeles, S. S. Why people seek dental care: A test of a conceptual formulation. *Journal of Health and Human Behavior*, 1963, *4*, 166.

Keller, E. F. Gender and science. In S. Harding, & M. B. Hintikka (Eds.), *Discovering Reality: Feminist Perspectives on Epistemology, Metaphysics, Methodology, and Philosophy of Science*. Dordrecht, Holland: D. Reidel, 1983, pp. 187–205.

Kelley, H. H. (1965). Two functions of reference groups. In H. Proshansky, & B. Seidenberg (Eds.), *Basic Studies in Social Psychology*. New York: Holt, & Rinehart, & Winston, 1965.

Kelly, J. A. Sex-role stereotypes and mental health: Conceptual models and issues for the 1980s. In V. Franks, & E. D. Rothblom (Eds.), *The Stereotyping of Women: Its Effects on Mental Health*. New York: Spring, 1983, pp. 11–29.

Kemper, T. D. Reference groups, socialization and achievement. *American Sociological Review*, 1968, *33*, 31.

Kennedy, C. W., & Garvin, B. J. The effect of status and gender on interpersonal relationships in nursing. *Nursing Forum*, 1981, *20*(3), 275.

Kerckhoff, A. C. *Socialization and Social Class*. Englewood Cliffs, NJ: Prentice-Hall, 1972.

Kerlinger, F. N. *Foundations of Behavioral Research* (2nd ed.) New York: Holt, Rinehart, & Winston, 1973.

Kerr C. Forward. In E. C. Hughes, B. Thorne, A. M. DeBaggis, & D. Williams (Eds.), *Education for the Professions of Medicine, Law, Theology, and Social Welfare*. New York: McGraw-Hill, 1973.

Kiesler, S. B., & Baral, R. L. The search for a romantic partner: The effects of self-esteem and physical attractiveness on romantic behavior. In J. Heiss (Ed.), *Family Roles and Interaction: An Anthology* (2nd ed.). Chicago: Rand McNally, 1976, pp. 105–115.

Killian, L. The significance of multiple-group membership in disaster. In E. E. Maccoby, T. M. Newcomb, & E. L. Hartley (Eds.), *Readings in Social Psychology* (3rd ed.). 1952, pp. 459–464.

Killian, L. The significance of multiple-group membership in disaster. In Proshansky, H., & Seidenberg, I. (Eds.), *Basic Studies in Social Psychology*, New York: Holt, Rinehart, & Winston, 1966.

Kim, H. S. *The Nature of Theoretical Thinking in Nursing*. Norwalk, Conn: Appleton-Century-Crofts, 1983.

Kim, H. S., & Schwartz-Barcott, D. A hybrid model. In Chinn, P. (Ed.), *Nursing Research Methodology: issues and implementation*. Rockville, Maryland: Aspen, 1986, pp. 92–102.

Kinch, S. W. A formalized theory of the self-concept. *American Journal of Sociology*, 1963, *68*, 481.

Kirscht, J. P. The Health Belief Model and illness behavior. In M. H. Becker (Ed.), *The Health Belief Model and Personal Health Behavior*. Thorofare, NJ: Slack, 1974, pp. 60–81.

Kirscht, J. P., Becker, M. H., Haefner, D. P., & Maiman, L. A. Effects of threatening communications and mother's health beliefs on weight change in obese children. *Journal of Behavioral Medicine*, 1978, *1*, 147.

Kirscht, J. P., & Haefner, D. P. Effects of repeated threatening health communications. *International Journal of Health Education*, 1973, *16*, 268.

Kirscht, J. P., Haefner, D. P., & Eveland, J. D. Public response to various written appeals to participate in health screening. *Public Health Reports*, 1975, *90*, 539.

Kirscht, J. P., Kirscht, K. L., & Rosenstock, I. M. A test of interventions to increase adherence to hypertensive medical regimens. *Health Education Quarterly*, 1981, *8*, 261.

Kirscht, J. P., & Rosenstock, I. M. Patient adherence to antihypertensive medical regimens. *Journal of Community Health*, 1977, *3*, 115.

Kitay, P. M. A comparison of the sexes in their attitudes and beliefs about women. *Sociometry*, 1940, *34*, 399.

Khanwalla, P. Mass output orientation of operations technology and organizational structure. *Administrative Science Quarterly*, 1974, *19*, 74.

Knutson, A. L. *The Individual, Society, and Health Behavior*. New York: Russel Sage Foundation, 1965.

Kohlberg, L. Development of moral character and moral ideology. In M. L. Hoffman & L. W. Hoffman (Eds.), *Review of Child Development Research* (Vol. 1). New York: Russel Sage Foundation, 1964, pp. 383–431.

Kohlberg, L. A cognitive-developmental analysis of children's sex role concepts and attitudes. In E. E. Maccoby (Ed.), *The Development of Sex Differences*. Stanford, Cal: Stanford University Press, 1966, pp. 82–173.

Kohlberg, L. Stage and sequence: The cognitive-developmental approach to socialization. In D. A. Goslin (Ed.), *Handbook of Socialization Theory and Research*. Chicago: Rand McNally, 1969.

Kohlberg, L. Continuities in childhood and adult moral development revisited. In P. B. Baltes, & K. W. Schaie (Eds.), *Life-span Developmental Psychology: Personality and Socialization*, New York: Academic Press, 1973, pp. 179–204.

Kohlberg, L. Moral stages and moralization: The cognitive developmental approach to socialization. In T. Lickona (Ed.), *Moral Development and Behavior: Theory, Research, and Social Issues*. New York: Holt, Rinehart, & Winston, 1976.

Kohlberg, L. Revisions in the theory and practice of moral development. In W. Damon (Ed.), *Moral Development* (New Directions for Child Development, No. 2). San Francisco: Jossey-Bass, 1978.

Kohlberg, L. *The Philosophy of Moral Development* (Vol. 1). San Francisco: Harper, Row, 1981.

Kohlberg, L., & Kramer, R. Continuities and discontinuities in childhood moral development. In D. R. Heise, *Personality and Socialization*. Chicago: Rand McNally, 1972, pp. 336–361.

Kohn, M. Bureaucratic man: A portrait and an interpretation. *American Sociological Review*, 1971, *36*, 461.

Kohn, M. L. Social class and parental values. *American Journal of Sociology*, 1959, *64*, 337.

Kohn, M. L. Social class and parent-child relationships: An interpretation. *American Journal of Sociology*, 1963, *68*, 471.

Kohn, M. L. *Class and Conformity*. Homewood, Ill: Dorsey Press, 1969.

Kohn, M. L., & Schooler, C. Class, occupation, and orientation. In D. R. Heise, *Personality and Socialization*. Chicago: Rand McNally, 1972, pp. 223–249.

Komarovsky, M. Cultural contradictions and sex roles. *American Journal of Sociology*, 1946, *52*, 184.

Komarovsky, M. Functional analysis of sex roles. *American Sociological Review*, 1950, *15*, 508.

Komarovsky, M. Cultural contradictions and sex roles: The masculine case. In J. Huber (Ed.), *Changing Women in a Changing Society*. Chicago: University of Chicago Press, 1973, pp. 111–122.

Komarovsky, M. Learning conjugal roles. In J. Heiss (Ed.), *Family Roles and Interaction: An anthology* (2nd ed.). Chicago: Rand McNally. 1976, pp. 129–143.

Komarovsky, M. *Women at College: Shaping Feminine Identity*. New York: Basic Books, 1985.

Koopman, C., Eisenthal, S., & Stoeckle, J.D. Ethnicity in the reported pain, emotional distress and requests of medical outpatients. *Social Science and Medicine*, 1984, *18*, 487.

Kornhauser, W. *Scientists in Industry: Conflict and Accomodation*. Berkely: University of California Press, 1962.

Kotarba, J.A. *Chronic Pain: Its social dimensions*. Beverly Hills, CA: Sage, 1983.

Kovner, A. R. *The nursing unit: A technological perspective*. Unpublished doctoral dissertation, University of Pittsburgh, 1966.

Kramer, M. Nurse role deprivation—a symptom of needed change. *Social Science and Medicine*, 1968, *2*, 461.

Kramer, M. Role models, role conceptions, and role deprivation. *Nursing Research*, 1968, *17*, 115.

Kramer, M. Collegiate graduate nurses in medical center hospitals: Mutual change or duel. *Nursing Research*, 1969, *18*, 196.

Kramer, M. Role conceptions of baccalaureate nurses and success in hospital nursing. *Nursing Research*, 1970, *19*, 428.

Kramer, M. *Reality Shock: Why Nurses Leave Nursing*. St. Louis: Mosby, 1974.

Kramer, M., & Schmalenberg, C. *Path to Biculturalism*. Wakefield, Mass: Contemporary Publishing, 1977.

Kritek, P. B. *Nursing faculty's sex role identity as it relates to selected perceptions of their college of nursing*. Unpublished doctoral dissertation, University of Illinois at the Medical Center, Chicago, 1980.

Kuhn, A. *The Logic of Social Systems*. San Francisco: Jossey-Bass, 1974.

Kuhn, M. Major trends in symbolic interaction theory in the past twenty-five years. In J. G. Manis, & B. N. Meltzer (Eds.), *Symbolic Interaction: A Reader in Social Psychology*. Boston: Allyn & Bacon, 1978.

Kuhn, M. The reference group reconsidered. In J. G. Manis & B. N. Meltzer (Eds.), *Symbolic Interaction: A Reader in Social Psychology*, Boston: Allyn & Bacon, 1972.

Kuhn, T. S. *The Structure of Scientific Revolution*. University of Chicago Press, 1968.

Kurdek, L. Perspective taking as the cognitive basis of children's moral development: A review of the literature. *Merrill-Palmer Quarterly*, 1978, *24*, 3.

Ladner, J. A. Becoming a woman in the black lower class. In J. Heiss (Ed.), *Family Roles and Interaction: An Anthology* (2nd ed.). Chicago: Rand McNally, 1976, pp. 72–89.

Lalonder, M. *A New Perspective on the Health of Canadians: A Working Document*. Ottawa, Canada, 1974.

Lamb, M. E. Effects of stress and cohort on mother- and father-infant interaction. *Developmental Psychology*, 1976a, *12*, 435.

Lamb, M. E. Interactions between eight-month-old children and their fathers and mothers. In M. E. Lamb (Ed.), *The Role of the Father in Child Development*. New York: Wiley, 1976b.

Lamb, M. E. The role of the father: An overview. In M. E. Lamb (Ed.), *The Role of the Father in Child Development*. New York: Wiley, 1976c.

Lamb, M. E. Father-infant and mother-infant interaction in the first year of life. *Child Development*, 1977a, *48*, 167.

Lamb, M. E. The development of mother-infant and father-infant attachments in the second year of life. *Development Psychology*, 1977b, *13*, 637.

Lamb, M. E. The development of parental preferences in the first two years of life. *Sex Roles*, 1977c, *3*, 495.

Lamb, M. E. The effects of divorce on children's personality development. *Journal of Divorce*, 1977d, *1*, 163.

Lamb, M. E. The father's role in the infant's social world. In J. H. Stevens & M. Matthews (Eds.), *Mother/Child, Father/Child Relationships*. Washington, DC: National Association for the Education of Young Children, 1978a.

Lamb, M. E. *Social and Personality Development*. New York: Holt, Rinehart, & Winston, 1978b.

Lamb, M. E. Paternal effects and the father's role: A personal perspective. *American Psychologist*, 1979, *34*, 938.

Lamb, M. E. The development of parent-infant attachments in the first two years of life. In F. A. Pedersen (Ed.), *The Father-Infant Relationship: Observational Studies in a Family Setting*. New York: Praeger, 1980.

Lamb, M. E. Paternal influence on child development: An overview. In M. E. Lamb (Ed.), *The Role of the Father in Child Development* (2nd ed.). New York: Wiley, 1981.

Lamb, M. E. What can "research experts" tell parents about effective socialization? In E. F. Zigler, M. E. Lamb, & I. L. Child, *Socialization and Personality Development* (2nd ed.). New York: Oxford University Press, 1982, pp. 268–273.

Lamb, M. E., & Bronson, S. K. Fathers in the context of family influences: Past, present, and future. *School Psychology Review*, 1980, *9*(4), 336.

Lamb, M. E., & Campos, J. J. *Development in infancy: An Introduction*. New York: Random House, 1982.

Lamb, M. E., Chase-Lansdale, L., & Owen, M. T. The changing American family and its implications for infant social development: the sample case of maternal employment. In M. Lewis & L. A. Rosenblum (Eds.), *The Child and Its Family*. New York: Plenum, 1979.

Lamb, M. E., & Sherrod, L. R. (Eds.). *Infant Social Cognition: Empirical and Theoretical Considerations*. Hillsdale, NJ: Erlbaum, 1981.

Lamb, M. E., & Stevenson, M. B. Father-infant relationships. Their nature and importance. *Youth and Society*, 1978, *9*, 277.

Lambertson, E. C. *Nursing Team Organization and Functioning: Results of a Study of the Division of Nursing Education*. New York: Teachers College, Columbia, University, 1953.

LaPiere, R. T. Attitudes versus actions. *Social Forces*, 1934, *13*, 230.

Larson, E. B., Olsen, E., Cole, W., & Shortell, S. The relationship of health beliefs and a postcard reminder to influenza vaccination. *Journal of Family Practice*, 1979, *8*, 1207.

Laslett, B. Family membership, past and present. In A. S. Skolnick & J. H. Skolnick, *Family in Transition* (4th ed.). Boston: Little, Brown, 1983, pp. 53–72.

Lauer, R. H., & Boardman, L. Role-taking: Theory, typology, and propositions. *Sociology and Social Research*, 1971, *55*(2), 137.

Lauer, R. H., & Handel, W. H. *Social Psychology*. (2nd ed.). Englewood, Cliffs, NJ: Prentice-Hall, 1977.

Lawler, E. E. *Pay and Organizational Effectiveness: A Psychological Review.* New York: McGraw-Hill, 1971.

Lawler, E. E., Kopkin, C. A., Young, T., & Fadem, J. Inequity reduction over time in an induced overpayment situation. *Organizational Behavior and Human Performance,* 1968, *3,* 253.

Lawrence, P. R., & Lorsch, J. W. *Organization and Environment.* Boston: Graduate School of Business Administration, Harvard University, 1967a.

Lawrence, P., & Lorsch, J. W. Differentiation and integration in complex organizations. *Administrative Science Quarterly,* 1967b, *12,* 1.

Laws, J. L. The psychology of tokenism: An analysis. *Sex Roles,* 1975, *1,* 209.

Laws, J. L. *The Second Sex.* New York: Elsevier, 1975.

Leatt, P., & Schneck, R. Work environments of different types of nursing subunits. *Journal of Advanced Nursing,* 1982, 7, 581.

Lebowitz, A. (Ed.). *Executive summary: A study of the participation of women in the health care industry labor force.* Washington, DC: Department of health, Education, and Welfare, Health Resources Administration, DHEW Publication No. HRA-77-644, 1977.

Lee, P. C., & Stewart, R. S. (Eds.). *Sex Differences: Cultural and Developmental Dimensions.* New York: Urizen, 1976.

Leff, H. S. Interpersonal behavior in a non-zero-sum experimental game as a function of cognitive complexity, environmental complexity, and predispositional variables. *Dissertation Abstracts,* 1969, *29,* 4103A.

Lein, L., & Blehar, M. C. Working couples as parents. In A. S. Skolnick & J. H. Skolnick, *Family in Transition* (4th ed.). Boston: Little, Brown, 1983, p. 420.

Leininger, M. The leadership crisis in nursing: A critical problem and challenge. *Journal of Nursing Administration,* 1974, *4*(2), 28.

Lemaku. Women and Employment. In Heckerman (Ed.), *The Evolving Female,* New York: Human Scuna Press, 1980.

Lemert, E. M. Human Deviance, Social Problems, and Social Control. Englewood Cliffs, NJ: Prentice-Hall, 1967.

Lemert, E. M. *Social Pathology.* New York: McGraw-Hill, 1951.

Lemons et al., v. City and County of Denver.

Lennard, H., & Bernstein, A. Expectations and behavior in therapy. In B. Biddle & E. Thomas (Eds.), *Role Theory: Concepts and Research.* New York: Wiley, 1966.

Lenney, E. Women's self-confidence in achievement settings. *Psychological Bulletin,* 1977, *84,* 1.

Lenski, G. *Power and Privilege: A Theory of Social Stratification.* New York: McGraw-Hill, 1966.

Leshan, L., & Margenau, H. *Einstein's space and Van Gogh's Sky.* New York: Macmillan, 1982.

Levenson, R. Intimacy and gender: Developmental differences and their reflection in adult relationships. *Journal of American Academy of Psychoanalysis,* 1984, *12*(4), 529.

Leventhal, H. Findings and theory in the study of fear communications. In L. Berkowitz (Ed.), *Advances in Experimental Social Psychology* (Vol. 5). New York: Academic Press, 1970, pp. 119–186.

Leventhal, H., Rosenstock, I. M., Hochbaum, G. M., & Carriger, B. K. Epidemic impact on the general population in two cities. In *The Impact of Asian Influenza on Community Life: A Study of Five Cities.* PHS Publication No. 776. Washington, DC: U. S. Government Printing Office, 1960, pp. 53–57.

Leventhal, H., Singer, R., & Jones, S. Effects of fear and specificity upon attitudes and behavior. *Journal of Personality and Social Psychology,* 1965, 2, 20.

Levin, L., Katz, H., & Holst, E. *Self-care: Lay Initiates in Health.* New York: Prodist, 1976.

Le Vine, R. Culture, personality and socialization: An evolutionary view. In D. Goslin (Ed.), *Handbook of Socialization Theory and Research*. New York: Rand McNally, 1969.

Levine, A., & Crumrine, J. Women and the fear of success: A problem in replication. *American Journal of Sociology*, 1975, *80*, 964.

Levine, A. J., & Trent, R. B. The swine flu immunization program: A comparison of innoculation recipients and nonrecipients. *Evaluation of the Health Professions*, 1978, *1*, 195.

Levine, D. M. Morlock, J. M. Mushlin, A., et al. The role of new health practitioners in a prepared group practice: Provider differences in process and outcomes of medical care. *Medical Care*, 1976, *14*, 326.

Levine, J. A. *Who Will Raise the Children? New Options for Fathers (and Mothers)*. New York: Lippincott, 1976.

Levine, R. A. Culture, personality, and socialization: An evolutionary view. In D. A. Goslin (Ed.), *Handbook of Socialization Theory and Research*. Chicago: Rand McNally, 1969.

Levine, S., & Kozloff, M. A. The sick role: Assessment and overview. *Annual Review of Sociology*, 1971, *4*, 317.

Levy, M. J. *The Structure of Society*. Princeton: Princeton University Press, 1952.

Lewin, K. Resolving Social Conflicts, Part III. New York: Harper, 1948.

Lewin, K. *Field Theory in Social Science*. New York: Harper, 1951.

Lewin, K., Dembo, T., Festinger, L., et al. Level of aspiration. In J. McV. Hunt (Ed.), *Handbook of Personality and the Personality Disorders*. New York: Ronald Press, 1944.

Lewis, C. C. The effects of parental firm control: A reinterpretation of findings. *Psychological Bulletin*, 1981, *90*(3), 547.

Lewis, J. D. A social behaviorist interpretation of the Meadian "I". *American Journal of Sociology*, 1979, *85*, 261.

Lewis, M., & Rosenblum, L. A. (Eds.). *The Effect of the Infant on Its Caregiver* (Vol. 1). New York: Wiley, 1974.

Lewis, R. A. A developmental framework for the analysis of premarital dyadic formation. In J. Heiss (Ed.), *Family Roles and Interaction: An Anthology* (2nd ed.). Chicago: Rand McNally, pp. 33–57.

Lieb, R. Power, powerlessness, and potential nurse's role within the health care delivery system. *Image*, 1978, *10*, 75.

Light, E., & Keller, S. *Sociology*. New York: Knopf, 1975.

Likert, R. A. A technique for the measurement of attitudes. *Archives of Psychology*, 1932, *140*.

Lindeman, C. A., & Aernam, B. V. Nursing intervention with the presurgical patient—the effects of structured and unstructured preoperative teaching. *Nursing Research*, 1971, *20*, 319.

Linder, F., & Bauer, D. Men's and women's perceptions of values and subsequent feelings of understanding or misunderstanding. *Perceptual and Motor Skills*, 1984, *58*, 773.

Lindesmith, A. R., & Strauss, A. L. *Social Psychology*. New York: Holt, Rinehart, & Winston, 1968.

Lindesmith, A. R., & Strauss, A. L. *Social Psychology* (3rd ed.). New York: Holt, Rinehart, & Winston, 1968, pp. 270–298.

Linn, L. S. Patient acceptance of the family nurse practitioner. *Medical Care*, 1976, *14*, 357.

Linton, R. *The Study of Man*. New York: Appleton-Century, 1936.

Linton, R. *The Cultural Background of Personality*. New York: Appleton-Century, 1945.

Linton, R. The status-role concept. In E. P. Hollander & R. G. Hunt (Eds.), *Classic Contributions to Social Psychology*. New York: Oxford University Press, 1972, pp. 111–114.

Lipman-Blumen, J. How ideology shapes women's lives. *Scientific American*, 1972, *226*, 34.

Lippa, R. Androgyny, sex typing, and the perception of masculinity-femininity in hand-writing. *Journal of Research in Personality*, 1977, *11*, 21.

Litterst, J. K. The impact of fatigue on communication: A study of the dual-career family (Doctoral dissertation, University of Minnesota, 1983). *Dissertation Abstracts International*, 1983, *44*, 610-A.

Locke, E., Mento, A., & Katcher, B. The interaction of ability and motivation in performance. An explanation of the meaning of mediators. *Personnel Psychology*, 1978, *31*, 269.

Locker, D. *Symptoms and Illness*. London: Tavistock, 1981.

Lodahl, J. B., & Gordon, G. The structure of scientific fields and the functioning of University Graduate Departments. *American Sociological Review*, 1972, *37*, 57.

Lodge, M. *Magnitude Scaling Quantitative Measurement of Opinions*. Beverly Hills: Sage, 1981.

Lodge, M., Cross, D., Tursky, B., et al. The calibration and cross-model validation of ratio scales of political opinion in survey research. *Social Sciences Research*, 1976, *5*, 325.

Loeb, J. W., & Ferber, M. A. Sex as predictive of salary and status on a university faculty. *Journal of Educational Measurements*, 1971, *8*, 235.

Loeb, J. W., & Ferber, M. A. Representation, performance, and status of women on the faculty at the Urbana-Champaign Campus of the University of Illinois. In A. Rossi & A. Calderwood (Eds.), *Academic Women on the Move*. New York: Russell Sage Foundation, 1972.

Loether, H. J. *Problems of Aging: Sociological and Social Psychological Perspectives*. Belmont, Cal: Dickenson, 1967.

Loewenstine, H. V., Ponticos, G. D., & Pauldi, M. A. Sex differences in graffiti as a communication style. *Journal of Social Psychology*, 1982, *117*, 307.

Lorber, J. Women and medical sociology: Invisible professionals and ubiquitous patients. In M. Millman & R. Kanter (Eds.), *Another Voice*, 1972, pp. 75–105.

Lorber, J. Good patients and problem patients: Conformity and deviance in a general hospital. *Journal of Health and Social Behavior*, 1975, *16*, 213.

Lorber, J., & Ecker, M. Career development of male and female physicians. *Journal of Medical Education*, 1983, *58*, 447.

Lortie, D. C. Layman to lawman: Law school, careers, and professional socialization. *Harvard Educational Review*, 1959, *29*, 352.

Lowery, B., & DuCette, J. Disease-related learning and disease control in diabetes as a function of locus of control. *Nursing Research*, 1976, *25*, 358.

Lum, J. L. J. Reference groups and professional socialization. In M. E. Hardy & M. E. Conway (Eds.), *Role Theory: Perspectives for Health Professionals*. New York: Appleton-Century-Crofts, 1978.

Luukkonen-Gronow, T., & Stolte-Heiskanen, V. Myths and realities of role incompatibility of women scientists. *Acta Sociologica*, 1983, *26*(3/4), 267.

Lyons, T. Role clarity, need for clarity, satisfaction, tension and withdrawal. *Org. Behav. Human Perf.*, 1971, *6*, 99.

Lynn, D. B. A note on sex differences in the development of masculine and feminine identification. *Psychological Review*, 1959, *66*, 126.

Lysaught, J. P. (Ed.). *An Abstract for Action*. New York: McGraw-Hill, 1971.

Lysaught, J. P., (Ed.). *From Abstract into Action*. New York: McGraw-Hill, 1973a.

Lysaught, J. P. An epistle to the new Corinthians. *Heart and Lung*, 1973b, *2*, 180.

Maccoby, E. E. Role-taking in childhood and its consequences for social learning. *Child Development*, 1959, *30*, 239.

Maccoby, E. E. The taking of adult roles in middle childhood. *Journal of Abnormal and Social Psychology*, 1961, *63*, 493.

Maccoby, E. E. *The Development of Sex Differences*. Stanford, Cal: Stanford University Press, 1966.

Maccoby, E. E. The development of moral values and behavior in childhood. In J. A. Clausen (Ed.), *Socialization and Society*. Boston: Little, Brown, 1968, pp. 227–269.

Maccoby, E. E. *Social Development: Psychological Growth and the Parent-Child Relationship*. New York: Harcourt Brace Jovanovich, 1980.

Maccoby, E. E., & Jacklin, C. N. *The Psychology of Sex Differences*. Stanford, Cal: Stanford University Press, 1974.

MacKay, R. Conceptions of children and models of socialization. In H. P. Dreitzel (Ed.), *Childhood and Socialization* (Recent Sociology, No. 5). New York: Macmillan, 1973, pp. 27–43.

Maier, R. A., & Lavrakas, P. J. Attitudes toward women, personality rigidity, and idealized physique preferences in males. *Sex Roles*, 1984, *11*(5/6), 425.

Maiman, L. A., Becker, M. H., Kirscht, J. P. et al. Scales for measuring Health Belief Model dimensions: A test of predictive value, internal consistency and relationships among beliefs. *Health Education Monographs*, 1977, *5*, 215.

Maines, D. R. Researching form and process in the Iowa tradition. In N. Denzin (Ed.), *Studies in Symbolic Interaction*, Supplement 2. Greenwich, Conn: JAI Press, 1985.

Malinowski, B. The group and the individual in functional analysis. *American Journal of Sociology*, 1939, *44*, 938.

Manicas, P. T., & Secord, P. Implications for psychology of the new philosophy of science. *American Psychologist*, 1983.

Manis, J. S., & Meltzer, B. N. *Symbolic Interactionism* (2nd ed). Boston: Allyn & Bacon, 1972.

March, J., & Simon, H. *Organizations*. New York: Wiley, 1958.

Marini, M. M., & Greenberger, E. Sex differences in the process of occupational aspirations and expectations. *Sociology of Work and Occupation*, 1978, *5*, 147.

Marini, M. M. Age and sequencing norms in the transition to adulthood. *Social Forces*, 1984, *63*(1), 229.

Marks, S. Multiple roles and role strain: Some notes on human energy, time and commitment. *American Sociologist Review*, 1977, *42*, 921.

Marram, G., Schlegel, M., & Bevis, E. *Primary Nursing: A Model for Individual Care*. St. Louis: C. V. Mosby, 1974.

Marrett, C. B. Centralization in female organizations: Reassessing the evidence. *Social Problems*, 1972, *19*, 348.

Martin, H., & Katz, F. the professional school as a molder of motivation. *Journal of Health Social Behavior*, 1961, *2*, 106.

Martin, M. W., Jr. Some effects of communication on group behavior in Prisoner's dilemma. *Dissertation Abstracts*, 1966, *27*, 231B.

Martindale, D. American sociology before World War II. In A. Inkles, J. Coleman, & N. Smeleer, *American Review of Sociology* (Vol. 6) Palo Alto, Cal: Annual Review, Inc, 1976, pp. 121–144.

Marwell, G. Why ascription? Parts of a more or less formal theory of the functions and dysfunctions of sex roles. *American Sociological Review*, 1975, *40*, 445.

Marx, K., & Engels, F. *Manifesto of the Communist Party*. New York: International Publishers, 1932.

Marx, K., & Engels, F. *Basic Writings on Politics and Philosophy*. (L. S. Feuer, Ed.). New York: Anchor Books, 1959.

Maslow, A. *Motivation and personality*. New York: Harper, 1954.

Mason, K. O., & Bumpass, L., L. U. S. women's sex-role ideology, 1970. *American Journal of Sociology*, 1975, *80*, 1212.

Mason, K., O., Czajka, J., & Arber, S. *Change in U.S. women's sex-role attitudes, 1964–1971*. Final report of Grant No. R01-MH25271, NIMH, 1975.

Masson, V. Nursing: Healing in a feminine mode. *The Journal of Nursing Administration*, 1981, *11*(10), 20.

Masters, J. C. Treatment of adolescent "rebellion" by the reconstrual of stimuli. *Journal of Consulting and Clinical Psychology*, 1970, *35*, 213.

Matza, D. Position and behavior patterns of youth. In R. E. L. Faris (Ed.), *Handbook of Modern Sociology*. Chicago: Rand McNally, 1964, pp. 191–216.

Mayhew, B. H. Structuralism versus individualism: Shadowboxing in the dark, Part I. *Social Forces*, 1980, *59*, 335.

McCall, G. J., & Simmons, J. L. *Identities and Interactions. An examination of human associations in everyday life*. New York: Free Press, 1978.

McCandless, B. R. Childhood socialization. In D. A. Goslin (Ed.), *Handbook of Socialization Theory and Research*. Chicago: Rand McNally, 1969, pp. 791–819.

McCloskey, H., & Sharr, J. Dynamics of Anomy. *American Sociological Review*, 1965, *30*, 14.

McCord, W., & McCord, A. *Power and Equity: An Introduction to Social Stratification*. New York: Praeger, 1977.

McCullock, S. J. The politics of nursing. *The Australian Nurses Journal*, 1982, *11*(3), 11.

McGee, R., et al. *Sociology: An Introduction*. Hinsdale, Ill: Dryden, 1977.

McGlothlin, W. J. *The Professional Schools*. New York: Center for Applied Research in Education, 1964.

McGrath, J., (Ed.), Social and Psychological Factors in Stress. New York: McGraw-Hill, 1972.

McGregor, D. *The Human Side of Enterprise*. New York: McGraw-Hill, 1960.

McInernay, K. Sexism is a social disease—And nursing is infected. *ANA Clinical Sessions*. Kansas City: American Nurses' Association, 1974, pp. 36–39.

McKee, J. P., & Sherriffs, A. C. The differential evaluation of males and females. *Journal of Personality*, 1957, *25*, 356.

McMichael, A. J. Personality, behavioral, and situational modifiers of work. In C. L. Cooper & R. Payne (Eds.), *Stress at Work*. New York: Wiley, 1978, pp. 127–148.

McNeil, K., & Minihan, E. Regulation of medical devices and organizational behavior in hospitals. *Administrative Science Quarterly*, 1977, *22*, 475.

McPherson, K. S., & Spetrino, S. K. Androgyny and sex-typing: Differences in beliefs regarding gender polarity in ratings of ideal men and women. *Sex Roles*, 1983, *9*, 441.

Mead, G. H. The genesis of the self and social control. *International Journal of Ethics*, 1925, *35*(3), 251.

Mead, G. H. *Mind, Self and Society*. Chicago: University of Chicago Press, 1934.

Mead, G. H. In C. W. Morris (Ed.), *Mind, Self and Society from the Standpoint of Social Behaviorist*. Chicago: University of Chicago Press, 1934.

Mead, G. H. The genesis of self. In G. Gordon & K. J. Gergen (Eds.), *The Self in Social Interaction*. New York: Wiley, 1968, pp. 51–59.

Mead, G. H. The development of the self through play and games. In G. P. Stone & H. A. Farberman (Eds.), *Social Psychology through Symbolic Interaction*. Watham, Mass: Xerox, 1970, pp. 537–545.

Mechanic, D. Some problems in developing a social psychology of adaptation to stress. In J. McGrath (Ed.), *Social and Psychological Factors in Stress*. New York: Holt, Rinehart, & Winston, 1972.

Mechanic, D. The concept of illness behavior. *Journal of Chronic Diseases*, 1972, *15*, 180.

Mechanic, D. *Medical Sociology* (2nd ed.). New York: Free Press, 1978.

Mechanic, D. Correlates of physician utilization: Why do major multivariate studies of physician utilization find trivial psychosocial and organizational effects? *Journal of Health and Social Behavior*, 1979, *20*, 387.

Mechanic, D. Response factors in illness: The study of illness behavior. *Social Psychiatry*, 1966, *1*, 11.

Mechanic, D., & Volkart, E. H. Illness behavior and medical diagnosis. *Journal of Health and Human Behavior*, 1960, *1*, 86.

Mechanic, D., & Volkart, E. H. Stress, illness behavior and the sick role. *American Sociological Review,* 1961, *26,* 51.

Meeker, R. J., & Shure, G. H. Pacifist bargaining tactics: Some "outsider" influences. *Journal of Conflict Resolution,* 1969, *13,* 487.

Meeker, B. F., & Weitzel-O'Neil, P. A. Sex roles and interpersonal behavior in task-oriented groups. *American Sociological Review,* 1977, *42,* 91.

Mehrens, W. A., & Lehmann, I. J. *Measurement and Evaluation in Education and Psychology.* New York: Holt, Rinehart, & Winston, 1973.

Meier, R. F. Perspectives on the concept of social control. In R. Turner & J. Short (Eds.). *Annual Review of Sociology,* (Vol. 8), 1982, p. 34.

Meile, R. L. Pathways to patienthood: Sick role and labeling perspectives. *Social Science and Medicine,* 1986, *22,* 35.

Meleis, A. I. Role insufficiency and role supplementation: A conceptual framework. *Nursing Research,* 1975, *24*(4), 264–271.

Meleis, A. I., & Dagenais, F. Sex-role identity and perception of professional self in graduates of three nursing programs. *Nursing Research,* 1980, *30,* 162.

Meleis, A. I., & Swendsen, L. A. Role supplemetation: An empirical test of a nursing intervention. *Nursing Research,* 1978, *27*(1), 11.

Meleis, A. I., Swendsen, L., & Jones, D. Preventive supplementation: A grounded conceptual framework. In B. C. Flynn & M. H. Miller (Eds.), *Current Perspectives in Nursing Social Issues and Trends.* St. Louis: C. V. Mosby, 1980.

Meltzer, B. N., Petras, J. W., & Reynolds, L. Y. Varieties of symbolic interaction. In J. G. Manis & B. N. Meltzer (Eds.), *Symbolic Interaction: A Reader in Social Psychology.* Boston: Allyn & Bacon, 1978.

Meltzer, M., Petras, J. W., & Reynolds, L. *Symbolic Interactionism: Genesis, Varieties and Criticism.* London: Routledge, Kegan Paul, 1975.

Merton, R. K. The normative structure of science. In R. K. Merton, *The Sociology of Science.* Chicago, University of Chicago Press, 1942, 1973.

Merton, R. Social structure and anomie. In R. K. Merton, *Social Theory and Social Structure.* New York: Macmillan, 1957.

Merton, R. The role set: Problems in sociological theory. *British Journal of Sociology,* 1957, *8,* 106.

Merton, R. *On Theoretical Sociology: Five Essays, Old and New.* New York: The Free Press, 1967.

Merton, R. K. *Social Theory and Social Structure* (Rev. ed.). Free Press, 1968.

Merton, R. K. *The Sociology of Science.* Chicago: Chicago University Press, 1973.

Merton, R. K. Structural analysis in Sociology. In P. M. Blau (Ed.), *Approaches to the Study of Social Structure.* New York: Free Press, 1975.

Merton, R. K. *Sociological ambivalance.* New York: Free Press, 1976.

Merton, R., & Barber, E. Sociological ambivalence. In R. Merton (Ed.), *Sociological Ambivalence.* New York: Free Press, 1963, 1976.

Merton, R. K., & Kitt, A. S. Contributions to the theory of reference group behavior. In R. K. Merton & P. F. Lazarsfeld (Eds.), *Continuities in Social Research: Studies in the Scope and Method of "The American Soldier."* Glencoe, Ill: Free Press, 1950.

Merton, R. K., Reader, J., & Kendall, P. (Eds.). *The Student Physician.* Cambridge, Mass: Harvard University Press, 1957.

Merton, R. K., & Rossi, A. Contributions to the theory of reference group behavior. In R. K. Merton (Ed.), *Social Theory and Social Structure.* New York: Free Press, 1968, pp. 279–334.

Messick, D. M., & Cook, K. S. (Eds.). Equity Theory. New York: Praeger, 1983.

Mikhail, B. I. The health belief model: A review and critical evaluation of the model, research, and practice. *Advances in Nursing Science,* 1981, *4*(1), 65.

Mikhail, B. I. *An investigation of the psychosocial factors that influence pregnant women's health behavior*. Unpublished doctoral dissertation, Boston University, 1984.

Miles, R. H. An empirical test of causal inference between role perceptions of conflict and ambiguity and various personal outcomes. *Journal of Applied Psychology*, 1975, *60*, 334.

Miles, R. H., & Pereault, W. D., Jr. Organizational role conflict: Its antecedents and consequences. *Organizational Behavior and Human Performance*, 1976, *17*, 19.

Milgram, S. *Obedience to Authority*. New York: Harper & Row, 1974,

Miller, D. "George Herbert Mead: Biographical notes". In Corti, R. (Ed.), *The Philosophy of George Herbert Mead*. Amriswiler Bucherei, 1975.

Miller, D. I. The meaning of role-taking. *Symbolic Interaction*, 1981, *4*, 167.

Miller, G. A. Profession in bureaucracies: Alienation among industrial scientists and engineering. *American Sociological Review*, 1968, *32*, 755.

Miller, J. The nature of living systems. *Behavioral Science*, 1971, *16*, 278.

Miller, J. Living systems: The organization. *Behavioral Science*, 1972, *17*, 1.

Miller, J. B. *Toward a New Psychology of Women*. Boston: Beacon Press, 1976.

Miller, L. K., & Hamblin, R. I. Interdependence, differential rewarding and productivity. *American Sociological Review*, 1963, *28*, 768.

Miller, P. H. *Theories of Developmental Psychology*. San Francisco: Freeman, 1983.

Millett, K. *Sexual Politics*. New York: Avon, 1969.

Milliken, R. Men and women in nursing: Do we need both? *The New Zealand Nursing Journal*, 1981, *74*(1), 21.

Mills, C. W. *The Power Elite*. New York: Oxford University Press, 1956.

Mills, C. W. *The Sociological Imagination*. New York: Grove Press, 1959.

Mills, J. Self-posed behaviors of females and males in photographs. *Sex Roles*, 1984, *10*(7/8), 633.

Minehan, P. L. Nurse role conception. *Nursing Research*, 1977, *26*, 374.

Minkler, M., & Biller, R. Role shock: A tool for conceptualizing stresses accompanying disruptive role transitions. *Human Relations*, 1979 *32*, 125.

Minnigerode, F. A., Kayser-Jones, J. S., & Garcia, G. Masculinity and femininity in nursing. *Nursing Research*, 1978, *27*, 299.

Mintzberg, H. *The Structure of Organizations*. Englewood Cliffs, NJ: Prentice-Hall, 1979.

Mischel, W. A social-learning view of sex differences in behavior. In E. E. Maccoby (Ed.), *The Development of Sex Differences*. Stanford, Cal: Stanford University Press, 1966, pp. 56–81.

Mischel, W. *Personality and Assessment*. New York: Wiley, 1968.

Mishler, E. Personality characteristics and the resolution of role conflicts. *Public Opinion Quarterly*, 1953, *17*, 115.

Mitchell, W. Occupational role strain: The American elective official. *Administrative Science Quarterly*, 1958, *3*, 210.

Mitroff, I., & Bonoma, J. V. Psychological assumptions, experimentation, and real world problems. *Evaluation Quarterly*, 1978, *2*, 235.

Mitroff, I. Norms and counter-norms in a select group of the Apollo moon scientists: A case study of the ambivalence of scientists. *American Sociological Review*, 1974, *39*, 579.

Mitroff, I., & Kilmann, R. H. *Methodological Approaches to Social Science*. San Francisco, Jossey-Bass, 1978.

Miyamoto, S. F. The Social Act: Reexamination of a concept. *Pacific Sociological Review*, 1979, *2*, 51–55.

Moore, D. S., Decker, S. D., & Dowd, M. W. *Nursing Research*, 1978, *27*, 291.

Moore, P., Conine, T., & Laster, T. E. Sex-role stereotyping in health care: Perceptions of physical therapists. *Physical Therapy*, 1980, *60*, 1425.

Moore, W. *The profession: Roles and rules*. New York: Sage, 1976.

Moore, W. E. Occupational socialization. In D. A. Goslin (Ed.), *Handbook of Socialization Theory and Research*. Chicago: Rand McNally, 1969.

Morais, H. M. *History of the Negro in Medicine*. New York: Publishers, 1968.

Moreno, J. L. Psychodrama. In Ariefi (Ed.), *American Handbook of Psychiatry*, (Vol. 2). New York: Basic Books, Inc., 1959.

Morris, J. H., Steers, R. M., & Koch, J. L. Influence of organization structure on role conflict and ambiguity for three occupational groupings. *Academy of Management Journal*, 1979, *22*, 58.

Moses, E., & Roth, A. Nursepower. *American Journal of Nursing*, 1979, *79*, 1745.

Moses, J. L., & Boehm, V. R. Relationship of assessment-center performance to management progress of women. *Journal of Applied Psychology*, 1975, *60*, 527.

Mulkay, M. *Science and the Sociology of Knowledge*. Boston: George Allen & Unwin, 1979.

Mumford, E. *Interns: From Students to Physicians*. Cambridge, Mass: Harvard University Press, 1970.

Murdaugh, C. Instrument development to assess specific psychological variables explaining individual differences in preventive behaviors for coronary artery disease. (Doctoral dissertation, University of Arizona). *Dissertation Abstracts International*, 1981, *43*, 680.

Murdaugh, C., & Hinshaw, A. S. Theoretical model testing to identify personality variables effecting preventive behaviors. *Nursing Research*, (in press).

Murphy, E. An examination of the relationship between perceived social support of a significant other and the maintenance of weight loss among successful reducers. Unpublished doctoral dissertation, Boston University, 1985.

Mussen, P. H. Some antecedents and consequents of masculine sex-typing in adolescent boys. *Psychological Monographs (No. 506)*, *75*, 1961.

Mussen, P. H. Long-term consequents of masculinity of interests in adolescence. *Journal of Consulting Psychology*, 1962, *26*, 435.

Mussen, P. H. Early socialization: Learning and identification. In T. M. Newcomb (Ed.), *New Directions in Psychology III*. New York: Holt, Rinehart, & Winston, 1967.

Mussen, P. H. Early sex-role development. In D. A. Goslin (Ed.), *Handbook of Socialization Theory and Research*. Chicago: Rand McNally, 1969, pp. 707–731.

Mutran, E., & Reitzes, D. C. Intergenerational support activities and well-being among the elderly: A convergence of exchange and symbolic interaction perspectives. *American Sociological Review*, 1984, *49*, 117.

Muus, R. E. Social cognition: Robert Selman's theory of role taking. *Adolescence*, 1983, *17*, 499.

Myrdal, G. *An American Dilemma: The Negro Problem and American Democracy*. New York: Harper, 1944.

Nagel, E. *The Structure of Science*. London: Routledge & Kegan Paul, 1961.

Nasstrom, R. R. The male attitude and affirmative action for women in education. *Kappa Delta Pi Record*, 1976, *13*, 3.

Natanson, M. *The Social Dynamics of George Herbert Mead*. The Hague: Martinus Nijhoff, 1973.

Nathanson, C. A. Illness and the feminine role: A theoretical review. *Social Science and Medicine*, 1975, *9*, 57.

Nathanson, C. A. Sex, illness and medical care: A review of data, theory, and method. *Social Science and Medicine*, 1977, *11*, 13.

National Center for Health Statistics. *Health Resources Statistics: Health Manpower and Health Facilities*. Washington, DC: U. S. Government Printing Office, 1976–77.

Neiman, L. J., & Hughes, J. W. The problem of the concept of role: A resurvey of the literature. *Social Forces*, 1951, *30*, 141.

Nelson, E. C., Stason, W. B., Neutra, R. R., et al. Impact of patient perceptions on compliance with treatment for hypertension. *Medical Care*, 1978, *16*, 893.

Newcomb, T. M. Attitude development as a function of reference groups: The Bennington study. In H. Proshansky & B. Seidenberg (Eds.), *Basic Studies in Social Psychology*. New York: Holt, Rinehart, & Winston, 1975.

Newton, L. H. In defense of the traditional nurse. *Nursing Outlook*, 1981, *29*, 348.

Noble, J. (Ed.). *Primary Care and the Practice of Medicine*. Boston: Little, Brown, 1976.

Norbeck, J. S. Social support: A model for clinical research and application. *Advances in Nursing Science*, 1981, *3*(4), 43.

Norbeck, J. S., Lindsey, A. M., & Carrieri, V. L. The development of an instrument to measure social support. *Nursing Research*, 1981, *30*, 264.

Norbeck, J. S., Lindsey, A. M., & Carrieri, L. Further development of the Norbeck Social Support Questionnaire: Normative data and validity testing. *Nursing Research*, 1983, *32*, 4.

Norman, J. C. *Medicine in the Ghetto*. New York: Appleton-Century-Crofts, 1969.

Norris, C. M. Direct access to the patient. *American Journal of Nursing*, 1970, p. 1006.

Nuckolls, K. B., Cassel, J., & Kaplan, B. H. Psychosocial assets, life crisis, and the prognosis of pregnancy. *American Journal of Epidemiology*, 1972, *95*, 431.

Nunnally, J. *Psychometric Theory*. New York: McGraw-Hill, 1978.

Nye, F. I., & Gecas, V. The role concept: Review and delineation. In F. I. Nye, (Ed.), *Role Structure and Analysis of the Family*. Beverly Hills, Cal: Sage, 1976, pp. 3–14.

Nye, F. I., & Hoffman, L. W. *The Employed Mother in America*. Chicago: Rand McNally, 1963.

Oleson, V., & Whittaker, E. *The Silent Dialogue*. San Francisco: Jossey-Bass, 1968.

Olmstead, A. G., & Paget, M. A. Some theoretical issues in professional socialization. *Journal of Medical Education*, 1969, *44*, 663.

Ondrack, D. A. Socialization in professional schools: A comparative study. *Administrative Science Quarterly*, 1973, *20*, 97.

Orden, S. R., & Bradburn, N. M. Working wives and marriage happiness. *The American Journal of Sociology*, 1969, *74*, 392.

Orphen, C. Type A personality as a moderator of the effects of role conflict, role ambiguity and role overload on individual strain. *Journal of Human Stress*, 1982, *6*, 8.

Ouchi, W., & Johnson, J. Types of organizational control and relationship to emotional well being. *Administrative Science Quarterly*, 1978, *23*, 293.

Overall, B., & Aronson, H. Expectations of psychotherapy in patients of lower socioeconomic class. In Biddle, B. & Thomas, E. (Eds.), *Role Theory: Concepts and Research*. New York: Wiley, 1966.

Overton, P., Schneck, R., & Hazlett, C. B. An empirical study of the technology of nursing subunits. *Administrative Science Quarterly*, 1977, *22*, 203.

Paige, S. *Alone unto the alone*. Unpublished doctoral dissertation, Boston University, 1980.

Palmer, F. H. Inferences to the socialization of the child from animal studies: A view from the bridge. In D. A. Goslin (Ed.), *Handbook of Socialization Theory and Research*. Chicago: Rand McNally, 1969, pp. 25–55.

Palola, E. *Organization types and role strains: A laboratory study of complex organization*. Unpublished dissertation, University of Washington, Seattle, 1962.

Parasuraman, S., & Alutto, J. A. An examination of the organizational antecedents of stressors at work. *Academy of Management Journal*, 1981, *24*, 48.

Park, R. E. Human nature and collective behavior. *American Journal of Sociology*, 1927, *32*, 733.

Park, R. E., & Burgess, E. W. *Introduction to the Science of Sociology*. Chicago: University of Chicago Press, 1921.

Park, R. E. Symbiosis and socialization: A frame of reference for the study of society. *American Journal of Sociology*, 1939, *45*, 1.

Parke, R. D. The role of punishment in the socialization process. In R. A. Hope, G. A.

Milton, & E. C. Simmel (Eds.), *Early Experiences and the Processes of Socialization*. New York: Academic Press, 1970, pp. 81–108.

Parke, R. D. Some effects of punishment on children's behavior. In W. W. Hartup (Ed.), *The Young Child: Reviews of Research*. Washington, DC: National Association for the Education of Young Children, 1972, pp. 264–283.

Parke, R. D. Perspectives on father-infant interaction. In J. D. Osofsky (Ed.), *Handbook of Infant Development*. New York: Wiley, 1979.

Parkes, K. R. Occupational stress among student nurses: A natural experiment. *Journal of Applied Psychology*, 1982, 67(6), 784.

Parsons, T. *The Structure of Social Action*. New York: McGraw, 1937.

Parsons, T. Age and sex in the social structure of the United States. *American Sociological Review*, 1942, 7, 604.

Parsons, T. *The Social System*. New York: Free Press, 1951.

Parsons, T. Youth in the context of American society. *Daedalus*, 1962, *91*, 97.

Parsons, T. Definitions of health and illness in the light of American values and social structure. In E. G. Jaco (Ed.), *Patients, Physicians and Illness* (2nd ed.). New York: Free Press, 1972, pp. 107–127.

Parsons, T. The sick role and the role of the physician reconsidered. *Milbank Memorial Fund Quarterly*, 1975, *53*, 257.

Parsons, T., & Fox, R. Therapy and the modern urban family. *Journal of Social Issues*, 1952, *8*, 31.

Parsons, T., & Shills, G. E. Values, motives and systems of action. In T. Parson & E. Shills (Eds.), *Toward a General Theory of Action*, 1951, pp. 47–243.

Pavalko, R. M. *Sociology of Occupations and Professions*. Itasco, Ill: Peacock, 1971.

Pear, R. Administration may challenge equal pay rules. *New York Times*, A1:16. January 22, 1984.

Pederson, F. A. (Ed.) *The Father-Infant Relationship: Observational Studies in a Family Setting*. New York: Praeger, 1980.

Pellegrino, E. D. Rationale for nursing education in the University. *American Journal of Nursing*, 1968, *68*, 1006.

Pennings, J. The relevance of the structural contingency model for organizational effectiveness. *Administrative Science Quarterly*, 1975, *20*, 393.

Perlman, B., & Hartman, E. A. The Community Health Care Administration Project. Oshkosh, Wisc: University of Wisconsin-Oshkosh, 1980.

Perloe, S. The relationship between category-rating and magnitude estimation judgements of occupational prestige. *American Journal of Psychology*, 1963, pp. 395–403.

Perrow, C. A framework for the comparative analysis of organizations. *American Sociological Review*, 1967, *32*, 194.

Perrow, C. *Organizational Analysis*. Belmont, Cal: Wadsworth, 1970.

Perrow, C. *Complex Organizations*. Glenview, Ill: Scott, Foresman, 1972.

Perry, S., & Wynne, L. L. Role conflict, role redefinition, and social change in a clinical research organization. *Social Forces*, 1959, *38*, 62.

Petersen, L. R., Lee, G. R., & Ellis, G. J. Social structure, socialization values, and disciplinary techniques: A cross-cultural analysis. *Journal of Marriage and the Family*, 1982, *44*(1), 131.

Peterson, G. W., & Peters, D. F. Adolescents' construction of social reality. The impact of television and peers. *Youth and Society*, 1983, *15*, 67.

Pettigrew, A. *The Politics of Organizational Decision-making*. London: Tavistock, 1973.

Petty, M. M., & Miles, R. H. Leader sex-role stereotyping in a female-dominated work culture. *Personnel Psychology*, 1976, *29*, 393.

Pfeffer, J., & Salancik, G. R. *The External Control of Organizations*. New York: Harper, Row, 1978.

Phelan, J. G., & Richardson, E. Cognitive complexity, strategy of the other player, and two person game behavior. *Journal of Psychology*, 1969, *71*, 205.

Pheterson, G. I. *Female prejudice against men.* Unpublished doctoral dissertation, Connecticut College, New London, 1969.

Piaget, J. *The Moral Judgement of the Child.* Glencoe, Il: Free Press, 1948.

Piaget, J. *On the Development of Memory and Identity.* Worcester, Mass: Clark University Press, 1968.

Pillette, P. Mentoring. In E. Hein & J. Nicholson (Eds.), *Contemporary Leadership Behavior: Selected Readings*, 1986, pp. 155–162.

Pinch, W. J. Feminine attributes in a masculine world. *Nursing Outlook*, 1981, *29*, 596.

Pines, A., & Kafry, D. Occupational tedium in the social services. *Social Work*, 1978, *23*, 499.

Poggi, G. A main theme of contemporary sociological analysis. Its achievements and limitations. *British Journal of Sociology*, 1965, *16*, 283.

Popper, K. R. *The Logic of Scientific Discovery.* New York: Harper & Row, 1959.

Poulton, E. C. Models for biases in judging sensory magnitude. *Psychological Bulletin*, 1977, *86*, 777.

Powell, B., & Reznikoff, M. Role conflict and symptoms of psychological stress in college-educated women. *Journal of Consulting and Clinical Psychology*, 1976, *44*, 473.

Practice and Academia. *Social Work*, 1973, *18*, 2.

Preiss, J. J. Self and role in medical education. In C. Gordon & K. Gergen (Eds.), *The Self in Social Interaction.* New York: Wiley, 1968, pp. 207–218.

Preiss, J. J., & Ehrlich, H. J. *An Examination of Role Theory: The Case of the State Police.* Lincoln, Nebr: University of Nebraska Press, 1966.

Promoting Health, Preventing Disease: Objectives for the Nation. (DHHS). Washington, DC: U. S. Government Printing Office, 1981.

Pruitt, D. G., & Johnson, D. F. Mediation as an aid to face saving in negotiation. *Journal of Personality and Social Psychology*, 1970, *14*, 239.

Psathas, G. The fate of idealism in nursing school. *Journal of Health and Social Behavior*, 1968, *9*, 52.

Psathas, G. Toward a theory of occupational choice for women. *Sociology and Social Research*, 1968, *52*, 253.

Psathas, G., & Plapp, J. Assessing effects of a nursing program: A problem in design. *Nursing Research*, 1968, *17*, 337.

Pugh, D. S., Hickson, D. J., Hinings, C. R., & Turner, C. Dimensions of organizational structure. *Administrative Science Quarterly*, 1968, *13*, 65.

Putnam, L., & Heinen, J. S. Women in management: The fallacy of the trait approach. *MSU Business Topics*, 1976, *14*(3), 47.

Quell, M., & Pfeiffer, I. L. Instances of sex bias rated by women administrators. *Journal of Educational Equity and Leadership*, 1982, *2*, 268.

Quint, J. Institutionalized practices of information. *Psychiatry*, *28*, 119, May 1965.

Rafky, D. M. Phenomenology and socialization: Some comments on the assumptions underlying socialization theory. In H. P. Dreitzel (Ed.), *Childhood and Socialization* (Recent Sociology, No. 5). New York: Macmillan, 1973, pp. 44–64.

Ragan, J. M. Gender displays in portrait photographs. *Sex Roles*, 1982, *8*(1), 33.

Rainwater, L. *Interim Report on Explorations of Social Status, Living Standards and Family Life Styles.* Cambridge, Mass: Joint Center for Urban Studies of the Massachusetts Institute of Technology and Harvard University, 1972.

Randolph, W. A., & Posner, B. Z. Explaining role conflict and role ambiguity via individual and interpersonal variables in different job categories. *Personnel Psychology*, 1981, 34.

Rappoport, R., & Rappoport, R. N. *Dual Career Families Reexamined.* New York: Harper, Row, 1976.

Raschke, H. J., & Raschke, V. J. Family conflict and children's self-concepts: A comparison of intact and single parent families. *Journal of Marriage and the Family*, May 1979, 367.

Reeder, L. G. The patient-client as a consumer: Some observations on the changing professional-client relationship. In H. D. Schwartz & C.S. Kart (Eds.), *Dominant Issues in Medical Sociology.* Reading, MA: Addison-Wesley, 1978, pp.111–117.

Reiber, R. W. *William Wundt and the Making of Scientific Psychology.* New York: Plenum, 1980.

Reich, C. A. *The Greening of America.* New York: Random House, 1970.

Reid, M. Marginal man: The identity dilemma of the academic general practitioner. *Symbolic Interaction*, 1982, *5*(2), 325.

Reimanis, G. Effects of locus of reinforcement control modification procedures in early graders and college students. *Journal of Educational Research*, 1974, *68*, 124.

Reisine, S. T. Theoretical considerations in formulating sociodental indicators. *Social Science and Medicine*, 1981, *6*, 745.

Reiter, F. The nurse clinician. *American Journal of Nursing*, 1966, *66*, 274.

Rheingold, H. L. The social and socializing infant. In D. A. Goslin (Ed.), *Handbook of Socialization Theory and Research.* Chicago: Rand McNally, 1969, pp. 779–790.

Rich, A. *Of Woman Born: Motherhood as Experience and Institution.* New York: Norton, 1976.

Rich, W. Special role and role expectations of black administrators of neighborhood health programs. *Community Mental Health Journal*, 1975, *11*, 394.

Richardson, D., Leonard, K., Taylor, S., Hammock, G. Male violence toward females: Victim and aggressor variables. *The Journal of Psychology*, 1985, *119*(2), 129.

Riehl, P. O., & McVay, J. W. *The Clinical Nurse Specialist: Interpretations.* New York: Appleton-Century-Crofts, 1973.

Riger, S., & Galligan, P. Women in management: An exploration of competing paradigms. *American Psychologist*, 1980, *35*, 902.

Riley, M. W. *Aging from Birth to Death: Interdisciplinary Perspectives.* Boulder, Colo: Westview, 1979.

Riley, M. W., Abeles, R. P., & Teitelbaum, M. S. *Aging from Birth to Death* (Vol. 2: Sociotemporal Perspectives). Boulder, Colo: Westview, 1982.

Riley, M. W., & Foner, A. *Aging and Society: An Inventory of Research Findings* (Vol. 1). New York: Sage, 1968.

Riley, M. W., Foner, A., Hess, B., & Toby, M. Socialization for the middle and later years. In D. A. Goslin (Ed.), *Handbook of Socialization Theory and Research*, Chicago: Rand McNally, 1969, pp. 951–982.

Ritter, K. V., & Hargens, L. L. Occupational positions and class identifications of married working women: A test of the assymetry hypothesis. *American Journal of Sociology*, 1975, *80*, 934.

Rizzo, A. M. Perceptions of membership and women in administration: Implications for public organizations. *Administration and Society*, 1978, *10*, 33.

Rizzo, J., House, R., & Lirtzman, S. Role conflict and ambiguity in complex oranizations. *Administrative Science Quarterly*, 1970, *15*, 150.

Roberts, M. M. *American Nursing: History and Interpretation.* New York: Macmillan, 1961.

Roche, G. R. Much ado about mentors. *Harvard Business Review*, 1979, *57*, 14.

Rock, P. *The Making of Symbolic Interactionism.* Totowa, NJ: Rowman & Littlefield, 1979.

Roethlisberger, F. J., & Dickson, W. J. *Management and the Worker.* Cambridge, Mass: Harvard University Press, 1939.

Rogers, M. E. *An Introduction to the Theoretical Basis for Nursing.* Philadelphia: Davis, 1970.

Rommetviet, R. *Social Norms and Roles.* Minneapolis: University of Minnesota Press, 1954.

Rose, A. M. *Human Behavior and Social Processes*. Boston: Houghton, Mifflin, 1962.

Rose, A. M. A systematic summary of symbolic interaction theory. In A. M. Rose (Ed.), *Human Behavior and Social Processes: An Interactionist Approach*. Boston: Houghton Mifflin, 1962.

Rosen, B., & Jerdee, T. H. The influence of sex-role stereotypes on evaluation of male and female supervisory behavior. *Journal of Applied Psychology*, 1973, *57*, 44.

Rosen, B., & Jerdee, T. H. Effects of applicant's sex and difficulty of job on evaluations of candidates for managerial positions. *Journal of Applied Psychology*, 1974a, *59*, 511.

Rosen, B., & Jerdee, T. H. Influence of sex role stereotypes on personnel decisions. *Journal of Applied Psychology*, 1974b, *59*, 9.

Rosen, B., & Jerdee, T. H. Sex stereotyping in the executive suite. *Harvard Business Review*, 1974c, *52*, 45.

Rosen, B., & Jerdee, T. H. Effects of employees sex and threatening versus pleading appeals on managerial evaluations of grievances. *Journal of Applied Psychology*, 1975, *60*, 442.

Rosen, G. The hospital: Historical sociology of a community institution. In E. Freidson (Ed.), *The Hospital in Modern Society*. London: Free Press of Glencoe, Collier-Macmillan, 1963, pp. 1–36.

Rosenberg, M., & Turner, R. H. *Social Psychology: A Sociological Perspective*. New York: Basic Books, Inc., 1981.

Rosenberg, R. *Beyond Separate spheres: Intellectual Roots of Modern Feminism*. New Haven, Conn: Yale University Press, 1982.

Rosenkrantz, P., Vogel, S., Bee, H., et al. Sex-role stereotypes and self concepts in college students. *Journal of Consulting and Clinical Psychology*, 1968, *32*, 287.

Rosenman, R. H., & Freidman, M. Neurogenic factors in pathogenesis of coronary heart disease. *Med. Clin. N. Amer.*, 1974, *58*, 269.

Rosenman, R. H., Brand, R. J., Jenkins, D., et al. Coronary heart disease in the Western Collaborative Group Study: Final follow-up experience of 8-1/2 years. *Journal of American Medical Association*, 1975, *233*, 872.

Rosenstock, I. M. Why people use health services. *Millbank Memorial Fund Quarterly*, 1966, *44*, 94.

Rosenstock, I. M. Historical origins of the Health Belief Model. In M. H. Becker (Ed.), *The Health Belief Model and Personal Health Behavior*. Thorofare, NJ: Slack, 1974, pp. 1–8.

Rosow, I. Forms and functions of adult socialization. *Soc Forces*, 1965, *44*, 35.

Rosow, I. *Socialization to Old Age*. Berkely: University of California Press, 1974.

Rosse, J. G., & Rosse, P. H. Role conflict and ambiguity: An empirical investigation of nursing personnel. *Evaluation and the Health Profession*, 1981, *4*, 385–405.

Rossi, A. S. Transition to parenthood. In J. Heiss (Ed.), *Family Roles and Interaction: An Anthology* (2nd ed.). Chicago: Rand McNally, 1976, pp. 268–294.

Rossi, A. S. Transition to parenthood. In P. I. Rose (Ed.), *Socialization and the Life Cycle*. New York: St. Martin's Press, 1979, pp. 132–145.

Rossi, A. S. Transition to parenthood. In A. S. Skolnick & J. H. Skolnick (Eds.), *Family in Transition* (4th ed.). Boston: Little, Brown, 1983, pp. 453–463.

Rossi, A. S. Gender and parenthood. *American Sociological Review*, 1984, *49*(1), 1.

Roth, J. A. Information and the control of treatment in tuberculosis hospitals. In E. Freidson (Ed.), *The Hospital in Modern Society*. New York: Free Press, 1963, pp. 293–318.

Rotter, J. B. Generalized expectancies for internal versus external control of reinforcement. *Psychological Monographs*, 1966, *80*(1), (Whole No. 609).

Rotter, J. B. Some problems and misconceptions related to the construct of internal versus external control of reinforcement. *Journal of Consulting and Clinical Psychology*, 1975, *43*, 56.

Rotter, J. B., Chance, J. E., & Phares, E. J. *Applications of a Social Learning Theory of Personality*. New York: Holt, Rinehart, & Winston, 1972.

Roy, D. Quota restriction and goldbricking in a machine shop. *American Journal of Sociology*, 1952, *57*, 427.

Rubin, J. R., & Brown, B. R. *The Social Psychology of Bargaining and Negotiation*. New York: Academic Press, 1975.

Ruble, T. L. Sex stereotypes: Issues of change in the 1970's. *Sex Roles*, 1983, *9*, 397.

Rudner, R. S. *Philosophy of Social Science*. Englewood Cliffs, NJ: Prentice-Hall, 1966.

Rundall, T. G., & Wheeler, J. R. G. Factors associated with utilization of the swine flu vaccination program among senior citizens in Tompkins County. *Medical Care*, 1979, *17*, 191.

Rushing, W. Social influence and the social psychological function of deference: A story of psychiatric nursing. *Social Forces*, 1962, *41*, 142.

Rushing, W. Two patterns of industrial administration. *Human Organization*, 1976, *4*, 32.

Rutter, M. Parent-child separation: Psychological effects on the children. *Journal of Child Psychology and Psychiatry*, 1971, *12*, 233–260.

Rutter, M. *Maternal Deprivation Reassessed*. Harmondsworth, England: Penguin, 1972.

Rutter, M. Maternal deprivation, 1972–1978: New findings, new concepts, new approaches. *Child Development*, 1979, *50*, 283.

Sackett, D. L., & Haynes, R. B. (Eds.). *Compliance with Therapeutic Regimens*. Baltimore, Md: Johns Hopkins Press, 1976.

Schaef, A. *Women's Reality: An Emerging Female System in the White Male Society*. Minneapolis: Winston Press, 1981.

Safilios-Rothschild, C. *Love, Sex, and Sex Roles*. Englewood Cliffs, NJ: Prentice-Hall, 1977.

Sales, S. Organizational role as a risk factor in coronary disease. *Administrative Science Quarterly*, 1969, *14*, 325.

Salisbury, R. The pharmacist's duty to warn the patient of side effects. *Journal of the American Pharmaceutical Association*, 1977, *17*, 97.

Saltzer, E. B. Locus of control and intention to lose weight. *Health Education Monographs*, 1978, *6*, 118.

Sampson, E. E. The study of ordinal position: Antecedents and outcomes. In D. R. Heise (Ed.), *Personality and Socialization*. Chicago: Rand McNally, 1972, pp. 86–122.

San Jose nurses reach settlement at three hospitals. *American Journal of Nursing*, 1983, *82*, 1026, 1036.

Sarbin, T., R., & Allen, V. L. Role theory. In G. Lindzey & E. Aronsen (Eds.), *Handbook of Social Psychology*, Vol. 1 (2nd ed.). Reading, Mass: Addison-Wesley, 1969, pp. 488–567.

Satow, R. L. Value-rational authority and professional organizations: Weber's missing type. *Administrative Science Quarterly*, 1975, *20*, 526.

Sayles, L. R., & Strauss, A. *Human Behavior in Organizations*. Englewood Cliffs, NJ: Prentice-Hall, 1966.

Scheff, T. J. Decision rules and types of error, and other consequences in medical diagnosis. *Behavioral Science*, 1963, *8*, 97.

Scheff, T. J. *Being Mentally Ill*. Chicago: Aldine, 1966, 1984.

Scheff, T. J. The labeling theory of mental illness. *American Sociological Review*, 1974, *39*, 444.

Scheff, T. Reply to Chauncey and Gove. *American Sociological Review*, 1975, *40*, 252.

Scheff, T. J., & Sundstrom, E. The stability of deviant behavior over time: A reassessment. *Journal of Health and Social Behavior*, 1970, *11*, 37.

Scheffler, I. *Science and Subjectivity*. New York: Bobbs-Merrill, 1967.

Schein, V. E. Sex role stereotyping, ability, and performance: Prior research and new directions. *Personnel Psychology*, 1978, *31*, 259.

Schlenker, B. R. Bonoma, T. V., Tedeschi, J. T., & Pivnick, W. P. Compliance to threats as a function of the wording of threat and the exploitiveness of the threatener. *Sociometry*, 1970, *33*, 394.

Schlueter, L. A. Knowledge and beliefs about breast cancer and breast self-examination among athletic and nonatheltic women. *Nursing Research*, 1982, *31*, 348.

Schneider, J. W., & Conrad, P. In the closet with illness: Epilepsy, stigma potential and information control. In P. Conrad & R. Kern (Eds.), *The Sociology of Health and Illness* (2nd ed.). New York: St. Martin's Press, 1986, pp. 110–121.

Schur, E. M. *Labeling Women Deviant: Gender, Stigma, and Social Control.* New York: Random House, 1984.

Schutz, A. *Collected papers: Volume 1.* The Hague: Martinuss Nijhof, 1971.

Schwartz, S. H., & Amos, R. E. Positive and negative referent others as sources of influence: A case of helping. *Sociometry*, 1977, *40*, 12.

Schwartz, T. Introduction. In T. Schwartz (Ed.), *Socialization as Cultural Communication.* Berkeley: University of California Press, 1976, pp. vii–xviii.

Scott, R. W. Professionals in bureaucracies-areas of conflict. In H. Vollmer & D. Mills (Eds.), *Professionalization.* Englewood Cliffs, NJ: Prentice-Hall, 1966.

Scott, R. Professional employees in a bureaucratic structure: Social work. In A. Etzioni (Ed.), *The Semi-professions and Their Organizations.* New York: Free Press, 1969.

Scott, W. R. *Social Processes and Social Structures: An Introduction to Sociology.* New York: Holt, Rinehart, & Winston, 1970.

Scott, R. Effectiveness of organizational effectiveness studies. In P. Goodman & J. Pennings (Eds.), *New Perspectives on Organizational Effectiveness.* San Francisco: Jossey-Bass, 1977, p. 90.

Sears, R. R. Relation of early socialization experiences to self-concept and gender role in middle childhood. *Child Development*, 1970, *41*, 267.

Seashore, S., & Vuchtman, E. A system resource approach to organizational effectiveness. *Amer. Soc. Review*, 1972, *32*, 89.

Secord, P., & Backman, C. W. *Social Psychology.* New York: McGraw-Hill, 1964.

Secord, P., & Backman, C. W. *Social Psychology* (2nd ed.). New York: McGraw-Hill, 1974, pp. 528–548.

Seeman, M. Role Conflict and ambivalence in leadership. *American Sociological Review*, 1953, *18*, 373.

Seeman, M. On the meaning of alienation. *American Sociological Review*, 1959, *24*, 783.

Selby, T. Court overturns ruling restricting NPs practice. *The American Nurse*, 1984, *6*, 3.

Segal, A. The sick role concept: Understanding illness behavior. *Journal of Health and Social Behavior*, 1976, *17*, 162.

Seigrist, H. E. The special position of the sick. In M. I. Roemer & J. M. Makintosh (Eds.), *On the Sociology of Medicine.* New York: M. D. Publications, 1960, pp. 9–22.

Selman, R. L. The relation of role-taking to the development of moral judgement in children. *Child Development*, 1971, *42*, 79.

Selman, R. L. Social-cognitive understanding. In T. Lickona (Ed.), *Moral Development and Behavior: Theory, Research, and Social Issues.* New York: Holt, Rinehart, & Winston, 1976.

Selman, R. L. *The Growth of Interpersonal Understanding.* New York: Academic Press, 1980.

Selman, R. L., & Bryne, D. F. A structural-developmental analysis of levels of role-taking in middle childhood. *Child Development*, 1974, *45*, 803.

Selman, R. L., & Bryne, D. F. A structural-developmental analysis of levels of role-taking in middle childhood. In L. D. Steinberg (Ed.), *The Life Cycle: Readings in Human Development.* New York: Columbia University Press, 1981, pp. 96–103.

Selman, R. L., & Jaquette, D. Stability and oscillation in interpersonal awareness: A clinical-developmental approach. In C. B. Keasey (Ed.), *Nebraska Symposium on Moti-*

vation: Social Cognitive Development (Vol. 25). Lincoln, Nebr: University of Nebraska Press, 1978.

Sennott, I. A. Value-expectancy theory and health behavior: An exploration of motivating variables. (Doctoral dissertation, University of Arizona). *Dissertation Abstracts International*, 1980, *40*, 6013A.

Sewell, W. H. Social class and childhood personality. *Sociometry*, 1961, *24*, 340.

Sewell, W. H. Some recent developments in socialization theory and research. In G. P. Stone & H. A. Farberman (Eds.), *Social Psychology through Symbolic Interaction.* Waltham, Mass: Xerox, 1970, pp. 566–583.

Shamberg, B. A. The relationship of wives' marital satisfaction to their perception of and behavioral responses to husbands' communications (Doctoral dissertation, Hofsted University, 1984). *Dissertation Abstracts International*, 1985, *45*, 3631-B.

Shantz, C. Social-cognitive development. In J. Flavell & E. Markham (Eds.), *Carmichael's Manual of Child Psychology* (Vol. 2) (4th ed.). New York: Wiley, 1983.

Sharp, W. H., & Anderson, J. C. Changes in nursing students' descriptions of the personality traits of the ideal nurse. *Measurement and Evaluation of Guidance*, 1972, *5*, 339.

Shaver, P. & Hendrick, C. (Eds.) *Sex and Gender: Review of Personality and Social Psychology.* Newbury Park, CA: Sage, 1987.

Shaw, M., & Wright, J. M. *Scales for the Measurement of Attitudes.* New York: McGraw-Hill, 1967.

Shaw, M. E., & Constanzo, P. R. *Theories of Social Psychology.* New York: McGraw Hill, 1970, 1982.

Sherif, M. *An Outline of Social Psychology.* New York: Harper & Row, 1948.

Sherlock, B., Cohen, A., & Pavalko, R. M. (Eds.), *Sociological Perspectives on Occupations.* Itasca, Ill: Peacock Publishers, 1972.

Sherohman, J. Conceptual and methodological issues in the study of role-taking accuracy. *Symbolic Interaction*, 1977, *1*, 121.

Sherriffs, A. C., & Jarrett, R. F. Sex differences in attitudes about sex differences. *Journal of Psychology*, 1953, *35*, 161.

Shibutani, T. Reference groups as perspectives. *American Journal of Sociology*, 1955, *60*, 562.

Shibutani, T. Reference group and social control. In A. M. Rose (Ed.), *Human Behavior and Social Processes.* Boston: Houghton, Mifflin, 1962.

Shibutani, T. Self-control and concerted action. In C. Gordon, & K. J. Gergen (Eds.), *The Self in Social Interaction.* New York: Wiley, 1968, pp. 379–381.

Shibutani, T. Reference groups as perspectives. In J. G. Manis & B. N. Meltzer (Eds.), *Symbolic Interaction.* Boston: Allyn & Bacon, 1978.

Shinn, A. M., Jr. An application of psychophysical scaling techniques to measurement of national power. *Journal of Politics*, 1969, *31*, 932.

Shinn, M. Father absence and children's cognitive development. *Psychological Bulletin*, 1978, *85*, 295.

Shorter, E. *Bedside Maneuvers: The Troubled History of Doctors and Patients.* New York: Simon & Schuster, 1985.

Shrauger, J. S., & Shoeneman, T. J. Symbolic interactionist view of self-concept: Through the looking glass darkly. *Psychological Bulletin*, 1979, *86*, 549.

Sieber, S. D. Toward a theory of role accumulation. *American Sociological Review*, 1974, *39*, 567.

Siegel, A. E., & Siegel, S. Reference groups, membership groups, and attitude change. *Journal of Abnormal Social Psychology*, 1957, *55*, 630.

Silberman, C. E. *Crisis in Black and White.* New York: Vintage House, 1964.

Silverman, D. *The Theory of Organizations.* Exeter, NH: Heinemann, 1970.

Simari, C. G., & Baskin, D. Sex-role acquisition, parental behavior, and sexual orientation: Some tentative hypotheses—A critique. *Sex Roles*, 1983, *9*, 1061.

Simmel, G. Der streit. In Sociologie: Untersuchungen uber die Formen der Vergesellschaftung. Leipzig: Verlag von Duncker und Humbolt. (Conflict. Published together with *The Web of Group Affiliations*). Glencoe, Ill: Free Press, 1908 (1955).

Simmel, G. *The Society of Georg Simmel*. K. Wolf (Ed.). New York: Free Press, 1950.

Simmons, R. The role conflict of the first-line supervisor, an experimental study. *American Journal of Sociology*, 1968, *73*, 482.

Simon, H. A behavioral model of rational choice. *Quarterly Journal of Economics*, 1955, *69*, 99.

Simon, H. *Administrative Behavior* (2nd ed.). New York: Macmillan, 1957.

Simon, H. *Administrative Behavior* (3rd ed.). New York: Free Press, 1976.

Simon, R., Clark, S., & Galway, K. The woman PhD.: A recent profile. *Social Problems*, 1967, *15*(2), 221.

Simpson, I. H. *From Student to Nurse: A Longitudinal Study of Socialization*. New York: Cambridge University Press, 1979.

Simpson, O. W., & Green, Y. N. Adrogynous nurses. *Canadian Nurse*, 1975, *71*, 20.

Simpson, R. L., & Simpson, I. H. Women and bureaucracy in the semi-professions. In A. Etzioni (Ed.), *The semi-professions and Their Organizations: Teachers, Nurses, Social Workers*, New York: Free Press, 1969, pp. 196–265.

Singer, E. Reference groups and social evaluaton. In M. Rosenberg & R. H. Turner (Eds.), *Social Psychology Sociological Perspectives*. New York: Basic Books, 1981.

Skipper, J. K., Jr. Communication and the hospitalized patient. In J. K. Skipper Jr. & R. C. Leonard (Eds.), *Social Interaction and Patient Care*. Philadelphia: Lippincott, 1965, pp. 61–82.

Skolnick, A. S., & Skolnick, J. H. Introduction: Family in transition. In A. S. Skolnick & J. H. Skolnick, *Family in Transition* (4th ed.). Boston: Little, Brown, 1983, pp. 1–19.

Skord, K. G., & Schumacher, B. Masculinity as a handicapping condition. *Rehabilitation Literature*, 1982, *43*, 284, 289.

Smelser, W. Dominance as a factor in achievement and perception in cooperative problem solving interactions. *Journal of Abnormal Social Psychology*, 1961, *62*, 535.

Smith, E. E. The effects of clear and unclear role expectations on group productivity and defensiveness. *Journal of Abnormal Social Psychology*, 1957, *55*, 213.

Smith, H. L. Two lines of authority: The hospital's dilemma. In E. G. Jaco (Ed.), *Patients, Physicians and Illness*. New York: Free Press, 1958.

Smith, M. B. Competence and socialization. In J. Clausen (Ed.), *Socialization and Society*. Boston: Little, Brown, 1968.

Smith, P. A., & Midlarsky, E. Empirically derived conceptions of femaleness and maleness: A current view. *Sex Roles*, 1985, *12*, 328.

Snoek, D. Role strain in diversified role sets. *American Journal of Sociology*, 1966, *71*, 363.

Sofer, C. *Organizations in Theory and Practice*. New York: Basic Books, 1972.

Solomon, E. Trends in female enrollment in health professions schools. *Journal of Dental Education*, November, 1982, *46*, 672.

Spence, J. T., Helmreich, R., & Stapp, J. Ratings of self and peers on sex-role attributes and their relation to self-esteem and conceptions of masculinity and femininity. *Journal of Personality and Social Psychology*, 1975, *32*, 29.

Spencer, T. D. Sex-role learning in early childhood. In W. W. Hartup & N. L. Smothergill (Eds.), *The Young Child: Reviews of Research*. Washington, DC: National Association for the Education of Young Children, 1967, pp. 193–205.

Spengler, C. Other women. In M. Grissum & C. Spengler (Eds.), *Woman-power and Health Care*. Boston: Little, Brown, 1976.

Spicker, S., & Gadow, S. (Eds.). *Nursing: Images and Ideals*. New York: Springer, 1980.

Spitzer, R. The nurse in the corporate world. In E. C. Hein & M. J. Nicholson (Eds.), *Contemporary Leadership Behavior* (2nd ed.). Boston: Little, Brown, 1986.

Staines, G., Tavris, A., & Jayratne, T. E. The Queen Bee syndrome. *Psychology Today*, 1974, *7*(8), 55.

Stanton, M. Political action and nursing. *Nursing Clinics of North America*, 1974, *9*, 579.

Staples, R., & Mirande, A. Racial and cultural variations among American families: A decennial review of the literature on minority families. In A. S. Skolnick & J. H. Skonick, *Family in Transition* (4th ed.). Boston: Little, Brown, 1983, pp. 496–520.

Starr, P. *The Social Transformation of American Medicine*. New York: Basic Books, 1982.

Stebbins, R. A theory of the definition of the situation. In A. Furnham & M. Argyle (Eds.), *The Psychology of Social Systems*. New York: Pergamon Press, 1981, pp. 146–361.

Stebbins, R.A. *Teachers and Meaning: Definitions of Classroom Situations*. Leiden, Netherlands: E. J. Brill, 1975.

Steckel, S. B. *Patient Contracting*. Norwalk, Conn: Appleton-Century-Crofts, 1982.

Steckel, S. B., & Swain, M. A. Contracting with patients to improve compliance. *Hospitals*, 1977, *51*, 81.

Steelman, L. C., & Mercy, J. A. Unconfounding the confluence model: A test of sibship size and birth-order effects on intelligence. *American Sociological Review*, 1980, *45*, 571.

Stein, L. I. The doctor-nurse game. *Archives of General Psychiatry*, 1967, *16*, 699.

Steiner, I. D. *Group Process and Productivity*. New York: Academic Press, 1972.

Steinmann, A. A study of the concept of the feminine role of 51 middle-class American families. *Genetic Psychology Monographs*, 1963, *67*, 275.

Steinmann, A., & Fox, D. J. Male-female perceptions of the female role in the United States. *The Journal of Psychology*, 1966, *46*, 265.

Stelling, J., & Bucher, R. Autonomy and monitoring in hospital wards. *Sociological Quarterly*, 1972, *13*, 431.

Stevens, C. M. Strategy and Collective Bargaining Negotiation. New York: McGraw-Hill, 1963.

Stevens, S. S. (Ed.). *Handbook of Experimental Psychology*. New York: Wiley, 1952, pp. 1–49.

Stevens, S. S. On the psychophysical law. *Psychological Review*, 1959, *64*, 153.

Stevens, S. S. The psychophysics of sensory function. *American Scientist*, 1960, *48*, 226.

Stevens, S. S. A metric for the social sciences. *Science*, 1966, *151*, 677.

Stevens, S. S. *Psychophysics*. New York: Wiley, 1975.

Stevens, S. S., & Mack J. D. Scales of apparent force. *Journal of Experimental Psychology*, 1959, *58*, 405.

Stewart, D. C., & Sullivan, T. J. Illness behavior and the sick role in chronic disease: The case of multiple sclerosis. *Social Science and Medicine*, 1982, *16*, 397.

Stewart, I. M. *The Education of Nurses: Historical Foundations and Modern Trends*. New York: Macmillan, 1949.

Stewart, J. Understanding women in organizations: Toward a reconstruction of organizational theory. *Administrative Science Quarterly*, 1978, *23*, 336.

Stillman, M. Women's health beliefs about breast cancer and breast self-examination. *Nursing Research*, 1977, *26*, 121.

Stolz, L. M. Effects of maternal employment on children: Evidence from research. *Child Development*, 1960, *31*, 749.

Stone, G., & Faberman, H. A. (Eds.) *Social Psychology Through Symbolic Interaction*. Boston: Genn-Baisdell, 1970.

Stone, G. P., & Faberman H. A. Social Psychology through symbolic interaction (2nd ed.). New York: Wiley, 1981.

Storer, N. *The Social System of Science*. New York: Holt, Rinehart, & Winston, 1966.

Story, D. Replication study of the Queen Bee syndrome. Unpublished manuscript, West Union, Iowa, 1986.

Stouffer, S. A., Suchman, E. A., DeVinney, L. C., et al. *The American Soldier: Studies in Social Psychology in World War II* (Vols. 1 & 2). Princeton, NJ: Princeton University Press, 1949.

Strauss, A. L., et al. *Psychiatric Ideologies and Institutions*. New York: Free Press, 1964.

Strauss, A. L. (Ed.), *George Herbert Mead on Social Psychology*. Chicago: Phoenix Books, 1964, c. 1934.

Strauss, A. L. *Negotiations: Varieties, Contexts, Processes, and Social Order*. San Francisco: Jossey-Bass, 1978.

Strauss, A. L. The hospital and its negotiated order. In E. Freidson (Ed.), *The Hospital in Modern Society*. New York: Free Press, 1963, pp. 147–169.

Strauss, A. L. *Mirrors and Masks*. San Francisco: Sociological Press, 1969.

Streissguth, A. P., & Bee, H. L. Mother-child interactions and cognitive development. In W. W. Hartup (Ed.), *The Young Child: Reviews of Research* (Vol. 2). Washington, DC: National Association for the Education of Young Children, 1972.

Strickland, B. Internal-external expectations. *Clinical Psychology*, 1978, *46*, 1192.

Stryker, S. *Symbolic Interactionism*. Reading, Mass: Benjamin/Cummings, 1980.

Stryker, S. In M. Rosenberg, & R. Turner (Eds.), *Social Psychology*. New York: Basic Books, 1981, pp. 3–29.

Stryker, S., & Macke, A. S. Status inconsistency and role conflict. *Ann Rev of Sociology*, 1978, *4*, 57.

Stryker, S., & Statham. Symbolic interaction and role theory. In G. Lindzey & E. Aronson (Eds.). *The Handbook of Social Psychology* (Vol. 1, 3rd ed.). New York: Random House, 1985, pp. 311–378.

Suchman, E. A. Stages of illness and medical care. *Journal of Health and Human Behavior*, Fall 1965a, *6*, 2.

Suchman, E. A. Social patterns of illness and medical care. *Journal of Health and Human Behavior*, 1965b, *6*, 2.

Suchman, E. A. Preventive health behavior: A model for research on community health campaigns. *Journal of Health and Social Behavior*, 1967, *8*, 197.

Sudnow, D. *Passing On: The Social Organization of Dying*. Englewood Cliffs, N.J.: Prentice-Hall, 1967.

Sullivan, H. S. *An Interpersonal Theory of Psychiatry*. New York: Norton, 1953.

Suppe, P. *The Structure of Scientific Theories* (2nd ed.). Urbana, Ill: University of Illinois, 1977.

Sutherland, E. H. *White Collar Crime*. New York: Holt, Rinehart, & Winston, 1961.

Sutton, S. R., & Eiser, J. R. The effect of fear-arousing communications on cigarette smoking: An expectancy-value approach. *Journal of Behavioral Medicine*, 1984, *7*, 13.

Swain, M. A., & Steckel, S. B. Influencing adherence among hypertensives. *Research in Nursing and Health*, 1981, *4*, 213.

Swendsen, L. A., Meleis, A. I., & Jones, D. Role supplementation for new parents. A role mastery plan. *The American Journal of Maternal Child Nursing*, 1978, *3(2)*, 84.

Symonds, A. Emotional conflicts of the career woman: Women in medicine. *The American Journal of Psychoanalysis*, 1983, *43*, 21.

Szasz, T. S. *The Myth of Mental Illness*. New York: Hoeber-Harper, 1961.

Szilagyi, A., Sims, H., & Keller. Role dynamics, locus of control, and employee attitude and behavior. *Academy of Management Journal*, 1976, *19*, 259.

Szinovacz, M. E. Female retirement: Effects on spousal roles and marital adjustment. *Journal of Family Issues*, 1980, *1*, 423.

Szymanski, A. *Class Structure: A Critical Perspective*. New York: Praeger, 1983.

Taft, J. *The women's movement from the point of view of social consciousness*. Unpublished dissertation, University of Chicago, 1916.

Taylor, D. W. A test of the Health Belief Model in hypertension. In R. B. Haynes, D. W. Taylor, & D. L. Sackett (Eds.), *Compliance in Health Care*. Baltimore, Md: Johns Hopkins Press, 1979, pp. 103–109.

Taylor, J., & Deaux, K. When women are more deserving than men: Equity, attribution and perceived sex differences. *Journal of Personality and Social Psychology*, 1973, *28*, 360.

Teevan, J. J. Reference groups and premarital sexual behavior. In J. Heiss (Ed.), *Family Roles and Interaction: An Anthology* (2nd ed.). Chicago: Rand McNally, 1976, pp. 90–104.

Tedeschi, J. T., Bonoma, T. V., & Brown, R. C., Jr. A paradigm for the study of coercive power. *Journal of Conflict Resolution*, 1971, *15*, 197.

Tedeschi, J. T., Schlenker, B. R., & Bonoma, T. V. *Conflict, Power and Games: The Experimental Study of Interpersonal Relations.* Chicago: Aldine, 1973.

Telles, J. L., & Pollack, M. H. Feeling sick: The experience and legitimation of illness. *Social Science and Medicine*, 1981, *3*, 243.

Temkin-Greener, H. Interprofessional perspectives on teamwork in health care: A case study. *Milbank Memorial Fund Quarterly*, 1983, *61*, 641.

Terborg, J. Richardson, P., & Pritchard, R. Person-situation effects in the prediction of performance: An investigation of ability, self-esteem and reward contingencies. *Journal of Applied Psychology*, 1980, *65*, 574.

Terhune, K. W. Motives, situation, and interpersonal conflict within Prisoner's dilemma. *Journal of Personality, Social Psychology*, (Suppl), 1968, *8*, 956.

Terman, L. M., & Miles, C. C. *Sex and Personality: Studies in Masculinity and Femininity.* New York: McGraw-Hill, 1936.

Terreberry, S. The evolution of organizational environments. In F. Baker (Ed.), *Organizational Systems.* Homewood, Ill: Irwin, 1973.

Tesch, S. A. Sex-role orientation and intimacy status in men and women. *Sex Roles*, 1984, *11*(5/6), 451.

The biennial. *American Journal of Nursing*, 1946, *46*, 728.

Thibault, J., & Kelley, H. *The Social Psychology of Groups.* New York: Wiley, 1959.

Thoits, P. A. Conceptual, methodological, and theoretical problems in studying social support as a buffer against stress. *Journal of Health and Social Behavior*, 1982, *23*, 145.

Thomas, E., & Biddle, B. Basic concepts for classifying the phenomena of role. In B. Biddle & E. Thomas (Eds.), *Role Theory: Concepts and Research.* New York: Wiley, 1979.

Thomas, E. J., & Biddle, B. J. The nature and history of role theory. In B. J. Biddle & E. J. Thomas (Eds.), *Role Theory: Concepts and Research.* Huntington, NY: Robert E. Krieger Publishing Co., 1966.

Thomas, W. I. *Sex and Society: Studies in the Social Psychologies of Sex.* Chicago: University of Chicago Press, 1907.

Thomas, W. I. Situational analysis: The behavior pattern and the situation. In M. Janowitz (Ed.), *W. I. Thomas on Social Organization and Social Personality*, Chicago: University of Chicago Press, 1966, pp. 154–167.

Thomas, W. I. The definition of the situation. In J. G. Manis & B. N. Meltzer (Eds.), *Symbolic Interaction.* Boston: Allyn & Bacon, 1978.

Thomas, W. I., & Znaniecki, F. *The Polish Peasant in Europe and America.* Chicago: University of Chicago Press, 1918. (5 vols., reprinted, 2 vols. Dover publications, 1958.)

Thomas, W. J., & Thomas, D.S. *The Child in America.* New York: Knopf, 1928.

Thompson, J. D. *Organizations in Action.* New York: McGraw-Hill, 1967.

Thompson, W. G. The relation of the visiting and house staff to the care of hospital patients. *New York Medical Journal*, 1906, *83*, 744.

Thornton, R., & Nardi, P. M. The dynamics of role acquisition. *American Journal of Sociology*, 1975, *80*(4), 870.

Thurstone, L., & Chave, E. *The Measurement of Attitude.* Chicago: University of Chicago Press, 1946.

Tillotson, J. L. (Ed). *Proceedings of the Nutrition Research Conference*, Publication No. (NIH) 76-978. Bethesda, MD: U.S. DHEW, 1976.

Tosi, H., Aldag, R., & Storey, R. On the measurement of the environment: An assessment of the Lawrence and Lorsch environmental subscale. *Administrative Science Quarterly*, 1973, *18*, 27.

Touraine, A. *The Post-industrial Society*. L. Mayhew (Trans). New York: Random House, 1971.

Tucker, C. W. Some methodological problems of Kuhn's self-theory. In J. G. Manis & B. N. Meltzer (Eds.), *Symbolic Interaction: A Reader in Social Psychology*, (2nd ed.). Boston: Allyn & Bacon, Inc, 1972, pp. 303–315.

Tuckett, D., & Kaufert, J. (Eds.). *Basic Readings in Medical Sociology*. London: Tavistock Publications Ltd, 1978.

Tumin, M. Some principles of stratification: A critical analysis. In R. Bendix & S. M. Lipset (Eds.), *Class, Status, and Power: Social Stratification in Comparative Perspective* (2nd ed.). New York: Free Press, 1966.

Tuminia, P. Teaching problems and strategies with male nursing students. *Nurse Educator*, 1981, *6*(5), 9.

Turner, J. H. *The Structure of Sociological Theory*. Homewood, Ill: Dorsey, 1982.

Turner, J. H. *The Structure of Sociological Theory* (2nd ed.). Chicago: Dorsey, 1983.

Turner, J. H. *The Structure of Sociological Theory* (3rd ed.). Chicago: Dorsey, 1985.

Turner, J. H. *The Structure of Sociological Theory* (4th ed.). Chicago: Dorsey, 1986.

Turner, R. H. Role-taking, role standpoint and reference group behavior. *American Journal of Sociology*, 1956, *61*, 316.

Turner, R. H. Role taking: Process versus conformity. In A. Rose (Ed.), *Human Behavior and Social Processes*. Boston, Mass: Houghton, Mifflin, 1962.

Turner, R. H. Role: Sociological aspects. In D. L. Sills (Ed.), *International Encyclopedia of the Social Sciences*, 1968a, *13*, 552.

Turner, R. H. The self-conception in social interaction. In C. Gordon & K. J. Gergen (Eds.), *The Self in Social Interaction*. New York: Wiley, 1968b, pp. 93–106.

Turner, R. H. The real self: From institution to impulse. *American Journal of Sociology*, 1976, *81*, 989.

Turner, R. H. The role and the person. *American Journal of Sociology*, 1978, *84*, 1.

Turner, R. H. Strategy for developing an integrated role theory. *Humbolt Journal of Social Relations*, 1979–80, *7*, 132.

Turner, R. H. *Family Interaction*. New York: Wiley, 1980.

Turner, R. H., & Shosid, N. Ambiguity and interchangeability in role attribution: The effect of Alter's response. *American Sociological Review*, 1976, *41*(6), 993.

Twaddle, A. C. Health decisions and sick-role variations: An exploration. *Journal of Health and Social Behavior*, 1969, *10*, 105.

Twaddle, A. C. *Sickness Behavior and the Sick Role*. Cambridge, Mass: Schenkman Publishing Co., 1981.

Uhlenberg, P. Death and the family. In A. S. Skolnick & J. H. Skolnick, *Family in Transition* (4th ed.). Boston: Little, Brown, 1983, pp. 92–101.

U. S. Bureau of the Census. *Statistical Abstract of United States*. Washington, DC: U. S. Government Printing Office, 1981.

U. S. Bureau of the Census. *Statistical Abstract of United States*. Washington, DC: U. S. Government Printing Office, 1984.

U. S. Department of Health, Education, Welfare. *The Supply of Health Manpower* (Publication No. (HRA) 75-38. Bethesda, MD: U. S. DHEW, 1971.

U. S. Department of Labor. *Careers for Women in the '70s*. Washington, DC: Department of Labor, Women's Bureau, 1973.

U. S. Department of Labor. Physicians. In *Occupational Outlook Handbook* (1982–83 ed.). Bulletin 2200. Washington, DC: Bureau of Labor Statistics, 1983, pp. 153–155.

U. S. Public Health Service. *A ten-year record of absences from work on account of sickness and accidents*. Reprint No. 1142, U. S. Public Health Reports, Washington, DC: U. S. Government Printing Office, 1927.

Vance, C. N. Women leaders: Modern day heroines or societal deviants. *Image*, 1979, *11*, 37.

Van de Ven, A., & Delbecq, A. A task contingent model of work-unit structure. *Administrative Science Quarterly*, 1974, *19*, 183.

Van Sell, M., Brief, A. P., & Schuler, R. S. Role conflict and role ambiguity: Integration of the literature and directions for future research. *Human Relations*, 1981, *34*, 43.

Vaughn, B., Egeland, B., Sroufe, L. A., & Waters, E. Individual differences in infant-mother attachment at 12 and 18 months: Stability and change in families under stress. *Child Development*, 1979, *50*, 971.

Vaughn, L. S., & Wittig, M. A. Occupation, competence, and role overload as evaluation determinants of successful women. *Journal of Applied Social Psychology*, 1980, *10*(5), 398.

Vecchio, R. A. Individual differences interpretation of the conflicting predictions generated by equity theory and expectancy theory. *Journal of Applied Psychology*, 1981, *66*, 470.

Veenendall, T. L. Male gender-role orientation as a predictor of confirmation/disconfirmation communicative behavior in marital dyads (Doctoral dissertation, University of Denver, 1982). *Dissertation Abstracts International*, 1982, *43*, 587A.

Vertinsky, P. A., Yang, C., MacLeod, P. J., & Hardwick, B. F. A study of compliance factors in voluntary health behavior. *International Journal of Health Education*, 1976, *19*, 16.

Vogel, S. R., Broverman, I. K., Broverman, D. M., et al. Maternal employment and perception of sex-roles among college students. *Developmental Psychology*, 1970, *3*, 384.

Volicer, B. Perceived stress levels of events associated with the experience of hospitalization. *Nursing Research*, 1973, *22*, 491.

Vollmer, H. M., & Mills, D. L. (Eds.). *Professionalization*. Englewood Cliffs, NJ: Prentice-Hall, 1966.

Von Bertalanffy, L. The theory of open systems in physics and biology. *Science*, 1950, *3*, p. 23.

Vroom, V. H. *Work and Motivation*. New York: Wiley, 1964.

Waite, L. J., & Stolzenberg, R. M. Intended childbearing and labor force participation of young women: Insight from nonrecursive models. *American Sociological Review*, 1976, *41*, 235.

Waitzkin, H. *The Second Sickness: Contradictions of Capitalist Health Care*. New York: Free Press, 1983.

Waldron, I. The coronary-prone behavior pattern, blood pressure, employment and socioeconomic status in women. *Journal of Psychosom. Res.*, 1978, *22*, 79–87.

Waldron, I. Employment and women's health: An analysis of causal relationships. *International Journal of Health Services*, 1980, *10*, 435.

Wallace, A. F. C. *Administrative Forms of Social Organizations*. Reading, Mass: Addison-Wesley, 1971.

Wallerstein, J. S., & Kelly, J. B. The effects of parental divorce: Experiences of the child in later latency. In A. S. Skolnick & J. H. Skolnick, *Family in Transition* (4th ed.). Boston: Little, Brown, 1983, pp. 438–452.

Wallston, B. S., & Wallston, K. A. Locus of control and health: A review of the literature. *Health Education Monographs*, 1978, *6*, 107.

Wallston, K. A., & Wallston, B. S. Health locus of control scales. In H. M. Lefcourt (Ed.), *Research with Locus of Control Construct: Assessment Methods* (Vol. 1). New York: Academic Press, 1981, pp. 189–243.

Wallston, K. A., Wallston, B. S., Kaplan, G. D., & Maides, S. Development and validation of the health locus of control (HLC) scale. *Journal of Consulting and Clinical Psychology*, 1976, *44*, 580.

Wallston, K. S., Wallston, B. S., & DeVellis, R. Development of multidimensional health locus of control (MHLC) scales. *Health Education Monographs*, 1978, *6*, 160.

Walster, E., Berscheid, E., & Walster, W. New directions in equity research. *Advances in Experimental Social Psychology*, 1976, *9*, 1.

Walster, E. Walster, G. W., & Berscheid, E. *Equity: Theory and Research*. Boston: Allyn & Bacon, 1982.

Waltz, C., Strickland, O., & Lenz, E. *Measurement in Nursing Research*. Philadelphia: F. A. Davis, 1984.

Ward, C. Differential evaluation of male and female expertise: Prejudice against women. *British Journal of Social and Clinical Psychology*, 1979, *18*, 65.

Wardwell, W. Reduction of strain in a marginal social role. *American Journal of Sociology*, 1955, *61*, 16.

Wardwell, W. I., & Pavalko, R. M., (Eds.). Sociological perspectives on occupations. Itasca, Ill: Peacock Publishers, 1972.

Waring, E. M., & Reddon, J. R. The measurement of intimacy in marriage: The Waring intimacy questionnaire. *Journal of Clinical Psychology*, 1983, *39*(1), 53.

Warner, W., Havighurst, R. J., & Loeb, M. B. *Who Shall Be Educated?* New York: Harper, Row, 1944.

Warner, W. L., & Lunt, P. S. *The Social Life of a Modern Community*. New Haven, Conn: Yale University Press, 1941.

Warner, W. I., Meeter, M., & Eels, K. *Social Class in America*. Chicago: Science Research, 1949.

Watts, R. J. Sexual functioning, health beliefs, and compliance with high blood pressure medications. *Nursing Research*, 1982, *31*, 278.

Webb, A. P. Sex-role preferences and adjustment in early adolescents. *Child Development*, 1963, *34*, 609.

Weber, M. *Essays on Sociology*. New York: Oxford University Press, 1946.

Weber, M. *The Theory of Social and Economic Organization*. New York: Free Press, 1947.

Webster, M., & Sobieszek, B. *Sources of Self-evaluation*. New York: Wiley, 1974.

Weick, K. Educational organizations as loosely coupled systems. *Administrative Science Quarterly*, 1976, *21*, 1.

Weiner, J. P., Steinwachs, D. M., & Williamson, J. W. Nurse practitioner and physician assistant practices in three HMOs: Implications for future US health manpower needs. *American Journal of Public Health*, 1986, *76*(5), 507.

Weinberger, M., Greene, J. Y., Mamlin, J. J., & Jerin, M. J. Health beliefs and smoking behavior. *American Journal of Public Health*, 1981, *71*, 1253.

Weiner, B., & Kukla, A. An attributional analysis of achievement motivation. *Journal of Personality and Social Psychology*, 1980, *15*, 1.

Weinstein, E. A. The development of interpersonal competence. In D. A. Goslin (Ed.), *Handbook of Socialization Theory and Research*. Chicago: Rand McNally, 1969, pp. 753–775.

Weinstein, E. A., & Deutschberger, P. Tasks, bargains and identities in social interaction. *Social Forces*, 1964, *42*, 451.

Weisman, C., Alexander, C., & Chase, G. Determinants of hospital staff nurse turnover. *Medical Care*, 1981, *19*, 431.

Weiss, C. S. The development of professional role commitment among graduate students. *Human Relations*, 1981, *34*(1), 13.

Weiss, S. M. Health psychology: The time is now. *Health Psychology*, 1982, *1*, 81.

Weiss, S. M. (Ed.). *Proceedings of the National Heart and Lung Institute working conference on health behavior*. Bethesda, Md. (DHEW) Publication No. (NIH) 76-868). Washington, DC: U. S. Government Printing Office, 1975.

Weitz, J. Job expectancy and survival. *Journal of Abnormal Social Psychology*, 1956, *40*, 245.

Werley, H. H., Zurich, A., Zajkowski, M., Zagornik, A. D. *Health Research: The Systems Approach*. New York: Springer, 1976.

West, C. *Routine Complications: Troubles with Talks Between Doctors and Patients.* Bloomington, Indiana: Indiana University Press, 1984.

Westley, W. A., & Elkin, F. The protective environment and adolescent socialization. *Social Forces*, 1957, *35*, 243.

Wheeler, S. The structure of formally organized socialization settings. In O. G. Brim, Jr. & S. Wheeler (Eds), *Socialization After Childhood: Two Essays*, New York: Wiley, 1966, pp. 51–116.

White, J. Women in the law. *Michigan Law Review*, 1967, *65*, 1051.

White, L., Jr. *Educating Our Daughters*. New York: Harper, 1950.

White, P. Motivation reconsidered: The concept of competence. *Psychol Rev* 1959, *66*:297.

Whitt, H. P., Meile, R. L., & Larson, L. M. Illness role theory, the labeling perspective and the social meaning of mental illness: An empirical test. *Social Science and Medicine*, 1979, *13A*, 655.

Whyte, W. F. The social structure of the restaurant. *American Journal of Sociology*, 1949, *54*, 302.

Whyte, W. F. Man and Organization. Homewood, Ill: Irwin, 1959.

Wilbur, J. A., & Barrow, J. G. Reducing elevated blood pressure. *Minnesota Medicine*, 1969, *52*, 1303.

Wilcox, B. L. Social support, life stress, and psychological adjustment: A test of the buffering hypothesis. *American Journal of Community Psychology*, 1979, *7*, 263.

Wilensky, H. *Intellectuals in Labor Unions*. Glencoe, Ill., Free Press, 1956.

Wilensky, H. The professionalization of everyone? *American Journal of Sociology*, 1964, *69*, 488.

Wilensky, H. *Women's Work: Economic Growth, Ideology, and Structure*. Institute of Industrial Relations, Reprint Series, No. 7, Berkeley: Institute of Industrial Relations, University of California, 1968.

Wiley, N. The rise and fall of dominating theories in American Sociology. In Snizek, W. E., Furman, E. R., Miller, M. K. (Eds.), *Contemporary Issues in Theory and Research*. Westport, Conn: Greenwood Press, 1979.

Wilson, F., & Neuhauser, D. *Health Services in the United States* (2nd ed.). Cambridge, Mass: Ballinger, 1982.

Wilson, M., Raney, M., & Norton, L. E. Myths about women: Medicine's nostalgic view. *Journal of the Medical Association of the State of Alabama*, 1982, *51*(12), 37.

Windsor, R. A., Heard, R., Reese, Y., et al. Smoking behavior and health beliefs of pregnant adolescents: An educational diagnosis. *Patient Education and Counseling*, 1984, *5*, 118.

Winstead, B. A., Derlega, V. J., & Wong, P. T. Effects of sex-role orientation on behavioral self-disclosure. *Journal of Research in Personality*, 1984, *18*, 541.

Wolinsky, F., & Wolinsky, S. Expecting sick-role legitimization and getting it. *Journal of Health and Social Behavior*, September 1981, *22*, 229.

Wolfe, D., & Snoek, J. D. A study of adjustment under role conflict. *Journal of Social Issues*, 1962, *18*, 102–127.

Woodruff, D. S., & Birren, J. E. (Eds.). *Aging: Scientific Perspectives and Social Issues* (2nd ed.). Monterey, Cal: Brooks/Cole, 1983.

Woods, N. F., & Earp, J. Women with cured breast cancer: A study of mastectomy patients in North Carolina. *Nursing Research*, 1978, *7*, 263.

Woods, N. F. Employment, family roles, and mental ill health in young married women. *Nursing Research*, 1985, *34*(1), 4.

Woods, N. F. Women's roles and illness episodes: Prospective study. *Research in Nursing and Health*, 1980, *3*, 137.

Woodward, J. *Industrial Organization: Theory and Practice*. London: Oxford University Press, 1965.

Wright, B. D., & Turner, S. A. Career dreams of teachers. In A. Theodore (Ed.), *The Professional Woman*. Cambridge, Mass: Schenkman, 1971.

Wylie, R. *The Self Concept*. Lincoln, Nebr: University of Nebraska Press, 1973.

Yarrow, L. J. Separation from parents during early childhood. In M. L. Hoffman & L. W. Hoffman (Eds.), *Review of Child Development Research* (Vol. 1). New York: Sage, 1964, pp. 89–136.

Yoder, J. D., Adams, J., Grove, S., & Priest, R. F. To teach is to learn: Overcoming tokenism with mentors. *Psychology of Women Quarterly*, 1985, *9*, 119.

Yogev, S. Do professional women have egalitarian marital relationships? *Journal of Marriage and the Family*, 1981, *52*, 865.

Yogev, S. Judging the professional woman: Changing research, changing values. *Psychology of Women Quarterly*, 1983, *7*(3), 219.

Youniss, J. Social construction of adolescence by adolescents and parents. In H. D. Grotevant & C. R. Cooper (Eds.), *Adolescent Development in the Family*. San Francisco: Jossey-Bass, 1983, pp. 93–109.

Yuchtman, E., & Seashore, S. A system resource approach to organizational effectiveness. *American Sociological Review*, 1967, *32*, 891.

Zborowski, M. Cultural components in response to pain. *Journal of Social Issues*, 1952, *8*, 16.

Zetterberg, H. L. *On Theory & Verification in Sociology* (3rd ed.). Totowa, N.J.: Bedminster Press, 1965, c. 1963.

Zey-Ferrell, M., & Aiken, M. *Complex Organizations: Critical Perspectives*. Glenview, Ill: Scott, Foresman, 1981.

Ziel, S. The androgynous nurse manager. *The Journal of Continuing Education in Nursing*, 1983, *14*, 27.

Zigler, E., & Child, I. L. Socialization. In G. Lindzey & E. Aronson (Eds.), *The Handbook of Social Psychology* (Vol. 3) (2nd ed.). Reading, Mass: Addison-Wesley, 1969.

Zigler, E., & Child, I. L. (Eds.). *Socialization and Personality Development*. Reading, Mass: Addison-Wesley, 1973.

Zigler, E. F. Lamb, M. E., & Child, I. L. *Socialization and Personality Development* (2nd ed.). New York: Oxford University Press, 1982.

Zigler, E., & Cascione, R. On being a parent. In E. F. Zigler, M. E. Lamb, & I. L. Child, *Socialization and Personality Development* (2nd ed.). New York: Oxford University Press, 1982, pp. 258–267.

Zigler, E., & Seitz, V. Future research on socialization and personality development. In E. F. Zigler, M. E. Lamb, & I. L. Child, *Socialization and Personality Development* (2nd ed.). New York: Oxford University Press, 1982, pp. 185–199.

Zola, I. Problems of communication, diagnosis and patient care. *Journal of Medical Education*, 1963, *10*, 829.

Zuckerman, D. M., & Sayre, D. H. Cultural sex-role expectations and children's sex-role concepts. *Sex Roles*, 1982, *8*, 853.

Index